SOCIAL PSYCHOLOGY
THEORIES, RESEARCH, AND APPLICATIONS

SOCIAL PSYCHOLOGY
THEORIES, RESEARCH, AND APPLICATIONS

ROBERT S. FELDMAN
University of Massachusetts—Amherst

McGRAW-HILL BOOK COMPANY

New York   St. Louis   San Francisco   Auckland
Bogotá   Hamburg   Johannesburg
London   Madrid   Mexico   Montreal   New Delhi
Panama   Paris   São Paulo   Singapore   Sydney   Tokyo   Toronto

As an additional learning tool, McGraw-Hill also publishes a study guide to supplement your understanding of this textbook. Here is the information your bookstore manager will need to order it for you: 20394-6   STUDY GUIDE TO ACCOMPANY SOCIAL PSYCHOLOGY

This book was set in Caledonia by Ruttle, Shaw & Wetherill, Inc.
The editors were David V. Serbun, Rhona Robbin,
and David Dunham;
the designer was Joan E. O'Connor;
the production supervisor was Phil Galea.
The photo editor was Randy Matusow;
the cover illustration was done by Lisa Young.
The drawings were done by Fine Line Illustrations, Inc.
Von Hoffmann Press, Inc., was printer and binder.

Chapter-Opening Photograph Credits

1 Hazel Hankin   2 Chris Steele-Perkins/Magnum   3 Hazel Hankin
4 Hazel Hankin   5 Chester Higgins, Jr./Photo Researchers
6 Charles Harbutt/Archive Pictures   7 Gilles Peress/Magnum   8 Mim
Forsyth/Monkmeyer Press   9 Sam Pierson, Jr./Photo Researchers
10 Randy Matusow   11 Michael Heron/Woodfin Comp   12 Louis
Goldman/Photo Researchers   13 Bill Bachman/Photo Researchers
14 Peter Marlow/Magnum   15 Hugh Rogers/Monkmeyer Press

SOCIAL PSYCHOLOGY
THEORIES, RESEARCH, AND APPLICATIONS

1 2 3 4 5 6 7 8 9 0 VNH VNH 8 9 8 7 6 5

ISBN 0-07-020392-X

Library of Congress Cataloging in Publication Data

Feldman, Robert S. (Robert Stephen), date
    Social psychology.

    Bibliography: p.
    Includes indexes.
    1. Social psychology: I. Title
HM251.F374 1985   302   84-19381
ISBN 0-07-020392-X

To Kathy,
with love and gratitude.

CONTENTS IN BRIEF

CONTENTS

PREFACE

There is a campaign-style button attached to the bulletin board above my desk which reads "I Like Social Psych." I picked it up at a convention a few years ago and, as I wrote this book, I found myself casting occasional glances at it. In a way, it began to symbolize for me why I was working on this book and what it was that I wanted to convey to students whose exposure to the discipline would come largely from this text. As I contemplated the button more and more, I realized that I wanted readers to come away with the same feelings of affection—and respect—for social psychology that I have, and to allow them to learn that the field could help them to understand the world in which they live in a fuller way.

To do this, I have tried to capture the essence of social psychology as the discipline exists today. In the book, I present social psychology as a dynamic, evolving scientific discipline with substantial relevance to people's lives. Congruous with current interest in applying social psychology, the book includes more material on applications than any other mainstream text. At the same time, basic theory has not been sacrificed. The result is a balanced integration of theory, research, and applications, providing a broad and up-to-date view of the field.

The text reflects the view that a strict theory–application dichotomy is a false one. Applications are not presented as devoid of theory; rather, they are placed within a theoretical context. Likewise, when theoretical material is discussed, practical implications are drawn. And presentation of both theory and applications is supported by classic and current examples of empirical research. Theory, application, and research, then, are integrated both within and between chapters throughout the text, and the result is a balanced view of social psychology in the mid-1980s.

The book is made up of five parts. The first part provides an introduction to the major theoretical schools of the field and gives an overview of the major methodologies. The second part, relating to how people define, understand, and evaluate their social world, is concerned with how people understand and judge themselves and others, communication processes, attitudes, and, in a chapter devoted to an applied aspect of attitudes, prejudice and discrimination.

In the third part of the book, the emphasis turns to positive and negative social interaction. First, in three separate chapters, we consider three types of behavior indicative of different kinds of caring relationships: interpersonal attraction, prosocial behavior, and caring behaviors in a health-related context. The part ends with a chapter on negative social interaction in the form of aggression.

Part Four is about larger-scale social processes. First, we discuss social influence, power, and leadership. Next, the topic of behavior in groups is addressed. Finally, we look at what social psychologists have to say about organizational behavior, particularly as it pertains to the workplace.

In the final part of the book, we discuss broad societal issues from a social psychological perspective. First, justice and the legal system are considered. Next, we discuss bargaining and negotiations, with particular reference to international relations and arms reduction strategies. Finally, the book concludes with a chapter on how the physical environment affects social behavior.

As can be seen from this brief overview and from an examination of the text's tables of contents, the book not only covers the traditional areas of study, but also features several new areas of interest, such as communication, health care, justice and law, and organizations and the workplace. These chapters are integrated into the text and provide instructors wishing to present the breadth of the field a comprehensive base from which to teach their course. At the same time, instructors who wish to teach a theory-oriented social psychology course could, with the deletion of the more applied chapters, use the book in their classes.

Throughout the text, I have tried to focus on the field in an objective, eclectic manner. No single theoretical position or idiosyncratic point of view is espoused; rather, theories, research, and applications are presented in a rational, orderly manner, representative of the dominant views of the discipline. The writing style is consistently open, clear, and direct. Moreover, the text emphasizes what is objectively known about the field, synthesizing findings in a way that makes them accessible and meaningful. Although the emphasis is on what is known, as opposed to contradictions between various studies and the uncertainties of the field, major findings and viewpoints that are controversial are included and used to show how social psychologists try to resolve such controversies by means of scientific approaches. The book includes both the promise and the problems of social psychology—but emphasizes the promise.

In order to make the book both effective from a pedagogical point of view and interesting and engaging to the reader, several features are common to each chapter. They include:

- *Chapter-opening interview.* These interviews were held with people who are involved in day-to-day activities that reflect relevant applications of social psychology. The interviewees are not, for the most part, social psychologists, but rather persons whose particular roles or occupations cause them to use, either explicitly or implicitly, theories, findings, and issues related to the field of social psychology. These informal discussions provide a springboard to the issues discussed in the chapter that follows. Some of the interviewees are well known— such as Penn State football coach Joe Paterno (in the chapter on groups), attorney Archibald Cox (the law and justice chapter), and former U.S. Representative Shirley Chisholm (social influence)— while others are not; but they all illustrate how issues of interest to social psychologists are pervasive.
- *Boxed material.* Each chapter contains highlighted boxes, labeled "Spotlights." Spotlights focus either on theory, applications, research, or methods, and they feature an area of particular interest or an alternate point of view.
- *Discussion of solutions to social problems.* Chapters typically provide information derived from social psychology that is relevant to the solution of pressing social problems. For example, the chapter on prejudice includes a section on reducing discrimination; the chapter on helping provides techniques for increasing prosocial behavior; and the chapter on social exchange and bargaining considers means for ending the arms race. Potential solutions are not discussed in terms of generalities; rather, they are based on implications drawn from specific applied studies.
- *Chapter summary, key terms, and annotated bibliography.* Each chapter ends with a summary, a list of key terms discussed in the chapter, and an annotated bibliography which refers to material of both theoretical and applied relevance.

In addition to the features common to each chapter, the book includes two other features of note:

- *Glossary.* There is a complete glossary at the end of the book, providing definitions of important terms.
- *Instructor's manual and student study guide.* The ancillary materials are among the best for *any* text available today. The *Instructor's Manual* includes chapter outlines, goals and objectives, discussion ques-

tions, field exercises, additional readings, lists of films and other au-
diovisual aids, and a very large test-item bank in which the items are
keyed directly to the text. The test-bank questions are also available
on *Examiner*, McGraw-Hill's computerized test-generation system for
the mainframe computer, and on *Microexaminer*, for the Apple II®,
TRS-80®, and IBM® PC. The *Study Guide* includes objectives, goals,
extensive self-tests, and chapter summaries. When used with the text,
the *Instructor's Manual* and *Study Guide* form an integrated, versatile
package.

These features are designed to achieve my goal of providing effective,
broad coverage of the field, at the same time conveying the excitement
and relevance of social psychology to people's everyday concerns. I will
be satisfied if, after using this text, readers are able to feel—and understand—the sentiment on the button I mentioned at the start of this
preface: "I like Social Psych."

ACKNOWLEDGMENTS

One does not write a book without amassing a long list of individuals
to whom one is indebted. To begin, I was graced with responsible,
insightful, and wise reviewers who commented on part or all of the
manuscript. I thank them. They include:

Icek Ajzen, University of Massachusetts
Tom Baranowski, University of Texas Medical School, Galveston
Paul A. Bell, Colorado State University
Eugene Borgida, University of Minnesota
Bert Brown, Rutgers University
Thomas P. Cafferty, University of South Carolina
Philip Costanzo, Duke University
Ebbe Ebbesen, University of California, San Diego
Howard S. Friedman, University of California, Riverside
Jeffrey H. Goldstein, Temple University
Alice M. Isen, University of Maryland
Christine H. Jazwinski, St. Cloud State University
Marianne Lafrance, Boston College
George Levinger, University of Massachusetts
Rosemary H. Lowe, Louisiana State University
Robert S. Miller, Plymouth State College
Richard C. Noel, California State College at Bakersfield
Miles Patterson, University of Missouri-St. Louis
James W. Pennebaker, Southern Methodist University
Janet Reohr, Russell Sage College
Jonathan Segal, Trinity College
R. Lance Shotland, Pennsylvania State University

Steve Slane, Cleveland State University
Elizabeth D. Tanke, University of Santa Clara
Dalmas A. Taylor, University of Maryland

I am very grateful to the extraordinary staff at McGraw-Hill. First and foremost, Rhona Robbin, developmental editor on this project, provided precise and adept critiques, comments, and editorial advice. Her influence can be found on every page of this book. Pat Nave and Dave Serbun, sponsoring editors, provided impetus to the project, and their continuing support was gratifying. David Dunham and others on the production staff were a pleasure to work with, and marketing representative Bob Schuyler was always ready to encourage me along. These people make up a first-class team, and I am proud to be a McGraw-Hill author.

Kate Cleary, who typed and retyped and then typed again the manuscript, probably should have her name somewhere on the cover of this book; her contributions were extensive. Not only did she provide editorial advice, but her moral support kept me writing at quite a few junctures. Jean Glenowicz also provided much needed secretarial help, and I am grateful to both of them.

There were others who provided research and editorial assistance. They include Carolyn Dash, John White, Janice Rose, and Kate Shildauer.

Two social psychologists, in particular, got me started in this field: Karl Scheibe and Vernon Allen. And my colleagues here at the University of Massachusetts provided a supportive, intellectually stimulating, and amiable atmosphere. I am very grateful to them.

Finally, I am part of a large family group that plays a welcome role in my life. My parents, Leah Brochstein and the late Saul D. Feldman, gave me love and support, and I am continually grateful to them. There are many others, as well; in roughly generational order, they include my nieces and nephews, brother, brothers-in-law, sisters-in-law, Ethel Radler, and Harry Brochstein. Mary Vorwerk warrants a special note of thanks, with utmost fondness, for her unceasing and most special contributions to me and many others. Ultimately, my greatest thanks go to the members of my immediate family. My children, Jonathan, Joshua, and Sarah, keep me young (in spirit, if not body) and happy. And to my wife, Katherine Vorwerk, I owe most everything.

Robert S. Feldman

PART ONE

INTRODUCTION
TO
SOCIAL PSYCHOLOGY

CHAPTER 1

THEORIES AND METHODS OF SOCIAL PSYCHOLOGY

THE FIELD OF SOCIAL PSYCHOLOGY

Three men were attacked and one of them beaten to death when their car stalled on a street in the Sheepshead Bay section of Brooklyn early yesterday morning. The victims, who were on their way home from work, were black, and the police said the attack was unprovoked and "racially motivated."

A 29 year-old unemployed father of eight children leaped onto the tracks of a Greenwich Village subway station yesterday morning and saved the life of a 75-year-old blind man who had stumbled and fallen between the cars of a train that was about to pull out.

"I wasn't thinking about the danger, just that, hey, somebody needs help," said Reginald Andrews, who tore ligaments in his right knee as he pulled the confused, bleeding victim into a narrow crawlspace under the edge of the platform while others tried frantically to halt the train.

"I'd do it again—I'd do it for anybody who needs help," said Mr. Andrews.

In a Kamikaze-like attack, a man drove a truck loaded with thousands of pounds of TNT into an American military headquarters in Beirut, leveling the building, and killing over 200 sleeping Marines.

After another fruitless round of negotiations, United States and Russian arms negotiators meeting in Geneva adjourned the 121st session without reaching agreement.

Although political fortunes rise and fall, few instances are as dramatic as the career of British Prime Minister Margaret Thatcher in the early 1980s. Just one year after a national public opinion poll showed that the British public thought she was the worst Prime Minister in history, she was swept back into office with the greatest landslide in forty years.

Despite the obvious dissimilarities among the five situations described above, they share an important commonality: each is an example of one of the central topics of the field of social psychology. In the first, we see people demonstrating racial bigotry in its most overt and violent form. The second situation illustrates a brighter side of human nature: someone risking his own life to aid someone else. The third demonstrates the kind of senseless aggression of which human beings are capable, and the fourth shows bargaining and negotiating with stakes that could not be higher. The last situation highlights the variability of human behavior by illustrating how attitudes and opinions can undergo major alterations over a relatively short period of time.

These particular examples only begin to cover the many areas of interest to social psychologists. To give you an idea of the scope of the discipline, let us consider the most commonly accepted formal definition of the field of social psychology: "An attempt to understand and explain how the thought, feeling, and behavior of individuals are influenced by the actual, imagined, or implied presence of others (Allport, 1968, p. 3). But a more informal definition captures the flavor of what social psychology is all about just as well: we shall consider the discipline as one which examines *how a person's thoughts, feelings, and actions are affected by others.*

Whatever definition one chooses, it is clear that social psychology covers a lot of territory and that there are many diverse topical areas that fit comfortably within the discipline. For example, some social psychologists focus on social influences on the individual, some on social interaction between two or more individuals, and still others on group processes.

As illustrated in Table 1-1, one focus of study is on social influences that have an effect on individuals and the way in which they understand the world. Even when we are alone, the way we think and behave is affected by others; and the effects of others are even more salient when they are physically present. Accordingly, social psychologists interested in the individual person study processes such as motivation, perception, learning, and the ways in which information is acquired and processed. Specifically, social psychologists concerned with individual processes might examine how achievement motivation is manifested, how attitudes are learned, and how we form our views of others.

Another major approach of social psychologists is related to interaction between and among individuals. The unique characteristics of social behavior when two or more people are talking, working, bargaining, planning, or engaging in any of the myrid activities that people do together are the primary interest of social psychologists taking this approach. Specific areas of investigation include communication processes (both verbal and nonverbal), social influence in attitude change, bargaining and negotiating, interpersonal attraction (identifying the determinants of liking), and aggressive and helping behavior. For example, social psychologists have considered how nonverbal behavior can be used to infer emotions, how attitudes can be changed by advertising, and how we form friendships and loving relationships with others.

The final major area of interest to social psychologists is group processes. Under this category fall studies of the unique properties of groups, such as status, roles, group pressure and norms, and communication patterns. On a larger scale, social psychologists study organizations, societal institutions such as governments and the legal system, and the physical environment in an attempt to determine how people respond to these influences. Questions relating to how to maintain one's independence in group situations, how to promote communication in organizations, and how to design buildings architecturally to promote user satisfaction illustrate the range of the group processes approach.

TABLE 1-1 Major Topics of Social Psychology: A Representative Listing

Category	Topic	Chapter in Which Topic Is Discussed	Example of Specific Researchable Question on the Topic	No. of Publications*
Individual processes				
	Achievement and task performance	2	What are the determinants of achievement and motivation relating to school performance?	19
	Attitudes and attitude change	4	What is the relationship between political attitudes and voting behavior?	50
	Attribution	2	To what factors do we attribute the behavior of others?	55
	Cognitive processes	2	How do we classify and categorize others' personality characteristics?	41
	Dissonance	4	When we are led to behave in a way that runs counter to what we believe, do our attitudes change?	7
	Person perception	2	How do we combine individual personality characteristics to form an overall opinion of others?	15
	Self-awareness	8	How does being made aware of ourselves as individuals affect the way we report symptoms to a physician?	13
	Social and personality development	5	What factors in childhood lead to prejudice in adults?	44
	Stress, emotion, and arousal	8	What factors lead to sexual arousal?	17
	Victims	9	Why are victims of crimes sometimes treated as if they deserved to be victimized?	5
Interpersonal interaction				
	Aggression	9	Do aggressive television shows promote violence?	24
	Attraction and affiliation	6	How does physical attractiveness affect the way people are treated?	31

Category	Topic	Chapter in Which Topic Is Discussed	Example of Specific Researchable Question on the Topic	No. of Publications*
	Bargaining and coalition	14	What is a good bargaining strategy when buying a car from a used-car salesperson?	12
	Conformity and compliance	10	Why do we conform to others' opinion?	11
	Equity, justice, and social exchange	13	What do we consider a just trial?	14
	Helping	7	In an emergency, what leads bystanders to intervene?	24
	Nonverbal communication	3	Can we accurately infer emotions from others' nonverbal behavior?	21
	Sex roles and sex differences	10	Do females conform more than males?	26
	Social influence	10	How can minorities influence the majority in a group?	13
	Social interaction	6	Why do we prefer the presence of others when we are anxious?	15
Group processes				
	Cross-cultural research	12	Do the Japanese have superior management systems in industry?	8
	Crowding and interpersonal distance	15	Why does performance decline in crowded situations?	16
	Environmental and population psychology	15	How can buildings best be designed to promote user satisfaction?	10
	Group processes	11	Is a group decision better than those made by individuals?	23
	Law and crime-related research	13	How well are judges' instructions understood by juries?	12
	Racial and ethnic issues	5	Does desegregation reduce prejudice?	9

* The figures in the last column refer to the number of journal articles published during 1979. Note that there is a substantial amount of overlap among the categories.
Source: Adapted from Smith, S. S., Richardson, D., & Hendrick, C. (1980). Bibliography of journal articles in personality and social psychology: 1979. *Personality and Social Psychology Bulletin, 6,* 606–636.

Interaction between people is a major focus of study by social psychologists. (Frank Siteman/ Stock, Boston)

WHAT SOCIAL PSYCHOLOGY IS NOT

As one can see, social psychology covers a wide range of behavior. But it does not encompass *all* instances of behavior; other related social science disciplines are better equipped to investigate certain phenomena from their particular vantage point. Take, for example, the related field of sociology. Sociology is the science of society and social institutions, focusing on how members of groups are subject to similar, culturally universal influences which determine how the group as a whole performs. Hence, the focus is considerably more on the group as a whole than on its individual members.

For example, sociologists would be best equipped to investigate the general role of schools in our society. On the other hand, if we ask how a child's performance in school is affected by his parents' attitudes, we should turn to social psychologists to explore this relationship. In the first case, we are looking at schools in a collective sense, while in the second we are investigating the individual within the school setting.

Another discipline related to social psychology is anthropology, which is generally defined as the study of men and women and their cultures. Anthropology takes an even broader approach to social phenomena than sociology does by concentrating on the universals in a given culture (such as family structure) and placing very little emphasis on the individual.

In sum, although there is overlap between social psychology and other social science disciplines, the major focus of interest and the approach to problems differ among these fields. The major focus of social psychologists is on people's individual psychological processes and their social interactions with others, while that of sociologists and anthropologists is on the larger groups to which people belong.

THEORIES OF SOCIAL PSYCHOLOGY

Intrinsic to an understanding of how social psychologists approach their field is the notion that social psychology is a **science.** As with any science, social psychologists seek knowledge to predict, control, and understand social behavior. What guides them through this search for knowledge are social psychological **theories,** which are explanations and predictions of phenomena of interest.

Almost all of us develop theories of social behavior. For example, we may assume that people conform to certain group norms of dress and behavior because of a wish to be popular. Whenever we develop such an explanation, we are actually building our own theories. However, our personal theories usually rest on unverified observations, collected in an unsystematic manner—hardly the stuff from which science is developed.

In constrast, theories developed by social psychologists are considerably more formal, consisting of a set of related **hypotheses**—predictions of phenomena which have not yet been observed (Shaw & Costanzo, 1982). Theories allow us to make sense of observations, putting them together in a way that both summarizes and organizes them. Moreover, theories permit the social psychologist to move beyond observations that have already been collected and make deductions that are not readily apparent from the individual pieces of data that already exist. Theories also provide a guide to the future collection of observations, suggesting the direction in which research should move.

In social pyschology, most sets of observations can be explained by alternate theoretical perspectives, and one of the major goals of the science is to determine which theory provides the best explanation of the phenomena. Theories còme and go, depending on how well observations support them. Indeed, the discarding of a theory, rather than being lamentable, merely shows that the science is evolving.

Characteristics of Theories

What makes a good theory? Shaw and Costanzo (1982) suggest that a theory must be consistent internally—i.e., the various propositions that are derived from it must fit together and not contradict one another. A second characteristic is that a good theory ought to agree with existing facts about the world, as well as being a good predictor of future happenings. Finally, good theories must be testable. It does us little good to develop a theory that cannot be tested; if the theory does not provide a means of collecting data that can at least potentially refute the theory, there is no way of evaluating its accuracy.

Many of the theories that social psychologists have developed are relatively narrow in scope, and we will be discussing these throughout the book in reference to particular topics. However, there are five major theoretical approaches which guide social psychological work—as well as the work of other kinds of psychologists—in a broad sense. These include genetic theories, learning theories, cognitive theories, psychoanalytic theories, and role theories. Each of these approaches provides a different perspective by emphasizing different kinds of variables used in explaining human social behavior. (Refer to Table 1-2 for a summary of the major theoretical approaches described below.) None of them alone is sufficient to understand all behavior, but when the theories are considered together they represent a comprehensive set of explanations for social psychological phenomena.

Genetic Theories: The Innate Qualities of Social Behavior

The phrase "people are social animals" captures the essence of genetic theoretical approaches, suggesting as it does that social behavior has its roots in biologically determined causes. Genetic theories generally assume that large components of social behavior are related to unlearned genetic causes. One of the major proponents of genetic theories is Konrad Lorenz, an ethologist who studied social phenomena in animals. He suggests that aggressive behavior is a manifestation of an instinctive, inborn aggressive drive stemming from a need to fight for self-preservation (Lorenz, 1966).

The work of one of the earliest social psychologists, William McDougall, was also based on genetic conceptions of social behavior. McDougall (1908) believed that many specific behavioral traits could be explained in terms of *instincts*, unlearned goal-directed behavior. He postulated a set of instincts that supposedly underlie behavior. If, for example, a mother acted protectively toward her child, McDougall explained such behavior in terms of a "parental instinct." Likewise, people conformed to others presumably because of a "herd instinct."

Today, most social psychologists reject the notion of instincts as explanatory mechanisms for social behavior. The major problem with such a belief is that instincts do not really explain the reasons behind a behavior; they simply provide an alternative label for observed behavior. Moreover, they do little in the way of providing accurate *predictions* of future behavior, something that any good theory should do.

Despite these limitations, the genetic approach is still with us today, primarily in an incarnation known as "sociobiology" (Wilson, 1978). Sociobiology represents an attempt to draw upon the fields of sociology, psychology, and biology to explain social behavior. In essence, sociobiology suggests that through a process of natural selection, social behaviors have evolved which provide the human species with certain

TABLE 1-2 Summary of Major Theoretical Approaches

Theoretical Approach	Major Concepts	Emphasis on Environment or the Individual	Major Outgrowths	Current Status
Genetic	Genetic, biological determinants of behavior; instincts	Individual	Sociobiology	Relatively little impact
Learning	Social behavior learned; stimuli, response, imitation, and reinforcement; black-box approach	Environment	Imitation, modeling	Strong impact
Cognitive	Phenomenological approach; field theory; impression formation	Individual and environment	Attribution theory Social cognition	Strong impact
Psychoanalytic	Unconscious determinants of behavior; developmental influences on adults' behavior	Individual	Explanations of aggression, prejudice, socialization	Minor impact
Role	Role; role expectations; role demands	Primarily environment	Self-presentation; impression management	Moderate impact

survival advantages. Thus, the sociobiologist might explain instances of altruistic behavior in terms of the survival value of altruism. Presumably, altruistic behaviors may have provided some kind of greater fitness to the human species as a whole by protecting the overall pool of genes, so those with the gene for altruism were more apt to survive and pass on that trait. In this way, altruistic behaviors are at least partially determined by an individual's genetic makeup.

The major proponent of sociobiology, Edmund Wilson, has provided many elegant explanations of social behavior that are based on the principles of the theory. Still, the approach suffers from deficits similar to those of other genetic theories: The theory lacks predictive power. Moreover, genetic theories in general minimize the role of situational, environmental factors in social behavior. For these reasons, they are probably the least popular of the theoretical approaches currently employed by social psychologists. While it is clear that any complete understanding of human social phenomena must take genetic predispositions into account, social psychologists generally agree that social behavior is not fixed and predetermined by instinctual factors.

Still, predictions derived from sociobiology can readily be used to explain social behavior. As an example, consider the news clip that began the chapter which reported about a group of blacks who were beaten in a racially motivated attack. A sociobiologist would approach this incident, as well as other instances of prejudicial behavior, by trying to determine the function of such an attack from a biological point of view. The sociobiologist might suggest that behavior discriminating against members of groups to which one does not belong might serve to strengthen one's own group by eliminating competitors, thereby providing one's own group with a greater chance of survival in evolutionary terms. Although speculative—and inherently untestable—such a hypothesis is congruent with the basic tenets of sociobiology.

Learning Approaches to Social Psychological Phenomena

At the opposite conceptual pole from genetic conceptions of social behavior stand learning theory approaches. Instead of explaining social phenomena by internal biological predeterminants, learning theories emphasize the roles of the situation and the environment in causing behavior. More specifically, these theories analyze social behavior in terms of learned associations between stimuli and responses.

In classical conditioning, as you probably recall from earlier psychology classes, learning occurs when a previously neutral stimulus evokes a conditioned response. Hence, we may learn that the presence of others (the stimulus) results in a decrease in anxiety (the response) when we are in an anxiety-evoking situation. The decrease in anxiety is the result of classical conditioning processes similar to those that taught Pavlov's dogs to salivate at the sound of a bell. In operant conditioning, learning is said to occur when a response is followed by reinforcement. Thus, a child who shares candy with a friend and is praised by his parents has been reinforced in his generosity, and is theoretically more likely to be generous in the future.

One straightforward example of the use of learning theory is **social exhange theory,** which views social interaction in terms of the rewards and punishments that accrue to the individuals involved in the interaction. According to George Homans (1958), if we consider the bare basics of social interaction, it is reasonable to predict that people tend to interact most with those who provide them with rewards—such as privileges, praise, and prestige—and avoid those who bestow punishment. As we shall see when we discuss the concepts of bargaining, equity, and justice, this simple concept provides a starting point for a good deal of sophisticated work on social interaction.

One further example of learning theory approaches regards the phenomenon of imitation, a primary means by which social behavior is learned. According to the theory, whose major proponent is Albert Bandura, children learn new behavior by viewing what others—models—are doing and observing the consequences of such behavior (Bandura, 1965, 1977). If the models are rewarded, the observers are more likely

Although this young girl's imitation of her mother is obvious, she also imitates—and learns—more subtle sorts of things, such as parental attitudes. (Abigail Heyman/ Archive Pictures Inc.)

to carry out the behavior in the future; but if they are punished, the observers are less likely to carry out such behaviors.

Learning theory has been used to explain many social psychological phenomena, including aggression, altruism, interpersonal attraction, communication, prejudice, and attitude formation. In some of these areas, learning theory is the dominant explanatory mechanism that has been employed. In others, however, learning theory is used only in a peripheral fashion.

Although its emphasis on scientifically observable behavior makes learning theory attractive to many social psychologists, some find learning theory objectionable because of its minimization of internal factors, such as thinking processes and an individual's genetic makeup. Indeed, most learning theories present what is frequently called a **black-box view** of human beings: Stimuli and responses are examined microscopically, but what goes on inside the person (the black box) is basically of no consequence to the "pure" learning theorist. To the many social psychologists interested in social thinking processes, this view is an especially inappropriate one. Another criticism that has been leveled against learning theories is that there are some clear instances in which social behaviors that are followed by *negative* consequences actually increase in frequency and strength. For example, we sometimes grow to like passionately someone who treats us miserably, as we shall discuss in Chapter 6.

Despite these criticisms, learning theories provide a reasonable explanation for many kinds of behaviors of interest to social psychologists.

If we return to our initial example of the unprovoked attack on the group of blacks, it is clear how learning theory can be used to explain how the attackers' negative attitudes may have been acquired. We could speculate that they may have imitated parental and peer prejudiced attitudes. Another speculation based on a learning theory approach might be that they had had negative experiences during past interactions with blacks and generalized them to blacks in general. As you can see, learning theories can provide us with a number of plausible explanations.

Cognitive Approaches

In contrast to learning theories, cognitive theories place particular emphasis on thinking processes and how people come to understand and represent the world. Much of current theorizing based on cognitive approaches stems from work done by an early group of German psychologists known as **gestaltists.** Although the primary interest of the gestalt psychologists lay in the area of perception, their work has had a very important impact upon social psychology throughout its history for two major reasons: First, the gestalt psychologists developed techniques that made experimentation on phenomena of interest to social psychologists amenable to laboratory study. Studies of group structure, interpersonal communication, and attitude change, for example, were first made possible by the gestalt approach to experimentation.

A second reason for the impact of the gestaltists on social psychology lay in their use of "naive experience"—the way in which a person understands and perceives a situation. While learning theorists posit that measurement of an objective situation, independent of how the person perceives it, is the most valid method for investigating social phenomena, the gestalt tradition suggests that a **phenomenological** approach—investigating how a person subjectively understands, interprets, and experiences the world—is most useful (Koffka, 1935).

The basic notions that guided the gestaltists are that psychological phenomena occur in a **field,** a system of interdependent factors that include perceptions and past experience, and that the individual elements of the field cannot be understood without knowing the field as a whole. Thus, when we view the objects in Figure 1-1, we do not see the parts as individual elements but rather as a whole (a *gestalt,* according to the original terminology). Hence, we view the first example in the figure as three pairs of dots, rather than six dots (which would be an equally plausible description).

The gestalt approach has been expanded to include not just perceptual sorts of issues but also **cognitions** (elements of thinking) in general. Cognitive theories assume that the appropriate approach to psychological phenomena is to study thinking processes and how people come to understand and represent the world. For example, one very direct application of the cognitive theoretical approach has been research on how

FIGURE 1-1

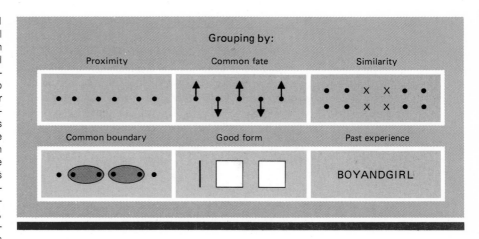

Examples of perceptual
grouping. Rather than
looking at the individual
parts of each set of fig-
ures, people tend to
group things together. For
instance, in the first example, "proximity" leads
to the perception of three
pairs of dots, rather than
simply six dots. In the
second example, dots
moving in the same di-
rection are grouped to-
gether; while in the third,
the dots are perceived together and the crosses
perceived separately.
Common boundaries de-
termine groupings in the
fourth figure. In the fifth
figure, we see two
squares—instead of the
individual lines that make
up each. Finally, if our
past experience is with
the English language, we
see the ten letters in the
last example as divided
into three words.

people form impressions of other people. As we shall see in Chapter 2, social psychologists following the gestalt tradition have examined how our knowledge of individual traits (i.e., elements in a gestalt sense) is combined to form overall impressions of people (Burnstein & Schul, 1982). Fritz Heider, an important pioneer in the field of social psychology, suggests that in an effort to make sense of their world, people put together their own "naive psychology" or explanations of why others behave as they do. His work has led to current work involving attribution theory—the systematic study of how observers determine the causes of behavior—and social cognition—the way in which people think about and understand their social world (Fiske & Taylor, 1983).

A cognitive approach to understanding the assailants of the blacks would focus on how they perceive members of different social groups and other objects of their prejudice. Their attributions regarding the behavior of the black men they attacked might be assessed to determine their reasoning and understanding—or misunderstanding—of the situation. In sum, the cognitive approach would look at how the attackers perceive and understand their world in order to explain their behavior.

Psychoanalytic Theory

To most nonpsychologists, Sigmund Freud's psychoanalytic theory represents what psychology is all about. To the social psychologist, however, psychoanalytic theory is among the least frequently employed of the major theoretical positions, and the theory itself represents a relatively minor influence over the field today. At the same time, some of Freud's major contributions have influenced the development of several important trends in the study of social behavior, and so his theory warrants scrutiny.

In its most basic form, psychoanalytic theory posits that adult behavior is in many ways a reflection of an individual's childhood experiences.

It maintains that all people move through a fixed series of stages during their early years of development, which relate to sources of sexual pleasure; these stages are labeled the oral, anal, phallic, and genital stages. The theory also introduces the concept of the **unconscious,** a part of personality in which desires, impulses, and conflicts are located and which can have a directive influence on behavior. People are not aware of the nature of activity occurring in their unconscious, and their behavior is motivated both by unconscious and conscious determinants.

Freud's psychoanalytic theory has led social psychologists in a number of diverse topical directions, although the common thread is that social behavior is examined in terms of unconscious processes. For instance, some theorists have suggested that aggressive behavior ought to be viewed as a manifestation of an innate, unconscious death instinct, as we shall discuss in Chapter 9 (Freud, 1930). Similarly, one approach to prejudice, presented in Chapter 5, suggests that prejudice toward minority groups may be due to childhood conflicts in which the demands of harsh, rigid parents are reflected in adult disliking of people who are dissimilar (Adorno, Frenkel-Brunswik, Levinson, & Sanford, 1950). Hence, in our initial example referring to the attackers of the blacks, a psychoanalytic theorist would focus on the attackers' childhoods and upbringing in order to understand the violent prejudice they displayed as adults.

The reason most social psychologists are not apt to make much use of psychoanalytic theorizing is basic to the theory: its reliance on the unconscious to explain and predict behavior. Given that unconscious processes are, by definition, unobservable, it is next to impossible to derive scientific tests that can demonstrate the validity of the theory. Indeed, one of the major failings of psychoanalytic theory as a theory is that there is no way of formally disproving or confirming it, a feature that strongly detracts from its efficacy in a formal sense. The theory is much stronger as an after-the-fact explanation than as a predictor of behavior. On the other hand, the view that social behavior is in part a function of an individual's past developmental history is unassailable, and any attempt to explain fully the complexities of human social interaction must take an individual's prior experiences into account.

Role Theory: The Many Faces of People

Of the theories we have discussed, role theory is the most overtly social in nature and, in fact, is derived from work done initially by sociologists. Its basic approach—that behavior is shaped by the roles that society provides for individuals to play—clearly takes into account the way in which social factors affect how people behave across different situations. On the other hand, it is the least formalized, the least structured, and among the least concerned with a person's motivations, genetic makeup, and personality of any major theoretical approach. Moreover, researchers have not been able to agree upon a definition of even the most central concept of role theory—the role.

Despite these difficulties, the central concepts of role theory are relatively straightforward. A **role** is typically defined as a set of behaviors that are related to a given position (Sarbin & Allen, 1968; Biddle & Thomas, 1966). Thus, a physician acts a certain way when in the physician role, but quite differently when in the role of a father, and still differently when he is playing the role of tennis player. The different roles permit different sorts of behavior to occur and be socially sanctioned; it is expected, for instance, that physicians will ask us to remove our clothes, but it is less acceptable if they do so while they are acting as our tennis partners. According to role theory, what makes the behavior appropriate in one situation and inappropriate in the other is relatively independent of the person occupying the role; what is significant is that the role he or she is occupying has changed. Hence, each role has associated with it a set of *expectations* regarding what is appropriate and acceptable behavior in that role.

Role theory has led to work on **impression management,** an area which studies the way in which people try to create specific—and positive— impressions about themselves (Schlenker, 1980). Work on this topic has shown that people actively engage in behavioral strategies to enhance others' impressions of themselves.

Role expectations affect behavior in ways that are both intuitively obvious and not so readily apparent. For instance, it is clear that people who are asked to play the role of teacher should be prepared, give coherent explanations, and treat their students well. But it is less obvious that when people learn the material they are going to teach to others, they do so in a way that is qualitatively distinct from the way they study the material to learn it on their own (Allen & Feldman, 1973). Hence, simply placing someone in a role can change his or her perceptions and ways of cognitively structuring the world.

Role theory can be applied readily to the case of the blacks' assailants. Using this theoretical perspective, we could speculate that the assailants held rigid—and negative—role expectations regarding blacks, and that they interpreted the sight of a group of blacks riding through a white neighborhood as a threat to the neighborhood. In other words, the attackers may have assumed that the blacks occupied the role of "criminals," as opposed to their actual role of "workers" on their way home from a day on the job.

Another way of viewing the situation from the perspective of role theory is to consider the role that the assailants felt they were playing; perhaps they looked at themselves as upholders of social values they felt were being threatened by the blacks. Whatever the analysis employed, the critical point to be derived from role theory is that behavior is seen to be influenced by the role that is being occupied at a given time.

Which Theory Is Right? The Wrong Question

A question that may appear inevitable following the presentation of a group of theories such as these is "Which theory is right?" In fact, this is an inappropriate query. As can be seen from our discussion of each of the five major approaches, the theories focus on social behavior at different levels of analysis, making different assumptions about human nature, observing different sorts of variables, and varying in degree of specificity. It is unlikely that we will find that any one of these theories is "right" in the same way that we know that the equation $2 + 2 = 4$ is right.

Rather, certain social psychological phenomena are more or less amenable to study, and ultimately to understanding, using one or the other of the theoretical perspectives. Indeed, it is unlikely that any one of the orientations is sufficient, in and of itself, to explain all of human social behavior. People are so varied and multifaceted that a theory which only looks at, for instance, their rational, cognitive thought processes is apt to be less useful when we consider the times that these same people act impulsively, without any apparent thought.

For these reasons, then, it is unlikely that any of the major theoretical approaches will evolve into the broad, all-encompassing theory that guides all of social psychological research and thinking. Instead, social psychologists will continue to draw upon each of the perspectives, using whichever is most relevant to a given phenomenon. In fact, most research that is reported in the literature today is guided by narrower, better defined, and more restricted theories—which can be thought of as "middle-range theories"—than the broader theoretical conceptions we have discussed. Yet each of these middle-range theories grows out of one of the five broad theories, giving the theoretical orientations a continuing and fundamental impact upon the field of social psychology.

ANSWERING QUESTIONS: RESEARCH METHODS IN SOCIAL PSYCHOLOGY

If social psychology relied solely on the development of theory to explain phenomena of interest, it could make little legitimate claim to being considered a science. Armchair philosophizing—a derisive term sometimes used to describe theorists who do not test their formulations except in their own heads and in the comfort of their own armchairs—has little acceptance among contemporary social psychologists as a means of answering questions of interest. To the social psychologist, the only acceptable means is to do **empirical research,** in which ideas are tested through the use of systematic data collection and observation.

To illustrate the point, we might try a little armchair philosophizing of our own. Suppose you were interested in what factors affect whether people help others in emergency situations. You might theorize, on the

BOX 1-1 SPOTLIGHT ON RESEARCH

SOCIAL PSYCHOLOGY THROUGH THE YEARS

All psychologists are fond of saying that their field is a new one; and in the case of social psychologists, this statement is particularly true. Although the field can trace its roots to Plato and Aristotle, who reflected on the social nature of people, social psychology did not really emerge as a science until the very end of the nineteenth century. At that time, the first laboratory experiment was conducted by Norman Triplett (1897), who investigated how performance alone on a given task was inferior to performance when in the presence of others—a topic (called **social facilitation**) that is still of interest to social psychologists today.

Just eleven years later, the first two American textbooks were published that were devoted solely to social psychology (McDougall, 1908; Ross, 1908). Both books emphasized the instinctual nature of social behavior, a focus which was to mark the early years of the field. Fairly soon, however, social psychology began to broaden its horizons by studying the influence of external factors on the individual; and with the publication of Floyd Allport's *Social Psychology* in 1924, many of the current foci of the field were established. For example, there was a strong emphasis on findings derived from formal experiments and an interest in how the individual was affected by group membership.

The end of the 1920s marked a rapid expansion of the field which continued into the 1930s. Two figures are particularly noteworthy: Muzafer Sherif and Kurt Lewin. Sherif's work on the transmission of social norms portended important advances in the study of social influence (Sherif, 1935). Lewin, a German who fled the Nazis to America, is often referred to as the father of applied social psychology. He was one of the first to argue that the field should take an active, problem-solving approach by applying social psychological experimental techniques to social problems.

The field was strongly influenced by the advent of World War II, and in the 1940s and 1950s, there was an increasing orientation toward practical issues, including the study of prejudice, group behavior, propaganda, and attitude change. The end of the 1950s brought a turn toward more theoretical issues, with particular emphasis being placed on a theory proposed by Leon Festinger (1957) which concerned how people's cognitions (or thoughts) are affected by inconsistencies between behavior and cognitions. In larger terms, there was a shift in interest in the 1960s toward *intra*individual social processes and away from *inter*individual processes. This culminated in a great deal of work on **attribution**: the processes by which we make inferences regarding the causes of others' behavior. Attribution and, more generally, social cognition became the dominant themes of the 1970s.

As for the present, social psychologists are moving increasingly back toward a problem-solving orientation, with work in applied settings outside the laboratory becoming more and more prevalent. As you will see in this text, social psychology is having an increasing impact on areas that are related to everyone's lives—medical care, the law, business, arms negotiations, and many other important topics. Moreover, there is an increasing concern over the cultural determinants of behvior and of the individual in his or her natural surroundings. At the same time, theoretical research continues to be done, providing the building blocks of the science. Perhaps the most encouraging phenomenon of the mid-1980s is the fact that both purely theoretical *and* applied research are seen as part of the mainstream of social psychology (Rosemberg & Gara, 1983; Oskamp, 1984).

The presence of bystanders does not ensure that helping behavior will occur in emergency situations. In fact, this person in need of assistance might have been better off if just one person had been present, rather than two. (Danny Lyon/Magnum)

basis of your own logic, common sense, and general experience, that the more bystanders there are viewing an emergency situation, the more likely it would be that a victim would receive help.

Interestingly enough, however, as we shall see when we discuss helping behavior in Chapter 7, just the opposite is true: the more bystanders present in an emergency situation, the *less* likely it is that a victim will receive help. Only through carrying out expirical research could we have known this to be true. At the same time, we cannot jump into empirical research without a firm theoretical base. Research and theory are inextricably intertwined.

Although probably all social psychologists would agree that research ought to be related to theory on some level, the degree to which it is based on theory varies dramatically. Some research is motivated primarily by a desire to test a theoretical derivation; this work is called **pure, basic,** or simply **theoretical** research. Research of this type is done only with the intention of building support for a particular theoretical view, and without regard for the practical implications of the work. Thus, a social psychologist might try to build a theoretical model of how various elements of someone's behavior are combined by an observer into an overall impression; the application of the research findings to actual social problems is left to others. On the other hand, work may be more applied in nature. Such research is directed at answering a practical question about an immediate problem. Thus, research of this type might examine how teachers form impressions of students based upon their classroom behavior with the goal of helping to improve the quality

BOX 1-2   SPOTLIGHT ON RESEARCH AND THEORY

THEORETICAL VERSUS APPLIED RESEARCH: A FALSE DICHOTOMY?

Although the terms **theoretical research** and **applied research** imply two distinct kinds of research, this is not the case. Instead, the difference between the two types of work is not a qualitative one, but rather a matter of degree.

Pure theoretical work in social psychology is aimed at the building of a basic body of knowledge and facts about the social world. At the other end of a continuum lies purely applied research, which is meant to provide immediate solutions to immediate problems (Bickman, 1980 +). But even applied research has relevance to theory-building efforts, for results of even the most applied studies are invariably used not only for their immediate applications to the problem at hand but also for their implications for theory. Moreover, work in applied areas can illuminate where there are gaps in theoretical formulations.

Similarly, theory is useful in leading to solutions to applied problems which might otherwise be overlooked. Theories are ble to suggest new approaches and strategies for dealing with the problems facing society.

Basically, then, while the methods that are used may differ—with theoretical research typically conducted in laboratories using experiments and applied research occurring more often in natural field settings—both kinds of research are carried out with similar underlying goals in mind. Whether it is made explicit or not, social psychologists tend to have an underlying commitment to building knowledge, a concern regarding the quality of life, and an interest in how knowledge of social psychology is ultimately utilized and employed (Mayo & LaFrance, 1981). While the paths to these goals may differ, depending on the orientation of a particular social psychologist, the interaction between theory and research is an accepted one. As Kurt Lewin, one of the towering figures in social psychology, said more than forty years ago:

> Many psychologists working today in an applied field are keenly aware of the need for close cooperation between theoretical and applied psychology. This can be accomplished in psychology . . . if the theorist does not look toward applied problems with high-brow aversion or with a fear of social problems, and if the applied psychologist realizes that there is nothing so practical as a good theory.
>
> (Lewin, 1951, p. 169)

---

of teaching. The crucial difference between the two examples is the desire of the more theoretically oriented researcher to answer a broad, abstract question, while the more explicit underlying aim of the second researcher is to improve educational practice. However, as is argued in Box 1-2, the difference between theoretical and applied research sometimes may be more apparent than real.

DOING RESEARCH: ASKING THE RIGHT QUESTIONS GUIDED BY THEORY

All research begins with the formulation of a question. Under what circumstances do we conform to group pressure? How do we encourage helping behavior? What is the best negotiating strategy? Typically, one has a tentative answer to the question in the form of a hypothesis which, as we referred to earlier, is a prediction of a phenomenon that has not yet been observed. For example, we might hypothesize that conformity is related to the size of the group providing group pressure, that the presence of helpful others will encourage helping behavior, or that maintaining a tough opening stance facilitates negotiation outcome.

Hypotheses are derived from theories and, like good theories, must be testable. That hypotheses are drawn form theory is a critical feature. Without an underlying theory to guide us, we would not be much better off than the armchair philosopher. Theories give us a background and basis for producing reasonable hypotheses, hypotheses which can fit together with other known explanations of social phenomena. In this way we can build up a body of knowledge that allows us to determine which is the most valid explanation.

Of course, social psychologists develop hypotheses from other sources. They may have hunches and intuitions like anyone else. But without a valid theoretical underpinning, a hypothesis will do little in the way of explaining human behavior in a larger sense, and thus will not advance our understanding of social behavior very far. Equally important to the development of hypotheses is that they be testable. As is true of theories, a hypothesis that is untestable cannot be used to carry out research and therefore cannot be confirmed (or disconfirmed) in a scientific sense. Hence, it makes little sense to speculate on the number of angels who can fit on the head of a pin, given our inability to test such a hypothesis.

After a hypothesis is derived, a strategy must be devised to test its validity. There are two major classes of research from which to choose: experimental research and correlational research. We will discuss each, but it is important to note at the outset the major difference between them: Experimental research is aimed at discovering *causal* relationships between various factors, while correlational research studies whether there is an association or relationship between two factors— without determining whether one factor causes changes in the other.

As we shall discuss in detail below, experimental research is distinguished by the fact that the investigator intervenes in a setting and *manipulates* or changes some part of the situation in order to determine the effects of the manipulation. In doing so, the investigator is able to learn how the manipulation *causes* changes in the situation. In contrast, in ocrrelational research the investigator does not intervene and does not manipulate the setting; because of this, factors are left to vary naturally; therefore, causality cannot be determined from correlational studies.

In sum, experimental research tests whether changes in one factor *cause* changes in another factor; correlational research tests necessarily caused by, changes in a second factor. As we shall discuss, the difference is crucial.

Experimental Research

Let us start with the hypothesis that anonymity leads to an increase in verbal aggression. (In fact, as we shall see in Chapter 9, research has shown that anonymity *is* associated with increases in aggression.) One way to test such a hypothesis might be to imagine yourself at a costume party at which the host hands guests a mask as they walk through the door. By the end of the party, you measure the level of verbal aggression and find that it is high. "Aha," you say, "I have confirmed my hypothesis—anonymity makes people behave more verbally aggressive.

Would you be correct in making such an inference? Not at all. Consider all the alternative explanations for the aggression. Alcohol and drug use may have decreased people's restraint, the music was loud and increased arousal, the dancing increased people's energy level, and so on. The list literally is endless. Hence, the problem with this kind of research is that we have no way of knowing whether aggression is higher than in a group that is not anonymous. The only way we can know if the anonymity has caused the level of verbal aggression that we observe is to compare this group's reactions with those of some other group that is not anonymous—or is anonymous to a different degree.

To state this point in more abstract terms, experimental research requires that at least two groups be compared with one another. One group receives some kind of **treatment** (the procedure provided by an investigator) and the other receives no treatment (or, in some cases, a different form of treatment). The group receiving the treatment is known as—unsurprisingly—the **treatment group;** the no-treatment group is known as the **control group.** The differeing treatments that are given to the two groups are referred to as the two **conditions** of the experiment.

In technical terms, treatment and control groups differ in terms of the **independent variable,** which is the variable that is manipulated in the experiment by the researchers. (A **variable** is a factor or event that is capable of change and may take on two or more levels.) In our example, the degree of anonymity could be manipulated by giving masks to half the people at the party and not giving masks to the other half. On the other hand, the **dependent variable** is the variable which is measured in an experiment. In our example, the amount of verbal aggression would be the dependent variable. Researchers assume that the dependent variable will be affected by the manipulation of the independent variable.

Clearly, there are a number of different ways in which the independent and dependent variables can be conceptualized. The way that is chosen is known as the **operationalization** of the independent and dependent variables. Operationalization is the way in which the abstract concepts of the hypothesis are translated into the actual procedures that are used in the study. There is no one "correct" means of carrying out the operationalization; rather, logic and ethical constraints dictate which will be chosen.

For instance, we may operationalize "verbal aggression" as the number of insults a person gives at a party or analyze a person's conversation for aggressive imagery. Both methods are adequate, although they do tap into somewhat different aspects of what is meant by verbal aggression. The way in which a variable is operationalized is crucial in determining the kinds of conclusions that may be drawn from a study.

Assigning Subjects to Conditions: Random Assignment   The most critical feature of an experiment has to do with how we decide to assign subjects to experimental and control groups. Let's consider one way initially: Suppose we take the first half of the people who walk into the party and assign them to the experimental condition by giving them masks and then assign the second half to the control condition. If we later find that those who had worn masks differed in aggression from those who had not worn masks, are we justified in concluding that our hypothesis has been confirmed? No, because there is a good chance that those people assigned to the treatment group differed along some important dimensions from those who were assigned to the control group. For instance, the early arrivals may have been more assertive, and their apparent greater verbal aggression at its end was simply a reflection of this higher initial assertiveness. In sum, a better means of assignment of subjects to condition is necessary.

Fortunately, there is a better way: random assignment. Called by some "one of the greatest intellectual achievements of our time" (Kerlinger, 1973, p. 123), **random assignment** is a simple but elegant method in which subjects are assigned to condition so that each potential subject in an experiment has an equal chance of being assigned to any one of the experimental conditions. Instead of letting subjects select their condition or having the experimenter assign subjects based on some characteristic of the subject, the laws of probability are used to ensure that no subject characteristic is more or less likely to occur in one condition than in any other. Hence, if subjects in our example were assigned to a condition on the basis of a coin flip when they came to the party, both those of high and low motivation would be represented in approximately equal numbers in each condition, as would early guests and latecomers, guests who are intelligent and unintelligent, short and tall, and all of the infinite other characteristics on which the subjects could vary.

Through random assignment to conditions, it is possible to avoid **confounding** results. Confounding refers to instances in which factors other than the independent variable are allowed to vary. If this occurs, one cannot determine if changes in the dependent variable are due to the manipulation of the independent variable or to the other, confounding factors. Random assignment of subjects to experimental condition ensures that any potential confounding factors are distributed fairly equally across the various experimental conditions, allowing us to interpret results unequivocally. For example, if only males were assigned to one condition in an experiment and only females into another, we would not be able to make sense of the results: any differences would be due either to the experimental manipulation *or* to the sex of subject. One could never determine which was the source of variation in the dependent variable.

In practice, random assignment can be complicated by the fact that subjects in real-world settings may not be constrained to remain in a condition. Thus, in our example, subjects who are assigned to the mask experimental condition may, through their own actions, place themselves in the no-mask control condition by taking off their masks after their arrival.

In an instance of this phenomenon occurring in an actual experiment, a group of researchers tried to learn about the effects of watching *Sesame Street* on television by creating a treatment group that watched the program and a control group that did not. Although subjects were assigned to condition at random, it soon became apparent that many of the nonviewers became viewers during the course of the experiment— something that obviated the initial random assignment. Based on this experience, the researchers used a different strategy the following year: They went to locations in which a VHF adaptor or cable was needed to view *Sesame Street*, used a group of subjects who initially had neither, and gave half the subjects—chosen at random—an adaptor or cable. In this way they could be considerably more confident that the subjects would remain within the condition to which they were assigned (Conner, 1982).

Nonexperimental Techniques: Correlational Research

Many problems of interest to social psychologists cannot be investigated by using experimental methods. We cannot, for example, assign subjects to a condition in which we tell them that a close relative has died in order to study the effects of anxiety, or cut off a hand in one condition in order to study a subject's reaction to being handicapped. Ethical and moral restraints clearly prevent the manipulation of variables in cases such as these. In addition, some factors simply cannot be manipulated, no matter how much a researcher would like to manipulate them. An investigator interested in reactions of victims following an earthquake would be unlikely to find the means to cause an earthquake. (As we will discuss in Chapter 5, one correlational study examined just this issue after an earthquake in California.)

When it is impossible to control and manipulate variables of interest, experimental research cannot be carried out. However, there is a research technique that can be used—correlational research. As explained earlier, correlational research examines the relationship between two (or more) variables to determine whether they are associated or "correlated" (hence the word "correlational"). As illustrated in Figure 1-2, correlational research basically has three possible outcomes: (1) As values of one variable rise, values of the second variable rise. (2) As values of one variable rise, values of the second decline. (3) There is no relationship between the two variables. In the first case the association is one of positive correlation; in the second case it is a negative correlation; and in the third case the two variables would be uncorrelated or, put another way, the correlation is zero. Correlations are typically expressed as figures ranging from -1.00 to +1.00. The plus sign indicates a positive correlation and the minus sign a negative correlation. The closer a

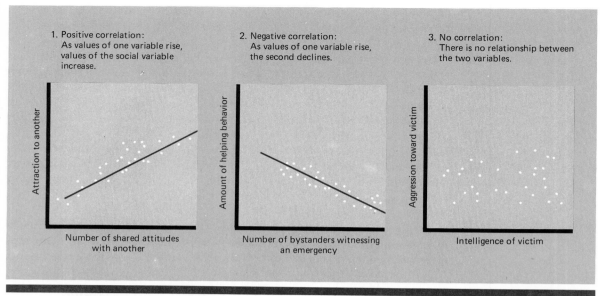

1. Positive correlation:
   As values of one variable rise, values of the social variable increase.

2. Negative correlation:
   As values of one variable rise, the second declines.

3. No correlation:
   There is no relationship between the two variables.

Attraction to another

Number of shared attitudes with another

Amount of helping behavior

Number of bystanders witnessing an emergency

Aggression toward victim

Intelligence of victim

FIGURE 1-2

Examples of correlational study outcomes. 1) Positive correlation: as values of one variable rise, values of the social variable increase; 2) Negative correlation: as values of one variable rise, values of the second decline; 3) No correlation: there is no relationship between the two variables.

correlation comes to positive or negative 1.00, the stronger the relationship between the two variables.

One of the most important points to be mastered in understanding the results of correlational, nonexperimental research is that finding a correlation between two variables does not in any way imply that the two are linked causally—only that they are associated with one another. It *may* be that one variable causes the changes in the other; but it is just as plausible that it does not. It is even possible that some third, unmeasured—and previously unconsidered—variable is causing both variables to increase or decrease simultaneously.

A concrete example can provide an illustration of the point that correlation does not imply causality. One of the important social issues that is continually studied by social psychologists is the possible relationship between television violence and viewer aggression. Because in most cases it is difficult to control adult viewers' television viewing habits—in a way that was possible to do in the *Sesame Street* example of experimental research we mentioned earlier—researchers by and large must carry out correlational studies, in which the aggressive content of television programs viewed by an individual is compared with the degree of aggressive behavior that person carries out.

The hypothesis generally being tested stipulates that there is a positive correlation between aggressive content of programs and aggressive behavior of viewers. Now suppose that the results are supportive of the hypothesis: that high aggressive content is associated with high viewer aggression and that low aggressive content is associated with low viewer aggression. While it would be tempting to conclude that the aggressive content *caused* the aggression, drawing such a conclusion would be inappropriate and quite possibly inaccurate.

Consider some alternative explanations shown in Figure 1-3. It is possible that people who exhibit high degrees of aggression prefer to watch shows which are high in aggressive content *because* of their own aggressive tendencies. It is just as possible that the third causal sequence illustrated is operative; an individual's socioeconomic status may cause both the choice of programs that are viewed *and* the level of aggression displayed. Using correlational techniques, we have no way of determining which, if any, of these possible sequences is correct.

It follows, then, that although the use of correlational techniques allows us to learn what associations exist between two variables, it does not inform us about causality. Moreover, experimental techniques allow greater control over variables; the experimenter can choose how to manipulate different levels of the independent variable, something that is not possible in correlational research, where variable values fluctuate without experimenter intervention. Given these limitations, experimental techniques—where they can be carried out—are generally the preferred means of doing research. Still, in instances in which experiments cannot be made, correlational research can provide valuable information.

Specific Research Techniques

We have described the differences between the two major classes of research—experimental and correlational. We now will consider some

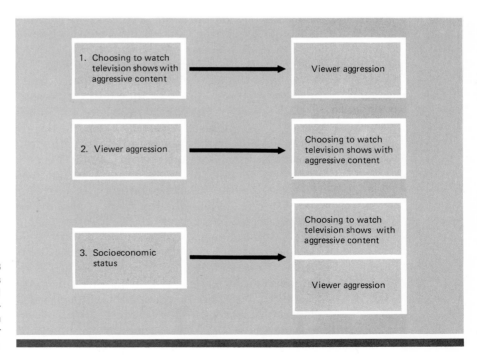

FIGURE 1-3
Possible causal paths found in a correlational study examining aggressive content of television shows and viewer aggression.

specific research techniques used by social psychologists, along with some of the advantages and disadvantages of each approach.

Laboratory and Field Experiments   One of the first decisions a researcher confronts when setting out to test a hypothesis using experimental methods is the choice of setting—the laboratory or the field. As the names imply, the essential difference between a laboratory and a field experiment rests on locale. The laboratory experiment takes place in a controlled environment where circumstances can be held constant down to the smallest detail, while field experiments take place in naturally occurring environments, such as the street, a bus, or a classroom— places where the experimenter has far less control over many aspects of the situation. For example, one set of investigators examining helping behavior used a New York City subway car to stage the collapse of a victim (Piliavin, 1973)—an environment over which the investigators had little influence, except for the behavior of the fake "victim."

Given that the field clearly is more amenable to occurrences over which the experimenter has no control and which, then, may interfere with the conclusions that can be drawn, it would seem that the laboratory would be the setting of choice, yet there are important drawbacks to laboratory experiments. Laboratory experiments can sometimes appear artificial and contrived to subjects. If this occurs, we have a problem with **generalization:** the ability to apply the results of a study to other settings and subject populations beyond those immediately employed in the experiment.

Laboratory experiments that are low in generalizability may produce findings that do not give us much information about social behavior in general. In such instances, unless we are interested in a social psychology of the laboratory, our findings will not be of much value to society. In addition, the knowledge that subjects have that they are participating in a study, which is inherent in laboratory experiments, is bound to have some effect upon the way subjects behave.

Still, the laboratory experiment remains the dominant technique for social psychologists. The reason is that the drawbacks can, to a large extent, be overcome through the use of a well-designed laboratory experiment. In a laboratory experiment, it is not necessary, or even appropriate, to recreate a situation exactly as it appears outside the laboratory in order to understand a naturally occurring phenomenon. Instead, a laboratory experiment attempts to isolate the component parts of a phenomenon in order to capture its essence.

Thus, laboratory experiments do not try to duplicate real-life circumstances; rather, they attempt to create a situation which captures subjects' attention and elicits behavior which is representative of the phenomenon in question. Events in a well-designed laboratory experiment can be controlled in a way that typically is impossible outside the laboratory; thus purer inferences about cause-and-effect relationships can be made. Of course, such purity sometimes must be bought at the expense of a somewhat lower degree of generalizability of the findings.

There is a constant trade-off between the advantages and disadvantages of laboratory versus field experiments. Neither one is inherently "better" than the other, and each individual experiment—whether it be a laboratory or a field experiment—must be evaluated on its own merits. Throughout this text, we will present findings from research that is carried out in both the laboratory and the field, using a variety of techniques. Where appropriate we will mention the limitations (and virtues!) of particular techniques. It is important to realize that even when such strengths and weaknesses are not explicitly spelled out, the kinds of issues that we have been discussing here are applicable.

Field Studies   Although it is a relatively straightforward procedure to control events experimentally in laboratory settings, field settings are often not amenable, for either practical or ethical reasons, to the kind of manipulation that is necessary to conduct a true experiment. Therefore, many studies done in field settings are correlational in nature and are generally known as "field studies." The essential difference between a field experiment and a field study is that the former includes appropriate control groups and experimental manipulation, allowing cause-and-effect relationships to be determined, whereas the field study is nonexperimental and generally a researcher does not intervene in the situation. (It should be pointed out that this sort of distinction also can be drawn in the laboratory: nonfield, laboratory work can be either correlational or—more typically—experimental.)

Field studies, because of their noninterventive nature, frequently employ observational methods in which the researcher intensively and carefully observes a set of individuals. Researchers doing such observation may either be **participant observers,** in which case they participate in the ongoing activities of the people being observed, or **nonparticipant observers,** in which case the observers record people's behavior but do not actually participate in their activities.

Participant observers are able to get close to the people being studied and may be in a better position to understand what is actually occurring in a field setting. For example, an investigator interested in studying friendship patterns in a college class might act as a participant observer, thereby learning firsthand the relationships among the students. On the other hand, an investigator may influence the activities of the people being studied, and the observed behavior may not be a reflection of what they would have done had the observer not been participating in their activities. Moreover, both participant and nonparticipant observers can evoke **reactive** behavior on the part of those being observed, and the behavior that is observed may reflect the influence of the observer being in a study. Although typically if a researcher observes over long enough periods, subjects' reactions to being observed decline to where they are no longer a threat to the validity of the observations, they can be a serious problem in short-term observational studies.

It should be noted that although research done in the field is most frequently correlational and research done in the laboratory is typically experimental, this need not always hold true. As we mentioned earlier, the essential distinction between experimental and nonexperimental research is whether the experimenter intervenes in a situation and manipulates an independent variable—not where it is done. Experimental research can be carried out in either the laboratory or the field—and correlational research can be done in either place as well.

Survey Research   One of the most direct ways of determining how people feel and think about a topic is simply to ask them. To do this in a formal way, social psychologists conduct **survey research.** In survey research, a group of people—respondents—are asked a series of questions regarding their behavior, attitudes, or beliefs. If the researcher has sampled respondents carefully, according to the laws of probability, the results can be generalized beyond the sample to the larger population of which the respondents are members. Thus, in order to learn about attitudes regarding the use of marijuana, we might sample a certain percentage of all students enrolled in college and use the results of the sample survey to infer the attitudes of the college population as a whole. If we are unable to draw a representative sample, however, our conclusions will be biased.

Although survey research methods seem to be a sensible method for learning about people's behaviors and attitudes, data obtained from surveys cannot always be taken at face value. For one thing, people do not always respond accurately. They may not remember past behavior adequately; they may not want to reveal something about themselves; or they may not even know how they feel and answer glibly, without considering the question fully. Because people may try to present themselves well, their answers may be dishonest. The great drawback to survey research, then, is that the research does not directly observe behaviors in question but instead relies on the accuracy of the response.

Evaluation Research   Governments spend literally billions of dollars annually on programs designed to do everything from getting people to stop smoking to conserving energy. How effective are such programs? The method that is typically used to find out is evaluation research, an important applied research technique in the repertoire of social psychologists. The basic purpose of evaluation research are to understand the effects of a program to determine whether the program is meeting its goals and to contribute information to facilitate improvement of the program in the future.

One good example of an evaluation study was a truly massive experiment called Project Follow-Through, which was designed to study children from disadvantaged backgrounds who had been involved in an innovative program aimed at helping their school performance. The study took more than eleven years to complete, had a budget of more than $100 million, and involved literally thousands of students. Among the variables evaluated were the nature of the physical environment in schools, student grouping arrangements (e.g., large- versus small-group teaching), and the nature of the interactions that occurred between adults and children. The results of the evaluation were so complex, as you might expect in a study this size, that the findings remain controversial today, with some interpreters of the data feeling that the program was effective and others viewing it as a failure.

The difficulty in interpreting evaluation results is not unique to Project Follow-Through. Because of the complexity of nonlaboratory situations, contradictory evidence regarding a program's effectiveness is often collected. In addition, social programs typically reflect a particular philosophy or political orientation. This means that it is not possible to conduct a "pure" evaluation; rather, political pressures must be taken into account. Finally, programs often have a set of advocates in the form of administrators who stand to lose their jobs if a negative evaluation is produced. Such program personnel are likely to resist any radical suggestions for program improvement that might be made. Although these very tangible real-world pressures can make the program evaluator's job a difficult one, program evaluation is an activity in which social psychologists increasingly are becoming involved.

Archival Research: Neither the Laboratory nor the Field   One kind of research, in which the researcher avoids both there laboratory *and* the field, is **archival research.** In archival research, existing records or documents are analyzed in an attempt to confirm a hypothesis. For example, if we hypothesized that the phases of the moon are related to criminal activity, we might consult the *Farmer's Almanac* for a five-year period to document when changes in the moon's phases occurred and then look at daily crime statistics printed in newspapers for the same period. By using preexisting records, we might be able to confirm our hypothesis.

Archival research has the advantage of being completely nonreactive; subjects do not know that they are bing observed, and their behavior will be uninfluenced by that fact. Even more important, hypotheses can be tested that span vast periods of time and history. Hence, the validity of principles derived from "here and now" data collection techniques such as experiments and observational studies can be confirmed in other contexts. However, there are disadvantages to archival techniuqes. Sometimes the data needed to confirm a hypothesis simply do not exist or are not available. When such data are available, the sheer mass may be so great that it is hard to tell what is and is not important. Moreover, the researcher is at the mercy of the original collectors of the material— if they have done a poor job, the results of further research will be inconclusive at best, and misleading at worst.

ON THE SOCIAL PSYCHOLOGY OF RESEARCH: THREATS TO THE VALIDITY OF EXPERIMENTATION

For most of this chapter, we have been discussing research as if subjects were fairly passive responders to stimuli, reacting to events in experiments without much awareness or concern that they are, in fact, participating in an experiment. Nothing could be further from the truth. If you have been in an experiment, you know the kinds of questions that typically run through subjects' heads: What is happening? What does this mean? Why am I being told this? What is the experimenter trying to prove? In the attempt to answer questions such as these, the subject may pose some serious threats to the validity of any findings the experiment produces.

Demand Characteristics: Sizing Up the Situation

If a person came up to you on the street and asked you to answer twenty pages of addition problems, you would probably refuse. But if an experimenter asked you to do the same thing, you might be considerably more likely to accede to the request. The reason? You would probably be imputing some meaning to what the experimenter was asking, as well as acquiescing to the experimenter's authority and supposed expertise as a representative of science.

Indeed, this is a general response of subjects; they come up with guesses and interpretations about what the experimenter is looking for. Worse yet—in terms of the validity of the results—they may act upon their interpretations. They may try to "help" experimenters by conforming to their guess of the hypothesis or—if so inclined—they may try to disprove the hypothesis. In either case, their behavior may not be a pure response to the experimenter's manipulation, but can be confounded by what the subjects think is expected of them.

The term **demand characteristics** refers to the cues that subjects use in an experiment that provide information regarding what is expected or appropriate behavior (Carlsmith, Ellsworth, & Aronson, 1976). They may be the location of the experimental laboratory, the demeanor of the experimenter, the kind of equipment involved in the study. Any of these factors—and others as well—might be sufficient to trigger the development of a hypothesis on the part of subjects, leading them to determine what kinds of behavior are appropriate in the experiment.

There are a number of ways of dealing with demand characteristics. One of the best is to provide subjects with a cover story that contains a false hypothesis about the true purpose of the experiment. If subjects then attempt to change their behavior in order to support (or refute) this fake hypothesis, their change in behavior is not likely to affect their responses to the hypothesis and experimental manipulations of actual interest. In many cases, social psychologists employ elaborate deceptive scenarios in experiments designed to mislead subjects about the true purpose of the experiment. Not only is the hypothesis concealed, but confederates—employees or colleagues of the experimenter who pose as subjects—may be used to produce a scene which is involving to subjects. (See Box 1-3 for a discussion of the ethical and methodological problems that arise with the use of deception.)

BOX 1-3 SPOTLIGHT ON METHODOLOGY

ON DECEPTION AND ETHICS

There is something inherently contradictory about a discipline that calls itself a science—which implies an open and public quest for knowledge—and yet uses deception as a major research tool, yet social psychologists continue to employ deception on a large scale. This technique is the source of a continual debate within the field.

Why is deception so prevalent? Most researchers argue that in many cases it is necessary to disguise the key elements of a study in order to avoid having subjects' behavior influenced by what they think is the study's true purpose. As we have discussed, subjects impute meaning to experimental procedures, and they may attempt to "help out" the experimenter after they decide what he or she is really after. If this is the case, the behavior we see in experiments is not necessarily a valid representation of real-life behavior; rather, it is an indication of how subjects feel they *ought* to behave. Hence, investigators have turned to deception in an attempt to produce more valid research findings.

Deception appears in many forms (Geller, 1981). **Implicit deception** occurs when the actual situation is so different from what the subjects expect that they behave under incorrect assumptions. In the most extreme cases, subjects do not even know that they are in an experiment when in reality they are. **Technical deception** occurs when the equipment and procedures of an experiment are misrepresented. Typically, this occurs when subjects are given a cover story about the purpose of the experiment when the real purpose is, in fact, very different. Finally, **role deception** occurs when other people in a study are misrepresented. Hence, another subject may actually be a confederate of the experimenter, or the experimenter may pose as a fellow student in a classroom.

Deception raises a number of ethical dilemmas, including the following issues (Cook, 1976):

- Should people be studied without their knowledge?
- Should the true purpose of experiments be revealed to subjects?
- Should research procedures place people under stress?
- Should subjects be actively deceived?
- Should researchers induce subjects to behave in a way that they otherwise would be unlikely to do?

Each of these issues is complicated, and the answers are not readily apparent (Rosenthal & Rosnow, 1984). The basic dilemma concerns the rights of the individual (the subject) versus the rights of society (the presumed ultimate beneficiary of the knowledge derived from social psychological research). To deal with these questions, the American Psychological Association developed a set of guidelines in 1981. These ethical principles suggest that subjects be told enough about the experiment to give their **informed consent**—agreement to proceed as subjects after the possible risks and benefits have been fully disclosed and explained. Moreover, the principles state that deception should be used only if no other techniques are available; subjects should not be harmed or placed in discomfort; a full debriefing following the study should be done; and the benefits of participation should outweigh the risks for people who act as subjects. Institutions in which research is carried out have review boards, composed of professionals not involved in the research, who evaluate the methods employed to ensure the ethical conduct of experimentation.

In sum, there is no simple solution to the problems raised by the use of deception. Until social psychologists have devised new methodologies—such as the use of role-playing subjects or nonintervtive field studies—deception will remain an important and basic tool of the field.

Other techniques for combating demand characteristics include disguising the dependent measures and, even more extreme, preventing subjects from even knowing that they are in an experiment. It is also possible to separate the measuring of the dependent variable from the experimental setting, thus disguising its connection to the experiment.

Experimenter Effects and the Danger of the Self-fulfilling Prophecy

Experimenters play an active role in the administration of experimental procedures. Therefore, their behavior, personal qualities, and expectations can have an effect upon how subjects behave. This is not a problem if experimenters treat all subjects similarly; experimenter effects will then exert roughly the same influence on all subjects. It *is* a problem if experimenter behavior and characteristics affect certain subjects in one way and others in a different way. If an experimenter treated attractive subjects one way and unattractive subjects a different way, the outcome of the experiment clearly could be affected.

Even more threatening to the validity of an experiment is what occurs when an experimenter sends out unintentional cues to subjects indicating the way in which they are to behave in a given condition. This phenomenon, known as the **experimenter expectancy effect,** acts as a type of self-fulfilling prophecy (Rosenthal & Rosnow, 1975). In such instances, the expectations of the experimenter about what is appropriate behavior are transmitted to the subjects and may actually bring about the expected behavior. For example, an experimenter who hopes subjects in one condition will be aggressive and in another passive may act in a way that evokes aggression from the subjects in the first condition and evokes passivity in the second. The experimenter may not be aware of his or her behavior, but the expectations may be communicated inadvertently from the kinds of things the experimenter says and does.

There are a number of ways in which experimenter effects can be reduced. The most obvious technique is to keep the people who carry out the experiment "blind" as to the experimental hypotheses that the social psychologist is testing. In this way, experimenters will be ignorant of what it is that they otherwise might communicate to subjects. An even more satisfactory solution is to keep experimenters blind to the *condition* in which a subject is being run, if the experimental procedure allows for this possibility. Finally, using tape-recorded instructions and other mechanical instruments to run an experiment, thereby eliminating the need for a human experimenter, is the ultimate remedy for experimenter effects. However, usually such a procedure is not practical.

FUTURE CHALLENGES TO SOCIAL PSYCHOLOGY

Despite the threats to the validity of experimentation that we have been discussing, most social psychologists hold an optimistic view regarding

In any social situation, we use the behavior of others as a guide to what is expected of us and the kinds of things we should do and say. (Sepp Seitz/ Woodfin Camp)

the future of the field and the value of research. Indeed, these "threats" typically are viewed as *challenges* that confront social psychology—challenges that to a large extent have been met successfully.

As we shall see in successive chapters, there is a wealth of valid, reliable knowledge that has been amassed in literally thousands of studies by investigators in the field of social psychology. This knowledge, both theoretical and applied, has the potential for addressing some of the most pressing problems that people face on both a personal and a societal level. Although the field has its limits—as is true for any growing young science—social psychology has begun to realize its potential for making significant contributions to many people's lives and to society as it evolves into a mature, "middle-aged" science.

A FEW COMMENTS ON THIS BOOK

Having read this introductory chapter, you are now ready to proceed to the body of the text. Before doing so, though, it seems appropriate for me to say a few words about the way in which the book is put together. The overall philosophy behind this text is that social psychology represents a dynamic, growing, constantly changing scientific discipline which has substantial relevance to everyday life. I have tried to capture this dynamism throughout the book by integrating in a balanced fashion the most current theory, research, and applications—following my earlier point that theory and applications are inextricably bound together.

The text includes traditional, core topics on which work has been done for years, but it also features topical areas that represent new directions to which social psychologists are turning—as, for example, in the chapters on communication, health, organizations and the workplace, and justice and the law. The field of social psychology is moving at a rapid pace toward an increasing emphasis and concern with applications, and this book reflects this trend. At the same time, theoretical innovations of import have not been sacrificed; advances in theory are detailed throughout the text. The result is a balanced view of the field of social psychology as it exists in the mid-1980s.

To emphasize the relevance of social psychology to people's everyday activities and the interface between theory and applications, each chapter begins with an interview with someone whose professional activities and accomplishments are directly tied to the content of the chapter. Most of these people are *not* social psychologists, but rather representatives of fields which are of relevance to social psychological research and theorizing. Some of the people I spoke to are well known (attorney Archibald Cox, former U.S. representative Shirley Chisholm, and Penn State football coach Joe Paterno), while others simply represent people whose everyday life has the potential for being affected and enhanced by the work being done by social psychologists.

Each chapter also includes a number of Spotlights, which are inserted boxes of four types: Spotlight on Theory, Spotlight on Applications, Spotlight on Methodology, and Spotlight on Research. Each Spotlight highlights a topic of particular interest and relevance or presents an alternate point of view from mainstream thinking on an issue. In addition, to clarify further the relationship between the subject matter of social psychology and everyday life, many of the chapters include explicit suggestions and techniques for improving the human social condition and solving social problems.

To cite a few examples, the chapter on helping includes ways of increasing prosocial behavior, the discussion of prejudice suggests means for reducing discrimination, and the chapter on the environment includes features that architects can employ to enhance the enjoyment of buildings they design. Moreover, each chapter concludes with a list of annotated references—directed toward both theoretical and applied topics—that will allow further investigation of areas of interest.

This book is designed to make the relevance of the field of social psychology apparent to the reader. The issues that social psychologists investigate—whether done from the vantage point of the laboratory or the field or from a theoretical or applied perspective—have the potential for improving all of our lives.

SUMMARY

Social psychology is the discipline that examines how a person's thoughts, feelings, and actions are affected by others. The field encompasses three major levels of analysis: individual processes affected by social factors, interactive processes between two or more people, and the study of social entities such as groups and organizations.

Social psychology is a science, and as such it seeks to predict, control, and understand social behavior. This process is guided by the development of theories—interrelated sets of hypotheses about a phenomenon. Hypotheses are predictions about phenomena that have not yet been observed. Good theories are internally consistent, agree with existing facts, and must be testable.

There are five major theoretical orientations which guide social psychological work. Genetic theories suggest that social behavior has its roots in biologically determined causes. Sociobiology, a major outgrowth of genetic theories, suggests that through an evolutionary process of natural selection, social behaviors have evolved that provide humans with certain advantages. However, most social psychologists agree that social behavior is not fixed and predetermined by instincts. Learning approaches emphasize environmental causes of behavior by analyzing social behavior in terms of learned associations between stimuli and responses. Work on social exchange and imitation which is based on learning theories has had an important impact on the field.

Cognitive theories are based on a phenomenological approach, investigating how a person subjectively experiences the world. Cognitive theories have led to work on attribution (how observers determine the causes of behavior) and social cognition (the way in which people think about and understand their social world).

Psychoanalytic theory, based on Freud's theory, posits that adult behavior reflects childhood experiences. The theory suggests that social behavior should be examined in terms of unconscious processes—a fact which makes it difficult to produce scientific evidence in support of the theory. Role theory, on the other hand, pays considerably more attention to the social environment. It predicts that behavior is shaped by the roles that society provides for individuals to play.

To determine which theoretical formulation provides us with the best understanding of a phenomenon, social psychologists carry out empirical research, in which ideas are tested through the use of systematic data collection and observation. Research begins with a hypothesis which is derived from theory and is testable.

In experimental research, causal relationships between two variables can be ascertained, while in correlational research, the association between two factors is determined. Experimental research includes at least two conditions: a treatment group and a control group. In an experiment, the independent variable is the variable that is manipulated, while the dependent variable is the variable that is measured.

Experiments vary in their operationalization, the way in which the abstract concepts of the hypothesis are translated into the actual procedures that are used in the study. Random assignment helps ensure that subjects are assigned to a condition without specific characteristics being overrepresented in that particular condition. In contrast, correlational research examines the relationship between two variables to determine whether they are associated. Even if variables are correlated, it is not necessarily true that the two are linked causally.

Laboratory and field experiments employ experimental methods in which subjects are assigned to condition randomly. The difference between the two is in the location, with laboratory research taking place in a controlled laboratory environment and field experiments occurring in natural settings. Field studies occur outside the laboratory and are correlational in nature. They are noninterventive, and frequently use participant or nonparticipant observation. In survey research, respondents are asked a series of questions regarding their behavior, attitudes, or beliefs. In evaluation research, programs designed to solve a social problem are studied to determine whether the programs are meeting their intended goals, as well as to facilitate the improvement of the programs. Archival research analyzes existing records or documents to confirm a hypothesis.

Among the threats to the validity of experiments are demand characteristics and experimenter expectancy effects. Demand characteristics are cues that subjects use in an experiment that provide information regarding what is expected or appropriate behavior. Experimenter effects occur when an experimenter transmits unintentional cues to subjects indicating the way in which they are to behave under a given

condition. Despite these threats to the validity of experimentation, however, social psychology has begun to realize its potential for making
significant contributions to society.

KEY TERMS

archival research
attribution theory
causality
classical conditioning
cognitive theory
confederate
confound
control group
correlational research
debriefing
deception
demand characteristics
dependent variable
empirical research
experimental research
experimenter expectancy effect
field experiment
field study
generalization
genetic theories

hypothesis
implicit deception
impression management
independent variable
informed consent
nonparticipant observation
operant conditioning
operationalization
participant observation
random assignment
role deception
role theory
social cognition
social exchange
social facilitation
social psychology
sociobiology
survey research
technical deception
treatment group

FOR FURTHER STUDY AND APPLICATION

Shaw, M. E., & Costanzo, P. R. (1982). *Theories of social psychology* (2nd ed.). New York: McGraw-Hill.

Deutsch, M., & Krauss, R. M. (1965). *Theories in social psychology.* New York: Basic Books.

Each of these books presents a detailed description of the major theories of social psychology. Although the Deutsch and Krauss book is somewhat outmoded, it has become a classic integration and overview of the field.

Allport, G. W. (1968). The historical background of modern social psychology. In G. Lindzey and E. Aronson (Eds.), *Handbook of social psychology* (2nd ed.). Reading, MA: Addison-Wesley.

The definitive history of the field of social psychology up to the point at which it was written. Very scholarly and detailed, it traces the scientific and philosophical roots of the field.

Bickman, L. (Ed.). (1980+). *Applied social psychology annual.* Beverly Hills, CA: Sage.

A continuing series of volumes, these books contain insightful and entertaining chapters on the progress and pitfalls of a series of applied research programs. They provide a better flavor for how research is really done than most articles.

Carlsmith, J. M., Ellsworth, P. C., & Aronson, E. (1976). *Methods of research in social psychology.* Reading, MA: Addison-Wesley.

A well-written, thoughtful account of how to do research in social psychology. Although the emphasis is clearly on traditional, laboratory experiments, it is written by masters of that genre.

Rossi, P. H., Freeman, H. E., & Wright, S. R.

(1979). *Evaluation: A systematic approach.* Beverly Hills, CA: Sage.

A primer on carrying out evaluation studies, this volume is also useful in terms of doing field research outside the laboratory.

Oskamp, S. (1984). *Applied social psychology.* Englewood Cliffs, NJ: Prentice-Hall.

A current and comprehensive overview of applied social psychology, replete with literally hundreds of applications. Also provides a cogent philosophical overview of the field and how it fits in with more traditional, theoretical social psychology.

PART TWO

DEFINING, UNDERSTANDING, AND EVALUATING THE SOCIAL WORLD

CHAPTER 2

PERSON PERCEPTION, SOCIAL COGNITION, AND ATTRIBUTION: UNDERSTANDING AND JUDGING OURSELVES AND OTHERS

A CONVERSATION WITH . . .

Barry Serafin
ABC News
Investigative Reporter

A national correspondent for ABC News, Barry Serafin is a veteran reporter. He has covered such major stories as the Iranian hostage crisis and the war between Great Britain and Argentina over the Falkland Islands. He was also ABC's principal correspondent assigned to cover the 1980 presidential campaign of Ronald Reagan. In this capacity, he came to know Reagan and his family well.

We spoke in Serafin's memento-filled office in Washington, D.C. The purpose of the conversation was to illustrate that many of the issues he deals with on a day-to-day basis in his professional life are questions of concern to social psychologists, who are currently investigating them through both laboratory and field studies. The discussion focused on identifying how he deals with understanding what other people are like and what the reasons are behind the actions they have taken—issues which are at the heart of investigative reporting. We began by discussing President Reagan, whom Serafin has covered extensively.

Q. Probably the most salient characteristic of President Reagan is the way in which he presents himself—as a warm, sincere, open, and friendly individual. Because of your experience on the campaign trail where you watched him day after day, you probably know him better than most other reporters. How do you get beyond the nice-guy image?

A. That is not an image. He *is* a nice guy. I don't think that he has much true meanness in him. I think that through the kind of life he has led he has been isolated from some things. He really has lived a good life almost all of his adult years. I think there are some things he is just not aware of—in terms of poverty, in terms of peo-

ple feeling desperate in their lives.

Q. As a reporter, how do you know what he is really like? Is there a general strategy you used to learn what to attribute people's behavior to? In other words, how do you move beyond surface behavior to understand the causes underlying what people do and say?

A. Every situation is different. Obviously, if I'm interviewing a housewife I assume that she's going to tell me pretty much what she feels. On the other hand, if I'm interviewing a senator or a corporate vice president for public relations or somebody in the State Department, I tend to be a little more cynical. People in public life, or people with a job in the government with a project or budget or policy to protect, obviously want to put the best face on what they are doing. In that kind of situation you go in as well prepared as you can in terms of research. Very often it means asking exactly the same question three, four, five times in a row. For example, I might say, "I'm sorry, senator, that really isn't what I was asking. What I really want to know is. . . ." I don't think there is any secret to it. It is just a matter of trying to listen carefully and gauging what you are hearing against what you know from other sources.

Q. So you examine people's consistency over time, as well as what you know about their behavior from others in order to make a closer approximation to what their underlying dispositions are.

A. Right—absolutely.

Q. There must be some political figures with whom you have become very friendly as you have covered them over the years. Is it difficult to maintain your objectivity when writing about these people?

A. That really is hard—and perhaps

44

PERSON PERCEPTION,
SOCIAL COGNITION, AND
ATTRIBUTION:
UNDERSTANDING AND
JUDGING OURSELVES AND
OTHERS

hardest in the context of a campaign. I have covered several political figures in the sense of being on the plane week after week, month after month, with the candidate and his staff and the press. You cannot be at close quarters over a period of months and avoid either coming to like somebody or to dislike him or her. Either way you face a terrible problem. You almost have to force yourself to step back at arm's length and keep a professional distance and try to be as fair as you can. If they stumble, you've got to report that they're stumbling whether you like them personally or not. If they're not stating facts, if they are distorting records, outright lying, pulling cheap shots—all of the things that politicians are capable of doing at times—you've got to be able to say that. On the other hand, if it's somebody that you really dislike personally but he's out there wowing them, doing a good job, and being fair, moderate, accurate, and all of those things, then you've got to have the professional ability to report that as well.

Q. My perception of the news media is that they sometimes produce their own self-fulfilling prophecies: that by their very coverage of an event, they make a story out of something that may not have otherwise amounted to very much. I'm thinking specifically about the early days of a presidential campaign, where the press treats even the smallest straw polls in obscure states as something very meaningful. By reporting the results, don't the media sometimes inordinately emphasize the candidacies of the winners of such polls, thereby helping to bring about the success of a particular candidate?

A. There are some events we cannot avoid reporting because they happen. If things happen, you've got to report them whether you think they're important or not. What you can do in

your reporting is try to keep things in perspective. But take the New Hampshire primary. In this small state, with just a tiny fraction of voters and a demographic background that is completely unrepresentative of the rest of the nation, we have an army of press corps and candidates who invade it every election year. It's outrageous, and yet we do it because it's happening and because it's one of the first tests and because the candidates themselves take it seriously. It *is* an example of a self-fulfilling prophecy, but not just on the part of the media.

Q. I've sometimes had the feeling that the media—and television in particular—are especially susceptible to consistently portraying people in either a very positive *or* a very negative light. Do you find this to be the case?

A. It may be. Television, particularly, has some severe time limitations. You are talking typically about a half hour of newscast. When you subtract commercials and station time, you have twenty-two minutes left. There's not much time to be sophisticated in your portrayals of people. On the other hand, I really do believe that the television medium consciously tries to be fair. For example, I was in Iran during the hostage crisis. It was a fascinating story. On any given night, we probably didn't get at what was really happening there, what was motivating the people, what people really felt about it, why it was going on—because of the time limitations. But over a period of time, I have a theory that we deposited an accumulation of knowledge with our audience. By the end of it, the audience had some feeling for why the Iranians behaved in the way they did, why they felt so passionately about the shah and the United States. We were able to get behind the overt behavior of the Iranians and present the reasons and motivations behind behavior that was so foreign to us.

OVERVIEW

As was touched upon in the interview with Barry Serafin, one of a reporter's most important tasks is to go beyond the surface appearance and behavior of people in order to understand the reasons for their actions. However, such activities are not limited to journalists; all of us constantly try to make sense of other people and their behaviors. We are not content to rely on surface descriptions of what people are like to arrive at an understanding of their behavior; rather, we look beneath appearances to explain the reasons behind their actions.

The way in which people come to an understanding of both others and themselves has become a major focus of study for social psychologists. The topic is critical for an understanding of social behavior, because how people process information and make judgments of others and how they explain the causes of behavior have an important influence on their own behavior. Moreover, as you will see in this chapter, social psychologists have found that learning how people understand their own and others' behavior provides a clear basis for solving a variety of everyday problems, ranging from insomnia to poor school performance.

In this chapter, we will first discuss person perception and social cognition: how people make sense of information they have about an individual to form an overall impression, and how that information is stored and organized in memory. Next, we will discuss attribution theory, which encompasses how people explain the causes of both their own and others' behavior. Finally, we will discuss the ways in which people act upon the impressions and attributions they have developed. By the end of the chapter, it should be clear what Fritz Heider (1958), a pioneering theoretician in this area, meant when he said that most people go through life behaving as if they were "naive psychologists."

PERSON PERCEPTION AND SOCIAL COGNITION: MAKING SENSE OF OTHERS

As Matt entered the classroom where his social psychology course was to meet this term and waited for the instructor to walk in, his thoughts centered upon the kind of person the instructor would be. Would this Mr. Andrews, about whom no one seemed to know very much (Matt had checked around), be a good teacher, genuinely interested in the students and the subject matter? Would he be strict, harsh, and unduly demanding or a person Matt would want to get to know? Eventually, Mr. Andrews came into the classroom. Matt scrutinized and classified his mannerisms, style of dress, age, sex, and race. He formed an initial impression just on these surface characteristics, but he tried to suspend judgment until he heard what Mr. Andrews had to say. Only then did he begin to formulate a firm judgment about what kind of person Andrews was.

PERSON PERCEPTION,
SOCIAL COGNITION, AND
ATTRIBUTION:
UNDERSTANDING AND
JUDGING OURSELVES AND
OTHERS

We tend to form an impression of others on the basis of limited information. Haven't you already formed an opinion about this person? (Timothy Eagan)

As the term wore on, Matt's impressions became more and more concrete and he began to feel confident that his assessments—which actually were pretty close to his first impression—were valid.

The situation described above happens over and over, not just in classroom settings, but in every sphere of our lives. We are constantly making judgments about what others are like, what personality traits best characterize them, and what motivates their behavior. We can begin our discussion of the processes underlying these judgments—known as person perception and social cognition—by considering the research on how people form initial impressions.

An early experiment on perceiving others actually used a scenario quite similar to the one described above. In the study, Harold Kelley (1950) gave a group of students one of two descriptions of a lecturer whom they had never met, and then had the lecturer lead a discussion. In one case, students were told that the lecturer was "a rather warm person, industrious, critical, practical, and determined." But in a second condition, a group of students was told that the same lecturer was "a rather cold person, industrious, critical, practical, and determined." The crucial difference, of course, was the substitution of the word "cold" for "warm" in the second description. You may be surprised to learn that the substitution made a drastic change in the way the lecturer was viewed in the two conditions. Students who were told that the lecturer was cold rated him far less positively after the discussion than those who were told that he was warm, although the behavior of the lecturer was invariant across the two conditions.

The Kelley experiment, now considered a classic, illustrates an early view of person perception, which concentrated on the way in which individuals focus on particular traits when forming overall impressions of others. According to this perspective, certain traits—known as **central traits**—play an unusually large role in determining a general impression (Watkins & Peynircioğlu, 1984). Central traits serve to organize the impression and provide a framework for interpreting information that is received subsequently. In fact, Solomon Asch (1946), who first conceived of the notion of central traits, suggested that the meaning of additional descriptive traits is altered by the presence of a central trait. Thus, the word "determined" when describing an individual means something very different, depending upon whether it is preceded by the word "warm" or "cold."

Cognitive Algebra: Adding (or Averaging) the Good and Bad

Subsequent work on impression formation has suggested more precise models for the way in which different personality traits are combined. Based upon information processing approaches to human cognitive processes which emphasize how data are considered and combined, these models have as a starting point the notion that mathematical models can be derived which are able to predict how separate bits of information—in the form of individual traits—can be combined into an overall impression.

At least two different models have been proposed: **additive** and **averaging.** The **additive model** (Anderson, 1965) suggests that we simply add together the bits of information we have about a person to form a judgment. For example, if we learn that a new acquaintance is adventurous, bold, and caring, we simply assign each one a value—on some hypothetical scale—and add them together. If, for instance, one rates adventurousness as 4, boldness as 5, and caring as 9 (on an 11-point scale), the overall impression can be expressed in mathematical terms as $4 + 5 + 9 = 18$. Of course, a consequence of such a model is that the inclusion of more positive traits on a list will lead to a more positive impression.

The **averaging model** (Anderson, 1974), on the other hand, suggests that although we start in the same way, there is an additional step in which we divide by the number of traits to form an average. Hence, we get $(4 + 5 + 9) \div 3 = 18 \div 3 = 6$. What is particularly important about his model is that the inclusion of additional information does not necessarily make the impression more positive; rather, it depends on the nature of the new traits. Hence, if we learn that the person is also neat and we scale neat as a 2, the overall impression drops: $(4 + 5 + 9 + 2) \div 4 = 5$. In contrast, a model employing addition would suggest that the additional information would result in a more positive impression.

49

PERSON PERCEPTION,
SOCIAL COGNITION, AND
ATTRIBUTION:
UNDERSTANDING AND
JUDGING OURSELVES AND
OTHERS

Which model—additive or averaging—is most accurate in predicting the nature of impressions that people form? Critical tests of the two models, directly comparing experimental outcomes with model predictions, have shown that averaging provides more accurate predictions—but some additional information is required to explain the process more fully (Kaplan, 1975). It turns out that the greatest accuracy in predicting an individual's impression comes when we weight the average to take into account both the importance of each piece of information and whether the information is positive or negative. The importance of the information refers generally to the source of the information: for instance, whether it comes from a high- or low-status person or a credible or unreliable source. Moreover, negative information is sometimes weighted more heavily than positive information (Kanouse & Hanson, 1972).

In sum, most evidence suggests that people use a weighted averaging model to combine trait information, although the process is a complex one. Indeed, there are serious methodological issues that can be raised concerning the applicability of research on cognitive algebra to nonlaboratory situations. The central issue concerns the degree of representativeness to situations outside the laboratory of an experimental method in which people are restricted to a small, finite set of traits when evaluating another person. Such an experimental paradigm tends to deemphasize the richness of actual social interaction, in which observers must infer traits on their own and are not limited to any specific set of traits. Despite such limitations, however, research on impression formation has provided important insights into how information about people is processed and combined.

Impression Formation: First Impressions Do Count

Although the weighted averaging model makes predictions about impression formation that most closely approximate findings in the general case in which people are given a list of adjectives and asked to make an overall judgment, it is less helpful when we consider the **order** in which information is presented. Does it matter if a person learns that another person is, for example, introverted initially but later acts extroverted—as compared with the case in which the individual first acts extroverted and later introverted?

The answer to this question is a clear "yes." In a classic study, Luchins (1957) gave subjects a two-paragraph description of a boy named Jim (presented in Figure 2-1). One paragraph described Jim walking to school with others and participating in a number of other activities. In short, he was portrayed as an extrovert. In the second paragraph, the activities described were similar, but Jim did them all alone, thus appearing introverted. Subjects were presented with the two paragraphs, but the order was reversed according to condition. When asked to form an overall impression of Jim, subjects' responses demonstrated a strong

> After school, Jim left the classroom alone. Leaving the school, he started on his long walk home. The street was brilliantly filled with sunshine. Jim walked down the street on the shady side. Coming down the street toward him, he saw the pretty girl whom he had met on the previous evening. Jim crossed the street and entered a candy store. The store was crowded with students, and he noticed a few familiar faces. Jim waited quietly until the counterman caught his eye and then gave his order. Taking his drink, he sat down at a side table. When he had finished his drink he went home.
>
> (Luchins, 1957, p. 35)

> Jim left the house to get some stationery. He walked out into the sun-filled street with two of his friends, basking in the sun as he walked. Jim entered the stationery store, which was full of people. Jim talked with an acquaintance while he waited for the clerk to catch his eye. On his way out, he stopped to chat with a school friend who was just coming into the store. Leaving the store, he walked toward school. On his way out he met the girl to whom he had been introduced the night before. They talked for a short while, and then Jim left for school.
>
> (Luchins, 1957, p. 34)

FIGURE 2-1
Paragraphs used to demonstrate primacy effect in Luchins (1957).

primacy effect (which refers to instances in which early information has a stronger impact than later information). If subjects had read the extrovert paragraph first, they found him considerably more extroverted than if they had read the introvert paragraph first, and vice versa.

More recent work confirms that indeed early information is weighted more heavily than later information. This holds true even when the later information is very salient and clearly contradicts early information. Thus, Jones and Goethals (1972) found that early performance on a thirty-item test was considered more indicative of a person's true ability than performance later on in the test—even if the person showed substantial improvement or decrement.

On the other hand, **recency effects,** in which *later* information is given more credence than early information, have been reliably produced under three sorts of conditions. First, when people are asked specifically to make a second evaluation following the presentation of new information, later information takes on more importance than earlier information (Stewart, 1965). Second, if there is a relatively large time span between the presentation of new information and the initial exposure, recency effects are likely to occur (Rosenkrantz & Crockett, 1965). Finally, later information is given heavier weight if the task is one in which people assume that practice might improve performance (Larkin, D'Eredita, Dempsey, McClure, & Pepe, 1983).

Schemas: Holding Our Impressions Together

Given the diversity of people and settings that one encounters passing through everyday life, we might suspect that people could easily become overwhelmed with the sheer quantity of information relating to what others are like. To avoid becoming overwhelmed, people need to

51

PERSON PERCEPTION,
SOCIAL COGNITION, AND
ATTRIBUTION:
UNDERSTANDING AND
JUDGING OURSELVES AND
OTHERS

organize their impressions of others. The way that they are able to do this is through the production of **schemas**, which are organized bodies of information stored in memory. The information in a schema provides a representation of the way in which the social world operates as well as allowing us to categorize and interpret new information related to the schema (Fiske & Taylor, 1983; Rumelhart, 1984).

We all hold schemas relating to everyday objects in our environment. We might, for instance, hold a schema for automobiles—we have an idea of what they look like, how they are used, what they can do for us, and how to differentiate them from other vehicles such as buses and horse and buggy. More importantly, from a social psychological point of view, we hold a schema for particular people (one's mother, girlfriend, boyfriend, brother, or sister) and for classes of people playing a given role (mail carriers, teachers, or librarians). Each of these schemas provides a way of organizing behavior into meaningful wholes.

The personality types that we derive in the case of person perception are organized into schemas known as **prototypes.** Prototypes are schemas that organize a group of personality traits into a meaningful personality type. For example, Nancy Cantor and Walter Mischel (1979) suggest a frequently held prototype concerns a person labeled on a general level as "committed." As shown in Figure 2-2, this prototype can be divided into different levels of a hierarchy which relates to the level of specificity at which the information within the prototype is held.

At the most specific level—called the subordinate level—the proto-

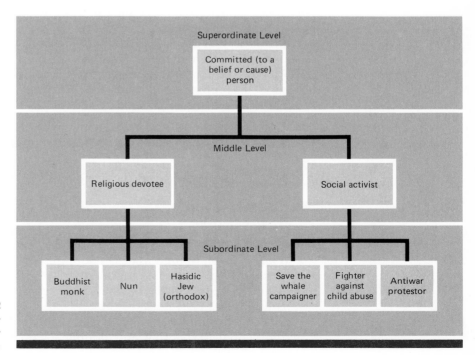

FIGURE 2-2
Prototype of the committed person. Source: Cantor and Mischel (1979).

type consists of different types of committed individuals: for example, monks, nuns, and activists for a particular cause. At the middle level of specificity, there are basic classes of individuals: the religious devotee or social activist. In turn, the subordinate and middle levels of specificity are subsumed under the broader superordinate level, which encompasses the prototype as a whole.

The importance of prototypes lies in two directions. First, prototypes allow people to recall more readily, recognize, and categorize information about others (Smith, 1984). In a sense, then, information processing capabilities are enhanced through the use of prototypes. Second, as with any schema, prototypes help us to organize the social world around us. By observing relatively few traits or behaviors, we are able to categorize people into certain prototypes, and this in turn allows us to form expectations about others' behavior. Ultimately, then, prototypes allow people to plan behavior in social interactions more readily (Snyder & Cantor, 1979).

ATTRIBUTION: EXPLAINING THE CAUSES OF BEHAVIOR

Up to this point, we have been discussing how an individual is given pieces of information about another person and combines them to formulate an overall impression about what that other person is like. Most of the time, however, information about others is not neatly dropped in our laps the way it is when someone is presented with a set of personality traits or descriptions of another's behavior. Instead, we must come up with our own inferences about others.

We turn now to an examination of how people observe behavior and draw inferences about what motivates behavior. The process of **attribution**—an individual's understanding of the reasons behind people's behavior—has represented the fastest growing area of social psychology throughout the last decade.

The First Attributional Issue: Situation or Disposition

Let us return for a moment to our hypothetical example of Matt's social psychology class with Mr. Andrews:

It is now later in the term, and Matt has grown to like Andrews quite a bit. To Matt, he is the epitome of a good teacher; he works hard, gives interesting lectures, and he grades papers and tests carefully and fairly. Even though Matt is not doing all that well in the class, he is a friendly person, and he decides he would like to get to know Andrews better. One day after class he goes up to Mr. Andrews and tells him how much he likes the class, that he thinks Mr. Andrews is a really fine teacher, and, in fact, is probably one of the best instructors at the school. Expecting and hoping for an unequivocally positive

53

PERSON PERCEPTION,
SOCIAL COGNITION, AND
ATTRIBUTION:
UNDERSTANDING AND
JUDGING OURSELVES AND
OTHERS

reaction, he is startled by Andrew's ambiguous and noncommittal thanks—and what appears to be a brush-off. Matt goes off, feeling he has made a fool of himself.

If Matt had been doing better in his social psychology class, he might have realized that he had placed Mr. Andrews in a clear attributional dilemma. There are two fundamental ways for Andrews to interpret Matt's behavior. One way is in terms of the **situation** ("He must be saying that in order to raise his grades; people always tell me they like my class—before the end of the semester") and the other is in terms of Matt's **disposition** ("He is saying that because he really is a friendly person and truly likes me and the course"). Because he cannot readily attribute Matt's behavior to dispositional forces, and because situational constraints against saying anything except what Matt did say are so strong, Mr. Andrews is most likely to attribute his remarks to situational (and less flattering) motives.

Indeed, this reasoning illustrates a general principle about attributions: Behavior will be attributed to an external cause when external reasons are more likely or plausible. Conversely, behavior will be attributed to dispositional factors when external causes are unlikely. In a clear experimental demonstration of this phenomenon, Jones, Gergen, & Davis (1961) asked subjects to rate the personality of a job applicant who presented himself as either having or not having the characteristics that were a prerequisite for the job. Subjects were confident about assessing the job candidate's true personality only when the candidate had displayed traits that were contrary to ones related to the job requirements.

If we refer to our interview with Barry Serafin that began this chapter, we can see how this attributional principle might be used. For example, we might consider the case of a Republican senator, who would normally be expected—because of external pressures—to support a Republican President's position. If the senator tells the reporter he supports the President's position, the reporter is apt to attribute his stance to external causes. On the other hand, if the senator tells the reporter he does not support the President's position, the reporter is likely to make an internal attribution, with a high degree of confidence, since the senator is acting contrary to the external pressures of the situation.

The Covariation Principle To describe the general process people use to explain behavior, Harold Kelley (1967) has introduced the principle of **covariation.** Kelley suggests that there are many possible cause-and-effect relationships inherent in a situation that provide a possible explanation for a behavior, and that we try to analyze these relationships in order to pinpoint a particular cause for a behavior. The covariation principle states that the cause that will be chosen to explain an effect is a cause that is present when the effect is present, and absent when the effect is also absent.

According to the covariation principle, an observer can use one of three specific types of causes to explain an effect: the actor (the individual who is demonstrating the behavior), the entity (the target person or thing at which the behavior is directed), and the circumstances (the setting under which the behavior occurs). Suppose, as an example, we see Rachel get angry with Josh and slap his face at a party. An observer could infer that the effect (the slap) was caused by one of the three potential causes: Rachel's behavior might be caused by something about Rachel (the actor), it might be caused by something about Josh (the target person), or it might be caused by the situation (something that happened at the party).

But how do we know which explanation is correct? According to Kelley, we consider three different kinds of information to figure out the answer. First, we use **consensus** information. Consensus is the degree to which other people react similarly in the same situation. For example, if people frequently get angry with Josh, we would have high consensus; if others rarely get angry with him, we would have low consensus. According to the consensus rule, Josh would be attributed with being the cause of the anger if there was high consensus.

The second kind of information we can use to make an attribution is **consistency,** which is the degree to which the actor behaves the same way in other situations. If Rachel often gets angry at Josh and slaps him at parties, we have high consistency; if she rarely gets angry with Josh, her behavior is of low consistency.

Finally, the third kind of information we can use is **distinctiveness** information. Distinctiveness refers to the extent to which the same behavior occurs in relation to other people or stimuli. Thus, if Rachel only gets angry at Josh—and doesn't get angry with anyone else—the behavior is high in distinctiveness. But if she frequently gets angry at her dates and reacts by slapping them, the behavior is low in distinctiveness.

By using the three kinds of information—consensus, consistency, and distinctiveness—Kelley suggests that we make attributions either to dispositional factors (something about the person) or to situational factors (something about the target person or the particular circumstances). As can be seen in Table 2-1, when consensus and distinctiveness are low and consistency is high, we tend to make dispositional attributions. But when consensus, consistency, and distinctiveness are all high, we tend to make attributions to external, situational factors.

Research concerning these predictions has largely been supportive of Kelley's theory (McArthur, 1972; Wells & Harvey, 1978; Zuckerman, 1978). Moreover, even when some of the sources of information are absent, people still make causal inferences similar to the ones predicted by Kelley. Just knowing that a behavior is of low distinctiveness is sufficient to lead people to make attributions of internal causality, and learning that there is high consensus, without any other information, is sufficient to produce attributions to external causes (Orvis, Cunningham, & Kelley, 1975).

55

PERSON PERCEPTION,
SOCIAL COGNITION, AND
ATTRIBUTION:
UNDERSTANDING AND
JUDGING OURSELVES AND
OTHERS

TABLE 2-1   An Example of Kelley's Model of Causal Attribution

Kind of Information	Example	Kind of Attribution
Low consensus	Others don't get angry with Josh	Dispositional (internal) attribution: Rachel's anger is due to something about herself
High consistency	Rachel often gets angry with Josh	
Low distinctiveness	Rachel gets angry with most of her dates	
High consensus	People frequently get angry with Josh	Situational (external) attribution: Josh is the source of Rachel's anger
High consistency	Rachel often gets angry with Josh	
High distinctiveness	Rachel gets angry only with Josh	

On the other hand, some evidence suggests that an important restriction must be placed on Kelley's theory. Sillars (1982) argues that although the theory of causal attributions holds up when people are presented with concrete, explicit information about consensus, distinctiveness, and consistency, it does not work quite so well when people must infer the information on their own.

For example, it is one thing to be presented with direct consensus information that Volvos are highly reliable cars in an experiment, and another to run across these facts in an issue of *Consumer Reports*. In the latter case, it is quite possible that the objective consensus information found in the magazine may be overlooked, especially if there are more salient sources of contradictory information—such as a neighbor who had a Volvo that turned out to be a lemon (Nisbett & Ross, 1980). In sum, although the general principles of Kelley's theory appear to be valid, the information on which the attributions are based must be clear enough to allow for the operation of the principles.

From Acts to Dispositions: Using Behavior to Understand What Others Are Like

Dan is sitting alone in his dorm room working on a term paper. There is a knock at the door, but Dan ignores it. The knock becomes louder and a voice outside the door says, "I know you're in there. I just want to talk to you for a minute about catching a quick movie." Finally, Dan answers the door, talks to the visitor for half an hour, and decides to go to the movie.

As an observer of the above scenario, what kind of judgment would you make about the motives behind Dan's behavior? Edward Jones and

BOX 2-1   SPOTLIGHT ON RESEARCH

MINDLESSNESS VERSUS MINDFULNESS IN SOCIAL INTERACTION

One of the major assumptions of attribution theorists is that people are active processors of information, continually asking questions about reasons for their behavior and that of others. Yet some social psychologists have challenged this assumption, suggesting that very often people are in a state of "mindlessness" in which they simply do not think about what they are doing. According to Ellen Langer (Langer, Blank, & Chanowitz, 1978), who has done pioneering work on the state of mindlessness, people often rely on **scripts**—well-learned patterns of behavior—that allow them to move through their daily activities. She believes that the more mundane and commonplace the activity, the more likely it is that a script will be used to guide behavior with a relative lack of awareness.

To test the hypothesis that when scripts exist for a given behavior pattern, mindlessness is likely to occur, Langer, Blank, and Chanowitz (1978) conducted a field experiment at a university copying machine. People who were about to use the copying machine were approached by the experimenter and

asked, in a way that varied according to the experimental condition, to let another person use the machine. In one group, subjects were asked to let a confederate use the machine but were given no reason for this request. In a second condition, they were again asked, but this time they were given a reason—although the reason was entirely redundant with the request. Thus the confederate said, "May I use the Xerox machine because I have to make copies?" (Why else would anyone want to use a copying machine?) Finally, in a third condition, subjects were given a real reason; they were told that the confederate needed to use the machine because he was in a rush.

The experimenters also varied whether the request required a small or larger sacrifice on the part of the subject by having the confederate say that he needed to copy just five pages or twenty pages. The result, displayed in Figure 2-3, showed a pattern of compliance that supports the mindless formulation. When the request required little sacrifice, subjects were more compliant when they were given a reason

FIGURE 2-3
Percentage of subjects complying with request. When there was little effort involved, more subjects were compliant, showing evidence of mindlessness. When greater effort was involved, considerably fewer subjects complied with the request. Source: Based on data from Langer, Blank, & Chanowitz (1978).

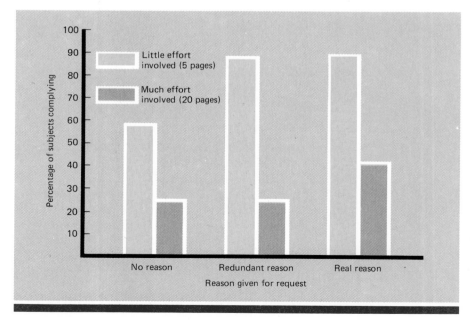

than when they were given no reason, regardless of whether the reason made any sense. It appeared that subjects had a script that went something like, "favor X + reason Y = comply," and they used the script without evaluating the reason. On the other hand, when the request required a greater sacrifice on their part, it seemed as if they were shaken out of their mindlessness and so did not use the automatic script. In this case, there was minimal compliance in the no-information and redundant-reason conditions, and considerably higher compliance in the real-information condition—a state of affairs that would be expected if subjects are actively attending to the nature of the request.

Langer and associates argue that much of social behavior follows regular, scripted patterns and proceeds in a state of mindlessness. Note how this view is quite different from what most attribution theorists would claim, suggesting as it does that people frequently—and perhaps even usually—do *not* actively place meaning upon their environment and make attributions about others' behavior. Indeed, Hastie (1984) suggests that there are relatively frequent occasions on which causal attributions are not made, and other researchers have found evidence against a completely rational view of human information processing. For instance, Taylor and Fiske (1978) examined what they call the "top of the head" phenomenon, in which trivial—but highly salient—information is given undue weight when responding to social stimuli. Even such a mundane factor as seating position can affect how others are perceived; a person sitting at the head of a table, for instance, may be perceived differently from one sitting in the middle—even if the behavior of the two is identical.

In sum, people do not always process information in a way that is in the least scientific. Further research is likely to illuminate just how often mindlessness and top-of-the-head phenomena are part of our daily lives.

Keith Davis (1965) have produced an attribution theory that helps us understand how an observer would answer this question and the general case of how a person's behavior can be used to make inferences about that person's personality traits and motivations. The theory examines **correspondent inferences,** observers' ideas of how closely an overt behavior or action represents a specific underlying intention, trait, or disposition. The more a behavior appears to reflect the underlying disposition, the greater the correspondence between these two factors is.

According to Jones and Davis, we learn the most from behaviors of others that lead to unique or **noncommon effects.** It is assumed that any behavior leads to some set of consequences but that the behaviors which are most helpful in forming correspondent inferences are those resulting in consequences or effects that alternative behaviors would *not* have produced.

For example, if we knew that Dan could work on his term paper equally well whether he was alone or chatting with a visitor, we would know little about his motivation for completing his term paper. However, the fact that he *cannot* continue writing as he chats with the visitor but *can* write if he does not answer the door shows that the two alternative behaviors have noncommon effects. The choice of behavior—to talk to the visitor—suggests that the motivation to write the term paper is not particularly high.

Another factor that colors the kind of attributions we make, and the confidence with which we hold them, is the social desirability of an action. Generally, the greater the social desirability of an action or behavior, the more difficult it will be to draw a correspondent inference between act and disposition. Since the visitor knew that Dan was inside his room, it would be an outright insult for Dan to refuse to open the door to the visitor. Therefore, Dan's chosen behavior of opening the door has an element of social desirability and is relatively uninformative about what it represents. On the other hand, if Dan had refused to answer the door, even in the face of the plaintive requests of the visitor, his behavior would clearly be low in social desirability. Consequently, it would tell us more about Dan's motivations and dispositions, suggesting that Dan was strongly committed to completing his term paper.

The Jones and Davis theory considers a somewhat different aspect of the attribution process than Kelley's model of causal attribution. Whereas Kelley's model focuses on the general direction from which to draw an explanation—dispositional versus situational causes—the Jones and Davis theory of correspondent inferences provides identification of the particular characteristics and traits which underlie behavior when a dispositional attribution is made. On the other hand, Kelley's theory has an important advantage: it considers behavior over an extended period of time (consistency information), whereas Jones and Davis do not take such information into account. Thus, neither theory alone is able to provide a complete account of the attribution process. But both theories do agree that people are logical, rational processors of information—a view disputed by some other theorists (see Box 2-1 on mindlessness).

Errors in Attribution: The Naive Psychologist Is Fallible

The basic attributional processes that we have discussed have been supported in many studies. The theories underlying these studies are similar in that they all paint a picture of human beings as thoughtful, systematic processors of information. On the other hand, people are not always as rational in making attributions as the theories might suggest; the "naive psychologist" that Fritz Heider described is susceptible to error. We turn now to some of the most frequent pitfalls.

The Fundamental Attribution Error: People Are Not Always What They Do—It Just Seems That Way   When we see someone acting friendly toward another person, our inclination is to assume that he or she is in fact, friendly and outgoing. Yet that person may think of himself or herself as introverted and shy, and attribute his or her friendliness to something about the situation—such as earlier gregarious behavior on the part of the person to whom he or she is acting friendly.

This situation exemplifies an attributional bias—labeled, because of its pervasiveness, the **fundamental attribution bias**—whereby people, when acting as raters of others, tend to attribute the behavior they view as indicative of stable trait dispositions but, when acting as self-raters, tend to perceive their own behavior as more affected by specific situational influences. Although there has been some controversy regarding

The fundamental attribution error, illustrated graphically in these two photos, reflects people's bias in placing undue weight on personal characteristics when explaining others' behavior (photo A), while focusing on situational factors in explaining the causes of their own behavior. (Randy Matusow)

the specific nature of the phenomenon (Harvey, Town, & Yarkin, 1981), most recent evidence points to its pervasiveness (Watson, 1982). For example, a field study that analyzed letters and responses to newspaper advice columns (such as "Dear Abby" and Ann Landers) lent support to the phenomenon; individuals were more likely to attribute the cause of their circumstances to situational factors than were people acting as observers (Schoeneman & Rubanowitz, 1983). Moreover, there is a good deal of laboratory research that directly confirms the viability of the fundamental attribution error.

Why are we apt to characterize others' behavior as due to dispositional causes, yet see our own as a reflection of the situation? Part of the explanation relates to the nature of information that is available to us. When we view the behavior of others, the information that is most perceptually salient is that which comes from the individual; typically, the environment is static and unchanging, while the person moves about—making the person the focus of attention. In contrast, to people observing their own behavior, any change in the environment is going to be most salient, and thus they are more likely to employ environmental, situational explanations (McArthur, 1981).

An alternative explanation for the fundamental attribution error stems from people's desire to interact effectively with others. According to

59

this view, observers increase their understanding and ability to make predictions about the world by differentially attending to the situation or person, depending on whether they are rating another person or themselves. For the observer, knowing the internal dispositions of others increases predictability of another's behavior, causing observers of others to focus on those dispositions. In contrast, understanding and predictability regarding appropriate behavior for people considering their own behavior are apt to be enhanced through attention, not to themselves, but to the environment; therefore, situational factors will be attended to more carefully.

Both of these explanations for the fundamental attribution error are plausible, and because they are not mutually exclusive it is likely that each contributes in varying degrees to the phenomenon. Indeed, each explanation has some experimental support, although the most conclusive evidence favors the information salience hypothesis. Moreover, recent work suggests that even when acting as self-raters, people may have a tendency to overattribute the causes of their own behavior to traits rather than to situations—although to a considerably lesser degree than they do when acting as raters of others' behavior (Watson, 1982). In sum, overuse of trait explanations in making attributions of others'— and sometimes even one's own—behavior is a pervasive source of bias in the accuracy of attributions.

The fundamental attribution error has important applied applications. For example, a husband complaining of his wife's purchase of second-hand clothing for their children may see the cause as his wife's inherent stinginess, while the wife may claim that her behavior is caused merely by the circumstances of her family's low income and has nothing to do with her personality traits. It is obvious how such differing attributions can lead ultimately to a deterioration in the relationship. The fundamental attribution error, then, can have clear and sometimes deleterious effects on interpersonal interaction.

Halo Effects: Assuming Consistency within a Person   One outgrowth of the overascription of dispositional factors to explain others' behavior is that we assume a certain consistency in their behavior which may be inaccurate. In fact, we frequently draw conclusions about an individual's personality on the basis of rather limited information, as we saw when we discussed schemas earlier in the chapter. This tendency is well illustrated by the **halo effect.**

The halo effect is the phenomenon in which the initial acknowledgment that a person has positive traits is used to infer other uniformly positive characteristics. (The converse is also true: observation of a single negative trait can be used to infer the existence of uniformly negative traits.) For example, finding that a person is friendly and clearheaded may lead us to believe that he is also helpful and sociable. Although this may be true, it is not necessarily the case. Our assumption that good traits are found together reflects our **implicit personality the-**

61

PERSON PERCEPTION,
SOCIAL COGNITION, AND
ATTRIBUTION:
UNDERSTANDING AND
JUDGING OURSELVES AND
OTHERS

ory, which is people's notions of what traits are found together in an individual. In many cases, this implicit personality theory may not be the least bit valid (Norman, 1963).

The halo effect is sometimes seen in media portrayals of various prominent figures, as we discussed with Barry Serafin. Individuals may be painted in black or white terms, with few shades of gray apparent. While Serafin suggests it is due partly to time constraints, at least in the case of television news, it may just as plausibly be considered a manifestation of the halo effect.

The Person-Positivity Bias: Looking for the Good in Others   When Will Rogers said, "I never met a man I didn't like," he was exemplifying another bias that colors people's views of others: the **person-positivity bias.** This bias, which has been shown to apply to a wide range of situations, reflects the tendency to rate others in a predominantly positive way. Stimulus persons in experiments tend to elicit positive ratings, and people tend to overattribute good outcomes to internal causes and bad outcomes to external causes.

Moreover, public figures are usually evaluated positively. For example, results of nationwide Gallup polls from 1935 to 1974 show that 83 percent of the public's evaluations of incumbent presidents were favorable, and 77 percent of those of other public figures were positive—findings that are congruent with current figures (Sears, 1982). Results such as these seem to reflect the fact that people have a tendency to view others positively.

Why should this be the case? One simple explanation is that a "Pollyanna principle" operates to color our perceptions (Matlin & Stang, 1978). According to this view, we enjoy being surrounded by a pleasant world, and thus we have a propensity to view people through rose-colored glasses. This argument would be compelling—except that there are limitations to the person-positivity bias. Not every person or social entity is rated favorably. For instance, although people tend to rate their own congressman favorably, they rate Congress as a whole negatively.

David Sears (1982) suggests that the reason for the positivity bias is that observers develop an extra degree of positive regard for *individuals* who are being evaluated which they do not develop when rating *groups* of people—even if the groups are made up of people who, as individuals, are evaluated positively. For example, examination of student ratings of instructors shows that college professors receive more favorable ratings as individuals than when they are rated in groups, and college professors are rated more highly than the courses they teach.

It seems that we tend to relax our evaluation standards a bit when making ratings of individual human beings, but become stricter as soon as the ratings shift away from the individual. Why should this be so? Sears suggests that this tendency is related to perceived similarity. As we will discuss below, when evaluating another person we tend to assume that he or she is similar to ourselves—and we are motivated to rate him or her more positively. On the other hand, when we rate nonperson social objects, aggregates of people, or groups, this assumption is not so salient, and our ratings, therefore, do not show a positivity bias.

Assumptions of Similarity: You're Like Me, and I'm Like You As we have indicated, people not only rate others in a generally positive way, but they tend to assume that others are similar to themselves—a tendency that constitutes another kind of attributional bias (Ross, Greene, & House, 1977). This predisposition—known as the **assumed similarity bias**—is particularly pronounced when obvious features such as sex and race are similar, but can even occur when there are overt differences between rater and ratee.

This phenomenon can lead to misperception of other people's personalities if they are, in fact, dissimilar to that of the rater. On the other hand, the assumed similarity bias can actually lead raters to appear to make very accurate judgments if the others actually are similar—not because the raters are unusually astute, but simply because they are categorizing the others as similar to themselves. In some cases, then, attributional biases can make judgments more, rather than less, accurate.

THE SELF AS SOCIAL OBJECT: UNDERSTANDING AND JUDGING ONE'S OWN BEHAVIOR

Who is the person you think about most? If modesty were to be cast aside, most of us would have to admit that it is in thinking about ourselves that we invest the most time and cognitive energy. In this section of the chapter we examine some of the most important processes involved in stepping back and viewing ourselves as social objects.

Social Comparison: Using Others to Understand Oneself

When Mayor Ed Koch of New York City travels around the city meeting his constituents, he often asks, "How am I doing?" While this query might be dismissed as campaign rhetoric, it illustrates an important constant in human curiosity: the need to evaluate one's own abilities, opinions, and emotions.

According to early theorizing by Leon Festinger (1954), there is a basic drive to evaluate one's opinions and abilities—a **need for social comparison.** In many cases, there is objective, physical evidence which can provide us with answers. For instance, if I think my route from home to the center of town is shorter than the route my wife takes, I can objectively determine whether my opinion is correct by using my car odometer and measuring the two routes. But suppose I want to find out how good a piano player I am. Here, objective means are lacking.

According to Festinger, I will probably turn to **social reality** to satisfy my needs for evaluating my ability. Social reality refers to understanding

BOX 2-2 SPOTLIGHT ON THEORY

MOTIVATIONAL BIASES: PRESENTING ONESELF WELL THROUGH IMPRESSION MANAGEMENT

The biases that we have been discussing up to this point all reflect inaccuracies in the ways information about others is processed; these are known as **cognitive biases.** But there is another category of attributional bias that exists called **motivational bias.** Motivational biases arise from a need to manage the impression one makes in order to present oneself well—either to others, or to oneself to maintain one's own sense of self-esteem.

A good example of a motivational bias comes from a study by Linda Beckman (1970). She asked experienced instructors to teach a lesson to pupils, and experimentally manipulated the degree and sequence of success of the pupils. When asked to attribute the cause of improving performance, the instructors tended to say it was because of their success as teachers. But when the pupils' performance declined, the instructors attributed the failure to the students. Interestingly, a group of non-ego-involved observers who had no responsibility for the students' performance attributed good performance to the students and bad performance to the teachers—just the opposite pattern. Thus, the nature of an individual's involvement in a situation can have a strong effect on the nature of the attributions that are drawn.

Indeed, there appears to be a general tendency to attribute our own success to internal factors—skill, ability, or effort—and failure to external factors—chance, or something about the situation. In fact, this bias, known as the self-serving bias, may even operate in terms of our attributions about others if we feel that we are responsible for the others' behavior.

A good example of this bias was presented in a field study of a football team (Carver, DeGregorio, & Gillis, 1980). In the experiment, attributions for the team's poor performance at midseason were taken from the head coach and assistant coaches. The researchers hypothesized that the head coach, whose major responsibility was recruitment, would be most concerned with the players' abilities, and would therefore try to protect his image by attribut-

ing the failure to some other factor, such as effort. On the other hand, the assistant coaches, whose primary job was to develop motivation and effort, would be more likely to protect their images by attributing failure not to the players' efforts, but rather to their low ability—after all, it was the head coach's job to find good talent, not theirs.

Measures of the head's and assistants' attributions confirmed these predictions precisely. The head coach felt that the players had greater ability at midseason than they did at the start of the season, but he thought their effort had decreased. In contrast, assistant coaches felt the players had less ability than they had originally thought, but expended more effort at midseason than during preseason.

While it seems clear that people do tend to take credit for their successes and blame others for their failures, the reason for this is not entirely clear (Van Der Pligt & Eiser, 1983). Most theoreticians suggest that people do so with the obvious goal of presenting a positive self-image—a goal which has a clear motivational basis.

On the other hand, Miller and Ross (1975) reject the motivational explanation and instead have put forward a cognitive view of the self-serving bias. They suggest that people generally hold expectations for success. Thus, when they fail, they do not claim responsibility because they do not see a clear relationship between what they have done and the outcome. Moreover, people assume they have control over situations in which they find themselves. They expect success and think they have control, but a failure implies that they never really were in control. Logically, then, they could not be responsible for a failure—since a failure inherently suggests that they were not in control.

What all this complicated reasoning provides is a logical and *cognitive* explanation for the self-serving bias. What appears at first to have a clearly motivational basis, then, may in reality be explained by cognitive factors. Which explanation is most accurate remains to be seen.

that is derived from how other people generally think, feel, and view the world. Hence, if I turn to social reality to discern my level of performance, I will examine how others play the piano. But who is included in an individual's social reality? It wouldn't help me very much to compare myself to a very dissimilar other. I already know I don't play as well as Vladimir Horowitz. For me, the most relevant information would come from similar others—people who have taken lessons for about the same amount of time, who are adults, and so forth. Thus, Festinger suggests that the people with whom we compare ourselves will be similar to us.

The fundamental propositions of the theory—that people have a basic drive to evaluate their opinions and abilities and that they use the social reality provided by similar others—have stood up well over time (e.g., Goethals & Darley, 1977; Trope, 1980; Olson, Ellis, & Zanna, 1983). For instance, Zanna, Goethals, and Hill (1975) led men and women to compete on tasks that were supposedly related to the sex of the person carrying out the task. As would be expected from social comparison theory, both the men and women tried to learn how others had done to determine how well they had performed. But men were most interested in finding out how other men had performed, while women wanted to know how other women had performed. Hence, similarity of others was an important factor in who was used as a comparison person.

Knowing Our Emotions: Same Feeling, Different Label   One important outgrowth of the notion that we evaluate our abilities and opinions by comparing them with those of others is the idea that the way we identify our emotional states might also be influenced by comparison with others. In fact, a classic experiment by Stanley Schachter and Jerome Singer (1962) found evidence for this hypothesis, showing that how we label our emotional experiences may be due in large part to the circumstances in which we find ourselves.

In the study, subjects were told that they would be given injections of a "vitamin" called Suproxin. In reality, they were given epinephrine, a drug which causes increases in physiological arousal such as increased heart rate and flushing of the face, responses that occur during natural emotional experience. One group of subjects was informed of these drug effects, while another was kept ignorant.

Subjects in both groups were placed in a situation in which a confederate acted either very euphoric—tossing papers into a wastebasket and throwing paper airplanes—or quite angry while completing a series of questionnaires. Subjects then were asked to describe their own emotional states. Those who had been informed of the effects of the epinephrine were generally unaffected by the confederate's behavior; they attributed their physiological arousal to the drug, and thus were not faced with the need to find a reason for their arousal. On the other hand, subjects who were uninformed of the drug's effect upon them were affected by the confederate's behavior: When the confederate acted

65

PERSON PERCEPTION,
SOCIAL COGNITION, AND
ATTRIBUTION:
UNDERSTANDING AND
JUDGING OURSELVES AND
OTHERS

euphoric, they reported feeling happy, but when he acted angry, they felt angry. Basically, then, subjects who experienced unexplained physiological arousal functioned as problem solvers. In attempting to explain their arousal, they turned to the environment and used external cues, in the form of the behavior of others, to label their own emotional state.

While others support the notion that the emotions we experience are a joint function of physiological arousal and labeling from the environment, the original experiment has been criticized on both methodological and conceptual grounds (e.g., Marshall & Zimbardo, 1979; Maslach, 1979; Reisenzein, 1983). For instance, the magnitude of the obtained effects was relatively small, and ratings in *all* groups of subjects fell on the positive end of an emotional self-report scale—contrary to what would be predicted. Moreover, some critics have suggested that appropriate control groups were not included in the original work.

On the other hand, the results have been replicated (Erdmann & Janke, 1978), and the theory has been extended in a number of ways that have direct relevance to such phenomena as passionate love (which will be discussed in Chapter 6). In sum, although the original work has proven to be controversial, it is well established that people make use of situational cues as a partial determinant of how they label their emotional experiences (Reisenzein, 1983).

Attributions Based on Our Own Behavior: Bem's Self-perception Theory

Schachter's work on emotions suggests that we can use a combination of internal arousal and situational cues to make inferences about the nature of our emotional state. What other sources of information can be used to come to an understanding of what we are like? One possible candidate is our own behavior. Daryl Bem, in a simple but elegant extension of the work we have been discussing, has proposed a theory of self-perception which relates to the attributions people make about the meaning of their own behavior (Bem, 1972).

According to Bem, people come to be aware of their own dispositions, emotions, attitudes, and other internal states in the same way they learn about other people—through observation of behavior. The theory suggests—to the extent that situational cues or past experience is irrelevant, weak, or ambiguous—that after viewing one's own behavior, a person applies the same attributional principles that are used in attributions of others to identify the causes of the behavior one has observed in oneself.

A few examples may clarify Bem's theory. If you saw someone patiently helping an old lady cross a busy road, it would be reasonable to infer that the helper is altruistic or perhaps favorably disposed toward the elderly. But suppose that person is *you*, and at an intersection you find yourself helping an old woman cross the road. When you look back to analyze your own behavior, Bem's theory suggests that you would make the same kind of attributions about your own behavior that you did about the other's behavior—i.e., that you have an altruistic streak and hold positive attitudes toward the elderly. (We discuss the role of self-perception in attitude change more fully in Chapter 4).

Consider another example: As part of an experiment, you are looking at a set of attractive nudes of the opposite sex. When you see some of them, your heart rate—which is amplified through a speaker—speeds up or slows down, while with others it stays the same. Which do you think you like best? Such a study, actually carried out by Stuart Valins (1966), suggests that you will later say you liked the ones for which your heart rate changed more than ones for which it remained stable. What is particularly intriguing about these results is that in the experiment, the heart-rate changes that the subjects experienced were false; the experimenter used a tape recording of an accelerating, decelerating, or unvarying heartbeat to lead subjects to believe that there had been actual variations in their own heartbeats.

In sum, Bem's theory of self-perception indicates that people will apply the same sort of attributional principles to their own behavior that they use with others. Through this process, they are able to understand and infer how they feel and why they have carried out certain actions.

The Practical Benefits of Attributional Errors   The Valins experiment, in which subjects were led to attribute the meaning of false heart rate to feelings of attraction, shows that attributions based upon one's behavior may not necessarily be accurate. Interestingly, this inaccuracy, known as **misattribution,** has some important applied implications. For example, work with insomniacs suggests that one of the reasons for their inability to go to sleep is the heightened emotionality that accompanies their going to bed. Indeed, insomniacs often attribute their insomnia to anxiety, unusually strong emotional responses, problems in general, or a host of other personality factors. These attributions tend to make it even harder to go to sleep.

Suppose, however, an insomniac was told that his inability to get to sleep easily was due not to anxiety or other internal factors, but to factors essentially beyond his control. It is conceivable that he might learn to fall asleep more quickly than usual, since the usual source of worry— himself—could not be blamed.

Using this reasoning, Storms and Nisbett (1970) told a group of insomniacs that they would be taking a pill that would either relax them and allow them to sleep more easily or, in another condition, would keep them awake. In reality, the pills were inert sugar pills which had no real physiological effects. The results of the study were supportive of the prior reasoning. Subjects who were told that they would be able to get to sleep more easily actually took about fifteen minutes *longer* to fall asleep than they usually did. In contrast, those who could attribute their initial sleeplessness to the side effects of the pill actually took *less* time—about twelve minutes less—to fall asleep than they usually did.

It thus appears that altering the cause to which a person attributes his

67

PERSON PERCEPTION,
SOCIAL COGNITION, AND
ATTRIBUTION:
UNDERSTANDING AND
JUDGING OURSELVES AND
OTHERS

or her behavior may be an important therapeutic technique. Instead of experiencing anxiety over a problem which is viewed as a personality failing, patients treated with **attribution therapy** learn to attribute the source of their problem to something outside of themselves, something that can be dealt with more effectively than if they attribute the problem to a long-term neurotic state (Ross, Rodin, & Zimbardo, 1969; Storms & McCaul, 1976).

Determining Responsibility for Success and Failure: Attributions of Achievement

One of the most frequently heard and fervent complaints made by college students to their professors is that a given test was "too hard," and that the students did poorly because the test was not properly written. Professors commonly respond, with equal fervor, that clearly the students had not studied hard enough—or (in a view that they may keep to themselves) that the students just weren't smart enough.

If we analyze the two sets of reasons for the students' poor performance, we can see that they are based on two kinds of attributional explanations. The students' explanation is based on the situation (an external cause), whereas the professor's explanation is based on factors that are dispositional (or internal) to the students. Bernard Weiner, who has done a great deal of work on how people explain the causes of success and failure, suggests that the internal–external dimension (which corresponds to the dispositional–situational distinction central to Kelley's theory) is a crucial one for understanding causal attributions (Weiner, 1974; Weiner, Frieze, Kukla, Reed, Rest, & Rosenbaum, 1972). But he also adds a second dimension: the *stability* of a given cause. He suggests that causes are either viewed as stable or unstable.

If we chart the two dimensions, which are considered independent of each other, we come up with the model shown in Figure 2-4. As can be seen, when performance is due to stable and internal causes, it is attributed to ability; when it is due to stable and external causes, it is

FIGURE 2-4
Weiner's model of causal attributions of ability. Source: Adopted from Weiner, Frieze, Kukla, Reed, Rest, & Rosenbaum (1972).

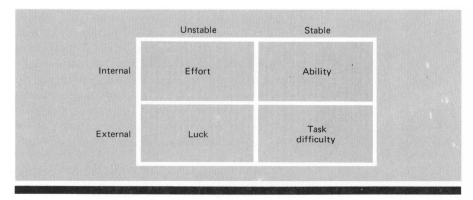

attributed to the task difficulty; when it is unstable and internal, the attribution is made to effort; and when it is unstable and external, it is made to luck.

What is of particular importance about this model is that feelings of pride and shame over one's performance are influenced by whether one attributes performance to internal or external causes. Pride over successful performance is enhanced when people perceive of their success as due to internal qualities (ability and/or effort) but diminishes if it is attributed to external events (luck and/or difficulty of task). On the other hand, feelings of shame increase when people perceive the cause of failure to be internal, but decrease if they attribute their failure to external causes.

While the internal–external dimension is particularly influential in terms of people's feelings of pride or shame regarding their performance, the stability dimension is related closely to a person's expectations regarding his or her future performance. For instance, if performance is attributed to stable causes (ability and/or task difficulty), people will tend to hold the expectation of similar performance in future—be it good or bad. On the other hand, attributions based upon unstable factors (effort and/or luck) are apt to indicate that future performance is likely to vary from earlier success or failure.

If we integrate these predictions, we come up with the model shown in Figure 2-5, which illustrates the emotional reactions and expectations that would be indicated as a function of the kind of attributions that are made to success and failure. For instance, a person who attributes successful performance to effort is likely to experience pride (since effort is internal), but is also likely to expect the possibility of change in the future (since effort is an unstable cause).

This model has been verified in a number of studies (Bar-Tal, 1978). Moreover, and perhaps most importantly, the kinds of expectations that people have as a result of their attributions are reflected in the success of their future performance. For example, Dweck (1975) found that students who tended to attribute their successful performance on a task to effort were apt to work longer and harder on a future task than those who attributed their success to ability. Analogously, those who attributed failure to lack of ability were likely to spend less time at future tasks than those who attributed their failure to lack of effort.

Weiner has recently expanded his model to include still a third dimension—**controllability**—which measures whether a cause for performance can or cannot be controlled by an individual (Weiner, 1979, 1980). Although confirmation for this new dimension is not extensive, preliminary evidence does support the reformulation.

The Stability of Attributions

One important outgrowth of work on attributions of success and failure is proof that people have stable patterns regarding which factor they use to explain their performance. For instance, some people tend to attribute success to internal causes while others habitually attribute success to external causes. Moreover, the kind of attributions one tends to make influences one's preference for different kinds of tasks. Thus, students who characteristically attribute their performance to ability prefer tasks in which competence is necessary to succeed, while those who characteristically attribute their performance to external factors such as luck prefer tasks in which chance plays an important role (Fyans & Maehr, 1979). These choices have a self-perpetuating quality to them: If people prefer ability-oriented tasks and choose to perform them more frequently, they are likely to do better on those tasks, given their greater practice and motivation. Conversely, those who prefer and choose tasks

FIGURE 2-5

Affective and cognitive reactions to success and failure. The figure shows the two sorts of reactions that follow from a given attribution for success or failure. Source: Bar-Tal (1978).

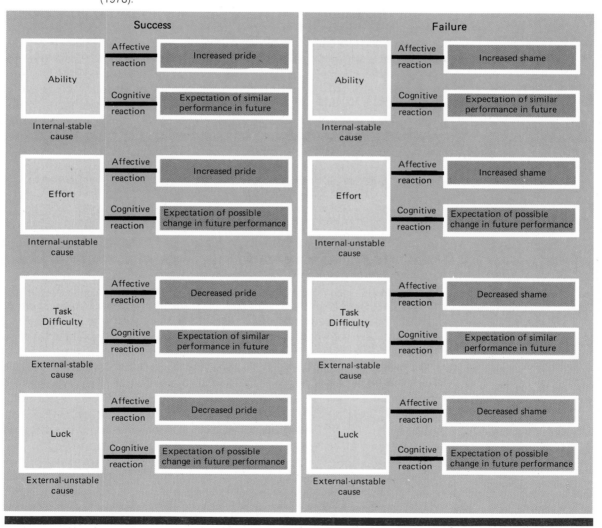

in which luck plays an important role may eventually perform more poorly in ability-oriented tasks, given their lower practice and motivation levels.

In addition to differences among people in how they attribute causality in achievement-related situations, there are some stable regularities related to membership in particular demographic groups, most likely due to differences in socialization and family-rearing practices. For instance, more blacks than whites tend to attribute success to external causes (Katz, 1976). Work with black children shows that task difficulty and luck—external causes—are thought to be the major cause of how well they perform. In contrast, white children tend to explain success in terms of ability and effort.

Attributional styles have been found to differ across sexes as well. Females tend to attribute poor performance to low ability, although, interestingly, they do not attribute good performance to high ability, but rather to external causes (Dweck & Bush, 1976; Frieze, Whiteley, Hansua, & McHugh, 1982). Such attributional patterns clearly are maladaptive, since they suggest that poor performance cannot be improved in the future. After all, if people assume they have low ability, they will feel that even future hard work is not going to ensure success. Thus, people who characteristically attribute their failures to low ability are unlikely to be particularly motivated to improve their performance through greater effort in the future.

Applying Attribution Theory: Training Attributional Styles

Given that people differ in the ways they explain success and failure, it might be possible to retrain people to develop more adaptive attributional styles. In fact, a field experiment conducted by Carol Dweck (1975) proved this assumption to be valid. In her study, she used elementary-school-age children identified as underachievers who attributed their failures to a lack of ability and, therefore, showed little persistence when given new tasks. In fact, their attributional patterns were so rigid that these students were characterized as suffering from **learned helplessness,** a belief that no matter what behavior they engaged in, they were doomed to failure.

Dweck's retraining program lasted for twenty-five sessions, during which the subjects were given a series of success and failure experiences on math problems. Whenever they made an error, they were taught specifically to attribute their failure to a lack of effort rather than to low ability (as customarily had been the case). Children who were retrained in this way showed better performance and greater effort after the program was over. In comparison, a control group, in which the subjects were not retrained and, in fact, had experienced unmitigated success, actually performed more poorly subsequent to the program.

Later research (Andrews & Debus, 1978), supports and extends Dweck's results. Not only did retraining to attribute performance to

71

PERSON PERCEPTION,
SOCIAL COGNITION, AND
ATTRIBUTION:
UNDERSTANDING AND
JUDGING OURSELVES AND
OTHERS

effort rather than ability result in higher persistence of children imme-diately following the end of the training program, but the results still held in a four-month follow-up posttest. Moreover, a direct assessment of how the children attributed performance showed that the attributions themselves had shifted in the direction of favoring internal causes over external ones. Other research has shown the success of attributional training even with college students, as discussed in Box 2-3.

ACTING ON PERCEPTIONS AND ATTRIBUTIONS: APPLICATIONS TO SOCIAL BEHAVIOR

We have spent a good deal of time discussing how people form impres-sions of others and attributions regarding their behavior. All this would be fairly academic if it were not for the fact that the decisions we make—and we have seen the many possibilities of bias inherent in such deci-sions—affect the way in which we interact with others.

Expecting Much—or Little—of Others

Suppose you were an elementary school teacher who was given the following message at the beginning of a new school year about a test that your students had taken:

> All children show hills, plateaus, and valleys in their scholastic progress. A study being conducted at Harvard with the support of the National Science Foundation is interested in those children who show an unusual forward spurt of academic progress. These spurts can and do occur at any level of academic and intellectual functioning. When these spurts occur in children who have not been functioning too well academically, the result is familiarly referred to as "late blooming."

> As part of our study we are further validating a test which predicts the like-lihood that a child will show an inflection point or "spurt" within the near future. This test which will be administered in your school will allow us to predict which youngsters are most likely to show an academic spurt. . . . The development of the test for predicting inflections or "spurts" is not yet such that every one of the top 10 percent will show the spurt or "blooming" effect. But the top 20 percent of the children will show a more significant inflection or spurt in their learning within the next year or less than will the remaining 80 percent of the children. (Rosenthal & Jacobson, 1968, p. 66)

What would your reaction be to such information? Would you treat your students differently, according to the nature of the information you received about them? Although most of us would want to feel that as teachers, we would treat our students in an unbiased manner, the infor-mation we discussed earlier in the chapter suggests that this might not be the case. As active perceivers and attributors of information, it seems probable that we would use the information to form impressions of

BOX 2-3 SPOTLIGHT ON APPLICATIONS

IMPROVING THE PERFORMANCE OF COLLEGE FRESHMEN

Most college freshmen feel some trepidation about their academic performance, how well they compare with their fellow classmates, and whether they are doing as well as they can. If they perform poorly early in their academic careers, they may see this as confirmation of their greatest fears, and assume that they are characteristically unable to do well in college. In turn, this attribution may cause further anxiety and distress, ultimately leading to even poorer academic performance.

In an attempt to break this cycle, Timothy Wilson and Patricia Linville (1982) devised a program based on attribution theory to change the nature of freshmen attributions regarding their own performance. Rather than attempting to change attributions from internal to external causes, as other programs have done, they tried to change attributions from stable to unstable causes. Basically, students were exposed to information that led them to attribute their problems to temporary factors that are amenable to change, instead of permanent, unchangeable causes.

To test their program, the experimenters assigned a group of freshmen at Duke University who had expressed concern over their first-semester performance either to an experimental treatment or to a control group. In the experimental group, sub-jects were given information showing that college students typically improve their grades over the course of their college career. To increase the salience of this information, they were also shown videotapes of actual interviews with juniors and seniors who stated that their grades had improved since their freshman year. The control group received no treatment at all.

Rather than simply looking at the direct effects of this one-time manipulation on students' attributions, the investigators examined factors which would be much more resistant to change but which would be expected to vary if attribution patterns were, in fact, altered: dropout rates, grade-point average, and academic ability. As can be seen in Table 2-2, students who received the attribution information were superior to the control group on each of these dependent measures. Whereas 25 percent of the control students had dropped out of college by the end of their sophomore year, just 5 percent of the subjects in the experimental condition dropped out. Moreover, experimental group subjects had raised their grade-point averages an average of .34 points by the second semester of their freshman year, while control subjects declined by .05 points—a significant difference. Finally, experimental subjects performed better on a set of sample items from the

TABLE 2-2 Comparison of Subjects Receiving Information That Freshman Performance Is Typically due to Unstable Factors versus Subjects Receiving No Information

Condition	Dropout Rate	Grade-Point Average Change	Scores on GRE Sample Items	Meaning of Results
No information control group	25%	−.05	3.50	Inferior performance on every measure
Information experimental group	5%	+.34	4.18	Superior performance on every measure

Source: Wilson & Linville, 1982.

Graduate Record Exams (GRE) than control group subjects did.

In sum, one-time exposure to information suggesting that first-semester performance is due to unstable rather than stable causes was sufficient to bring about changes in student performance. Although some evidence suggests that these findings may not be entirely unequivocal (Block & Lenning, 1984), the results of a recent replication (Wilson & Linville, 1984) still suggest that the procedure is a practical and inexpensive method for helping students who are concerned about their academic performance and illustrate the potential that attribution theory has for solving social problems.

students' underlying abilities and might even treat students differently on the basis of our newly formed impression.

Evidence that this reasoning is valid comes from a field study by Rosenthal and Jacobson (1968), who actually gave teachers in a school information regarding their students' likelihood of future success. Attached to the passage quoted above were the names of five children who were described as being ready to "bloom" during the next year. In reality, however, the names were simply chosen at random from the class list. Providing the student names to the teacher was the sole experimental manipulation employed; there was no reinforcement of these facts at any point in the school year.

At the close of the term, all the children in the school took a battery of tests. According to the investigators, the results were clear: In comparison to their scores of a year earlier, children who had been designated as "bloomers" gained significantly more than students about whom teachers had received no information. The gains were not uniform, however; students in the earliest grades increased more than children in grades three through six.

Teachers who hold high expectations regarding their students may actually bring about better student performance. (Charles Gatewood/Magnum)

These results were startling enough to pique the interest of the news media, and there were front-page stories in major newspapers describing them. Soon, however, they became controversial, and a scholarly review of the results suggested that there were some potential statistical difficulties—such as the reliability of the measures of student performance—that made the results less than conclusive (e.g., Snow, 1969; Elashoff & Snow, 1971).

Although the validity of the initial study has been questioned, subsequent work has shown that teachers' expectations about their students can, in fact, influence the students' performance (Dusek, Hall, & Meyer, 1984). Indeed, these findings are a special case of a broader phenomenon known as the **self-fulfilling prophecy,** a phenomenon in which an individual's expectation leads to behavior that brings about the expected outcome (Archibald, 1974).

Self-fulfilling prophecies operate in many contexts, such as when a physician prescribes a sugar pill to a patient who is cured not by the pill itself but rather by the expectation that the pill *ought* to work. Similarly, the experimenter expectancy effect that we described in Chapter 1—in which experimenters' hypotheses lead to behavior that ultimately brings about the expected behavior on the part of subjects—is a further example of expectation effects.

Sending the Message   Once an initial expectation is developed, how is it communicated to others? In the case of teacher expectations, Rosenthal (1974) suggests that there are four primary means by which expectations are communicated to the student. First, the overall social–emotional climate is pleasanter for students of whom teachers have high expectations than for the other students. With the high-expectation students, teachers smile and nod their heads more and act generally more friendly (Chaiken & Derlega, 1979). Second, teachers' feedback to students they expect to do well is more concrete and differentiated. Even when low-expectation students do well, the kind of feedback teachers give is less positive than when a high-expectation pupil does well (Cooper, 1979).

A third factor in differential teacher behavior concerns the amount and kind of material that teachers assign. Teachers give low-expectation pupils less opportunity to perform well than they do high-expectation students (Cornbleth, Davis, & Button, 1974). Finally, a fourth dimension in which teacher behavior varies toward high- and low-expectation students relates to the kinds of responses the teacher elicits. Teachers interact with high-expectation students at significantly greater levels than with low-expectation students and, therefore, the former are given greater opportunities to respond in class (Gay, 1975).

In sum, attributions and perceptions regarding students can lead to the formation of differential expectations. Teachers treat their students according to these expectations. What happens next is obvious: The students respond differently to the teacher because of the treatment

75

PERSON PERCEPTION,
SOCIAL COGNITION, AND
ATTRIBUTION:
UNDERSTANDING AND
JUDGING OURSELVES AND
OTHERS

they have received. They do better when they are treated as bright pupils, and worse when they are not. Their performance is thereby brought about *because* of their teachers' behavior.

We should note that the transmission of expectations is not a one-way street; it is not just a matter of teachers communicating their expectations to students. Research also shows that students transmit their expectations about teacher competence or incompetence to teachers, and actually make teachers they think are competent appear more competent— and those they think are incompetent act accordingly (Feldman & Prohaska, 1979; Feldman & Theiss, 1982).

Expectation effects and self-fulfilling prophecies are not limited to the classroom, but can also be found in other everyday contexts. For example, in a study by Snyder and Swann (1978), subjects were told that a partner with whom they would be holding a discussion was either hostile or nonhostile. In reality, this label was assigned randomly and bore no relation to what the person was like. But assigning the label did have an effect upon the people who were told about it. They acted in accordance with the label, speaking more loudly to the supposedly hostile partner. And how did the partner respond? As you might have guessed, he actually began to act hostile as the discussion proceeded.

What happened next was even more startling. The partner who had the "hostile" or "nonhostile" label unknowingly planted upon him was introduced to a third party, who also knew nothing about the label. At this stage in the experiment, the partner actually acted hostile to the new person. Thus, the chain that had been started with the initial labeling was complete: The first person acted as if the partner were hostile, which led the partner to act congruently with the expectation. And this behavior continued, even when the original holder of the expectation was no longer present.

In sum, the impressions and attributions that people form and believe about others can have important consequences on the nature of subsequent social interaction. As we shall see, the nature of our self-attributions can be an important determinant of even our own future behavior.

Self-handicapping: Protecting Ourselves from Our Failings

Most of us experience anxiety and insecurity about the extent of our own abilities from time to time. One way of dealing with this uncertainty is to develop what Edward Jones has called a **self-handicapping strategy** (Jones & Berglas, 1978). To use this strategy, we try to set up circumstances in which we can blame future failures on external causes—as opposed to our own internal lack of ability. For example, consider the student who says, "I don't think I'm going to do very well on today's test; I was up all night feeling upset." If, in fact, he doesn't do well, he will be quick to attribute his failure to being up all night—and not to any internal shortcomings.

An interesting point about self-handicapping strategies is that they seem to prevent the negative attributions that we have formed about ourselves from making us feel bad. Paradoxically, they may also lead us to continuing, unending failure since we are always setting up conditions under which it is nearly impossible to succeed.

What are the conditions under which self-handicapping is most likely to occur? Jones and Berglas (1978) suggest that self-handicapping is most likely to occur when we think that past successes have been caused by unstable factors, such as chance, or by external factors as opposed to stable, internal factors, such as ability. In such cases, we are apt to provide ourselves with a ready excuse for potential failure. In some instances, self-handicapping may become chronic, as in the case of a person who consistently takes a few too many drinks and whose performance in many areas of life suffers. The alcohol provides a ready excuse for explaining failures which might otherwise be attributed to internal factors.

A study by Smith, Snyder, and Handelsman (1982) provides a clear example of how psychological symptoms may serve as part of a self-handicapping strategy. These researchers hypothesized that highly test-anxious people—people who report chronic debilitating anxiety whenever they take a test—may use their symptoms in a self-protective fashion. In support of this logic, highly test-anxious people tended to exaggerate their reports of how anxious they felt when taking a test on which they were told that anxiety could adversely affect performance. On the other hand, reports of anxiety were considerably lower when they were told that anxiety had no effect.

Interestingly, when subjects were not allowed to use anxiety as a self-handicapping strategy (i.e., they were told anxiety would not have an effect), subjects employed another self-handicapping strategy: they reported putting in lower effort than when they were told anxiety could have a deleterious effect. It appears, then, that they may have substituted one handicap for another.

The work on self-handicapping provides a good example of how work on attribution theory can help us understand people's behavior in a variety of situations. Moreover, it is clear in indicating that the kind of attributions we make about others' past behavior can shape how we behave toward them. In the next chapter, we consider some of the ways in which these attributions—as well as other social phenomena—are transmitted from one individual to another, as we discuss communication processes.

SUMMARY

In this chapter we have discussed the processes by which individuals come to understand both themselves and others. We focused on how overall impressions are formed and attributions are made, and how such attributions ultimately influence the behavior of the observer.

77

PERSON PERCEPTION,
SOCIAL COGNITION, AND
ATTRIBUTION:
UNDERSTANDING AND
JUDGING OURSELVES AND
OTHERS

Person perception refers to the way in which individuals focus on specific traits to form an overall impression of others. According to Asch, particular traits—known as central traits—serve to organize a person's impression and provide a framework for interpreting information that is subsequently learned. Later approaches have suggested that mathematical models can provide more precise predictions of how information is combined. Additive models suggest that people add bits of information together to form an overall judgment, while averaging models suggest that the mean of the information is most appropriate. Tests comparing the two models show that a weighted averaging model, which takes into account both the importance and positivity of the information, provides the best predictions. Moreover, impressions are influenced by the order in which information is presented; there are both primacy and recency effects in person perception.

Schemas are organized bodies of information stored in memory. They allow us to categorize and interpret information related to the schema. In the case of personality traits, we organize information into schemas called prototypes, which are general personality types developed on the basis of prior experience and our understanding of the world.

Attribution theories explain how people come to understand the reasons behind their own and others' behavior. One of the basic issues of attribution concerns whether a behavior is due to the situation or to the disposition of the person being observed. According to Kelley, we consider three types of information to make this determination: consensus (the degree to which other people react similarly in the same situation), consistency (the degree to which the actor behaves the same way in other situations), and distinctiveness (the extent to which the same behavior occurs in relation to other people or stimuli). When consensus is low, consistency high, and distinctiveness low, we tend to make dispositional attributions; when consensus, consistency, and distinctiveness are all high, we tend to make situational dispositions. Jones and Davis's theory of correspondent inferences examines how behavior is attributed to a specific underlying intention, trait, or disposition. The theory states that we learn the most from uncommon effects—those effects that other, alternate behaviors would not have produced.

Attribution theory posits that people are fairly rational and logical processors of information. Still, people are prone to some systematic biases. In the fundamental attribution error, people tend to attribute the behavior of others to stable trait dispositions, but tend to view their own behavior as more affected by specific situational influences. The halo effect is the phenomenon by which the initial acknowledgment that a person has positive traits is used to infer the existence of other uniformly positive traits, while the person-positivity bias reflects the tendency to rate other people predominantly positively. Finally, people tend to assume that others are more similar to themselves than is actually the case.

Research on person perception shows that we often view ourselves as social objects in a way that is analogous to what we do when perceiving others. Social comparison theory suggests that there is a basic drive to evaluate our opinions and abilities. If objective means are impossible, we turn to social reality—in the form of similar others. Schachter and Singer suggest that we identify our emotional states by the nature of the situation around us. Finally, Bem proposes that people come to be aware of their own dispositions, emotions, attitudes, and other internal states in the same way that they learn about other people—through observation of behavior.

Weiner's theory of achievement-related attributions suggests that people explain success and failure by means of two independent dimensions: (1) internal or external and (2) stable or unstable causes. The factors are assumed to affect both affective reactions and expectations for future success. Attribution retraining programs have shown some success.

The last part of the chapter discussed how people act upon their perceptions and attributions once they are formed. Expectation effects lead to the development of self-fulfilling prophecies in which an individual's expectation alone is capable of bringing about the expected outcome. Self-handicapping strategies are used to set up circumstances under which people can blame future failures on external causes—as opposed to their own internal shortcomings.

KEY TERMS

additive model
attribution
averaging model
Bem's self-perception theory
bias
central traits
cognitive algebra
consensus
consistency
correspondent inferences
covariation principle
disposition
distinctiveness

fundamental attribution error
halo effect
impression formation
person perception
person-positivity bias
primacy effect
prototype
recency effect
schema
self-handicapping strategy
social comparison
social reality

FOR FURTHER STUDY AND APPLICATION

Heider, F. (1958). *The psychology of interpersonal relations.* New York: Wiley.
Jones, E. E., & Davis, K. E. (1965). A theory of correspondent inferences: From acts to dispositions. In L. Berkowitz (Ed.), *Advances in experimental social psychology* (Vol. 2). New York: Academic Press.
Kelley, H. H. (1967). Attribution theory in social psychology. *Nebraska Symposium on Motivation, 15,* 192–238.

Not for the fainthearted reader, these scholarly articles present the seminal attribution theories. Quite technical, but they give a flavor that cannot be obtained from secondary sources.

Shaver, K. G. (1984). *An introduction to attribution processes.* Hillsdale, NJ: Erlbaum.

Harvey, J. H., & Weary, G. (1981). *Perspectives on attributional processes.* Dubuque, IA: W. C. Brown.

Both are well-written, straightforward introductions to attribution theory. Very accessible, using everyday examples.

Schneider, D., Hastorf, A., & Ellsworth, P. (1979). *Person perception* (2nd ed.). Reading, MA: Addison-Wesley.

A fine introduction to the area of person perception, written at an undergraduate level. Provides some interesting applications of the work in the area.

Jones, E. E., Kanouse, D., Kelley, H. H., Nisbett, R. E., Valins, S., & Weiner, B. (Eds.). (1972). *Attribution: Perceiving the cause of behavior.* Morristown, NJ: General Learning Press.

A series of provocative technical articles that had an important influence upon the development of work on attribution theory.

Fiske, S. T., & Taylor, S. E. (1983). *Social cognition.* Reading MA: Addison-Wesley.

A clear, readable introduction to the area of social cognition. Written with many examples and implications for future work.

Turiel, E. (1983). *The development of social knowledge.* Cambridge: Cambridge University Press.

A technical description of how children and adolescents learn about their social world, and how their social judgments affect their interactions with others.

CHAPTER 3

SOCIAL ASPECTS OF NONVERBAL AND VERBAL COMMUNICATION

A CONVERSATION WITH . . .

Susan Greenlee
Actress

Susan Greenlee is a professional actress with a good deal of experience in different kinds of productions. Her acting credits range from a leading role in *Othello* to the star of a punk-rock musical to smiling in breakfast cereal commercials. She has also studied and taught at The Drama Studio, a well-known acting school in London. We began our discussion by examining the methods she uses to communicate emotions to an audience.

Q. How do you prepare yourself to take on the emotions of the character you are playing?

A. I think it depends on the kind of role. Sometimes I actually do feel, after the show has run for a while, the emotion that the character is experiencing, although I may not be getting the same kinds of images. For instance, in the show I'm doing now, there is a place where my character gives up all hope for the future. Now I've never given up in my life, but I've experienced similar kinds of emotions, such as severe despair. Although it's not the same thing that the character is experiencing, it is close enough to bring about the same emotions as those of the character.

Q. So you actually feel the emotion? It's not a matter of just "putting on" the appropriate facial expressions, while at the same time you might be thinking about what you had for lunch or what you are going to do the next day?

A. Oh, no. I would feel the emotion. Now there are times, if you are in the same show for years, when it would be impossible for you to feel heavy emotion night after night—and that is where technique comes in. That is where you learn, by doing it a lot, what you do physically to communicate an emotion to an audience without feeling anything.

Q. Is the general pattern you follow one in which you think about an emotional situation which is congruent with what you are doing in the play and begin to feel that emotion, and then the behavior that you display comes naturally from that emotion you are experiencing?

A. Yes. That's what *I* do. But there are other schools of thought. Some actors work from the inside out—like myself—where they have to feel the emotion first, and from that feeling comes a physical manifestation of the emotion. Other actors like Laurence Olivier work from the outside in. Olivier is famous for his great makeup jobs and elaborate costumes that he uses to make himself look different. A lot of actors do that—anything that they can do to make themselves feel different from the way they are. Similarly there are technical tricks to making an emotion come from "out"—tightening up the stomach, tightening up the face, whatever makes you feel a certain way. It's all technical. For example, some actors stare into space without blinking when they need to cry on stage. This causes tears to flow; and as soon as the tears start to flow, *then* they start to feel the emotion. But they have got to work from the outside in.

Q. When you try to communicate a particular emotion, is there any special part of your body you rely on more, such as your face, body movements, or hand gestures, or is it a matter of everything working together?

A. Ideally, everything should work together, although this is something that I still have to learn. My stamp on every role is my face. It's very expressive. I use my face and my mouth, but those are things that an actress shouldn't rely on too much. After you get the face down, you should be concentrating on other channels of communication.

Q. How do you do that?

A. One of the things I do is keep a file of emotions that I have experienced in which I write down the things I did physically. I have a large file on what I do when I cry, when I'm really happy, when I'm in love, when I hate somebody. People don't really know what they do when they experience an emotion. If people have an idea, it is usually nothing like what they really do. For instance, people think they know what they do when they cry, but it is usually not very accurate. When I was really crying once, I looked in a mirror, and I found where the tension was, where my hands went, how large my mouth got. I think you have to draw on this kind of experience to communicate to an audience. You need to be able to show to an audience the way an emotion is really displayed—not the way that they think it is displayed, which may be incorrect.

OVERVIEW

Communication is at the heart of human social interaction. Indeed, one of the primary characteristics that distinguishes human beings from other species is the ability to communicate on a structured, symbolic level through the formal use of language. But communication also occurs via other means, including a host of nonverbal behaviors such as facial expressions, body movements, gestures, and tone of voice.

In this chapter, we consider social psychological approaches to **communication**, which consists of the ways in which individuals transmit intended or unintended messages to others. Because it is necessary for people to be able to communicate their attitudes, feelings, and thoughts in order to carry out social activities, communication is a uniquely social process which underlies many of the topics we discuss throughout this book. Whether one is considering, for example, how we show attraction for others, how negotiations proceed, or how aggression and anger are demonstrated, communication is the underlying vehicle which permits social interaction to occur.

Because most work done by social psychologists has emphasized the nonverbal aspects of communication, in this chapter we will pay particular attention to nonverbal behavior, a form of communication that is at the heart of actress Susan Greenlee's profession. We explore the role of facial expressions, eye gaze, and body movements in social interaction, as well as theories that explain how individuals combine such different kinds of behaviors to produce a specific message.

We will also examine some selected aspects of verbal communication. However, rather than focusing on its formal properties, as a linguist might, we examine the social psychological functions of language. First, we discuss a model of communication. Then we proceed to consider techniques for structuring conversations and indicating status differentials. Finally, we conclude with a discussion of the relationship between language and thought and the ways in which language is affected by social and cultural factors.

NONVERBAL COMMUNICATION: SHOWING WHAT WE MEAN

From Shakespeare, who writes that Macbeth's face is "a place where men may read strange matters," to old torch songs which say things such as "your eyes are the eyes of a woman in love," nonverbal behavior has had the reputation of revealing the thoughts and feelings of an individual. In support of this anecdotal evidence, there is a large and growing body of scientific work that shows, with certain qualifications, that nonverbal behavior *can* be used to make inferences about others with a surprising degree of accuracy.

A number of different nonverbal communication *channels* will be considered in this chapter. The term **channel** refers to the various paths along which messages flow. For example, facial expressions, eye gaze, body movements, and even such less obvious behaviors as the positioning of the eyebrows can be conceptualized as separate channels of communication. Furthermore, each separate channel is capable of carrying a particular message—which may or may not be related to the message being carried by the other channels (Dittman, 1972). Although there are potentially dozens of separate channels to examine, we will consider the major ones, beginning with facial expressions.

The Face as Mirror of the Soul: Facial Expressions

One of the first, and still the most active, areas of research on nonverbal behavior concerns the expression of emotion through the face. Going back as far as Darwin, theorists have suggested that the face reveals a set of basic emotions that can be identified and distinguished reliably by untrained observers. Consider, for example, the six faces depicted in Figure 3-1. Can you apply an emotional label to each of the photographs?

Most people who are shown these faces conclude that each one expresses a different emotion, and they are fairly accurate in matching a particular emotion category with the following labels: surprise, sadness, happiness, anger, disgust, and fear. These categories, in fact, represent the emotions that emerge reliably over literally hundreds of experiments as being consistently identifiable and distinguishable from one another (Ekman, Friesen, & Ellsworth, 1982). Of course, it is possible to identify other emotions from facial expressions; this list represents the minimum. In sum, a large body of research (see Box 3-1) shows that the face can be a rich source of information, on which emotions *are* reliably revealed.

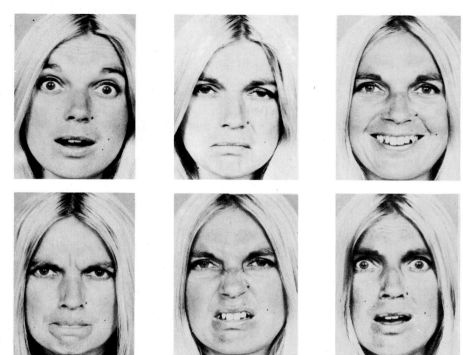

FIGURE 3-1
Faces representing the
primary emotions of sur-
prise, sadness, happi-
ness, anger, disgust, and
fear. Photograph courtesy
of Paul Ekman.

On the other hand, observers frequently are inaccurate when they attempt to decode the meanings of others' facial expressions. There are at least two sources of this inaccuracy—one relating to the person displaying the facial expressions and the second having to do with the observer. Let us consider sources of error due to the person displaying the emotion.

Controlling the Expression of Emotions   When we are given a gift that turns out to be terribly disappointing, we rarely frown, pout, or otherwise outwardly display the unhappiness we really feel. Instead, we are likely to smile and proclaim how pleased we are to have received, for instance, a package of socks and underwear. What prevents us from revealing how we actually feel are the social norms that govern appropriate behavior, the set of expectations that we learn at a young age that say gift givers should be thanked and made to feel that their gifts are appreciated. Such norms influence not just verbal behavior, but nonverbal behavior as well.

In the case of nonverbal behavior, these norms are known as **display rules** (Ekman & Friesen, 1975). Display rules are the implicit rules that govern a given situation or interpersonal relationship regarding the appropriateness of showing a particular emotion by means of facial expressions. These display rules are learned as part of childhood socialization experience as children's cognitive abilities and control over their facial musculature increase (Feldman, 1982).

There are at least four ways in which display rules can modify the expression of emotion (Ekman, Friesen, & Ellsworth, 1972): **intensifying, deintensifying, neutralizing,** or **masking** a felt emotion with another. To convey the appearance of a more intense emotion than is actually felt, one can exaggerate an expression, such as a smile, to show a greater degree of feeling than is actually being experienced. In deintensification, the opposite occurs: the expressed emotion is minimized. When, for example, we have bested someone in a business negotiation, we do not show how happy we are; rather, we try to minimize our true delight.

When people neutralize an expression, they attempt to withhold an indication of how they actually feel. The term "poker face" is derived from situations in which someone attempts to show little or no emotion of any sort through a neutralization of the nonverbal expressions representative of those actually being experienced. The most extreme form of modification of nonverbal behavior occurs when someone masks one expression with another. For instance, you might mask your glee at the funeral of an old and hated rival with appropriate expressions of grief, or you might smile and congratulate the winner of a race for which you had trained for more than a year. In both examples, the expression that is being displayed is just the opposite of the feeling being experienced.

How successful are people at modifying their facial expressions to conceal an emotion they are experiencing? Although there is no definitive answer, it does seem that in many cases people are able to mask their nonverbal behavior successfully (Zuckerman, DePaulo, & Rosenthal, 1981). However, this appears to be the case primarily for facial nonverbal behaviors; as we discuss in Box 3-2, nonfacial nonverbal behaviors such as body movements and tone of voice tend to be more revealing of hidden emotions than the face.

The display rule that will be used in a given situation comes from one of three different sources: those rules that are elicited by a specific situation, those that are cultural in nature, and those that are specific to an individual (Ekman, Friesen, & Ellsworth, 1982). Situational display rules relate to the social definition of the setting. For example, it is appropriate to display grief at funerals, happiness at weddings, and relative neutrality while waiting for a bus. Cultural display rules refer to the norms that are shared by most members of a culture regarding general displays of emotion, relatively independent of the specific situation. Thus, in many Oriental cultures it is considered inappropriate to display emotions, while in Mediterranean and Latin cultures volatile displays are expected.

People also have their own idiosyncratic display rules that relate to the ways in which they show emotions. For instance, some parents may teach their sons that it is "unmanly" to display sadness; thus their sons may learn habitually to show some other emotion—such as anger—when they are feeling unhappy. Hence, because of the nature of their social-

BOX 3-1 SPOTLIGHT ON METHODOLOGY

ON MEASURING EMOTIONS VIA FACIAL EXPRESSIONS

When researchers first began to study facial expressions to determine the accuracy of observations, they went about it in a very straightforward way. The typical procedure of the 1920s, when research of this sort first began, was to hire actors or actresses, have them show an emotion, take their picture, and then ask subjects to identify the emotions that were being expressed. This was a very simple and straighforward procedure—but not an accurate one.

The drawback of this methodology was its reliance on the actors and actresses to produce facial expressions that were identical to those of people who were not posing. If we could be certain that actors and actresses were capable of mimicking the facial expression of, for instance, a sad person accurately, such a procedure might be effective. However, this is not the case. Congruent with the observations of actress Susan Greenlee at the start of this chapter, there is a good deal of current evidence that posed facial expressions are dissimilar to naturally occurring ones in many respects (e.g., Allen & Atkinson, 1981; Rinn, 1984).

One potential solution to the problem of obtaining representative facial expressions relating to emotions has been found in a technique devised by Ross Buck (1976). In this procedure, an individual is exposed to a series of slides or videotapes of an emotion-evoking scene. Thus, for instance, people may be shown a tape of a very sad scene from a movie. As they are watching the tape, a videotape of their nonverbal behavior is made. An investigator is then entitled to claim that the facial expressions are representative of spontaneous, rather than posed, emotional reactions.

Although such a procedure brings us closer to

obtaining a true representation of facial expressions to use in experimental research, it still does not solve the problem completely. For instance, the emotion-evoking videotape may not be involving enough to bring about appropriate emotional displays. Worse yet, the tape may produce an emotion other than what the experimenter intended or the viewer's expressions may be unrelated to the content of the tape.

Even if the investigator succeeds in obtaining an accurate representation of a facial expression to use in an experiment, there are further methodological hurdles to overcome. The method of measuring the emotion that is perceived by the observers is critical. Should observers be allowed simply to write down the specific emotion they think they see? Should they be given a list of emotions from which to choose and be restricted to that list? Or should they be asked to rate the expressions along dimensions such as "positive–negative" without being required to categorize the expressions into specific emotions? In addition, there is an artificiality to procedures that ask observers to make ratings of faces devoid of context. For instance, without knowing that the two people who are displayed in Figure 3-2 have just won a lottery, an observer would find their facial expressions contradictory and misleading.

FIGURE 3-2
The nature of the situation must be considered when we determine the meaning of a particular facial expression. While we might at first think that the man and woman pictured here are experiencing very different emotions, in fact they are both responding to a very happy situation—winning a million-dollar lottery. (Neal Boenzi/ The New York Times)

Finally, it is always difficult to pinpoint the source of any results that one does obtain. Is it something about the observers or something about the people whose expressions are being rated? Suppose we found that a group of observers correctly identified the emotion of gratitude only 25 percent of the time. Logically, this result could mean one of two things. It might mean that observers in general are able to judge expressions of gratitude with only minimal accuracy. But it also might mean that people's facial expression of gratitude has only a minimal degree of clarity. If this is the case, it is not that the observers are poor judges; rather, the emotion of gratitude simply is not expressed through facial, nonverbal behavior. Both explanations are plausible.

There are, then, a number of difficult methodological issues involved in the study of nonverbal behavior; indeed, we have only scratched the surface here. Still, the field is progressing rapidly, and a number of new techniques have recently been devised. For example, one approach focuses on tiny muscle movements in the face that can be viewed only through special photographic techniques, while another involves computer-assisted coding and scoring procedures—a far cry from the use of posed actors (Scherer & Ekman, 1982).

---

ization experiences, people develop their own idiosyncratic set of display rules that operate in addition to situational and cultural rules.

In summary, display rules govern the way in which an emotion will be displayed in a particular situation, and they may bring about substantial differences in the way in which emotions are displayed between different people. We turn now to research that focuses on the *similarities*, rather than the differences, across individuals' expressions of emotion.

The Universality of Facial Expression: Do New Guineans and New Yorkers Behave the Same Nonverbally?   One of the most important issues under investigation in the area of nonverbal behavior is the degree to which nonverbal behavior is universal. Many theoreticians have argued that the relationship between nonverbal displays and particular emotions is innate within all human beings. Others, with a different orientation, have suggested that shared learning experiences, common to most people, result in similar nonverbal expressions being related to particular emotions. If either of these views is correct, we would expect to find similarity in emotional expression across members of different cultures. On the other hand, the opposite hypothesis has been argued: many researchers have suggested that the relationship between the display of particular nonverbal behavior and an emotional state is specific to a culture or subculture and shows distinct variations.

The most convincing evidence to shed light on this controversial issue comes from work carried out by Paul Ekman (1972, 1973). In the late 1960s, Ekman and colleagues traveled to New Guinea to study members of a jungle tribe that had had almost no contact with Western culture. They did not speak or understand English, had never seen movies or magazines, and had never worked with Caucasians.

To avoid the methodological difficulty of labeling emotions in different languages, Ekman used a procedure in which subjects were shown three photographs of Caucasian faces, each of which expressed a different emotion, and then told them a story which involved only one emotion. The subjects were asked to match the appropriate face with the story.

Most of the New Guineans chose the face that was the choice of most Western observers. As illustrated in Table 3-1, for the most part there were close similarities between the kinds of judgments made by the New Guineans and those made by the Western subjects, with just one minor exception (fearful faces were often confused with surprise by the natives). Interestingly, children were even more accurate than adult New Guineans.

Ekman also obtained results demonstrating that in addition to similarities in decoding facial expressions, there were similarities in the use of given expressions across different cultures. Ekman asked other New Guineans to show the expression that would appear on their faces if they were the person in the stories used in the earlier part of the study. These expressions were videotaped and shown to a sample of Western observers in the United States. These observers, asked to identify the emotion being displayed, were accurate in their judgments—except for the emotions of fear and surprise, with which they had some difficulty.

Taken together, the findings from this ambitious cross-cultural study support the idea that there are similarities in nonverbal behavior that run across cultures. Because of their isolation, the New Guineans could not have learned to recognize or produce the facial expressions of Westerners; the recognition and production capabilities seem to have been present either innately or through similar learning experiences in both cultures. For either reason, the expression of emotions, both facially and in other nonverbal behavior, appears to be basically similar across cultures.

The Facial Affect Program: A Link between Emotion and Nonverbal Behavior To provide an explanation for the apparent universality of emotion-related expressions, Ekman (1972, 1982) suggests that the expression of emotions is guided by a **facial affect program.** This program, which acts in a way analogous to a computer program, is activated when

TABLE 3-1 Percentage of New Guinean Subjects Correctly Identifying Photos of Westerners Described in Story

Emotion Category Described in the Story	Adults	Children
Happiness	92	92
Sadness	79	81
Anger	84	90
Disgust	81	85
Surprise	68	98
Fear: From anger/disgust or sadness	80	93
From surprise	43	—

Source: Ekman & Friesen (1971).

Can we make accurate inferences regarding the meaning of the facial expressions of people from very different cultures? Research suggests that, at least in terms of fundamental facial expressions, the answer is "yes." (*Left,* Phillip Jones Griffiths/ Magnum; *right,* Elliot Erwitt/Magnum)

a particular emotion is experienced. As soon as the emotion is felt, the program elicits a particular set of neurological impulses that activate facial muscles displaying a unique facial expression. According to this view, each primary emotion has a characteristic kind of muscular activation which results in a particular facial expression. For instance, happiness may produce a smile, which is actually the activation of a muscle—the **zygomatic major**—that raises the corners of the mouth.

The process invoked can be summarized as the sequence shown in Figure 3-3. The first step is some environmental or situational occurrence, or an internal memory, fantasy, or physiological event (such as a sudden pain) activating an appraisal mechanism. The process of appraisal next evokes the experience of a particular emotion. Then, the facial affect program is "turned on"—and the emotional experience is displayed as a representative facial expression due to the activation of particular muscles.

Of course, the facial expression that is displayed may not directly reflect the emotion being experienced because of the existence of display rules. These display rules, as we have seen, may prevent the facial affect program from being carried out in its pure form.

The Facial Feedback Hypothesis: Facial Expressions May Be a Cause of Emotional Experience

One of the most intriguing implications of the universality notion in emotional expression is the hypothesis—called the **facial feedback hypothesis**—that facial expressions not only *reflect* emotional experience, but are important in *determining* how we actually experience and label emotion. Specifically, as actress Susan Greenlee mentioned at the beginning of the chapter, it is possible that "wearing" a particular facial expression at a given time may cause us to

BOX 3-2   SPOTLIGHT ON APPLICATIONS

USING NONVERBAL BEHAVIOR TO DETECT DECEPTION: THE TRUTH ABOUT TELLING LIES

An issue that arises in almost all courtroom trials is the credibility of testifying witnesses. Because factual information is often lacking, and because witnesses may contradict one another, jurors are sometimes forced to evaluate whether or not witnesses are telling the truth from the way they appear—i.e., from their nonverbal behavior. Is it possible to winnow out the truth from the lies by using such nonverbal cues?

Research suggests that a cautious "yes" is the appropriate answer to such a question. Under certain conditions people are able to detect deceptive responses at better-than-chance levels—but not much better than chance. In an extensive review of the literature, Zuckerman, DePaulo, and Rosenthal (1981) found that at least in laboratory studies in which a group of stimulus persons are led to be truthful or deceptive and then observers are asked to distinguish those who tell the truth from the liars, there is a moderate degree of success. Overall, observers accurately discern truthfulness or deceit between 40 percent and 60 percent of the time (Miller, Bauchner, Hocking, Fontes, Kaminski, & Brandt, 1981).

What specific types of nonverbal behavior indicate that a person is being deceptive? Researchers have approached this question in two ways: (1) by measuring the kinds of behaviors that occur when a person is actually being deceptive and (2) by determining what behaviors people *think* are associated with people who are deceptive. The results of these two approaches, although overlapping considerably, are not always the same.

Researchers who have measured the nonverbal behavior of deceptive people have found a number of consistencies, although it should be noted that there are exceptions to almost every generalization one can draw. Overall, though, lying, compared with nondeceptive communications, seems to involve less eye contact, fewer head nods, less smiling, fewer gestures, more frequent shifts in body movements, less directness in postural orientation, changes in speech speed and pitch, and—in general—more discrepancies among various nonverbal behaviors (Miller & Burgoon, 1982). Observers expect to find deception in people who display by less eye gazing, less smiling, more postural shifts, slower speech rate, more speech errors, more hesitations during speech, higher speech pitch, and longer response times to questions (Zuckerman, DePaulo, & Rosenthal, 1981).

Given that there is so much overlap between nonverbal behavior that indicates deception and nonverbal behavior that is perceived as deception, why are people not better at decoding lying? The reason is that many of the same behaviors occur under conditions that are unrelated to deception. For instance, people may smile less and their speech pitch may rise when they are nervous for reasons having nothing to do with being deceptive. Hence, truthful people who are testifying in court may be perceived—inaccurately—as lying because their nonverbal behavior, which is actually a sign of their anxiety, is similar to that displayed by people who are being deceptive.

Of course, when we apply this research to courtroom assessments of witness credibility, we must do so with caution. As Miller et al. (1981, p. 177) point out, "Attributions of truthfulness and deceitfulness, which jurors must frequently make to weigh testimony and reach decisions, may be of questionable validity. In general, jurors probably have difficulty assessing the veracity of witnesses. This difficulty, in turn, suggests that certain assumptions regarding the jurors' *abilities* to contribute actively to the administration of justice may warrant re-examination."

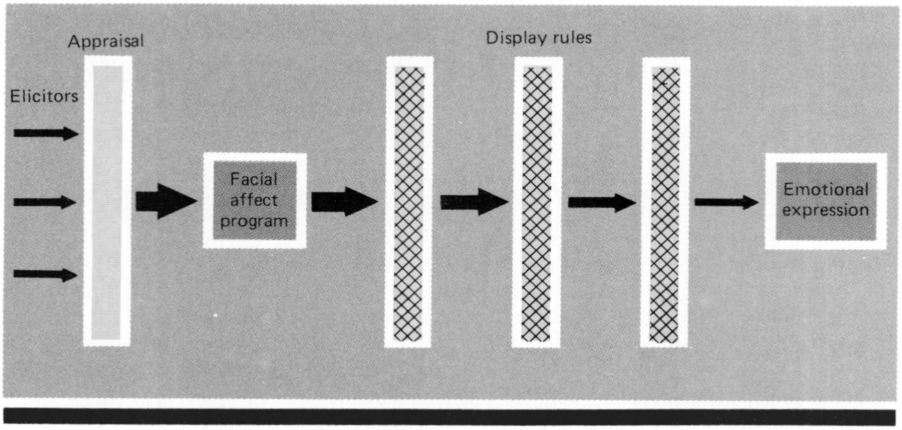

FIGURE 3-3
The facial affect program,
showing a model of how
emotions are displayed
nonverbally. Source:
Ekman (1972).

experience the emotion consistent with the expression. For instance, researchers have hypothesized that the muscular feedback from the facial muscles involved in the sad expression may actually help produce the emotion of sadness.

An even stronger version of this argument is possible. It is conceivable that an appropriate facial expression may be *necessary* for an emotional experience to occur, and that without such an expression, there will be no emotional experience. Another form of the argument suggests that even if *no* stimulus capable of evoking an emotion is present, adoption of a facial expression that is related to a specific emotion may be sufficient to produce an emotion (Tomkins, 1962; Izard, 1977). A popularized form of this argument is found in the lyrics of an old song—"Smile, though your heart is breaking"—which suggests that one just might feel better by adopting the demeanor of someone in a positive emotional state. (You might try something similar yourself: what emotion do you experience if you clench your teeth, narrow your eyes, and scowl?)

Although such hypotheses are intriguing, they enjoy only mixed support at the present time (Rinn, 1984). One of the few attempts to confirm them was carried out by Tourangeau and Ellsworth (1979), who had subjects watch films that were meant to be sad, fear arousing, or emotionally neutral. While they were watching, subjects were told to produce and maintain a fearful, sad, or grimacing expression (or, in a control condition, no expression). The rationale for this request was based on a cover story in which subjects were told that the purpose of the experiment was to measure various subtle physiological reactions which would necessitate their adopting a particular expression in order not to disturb the measurement of the various physiological factors.

After the experimental procedure, subjects' emotional experiences were assessed. The results showed that the content of the films had a powerful effect upon subjects' emotional reactions, but the particular expression that they had been instructed to adopt had essentially no influence on their emotions. Production of a particular emotional expression did not result in the experience of the emotion, and even if the face was not allowed to show the proper emotion, subjects experienced emotions appropriate to the external, emotion-evoking film stimuli—suggesting that people's emotional responses are not affected by the nature of their facial expressions.

However, before rejecting the notion that facial expressions can influence the experience of emotion, we should note that there are a number of methodological difficulties with the Tourangeau and Ellsworth (1979) experiment. As Hager and Ekman (1981) point out, it is unlikely that the subjects who were instructed to produce particular emotional expressions could do so with enough precision to give close representations of the equivalent spontaneous expressions. It could be argued, then, that subjects did not experience emotions equivalent to their facial expressions because they were unsuccessful in portraying the appropriate expressions accurately. Moreover, it is quite possible that the films that subjects were viewing elicited spontaneous emotional facial expressions which interfered with subjects' successful production of the specific emotion that they had been asked to produce.

In fact, recent research done by Ekman, Levenson, and Friesen (1983) found support for this hypothesis. In their experiment, they asked professional actors to follow instructions that were very explicit, such as "Raise your brows and pull them together; now raise you upper eyelids; now also stretch your lips horizontally back toward your ears." When the actors carried out these actions—which, in this case, turn out to produce expressions of fear—their heart rates rose and their skin temperatures went down, physiological reactions that usually accompany fear. In general, it appeared that the production of facial expressions characteristic of a fundamental emotion resulted in physiological effects that typically accompany the particular emotion.

Given the contradictory evidence, it is still too early to say that the facial feedback hypothesis has been confirmed. However, it remains a viable theory regarding the relationship between facial expressions and emotional experience, and it suggests that the old platitude that tells people to "smile your troubles away" just may be valid.

The Eyes as Windows to the Soul: Eye Gaze

Poets, lyricists, and playwrights have all paid homage to the power of the eyes in signifying love, interpersonal attraction, anger, power, and an assortment of other emotions and feelings. No less than others, social psychologists have also found that eye gaze plays an important role in indicating a variety of emotional states.

One of the stablest and best-replicated findings regarding eye gaze concerns liking: as we discuss in Chapter 6 when we examine interpersonal attraction, the degree of eye contact between two individuals is related directly to the intensity of their feelings for each other. This relationship holds not just for romantic lovers, but for friends as well (Rubin, 1973; Exline & Winters, 1965).

Gaze not only functions as a measure of interpersonal attraction, but its use by an individual can actually promote attraction by others. Salespeople have banked upon this fact for some time; one frequently employed sales tactic is to maintain eye contact with a potential buyer of one's product in the hopes of increasing one's likability. Research has confirmed this notion, although not without some clarification. People do rate others who look at them more frequently and for longer periods of time more positively than others who spend proportionally less time looking at them—but only when the situation and the topic being discussed are pleasant ones (Ellsworth & Carlsmith, 1968). If the topic under discussion is unpleasant to the subject, more eye contact can lead to reduced attraction.

There are other exceptions to the eye contact–attraction relationship. An important one concerns extremes of eye gaze, when one person gazes at another for an extended period of time. Consider your own reaction if you were to find a stranger on a subway gazing at you unfalteringly. Rather than being attracted to the stranger, you would be more likely to experience emotions of a negative nature. The reason? Most of us would interpret the eye contact as a hostile stare—a signal of aggression and dominance that exists throughout the animal kingdom (e.g., Greene & Reiss, 1984).

The aversive qualities of stares were illustrated quite imaginatively in a series of field studies carried out by Ellsworth, Carlsmith, and Henson (1972). In one study, automobile drivers pulled up to a red light at a busy intersection and found another motorist already in the inside lane, ostensibly waiting for the light to change. The other driver was actually an experimenter who in one condition stared directly at the driver's face or, in another condition, did not stare at the driver at all. When the light changed to green, the time it took for the driver to cross the intersection was measured.

As anyone who has ever been stared at by a stranger in an adjacent vehicle might guess, the results were clear and unequivocal: drivers who were stared at sped through the intersection in significantly less time (an average of 5.5 seconds) than those who were not stared at (an average of 6.7 seconds). The drivers who were stared at also engaged in a number of behaviors indicative of anxiety. They played with their car radios, touched their clothing, revved up their engines, paid undue attention to the traffic light, glancing at it frequently, or began to speak to the other occupants of their cars.

It appears, then, that staring can be interpreted as an aversive stimulus which brings about avoidance behavior. Of course, that is not the only explanation for the results of the Ellsworth, Carlsmith, and Henson (1972) experiment. It is possible, for instance, that subjects viewed the stare as an interpersonal signal of some sort—not necessarily an aversive signal—but one which required a response. Since the situation was one in which no obvious response was apparent, it is plausible that subjects chose to escape the situation because of their lack of understanding of what an appropriate response might be. Still, whatever the specific reason, staring evokes negative responses and provides a clear exception to the typical association between eye contact and liking.

Body Movements: Nonverbal Behavior in a Broader Context

As actress Susan Greenlee commented, the movements of the entire body have important communicative value. **Kinesics** is the study of how body language, movements of the hands, feet, and trunk, are related to communication. It should be noted that the nature of communication via body channels is qualitatively different from that of the face. Lacking the muscular complexity of the face, the rest of the body tends to provide information that is somewhat less specific in meaning. Nonetheless, body behaviors can sometimes be of greater use in identifying particular psychological states—such as when an individual is being deceptive—than facial nonverbal behaviors, since people tend to have less experience in consciously manipulating nonfacial behaviors (Ekman & Friesen, 1974).

One particularly well-defined type of body behavior is called an **illustrator.** It acts to modify and augment spoken messages (Hager, 1982). For instance, if you are asked to describe how to get to your dormitory, you are likely to point in the appropriate direction. Similarly, if you were asked to describe how big a new radio is, you would probably illustrate its size by indicating its dimensions in the air. Illustrators can also be used for emphasis: a finger pointed at you, accompanied by the statement "I want you to know how angry I am with *you*," leaves little chance that you would miss the emotion behind the statement.

Another type of body movement is termed the **adaptor.** Adaptors are specific behaviors that, at some point in a particular individual's development, served a special function or purpose but are no longer part of the individual's behavioral repertoire. For example, people under stress sometimes rub their eyes, as if to avoid viewing an unpleasant sight. They may also cover or pick at their ears, symbolically avoiding an unpleasant message. Adaptors occur largely outside of people's conscious awareness, but they may be useful as cues indicating emotional states.

One type of body movement with which we are all familiar is the **emblem.** Emblems are body movements that replace spoken language. They tend to be specific to particular cultures, and they are understood by most members of a culture in the same way that most everyone understands the verbal language.

Some of the most common emblems are illustrated in Figure 3-4. Many of them have complicated histories, and their meanings vary from culture to culture. Take, for instance, the A-OK sign, with the thumb and forefinger forming an "O" (Harrison, 1974). In America, this gesture was built upon the verbal phrase "OK," which in turn grew out of

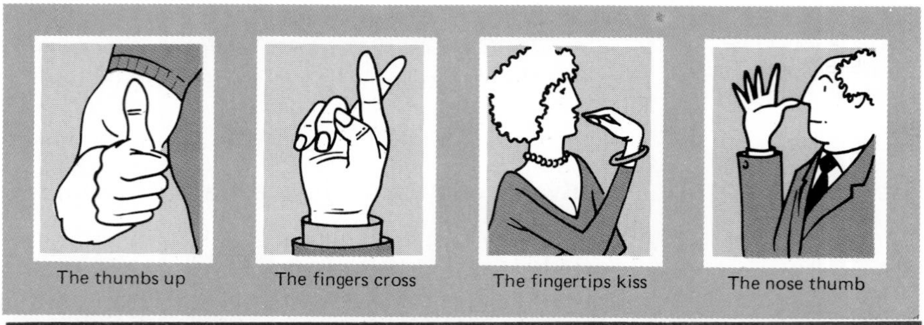

FIGURE 3-4
Common emblems.
Source: Morris (1979).

The thumbs up   The fingers cross   The fingertips kiss   The nose thumb

political terminology of the 1840s having to do with Martin Van Buren's birthplace, Old Kinderhook, N.Y.! (Most Americans would have little trouble identifying the meaning of the gesture, although clearly they would have little inkling of its origins.)

What is particularly interesting about the A-OK sign is that its meaning is completely different to non-Americans. In many cultures, the gesture represents the female sexual anatomy. If a male uses the sign toward a female, it is a sexual proposition. If a male gestures in the same way toward another male, it is insulting the recipient's masculinity. It is easy to envisage how cross-cultural misunderstandings can occur when people with such diverse understandings of a common gesture interact with one another.

The Body in Space: Where It Is Can Be as Important as What It Does
Not only can a person's body provide information by the way it moves, but the positioning of the body is informative as well. Imagine how you would behave if you were to meet the President of the United States in the Oval Office. Rather than rushing up to him, it is likely that you would stand back, keeping a respectful distance and waiting for him to ask you to sit down. Even if he did say to pull up a chair, you would probably maintain a distance between yourself and him.

An explanation for such behavior can be found in **proxemics,** the regularities that occur in interpersonal spacing. Much of the work on proxemics has centered on how spacing reflects the status and intimacy of the individuals who are interacting with each other, and it now appears clear that the greater the difference in status between two people, the larger the amount of space that they maintain between them will be (Lott & Sommer, 1967).

A good example of the relationship between status and spacing comes from a study by Dean, Willis, and Hewitt (1975) of military personnel—where status differentials are particularly obvious. In the field study, they clandestinely observed pairs of navy personnel in nonwork settings such as the cafeteria, the lobby of a hospital, and a recreation center. By counting the standard-size floor tiles that separated the members of each of the pairs, it was possible to make fairly precise measurements of the distance between each pair without intruding.

The findings indicated that military rank was clearly related to the distance by which the military men spaced themselves. When a subordinate initiated an interaction with a superior, he stood further apart than when interacting with a peer. And the greater the discrepancy in rank, the greater the distance between the two. However, when the interaction was initiated by a superior, interaction distance was unrelated to the discrepancy in rank. It seems as if the higher status superiors felt they had the freedom to interact with subordinates at whatever distance they desired. In contrast, a person who initiates an interaction with someone of higher status is constrained by social norms; he or she must maintain an interpersonal distance that is deemed appropriate to the situation.

Just what is an appropriate distance? In American society, there appear to be fairly universal standards for spacing, depending on the intimacy of the interaction. According to anthropologist Edward Hall (1966), middle-class Americans tend to interact with one another at a distance of 18 inches or less for the most intimate interaction. Casual interactions with friends are held at 18 inches to 4 feet, and people tend to space themselves from 4 to 12 feet apart when conducting impersonal business. Finally, there is a "public zone," which goes from 12 feet to the limits of hearing, generally about 25 feet. Formal occasions, such as lectures and judicial proceedings, occur at this distance.

Not only do regularities in spacing occur during social interaction, but people use distance to draw inferences about how much others are attracted to them. For instance, one experiment found that people who were asked to imagine that another person was standing 3 feet away thought that they would be liked significantly more than when the other person was imagined to be 7 feet away (Mehrabian, 1968a). Another experiment, in which subjects were asked to space themselves as if they liked (or disliked) another individual, revealed that subjects chose to stand considerably closer to the person they liked (Mehrabian, 1968b). Of course, such data suffer from a methodological drawback: subjects' *perceptions* of how they space themselves might be quite different from what they would do when interacting with an actual person (Love & Aiello, 1980).

As is true of the relationship between eye contact and interpersonal attraction, extremes of closeness are not always related positively to interpersonal attraction. If the interaction between two people is basically positive, increased proximity is related to enhanced liking. But if the interaction is initially negative, nearness can lead to increased negativity on the part of the interactants (Schiffenbauer & Schiavo, 1976). Hence, increased proximity does not invariably lead to enhanced attraction between two interactants.

One of the intriguing findings related to interpersonal spacing is that different cultures seem to have very different norms regarding what the appropriate distance to maintain when conversing is. For instance, Arabs tend to sit closer to one another than Americans do when conversing (Watson & Graves, 1966). In fact, Arabs tend to converse casually at a distance of just 1 foot—whereas Americans tend to hold conversations with nonintimate friends at distances of 4 to 12 feet, as was mentioned earlier. It is not hard to imagine the discomfort that a newly acquainted American and Arab would feel conversing with each other, each trying to maintain an "appropriate" distance. As the Arab tried to edge closer, the American would be likely to try to back away. Eventually, of course, some equilibrium would be found, but not without some initial cross-cultural misunderstanding and tension.

Arabs and Americans are not the only people to have well-entrenched norms regarding appropriate spacing when conversing. For example, members of English-speaking cultures in general (England, Canada, and America) tend to space themselves further apart than members of South American and Mediterranean cultures (Montagu, 1971; Aiello & Thompson, 1980). Moreover, these cross-cultural differences are not just limited to interpersonal spacing: members of South American and Mediterranean cultures also tend to touch each other more, use gestures more frequently, and be more demonstrative with affection in public.

Combining Channels of Communication: Is the Whole Greater than the Sum of the Parts?

Although we have been discussing different channels of nonverbal behavior as if each were independent of one another, nonverbal communication, of course, occurs along multiple channels simultaneously. As Susan Greenlee remarked, communication is a function of many stimuli being emitted at the same time. Surprisingly, though, relatively few theories have been put forward to explain how behaviors along the various channels are related to one another.

One approach that has been taken to explain cross-channel nonverbal behavior is an equilibrium model proposed by Michael Argyle (Argyle & Dean, 1965; Argyle & Cook, 1976). According to the model, intimacy toward others is represented by a combination of eye contact, interpersonal distance, body lean and orientation, facial expressions, and other related nonverbal behaviors. Each of these behaviors is assumed to be linked to the others and to the overall degree of interpersonal intimacy that exists between two people.

Most central to the theory is the notion that an *increase* in the level of intimacy along one nonverbal behavioral dimension—which would otherwise tend to increase the overall level of intimacy—will tend to be accompanied by a compensatory *decrease* in intimacy along another nonverbal dimension. The decrease acts to maintain a general equilibrium among the various indices of nonverbal intimacy as well as to maintain the desired overall level of intimacy toward the other person.

Equilibrium can either be maintained within an individual (as when person A stands closer to person B but at the same time looks less at person B) or exist between two people (as when person A stands closer to person B, but person B reacts by looking less at person A).

Let us take a concrete example of equilibrium maintenance between two people. Suppose Sarah has a friend, Matthew, and over the course of their relationship they build up a fairly stable pattern of nonverbal interactions, based upon a particular level of casual friendship that they both share. But suppose that Matthew begins to be romantically interested in Sarah and shows his newfound desire for closer friendship by gazing at Sarah for greater periods of time than he had in the past.

According to the equilibrium model, if Sarah does not share Matthew's desire for intimacy, her probable reaction will be to compensate for the increase in eye contact (a signal of greater intimacy) by *reducing* signs of intimacy, either along the same dimension or by modifying nonverbal behavior along some other dimension—perhaps by increasing the space that is maintained between the two of them. In this way, the overall degree of intimacy displayed between Sarah and Matthew will remain relatively invariant.

The equilibrium model has received a good deal of confirmation from experimental studies, although certain aspects have been more strongly supported than others (Patterson, 1973, 1983). For instance, there is clear evidence that as eye contact increases, body orientation becomes less direct and people may even leave the setting (Heslin & Patterson, 1982)—as the cartoon in Figure 3-5 illustrates quite well.

On the other hand, occasional exceptions to the equilibrium model have been found. For example, in some cases when equilibrium between nonverbal indices of intimacy is disturbed, an individual's reaction is to reciprocate the change in level by maintaining, or sometimes even increasing, the signals of intimacy (Breed, 1972; Jourard & Friedman, 1970). For instance, if Sarah from our earlier example becomes more interested in Matthew, she might reciprocate his heightened level of eye gaze by increasing her eye contact or by moving closer to him. Hence, rather than compensating by decreasing signals of intimacy, she may respond by raising the general level of intimacy of the interaction.

Arousal and Nonverbal Intimacy: A Labeling Theory   In an attempt to explain under what circumstances reciprocity, as opposed to compensation, of nonverbal signals of intimacy occurs, Miles Patterson (1976) proposed a model based upon the concept of physiological arousal and the way that arousal is labeled. The model suggests that the nature of changes in arousal determines whether intimacy will be reciprocated or compensated for.

According to Patterson, the first step in the model is noticing that the person with whom you are interacting (labeled "A" in Figure 3-6) has changed the nonverbal signs of intimacy being emitted. If you do not

FIGURE 3-5

Responding to unwelcome eye contact. Source: G. B. Trudeau, copyright © 1977. Reprinted with permission of Universal Press Syndicated. All rights reserved.

notice such a change, then of course you will not experience a change in your level of arousal, and consequently will neither compensate nor reciprocate in terms of your own nonverbal behavior.

But suppose that you (labeled "B" in the figure) *do* notice the change in nonverbal behavior and consequently do become physiologically aroused. According to the model, you will then try to assign a label to the source of the increased arousal in order to explain it. Whether you place a positive or negative label on the source of arousal will depend upon situational cues, past experience, and, perhaps, the nature of the prior relationship between you and the other person.

In any case, you will consider the arousal to be basically either positive or negative. If you assign a positive emotion—such as liking, loving, relief, or satisfaction—the model suggests that you will reciprocate the nonverbal signs of intimacy by producing nonverbal behaviors indicative of greater intimacy. On the other hand, if the label assigned the arousal is negative in nature—such as disliking or discomfort—you will be more apt to compensate by reducing signs of nonverbal intimacy.

The final stage in the model is a feedback loop, in which your nonverbal behavior then affects the person with whom you are interacting. Depending upon the nature of your reaction, the other person may modify his or her behavior to achieve congruence with the level of intimacy produced by his or her initial changes. Theoretically, such a sequence could proceed indefinitely, and it is likely, in fact, that interactants continually adjust and readjust their nonverbal behavior during ongoing social interactions.

Although the arousal model proposed by Patterson is reasonable, the

FIGURE 3-6
M. L. Patterson's arousal model of interpersonal intimacy. Source: Patterson (1976).

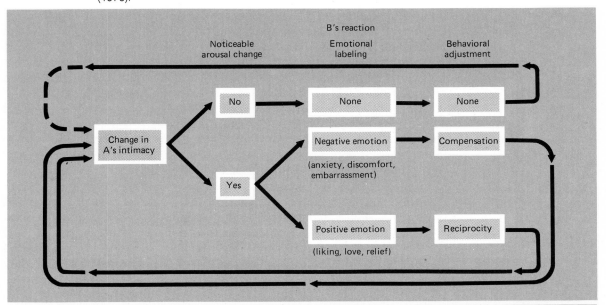

experimental support it has received is somewhat limited. Some support comes from a study in which a child was asked to watch a cartoon with either a friend or a stranger (Foot, Chapman, & Smith, 1977). Children in friendship pairs showed a significantly higher degree of similarity in their smiling, looking, laughing, and talking responses than did children in stranger pairs, suggesting that there was greater reciprocity among the friends than among strangers.

Recent work that has tested the arousal model more directly has produced some support for the theory, although the results have not been unequivocal (Patterson, Jordan, Hogan, & Frerker, 1981; Patterson, 1983). For instance, it appears that the social context in which intimacy occurs is taken into account more strongly than the model originally assumed. Moreover, it seems that compensation is apt to occur only under conditions in which there are moderate levels of initial changes in intimacy. Minor fluctuations may not warrant a compensatory change in another channel, whereas very large fluctuations may throw the entire intimacy equilibrium into such imbalance that there are major disruptions in communication (Hayduk, 1983).

Still, arousal theory and the equilibrium model represent an important advance in the study of nonverbal behavior, indicating as they do that nonverbal channels should not be looked at in isolation, but rather must be understood as they interact with one another.

Using Communication Channels in Social Interaction: The Case of Married Couples   One of the most promising avenues of work on communication across disparate channels is its potential applicability to a variety of areas. For instance, some clinical psychologists have theorized that one potential cause of schizophrenia in children might be discrepancies between nonverbal communication channels in the messages that come from their parents (Bateson, Jackson, Haley, & Weakland, 1956). Other research has shown that there are communication channel inconsistencies within pairs of mothers and children who show disturbances in their relationships (Bugental, Love, Kaswan, & April, 1971).

A recent line of work has found evidence that the state of marital adjustment in couples is related to the degree and nature of channel consistency between husband and wife. Patricia Noller (1982) videotaped married couples while they were discussing aspects of their married life and subsequently analyzed whether the messages being transmitted were basically positive, negative, or neutral from four separate channel combinations: the verbal channel (what was said, using a typed transcript), visual channel (using the face alone), vocal channel (verbal content using specific wording plus tone of voice while saying it), and the total channel (using all available cues). The couples also completed a battery of questionnaires assessing their marital adjustment, and they were divided into high, moderate, and low marital adjustment groups.

Noller found a number of differences regarding the nature of communications among the three groups. Across all channels, positive mes-

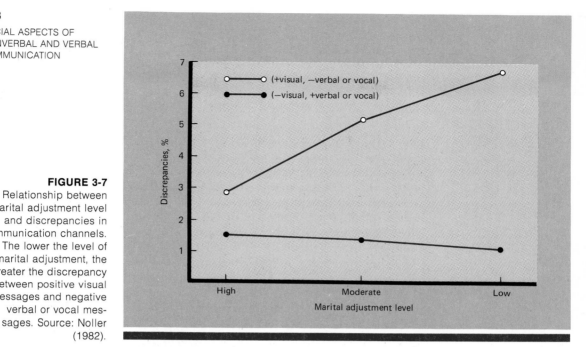

FIGURE 3-7
Relationship between
marital adjustment level
and discrepancies in
communication channels.
The lower the level of
marital adjustment, the
greater the discrepancy
between positive visual
messages and negative
verbal or vocal mes-
sages. Source: Noller
(1982).

sages were conveyed more frequently by high- and moderate-adjust-
ment couples, while negative messages were used more by subjects low
in marital adjustment. Even more interesting were discrepancies among
the various channels in the nature of the message being communicated.
One of the most frequent sorts of discrepancy consisted of a positive
message in the visual channel combined with a negative message in the
verbal or vocal channel. The opposite pattern (negative visual message
with a positive verbal or vocal message) was also prevalent.

As can be seen in Figure 3-7, the percentage of discrepancies related
to positive visual and negative verbal or vocal channels was strongly
related to marital adjustment levels, while the opposite pattern was not.
In high-adjustment couples, then, positive visual behavior was more
likely to be closely related to positive verbal and visual messages, while
in couples with lower adjustment, a positive visual message was more
likely to be accompanied by a negative verbal or vocal message.

The important point to be drawn from these findings is not so much
the specific nature of channel inconsistencies as the fact that certain
inconsistencies are systematically related to marital adjustment. Of
course, these findings come from a correlational study; subjects were
not randomly assigned to condition. Hence, channel inconsistency could
potentially be the cause *or* the result of marital adjustment. Still, the
findings are suggestive that cross-channel communication discrepancies
are a potential factor in marital discord.

VERBAL COMMUNICATION: SAYING WHAT WE MEAN

One of the primary characteristics that distinguishes human beings from other species is our use of a spoken language to communicate on a verbal level. While nonhumans are limited to nonverbal communication, people have developed complex and diverse sets of languages to communicate with one another. But to social psychologists who study verbal behavior, it is not so much the structure and formal properties of language that are of interest (as they might be to a linguist or literary scholar); rather, the focus is on those aspects of language that relate to the social nature of verbal interaction. In this view, considering just the overt, verbal content of an interchange may lead to a loss of an important part of the meaning of a dialogue, for verbal interaction is not just a matter of considering the definitions and grammatical structure of verbal discourse. Instead, there are several meanings that lie below the surface, predicated upon the prior social history of the interactants.

In the remainder of the chapter, we focus on the major issues of interest to social psychologists relating to verbal communication. To understand how verbal communication proceeds, we will use a variant of a model of communication that was first proposed by Shannon and Weaver (1949). Illustrated in Figure 3-8, the model traces the various stages through which communications proceed as they move from the person sending the message—the **encoder**—to the person receiving the message—the **decoder.** As can be seen, even the simplest of human interchanges can represent a high level of sophistication.

Before we discuss the model, it should be noted that this is but one of a number of models of communication that have been developed; other models emphasize the information processing, sociological, or anthropological aspects of communication. While early models were one-directional, stressing the ways in which an encoder develops and transmits his or her message and more or less ignoring the recipient of the message, more recent work has acknowledged that the nature of successful communications is very much dependent upon the characteristics and expected reactions of the listener. Moreover, while we will use the model to consider verbal behavior, it is also applicable to nonverbal channels of communication.

FIGURE 3-8
A model of communication processes.

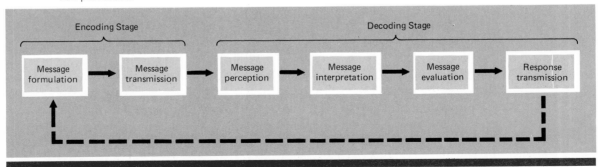

Encoding: Getting the Message Across

The first task facing someone who desires to communicate is to formulate the message. In the encoding phase of communication, the first stage consists of **message formulation,** in which the message is encoded according to the specific characteristics of the decoder or person to whom the communication is directed. The second stage is the **transmission** of the message.

Formulating the Message: Knowing to Whom You Communicate

One of the first steps in preparing to communicate with someone else is to assess that person's characteristics and the social constraints operating in a given situation. According to John Flavell and his associates (1968), speakers initially decide upon the nature of the message using language that is most accurate from their own point of view. However, if they are adept at what Flavell refers to as **role-taking**—understanding that others have a different point of view and set of perceptions about the world and that messages must take into account the decoder's perspective— the encoder will try to judge the characteristics of the listener and situation. The encoder will use his or her assessment as the basis for reformulating the message if it appears that such reformulation is necessary.

Although the reformulation of the message is typically viewed in terms of the impression that the encoder wants to convey to the decoder, an even more fundamental approach to formulation and reformulation of messages can be seen in terms of the relative levels of linguistic competence of encoder and decoder. For instance, people tend to simplify their speech when they are talking to young children or to foreigners—both of whom are assumed to understand language poorly (Freed, 1980). Even children tend to reformulate their messages when speaking to children younger than themselves. For instance, Shatz and Gelman (1977) found that 4-year-olds spoke very simply when trying to teach a concept to a 2-year-old—but they used considerably more sophisticated speech when teaching an adult.

It is therefore important to distinguish between **linguistic competence** and **social communicative competence** (Scott, 1977; Turiel, 1983). Linguistic competence is the highest level of linguistic ability a person can muster, and it is reflected in the initial formulation of a message. On the other hand, social communicative competence is the degree to which people take into account the characteristics of the audience to whom they are speaking and produce a message which is understood in the way they intend for it to be understood.

Clearly, linguistic competence and social communicative competence may be quite independent of each other. For example, we can conceive of someone who has a beautiful command of the English language, but who is totally inept at taking into account the characteristics of listeners and the social situation—thereby reflecting a low level of social communicative competence. Skill in communicating, then, requires both linguistic and social communicative abilities.

Transmitting the Message: Getting the Meaning Across Once the message has been formulated and, potentially, reformulated, the next step in the communication process is transmitting it. Although we are concentrating on verbal or spoken communication in this section of the chapter, the message can, of course, also be transmitted via nonverbal channels of communication. For example, facial expressions, eye contact, and interpersonal spacing each can provide important information to the decoder about the nature of the message.

Decoding: Perceiving, Interpreting, and Responding to the Encoder

The transmission of the message marks the end of the encoding phase—albeit temporarily—and the start of the decoding phase. Decoding involves at least four major subphases, which will be discussed separately: perception of the message, interpretation of the message, evaluation of the message, and, finally, feedback to the encoder (Hurt, Scott, & McCroskey, 1978).

Perceiving the Message: Communication on a Sensory Level Initially, the recipient must perceive a message on a sensory level in order for communication to occur. In other words, a fundamental requirement is that the appropriate sense organs be stimulated. In the case of verbal communication, auditory arousal would be a minimum. But nonverbal communication can require stimulation on a visual level as well.

Interpreting the Message Once the decoder has perceptually received the message, he or she must place some meaning on it. At a fundamental level, it is necessary to understand the linguistic code that is being used. Hence, if the encoder has spoken in English, it is obviously necessary for the decoder to understand the English language.

But in order to decode the message successfully, it is necessary to go beyond its absolute meaning. In the same way that encoders have to take into account the nature of the social situation and the personal characteristics of the decoder, the decoder must consider the social situation and characteristics of the encoder in order to understand what is being conveyed in the message. This underlying meaning of a message is known as its **metacommunicative content** (Foss & Hakes, 1978). Metacommunication may or may not be reflected in the literal content of the message; the nonverbal behavioral channels provide rich opportunities for the transmission of metacommunications.

Evaluating the Message: Deciding How to Respond After the decoder has determined how to interpret the message, the next step in the sequence is to evaluate it and determine an appropriate response. The nature of the evaluation of an individual's message rests on the communicative competence of the listener, which encompasses the listener's

Although conversation usually appears to be natural and spontaneous, in fact it usually follows an unspoken but intricate set of rules about speaking order and turn-taking. (Abigail Heyman/Archive Pictures)

linguistic and social skills in a way that is analogous to the requirements that the speaker be linguistically and socially competent. At this stage in the sequence, the listener determines what the appropriate response is—and, in fact, whether or not a response is called for.

Providing Feedback: Transmitting a Response   The final step in the communication sequence that we have been discussing involves the actual transmission of the response back to the initial communicator. As with the communication of the original message, the response can be transmitted by means of any one of the verbal or nonverbal communication channels available to the speaker and listener.

Starting Over: The Sequence Repeats   As the dotted line in Figure 3-8 indicates, the model assumes that most communicative interactions do not end with one speaker–listener exchange. Instead, the communication sequence repeats itself until one or both of the communicators stop the sequence. Up to that time, though, speaker and listener alternate through both roles.

Taking Turns: Determining Who Speaks When

Although most communication appears to occur relatively spontaneously, without much planning or adherence to social norms and conventions, in reality this is not the case. Communicative social interchanges follow a carefully determined, intricate set of rules which are implicitly understood by most members of a given society or culture. Indeed, failure to follow such rules can result in serious communicative difficulties.

Let us take one example of such rule setting: taking turns in conversations. As we have already noted, communicators have particular messages that they are trying to get across. Because both participants in a two-person interchange have their own goals, the problem they must both solve is one of trying to develop and organize a conversation that will allow each to attain his or her own personal goals.

One way they do this is to agree upon a series of "rules" to order the conversation (Sacks, Schegloff, & Jefferson, 1974). These rules must meet a number of requirements: each person must have a turn to talk, only one person should talk at a time, there should be only minor gaps in the conversation, the order in which the speakers talk cannot be fixed ahead of time, and there has to be a method to determine who speaks when (Clark & Clark, 1977).

When just two people are conversing, it is relatively easy to meet these requirements; the conversation simply alternates back and forth. But when more than two people are conversing, the interaction becomes much more complicated. According to Sacks, Schegloff, and Jefferson (1974), the coordination of conversation can be carried out through the application of one of the three following rules:

- Rule 1: The next turn goes to the person who is being addressed by the current speaker.
- Rule 2: The next turn goes to the person who speaks next.
- Rule 3: The next turn goes to the current speaker if he or she resumes prior to anyone else beginning to speak.

These three rules are hierarchical, with rule 1 taking precedence over rules 2 and 3; and if rule 1 is inoperative, rule 2 takes priority over rule 3. In a concrete example, suppose that Ellie, Jeri, and Barbara are holding a conversation. If Ellie asks Jeri a question, then Jeri should answer next, and Barbara is not supposed to respond—all according to rule 1. But if Ellie does not ask a question or addresses no one in particular, either Jeri or Barbara has the next turn (rule 2). And if neither Jeri nor Barbara says anything, it is permissible for Ellie to start speaking once again, following rule 3. But because rule 2 has precedence over rule 3, Jeri and Barbara have priority over a case in which Ellie desires to resume speaking immediately after her initial statement.

Taken together, these rules meet the requirements we mentioned earlier for ordering conversation. They give everyone a chance to talk, with just one person speaking at a time. The conversation is efficient, with only minor gaps, because in order to get a turn a person must start speaking before anyone else has. The rules provide a method of determining who should speak and at what point, without the participants having jointly to map out the conversational turn-taking before it happens.

Adjacency Pairs Many conversations are structured according to the first rule, in which the first speaker addresses a second one, and the second one answers. This type of sequence is known as an **adjacency pair**. It refers to two sequential turns, the second of which is a reaction to the first. There are a number of types of adjacency pairs, including the question–answer sequence (A: "How's the weather?" B: "Hot."); greeting–greeting sequence (A: "Hi." B: "Hi."); offer–acceptance/rejection sequence (A: "Want to get a pizza?" B: "Sure."); assertion–acknowledgment sequence (A: "Jim is getting fat again." B: "You're right."); compliment–acceptance/rejection sequence (A: "You sure look pretty." B: "Thanks—it must be my new dress."); and request–grant sequence (A: "Don't make me eat my spinach." B: "Alright, but eat your peas.") (Clark & Clark, 1977).

Each of these adjacency pairs goes beyond a simple exchange of information and implicitly carries with it the notion that B is cooperating in the conversation by responding to A's first statement. Moreover, B's response usually includes an implicit indication that the conversation can go forward cooperatively.

In sum, conversations carry well-developed strategies for taking turns. Rather than being a random process, the determination of who speaks when follows a set of norms about which there is a high degree of agreement within a particular society. And taking turns is not the only aspect of conversation that is regulated by social convention; practically every part of verbal communicative interchange is governed by normative restrictions, down to the opening and closing of a conversation.

The Power of Language: Indicating Status by What and How Much We Say

The choice of language that people employ is related to the nature of the social relationship between two speakers. For example, differences in status between two speakers is often represented in the way that the two address each other, with close friends using first names, and formal titles (Dr., Sir, Mr.) and last names reserved for others of higher status. Within a status level, there is also a fairly strong tendency to reciprocate the level of address: they both may use their last names, or they both may use first names.

With people at different status levels who have been addressing each other at disparate levels of intimacy, such as Mr. Langdon (the boss) addressing his employee as "Karl," there can be eventual changes in the formality with which the higher-status person is addressed—but such changes usually occur only at the behest of the higher-status person. It is more likely that Mr. Langdon would need to ask Karl to drop the "Mr." and start using his first name than that Karl would do so spontaneously.

The choice of address is based upon what Brown and Gilman (1960) have called the **power semantic** and **solidarity semantic**. The power semantic is the power or status level that a conversant holds. The solidarity semantic refers to the degree of shared social experience between two people. The power semantic suggests that people of greater power or status ought to be addressed with greater formality, while the solidarity semantic operates to allow greater familiarity between people who, for example, are close neighbors or friends or attend the same school.

In many languages other then English, the power and solidarity semantics are reflected in the use of "you" when referring to a listener, since there are two distinct words for "you"—one formal and one informal. In French, a speaker must choose between *tu* (familiar) and *vous* (formal); in German, the choice is *du* (familiar) and *Sie* (formal). Each language has its own set of rules. For example, French speakers use *tu* for intimate friends, family, and children, and *vous* for nonfamilial adults. And children use *vous* for all adults except their closest family members.

There have been a number of shifts in the use of the formal and the informal "you" which seem to be reflective of historical changes. In societies in which there has been movement toward greater egalitarianism, the trend has been toward less distinction being made between use of the formal and the informal "you." In France today more people are addressed by the informal *tu* than ever before. And at one time, even English speakers had a choice between "you" and "thou," which of course has long since disappeared from normal conversation.

In addition to causing differences in form of address, status differentials between speakers are related to the *quantity* of speech produced by the various participants. Higher-status speakers tend to talk more than others and, in group settings, more communications are addressed to them (Berger, Cohen, & Zelditch, 1973). Moreover, the nature of communications received by high-status people is more positive than those directed at lower-status people (Forsyth, 1983).

Why should high-status people be allowed, and even expected, to speak more? One possible reason is that their higher status is assumed to be associated with greater knowledge, and so their opinion is sought out more frequently. It is also conceivable that high-status people try to maintain their position by speaking more frequently. Thus, their greater level of talking may be a self-presentational strategy. Whatever the specific reason, it is clear that status—as well as other social and cultural factors (see Box 3-3)—affect both qualitative and quantitative aspects of the type of language employed in conversations.

Language as Thought: The Sapir-Whorf Hypothesis

One of the most interesting—and controversial—questions surrounding language concerns its relationship to our understanding of the world. Some investigators, notably linguists Benjamin Lee Whorf and Edward Sapir, suggest that the kind of language someone employs determines the nature of that person's thinking. Dubbed the "Sapir-Whorf hypoth-

BOX 3-3 SPOTLIGHT ON APPLICATIONS

CULTURAL VARIATIONS IN THE USE OF THE VERBAL CHANNEL

Consider the following dialogue held between a black 15-year-old named Larry and a researcher who asks Larry about his feelings about God and life and after death:

Q. What happens to you after you die? Do you know?

Larry. Yeah, I know.

Q. What?

Larry. After they put you in the ground, your body turns into ah—bones. . . .

Q. What happens to your spirit?

Larry. Your spirit—soon as you die, your spirit leaves you.

Q. And where does this spirit go?

Larry. Well, it all depends. . . .

Q. On what?

Larry. You know, like some people say if you're good . . . your spirit goin' to heaven . . . 'n' if you bad, your spirit goin' to hell. Well, [no]. Your spirit goin' to hell anyway, good or bad.

Q. Why?

Larry. Why. I'll tell you why. 'Cause, you see, doesn' nobody really know that it's a God, y'-know, 'cause I mean I have seen black gods, pink gods, white gods, all color gods, and don't nobody know it's really a God. An' when they be sayin' if you good, you goin' t'heaven, tha's [wrong] 'cause it ain't no heaven for you to go to.

(Labov, 1973, pp. 36–37)

While on the surface this sequence represents an example of illogic and poor thinking, it in fact illustrates an important social problem related to the place of minorities in American society. The dialogue contains an example of what is called nonstandard English or sometimes "black English," a form of English spoken fairly consistently by lower-class, urban blacks.

Nonstandard English is characterized by a lack of linking verbs ("she goin'" instead of "she is going"), improper verb agreement ("he go home" instead of "he is going home"), and omission of

prepositions ("he teach Washington School" instead of "he teaches at Washington School"), among other departures from standard English (Baratz, 1969). The social issue emerges when one considers whether the use of nonstandard English should be allowed—perhaps even encouraged—in the education of children who come to school speaking it.

Among those who argue the virtues of nonstandard English is William Labov, a linguist who conducted the interview related above. To Labov (1973), the arguments presented by Larry are actually quite logical, suggesting the following notions:

1. Everyone has a different idea of what God is like.
2. Therefore nobody really knows that God exists.
3. If there is a heaven, it was made by God.
4. If God doesn't exist, he couldn't have made heaven.
5. Therefore, heaven doesn't exist.
6. You can't go somewhere that doesn't exist.
7. Therefore, you can't go to heaven. Therefore, you are going to hell (Labov, 1973, pp. 36–37).

Labov's point is that people ought to be considered competent in their use of language if they can communicate effectively, and it does not matter whether that communication occurs in standard or nonstandard language. However, this is a point that is clearly open to dispute. For instance, Baratz (1969) has suggested that the use of nonstandard English may be disruptive in learning to read. Perhaps even more telling is the argument that people who do not use standard English are at a clear disadvantage when it comes to interacting with the majority who do use standard English or when doing such things as taking standardized tests. Listeners use language as an important cue to a speaker's social status, and speakers of nonstandard English are apt to be at a disadvantage when it comes to competing in a society that holds their language against them.

In sum, the use of nonstandard English boils down to a social issue. On the one hand, there are those who argue that to discourage the use of nonstandard

English is to denigrate an important part of a speaker's cultural heritage. On the other hand, there are those who suggest that the use of nonstandard English represents a deficit that society should strive to remediate. The solution to this problem is not obvious, but it is clear that there are important cultural differences in the use of language.

esis," this notion is made up of two related propositions. The first, and milder, statement suggests that language tends to *influence* the way people in a given culture understand and experience the world. The more extreme proposition suggests that language actually *determines* how people think about the world (Whorf, 1956; Brown, 1976).

One of the main lines of evidence used to support this hypothesis is based upon differences in vocabulary between different languages. For example, the Eskimo language has twenty or thirty different words for snow; in comparison, English has only one. Another example comes from the Hanunóo tribe, which has ninety-two names for different kinds of rice. On the other hand, there are examples of English being considerably more differentiated than other languages. For example, while the Hopi have only one word to describe all flying things other than birds, we make a distinction between airplanes, butterflies, helicopters, and so forth.

The importance of these vocabulary differences lies in Sapir and Whorf's view that the linguistic categorization system available to a speaker of a given language has an important effect on, and indeed is a major determinant of, the way in which that person thinks about the world. According to this perspective, an Eskimo perceives and thinks about snow in a way that is qualitatively more sophisticated than that of an English speaker—precisely because the Eskimo language provides more categories.

Differences in linguistic complexity do not, in and of themselves, confirm the Sapir-Whorf hypothesis. Indeed, they suggest a direct alternative: rather than language determining thought, the opposite sequence is plausible—that the language which is produced *reflects* an individual's thinking processes, which are determined by the environmental stimuli and social situations that are particularly relevant in a given culture.

For instance, the Eskimo is likely to require knowledge about different types of snow in order to function effectively; in turn, the Eskimo's thinking about and attending to snow may have produced the many related words in the Eskimo language. In contrast, most English speakers have little need to differentiate between types of snow, other than to know that it is or isn't snowing—and, for the most part, separate words for different kinds of snow have not been devised. In sum, this argument suggests that contrary to the Sapir-Whorf notion that language leads to particular ways of explaining the world, cultural experiences determine the linguistic categories that are used in a culture's language.

Most current evidence suggests that, in its strongest form, the Sapir-Whorf hypothesis does not stand up; language does *not* determine think-

According to one hypothesis, the language that people speak tends to influence the way they think about the world. For example, Eskimos, whose language contains many words for different types of snow, may actually perceive and think about snow differently from English-speakers, who are restricted to essentially the one word—"snow." (Alex Harris/Archive Pictures)

ing (Cairns & Cairns, 1976). People speaking different languages are able to make similar perceptual discriminations, even if a linguistic category is not readily available. For example, English speakers would, after suitable training, be able to discriminate among different types of snow, although in a less linguistically sophisticated manner than the Eskimo. Where an English speaker would have to say "hard-packed, crunchy, and crystallized snow," an Eskimo might need only one word to convey the same meaning. Still, verbal language clearly does have an influence upon how information is stored in memory and how easily it is remembered (Brown & Lenneberg, 1954; Brown, 1976). And, as we will see in our discussion of stereotypes in Chapter 5, the nature of the categories in which information is stored has an important effect on social relationships.

SUMMARY

Communication is at the core of social interaction. Verbal language in particular is a feature which differentiates human beings from other species. Nonverbal communication also provides an important mediator of social behavior.

One of the most active areas of research is in the expression of emotions via facial expressions. Seven emotions are consistently identifiable and distinguishable from one another; these are happiness, surprise, fear, sadness, anger, and disgust. However, errors in identifying these are sometimes made due to the use of display rules, implicit rules that govern a situation or interpersonal relationship regarding the appropriateness of showing a particular emotion. Display rules may either intensify, deintensify, neutralize, or mask an emotion that is being experienced.

Research that has investigated cross-cultural displays of emotion has found that there are universalities in the display of basic emotions. One explanation for these commonalities is the existence of a facial affect program, which activates particular musculature when a particular emotion is experienced. Some theorists even suggest that facial expressions not only reflect emotional experience, but are also important in determining how people experience and label emotion; this is known as the facial affect hypothesis.

Eye gaze also plays an important role in indicating a variety of emotional states. For instance, eye gaze is positively related to interpersonal attraction, although there are exceptions under certain circumstances.

Kinesics is the study of how movements of the hands, feet, and trunk are related to communication. Particular body movements include illustrators, adaptors, and emblems. There are also regularities in interpersonal spacing; this area of study is known as proxemics. Interpersonal spacing is related to status, the nature of the relationship between two interactants, and cross-cultural factors.

Two theories have attempted to explain the relationship between various nonverbal channels. Equilibrium theory suggests that increases in intimacy in one nonverbal channel are going to be accompanied by a compensatory decrease in intimacy along another nonverbal dimension. An alternative model is based on the concept of physiological arousal and the way in which that arousal is labeled.

Verbal communication can be conceptualized as following an encoding and decoding sequence. In encoding, the first stage is the formulation of the message and the second stage is the transmission of the message. Decoding consists of perceiving the message, interpreting it, and responding to the encoder.

Communicative social interaction follows an intricate set of rules which are implicitly understood by most members of a given society or culture. One example of such rule setting is taking turns in conversations. In addition, the choice of language that people employ is related to status factors.

The Sapir-Whorf linguistic relativity hypothesis suggests that language tends to influence the way people in a given culture understand and experience the world, and—in a stronger version—that language actually determines how people think. Most evidence now suggests that the hypothesis does not hold, although it does appear that language has an influence on how information is stored in memory and how easily it is remembered.

KEY TERMS

adaptors
adjacency pair
communication channel
display rules
emblem
equilibrium theory
facial affect program
facial feedback hypothesis
illustrator

kinesics
linguistic competence
metacommunicative content
power semantic
proxemics
role-taking
Sapir-Whorf hypothesis
social communicative competence
solidarity semantic

FOR FURTHER STUDY AND APPLICATION

Ekman, P. (Ed.). (1982). *Emotion in the human face.* New York: Cambridge University Press.
Written by experts in the area of nonverbal behavior, the chapters in this book provide a comprehensive look at current work on facial expression.

LaFrance, M., & Mayo, C. (1978). *Moving bodies.* Monterey, CA: Brooks/Cole.
A well-written lively introduction to nonverbal behavior, covering the major channels of communication. Fun to poke through because of the insights it offers.

Heslin, R., & Patterson, M. L. (1982). *Nonverbal behavior and social psychology.* New York: Plenum.
An integrative review of work on nonverbal behavior. Provides some interesting practical speculations on how nonverbal behavior operates in politics and intercultural relations.

Clark, H. H., & Clark, E. V. (1977). *Psychology and language: An introduction to psycholinguistics.* New York: Harcourt Brace Jovanovitch.

Dittmar, N. (1976). *Sociolinguistics.* London: Edward Arnold.
These two volumes provide a fine introduction to how language functions during social interaction and the role of language in communication.

Buck, R. (1984). *Nonverbal behavior and the communication of affect.* New York: Guilford.
Written by one of the major research figures in the field of nonverbal behavior, this book provides a comprehensive, current, and fascinating look at the state of the art in the area.

CHAPTER 4

FORMING, MAINTAINING, AND CHANGING ATTITUDES

A CONVERSATION WITH . . .

David Berger
Advertising Executive

David Berger makes his living largely by studying ways to change people's attitudes and behavior. As Director of Research at Foote, Cone & Belding, one of the country's leading advertising agencies, he has spent much of his professional life devising strategies to persuade people to adopt new attitudes and, ultimately, to change their behavior.

I first asked him a general question about the approaches used by advertisers.

Q. How do you go about putting an advertising campaign together?

A. For us, the most important thing to look at and understand is how people being advertised relate themselves to the product, how they buy it, use it, think about it, feel about it—their attitudes toward the product. In addition, one of the important things that we have to consider is that in many cases consumers don't care or think about the product—even though they may buy it. That's terribly important; so much of our advertising strategy is based on first assessing where a product fits in with a consumer's thoughts, feelings, and behavior. Once we know that, we are able to produce a specific strategy.

One of the things we have developed, then, is a method for assessing how consumers think and feel about a product and how involved they are with it. We can then graphically represent on a grid where a product falls in relationship to other products, and we can use this information to devise a specific strategy. For instance, on some products, involvement is so low that the feelings and thinking about the product make little difference; purchasing is done more out of habit than anything else. Consumers may not think or feel much about the product—something like barbecue

sauce, for instance—and the advertising challenge is to get them to begin thinking about the product and learning new habits. That's a very different kind of challenge from one in which involvement with the product is already high—such as with a television or automobile—when your concern would be more with changing thoughts and feelings.

Q. Do people in your firm actually keep these sorts of research-based considerations in the back of their minds when they are devising an advertising campaign?

A. They keep them in the back of their minds and the front of their strategies. We have done extensive research in twenty-one countries. Having the research base makes it much more efficient in terms of searching for creative ideas. It helps us know the kind of idea we are looking for—and the kind we're not looking for.

Q. Are there people in your agency who feel that advertising is 99 percent creativity and that the research guides that you provide are unnecessary?

A. I'm sure there are people who believe it but there aren't many who say it, because everybody at least pays lip service to the notion that you have to understand the consumer. Something in addition to your intuition is required.

Q. How do you go about choosing a specific kind of person to deliver an advertisement?

A. First you have to start with the rule that not every advertisment uses spokesmen. The decision to use a spokesmen is a conscious, reasoned decision. But if you decide to use one, there are a couple of general principles to follow. One is relevance to the product or to the audience. The other is whether to use a recognized spokesman. If the decision is yes, because you want to borrow some authority or recognition, you have to find out how well known that person is among your target audience—and that is readily ascertainable by research such as name recognition, face recognition, and so forth.

Q. Is there a kind of "average consumer" that you shoot for when you are putting together a campaign, or is it more precisely targeted to a specific group?

A. It is targeted. We believe in starting with a given product and its relationship to the consumer. Then we study attitudes and market segment for that particular product. We don't have a universal typology; it depends on the specific product.

Q. You tailor the content of the message, then, to the product and the specific consumer that you're hoping to purchase that product.

A. Right.

Q. How do you know when your advertising has been successful?

A. Sometimes you can know, and sometimes you can't. And when you can't know, it doesn't necessarily mean that you haven't been successful—you just may not be able to tell. Sales figures are certainly a relevant

criterion. But other measures are used; it is quite common to periodically assess the awareness of your product, its use, likes and dislikes about the product, and awareness of the advertising.

Q. Why do you bother with those other measures; isn't sales the only thing that really matters to an advertiser?

A. It depends on what your objective is. Greater awareness of the product may be the objective. The trouble with just measuring sales, is that all kinds of things are going on in the marketplace simultaneously. Because your're not running a controlled experiment, you often don't know for sure whether you've been successful. For instance, maybe last year's sales were affected by extreme competitive activity, or something else went on.

Q. I would think that the areas of attitude assessment and change, particularly as they relate to changes in behavior, are central to the field of advertising. Am I right?

A. One way I can respond is to suggest that to a large degree, the people who are involved in advertising are practicing social psychologists. They are working on affecting the behavior of people—in this case in the interest of the client.

OVERVIEW

- When Patricia Hearst, heiress to the Hearst publishing fortune, was abducted from her apartment, it seemed at first to be a simple kidnapping. But sixty days later, after her parents had paid millions of dollars in ransom for her return, Hearst decided to remain with her captors, adpoted a new name—Tania—and embraced the far-left philosophy of her kidnappers, the Symbionese Liberation Army. Over the next year and a half, she became involved in robberies and other criminal activities, until captured by the FBI. Then, at her trial, she renounced her new-found philosophy, saying she had been brainwashed.

• Tylenol was the leading brand of nonaspirin pain reliever in the world—until a handful of bottles that had been tampered with were found that contained a quick-killing poison which led to the deaths of a number of innocent victims. Tylenol was removed from drugstore grocery shelves all over the country, and consumer confidence in the product plummeted. Although most advertising executives thought the brand name could never be used again, one year after the incident consumers were buying the product (in tamper-proof bottles) in droves, following an extensive advertising campaign which played up the manufacturer's message that "we want you to continue to trust Tylenol."

• Results of surveys at the height of the Arab oil embargo showed that about half of all Americans believed that there was a real and serious energy crisis, yet there was no evidence that general attitudes and beliefs about the energy crisis or about the desirability of conservation policies were related to the adoption of energy-saving behaviors (Olsen, 1981).

Each of the three instances described above can be explained by considering the concept of attitudes, the topic of this chapter. As we shall discuss, social psychologists—as well as those focused on applications of attitude theory and research, such as advertiser David Berger—are interested in understanding how attitudes change, how to be persuasive, and how to measure attitudinal change. But more fundamentally, interest in attitudes lies beyond attitudes per se and rests instead on the way that attitudes are related to behavior.

In this chapter, we discuss these issues. Beginning with a review of various basic approaches to defining attitudes, we will then examine two major approaches to attitudes: learning and reinforcement theories and cognitive consistency theories. We will also present some of the ways in which persuasion has been studied and how it can be used to change attitudes. Finally, we address the basic and crucial issues of the relationship between attitudes and behavior.

WHAT IS AN ATTITUDE?

Just what is an attitude? Because of the prevalence of the term in our everyday lives, we probably all have a good commonsense notion of what is meant by the term. However, there is no one agreed-upon scientific definition of the concept.

The most common approach among social psychologists to defining attitudes stresses their evaluative aspects. For example, Fishbein and Ajzen (1975) call an attitude "a learned predisposition to respond in a consistently favorable or unfavorable manner with respect to a given object" (p. 6). In this view, attitudes are basically evaluations of a particular person, group, action, or thing.

Other theorists have suggested that attitudes should be considered in terms of their component parts. Specifically, attitudes are assumed to have three major components, known as a cognitive (thought) component, an affective (feeling) component, and a behavioral (action) component (Katz & Stotland, 1959; Rajecki, 1982). The **affective component** encompasses the direction and intensity of an individual's evaluation or the kind of emotion experienced toward the object of the attitude. The **cognitive component** refers to a person's system of beliefs about the attitudinal object. Finally, the **behavioral component** is a predisposition to act in a certain manner toward the attitudinal object.

Consider, for example, someone's attitude toward comedian Richard Pryor. The affective component might consist of attraction to, and positive feelings for, Pryor; the cognitive component might consist of the view that he is a brilliant, innovative comedian, is black, and has had a difficult and controversial private life; and the behavioral component could be manifested through the purchase of Pryor's records, the viewing of his movies, and attendance at his live performances.

One of the central notions that has followed from the component view of attitudes is the idea that attitudes are organized, both internally (among the three components) and in relation to other attitudes. The three components of attitude (affective, cognitive, and behavioral) are generally assumed to be interrelated and consistent with one another. Thus, if I think there is an energy crisis (the cognitive component) and my affective component toward energy conservation is positive, one might assume that my behavioral component will be consistent—that is, I ought to try to conserve energy (a manifestation of the behavioral component). On the other hand, if I do not think there is a crisis and I dislike conservation activities, I may avoid taking energy-saving steps—thereby maintaining consistency among the various parts of the attitude.

Related to the concept that there is internal organization among the three parts of attitudes is the idea that attitudes form interconnections with other attitudes to create organized patterns, rather than standing in isolation from one another. Hence, we might assume that someone's attitude about energy conservation is related to other attitudes regarding solar energy, nuclear power, wilderness conservation, and so forth. Such notions of consistency form the basis of a number of theories of attitudes, which we will examine more fully later in this chapter. First, however, we will consider how attitudes are acquired.

FORMING AND MAINTAINING ATTITUDES: LEARNING AND REINFORCEMENT APPROACHES

Form the moment of birth onward, we are exposed to both direct and indirect stimuli which can teach us to hold particular attitudes toward an attitudinal object. Parents, other family members, media, peers, and teachers all provide attitudinal *socialization* experiences by which people come to learn appropriate attitudes and behavior. Children learn to develop positive attitudes toward certain people, foods, and toys, and hold negative attitudes toward other people and things. By the time we are adults, these attitudes may have been modified, but the process of acquisition and development of attitudes continues. Learning and reinforcement theories approach attitudes as learned responses to particular stimuli, and the focus of these theories has been on identifying the nature of the stimuli that lead us to develop and hold specific attitudes.

Conditioning of Attitudes

That basic learning processes can describe how attitudes are formed has clearly been demonstrated by the research of Arthur Staats (Staats, 1975; Staats & Staats, 1958). You probably are familiar with the classical conditioning processes described by Pavlov. He found that after pairing an unconditioned stimulus (UCS) such as meat with a conditioned stimulus (CS) such as a bell, simply ringing the bell began to elicit a new response of salivating. This new response, which was called the conditioned response, or CR, was similar to the old, unconditioned response (UCR) of salivating to the meat (see Figure 4-1).

To Staats, an attitude is the equivalent of a conditioned response, something that can be elicited by the introduction of a conditioned stimulus. To demonstrate that attitudes can be classically conditioned, Staats conducted an experiment in which the goal was to condition positive and negative attitudes to the names of countries (Sweden and Holland) and people (Tom and Bill) which previously were regarded neither positively nor negatively.

Subjects were told that the purpose of the study was to investigate auditory and visual learning. The procedure consisted of flashing the names of one of six nationalities on a screen in a random order, and each time saying a word aloud. In one condition, two of the nationality labels were always followed by words that had positive connotations

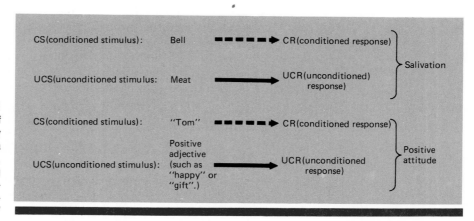

FIGURE 4-1
Classical conditioning of attitudes: in the same way that a bell can evoke a physiological response, classical conditioning produces a positive attitude toward the previously neutral name "Tom."

(e.g., happy, gift), while the others were followed by neutrally connotative words. In another condition, the two target nationalities were always followed by a word with negative conotations, with the rest of the nationalities once again being followed by neutral words.

After 108 conditioning trials in which each of the nationalities appeared eighteen times, the experimenter assessed the subjects' attitudes about each of the nationalities. With some exceptions, the results showed basically that subjects held more positive attitudes toward the nationalities associated with positive words and more negative attitudes toward those associated with negative words. Moreover, the analogous procedure using individuals' names instead of nationalities led to similar findings. According to Staats, the nationalities and names became conditioned stimuli when they were paired with the unconditioned stimuli of the positive or negative words, and the conditioned stimuli then evoked the new conditioned response (see Figure 4-1), just as the sound of the bell evoked the conditioned response of salivation by the dog in Pavlov's experiments.

The work of Staats and other theorists using classical conditioning approaches came under fire because of the possibility that subjects' responses were not caused by conditioning processes, but rather were due to awareness of what the experimenter was looking for (Page, 1969). This explanation, based on the concept of demand characteristics discussed in Chapter 1, is not easily dismissed. It is certainly plausible, for example, that in the Staats and Staats (1958) experiment (where conditioning took place over 108 trials) subjects might catch on and respond in a way that they thought was desired of them by the experimenter.

On the other hand, a number of experiments that specifically addressed the issue of subject awareness seem to rule out this alternative explanation (e.g., Zanna, Kiesler, & Pilkonis, 1970). Moreover, recent evidence has shown that persons associated with threatening circumstances tend to take on negative qualities simply through association, thus directly supporting classical conditioning explanations of attitude formation (Riordan & Tedeschi, 1983).

The importance of classical conditioning as a mechanism for attitude formation lies in the fact that through classical conditioning, people may come to have powerful attitudinal reactions to social objects even in the absence of firsthand experience. Hence, children who overhear repeated pairings of words in their parents' conversations (such as black–ignorant, black–lazy, black–incompetent) throughout their early years of development may come to adopt such negative attitudes themselves—even if they have never met a black person.

Reinforcement Approaches

Ethel: Look at that dress Sherry is wearing. It just looks awful. She really doesn't know a thing about dressing herself.

Denise: You are absolutely correct. I've felt that for a long time now and was wondering when you would agree with me. You're really catching on.

While not exactly showing the brighter side of human nature, this snippet of conversation, heard in a college dining commons, illustrates quite clearly the role of reinforcement in attitude formation. Following Denise's agreement, it is likely that Ethel's initial espousal of a negative attitude about Sherry will be reinforced. Of course, had Ethel remarked upon how nice Sherry looked, Denise might have reacted with disagreement, thereby punishing the remark. The important point is that following reward, Ethel's attitude is likely to be strengthened, whereas punishment would probably lead to a weakening of the attitude.

Processes of reward and punishment are examples of another learning theory approach, which suggests that a critical factor affecting the acquisition and maintenance of attitudes relates to the degree to which attitudes are verbally or nonverbally reinforced by others. In an early demonstration of reinforcement approaches, Verplanck (1955) found he could get subjects to increase their rate of emission of opinion statements by verbally agreeing with them and to decrease the frequency of such statements by disagreeing with them.

Likewise, the word "good" has been shown to have powerful reinforcing properties: judicious "goods" interspersed in conversations lead people to hold reinforced attitudes more strongly and actually to modify their attitudes in reinforced directions in much the same way that we are able to shape the behavior of pigeons to peck a key (Insko & Nelson, 1969; Krasner, Knowles, & Ullman, 1968).

On the other hand, some research points to the situation being more complicated than a simple reinforcement model suggests. Insko and Cialdini (1969) have proposed a two-factor model that suggests that a person who is reinforced with the word "good" by an interviewer uses the interviewer's behavior first to make an inference about the interviewer's attitude, which is assumed to be similar to the individual's response. In turn, this leads to liking for the interviewer, and subsequent strengthening of the attitude due to the interviewer's increased attractiveness. Hence, the underlying mechanism is the attraction to the person providing the reinforcement, and not the reinforcement itself.

Vicarious Learning

In both the classical conditioning and reinforcement approaches to attitudes, the person generally has direct contact with the attitudinal object or, at the very least, with verbal labels for the object (as in Staats's experiment). However, in many cases a person not only has no real contact with the attitudinal object, but apparently also receives no direct reinforcement. Specifically, it appears that subjects acquire attitudes simply by observing the rewards and punishments that others get for their espousal of those attitudes.

BOX 4-1   SPOTLIGHT ON METHODOLOGY

MEASURING ATTITUDES

Attitudes measurement has taken many forms over the years, and it continues to be a challenging problem. The reason for the myriad techniques is that attitudes themselves are **hypothetical constructs**, abstract concepts that do not exist in a concrete or directly observable way. Thus, every attempt to measure them is, in a sense, indirect. Still, most measurement procedures are related to one of a few basic kinds, which we will discuss briefly below.

Likert-type Scales: Going by the Numbers

It is unlikely that any type of measurement technique has been used more frequently than the Likert-type scale, which is a direct method of measuring an individual's evaluation of an attitudinal object (Likert, 1932). Although formal Likert scales have a complicated item selection process, in practice most researchers simply ask a question about the attitudinal object and supply the rater with a numbered response scale.

Suppose, for instance, that you wanted to measure attitudes toward nuclear disarmament. Using the Likert technique, you would present people with a statement such as "I think nuclear disarmament should be carried out," and then ask them to rate the degree of agreement on a sale such as this:

1	2	3	4	5
Strongly agree	Agree	Undecided	Disagree	Strongly disagree

By having people respond to a series of such statements, it is possible to sum the ratings across scales and get a summary score for attitude toward the issue. It is also possible to use more (or sometimes fewer) than five categories; and on occasion, Likert scales are labeled only at each end. Thus, the following measure also would be considered a Likert scale:

Strongly disagree $\quad -3 \; -2 \; -1 \; 0 \; +1 \; +2 \; +3 \quad$ Strongly agree

Thurstone Scales: Equal-appearing Interval Scales

Another influential scale is named after its developer, L. L. Thurstone. Thurstone (1928) suggested that as a preliminary step, judges read a large number of statements relating to the attitudinal object and place them into eleven categories representing degree of favorability to the object. By using many judges and a large number of statements, certain statements for which there is good agreement on category membership can be found.

After an item is reliably categorized, subjects can be asked to show their agreement with each item; then scale values from 1 to 11, as ascertained from the judgment categorization process, can be determined for each subject. Thus people might be asked to indicate whether they agree or disagree with the following statements, which vary in their degree of positivity:

- Nuclear disarmament is crucial to world peace.
- Planning for the use of nuclear weapons in a small-scale war increases the probability of an all-out nuclear war.
- Civil defense planning for a nuclear war is a futile effort.

The value of this technique is that we can be fairly confident that the resulting scale has mathematically equal intervals between each point. The drawback, however, is its lack of economy: Thurstone suggested that a large number of judges be employed in order to validate the scale. Most researchers, faced with constraints in time and money, are apt to rely on Likert-type scales.

Semantic Differential Scaling: Using Bipolar Adjectives

Semantic differential scaling is used to obtain a direct measure of the evaluation of an attitudinal object (Osgood, Suci, & Tannenbaum, 1957). In this technique, the meaning of an object is rated on a series of what are called bipolar adjectives, meaning that they are opposite to one another. For example, nuclear disarmament might be rated along the following dimensions:

Good __ : __ : __ : __ : __ : __ Bad
Attractive __ : __ : __ : __ : __ : __ Unattractive
Worthless __ : __ : __ : __ : __ : __ Valuable
Fair __ : __ : __ : __ : __ : __ Unfair

By giving each point a value, it is possible to quantify a subject's overall reaction to the attitudinal object being evaluated. The virtue of such a technique is that it taps into a respondent's general understanding of an attitudinal object, rather than specific aspects of the object.

Attitude Measures in General

The major value of the measurement techniques that we have discussed is that they allow quantifications of people's attitudes. By using these methods—which, it turns out, are fairly highly correlated with one another (Fishbein & Ajzen, 1975)—it is possible to assess the attitudes people hold toward other people, objects, and ideas accurately. But, as we shall discuss later in the chapter, assessing attitudes accurately is just the first step in learning about the ways in which attitudes are related to social behavior.

The phenomenon by which a person learns something through the observation of others is known as **vicarious learning.** It accounts for how a person who has no direct experience with an attitudinal object can hold firmly entrenched attitudes about the object. For example, the rationale behind beer commercials which show someone ordering and then obviously enjoying a beer is that viewers will form a positive attitude vicariously and imitate such behavior in the future.

The notion that people acquire attitudes vicariously, through observations of others, is well documented (Bandura, 1977). In fact, there is even physiological evidence that we can react affectively to the emotional experiences of others (Englis & Lanzetta, 1984). For example, Berger (1962) had subjects observe a person who was exposed to a cue that signaled that he could receive an electric shock. Observers (who were in no danger of being shocked themselves) showed physiological responses that were indicative of the affect being experienced by the model. Thus, they vicariously adopted the emotional response of the model to the signal.

A good deal of acquisition of attitudes occurs through vicarious learning processes. Consider, for instance, a person viewing Governor George Wallace of Alabama attempting to bar the way of a small group of black students trying to enroll at the University of Alabama. Although unsuccessful in his attempt to halt integration, Wallace drew much local public acclaim for his stance, and in the eye of the observer watching the scene, the message was clear: racism has its rewards. It is certainly plausible that someone watching the confrontation would vicariously acquire negative attitudes toward blacks.

(Times change, of course. Some twenty years later, Governor Wallace could be seen crowning a black homecoming queen at the same university he tried to keep segregated. Whether such behavior represents real attitude change, however, is difficult to ascertain, since public dis-

When Governor George Wallace of Alabama refused to let black students enter the then-segregated University of Alabama in 1963, he probably did not envision that twenty years later attitudes—and consequent political realities—would have changed sufficiently to lead him to warmly greet black leader Jesse Jackson in the governor's mansion. (*Left,* UPI/Bettmann Archive; *right,* AP/ Wide World)

plays of prejudice made much less political sense, given that the number of black voters in the state had increased substantially by then. As we mentioned earlier, the particular behaviors we use to infer attitudes are problematic when we want to determine whether there is a linkage between behavior and attitudes.)

MAKING SENSE OF ATTITUDES: COGNITIVE CONSISTENCY APPROACHES

In contrast to learning and reinforcement approaches to attitudes, which are basically concerned with the way in which a person acquires an attitude and the various components of that attitude, cognitive consistency approaches typically start with an existing attitude and try to explain how the attitudinal components fit together with each other and with other attitudes. Cognitive consistency theories view human beings as active information processors, trying to make sense out of what they think, feel, and do, and actively constructing and interpreting the world to bring congruence to inconsistencies that may occur between and within attitudes.

Although a number of theories fall under the rubric of cognitive consistency approaches, each shares the fundamental principle that inconsistency is a psychologically unpleasant state and that it prompts the person actively to seek to reduce this unpleasantness by decreasing the inconsistency. Inconsistencies can occur between cognitions about and affect toward an attitudinal object, between affect toward a person and his or her position on an issue, or between a person's cognitions, affect, and behavior toward an attitudinal object (Himmelfarb & Eagly, 1974). Whatever the source of the inconsistency, the person is motivated to reduce it; and the mechanism by which it is reduced is central to each of the cognitive consistency theories we shall discuss.

Heider's Balance Theory

The grandfather of all the cognitive consistency theories is Fritz Heider's **balance theory** (Heider, 1946, 1958). Basically, the theory is concerned with how we make our attitudes regarding people and an attitudinal object consistent. The principal element in the theory is the person or perceiver, notated as P by Heider. There are two other elements in the model: another person called O, and another entity (which may be an object or a person) called X.

Given the three elements (P, O, and X), it is possible to arrange them in a number of different combinations, depending on the nature of the relationship between each individual pair of elements. Heider differentiated between two different types of relationships—**unit relationships** (the degree to which the elements are perceived to belong together, due to similarity, ownership, or similar membership in a class) and **affective relationships** (the nature of liking between the elements). Heider's theory goes on to posit that the nature of relations between elements is either positive ($+$) or negative ($-$). The model's predictions are the same for both unit and affective relationships; we will only discuss affective relationships.

With these basics, it is possible to diagram eight different possible P-O-X combinations of relationships, as shown in Figure 4-2. The basic

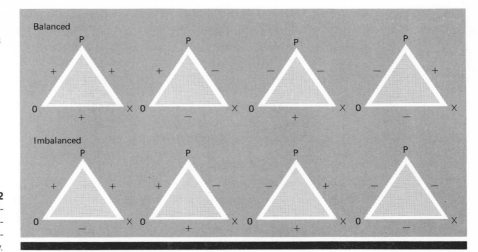

FIGURE 4-2
Balanced and imbal-
anced relationship ac-
cording to Heider's the-
ory.

prediction of the theory is that if one takes the signs of the three relationships and multiplies them together, a balanced state exists if the
result if positive, and an imbalanced state exists if the result is negative.
(Another way of saying this is that a system with three positive relations
or one positive and two negative relations is balanced, while a system
with three negative or a negative and two positive relations is imbalanced.)

Just what is balance? According to Heider, it is a stable cognitive state
which is comfortable to the perceiver. Imbalance, in contrast, is unstable, and it motivates the perceiver to change the nature of one of the
relationships to attain a balanced state. Let's examine an instance of
how this might work. Suppose, for instance, that I (as P) hold Jill (O) in
high regard; i.e., the affective relation is positive. And suppose that I
also like Jack (X), thus making another positive relation. But suppose
that I perceive that Jill doesn't like Jack (a negative relation). According
to balance theory, we then have an imbalanced state (two pluses and a
negative relation), and I should be motivated to bring the system into
balance—by changing my view either of Jill, *or* of Jack, *or* of the nature
of the relationship between Jack and Jill.

While intuitively appealing, Heider's theory has some clear limitations. Most obviously, it does not allow for distinctions between degree
of affect in a relationship or for consideration of the importance of the
particular elements to a perceiver. For instance, in our example, it is
completely plausible that I might have a strong, important relationship
with Jill, while only vaguely knowing Jack; consequently, it would not
bother me much that Jill doesn't like Jack.

Finally, another difficulty with the theory is that it does not predict
which of several ways of restoring balance will occur. At least three
possibilities for reducing imbalance are possible (Leventhal, 1974). A
first, and the most direct, way would be to effect a change in attitude.

("I never really liked Jill after all.") A second way is to deny that a relation even exists. ("Jill really didn't mean it when she told me that she didn't like Jack.") Finally, it is possible to modify and differentiate the attitudinal object to include attributes that would be consistent with a balanced relationship. ("Jill's right; there is a side of Jack that I don't like much, even though most of the time I do like him.") Balance theory does not provide us with predictions as to which of these ways of reducing imbalance will be chosen.

Even with these drawbacks, balance theory has had a marked influence on the study of attitudes and, with some exceptions, the major predictions of the theory have held up remarkably well (Jordan, 1953; Rodrigues, 1967; Steiner & Spaulding, 1966; Lusko & Adewole, 1979). Moreover, balance theory has spawned a number of extensions that have remedied some of the deficiencies of the model (Osgood & Tannenbaum, 1955; Harary, 1983). Thus, it remains an important cognitive consistency model.

Festinger's Theory of Cognitive Dissonance: Striving for Consistency

It is unlikely that when Leon Festinger wrote his 1957 book, *A Theory of Cognitive Dissonance*, he could have imagined the vast amount of work that his theory would spawn over the next decade. You could not pick up a major social psychological journal in the early 1960s without reading a number of articles designed to test one or more propositions of the theory, and a whole generation of social psychologists was trained with research on cognitive dissonance as the primary exemplar of theory-based experimental laboratory work.

Clearly the most influential of the cognitive consistency models, cognitive dissonance theory is deceptively simple in its fundamental assumptions. The basic notion is that when a person holds two cognitions (which, as we mentioned earlier, are ideas or thoughts) simultaneously that contradict one another, that person experiences a state of cognitive dissonance. A familiar example of two contradictory cognitions is that of a smoker who knows that smoking leads to lung cancer. The cognition "I am a smoker" does not fit with the cognition that "smoking causes lung cancer," thereby creating a state of dissonance.

Dissonance produces a state of psychological tension, which motivates the person to reduce the dissonance. There are a number of ways in which it can be reduced. The person can modify one of the cognitions (or the behavior or affect underlying it); he or she can change the perceived importance of the cognition; additional elements can be added; or the cognitions can be deemed psychologically irrelevant to one another (in the same way that balance could be achieved through the mechanism of denial). We turn now to some of the specific approaches that have been taken to understanding dissonant states.

Insufficient Justification: Where Less Results in More   Put yourself in the following situation:

> You've just spent an hour at a very boring, seemingly pointless and trivial task in an experiment, and you've grown to hate the whole situation. But just as you're about to leave, the experimenter asks your help. Because of a scheduling problem, he needs the services of a confederate for the next subject, and asks if you might like to help out. Indeed, he wonders if you could be "on call" to participate as confederate for future experiments. Your job as a confederate? All you have to do is to tell subjects that the task you've just finished is interesting, involving, and a lot of fun.

To make the above scenario complete, you need one additional fact: the amount of money the experimenter offers you to participate. Based upon what happened in an actual experiment using this scenario (Festinger & Carlsmith, 1959), there are two options, corresponding to two conditions of the experiment. In one condition, you would be paid $20; in the other, you would be paid just $1 for espousing an attitude that was clearly contrary to what you believed.

The basic question of interest here is which of the two conditions produced the greatest cognitive dissonance. To answer this question, we need to analyze the question from the dissonance theorist's point of view. According to Festinger and Carlsmith (1959), when people, with very little inducement, say something they do not agree with, they are left holding two contradictory cognitions:

Cognition 1   I believe X, and
Cognition 2   I said I don't believe X.

According to the theory, this inconsistency between cognitions should arouse dissonance.

But how much dissonance will be aroused? To answer that question, we need to consider the inducement used to bring about the counter-attitudinal behavior. Suppose, in one case, a person is paid $20, a relatively large amount of money, to say he does not believe X, while in another case, he is paid just $1. According to the theory, the greater the justification for saying something a person doesn't believe, the more reason there is to carry out this counterattitudinal behavior—and, thus, the smaller the dissonance. Hence:

Cognition 1   I believe X, and
Cognition 2   I said I don't believe X for a good reason ($20)   } Relatively low dissonance

Cognition 1	I believe X, and	
Cognition 2	I said I don't believe X for not much of a reason ($1)	Relatively high dissonance

Now that we have established that the dissonance will be greater in the $1 condition than in the $20 condition, we must posit some mechanism to reduce the dissonance. It is fairly difficult to change the second cognitive element; after all, it is clear that the statement was made. But the first element is considerably easier to change; hence, any likely reduction in dissonance will occur through a shift in attitude in a way that will make the attitude more congruent with the statement. In addition, the theory suggests that the greater the change in attitude, the greater the reduction of dissonance will be.

Putting all this together, we can predict that a person paid $1 for advocating a counterattitudinal position will experience more dissonance and, consequently, greater attitude change than a person paid $20. The results of the Festinger and Carlsmith (1959) study were remarkably in line with this prediction. In the original study, college students were first asked to spend an hour carrying out the most boring tasks the experimenters could think of: turning 48 pegs a quarter turn consecutively, and placing spools on a tray, emptying it, and filling it again.

After subjects completed these tedious tasks, the experimenter made what he said was a rather unusual request. He said that his experimental assistant had not shown up, and in order to use the next subject, waiting outside the room, it was necessary for someone to fill in for the missing confederate and tell the subject that the task was, in fact, very interesting, intriguing, exciting, and fun.

The experimental manipulation then occurred: the subject was promised a reward of either $1 or $20 if he would agree to act as confederate for the next subject as well as agree to being available if needed for future experimentation. Almost all subjects agreed to this request and told the next subject (in reality, a confederate) that they had indeed enjoyed the experiment. Finally, subjects were asked to indicate their actual attitude toward the task.

If the dissonance theory interpretation of the situation is correct, in both the $1 and $20 conditions dissonance will be aroused due to what has been termed the counterattitudinal advocacy of the subject. But greater dissonance will occur in the $1 condition, producing more vigorous attempts at its reduction; the result, as we have said, ought to be greater attitude change in the $1 condition. And this is just what happened. When asked to indicate after the experiment how much they enjoyed the task, the scientific importance of the experiment, and whether they would like to participate in similar experiments, all responses were more positive in the $1 condition than in the $20 condition (see Table 4-1), clearly appearing to support dissonance theory predic-

TABLE 4-1 Results of Insufficient Justification Experiment
These figures show that subjects paid just $1 were uniformly more positive about the experimental task than those paid $20.

	Paid $1	Paid $20
How enjoyable tasks were (−5 to +5)	+1.35	−.05
Scientific Importance (0 to 10)	6.45	5.18
Participate in future experiments (−5 to +5)	+1.20	−.25

Source: Adapted from Festinger & Carlsmith (1959).

tion of greater attitude change under conditions of insufficient justification.

The Festinger and Carlsmith (1959) study became one of the classic experiments showing support for dissonance theory, and it illustrates the major characteristics of the theory of cognitive dissonance. It is also illustrative of the nonintuitive nature of many dissonance theory predictions, which made the theory quite controversial—and appealing—to social psychologists sometimes accused of only finding out things that common sense already supported.

We should note that common sense, as well as a straightforward learning theory approach, would make just the opposite prediction from dissonance theory. We might expect that the more a person was paid for doing something, the more he would come to hold a positive attitude toward that activity. Hence, a plausible alternative prediction would have been that subjects in the $20 condition would undergo greater attitude change than those in the $1 condition. But this didn't happen, suggesting the efficacy of the dissonance interpretation.

Alternative Explanations Critics were quick to rush to the defense of both common sense and reinforcement theory, and the results of Festinger and Carlsmith's (1959) study came under heavy attack, making for what has been called a debate which "has undoubtedly been one of the liveliest within contemporary social psychology" (Himmelfarb & Eagly, 1974, p. 19). A number of critiques suggested that there were methodological flaws in the original experiment (Chapanis & Chapanis, 1964). For instance, one argument revolved around the concept of evaluation apprehension, which refers to subjects' concern that the experimenter in a study will evaluate them positively (Rosenberg, 1965). According to this view, the $20 payment offered to subjects was inordinately large and could have led to suspicion on the part of the subjects that the experimenter was in reality trying to "buy" attitude change. In order to be evaluated positively by the experimenter, subjects may have actively tried to resist attitude change in that condition.

Bem's Theory of Self-perception   Another alternative explanation was suggested by Daryl Bem (1967, 1972) in his theory of self-perception that we first encountered in Chapter 2. Bem, building upon a learning theory framework, suggests that people form and develop attitudes by observing their own behavior, analogous to the way in which an individual uses other peoples' behavior to infer an understanding about what their underlying attitudes are.

Applying this principle to the Festinger and Carlsmith (1959) study, Bem argued that it is not necessary to posit an internal motivational state of dissonance to explain subjects' behavior. Rather, subjects' behavior can be seen as entirely plausible if we view the situation from their point of view. A subject who is paid $20 may feel that there is a clear external reason for his behavior: the $20 justification. But the subject who is paid $1 looks at his behavior—the same way an outside viewer would—and could reason that making a positive statement for so little an external incentive must imply that he really did enjoy the task. The end result would be the same as in dissonance theory (a more positive attitude in the low-incentive condition), but the mechanism would be quite different.

Self-perception theory suggests, then, that subjects act as problem solvers, asking themselves what kind of attitude must underlie a behavior that they have evinced. This is not due, as dissonance theory would say, to an aversive motivational state, but rather to an active search for understanding of one's own behavior, in the same way that we try to understand the causes of other people's behavior.

To test self-perception theory, Bem (1967) carried out an "interpersonal replication" of the Festinger and Carlsmith (1959) study in which he presented a careful description of the original study and asked subjects to predict the attitude that an imaginary subject would hold at the end of the study. Bem's findings matched those of the original study precisely: the observers guessed that the subjects in the $1 condition would hold more positive attitudes than those in the $20 condition. According to Bem, when the external inducement is low (the $1 condition), the observer takes the behavior as an indication of the subject's true attitude. More crucially, he argues that the subjects themselves went through the same logical process, inferring their attitude on the basis of their behavior.

We should note, however, the difficulty in accepting Bem's argument: even though the results of an interpersonal simulation match those of an original experiment, there is no guarantee that the underlying psychological processes that produce those results are identical. Unfortunately, dissonance and self-perception theories make nearly identical predictions—except regarding the presence (dissonance theory) or absence (Bem) of an internal and hence unobservable aversive internal motivational state of dissonance. Thus far it has proven impossible to design a critical experiment that can distinguish between the two theories, although Fazio, Zanna, & Cooper (1977) suggest that Bem's theory

BOX 4-2 SPOTLIGHT ON APPLICATIONS

OVERJUSTIFICATION EFFECTS: DON'T REWARD PEOPLE FOR DOING WHAT THEY ALREADY LIKE TO DO

Consider this situation:

Bob's son, Jonathan, is 6 years old and loves to use machinery of any kind. Each week he begs Bob to be allowed to use the power lawnmower. Bob usually agrees, despite some qualms about his son's ability to handle the equipment safely. It turns out that Jonathan does quite a good job—so good, in fact, that Bob is considering paying Jonathan so that he'll continue to mow the lawn enthusiastically. Should he pay him?

A person familiar with Bem's theory of self-perception would be quick to answer "no," for a derivative of the theory clearly suggests that Jonathan would soon lose his intrinsic motivation to use the lawnmower and would begin to dislike, like most of us, mowing the lawn. The effect is known as **overjustification,** and it occurs when incentives are used to bring about behavior that would have been done voluntarily without the incentive (Lepper, Greene, & Nisbett, 1973).

When people are rewarded for something they would have done anyway, they are left with two possible explanations for why they carried out the behavior—intrinsic, self-generated motivation or the reinforcement provided by someone else. If the reinforcement is clear and unambiguous, the reinforcement provides the most reasonable cause of the behavior. But if no external reinforcement is present, the person's own interests, dispositions, or motivations provide the most reasonable explanation of the behavior. Thus, in our example, payment to Jonathan might make him feel that he is mowing for monetary reward, and not for the joy of using the machine.

Overjustification effects have been demonstrated in a number of experiments. For example, Morgan (1981) showed how children's play with jigsaw puzzles could be reduced after they were promised a reward for it. In the field experiment, teachers in one condition told students that they would receive a reward of candy for working on a jigsaw puzzle for ten minutes. In the control condition, children were simply asked to work on the puzzle; no mention of the reward was made.

The major dependent measure concerned the amount of free time the subjects spent later on solving jigsaw puzzles when alternative activities were available. Two to three weeks after the first session, subjects were given their choice of a number of activities, which included working on jigsaw puzzles. As was predicted, subjects who had received a reward earlier tended to choose jigsaw puzzles significantly less than those in the control group. Apparently, having received a reward earlier made the task less intrinsically interesting and enjoyable to the subjects.

Work on overjustification effects thus suggests that we should, in certain cases, avoid rewarding people for doing things that they already like to do—unless we want them to stop liking it. In fact, results of a recent field experiment provides strong support for this conclusion. Caldwell, O'Reilly, and Morris (1983) examined the attitudes of students enrolled in an evening M.B.A. program while being employed full time during the day. In all cases, their employer was subsidizing their tuition—but for different reasons and for varying amounts.

The researchers found that those people who saw their subsidy as an unusual employee benefit, given to them as a special reward, rated their interest in the M.B.A. program as lower when they received a high subsidy than when they received a low subsidy—the overjustification effect. Interestingly, when the students felt that the subsidy was a normal employee benefit, unrelated to any special reward, the opposite was found: the higher the subsidy, the greater their interest in the program. Thus, the way in which a reward is perceived seems to determine whether overjustification effects will occur.

provides the best explanation when behavior is only slightly discrepant from existing attitudes, whereas dissonance-produced change is the result of highly discrepant behavior. However, the controversy is likely to continue for some time.

Applications of Dissonance Theory

Cognitive dissonance theory has been incorporated into a number of important areas of application. These include decision-making processes and selective exposure to information.

Dissonance and Decision Making: Why Our Decisions May Seem for the Best   Consider for a moment someone who has a number of alternatives to choose from when making a decision, such as deciding between the purchase of a Ford, Chrysler, or Volvo. Each alternative has various positive and negative aspects to it: the Ford may be cheaper, but it also may be less attractive; the Chrysler has a long warranty, but gets worse gas mileage; the Volvo is durable, but very expensive; and so forth. Now suppose, after weighing the options, the purchaser finally decides to purchase a Volvo. According to the dissonance theory, at that point the decision maker is likely to experience dissonance. The reason? The choice will be dissonant with the positive features of the nonchosen alternatives (the Ford and Chrysler) and dissonant with the negative features of the chosen Volvo.

According to dissonance theory, a person has two likely options for reducing the dissonance. He or she can increase the importance assigned to the negative features of the nonchosen alternatives or increase the importance of the positive features of the chosen alternative. In either event, the result is essentially the same: the attitude toward the nonchosen alternative will be more negative and the attitude toward the chosen one should become more positive. In practice, this means that the difference between attitudes toward the Volvo and the nonchosen Ford and Chrysler will increase, making the choice seem clearly to be the right one.

There has been a good deal of experimental support for this particular derivation of the theory (e.g., Converse & Cooper, 1979), and we now know not only that dissonance occurs when an individual makes a decision, but also that its magnitude is related to how similar in attractiveness the options are and how many nonchosen attractive alternatives exist (Brehm, 1956; Brehm & Cohen, 1959). Dissonance theory, then, helps explain why we may come to feel that our choices are always for the best—at least after we have made them.

Selective Exposure to Information   One hypothesis derived from dissonance theory that has not fared well relates to the nature of selective exposure to information. The theory suggests that in order to minimize dissonance, people will selectively expose themselves to material and information that supports their own point of view, and attempt to avoid information that is contrary to their attitudes.

After someone has purchased a Volvo, for example, dissonance theory would predict that that person would seek out information extolling the virtues of the Volvo while avoiding information that casts aspersions upon the car. Indeed, an early study showed just this effect: people who had purchased new automobiles were asked to choose to read advertising information about either their own or other cars, and most chose to look at advertisements about their new car (Ehrlich, Guttman, Schonbach, & Mills, 1957).

Later research is far less clear-cut in its support for the selective exposure hypothesis, and it almost seems that for every study that supports the concept, there is one that does not (Sears, 1968). There are, however, certain factors that tend to increase the likelihood of selective exposure operating. For instance, information that is high in value and utility to an individual is more likely to lead to selective exposure effects, and a person's degree of commitment to and confidence in his or her initial choice also is crucial (Freedman, 1965; Mills & Ross, 1964). Most important is how much choice people feel they had in the initial decision. When that choice is perceived as having been made freely, it is most likely that people will seek out supportive information and avoid discrepant information (Frey & Wicklund, 1978).

A Final Word on Dissonance Theory   In a 1978 review entitled "Twenty Years of Cognitive Dissonance," Greenwald and Ronis state that "dissonance theory has been an extremely stimulating force within and beyond social psychology. The enigmas posed by the original statement of dissonance theory and later by the juxtaposition of that statement with research results have motivated research that has advanced greatly the understanding of human cognition" (p. 56). But they also note a number of revisions and exceptions to the theory, especially that dissonance occurs only when dissonant cognitions are brought together because of the personal responsibility of the person experiencing dissonance (Wicklund & Brehm, 1976).

Recent work on dissonance theory has begun to investigate the physiological aspects of dissonance (e.g., Croyle & Cooper, 1983) and has shown that dissonance reduction may occur in ways other than modifying relevant cognitive elements. For instance, Steele, Southwick, and Critchlow (1981) found that social drinkers who had the opportunity to drink alcohol following the arousal of dissonance tended to display less attitude change than those who did not drink. Apparently, alcohol acted to reduce the aversive affects of dissonance, allowing dissonant cognitive elements to be held without experiencing the unpleasant feelings of cognitive conflict. Thus, people may not strive for consistency if they can drink their dissonance away!

CHANGING ATTITUDES: THE SCIENCE OF PERSUASION

We need look no further than our daily newspaper, television, magazines, or radio to see and hear attempts to persuade us to change our attitudes. Businesses extol the virtues of their products; politicians, the correctness of their views. We are urged to buy cars, save energy, and eat nutritiously. As we discussed with David Berger at the start of the chapter, the base of all these attempts at persuasion is the desire either to change our existing attitudes or to teach us new ones, with the hope that these attitudinal modifications will lead to similar changes in behavior.

In the remainder of this chapter, we will discuss the factors that have been identified as being important and useful in bringing about attitude change through persuasive communication, and how that attitude change is reflected in behavioral outcomes. As David Berger mentioned, there is no formula that invariably results in successful persuasive communication. But there is a good bit known about the factors that lead to attitude change.

To guide our discussion, we will use a model which suggests that there are three major factors involved in persuasive processes (see Figure 4-3): the source of a persuasive message, the nature of the message, and characteristics of the recipient of the message (the target).

Message Source

Anyone who has ever watched Bill Cosby discussing the merits of Jell-O or seen James Garner taking pictures with his Polaroid camera

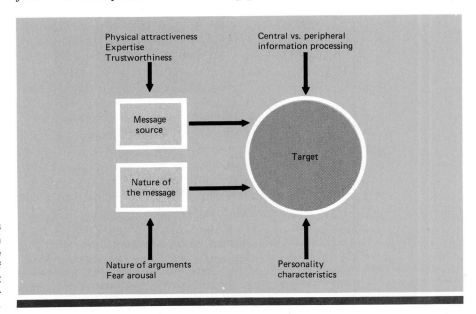

FIGURE 4-3
A model of persuasion. In this model, the message source and the nature of the message affect whether the target is persuaded.

Advertisers frequently use celebrities as message sources to persuade consumers to use their product.

knows that advertisers, at least, consider the source of a persuasive message crucial. This view is based on a good deal of experimental research that shows that the nature of a communicator is, in fact, quite important in determining whether the message will be accepted.

One factor relating to the message source that is particularly powerful is the attractiveness of the communicator, as perusal of television and magazine advertisements would have us infer. Research in both laboratory and field settings shows that physical attractiveness enhances an individual's ability to persuade others. For example, in a field study by Shelley Chaiken (1980), communicators who were high or low in attractiveness stopped students on a college campus and presented arguments in favor of the proposition that the "university should stop serving meat at breakfast and lunch at all dining commons." Subjects were more persuaded by the attractive communicators, as judged by a written assessment of subjects' agreement with the (rather unusual) position.

The critical factor may not be the physical attractiveness of the communicator per se, however. In a subsequent analysis, Chaiken found that the physically attractive communicators also were more fluent speakers, had higher SAT scores and grade-point averages, and rated themselves as more persuasive, attractive, and optimistic about future career success. It is possible that these attributes, which correlated with physical attractiveness, were the source of the greater persuasive effectiveness of the attractive communicators.

It is not just what a person says but the way it is said and the physical characteristics of the communicator that affect attitude change. In this photo we see William Jennings Bryan, a famed orator, at the Scopes evolution trial in the 1920s. (UPI/Bettmann Archive)

Other research on communicator attributes has shown quite clearly that the expertise and trustworthiness of a communicator is related to the impact of a message (Hovland, Janis, & Kelley, 1953). We are more likely to be swayed by a Nobel Prize–winner's physics theory than by a high school student's theory. Interestingly, an expert is effective in producing attitude change even when the message is irrelevant to his or her area of expertise (Aronson & Golden, 1962).

But even communicators high in expertise may not be persuasive if one believes they have an ulterior motive (Eagly, Wood, & Chaiken, 1978). For example, the Nobel Prize–winning biologist who argues in support of opening a genetic laboratory in your hometown is likely to have less credibility and, hence, be less persuasive if it is revealed that he would be a major shareholder in the laboratory and stands to make a good deal of money if it opens. Thus, messages that are seen primarily as serving the interests of the communicator are likely to be disregarded, despite the level of the communicator's expertise. The converse is true as well: communicators who are seen as arguing *against* their own best interests are seen as highly credible.

One other exception to the general finding that persons low in credibility are less likely to produce attitude change is a phenomenon known as the **sleeper effect.** The sleeper effect is an increase in the persuasive impact of a message from a low-credibility source that occurs over time (Hovland & Weiss, 1951). The effect is an interesting one, because it suggests that an apparent initial lack of attitude change is misleading and that a person can eventually show that he or she has been affected by the message if enough time elapses.

Sleeper effects have been explained by what has been called the "discounting cue hypothesis," which states that when initially an effective persuasive attempt is paired with a "discounting" cue such as a low-credibility source, the likelihood of immediate persuasion is low. However, with the passage of time, the message and discounting cue become disassociated in memory, and all that can be recalled is the persuasive message. The result is a delay in attitude change congruent with the message.

Unfortunately, the sleeper effect has proven an elusive phenomenon, and many attempts at replication of the initial findings have failed (Cook, Gruder, Hennigan, & Flay, 1979). Indeed, for many years in the 1970s, the effect was discounted entirely, until studies by Gruder, Cook, Hennigan, Flay, Alessis, and Halamaj (1978) and Pratkanis and Greenwald (1983) demonstrated its existence in a series of experiments. Problems remain in obtaining reliable sleeper effects, however, and the present status of the phenomenon has been summed up this way: "The sleeper effect will not be truly awakened from its slumber until it can be reliably produced and its determinants specified" (Pratkanis & Greenwald, 1983, p. 4).

In sum, communicator characteristics have an important effect upon the persuasiveness of a communication. Still, specific characteristics of

140

the communicator are not related to persuasion on an invariant basis. As Eagly (1983) points out, a number of characteristics of a communicator are likely to be processed cognitively simultaneously, and in a number of different ways, by the target of a persuasive message.

Characteristics of the Message: How Things Are Said Makes a Difference

The characteristics of the message itself, as well as the nature of its source, are likely to have an effect upon the ultimate persuasibility of people. We will discuss two of the most important characteristics: the kind of arguments that are made and the use of fear-inducing appeals.

The Nature of Arguments Made It should come as no surprise that the nature of arguments made in a message is related to its persuasibility. One line of work has examined the effects of increasing amounts of information in an argument, and has come to an interesting conclusion: although adding more information to an argument increases its persuasiveness, each additional amount of information has a smaller effect than the previous bit. Thus, the salesman who adds fact after fact about the virtues of the washing machine he is selling is probably wasting his (and your) time—assuming that each fact is consistent with all the others; it is the initial information that is going to make you buy it, if indeed you decide to (Calder, Insko, & Yandell, 1974).

A good deal of work has also gone into attempts to find whether one- or two-sided messages are most effective in producing attitude change. Is it best to ignore the opposition and just present the positive arguments in favor of a position or to present both sides? The answer to this question depends, it seems, on a number of factors (Karlins & Abelson, 1979). If the audience is favorable to the speaker's point of view or if it will only hear from the communicator and not hear from anyone holding an opposing view, a one-sided argument is probably best. But if the audience initially disagrees with the speaker's argument or is sure to receive a message from the opposition, two-sided communications are best. The reason seems to be that two-sided messages are perceived as fairer and, hence, people are less likely to feel that they are being coerced.

Fear Appeals Suppose you wanted to teach your child the virtue of brushing his teeth. Would it be wise to show him pictures of yellowed, crooked, decayed teeth and assure him that unless his habits change, such will be the fate of his teeth in the future? Or would it be better to describe the positive aspects of dental hygiene that come from brushing, such as a beautiful smile, fewer cavities, fresh breath, and fewer trips to the dentist?

Research examining questions such as these are representative of work that focuses upon what characteristics of a message make the most effective persuasive agents. One area in particular that has been of interest is fear-arousing appeals. The earliest work showed that lower levels of fear were most effective in producing attitude change. The explanation seemed to be that fear messages simply raised subjects' defense mechanisms, and they basically were not responsive to the message (Janis & Feshbach, 1953). Later work, however, showed the opposite result, with high fear appeals leading to greater attitude change (Leventhal, 1970).

A resolution has been suggested by Leventhal (1970), who suggests high fear-arousing messages will be effective only if they are accompanied by precise recommendations for actions to avoid the danger. Basically, it appears that three related aspects affect the success of fear-inducing messages: the magnitude of the fear induced, the probability of the undesired event occurring if nothing is done, and the probability of success in following the recommended regimen (R. W. Rogers, 1975; Mewborn & Rogers, 1979).

Receiving the Message: When Persuasion Is Accepted

The message has been delivered. But will it be accepted? Two approaches to this question can be discussed: one looks at situational characteristics related to message receipt and the other at personality characteristics of the receiver.

Central versus Peripheral Routes to Persuasion: Thoughtfulness versus Mindlessness

It is becoming increasingly clear that persuasion can occur along two different routes, what Petty and Cacioppo (1984) call **central** and **peripheral** routes to persuasion. Taking the central route, a person thoughtfully considers the issues related to the persuasive attempt because he or she is motivated and able to reflect upon the issue. In the peripheral route, in contrast, the recipient uses more easily assimilated information, such as the nature of the source or other noncontent sorts of information in deciding to accept a message. Basically, then, peripheral route persuasion occurs when the recipient is in a state we discussed as "mindlessness" in Chapter 2 in reference to attribution theory.

The most persistent and lasting persuasion occurs in the central, as opposed to the peripheral, route. For example, Shelley Chaiken (1980) carried out an experiment in which subjects received a message from a likable or dislikable source and which combined either six or two arguments. To vary whether central or peripheral routes would be operative, some subjects were told that they would discuss the topic later, while others expected to discuss a different topic. Chaiken anticipated that variation in the subjects' involvement in the topic due to the expectation of later discussion would be reflected in their susceptibility to persuasion: those expecting later discussion of the same topic (high consequences) would be more involved and thus process the informa-

FORMING, MAINTAINING,
AND CHANGING ATTITUDES

FIGURE 4-4
Opinion change due to
communicator likeability
and number of argu-
ments. Depending upon
whether they expected to
discuss the topic in the
future, subjects were differentially affected by the
likability of the communicator and number of ar-
guments used. (Sourse: S.
Chaiken, 1980.)

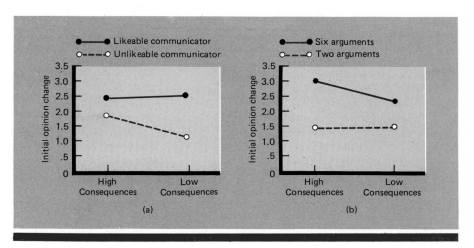

tion centrally. In the low-consequence condition (in which discussion
of a different topic was expected) peripheral processing was expected
to occur.

The results of the study confirm these predictions. As shown in Figure
4-4, subjects in the high-consequence condition were relatively unaffected by the manipulation of the likability of the message source; what
mattered was the number of arguments presented by the source. On the
other hand, subjects in the low-consequence condition, in which peripheral processing was expected, were more affected by the likability
of the communicator than by the number of arguments. Moreover, the
effects of attitude change were stabler for subjects in the high-consequence condition than for those in the low-consequence condition.

What these results suggest is that persuasive messages that are of high
quality will be most successful when the recipient is involved and when
the content of the message will be considered carefully—i.e., central
route processing is used. On the other hand, low-quality messages can
be persuasive if people are relatively uninvolved, because they will be
more likely to attend to peripheral information such as the likability or
attractiveness of the source.

This conclusion has important practical implications. For example, it
suggests that advertisers who use celebrities in their television commercials need not be terribly concerned with the quality of the message
(and, in fact, might well avoid complex messages) if the consumer is
relatively inattentive to the commercial, since peripheral cognitive processing is most likely to occur.

On the other hand, if the message in a commercial is well-reasoned
and involving or if the viewer happens to be highly attentive, it is less
important to use celebrities or other attractive message sources, since
processing can proceed along central routes. Because we can safely
assume that most viewers are not going to be highly attentive to commercial messages, the strategy of using celebrities to pitch products
seems reasonable.

Personality Factors: Who Is Most Easily Persuaded?   An enduring question that has been asked by people interested in attitude change is whether certain people are more prone to persuasion than others. When the question was first asked, researchers focused on particular variables, such as sex, self-esteem, and intelligence, and attempted to see whether, by themselves, they were systematically related to persuasibility. Results of such investigations were, for the most part, unsuccessful. For instance, although it was originally thought that women could be influenced more easily than men, research has not supported this contention (Eagly, 1978).

A more fruitful approach has been to look at personality characteristics in conjunction with variations in factors having to do with the nature of the message and arguments. For example, Eagly and Warren (1976) suggested that more intelligent people would understand more complex messages better than less intelligent ones, and thus would be more apt to be persuaded by a complex message. On the other hand, more intelligent people would also be expected to be less yielding because of their greater critical faculties. In support of this reasoning, they found a small, but positive, relationship between attitude change and intelligence when a complex message was employed. On the other hand, they found a strong negative relationship between persuasibility and intelligence when the message was not supported by complex arguments.

In sum, there are individual differences in persuasibility, but no one personality characteristic has been identified that is universally predictive of persuasibility across different situations.

ATTITUDES AND BEHAVIOR: ARE THEY RELATED?

To a scientist interested in social behavior, as well as to people like advertiser David Berger, who tries to change attitudes outside the laboratory, attitudes would be of little interest if they were not ultimately linked to behavior in one form or another. It should come as no surprise, then, that the question of how attitudes and behavior are related to one another has been a central issue in the study of attitudes.

Much of the early work on the attitude–behavior relationship was disappointing in that it seemed to show rather profound discrepancies between the two. One study in particular has come to represent this line of work, and we will discuss it in detail because not only is it illustrative of the kind of work done to investigate the attitude–behavior relationship, but it also shows some of the potential pitfalls in interpreting the results of such studies.

Discrepancies between Attitudes and Behavior: Discrimination Only in Writing?

Back in the 1930s, prejudice against the Chinese was rampant and overt on the west coast of the United States. It was not uncommon for people

BOX 4-3   SPOTLIGHT ON APPLICATIONS

FROM BRAINWASHING TO TOOTHBRUSHING: RESISTING PERSUASION

During the Korean War of the 1950s, the North Koreans and Chinese were involved in large-scale efforts to change the attitudes of American prisoners of war. Although by no means totally successful, they converted quite a few prisoners; these Americans embraced the Communist system and made public statements berating capitalism. More recently, Patty Hearst—whose case we mentioned at the start of this chapter—claimed that she had been brainwashed into accepting the views of the Symbionese Liberation Army.

Whether or not we accept her contention that she had been brainwashed, she, like many of the American prisoners of war before her, was placed in a situation that made her a relatively good candidate for **brainwashing**, which is the use of coercion to bring about attitude change. In both examples, the targets of persuasion were removed from their normal physical and social surroundings; they were deprived of sleep, food, and other physiological needs; they were made to feel guilt over any previous transgressions; and their beliefs were challenged with carefully crafted arguments and logic (McGuire, 1969; Schein, 1957).

Few of us will have to face such all-encompassing efforts to change our attitudes, and if we do, there is little research to provide guidance on how to resist such persuasion. However, there has been some work on resistance to persuasive attempts that occur in a more conventional manner: three major approaches can be identified.

Inoculation Theory

To provide immunization against smallpox, people are injected with a small amount of smallpox germs in order to encourage the formation of antibodies that can repel a future larger attack of the disease. Using this model, William McGuire (1964) suggested that people's beliefs about cultural truisms (such as "everyone should brush his teeth after every meal if at all possible") could be made more resistant to persuasive attacks if the people are exposed to a sample of opposing arguments and strategies for refuting them. The results of an extensive

series of experiments showed that the combination of opposing arguments and refutational examples was significantly more effective in reducing attitude change than providing supportive information alone. Thus, at least in terms of cultural truisms, innoculation leads to resistance to persuasion (Suedfeld & Borrie, 1978).

Forewarning: Forewarned Is Forearmed

When we consider issues other than cultural truisms, forewarning about the topic and position of a counterattitudinal persuasive message by itself (without providing actual counterarguments) is sufficient to reduce persuasion, at least when the issues are involving and relatively large amounts of information are available (Petty & Cacioppo, 1977; Cacioppo & Petty, 1979). By providing people with the knowledge that they are going to receive a message which is discrepant from their own point of view, you are allowing them to develop counterarguments prior to the persuasive message; thus, they are more resistant to persuasion. Forewarned is forearmed.

Warning of Persuasive Intent

In contrast to forewarning about the nature of the topic and the position of an upcoming message, it is also conceivable to provide forewarnings regarding the **persuasive intent** of the future message. It turns out that warning people that a persuasive message is coming is effective in reducing persuasion—but only for involving issues. On involving issues, people are more motivated to assert their freedom to hold their initial attitudes. Noninvolving issues are more amenable to change, and thus forewarnings of persuasive intent are less apt to be effective (Petty & Cacioppo, 1979). Simply telling people, then, that they are about to be the target of a persuasive message may be enough to reduce their persuasibility, at least for high-involvement issues.

Although these three approaches do not provide guidance on how to avoid being brainwashed, they do at least offer ways to reduce attitude change.

of Chinese extraction to be denied lodging and service at hotels and restaurants simply on the basis of their ethnic heritage. To sociologist Richard LaPiere, this state of affairs represented a useful opportunity to test the relationship between attitudes and behavior. LaPiere arranged a three-month, 10,000-mile trip with a Chinese couple that took him up and down the west coast, across the country. In all, the three stopped at some 250 hotels and restaurants and, somewhat to his surprise, they received service at all but one establishment.

To see how well the proprietors' attitudes matched their behavior, after their return LaPiere sent a questionnaire to all the hotels and restaurants they had stopped at which inquired if they would serve Chinese patrons. About 50 percent of the establishments responded and, contrary to the couple's actual experience, of those responding almost 92 percent flatly said "no"—with the rest saying "maybe." LaPiere (1934) took these results as a clear indication of attitude–behavioral discrepancy, and for many years the study was cited as evidence for the position that attitudes and behavior are unrelated.

Some Alternative Explanations   Before accepting LaPiere's results at face value, however, we should examine some alternative explanations. It might be, for example, that LaPiere's methodology was insensitive or flawed in some way. The most obvious methodological difficulty with LaPiere's study is that there is no way of ascertaining whether the respondents who answered LaPiere's survey (and remember that only about 50 percent bothered to reply) were the same ones who allowed them to stop at their establishment. It is possible, and perhaps even likely, that the people who served them were not the ones who responded to the questionnaire. Hence, a discrepancy between attitude and behavior should not be surprising if the attitude and the behavior were elicited from different people (Dillehay, 1973).

Another reason attitude–behavior congruence may be difficult to attain is the general relative insensitivity with which the behavior is measured. For instance, in studies of attitude–behavior congruence relating to consumer purchases, the behavioral measure is typically dichotomous: the consumer either buys or does not buy a product (Bogart, 1967). In constrast, we are able to measure attitudes using paper-and-pencil techniques much more precisely. Written scales may contain many more categories than behavioral measures. Consequently, people who fall into separate categories on a written measure may be lumped together on the more imprecise behavioral measure and, therefore, obscure possible congruence between attitudes and behavior.

Thus, one possibility is that even though the Chinese couple received only one outright rejection, more subtle signs of rejection (such as unpleasant verbal or nonverbal behavior or assignment of the couple to poorer table or room locations) occurred. Had this been the case, the results of the attitude and behavior measures would have been more congruent than LaPiere's study indicated (Kiesler, Collins, & Miller, 1969).

What this alternative explanation points out is that it is necessary to equate thresholds between written and behavioral measures of attitude in order to be able to ascertain the congruence between the two measures accurately. In other words, we must be sure that it is just as easy to say something negative (or positive) in written form as it is to act negatively (or positively). In LaPiere's study, it was fairly easy to respond negatively when writing a letter, but difficult to respond negatively when the Chinese couple was standing in front of the proprietor.

An approach which has greater methodological soundness might have been to compare responses to a pleading letter with the original behavioral measure (an in-person request) used by LaPiere; in this case, it would have been difficult to refuse either request. Alternatively, two measures on which it would have been relatively easy to refuse could have been employed: one in which the Chinese couple called the establishment, saying that they were 50 miles away and asking if they could come, and the other the survey letter that LaPiere employed originally. In this case, both the attitudinal and behavioral measures would have been designed to elicit an easy refusal. In sum, in order to be able to compare the relationship between attitudes and behavior meaningfully, it is necessary to use measures that are comparable in ability to elicit acceptance or rejection of the attitudinal object.

More generally, a high degree of **correspondence** between attitudes and behavior is a prerequisite for identifying a strong relationship between the two (Ajzen & Fishbein, 1980). Correspondence refers to the degree to which measures of attitudes and behaviors match in terms of action, target, context, and time. For example, as Cialdini, Petty, and Cacioppo (1981) point out, it is not surprising that attitudes toward driving (an action) might not be related to whether someone will drive a two-ton truck (target) on a highway blanketed with snow (context) on New Year's Eve (time), given the low degree of correspondence between the very general "driving" and the very specific "driving a two-ton truck on a snowy highway on New Year's Eve." Unless attitudes and behaviors are carefully specified and correspond to one another, the likelihood of finding an attitude–behavior linkage is quite low.

Whether Attitudes and Behavior Are Related: The Wrong Question?

Clearly, methodological pitfalls abound when we attempt to determine the relationship between attitudes and behavior. But the issue has been pursued doggedly because of the importance of the assumption, found in so many disparate approaches, that attitudes are organized and related to behavior.

Most researchers in the area of attitudes now reject the question of *whether* attitudes and behavior are congruent and instead concentrate on the issue of *under what circumstances* the two are related to one another. In contrast to the early skepticism of social psychologists like Wicker (1969), who concluded after a careful and influential review that

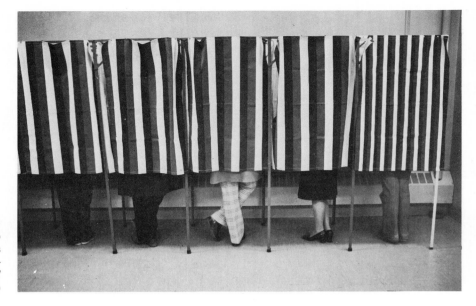

Using voter attitudinal
data, surveys are able to
predict election outcomes
with considerable accu-
racy. (Jim Anderson/
Woodfin Camp)

correlations between attitude and behavior were "rarely above .30" (which is quite modest), more recent evidence suggests in a clear-cut fashion that a high degree of congruence can be found if appropriate conditions are met (e.g., Schuman & Johnson, 1976). For instance, when people are more attentive to their own behavior (and presumably more aware of their internal states), attitude–behavior congruence increases (Snyder & Tanke, 1976; Ajzen, Timko, & White, 1982). In addition, attitudes that are formed through direct behavioral experience with the attitudinal object tend to be more congruent with behavior relevant to the object. Zanna, Olson, and Fazio (1981) argue that people frequently do not have a clear basis for articulating an attitude unless their prior experience with the attitudinal object is made clear-cut to them, and they therefore suggest that one way of increasing the link between attitudes and subsequent behavior is to ensure that people recall their past behavior at the time their attitudes regarding the attitudinal object are assessed.

In support of this hypothesis, subjects in an experiment were asked to indicate their attitude toward being religious on a number of items (Zanna, Olson, & Fazio, 1981). For some subjects, the items were preceded by a ninety-item checklist that inquired as to their religious behavior over the last year, thus making their prior behavior highly salient, while for other subjects the religious behavior checklist *followed* the attitude assessment. About one month later, all subjects were asked to indicate their religious behavior over the past month. As was predicted, the attitude–behavior correlations were generally higher for the subjects whose earlier religious behavior had been pointed out to them, and significantly lower for subjects whose attitudes were measured without the advantage of having their prior behavior made salient. It seems, then, that attitudes can be linked more closely to behavior when they are based on concrete past behavior.

The most definitive answer to the question of the nature of the correspondence between attitudes and behavior comes from the successful predictions made by pollsters. Except for the 1980 election, major polls have had percentage error rates of around one point (see Table 4-2) in predicting presidential election voting patterns. Although these are aggregate figures and do not predict individual behavior, they still lend support to the assumption underlying social psychological research that attitudes and behavior are correlated.

Do Attitudes Determine Behavior?

If we can assume that attitudes and behaviors are related to one another, the next question to be answered regards the issue of causality. Do attitudes determine behavior?

The most comprehensive answer to this question comes from findings that are based on a model proposed by Ajzen and Fishbein (1980) called a "theory of reasoned action." In their model, which has proved to be the most influential theory regarding the attitude–behavior linkage, they suggest that behavior is primarily a function of an *intention* to carry out the particular behavior relevant to an attitudinal object. As can be seen in Figure 4-5, the intention is determined by two factors: the attitude toward the behavior and the perceived social pressure to carry out the behavior, termed a **subjective norm.** It is only by examining the attitude

TABLE 4-2 Accuracy of Gallup and Harris Polls in Recent Presidential Elections

1972 Election	Sample Size	Predicted		Actual Result		Error, %
		Nixon	McGovern	Nixon	McGovern	
Gallup	3500	62.0	38.0	61.8	38.2	0.2
Harris	NA	60.0	37.0	61.8	38.2	1.8
1976 Election		Predicted		Actual Result		
		Carter	Ford	Carter	Ford	
Gallup	3500	48.0	49.0	50.0	48.3	2.0
Harris	NA	49.0	48.0	50.0	48.3	1.0
1980 Election		Predicted		Actual Result		
		Carter	Reagan	Carter	Reagan	
Gallup	3500	44.0	47.0	41.6	51.7	4.7
Harris	NA	41.6	46.8	41.6	51.7	4.9

Source: Adapted from Hennessy, (1981).

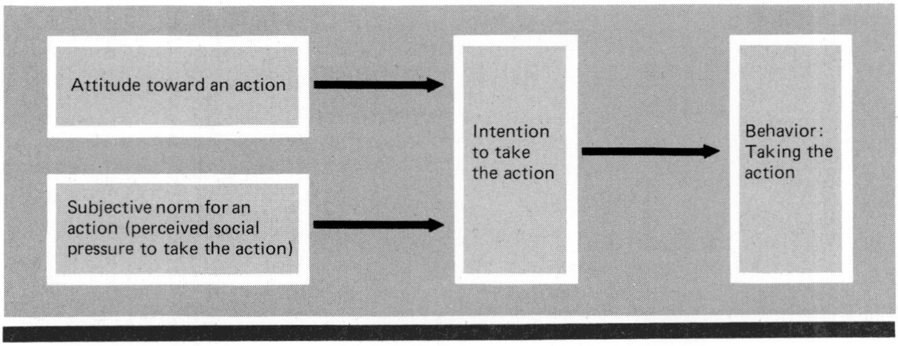

Attitude toward an action

Subjective norm for an
action (perceived social
pressure to take the action)

Intention
to take
the action

Behavior:
Taking the
action

FIGURE 4-5
The Ajzen and Fishbein
theory of reasoned action.

and subjective norm that we can successfully predict a person's behavioral intentions, and it is ultimately their behavioral intentions that can allow us to predict their behavior accurately.

Basically, then, Ajzen and Fishbein say that attitudes do lead to behavior—but that subjective norms and behavioral intentions must also be considered. The model has proven quite accurate in relating attitudes to behavior in a number of areas, including voting, political, and family planning behavior (Vinokur-Kaplan, 1978; Ajzen & Fishbein, 1980). For example, Bowman and Fishbein (1978) studied voting intentions and reported voting behavior on the 1976 Oregon nuclear safeguards initiative on which voters had the opportunity to place limits on the construction of nuclear plants. As would be predicted by the model, people who voted "yes" on the referendum (the behavior) were apt to have intended to vote that way (the intention). Moreover, both attitude and subjective norm (as measured by questions concerning the evaluation of voting and perceived social pressure for voting in a particular way) were highly correlated with voting intention.

The Ajzen and Fishbein model has been particularly important in pointing out the conditions under which attitudes do result in subsequent behavior. Probably the most important factor relates to the degree of specificity of attitude and behavior. In general, it is clear that specific attitudes can be used to predict specific behaviors, while general attitudes are useful primarily for predicting general classes of behaviors.

Ajzen and Fishbein's model is not the only one that has produced evidence that attitudes determine behavior. For instance, further evidence for this relationship comes from a study by Kahle and Berman (1979). Using a sophisticated technique known as "cross-lagged panel correlations," they assessed attitudes and behavior relating to four issues: Jimmy Carter's presidential candidacy, Gerald Ford's candidacy, drinking, and religion. For example, subjects responded to the following attitudinal item regarding drinking: "I like to drink," and the behavior assessed was the number of times in the past two weeks that subjects said they had had at least one drink. An example of the attitude toward religion was "Being active in church is important;" the behavior was the number of times the respondent had prayed in private or been with people from his or her church in the past two weeks.

By assessing these attitudes and behaviors at two sessions separated by two months, it was possible to infer whether the attitudes subjects held led to their subsequent behaviors. The results were clear: on each of the four issues, attitudes were shown to be the cause of behaviors. The authors conclude that, at least with regard to the issues studied in the experiment, "for the politicians, theologians, and alcoholism therapists who may be interested in knowing whether their efforts to change attitudes will help them to achieve their ultimate goals of changing behaviors, the answer appears to be 'yes' " (Kahle & Berman, 1979, p. 320).

An Alternate View: Does Behavior Determine Attitudes?

Although there is a great deal of positive evidence in support of the attitudes-determine-behavior school of thought, a number of theorists have instead suggested an opposite causal link: that behavior determines attitudes. For instance, as we mentioned earlier, Bem has argued that in some cases the behavior in which people engage becomes the determinant of their attitude (Bem, 1972). He suggests that when people's internal cues regarding the attitudinal object are weak or ambiguous, people act as observers of their own behavior.

For instance, we can imagine going to a movie about which we know very little and finding ourselves yawning, nodding our heads, and finally dozing off in the middle. Although we may still know very little about the movie, having fallen asleep in the middle of it, we probably have developed well-defined attitudes about it: it is boring, uninteresting, and dull. According to Bem, the mechanism by which we have developed these attitudes is analogous to the way in which we infer the attitudes of others: we observe our own behavior. In Bem's opinion, we would view our reactions to the movie and form an attitude based on those behaviors. (Similarly, we might come to the conclusion that the people who accompanied us to the movie disliked it as much as we did if they, too, fell asleep in the middle.)

Although Bem's theory of self-perception has received support, none of it has been definitive enough to rule out alternative explanations (Greenwald, 1975). It is clear that when behavior is congruent with an initially held attitude, the attitude can be strengthened, reevaluated, or modified, and we can say that the behavior has caused the attitude to be refined in a particular way (Fazio, Zanna, & Cooper, 1977). In at least some cases, then, behavior *does* lead to attitude change.

SUMMARY

Although there are many definitions of attitudes, one of the most universally acceptable definitions stresses their evaluative aspects. Other approaches suggest that attitudes have three major elements—a cognitive (thought), affective (feeling), and behavioral (action) component. The assumption generally is made that there is consistency both within and between attitudes.

Learning and reinforcement theories approach attitudes as learned responses to stimuli. Some attitudes are learned through conditioning processes in which a previously neutral stimulus takes on emotion-arousing properties through pairing with an unconditioned stimulus. Reinforcement approaches suggest that the acquisition and maintenance of attitudes are learned through reward and punishment. In addition, simple observation of others receiving rewards and punishments can result in vicarious learning, another form of attitude acquisition.

Cognitive consistency approaches to attitudes are used to explain how attitudinal components fit together and how they fit with other attitudes. Inconsistency is seen as a psychologically unpleasant state resulting in attempts to decrease the inconsistency. Heider's balance theory was the first of the cognitive consistency theories, and it is concerned with how we make our attitudes regarding people and an attitudinal object consistent. It suggests that relationships will either be balanced or unbalanced, depending on the nature of attitudes held, and that balance must be restored to achieve cognitive consistency.

Cognitive dissonance theory states that when two cognitions that contradict one another are held simultaneously, a state of dissonance is experienced. Dissonance produces psychological tension which can be reduced by modifying a cognition, changing the perceived importance of elements, adding more consonant elements, or determining that the cognitions are irrelevant to one another. Insufficient justification experiments produce dissonance by creating a situation in which people do things with which they do not actually agree for small justification. Dissonance is typically reduced by changing one's attitude to become more congruent with the behavior.

On the other hand, self-perception theorists suggest that dissonance is not aroused by counterattitudinal behavior; rather, attitude change occurs when people view their own behavior and attempt to understand the reasons behind it. Although the competing explanations have not been resolved, dissonance theory has been applied to other areas, such as decision making and selective exposure to information.

Work on persuasion has looked at three major factors: the source of the message, the nature of the message, and the characteristics of the message recipient. Message sources that are physically attractive and have greater expertise and trustworthiness are more persuasive, although work on the "sleeper effect" suggests that there may be an increase in the persuasive impact of a message from a low-credibility or disliked source over time. The nature of the argument made, including the amount of information and whether the message is one- or two-sided, has an effect on persuasiveness, as does the degree to which appeals to fear are invoked. Finally, use of central versus peripheral cognitive processes and the target's personality characteristics also affect persuasibility.

One of the first looks at the question of whether attitudes and behavior are related was the LaPiere study, which suggested that there is no relationship. However, more recent research suggests a relation between attitudes and behavior and concentrates on the circumstances that influence the strength of this relation. There is also good evidence suggesting that attitudes determine behavior. On the other hand, Bem's theory of self-perception suggests that behavior may determine attitudes, at least under some circumstances.

KEY TERMS

affective relationships
Bem's theory of self-perception
brainwashing
central routes of persuasion
classical conditioning
cognitive dissonance
counterattitudinal advocacy
discounting cue hypothesis
evaluation apprehension
forewarning
Heider's balance theory
innoculation theory

Likert-type scales
overjustification effect
peripheral route of persuasion
reinforcement
semantic differential scale
sleeper effect
sociogram
sociometric
subjective norm
Thurston scale
unit relationship
vicarious learning

FOR FURTHER STUDY AND APPLICATION

Rajecki, D. W. (1982). *Attitudes: Themes and advances.* Sunderland, MA: Sinauer Associates.
A current, readable, and sophisticated view of attitudes. Rich in contemporary work, the volume integrates research and theory into a series of meaningful themes.

Himmelfarb, S., & Eagly, A. H. (1974). *Readings in attitude change.* New York: Wiley.
A high-level comprehensive review of the research and theory on attitudes. It reprints the major articles in the field, preceded by a masterful and scholarly introduction.

Zimbardo, P., Ebbesen, E. B., and Maslach, C. (1977). *Influencing attitudes and changing behavior* (2nd ed.). Reading, MA: Addison-Wesley.

This book provides a clear, interesting introduction to the area of attitudes. Written for the person with little background in the area, it is a good first text.

Cialdini, R. (1984). *Influence.* New York: W. J. Morrow.
An up-to-date, lively introduction to techniques for persuading others to modify their behavior and attitudes. Includes very practical suggestions, at the same time explaining the theory behind them.

Campbell, A. (1981). *The sense of well-being in America.* New York: McGraw-Hill.
Provides a good example of how large-scale surveys are done and the degree to which they can be informative.

CHAPTER 5

PREJUDICE AND DISCRIMINATION

A CONVERSATION WITH . . .

Frederick B. Routh
*Director, Community
Relations,
U.S. Civil Rights
Commission*

Fred Routh served for many years as one of the principal administrators of the U.S. Civil Rights Commission, which was formed by Congress to further the end of prejudice and discrimination in the United States. Because of his position, Mr. Routh was aware of activities and trends in the area of civil rights throughout the country and was able to provide a broad overview of the state of prejudice and discrimination in America.

We spoke in his Washington office shortly before his untimely death at age 58. We began our conversation by discussing his specific activities as director:

Q. Could you describe briefly what you do at the commission?

A. My position is director of the community relations division, which acts as liaison with a selected number of federal agencies, state government agencies, and city agencies, and also with national private agencies, such as the NAACP, LaRasa, and others. We try to keep them informed on what the commission is doing and to keep track of what they are doing.

Q. Can you give me an example of the specific kinds of activities you are involved in?

A. They're endless. For instance, we have just completed a report of hearings in Miami. If you recall, there has been severe racial violence in Miami off and on over the past few years. We looked into the whole situation, trying to determine what some of the causes were and what might be learned by other communities. We recently held a hearing in Baltimore— where there have not been any riots—on economic development and the role of minorities. Another type of thing we've done recently is a survey of police activities in this country. We've held hearings and done a

number of studies on the tensions that exist between the police and minorities and, based on our findings, we issued a report called "Who Is Guarding the Guardians?" Another type of study dealt with the rights of American Indians and the whole question of tribal survival. So it's a wide variety of things we cover. The jurisdiction of the agency includes race, religion, national origin, sex, age, and handicap, and the areas that we cover are employment, education, housing, the administration of justice, and voting rights.

Q. With your familiarity with the area of civil rights, you must have a broad overview of the trends and changes occurring in this country. Do you have a sense that things are getting better or worse in the area of prejudice and discrimination?

A. This field, like most fields, has its ups and downs. Overall, in the last twenty-five years, I think we've made amazing progress. It's not been even, but if you compare where we are today with where we were twenty-five years ago, we've come a long, long way. We still have a long, long way to go, and the federal government in the next few years will not have the type of vigorous, aggressive role that it has had since 1964 to roughly 1980. There has been a trimming back and a cutback.

Q. So you're less optimistic than you once were?

A. I am less optimistic about what is being done now than I was, say, five or ten years ago. But I do not think the momentum for civil rights and for equal opportunity can be stopped. We're not going back to where we were before the civil rights movement really got under way. A good example of this is the recent extension of the Voting Rights Act for twenty-five years. The support of the administration was lukewarm at best, but then Congress came through.

Q. Do you think that reflects an underlying grassroots change in opinion about prejudice? Has there been an attitudinal change in that there is greater support for vigorous kinds of actions to end discrimination?

A. I don't think there is any question but that there is much more support among the general population in the United States today than there was twenty-five years ago for civil rights. In a number of southern states, the support for the extension of the Voting Rights Act was very strong, and if you look at the final vote in the Senate, there were only eight votes against the extension of that act. Overall, support for civil rights has increased very considerably.

Q. Why do you think that is so?

A. You're probably familiar with the notion that if you want to change attitudes, it is sometimes easier to change behavior, and the attitudes will follow. I think we have found that with the passage of various civil rights legislation in this country, the great difficulties that were anticipated did not take place—that, indeed, this legislation worked, and worked rather well. Not perfectly, by any means, but overall it worked pretty well. And as people adjusted to new behavior patterns, their attitudes followed. Now where we fell short in part was due to the fact that we did not sufficiently undergird the changed behavior by working on changes of attitudes. On the other hand, this is not a proper role for government—that would be the responsibility of the private agencies in the field. Government deals with discrimination in behavior patterns. You can outlaw discriminatory behavior, but you cannot outlaw prejudicial attitudes.

Q. One of the difficulties I have is that when you look at the scientific literature on, for instance, desegregation, the results are far from consistent. Sometimes positive results are found, sometimes negative, and sometimes no changes occur at all. How do you deal with this?

A. This may be a problem in any area of social science research. I've been involved in school desegregation for a long time, and at first desegregation was of a token nature. But after the 1964 Civil Rights Act and after the Supreme Court decided that desegregation should go forth with "all deliberate speed," the process sped up. And in those school systems where advance preparations were made with the faculty, staff, and children, and where the local authorities (mayor, town manager, chief of police, and others) said there will not be interference with the decisions of a court to desegregate, or where it was voluntarily done, by and large desegregation worked.

Q. So where there are supportive conditions, desegregation can be effective.

A. No doubt about it.

Q. What do you see for the future of the Civil Rights Commission?

A. It is my hope that this commission can continue to function both as the conscience of the federal government in the field of civil rights and as a goad to the other agencies. We have no enforcement powers. But by finding the facts and publishing those facts, we often can do a great deal.

OVERVIEW

Although, as Mr. Routh pointed out, there have been remarkable strides made in the area of civil rights, prejudice and discrimination have remained serious problems. Consider, for example, the following three recent news items:

- A former member of the Ku Klux Klan and the American Nazi Party was indicted by a Federal grand jury for the 1980 ambush shooting of Vernon E. Jordan, then president of the National Urban League. Though subsequently acquitted, the assailant is currently serving four life sentences for the murder of two young black men who were jogging in a Salt Lake City park with two white women. At his trial for these murders, the suspect was quoted as saying that the two blacks deserved to die for "race mixing." He has also been charged with the racially motivated slayings of a black man and his white wife in Oklahoma City and of two black men in Indianapolis.

- A Jewish female student was shot five times with a BB gun on the University of Maryland campus at College Park, Maryland. The attacker shouted "Heil Hitler" as he fired and used other epithets that indicated anti-Jewish feelings. An underground campus newspaper hailed the assailant as a hero and suggested that next time he use a flamethrower on the victim.

- A female applicant for a job of attorney for the town of Northampton, Massachusetts, was turned down because the hiring authority felt that having a male lawyer would bring greater prestige to the job.

These articles relate three different manifestations of prejudice and discrimination—racial, religious, and sexual—and illustrate that such problems remain part of a vital social issue that has defied an easy solution. In this chapter, we will discuss many of the topics alluded to in our conversation with Fred Routh by examining the social psychological principles underlying prejudice and discrimination, particularly in terms of individuals' attitudes toward members of their own and other groups. Because there generally is a link between attitudes and behavior (as we saw in the chapter on attitudes), we will discuss how prejudicial attitudes can be manifested in discriminatory behavior. We will also examine the major approaches that have been taken to gain an understanding of prejudice, particularly in respect to racial, religious, sex, and age discrimination. Finally, we will examine techniques that have been developed for promoting the reduction of prejudice and discrimination. Because of social psychologists' fundamental interest in attitudes and attitude change, it is natural that the topic of prejudice and discrimination is of critical interest to the field.

BASIC CONCEPTS: DEFINING PREJUDICE, DISCRIMINATION, AND MINORITY GROUPS

We need to distinguish between a number of basic concepts relevant to the area of intergroup interaction: prejudice, discrimination, and minority groups. **Prejudice** refers to positive or negative evaluations or judgments of members of a particular group which are based primarily on the fact of their membership in the group, and not necessarily because of particular characteristics of individual members. For example, sex prejudice occurs when an individual is evaluated on the basis of membership in a particular group—i.e., as a male or female—and not because of his or her own specific characteristics.

Although prejudice is generally thought of as a negative evaluation of group members, it can also be positive: at the same time people dislike members of another group, they may also positively evaluate members of their own group—solely on the basis of their group membership. In both cases, the affect is unrelated to qualities of particular individuals; rather, it is due to the group to which the individuals belong.

Discrimination is the behavioral manifestation of prejudice. In cases of discrimination, members of particular groups are treated either positively or negatively because of their membership in a particular group. People who harbor prejudicial attitudes do not necessarily engage in overt discriminatory action, since the target of their prejudice may not be present (someone may dislike Turks without ever having had an opportunity to interact with them). Moreover, strong social norms may prevent overt discrimination, although it may occur in subtler ways. Thus, the presence of prejudice does not always lead to discrimination. On the other hand, the manifestation of discrimination more readily allows the inference that prejudice is also present, although even this relationship does not always hold. For instance, a white real estate salesman who is not prejudiced toward blacks may still refuse to show a black house hunter particular homes because of his fear of offending the white neighbors.

Common sense might suggest that the term **minority group**, at least on the surface, is the clearest of the concepts we have discussed—if we focus only on the size of a group. From a social psychological standpoint, however, numbers often do not tell the whole story (Simpson & Yinger, 1972). For instance, in some parts of the south, blacks far outnumber whites; in South Africa whites make up only a small percentage of the population; and there are slightly more females than males in the United States. But we can make a good argument that those in the numerical minority should actually be considered the majority. The reason? The salient defining characteristic which distinguishes a minority from the majority group is the relative *power* wielded by the two groups, and in both examples, the minority holds considerably more power than the majority.

Thus, social psychologists consider minority groups in terms of psychological, as opposed to strictly numerical, characteristics. Specifically, Wagley and Harris (1958) suggest that minorities make up subordinate parts of a society, have physical or cultural characteristics that are held in relatively low esteem by dominant groups, and are aware of their minority status. Moreover, minority membership is passed on through norms that encourage affiliation and marriage with other minority group members. In many ways, then, being a minority (or majority) group member is something of a state of mind, regardless of what the absolute numbers imply.

THE BUILDING BLOCKS OF PREJUDICE AND DISCRIMINATION: STEREOTYPES

One of the reasons behind the development and maintenance of prejudice and discrimination relates to the general beliefs in a society about the characteristics and traits, known as stereotypes, of members of particular social and ethnic groups. **Stereotypes** are the cognitions and expectations assigned to members of groups simply on the basis of their membership in those groups (Weber & Crocker, 1983). As we will discuss in more detail later, stereotypes are oversimplifications that we use in an attempt to make sense out of a complex social environment. In the process, we can lose sight of the important differentiations that distinguish one person from another.

Racial and Ethnic Stereotypes

The classic study of stereotypes was carried out by David Katz and Kenneth Brayly (1933), who assessed Princeton University undergraduates' beliefs about which of a list of eighty-four adjectives best described members of ten different ethnic groups. They found extraordinarily high agreement on the first ten traits chosen for each group, showing that there was a commonly agreed-upon stereotype. As you can see from the lists in Table 5-1, some of the results are surprising; the subjects had no hesitancy in using adjectives with negative characteristics to describe a group. For instance, blacks were more frequently called superstitious (84 percent), lazy (75 percent), and ignorant (38 percent).

What is particularly important about the Katz and Brayly (1933) study is that it has been replicated twice in the years following its publication, once in 1951 and again in 1967, which allows us to trace the changes in stereotypes over time (Gilbert, 1951; Karlins, Coffman, & Walters, 1969). One change that occurred concerned the nature of the specific adjectives chosen over the years. Specifically, there was a trend for students to attribute more positive characteristics to most groups in later years. Hence, by 1967 blacks were most frequently called musical (47

TABLE 5-1 Stereotypes of American College Students from 1933 to 1967

AMERICANS	1933	1951	1967	GERMANS	1933	1951	1967
Industrious	48	30	23	Science minded	78	62	47
Intelligent	47	32	20	Industrious	44	10	9
Materialistic	33	37	67	Stolid	44	10	9
Ambitious	33	21	42	Intelligent	32	32	19
Progressive	27	5	17	Methodical	31	20	21
Pleasure loving	26	27	28	Nationalistic	24	50	43
Alert	23	7	7	Progressive	16	3	13
Efficient	21	9	15	Efficient	16	—	46

CHINESE	1933	1951	1967	NEGROES	1933	1951	1967
Superstitious	34	18	8	Superstitious	84	41	13
Sly	29	4	6	Lazy	75	31	26
Conservative	29	14	15	Happy-go-lucky	38	17	27
Tradition loving	26	26	32	Ignorant	38	24	11
Loyal to family ties	22	35	50	Musical	26	33	47
Industrious	18	18	23	Ostentatious	26	11	25
Meditative	19	—	21	Very religious	24	17	8
Reserved	17	18	15	Stupid	22	10	4

Note: Entries in the table are the percentages of respondents who indicated that trait was characteristic of the group. Blanks (—) in the table indicate that those data were not reported in the 1951 study, *not* that the percentage is zero.
Source: Based on Karlins, Coffman, & Walters (1969).

percent) and happy-go-lucky (27 percent)—still not particularly flattering attributes, but improvements over descriptions used in earlier years. In addition, the degree of agreement for the most often cited adjectives was lower in later replications, suggesting that shared agreement regarding the nature of stereotypes was weaker than in the initial study, which showed relatively high levels of consensus.

Subjects' reactions to the experimental task reflected another change that had occurred over time. When Katz and Brayly (1933) first carried out the study, subjects readily assigned traits to the various groups. But in later replications, they often complained about the procedure, in some instances declining to carry out the task. Hence, it is possible that subjects may have become more sensitive to the negative implications of stereotyping.

Still, we cannot say with confidence that stereotyping about racial and religious minority groups has declined over time. It is possible that subjects are becoming more circumspect about their expression of negative beliefs about a group, and that underlying their more positive choice of adjectives are less benign perceptions. It is also possible that language usage has changed somewhat over the years, so that the meaning of the same adjective applied to an ethnic group has shifted.

Yet there is some evidence that racial and ethnic stereotypes are not as prevalent as in earlier times. Indeed, it appears that the targets of stereotypes may shift from members of racial and ethnic groups to members of social and economic classes. Smedley and Bayton (1978), for instance, found that beliefs about social class provided more powerful stereotypes than did beliefs about race.

Sex Stereotypes

Although most of the classic work on stereotyping concerns beliefs and attitudes about racial and religious groups, more recent work has focused on the areas of sex and age stereotyping. A little thought will bring to mind society's traditional view of appropriate male behavior (for instance, aggressive, competitive, independent, ambitious) and appropriate female behavior (for example, gentle, quiet, home loving). Likewise, if told that someone is a nurse or a secretary, most people initially assume that the person in question is a female; but if told that someone is a steamfitter or physician, people typically assume that the person is a male.

Traditional sex stereotypes seem to fit into very regular categories (e.g., Wallston, De Vellis, & Wallston, 1983). For instance, in one study subjects were asked to rate the "typical male" and "typical female" over a series of dimensions, such as "very passive" to "very active." They were also asked which end of the dimension was most desirable. Results showed that the traits could be grouped into two clusters, one relating to competence and one relating to warmth and expressiveness. Traits

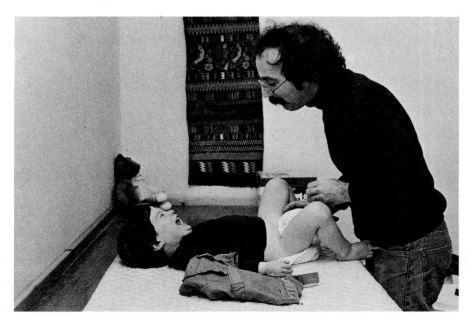

The sight of a man changing a child's diaper may still strike some as inappropriate—at least to holders of traditional sex stereotypes. (Hazel Hankin)

The stereotype of the passive, physically decrepit elderly is shattered by a scene such as this, taken at a five-mile race. (Ira Berger/Woodfin Camp)

relating to warmth and expressivity were judged most appropriate for females, while competency traits were seen as being most appropriate for males (Broverman, Vogel, Broverman, Clarkson, & Rosenkrantz, 1972).

As in the case of other stereotypes, there is little evidence that such stereotypes are valid (Eagly & Steffen, 1983). Indeed, over the past decade there has been a remarkable shift in stereotypes regarding what behaviors are viewed as masculine or feminine (e.g., DerKarabetran & Smith, 1977; Yoger, 1983). It is much less expected that a married woman will remain at home, taking care of the children, while the man is the breadwinner of the family—a view that is congruent with the reality that 52 percent of all women over the age of 16 now hold jobs (Bureau of Labor Statistics, 1981). Moreover, as women enter fields traditionally considered male-oriented (and vice versa), sex stereotypes are likely to undergo continuing modification.

Age Stereotypes: The Myth of the Senile Elderly

One of the most prevalent stereotypes of the elderly is that of passivity, unsociability, and senility (Rodin & Langer, 1980). Such views are manifestations of what Robert Butler, head of the National Institute of Aging, calls "ageism" (Butler, 1980). According to him, **ageism** consists of negative attitudes toward older people and toward the aging process, discrimination against older people, and institutional policies that maintain stereotypes about the aged. Indeed, even some physicians, who might otherwise be expected to be sympathetic to the elderly, use the terms "crones" or "trolls" when talking about their older patients.

How accurate are stereotypes of the elderly? In many cases they are quite off the mark. For example, some older people viewed as irreversibly senile are actually suffering from short-term depression, which may be reversed with psychotherapy (Wolinsky, 1983). Moreover, many elderly have active sex lives well into their eighties, a fact that hardly fits the typical stereotype.

DETERMINING WHO IS PREJUDICED

Thirty years ago, Gordon Allport included a now-classic conversation between a Mr. X and a Mr. Y in seminal work on the origins of prejudice. The dialogue went like this:

Mr. X: The trouble with Jews is that they only take care of their own group.

Mr. Y: But the record of the Community Chest campaign shows that they give more generously, in proportion to their numbers, than do non-Jews.

Mr. X: That shows they are always trying to buy favors and intrude

163

BOX 5-1 SPOTLIGHT ON RESEARCH

ON THE SELF-FULFILLING NATURE OF STEREOTYPES: ACTING IN ACCORDANCE WITH WHAT OTHERS WANT TO SEE

One of the more disturbing aspects of stereotyping is the possibility that holders of a stereotype can behave in a way that actually brings about confirmation of the stereotype. This phenomenon, in which the holder of a stereotype causes members of the stereotypical group to act in accordance with the stereotype, is an example of a self-fulfilling prophecy. As we mentioned in Chapter 2, **self-fulfilling prophecies** are expectations about the possibility of future events or behaviors that act to increase the likelihood that the event or behavior will occur (Archibald, 1974). Thus, if people think that members of a certain group are lazy, they may act in a way that actually elicits laziness on the part of members of that group (e.g., Word, Zanna, & Cooper, 1974; Skrypnek & Snyder, 1982).

Perhaps even more surprising is the possibility that knowing that another person holds a certain stereotype about oneself could lead one to behave in a way that is congruent with the stereotype—even if it is not the way that one normally behaves. A graphic example of this phenomenon was found in a study by Zanna and Pack (1975). Interested in how people are affected by the knowledge that an-

other person holds a certain type of stereotype, they first assessed a group of university women's self-concepts, particularly focusing on dimensions related to sex-role stereotypes. Thus, the women were asked how career-oriented, dependent, aggressive, and believing in women's liberation they were.

The next step in the experiment was for each subject to return, ostensibly to meet another person as part of an experiment on person perception. But before they met, the woman was given a description of the other individual, said to be a college-age male. The rest of the description varied according to experimental condition. However, half of the subjects were told that the man was attractive and desirable, and half that he was unattractive and undesirable. In addition, subjects were led to believe either that he held traditional sex-role stereotypes or untraditional stereotypes.

Zanna and Pack reasoned that when the man was described as desirable, the female subjects would be motivated to present themselves as being more like the male's stereotype than they might actually be. But when he was said to be undesirable, it was thought the subjects would not be interested in pre-

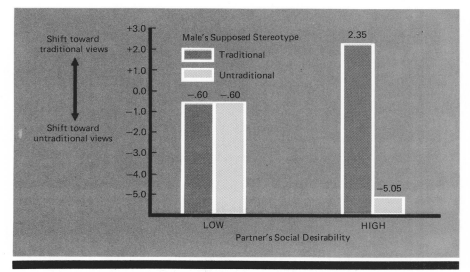

FIGURE 5-1

Changes in self-presentation regarding sex-role-related attitudes. With a male partner low in social desirability, the male's supposed stereotype about female behavior had no effect on the female subject's self-presentation. But when the partner was high in desirability, there was a large self-presentation effect. Source: Zanna & Pack (1975).

164

senting themselves according to the male's stereotype, and thus they would not be affected by the knowledge of his stereotypes regarding appropriate female behavior.

To test this hypothesis, the female subjects were asked to fill out another questionnaire after learning of the man's desirability and the nature of his stereotypes. This time the questionnaire asked about the women's view of the "ideal woman"—which the researchers felt would best tap into how the women would be affected by the knowledge of the man's stereotype.

The results supported this reasoning. As can be seen in Figure 5-1, when the women felt the man was unattractive, there were no changes relating to the man's stereotypes (both scores at the left of the figure are identical). But when the man was thought to be desirable, there was a large effect relating to the man's stereotypes. Women's responses became considerably more traditional when they thought the desirable male held traditional stereotypes; conversely, they became considerably more untraditional when they thought he held untraditional stereotypes.

The results of this study indicate quite clearly that people can be affected by the stereotypes that others hold about them. However, the results also show that stereotypes do not *invariably* affect the stereotyped individual; in some cases, at least, it appears to be at the discretion of the target of the stereotype.

---

into Christian affairs. They think of nothing but money; that is why there are so many Jewish bankers.

Mr. Y: But a recent study shows that the percentage of Jews in the banking business is negligible, far smaller than the percentage of non-Jews.

Mr. X: That's just it; they don't go in for respectable business. They are only in the movie business or run night clubs.

(Allport, 1954, pp. 13–14)

Anyone hearing this dialogue would have no difficulty in identifying Mr. X's prejudice. But in most instances prejudice is not expressed in nearly as overt and clear-cut a manner as this. Therefore, it has been necessary to devise a variety of means to assess prejudice, which we will discuss in this part of the chapter.

Measures of Prejudice

The most direct way of measuring prejudice would be to assess attitudes using written measures, employing some of the techniques that we discussed in our chapter on attitudes. However, attitudes toward potential objects of prejudice are particularly tricky to tap, primarily because in many social circles—and especially on college campuses—there is a high degree of social desirability in professing liberal, unprejudiced attitudes. Thus, even people who harbor prejudice toward a group may not be willing to express it because they may expect social sanctions to be brought against them. Therefore, social psychologists sometimes require subtler measures to measure prejudice.

Nonverbal Behavior as a Measure of Prejudice   One of the most revealing and yet unobtrusive measures of prejudice is the nonverbal

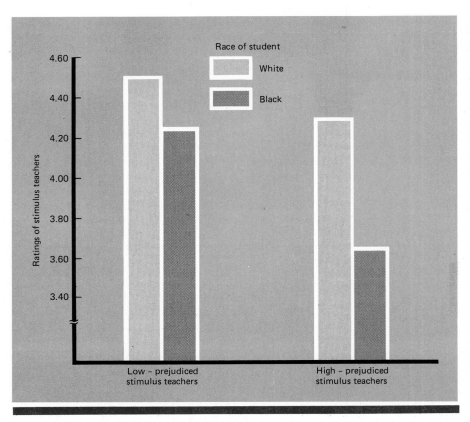

FIGURE 5-2
Ratings of how pleased stimulus teachers appear with their students. Low-prejudiced teachers showed little difference in nonverbal positivity to white or black students, while high-prejudiced teachers were considerably more positive to their white than their black students. Source: Feldman & Donohoe (1978).

behavior of people interacting with targets of their prejudice. While prejudiced people may censor what they are saying fairly readily, it is considerably more difficult to control one's nonverbal behavior (Zuckerman, DePaulo, and Rosenthal, 1981). For instance, Feldman and Donohoe (1978) placed white subjects, identified from a written test as highly or little prejudiced, in a situation in which they were to act as teachers to a third-grade student. In actuality, the student was a confederate who was either white or black. The confederate was trained to perform exceptionally well on a test administered by the subject, and the subject was told to praise correct responses with the phrase, "Right—that's good." (This ensured that the verbal behavior of the subjects was consistent.) While the subjects were praising their seemingly successful subjects, secret videotape recordings were made of their face and shoulders.

Later, groups of white observers rated the degree to which each subject appeared pleased with the student, using only short, twenty-second samples of the nonverbal behavior of the subjects to make their judgments. Results of the study, shown in Figure 5-2, revealed that, in fact, there were differences in nonverbal behavior displayed by the highly and little-prejudiced subjects according to the race of their student. Despite the fact that all "students" were performing equally well, highly-prejudiced subjects acted significantly more positively on a nonverbal level to white students than to black ones. (Interestingly, though, even the little-prejudiced subjects were judged to be somewhat more pleased with white than with black students—although to a significantly smaller degree than the highly prejudiced subjects.) The basic conclusion of the study is that nonverbal behavior of individuals can be used to infer their degree of prejudice toward the people with whom they are interacting. Even when the verbal behavior is of a highly positive nature, the nonverbal behavior may reveal when someone actually harbors negative feelings toward an interactant.

Other Behaviors as Measures of Prejudice   Subtle nonverbal behaviors are not the only measures of prejudice; more obvious behaviors can serve as indicators as well. For instance, differential helping and aggressive behaviors toward whites and blacks provide evidence of prejudice among the people carrying out the behaviors (Donnerstein & Donnerstein, 1976; Crosby, Bromley, & Saxe, 1980).

The nature of behavior used to infer prejudice is critical in making appropriate inferences, however. For instance, Dutton and Lennox (1974) showed that while most people readily carried out relatively simple, low-effort acts aiding a minority group member, more meaningful, important, and high-cost activities which would help minority group members occurred far less frequently. This finding suggests that **tokenism** is operating—a behavior which means that someone's relatively unimportant positive actions toward a minority group member may allow that person to avoid carrying out tasks of greater importance later. Indeed, the early token activity gives the person an excuse to avoid taking more vigorous positive action later. Thus, it is important to employ meaningful, involving tasks—such as asking for a large commitment of time—if we want to infer a person's underlying prejudice from behavioral measures. Employing simple, low-cost measures—such as observing whether someone helps pick up some dropped papers from the ground—proves little.

UNDERSTANDING THE ORIGINS OF PREJUDICE AND DISCRIMINATION

In examining the origins of a problem as widespread and complex as prejudice and discrimination, it is necessary to consider explanations that span a number of different levels of specificity. We will examine four levels, based on Allport's (1954) classic outline of theories of prejudice (see Figure 5-3): cognitive, psychodynamic, situational, and historical and sociocultural approaches.

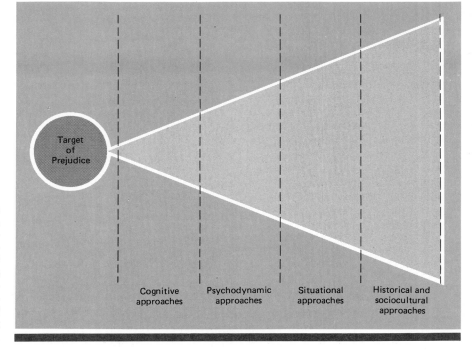

FIGURE 5-3
Approaches to the origins
of prejudice. The four major approaches to ex-
plaining the origins of
prejudice encompass
cognitive, psychodyn-
amic, situational, and his-
torical-cultural levels of
analysis. Source: Allport
(1950).

Cognitive Approaches: How People Think about the Targets of Prejudice

Most current approaches to the study of prejudice take a cognitive view, stressing the way prejudiced people perceive and process information regarding the target of prejudice. Such an approach is concerned less with the objective reality of the situation, and more with the prejudiced person's subjective understanding of the world and of the people in it (D. L. Hamilton, 1979). We will discuss two cognitive approaches, one based on attribution theory and the other on the distinctions that people make between in-group and out-group members.

Attributional Approaches   The attributional approach to understanding prejudice suggests that we concentrate on how people form an understanding of the reasons behind the behavior of minority group members. It suggests that prejudiced people may systematically bias their attributions, making favorable attributions to majority group members and unfavorable ones to minority group members.

Thomas Pettigrew (1979; Jemmott, Pettigrew, & Johnson, 1983) has suggested that prejudiced people are prone to what he calls the **ultimate attribution error,** which is an extension of the **fundamental attribution error,** mentioned in our discussion of attribution theory. You will recall from Chapter 2 that the fundamental attribution error refers to the tendency of observers to attribute behavior of others to stable traits and dispositions, but to perceive their own behavior as more affected by situational factors. The ultimate attribution error suggests that when prejudiced people view a target of prejudice carrying out a negative action, they will tend to attribute it to dispositional characteristics of the minority group member: "That's the way those people are," or "They're born like that." This, of course, is not all that different from what typically occurs with fundamental attribution error.

But things are different when a minority group member is seen engaging in a positive action. If prejudiced people were consistent, they would also view behavior with positive outcomes as being caused by internal dispositions. But, in fact, they don't—because this would be inconsistent with their basic negative view of the object of prejudice. The problem becomes one, then, of explaining away the positive behavior. Pettigrew suggests four ways in which the prejudiced person can deal with this problem:

1. *Exceptional case.* First, the positive act can be viewed as an exceptional case, and the actor can be differentiated from other members of the minority groups ("He's the exception that proves the rule," or "She's so different from most other blacks."). In some ways, in fact, the behavior of that person might even be considered deviant by the perceiver.

2. *Special advantage or luck.* A second way in which positive minority group behavior can be explained is by deciding that the behavior is due to receiving some kind of special advantage or simply to luck ("She only got where she is because of affirmative action policies," or "It must have been sheer luck that got him into medical school."). Thus, the minority member is viewed as receiving benefit from being a minority, something the prejudiced person may view with envy.

3. *Situational context.* Positive acts on the part of minority group members can be explained a third way: their actions are caused by situational factors outside their control, rather than by some personality or dispositional factors ("Anyone in that position would have done well."). In other words, the minority person's membership in the minority group is overlooked as a causal explanation, and it is assumed that the particular role or position that that person occupies can explain his or her behavior.

4. *High motivation and effort.* Attributing unusually high motivation to succeed and extraordinary effort on the part of the successful minority member to "compensate" for the handicap of being part of a minority group represents the last example of the ultimate attribution error. According to this explanation, the underlying negative characteristics of the minority group are still present, but exceptional motivation has enabled this person to overcome his or her "true" state. Curiously, though, the success of these people allows the prejudiced person to deny that prejudice and discrimination have negative consequences for the targets of prejudice, since some people do "make it."

Heads, I Win; Tails, You Lose The four possible attributions made regarding the behavior of someone who is a member of a minority group suggest a no-win situation. If that person engages in a negative act, his or her behavior is seen as a confirmation and manifestation of an underlying bad personality. If the action happens to be positive, any one of four unflattering causes will be adopted, none of which acknowledges the underlying positive nature of the act.

Although not thoroughly tested at this point, Pettigrew's theory has been supported in a number of studies. For instance, Taylor and Jaggi (1974) asked a group of Hindu office clerks in southern India to choose the reasons for the behavior of an individual described in a short passage. The passage described a shopkeeper being either generous or cheating, a teacher rewarding or punishing a student, an individual helping or ignoring an injured person, or a householder sheltering or ignoring a person caught in the rain. For each situation, subjects were to choose a reason for the behavior that represented either a primarily internal or a primarily external attribution.

The crucial variable was whether the actor in the passage was identified as a member of the observer's own ethnic group (Hindu) or as a member of another group (Muslims), which tended to be discriminated against and held in low esteem by Hindus. As the results in Table 5-2 indicate, the findings were clear-cut. When the behavior in question was attributed to the observer's own group, positive behavior was generally attributed to internal causes and only rarely to external causes; negative behavior tended to be perceived as due to external causes. In contrast, when the actor was a member of the disliked Muslim group, positive behavior was attributed to internal causes much less frequently than negative behavior was.

The findings of Taylor and Jaggi unequivocally support Pettigrew's

TABLE 5-2 Internal Attributions of Hindu Subjects

When Hindu subjects read about positive behavior on the part of an in-group (Hindu) actor, they tended to make internal attributions, while negative behaviors were not seen as indicative of internal characteristics. In contrast, attributions were made in an opposite direction when the actor was an out-group member. Percentages in table refer to percentage of subjects making internal attributions.

Situation	HINDU (IN-GROUP) ACTOR		MUSLIM (OUT-GROUP) ACTOR	
	Positive Behavior, %	Negative Behavior, %	Positive Behavior, %	Negative Behavior, %
Shopkeeper	43	3	10	40
Teacher	43	3	10	23
Help to Injured	67	3	10	33
Householder	80	0	20	33

Source: Adapted from Taylor and Jaggi (1974, Table 2).

attributional analysis, and suggest that no matter how exemplary the behavior of a minority group member, prejudiced observers may not alter their underlying negative views of the group to which the member belongs (Wilder, 1984). The ultimate attribution error puts the target of prejudice in a clear, no-win situation from which escape is seemingly impossible: nothing he or she can do can change the observer's perception.

In-groups and Out-groups: Minimal Distinctions Lead to Maximal Discrimination

Suppose you were part of a group of ten people, and someone came along and pulled five of your names randomly out of a hat in order to create two teams. Those five names would comprise team A and the remaining five would make up team B. Would you immediately react more positively toward members of your own team, and ultimately come to discriminate in favor of them?

A good deal of scientific evidence suggests that an affirmative answer is in order, for merely categorizing people into two groups, to one of which a person belongs (the **in-group**) and the other to which he does not belong (the **out-group**) influences the individual's behavior and interpersonal perception (Brewer, 1979; D. L. Hamilton, 1979; J. F. Evans & Dovido, 1983).

In what has come to be the typical procedure for eliciting in-group–out-group differences (e.g., Allen & Wilder, 1975; Billig & Tajfel, 1973), subjects are divided into two groups, supposedly on the basis of their preferences for one of two artists. In reality, they are randomly assigned to one of the two groups. Subjects are later asked to distribute money to a member of their own group and a member of the out-group, using various combinations of allocation: equality (choosing a combination that gives each person the same amount); maximizing the outcome so that the total amount is highest without regard to groups; or bias toward the in-group (in which the in-group's rewards are maximized). Results of these studies show a consistent effect: not only do subjects tend to reward members of their own group at the expense of members of other groups, but they try to do it in a way that magnifies the differences in reward between the two groups.

What is particularly interesting about results such as those described above is that the in-groups and out-groups are so minimally differentiated from one another (Tajfel, Billig, Bundy, & Flament, 1971). There is no direct, face-to-face interaction between subjects, either within their own group or with members of the other group; the subject is anonymous; and the categorization is based on a criterion that is unrelated to the subjects' responses. If discriminatory behavior toward out-groups occurs in situations such as these, we would expect that discrimination against out-groups would be even stronger when the out-groups have very obvious and salient differences from in-groups, and this is, in fact,

BOX 5-2   SPOTLIGHT ON RESEARCH

RACE OR BELIEF DIFFERENCES: WHAT UNDERLIES PREJUDICE?

Most work on racial prejudice suggests that it is the race of a target individual that elicits prejudice. But Milton Rokeach, a well-known expert on prejudice, began a lingering controversy in 1960 by suggesting that prejudice is determined more by the perception of belief dissimilarity than by racial background itself. In other words, we assume that people who are racially different from ourselves have different beliefs from ourselves, and it is these different beliefs that lead us to dislike them.

According to this reasoning, if we think that people of another race hold beliefs similar to our own, we are likely to view them positively. In support of this argument, Rokeach (1960) gave subjects descriptions of another person who was either white or black and who either believed or did not believe in God. When asked to judge the probability that they would become friends, similarity of beliefs had significantly greater impact than race (although race did have a small effect). Basically, then, the results supported Rokeach's position.

While later studies of Rokeach and others (e.g., Hendrick, Bixenstine, & Hawkins, 1971; Silverman, 1974) found that beliefs were more influential than race in determining attitudes, other researchers have found just the opposite (Triandis & Davis, 1965; Triandis, Loh, & Levin, 1966). One explanation for the discrepancy is based on the degree of intimacy or sensitivity of interaction required between an individual and a cross-race person. For nonintimate interaction, belief similarity seems most influential. But for more intimate and sensitive contact, racial considerations seem to predominate. In addition, there is evidence suggesting that as the general level of cross-race contact increases, race becomes a less salient factor, while belief similarity increases in importance (Moe, Nacoste, & Insko, 1981). Thus, the nature of interracial interaction has an effect upon whether race or beliefs have a greater effect on cross-racial prejudice.

the case. For instance, Downing and Monaco (1982) found that the greater the differential in contact between in-group and out-group members, the stronger the prejudice against out-group members.

Reasons for In-group–Out-group Differentiations   The cognitive approach suggests that one reason for prejudice is related to the need that people have to reduce the extraordinary complexity of the world around them. Because of the complexity, people frequently group others into organized classes or categories, which makes understanding the world more manageable. The problem comes when the categories are too broad and similarities that may not exist are assumed to be present (D. L. Hamilton, 1979). The process in which belief categories are formed leads to the use of stereotypes, which develop not because of some learned like or dislike for a particular individual or group, but because social categorization processes allow a person to deal more easily with what otherwise would be an overwhelming amount of information.

Out-groups present instances in which stereotyping or social categorization processes are particularly prone to occur. Research on perception makes it clear that perceivers pay more attention to stimuli that are unusual, novel, or distinct than those that are typical, familiar, and nondistinctive. Because these findings hold for human stimuli as well as inanimate stimuli, it is reasonable to assume that characteristics of minority groups (such as race, facial configuration, and dialect or accent) that differentiate them from majority group people will be particularly salient to the majority group member (Zareh & Mayer, 1983). In turn, it is plausible that these perceived differences in appearance will be used to develop other differentiations between majority and minority groups, leading to the development of stereotypes.

A further cognitive process is involved in in-group–out-group categorization. Park and Rothbart (1982) found that in-group members tend to view out-group members as more homogeneous and less differentiated than members of their own group. Thus, young people may tend to view the elderly as holding more similar views, acting in more similar ways, and generally sharing more attributes with one another than is necessarily valid (Linville, 1982). Conversely, other young people may be seen as being relatively heterogeneous and differentiated from one another. The reason for this **out-group homogeneity principle** seems to be that people are more likely to remember traits and characteristics of in-group members than of out-group members, with whom they typically have less contact. Thus, E. E. Jones, Wood, and Quattrone (1981) found that members of undergraduate eating clubs at Princeton University tended to rate their own clubs (where they knew most of the members) as being significantly more heterogeneous than members of clubs to which they did not belong.

Basically, then, cognitive approaches to prejudice argue that prejudice is the result of information processing that differentiates between majority and minority—or in-group and out-group—members. Not only are the characteristics of minority group members categorized and lumped together, but attributions vary according to the category in which a minority group member is placed.

Psychodynamic Approaches

Instead of looking at how prejudiced people perceive and process information, the psychodynamic approach contends that deficits in an individual's level of psychological functioning lead to prejudice. Using Freud's theory of psychoanalysis, such approaches attempt to identify the psychological conflicts and maladjustments that underly a person's overt displays of prejudice.

One of the most frequent uses of psychodynamic approaches is frustration theory, which suggests that prejudice is a manifestation of displaced hostility due to frustration. It is assumed that when someone's goals are thwarted or blocked, he or she experiences frustration. In turn, this frustration leads to feelings of hostility toward the source of frustration. In many cases, however, it is either impossible or socially unacceptable to vent the hostility toward the source. According to psychodynamic theory, the result of such circumstances can be a kind of "free-floating" hostility, ready to vent itself at an alternate, more convenient target. In many cases, a minority group represents a likely scapegoat, as it will probably be less powerful than the original thwarting agent.

The most elaborate use of psychodynamic theory is found in a classic book, *The Authoritarian Personality* (Adorno, Frenkel-Brunswick, Levinson, & Sanford, 1950). Based upon hundreds of interviews and the results of batteries of personality assessments, the theory reported in the book suggests that prejudice is the result of a particular set of characteristics shared by what was termed the "authoritarian" personality. According to this theory, authoritarians have developed hostility toward rigid and demanding parents, but are unable, because of a strong feeling that authority is always right, to direct hostility toward their parents. Instead, authoritarians displace their hostility toward groups that they perceive as weak or unconventional. Typically, this means the hostility is directed toward members of minority groups. Authoritarians also tend to be politically and socially conservative and view the world in rigid categories in which the weak are expected to be dutifully obedient to the powerful.

In order to test this theory, Adorno et al. devised a personality scale to measure authoritarianism, and they discovered, during extensive interviewing, that people with high scores tended to have the family backgrounds predicted by the theory, and to be prejudiced as well. Unfortunately, later researchers found a number of difficulties with the theory and the research supporting it, since it turns out that not all prejudiced people share a background of harsh, demanding parents. Moreover, even people who score low on the authoritarian scale may be very prejudiced. Thus, the theory is not entirely consistent with the original formulation (Cherry & Byrne, 1977).

One problem that is common to both the frustration theory and the authoritarian personality conception is that neither formulation is very precise in allowing us to predict in what way (or even why) the prejudiced person's hostility will be displaced. Still, it does appear that certain personality characteristics are systematically related to prejudice.

Situational Approaches

Situational approaches to prejudice emphasize the ways in which a person's immediate environment produces prejudicial attitudes. Many of the major topics of social psychology are related to this approach: how people acquire attitudes toward the objects of prejudice, how they are maintained through social influence processes, and what the results of prejudice are on both the prejudiced person and the target of the prejudice.

There is clear evidence that prejudiced attitudes in children are acquired from parents, other adults, and peers through the processes of direct reinforcement and vicarious learning during socialization (discussed in our chapter on attitudes), and that such attitudes regarding objects of prejudice are learned at an early age. For instance, P. A. Katz (1976) found that by the age of three or four, children are able to distinguish between blacks and whites, and even at that age can possess differential affective feelings regarding blacks and whites. Children of prejudiced parents are apt to be rewarded for espousing prejudiced attitudes of their own, and they can vicariously experience the rewards that may accrue to others who articulate prejudice (recall our example of George Wallace, whose actions of refusing entrance to blacks trying to enroll at the University of Alabama were widely hailed by local citizenry and the press).

Investigators taking a situational approach also have focused on demographic characteristics as a means to understanding prejudice. Such work is based on the premise that there are specific norms that develop in particular areas and among certain groups of people that may act to support prejudiced attitudes.

Research along these lines has shown that three demographic features systematically relate to prejudice against blacks: geographic region, educational level, and age (Maykovich, 1975). On a general level, people in the south are more prejudiced against blacks than northerners are; people with less education show higher prejudice; and older people are more prejudiced than younger ones.

However, when the three variables are considered simultaneously, the relationship among them turns out to be complex. For example, using survey techniques, Maykovich (1975) found that the most prejudiced people were likely to be poorly educated southerners; the second most prejudiced were poorly educated, but not very old, northerners; and the third most prejudiced were older and better-educated southerners. In contrast, the least prejudiced people were college-educated young people in the north; and the second least prejudiced were younger, poorly educated northerners.

Although the demographic approach is useful in identifying characteristics likely to be associated with prejudice, its drawback is that it does not provide an underlying explanation for the acquisition and maintenance of prejudiced attitudes. Thus, its explanatory powers are limited.

Historical and Sociocultural Approaches

KKK gains momentum as the economy sours. The hooded empire of the Ku Klux Klan, carrying the banner of white supremacy since the Civil War, is gaining momentum from economic hard times, new leadership and a backlash to civil rights advances, concerned opponents say.

"The Klan does well in times of social upheaval and turmoil," said Randall Williams of Klanwatch, an arm of the Southern Poverty Law Center in Montgomery, Alabama, which monitors Klan activity in the United States. "We're

in just such a period now. We have people out of work and looking for scapegoats as to why they lost their jobs," Williams said Tuesday. "We have a backlash against affirmative action and people are unhappy about busing."
(From an Associated Press dispatch, June 18, 1982)

As the newspaper clipping above indicates, one underlying reason for prejudice is the economic environment which exists at a particular time. Historical and sociocultural approaches to the study of prejudice examine this possibility.

Historical Approaches   An example of the historical approach can be seen in the case of prejudice against women. Certain occupations have been viewed historically as more appropriate for men than for women. For example, truck driving is typically viewed as a "masculine" profession, perhaps stemming from times in which the sheer physical effort in driving was high. However, with the advent of technological innovations such as power steering and brakes, the original rationale given for discouraging female truck drivers no longer holds. Yet there are still very few women truck drivers, due, in part, to these historical factors.

In a slightly different version of the historical approach, the development of prejudice is explained not so much by events relating to the objects of prejudice, but rather by historical attitudes that have served an important function for those doing the discriminating. For instance, Karl Marx devised an exploitation theory that held that the dominant class in society propagated prejudicial attitudes in order to justify the exploitation of the object of prejudice. Similarly, phrases such as "the white man's burden" in reference to colonized peoples imply a childlike dependence on the part of the objects of prejudice, rather than acknowledging the fact that colonialism often offered a relatively inexpensive source of labor and raw materials.

Sociocultural Approaches   Sociologists and anthropologists who study prejudice emphasize sociocultural factors, examining the impact of society on the individual's prejudice. For instance, the sociocultural approach suggests that such factors as the increasing urbanization and complexity of society, increasing population density, and the competition for scarce jobs between members of various ethnic groups operate in various ways to increase prejudice toward minority groups.

Consider the specific example of increasing urbanization. Cities represent environments which are less than ideal in many respects: they are perceived by many as noisy, dirty, unsafe, and impersonal. According to some sociologists, people can blame the difficulties of urban life on the presence of a particular minority group, which is seen as symbolizing the problems of urbanization (Simpson & Yinger, 1972). In some cities today, for example, blacks and Puerto Ricans are blamed for the ills of the city; in the past it was the Jews; and before them, the Irish and members of earlier immigrant groups.

Similar reasoning suggests that in times of high unemployment, in which there is competition for few available jobs, prejudice will be directed toward members of minority groups whom majority group members believe are taking jobs away from them. This is particularly true in cases in which affirmative action goals mandate that certain minority groups be given extra consideration in hiring or in admission to educational programs. For example, Alan Bakke sued the University of California at Davis Medical School, saying that he was denied admission to the medical school because he was white, despite the fact that his qualifications were objectively better than those of a number of minority group members who were admitted as part of the school's affirmative action policy. It would not be unreasonable to assume that societal factors such as these would ultimately increase prejudice on the part of people who feel they are being denied a resource that is "rightfully" theirs.

One difficulty with the historical and sociocultural approaches to prejudice is that they do not explain why certain groups are more discriminated against than others, when almost all minority groups have suffered from exploitation at some point in the past. Moreover, prejudice exists even when there are few historical, cultural, or economic reasons that can be identified. Still, it is clear that historical and sociocultural considerations must be taken into account when studying prejudice, as they provide at least part of the explanation for prejudice.

Studying the Targets of Prejudice

A last approach to the origins of prejudice and discrimination examines the targets of prejudice. Do the actual characteristics of the target promote prejudicial attitudes and discriminatory behavior? To answer this question, it is necessary to examine the relationship between beliefs about a target and the characteristics of the group in question. Earlier we discussed the existence of stereotypes, which are beliefs about members of a particular group about which there is a fairly high degree of agreement. But one critical question that we did not touch upon in depth is the degree of accuracy of such stereotypes. Are stereotypes accurate descriptions of targets of prejudice?

Most theorists suggest that there is a "kernel of truth" in stereotypes, at least for stereotypes that are held by people who are in close contact with the object of the stereotype. For instance, Triandis and Vassiliou (1967), who studied beliefs about Greeks, suggested that "there is a 'kernal of truth' in most stereotypes *when they are elicited from people who have firsthand knowledge of the group being stereotyped*" (p. 324, italics in the original). Supporting this view, R. A. Levine and Campbell (1972) suggest that stereotypes are not totally invalid, but that the cognitive processes involved in the development of stereotypes initially tend to exaggerate differences that already exist.

In sum, most research suggests that there is sometimes a degree of accuracy in stereotypes, but only in limited circumstances (McCauley & Stitt, 1978). Moreover, because stereotypes are basically oversimplifications, they do not permit accurate predictions of others' behavior.

What's Good for Me Isn't Good for You   To further complicate the question of the degree to which stereotyped groups reflect the traits assigned to them, Donald Campbell has suggested that when real group differences exist, there may be a distortion of the *meaning* of the differences. Campbell's (1967) analysis goes as follows: First, it is reasonable to assume that there are, in fact, at least some differences between members of different ethnic and racial groups. Otherwise there would be no reason for distinguishing between the two groups in the first place. Moreover, there can be a shared sense of what some of these differences are. As an example, we might agree that Englishmen tend to be formal and reserved, while Americans tend to be outgoing and friendly; and these descriptions might basically be agreed upon by both Americans and the English.

However, Campbell suggests that these traits become caught up in a process he calls reciprocal description. When Englishmen view themselves as formal and reserved, these are seen as positive traits. But when viewed by Americans, they take on negative connotations. ("The English are cold and unfriendly.") Similarly, when Americans view themselves as outgoing and friendly, the traits are seen as positive ones. But when these traits are viewed by the English, they are seen negatively. ("Americans are pushy and nosy.") Thus, beliefs about a particular group may be based upon a "kernel of truth," but the meaning given to the trait may differ greatly, depending on whether it pertains to our own or to another group.

REDUCING PREJUDICE AND DISCRIMINATION

Are we destined to live with prejudice and discrimination, or are there ways to reduce and eventually eliminate them? In the remainder of the chapter, we will try to answer this question by discussing some of the approaches that have been taken by social psychologists to bring about reductions in prejudice and discrimination against minority groups in society. Three major techniques will be examined: the use of contact between prejudiced people and the targets of prejudice, cognitive approaches, and educational approaches.

Contact: Interacting with the Target of Prejudice

No strategy for reducing prejudice has received greater attention from social psychologists than that of the idea that contact between a preju-

Contact between majority
and minority groups can
be effective in reducing
prejudice, if the group
members have equal sta-
tus and are interdepen-
dent and involved.
(Michael Heron/Woodfin
Camp)

diced person and the target of prejudice will lead to more favorable attitudes. First suggested by Allport (1954), the contact approach suggests that intergroup contact can reduce prejudice if it is structured in appropriate ways. The key to the issue is, of course, identifying the characteristics of "appropriate" contact, because contact by itself does not necessarily lead to reductions in prejudice. In fact, some of the most profound instances of prejudice are found in areas in which there is a high degree of interaction between majority and minority group members.

What, then, is the key to successful intergroup contact? One factor that is of crucial importance regards status: contact is most effective when there is equal status within a setting for people belonging to both groups (Amir, 1976; Norvell & Worchel, 1981). Thus, a prejudiced man who hires a female janitor to clean his factory would not be expected to become less prejudiced from the contact he experiences. But if he worked with the woman in some equal status setting, the possibilities for a reduction in prejudice would be greatly enhanced.

A second important factor revolves around the intimacy of contact between members of the two groups, with greater intimacy leading to a greater reduction in prejudice. But it is not just a matter of close spatial proximity; the people must be involved interactively in some activity. Superficial contact is ineffective in reducing prejudice and may even act to maintain a prejudiced person's intergroup hostility. Intimate contact helps to individualize the disliked group member, which means that he or she will be perceived less in terms of a stereotype and more in terms of an individual (Blake & Mouton, 1979; S. W. Cook, 1969). For example, we might not expect a prejudiced white male to lose his negative attitudes toward a female colleague until they had worked closely together on a project in which she could demonstrate her unique characteristics and capabilities.

Finally, contact is most effective when the two people must cooperate in a mutually interdependent activity whose success depends on both their contributions. In addition, holding a shared goal will facilitate the development of positive intergroup attitude—something we will discuss further in our chapter on group processes (Blanchard, Adelman, & Cook, 1975; Worchel, Andreoli, & Folger, 1977; Sherif, Harvey, White, Hood, & Sherif, 1961).

Both laboratory and field experiments have demonstrated the effectiveness of contact that meets the three criteria of equal status, intimacy, and interdependent interaction. For instance, S. W. Cook (1969) had prejudiced white women play a simulation game for a total of forty hours over a one-month period. The other participants included white and black confederates. In order to play the game, participants had to cooperate with each other, and there was a good deal of fairly intimate contact in which all players were of equal status. There were also breaks during the games in which the subjects could hold conversations with the confederate. Pre- and postexperiment measures of attitudes showed quite clearly a positive change on the part of about 40 percent of the participants.

In an even more elaborate experiment, Clore, Bray, Itkin, & Murphy (1978) studied interracial attitudes and behavior during sessions at a summer camp. The camp was set up so that each child had one white and one black counselor, and there were equal numbers of white and black campers in a group. The situation provided for intimate, equal status contact over a one-week period. As would be expected from the contact hypothesis, interracial attitudes tended to improve, and a number of behavioral measures showed increased attraction to cross-race individuals.

Applications of Contact Theory: Desegregation   While the results of laboratory studies testing the contact approach to the reduction of prejudice have generally been positive, not all efforts at introducing contact have been successful. As mentioned in the interview with Fred Routh, one area in which contact seems to have produced mixed results is school desegregation. In a comprehensive review of the literature, Stephan (1978) was unable to find unequivocal evidence that desegregation led to more positive attitudes or behavior toward cross-racial people (a conclusion supported by a review done by Schofield, 1978). After weighing the evidence, Stephan (1978) concluded desegregation generally did not reduce white prejudice toward blacks. Moreover, black self-esteem typically did not rise in desegregated schools, and studies that showed changes in black prejudice toward whites were about equally divided between those that showed increases and those that showed decreases in prejudice. Basically, then, the results are quite mixed (Amir & Sharan, 1984).

BOX 5-3   SPOTLIGHT ON APPLICATIONS

SOCIAL PSYCHOLOGISTS AND THE SUPREME COURT RULING ON SCHOOL DESEGREGATION

Not only was the 1954 Supreme Court ruling in the case of *Brown v. Board of Education* a landmark decision requiring school desegregation, but it also represented something of a milestone for social psychologists, who saw their findings and testimony cited as evidence for the negative effects of racial segregation.

Part of the Court's ruling was based on the work of Kenneth Clark, who later became president of the American Psychological Association. He testified about his research on racial preferences in young black children (Clark & Clark, 1947), stating:

> I have reached the conclusion . . . that discrimination, prejudice and segregation have definite detrimental effects on the personality development of the Negro child. The essence of this detrimental effect is a confusion in the child's concept of his own self-esteem—basic feelings of inferiority, conflict, confusion in his self-image, resentment, hostility towards himself (and) hostility towards whites.
>
> (Kluger, 1976, p. 353)

Clark reached these conclusions using a method in which a black child was shown a white and a black doll and then was given a series of directions such as "Give me the doll that looks bad" and "Give me the doll that is a nice color." In every case he studied, Clark found that the black children preferred white dolls over black ones, suggesting that the self-esteem of blacks was low in segregated schools.

Another social psychologist, David Krech, argued in court that the fact that blacks were placed in inferior schools apart from whites served to reinforce beliefs of whites that blacks were both different and inferior. Finally, Louisa Holt and Horace English, both psychologists, testified on the negative effects of segregation on school performance of blacks, referring to the effects of self-fulfilling prophecies:

> If we drive it into a person that he is incapable of learning, then he is less likely to be able to learn. . . . There is a tendency for us to live up to—or perhaps I should say down to—social expectations and to learn what people say we can learn, and legal segregation defi-

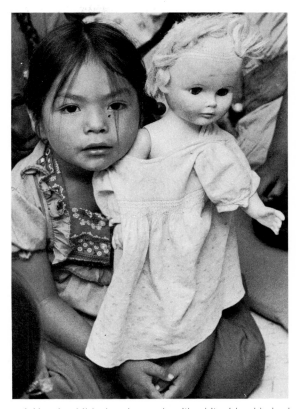

A Navajo child who plays only with white, blond-haired dolls is likely to experience, at the least, cultural confusion and possibly even lowered self-esteem as a result.
(Paul Conklin/Monkmeyer Press)

nitely depresses the Negro's expectancy and is, therefore, prejudicial to his learning.

(Kluger, 1976, p. 415)

Using arguments such as these as part of the basis for its decision, the Supreme Court ruled that "in the field of public education the doctrine 'separate but equal' has no place. Separate educational facilities are inherently unequal" *(Brown v. Board of Education).* The evidence of social psychological research thus had a tangible effect in an area of critical social policy.

181

Before we can conclude that desegregation is a failure and that the contact approach to reducing prejudice is ineffective, the difficulties in conducting research on this topic should be noted (Schofield, 1982; Patchen, 1982). "Desegregation" has many definitions, and generalizing across studies necessitates combining results from very diverse situations. Thus, a school in which only 5 percent of the students are black could be considered desegregated if it is a suburban school that has never enrolled blacks before, whereas in some cases it would take a much higher percentage of minority group enrollees for a school to be thought of as desegregated. In addition, there are differences between how even similar desegregation programs are implemented, rendering generalizations quite difficult to make. There are also variations in how eager the community and school leaders are to integrate their schools, in the characteristics of the particular students involved, and in how interracial attitudes and behavior are measured. Thus, as Fred Routh suggested, it is necessary to define the specific conditions under which desegregation occurs in order to be able to draw definitive conclusions about its success.

Applications of Contact Theory: The Jigsaw Technique   Some specific techniques that are derived from the contact approach appear to be quite effective in reducing prejudice. One approach is called the **jigsaw technique** because it is built upon the principle of putting a jigsaw puzzle together (Aronson, Stephan, Sikes, Blaney, & Snapp, 1978). In the same way that a jigsaw puzzle is constructed by taking small pieces and placing them together, students who participate are each given a small amount of information and then are required to teach the material to a set of partners in a group. When the information from all the students is put together, it forms a meaningful whole, enabling the group to understand the lesson in its entirety.

An example might be a lesson on the life of Freud. Each student in a group might be assigned by the teacher to study a different period or facet of Freud's life and then would be expected to teach the material to the other members of the group. After each member of the group has taught his or her part of the lesson, the group as a whole has learned about the entire life of Freud, and the students then are tested on the material.

A number of studies have shown that the jigsaw technique not only results in effective learning, but also promotes self-esteem, interpersonal attraction, and empathy for members of different ethnic and racial groups (Aronson & Bridgeman, 1979). The reasons for the success of the technique, which has been demonstrated in both laboratory and field settings, is clear: the method includes all the elements that have been identified as crucial in making intergroup contact effective in reducing prejudice—equal status, intimate contact, and interdependent interaction (Sharon, 1984). Thus, its usefulness in reducing prejudice is not surprising.

Martin Luther King used moral appeals in his effort to reduce prejudice. (Bob Henriques/Magnum)

Cognitive Approaches to Reducing Prejudice: Changing Attitudes and Attributions toward Objects of Prejudice

Cognitive approaches to reducing prejudice reflect the view that changes in attitudes and attributions about minorities and out-groups will bring about a concomitant change in behavior toward members of such groups. Drawing upon the general principles of persuasion, attitude change, and attribution that we discussed in Chapters 2 and 4, a number of techniques have been employed, including what has been termed **exhortation** (Simpson & Yinger, 1972) and the use of antiprejudice propaganda.

Exhortation: Making Values Salient   Although it has an old-fashioned ring to it, recalling as it does a preacher at a tent rally, exhortation is at the heart of the most frequently used approach to reducing prejudice. Demonstrations and rallies against prejudice and discrimination, such as the one led by Martin Luther King in 1963, which drew over 200,000 persons, are designed primarily to show the underlying value and moral rightness of the cessation of prejudice and discrimination.

The strategy of exhortation attempts to show that inherent in the basic values of democracy, freedom, and the rights of the individual is the notion that people should not be discriminated against on the basis of their ethnic or religious group membership. In addition to providing moral and logical appeals, demonstrations may be useful for showing that there is a broad base of support against prejudice and for suggesting that there are shared norms in favor of an end to prejudicial discrimination.

At the base of exhortation is the notion that making an individual's values explicit can lead to changes in behavior. In support of this notion, Rokeach (1971) showed that simply pointing out inconsistencies between a person's values, attitudes, and behaviors could be sufficient to bring about changes in attitudes and behaviors related to race. For instance, in one experiment, subjects were informed that most students at their university tended to rate the value of "freedom" significantly higher than the value of "equality." Subjects were then told that this implies that "students, in general, are much more interested in their own freedom than they are in freedom for other people" (p. 454). Next, they were told that students who rank equality high are likely to be in favor of civil rights demonstrations, while people who are against civil rights value their own freedom highly, but not the freedom of others.

This information produced a number of significant changes in behavior. In contrast to subjects who did not receive information regarding inconsistencies between values, subjects who were informed about such inconsistencies were considerably more likely to join the NAACP about a year and a half later and to register for a class in ethnic relations almost two years later. These findings suggest that making values explicit may be useful in reducing prejudice.

Propaganda: Unobtrusive Appeals to End Prejudice   While techniques which use exhortation are obvious in their attempts to reduce prejudice, propaganda is subtler. Indeed, the defining characteristics of propaganda are that controversial elements may be disguised, there can be distortion of relevant facts, and the motives behind the propaganda may be hidden (Simpson & Yinger, 1972).

One old example of propaganda is a cartoon series that appeared in the late 1940s, in which a buffoonish "Mr. Biggott" is shown displaying absurd prejudices. For instance, in one cartoon he is seen telling an American Indian, "I'm sorry, Mr. Eaglefeather, but our company's policy is to employ 100 percent Americans only" (Kendall & Wolf, 1949). The goal of such cartoons was to emphasize the absurdity of the situation in an effort to discourage prejudice.

The difficulty with this and other forms of propaganda is that it tends to reach those people who already agree with the message. Alternatively, people who are prejudiced may ignore or misinterpret the message, feeling that it is not directed toward them. An example of this can be seen in the television series featuring Archie Bunker. Although the intention of the writers of the show may be to present Bunker's prejudices as comically absurd, Bunker may have served as a model to prejudiced viewers, who had their own prejudice reinforced. Thus, both exhortation and propaganda attempts may sometimes backfire.

Direct Education: Teaching People to Like and Understand Others

The final approach that has been used to combat prejudice and discrimination is the use of direct educational techniques. Is it possible to teach people to hold more positive attitudes toward people belonging to different groups?

The problem is a difficult one. Although many schools, universities, and communities have set up education programs of some sort, there have been no systematic attempts at evaluating such programs (e.g., Oddou & Claijo, 1983). Moreover, the programs have been quite varied, including approaches that try to increase knowledge about minority groups (for example, black studies courses), as well as those that try to change affect toward minority groups directly (as in "human relations" courses). To date, the success of such programs has not been demonstrated.

The Cultural Assimilator One technique that has been effective in at least sensitizing people to the meaning of subtle cues that occur during social interaction between members of different groups is the **cultural assimilator** method. In this technique, people receive direct instruction (using written material) in ways of interpreting the meaning of others' behavior. Specifically, trainees are taught the norms and lifestyles of another group in an effort to allow them to make more accurate attributions regarding the behavior of the members of the other group and to drop any previous misconceptions that they may have held.

Based on the work of Harry Triandis, an authority on cross-cultural relations, the cultural assimilator used "critical incidents," which are episodes that are relevant to intergroup interaction, that are fairly common, and that can be misinterpreted by people unfamiliar with the target population but are quite clear to those who know the culture (Fiedler, Mitchell, & Triandis, 1971; Triandis, 1972). In the basic method, the trainee reads the episode describing an intercultural interaction and interprets the interaction. The assimilator then explains why the trainee's answer is right or wrong. If the answer is wrong, the trainee must return to the episode and choose another response.

An example of an episode used in an assimilation designed to decrease racial prejudice in the army is shown in Figure 5-4. In the episode, an officer attempts to understand why he is asked to review negative promotion decisions more often by blacks than by whites. Trainees are given four choices, and after making their response, are given a specific explanation as to why they are correct or incorrect. In the assimilator from which this sample item was drawn, there are a total of 100 items pertaining to white and black interactions.

Does the cultural assimilator technique work? There is no definitive answer to this question, but it does appear that the performance of

The white CO of a racially integrated unit tried to recommend promotions on the basis of his men's work and proficiency scores. After the list of promotions was posted, a black Spec 4 entered his office and asked why he had not been promoted. The Spec 4 claimed that he had fairly good scores and asked the CO to review his decision. The CO was surprised at this behavior, but promised to give some attention to the complaint. Upon reflection, the CO noted that promotion reviews were requested much more frequently by blacks in his unit than by whites. The CO was puzzled and surprised by this realization.

Why did more blacks than whites request reviews of promotion decision?

Option 1. Blacks feel they won't be given a promotion unless they ask for one. (Yes)
Rationale: Many blacks feel that a good mark record alone is not sufficient for a promotion. They feel that unless they call attention to their case, it will not be acted upon. This action is not to be taken as disrespectful, but rather as an action which is assumed to be necessary for promotion.

Option 2. The CO was prejudiced and promoted more whites than blacks. (No)
Rationale: There is no evidence to support this. Reread the incident and select another response.

Option 3. Blacks are troublemakers more often than whites are. (No)
Rationale: There is nothing in the incident to suggest that the blacks were troublemakers. Try again.

Option 4. Many blacks hope to get promotions they don't deserve by intimidating their COs and getting them to give in to avoid being called "prejudiced." (No)
Rationale: The blacks' behavior was not intimidating. There were no threats or insinuations. You're reading too much into this incident. Reread the incident and try again.

FIGURE 5-4
An example of a cultural assimilator. Source: Landis, Day, McGrew, Thomas, & Miller (1976).

trainees in cross-cultural groups is superior to that of untrained people. Moreover, trainees tend to hold more positive attitudes toward members of the other group after taining than do people who have not been trained. While the drawback to such data is that they do not indicate whether there are concomitant behavioral changes, they are encouraging, suggesting that increased understanding can be produced through direct educational techniques.

SUMMARY

Prejudice refers to a positive or negative evaluation or judgment of members of a particular group which is based on their membership in the group, while discrimination is the behavioral manifestation of prejudice. Minority groups are defined not just in terms of numbers, but also in terms of their psychological relationship to dominant groups.

Prejudice is often measured by assessing people's shared beliefs about particular groups, known as stereotypes. Such beliefs may be assessed overtly or they may be determined by disguised means. Behavioral measures of prejudice are particularly effective in identifying prejudice in people concerned with the social desirability of appearing unprejudiced. Thus, nonverbal, aggressive, and helping behavior all have been shown to reflect whether prejudice is present.

Cognitive approaches to prejudice stress the way in which prejudiced people perceive and process information regarding the target of prejudice. Attribution theory suggests that prejudiced people may systematically bias their attributions, making favorable attributions to majority group members and unfavorable ones to minority group members in the ultimate attribution error. Cognitive approaches also have shown that simply categorizing people into in-groups and out-groups is sufficient to cause distinctions in behavior and interpersonal perception. Perceived differences between in-group and out-group members are augmented when out-group members are seen as more homogeneous and less differentiated than members of one's own group.

Psychodynamic approaches to prejudice suggest that prejudice is a manifestation of displaced hostility due to frustration. The most elaborate use of psychodynamic theorizing is found in *The Authoritarian Personality,* which attempted to identify consistent personality traits in prejudiced people. In contrast, situational approaches have emphasized the ways in which a person's immediate environment is related to prejudicial attitudes. These approaches look at acquisition of prejudiced attitudes and at demographic factors relating to prejudice. Historical approaches look at how historical events and facts, such as the past slavery of blacks, are related to prejudice, while sociocultural approaches examine the impact of society on the individual's prejudice.

It is also possible to examine the targets of prejudice to determine if they have particular characteristics that are reflected in prejudicial attitudes and discrimination. Most theorists suggest that there is a "kernel of truth" in stereotypes, but that the differences between groups become exaggerated. In addition, the meaning attributed to differences may vary according to the group in which they are found.

One strategy for reducing prejudice and discrimination is the use of contact between a prejudiced person and the target of prejudice. Contact that is most effective involves equal status, intimacy, and interdependent interaction. One application of contact theory that has not been shown to be notably successful is school desegregation, although the jigsaw technique has been successful in reducing prejudice.

An alternative to contact is the use of persuasive techniques, including exhortation and propaganda. In some cases, making values salient has been enough to reduce prejudice. Finally, although direct education approaches have not been demonstrably effective, the cultural assimilator technique has been effective in at least sensitizing people to the meaning of behavioral differences during social interaction between members of different groups.

KEY TERMS

ageism
authoritarian personality
cognitive approach to prejudice
contact hypothesis
cultural assimilator
desegregation
discrimination
exhortation
frustration theory
fundamental attribution error
historical and societal approach to prejudice
in-group
minority group

norms
out-group
prejudice
propaganda
psychodynamic approach to prejudice
self-fulfilling prophecy
situational approach to prejudice
socialization
sociocultural approach
stereotype
tokenism
ultimate attributional error

FOR FURTHER STUDY AND APPLICATION

Allport, G. W. (1954). *The nature of prejudice.* Reading, MA: Addison-Wesley.
A classic in every respect. Although many of the applications and examples are dated, the major theoretical approaches are still influential. Makes for fascinating reading.

Simpson, G. E., & Yinger, J. M. (1972). *Racial and cultural minorities: An analysis of prejudice and discrimination* (4th ed.). New York: Harper & Row.
A classic, comprehensive text, covering research and theory on prejudice and discrimination exhaustively.

Tajfel, H. (1982). Social psychology of intergroup relations. *Annual Review of Psychology, 33.*
Sophisticated, yet readable, this paper is a chapter which reviews major trends in the area of intergroup interaction, particularly in terms of in-groups and out-groups.

Fiedler, F. E., Mitchell, T. R., & Triandis, H. C. (1971). The cultural assimilator: An approach to cross-cultural training. *Journal of Applied Psychology, 55,* 95-102.
Provides careful direction on devising and testing a cultural assimilator which can be used to increase intergroup sensitivity.

Katz, P. (Ed.). (1976). *Towards the elimination of racism.* New York: Pergamon.
A distinguished group of authors has contributed to this book. The authors report research findings and theorizing on the topic of reducing prejudice and discrimination.

Amir, Y., & Sharan, J. (1984). *School desegregation.* Hillsdale, NJ: Erlbaum.
A comprehensive set of chapters on the effects of school desegregation, especially in terms of its impact on social behavior and school performance.

PART THREE

CARING AND UNCARING
BEHAVIOR: POSITIVE AND
NEGATIVE INTERACTIONS IN A
SOCIAL WORLD

CHAPTER 6

INTERPERSONAL ATTRACTION: LIKING AND LOVING OTHERS

A CONVERSATION WITH . . .

Kathie Berlin
Public Relations
Executive

For actors and actresses, being popular with the public can spell the difference between success and failure. For this reason, many movie and television stars hire public relations firms for the sole purpose of enhancing their likability and attractiveness.

Kathie Berlin heads the New York office of Rogers and Cowan, a major public relations firm that specializes in favorable media coverage of many television and movie stars. Among the firm's clients are Paul Newman, Victoria Principal, Robert Redford, and Olivia Newton-John. In a discussion with Ms. Berlin, we focused on some of the issues relating to the ways in which people can be made likable and attractive to the public.

Q. Because of media exposure, many well-known individuals evoke very strong feelings of attraction—or, in some cases, repulsion—on the part of the public at large. Does the public image of a well-known individual typically match the private person?

A. It's hard to generalize. People who are admired, like Paul Newman, Robert Redford, and Dudley Moore, are very similar to the image presented in the media. In other cases, images have been built up. Take the image of Henry Kissinger as a swinger. Who would ever consider Henry Kissinger attractive and sexy? But he was powerful, and he made sure that he was seen with exciting women.

Q. Does that mean that Kissinger deliberately manipulated his image?

A. Well, he understood the public. And the women he was seen with were very bright: Liv Ullman and Marlo Thomas and Jill St. John.

Q. Let's take an extreme situation where people come to you and say that the public doesn't like them or that the public holds some kind of misperception about them. Can people like this increase their attractiveness?

A. No one comes to us saying just those things, but they do come and say they have gotten bad press coverage through no fault of their own and they want to know how to change it. For example, a star of a former television series came to us a few weeks ago. She said that she had been a replacement on the show for a popular star, and that the other stars of the show were loved and had gotten great press but that she had gotten horrible press.

Our advice to her was to wait until she had a really good project and to present herself as an *actress,* in contrast to her image as a television star. We also decided to choose the areas in which she was seen publicly. She is not going to be seen at big film openings; you are going to see her at more sedate theater openings. We're going to divorce her from television totally and focus on her as a stage and movie actress. We're going to have her give lectures at UCLA on method acting. The photos we take are not going to be sexy and cheesecake; we're going to give her a tailored, very classic look. You'll never see a sexy photo of her again.

Q. Did she get such a negative image because she was, in fact, a poor actress?

A. Probably yes. She was a model turned actress, and was thrown into acting. But that's not as important as some other things. People are going to see a totally different look. It's a total revamping.

Q. In your line of work, is there any systematic way in which information about how much a person is liked is used?

A. One factor is TV cues. TV cues are used by producers and television networks to a tremendous degree. It is a test system that asks the public the following two questions: "Do you know this person?" and "Do you like this person?" Now, suppose you are casting, and you have the names of five women on a piece of paper. Any one of those five will be fine. They all have the same amount of talent. But you will choose the one with the highest TV cue ratings because you know that your ratings are going to be big. There may even be someone else that you like better, but you won't use her without the right TV cue ratings.

Q. In a series of legal battles between newscaster Christine Craft and the television station that had employed and then fired her, one court ruled that the station had discriminated against her when she was fired for being "too old, unattractive, and not deferential enough to men." Apparently the station management felt that news anchors had to be physically attractive to be successful. Do you think that physical appearance is an important part of the success of television journalists who are female?

A. Unfortunately, yes. I'm not sure that this is due to the public's perception of who is good or bad—but it is part of the thinking of station managers.

Q. What would you advise a female client who wanted to be a success in television broadcasting about her appearance?

A. I'd say—as I would say to an actor or actress or anyone else—that your appearance is a selling point and is one of the areas of importance.

Q. There is a good deal of research suggesting that physical attractiveness is, in fact, linked to how much a person is liked. But in the case of television journalists, do you think it makes a difference in the degree of credibility and how much they are believed?

A. No, not at all. I think if you got on the air and covered a story well, that no one would even think if you were attractive or not—there would be no problem at all. But if you weren't attractive you would never get there in the first place—the people who make the decisions would never give you a shot to get on the air. There are many examples of this: there are top reporters for the *New York Times* and other papers whom you never see on television. They're bright, brilliant people, but they lack the physical attractiveness to make it big on the talk show circuit.

OVERVIEW

When Judy Woodruff became a TV news anchor in Atlanta in 1972, the station ordered her to cut her shoulder-length hair. Mary Alice Williams was urged in 1979 by NBC's New York station to change her eye color with tinted contact lenses. Dorothy Reed was forbidden in 1980 by ABC's San Francisco station to plait her hair in corn rows.

The reason behind the actions cited above had little to do with the journalistic skill of the news anchors. Rather, in each instance—as with the case of Christine Craft, who brought a lawsuit against her former television station employer for similar behavior—the reason was to increase the physical attractiveness, and ultimately the likability, of the newscaster. And male anchors face the same pressures: physical attractiveness is often an unstated requirement of the job of television journalists, particularly younger ones.

Were the importance of physical appearance in determining attraction related solely to the world of television journalism, it would be of little concern to most of us. But research has shown it is also a determinant of liking in everyday social interaction. Indeed, physical attractiveness is just one of a number of factors that social psychologists have identified as relating to **interpersonal attraction,** the area of social psychology that deals with the ways in which people form social relationships and develop liking for one another.

Although the average person is unlikely to hire a public relations firm to shape his or her image, interpersonal attraction remains an important issue for most people. We begin this chapter by examining the needs that underlie social interaction and the reasons people have a general desire to associate with others. Next, we discuss how situational factors, such as physical proximity and frequency of exposure, affect attraction. We then examine the particular qualities and behaviors that evoke interpersonal attraction between specific individuals. Finally, we will focus on the most meaningful type of interpersonal attraction—love—from a social psychological perspective.

THE NEED FOR SOCIAL INTERACTION: THE REWARDING NATURE OF THE PRESENCE OF OTHERS

Although for most of us social interaction is an important component of our day-to-day existence, theoretically this need not be the case. People can and have lived alone for extended periods of time, with little or no interaction with others. Consider, for example, the advantages of being a hermit: one develops a sense of self-sufficiency; there are no interruptions; there is no need to accommodate the idiosyncrasies of others; one is never asked to help with the dishes, take out the garbage, or pick up some milk at the grocery store. In short, many of life's minor irritations would be eliminated by avoiding other people.

Yet few of us would choose to live in total isolation. The phrase "people are social animals," despite its triteness, still provides an apt description of the way in which the vast majority of us choose to live. Indeed, reports of those such as hermits, prisoners of war, and shipwrecked castaways who have experienced long periods of voluntary or involuntary isolation indicate a number of major difficulties that arise (Schachter, 1959).

First, there is typically psychological pain due to the isolation, which increases with time. Ultimately there may be a change toward extreme apathy or something akin to a schizophrenic state of withdrawal. Second, isolated persons frequently spend long periods of time thinking and dreaming about other people and may also hallucinate about others. Finally, if the isolated person is unable to think about or engage in

Because physical isolation is often an unpleasant state, people frequently prefer the company of others. (Jean-Claude Lejeune/Stock, Boston)

distracting activities of some sort, the psychological suffering becomes profound.

It is clear, then, that physical isolation is an unusually aversive experience. (See Box 6-1.) Why is the presence of others so important? To find an answer to this question, social psychologists have focused on two specific types of needs that are fulfilled by the presence of others, the need for affiliation and the need for comparison.

The Need for Affiliation: Reducing Fear and Isolation

Suppose you agreed to be a subject in an experiment and were greeted by a professor of neurology and psychiatry who introduced himself as Dr. Gregor Zilstein. And suppose he told you that the experiment concerned the effects of electric shock, and after a seven- or eight-minute lecture on the importance of research on shock, he concluded with this summary:

> What we will ask each of you to do is simple. We would like to give each of [you] a series of electric shocks. Now, I feel I must be completely honest with you and tell you exactly what you are in for. These shocks will hurt; they will be painful. As you can guess, if in research of this sort we're to learn anything at all that will really help humanity, it is necessary for our shocks to be intense. (Schachter, 1959, p. 13)

Even if Dr. Zilstein assured you that there would be no "permanent damage" from the shocks—as he, in fact, went on to say—it is likely that you would be in a high state of fear as you anticipated participation in

BOX 6-1   SPOTLIGHT ON RESEARCH

LONELINESS AS A SOCIAL STATE

Loneliness is typically considered among life's most unpleasant experiences. Surprisingly, though, social psychologists have only recently begun to examine loneliness, defined as the unpleasant emotional outcome of the perceived lack of social relationships with others.

When we discuss loneliness, we are describing a *subjective* state. One can be alone and still not be lonely; it is only when being alone is interpreted as negative that it becomes loneliness. Moreover, there are at least two forms of loneliness: emotional isolation, in which there is a lack of deep emotional attachment to one specific individual, and social isolation, in which there is a lack of friends, associates, or relatives (Peplau & Perlman, 1982).

In many cases, these two kinds of loneliness are not found together. For example, it is possible to conceive of a person who is a popular dormitory roommate with many friends, who goes to parties frequently, and who participates in a number of extracurricular activities, yet who lacks any one special, meaningful relationship. In a case such as this, the person may be suffering from deep loneliness despite surface appearances.

Who suffers most from loneliness? While a popular stereotype holds that it is mainly the elderly who are lonely, in fact, it is the young—and particularly adolescents—who report themselves most lonely. For example, in an ingenious study, Larson, Csikszentmihalyi, and Graef (1982) had a large group of subjects carry an electronic pager for one week. At variable intervals, subjects were paged and asked to complete a short questionnaire that measured what they were doing, their preceived loneliness, and a number of other factors. The results were clear in showing that the reported happiness and sociability were lowered significantly more by being alone by adolescents than by adults. Moreover, adolescents tended to relate being alone with passivity, while adults did not. In sum, the adolescents appeared to perceive being alone in a more negative light than older people did, and seemed to experience loneliness at considerably higher levels.

In fact, the way in which one perceives being alone seems to make a major difference in whether one is lonely. People who see being alone as their own fault or as due to their deficiencies are apt to remain lonely; in a sense, it becomes a self-handicapping strategy of the sort we discussed in Chapter 2. In contrast, people who view being alone as a transitory state are apt to feel less lonely, and they are more likely to try to overcome their feelings of loneliness by seeking out friendships. Indeed, a survey by Cutrona (1982) found that the most critical factor that differentiates lonely from nonlonely college students is the establishment of strong relationships with peers—as opposed to relationships with family members or romantic partners.

---

the procedure. In fact, this is just what Stanley Schachter wanted his subjects to experience when he carried out a classic series of studies on affiliation some twenty-five years ago (Schachter, 1959). In order to understand the affiliative tendencies of subjects who were experiencing high fear, he arranged the preceding situation. For a comparison, subjects in a low-fear condition were told that the shocks would be mild, resembling "a tickle or a tingle."

Subsequent to the induction of high or low fear, subjects were told that there would be a ten-minute delay in setting up the equipment. They were then asked the crucial question: Would they prefer to wait by themselves or would they rather wait with others? Results on the

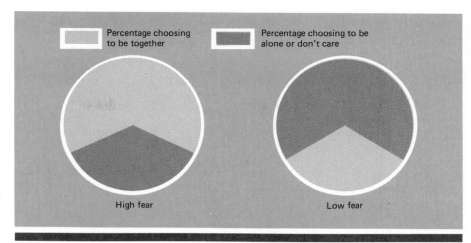

FIGURE 6-1
Relationship between fear and desire to affiliate. Under conditions of high fear, more people chose to wait with others; but under low-fear conditions, most people chose to wait alone.

measure were clear. As shown in Figure 6-1, subjects who were in the high-fear condition tended to choose to wait in the presence of others, while those in the low-fear condition tended either to want to wait alone or not to care. Why should this be the case?

Schachter reasoned that the presence of others is desired for at least two different reasons. One is that being with others can prompt a direct reduction of anxiety; the others may provide comfort, consolation, and reassurance. A second factor relates to self-evaluation processes. Others provide us with information about what to expect, how to feel, and how to react to the fear-producing situation. Thus, we may seek them out in order to understand the meaning of our emotions and feelings better.

Later research has shown that the relationship between fear and affiliation is a bit more complicated than originally thought. For instance, Schachter subsequently discovered that it is not just *any* company that is sought out by fearful others; it is the presence of others who are in a similar position. Subjects who think that they will receive a severe shock are likely to choose to affiliate with another individual, but only if they know the other person is also expecting to be shocked (Schachter, 1959). In Schachter's words, this finding "removes one shred of ambiguity from the old saying 'Misery loves company.' Misery doesn't love just any company; it loves only miserable company" (p. 24).

But even this generalization is a bit too broad, for it turns out there are a few exceptions. For instance, Shaver and Klinnert (1982) suggest that it is less important that others be equally miserable—only that the others be in the same situation. The reason is that people seek cognitive clarity by understanding more about the situation, understanding that others faced with a similar situation can provide. Hence, others provide information about what to expect, and it is not always necessary for them to feel miserable themselves.

Another instance in which the generalization that "misery loves miserable company" does not hold is for situations that provoke very strong negative emotions. In these cases, people prefer to remain alone. For instance, Sheatsley and Feldman (1964) found that people who were the most upset by President John Kennedy's assassination (as measured by the degree of admiration they held for him) were the ones who most wanted to be alone after his death. It may be that when they are very deeply distressed, people feel that their unhappiness will be increased or that they will be embarrassed or depressed by the presence of others. Moreover, when the emotion is strong and thus unambiguous, there is clearly no need to obtain information about the appropriateness of the emotion being experienced (Wheeler, 1974). Hence, at times of very deep emotional turmoil, we may turn away from others.

Fear versus Anxiety: They're Not the Same   Another important clarification that has been made to the original work done on affiliation and anticipation of aversive consequences regards the specific nature of the anticipated consequences. To understand this, it is necessary to distinguish between **fear** and **anxiety.** Fear is emotional arousal that is caused by the anticipation of an actual physical stimulus or danger, such as an electric shock or an injection. (Thus, fear is the emotion experienced by subjects exposed to the Dr. Zilstein stimulus in Schachter's early work.) In contrast, anxiety is emotional arousal that is caused by anticipation of a situation that is not physically painful but that promises to be psychologically unpleasant due to embarrassment or self-consciousness. Situations that have been used in experiments to provoke anxiety include anticipation of having to suck a nipple publically or having one's sexual arousal measured (L. Friedman, 1981; Sarnoff & Zimbardo, 1961).

It turns out that only *fearful* individuals tend to seek out and affiliate with others. People who are *anxious* tend to avoid being with others. Indeed, the presence of others seems to intensify a person's emotional arousal in situations that produce anxiety (Cottrell & Epley, 1977). One reason that anxious individuals do not find the presence of others helpful seems to be that their attention is inwardly directed, focusing upon their embarrassment and concerns about their self-presentation. Instead of using others as a calming influence, gaining information about the impending situations and others' feelings toward them, people in anxiety-producing situations are apt to become preoccupied with themselves (L. Friedman, 1981).

In sum, low and moderate levels of fear lead people to seek out the presence of others. However, at very high levels of fear, or when a person is experiencing anxiety, the presence of others is not only not sought out, but may actually be avoided.

Birth Order and Affiliation: Firstborns Need It Most   One of the striking and unexpected findings to come out of Schachter's early work on affiliation was the fact that birth order (the position in the family relative to one's brothers and sisters) is related to affiliative tendencies; firstborns and only children tend to have higher desires to affiliate than later-born

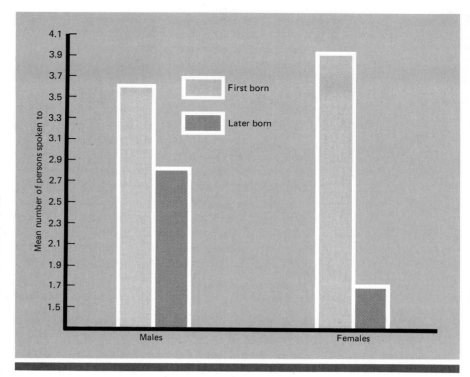

FIGURE 6-2
Number of persons spoken to following an earthquake. As predicted, both male and female firstborns tended to seek out the company of others in the fifteen minutes following the earthquake more than later-borns—although the phenomenon was more pronounced for the females. Source: Hoyt & Raven (1973).

children. Subsequent work has confirmed this finding (Darley & Aronson, 1966; Zimbardo & Formica, 1963), and it now seems clear that when faced with a stressful situation, firstborns prefer to be in the presence of others to a greater degree than later-borns.

One demonstration of the effects of birth order on affiliative behavior was provided in the aftermath of a large earthquake that struck southern California in February 1971. The quake, which lasted a full minute, caused the loss of fifty lives and millions of dollars worth of property. Clearly, it was a major event, and it provided an unexpected (if unwanted) opportunity to study affiliative behavior.

The day after the earthquake, Hoyt and Raven (1973) administered a questionnaire to some 400 undergraduates who had experienced the earthquake, asking about their affiliative behavior following the quake, as well as for demographic data, including their birth order. Those persons who were alone at the time of the earthquake offered clear support for the notion that firstborns would shortly thereafter be more affiliative than later-borns. Firstborns spoke to more people within fifteen minutes after the quake than did later-borns (see Figure 6-2), although the effect was stronger for females than for males. Other measures of affiliative tendencies tended to support this finding, at least for people who were alone at the time of the earthquake.

Why should firstborns have stronger needs for affiliation than later-borns? One cause may be socialization practices. Parents of firstborns tend to be more concerned about their infants than parents of later-borns, and this concern might be translated into fairly indiscriminate responding to signals of fear and distress in their firstborns (Schachter, 1959). In turn, this could lead the firstborn to learn that the presence of others (in this case, the parents) is rewarding through the reduction of anxiety, and thereby to associate affiliation with a pleasant emotional state.

On the other hand, the more experienced (and exhausted) parents of later-borns are likely to respond less quickly to their offspring, and thus later-borns do not learn to associate the presence of others with anxiety reduction as readily as firstborns. Moreover, older siblings may act as intimidating aggressive figures in their younger siblings' environment, thereby preventing the development of positive associations between the presence of others and anxiety reduction. For these reasons, then, we might expect firstborns to be more affiliative than later-borns in situations of fear and stress.

The Need for Social Comparison: How Others Help Us Know Ourselves

Another need that affiliation with others can help fulfill is the **need for social comparison** (Festinger, 1954). As you may recall from our discussion in reference to attribution theory in Chapter 2, according to this theoretical view, people are dependent upon others for information about the social and physical world around them, and they use the views and opinions of others to evaluate their own behavior, abilities, expertise, and opinions. Why is this necessary? Simply because, in many cases, the objective reality of a situation is either ambiguous or unknowable.

For instance, a young man may fancy himself a good tennis player, but since there are few objective tests of tennis-playing ability, there is little opportunity to ascertain unambiguously just how good he is. But there is one source of information available to him: he can compare this performance with those of other tennis players and see how he stands up against them. According to Festinger's theory of social comparison, which posits that there is a motivational drive to evaluate one's abilities and opinions, the tennis player may, in fact, seek out others for the sole purpose of being able to evaluate his performance.

Of course, the person chosen will be crucial to the usefulness of the comparison. If the individual in our example were to choose professionals Chris Lloyd or John McEnroe, he would be likely to obtain a discouraging view of his prowess at tennis. On the other hand, if he chooses his 7-year-old son, who has just started tennis lessons, he will naturally find that his own playing is superior—although he is likely to be dissatisfied with the viability of his comparison. A much more reasonable choice is someone at a similar level of expertise and training. Indeed,

BOX 6-2   SPOTLIGHT ON THEORY

THEORETICAL ORIENTATIONS TO INTERPERSONAL ATTRACTION

Underlying social psychologists' examination of the factors relating to interpersonal attraction are a number of general theoretical approaches. Among the major models that have been used to explore interpersonal attraction are three broad ones: learning theory models, comparison level models, and equity theory models. Although all of these theories are described in greater detail in other sections of the book, it is important to have at least a general sense of them at this point.

Learning Theory Models

One general approach to determining whom we find attractive is provided by learning theory, which, as we mentioned in Chapter 5 when discussing attitude formation, suggests that we like those who provide us with rewards and dislike those who punish us (Byrne & Clore, 1970; Byrne, 1971). Through basic classical conditioning learning processes, others become associated with rewarding or punishing circumstances, and we transfer our feelings about the circumstances to the people themselves in a way that is analogous to a dog who learns to salivate at the sound of a bell that has in the past been associated with the presence of food (Lott & Lott, 1974).

More directly, others can provide us with rewards—they tell us they like us, they do things for us, they help us, and so forth. According to the basic tenets of reinforcement learning theory, rewarding stimuli (including other people) arouse positive feelings, and thus we come to like them. Similarly, punishing stimuli evoke negative feelings, and we can come to dislike stimuli associated with such circumstances. In this way, people who hurt, annoy, or bother us in some way can come to be disliked because of their punishing qualities.

Comparison Level Models

Unlike learning theories, which examine the absolute degree of rewards and punishments provided by another individual, comparison level theories suggest that our attraction to others is based on comparison to some hypothetical baseline (Thibaut & Kelley, 1959). This baseline, known as a **comparison level,** is a kind of summary of the past outcomes that an individual has experienced or that are salient. If the rewards someone receives from a relationship are above the person's comparison level, he or she will be satisfied with the relationship; if they fall below it, he or she will be dissatisfied.

But whether people actually maintain the relationship depends upon the alternatives available. Thus, a person may continue in an unsatisfying relationship if no better alternative relationship is available. Likewise, an unpleasant relationship may be terminated if a better one comes along. As we shall discuss in greater detail in Chapter 14, comparison level models view interpersonal attraction in the form of economic exchange between two people who assess the rewards and costs of maintaining the relationship, and they are particularly useful when considering ongoing, long-term relationships (e.g., Berg, 1984).

Equity Theory Models

Equity theory explanations move a step beyond comparison level models by taking into account not only an individual's own outcomes, but also the outcomes that are perceived to be attained by a partner in a relationship (Walster, Walster, & Berscheid, 1978). The theory suggests that we try to maintain a balance between the rewards and costs we experience and those our partner experiences. If the partner is felt to be receiving more (or less) than his or her just due, we will experience distress and try to restore equity—potentially by modifying our perception of what we are getting out of the relationship or by modifying our feelings for the partner. Thus, if a working wife feels that her husband leaves an inordinate amount of housework for her to do, she may experience feelings of inequity and reevaluate the relationship.

this is a further assumption of Festinger's theory of social comparison: people tend to seek out others who are similar to themselves for purposes of evaluation.

Basically, then, social comparison theory suggests that there is a motivational drive to evaluate one's abilities and opinions, and that people tend to choose similar others to make such comparisons. Although the theory has largely been supported, recent reformulations (e.g., Goethals & Darley, 1977) have suggested a number of modifications. For instance, under conditions of competition, similar others may be rejected as sources of information—simply because we don't want to damage our self-esteem through the possibility of coming out second best in the comparison (Conolley, Gerard, & Kline, 1978; Fazio, 1979). Despite these modifications, though, social comparison theory provides a reasonable explanation for why people may seek out the presence of others.

SITUATIONAL INFLUENCES ON ATTRACTION

Although findings that there are basic needs for social interaction help to explain why the presence of others is rewarding, they do not help us to answer more explicit questions about the particular people to whom we are attracted and why certain people are chosen as friends and lovers over others. We begin discussing this line of query by examining two general situational factors associated with interpersonal attraction: geographical proximity and frequency of exposure.

Proximity: Liking the One You're Near

Accidents of geography frequently determine who our friends are. Think, for instance, about who your closest friends were when you were growing up. In most cases, they were probably children who lived near you. This phenomenon often occurs in college dormitories; we tend to be friendliest with those who are located closest to us, and least friendly with people who are assigned to rooms farthest from our own. The same relationship is found in marriages: an examination of 5000 marriage license applications in an early study showed that 33 percent of the couples consisted of people who had lived within five blocks of each other and that the number of marriages decreased as geographical distance increased (Bossard, 1932). And these findings don't include the 12 percent who shared the same address *before* they were married!

One of the earliest demonstrations of the importance of geographical proximity in determining interpersonal attraction remains one of the most graphic. Festinger, Schachter, and Back (1950) studied the development of friendships in an MIT housing project for married students. Festinger et al. found that there were several architectural features relating to proximity between people that were associated with the development of friendships (a typical building is shown in Figure 6-3).

For instance, there was a close association between friendship choices

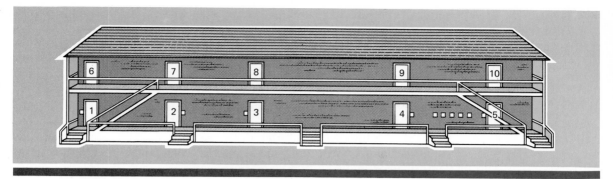

and the proximity of apartments. Couples who lived one door apart were more likely to be friends than those living two doors apart, and so on. People who lived near mailboxes or stairways (e.g., apartments 4, 5, and 1) had more friends in the building than those who lived farther from such architectural features. Indeed, any design feature that involved more traffic brought nearby people more popularity.

More recent evidence has confirmed these early findings, and it is clear that proximity is an important determinant of attraction (Nahemow & Lawton, 1975; Segal, 1974). But proximity does not *invariably* lead to attraction, as police statistics indicate. Berscheid and Walster (1978) point out that, in many cases, robberies are perpetrated against people who are either acquainted with or related to the robber. Assaults are also frequently committed against relatives and acquaintances, and close to one-third of all murders occur during family quarrels. Thus, in some instances, proximity can lead to hostility.

Most of the time, though, proximity is a precursor of liking. One explanation for the phenomenon is that people can obtain social rewards (such as companionship, social approval, and help) from others who are nearby at relatively little cost, and thus closer friends tend to be more rewarding than those who require greater effort and time to be with. Moreover, we tend to acquire more information about people who are in closer proximity to us. If Newcomb's (1956) suggestion that the amount of rewarding information tends to be greater than the amount of punishing information is correct, we are more likely to be attracted to those about whom we have the most information.

Although plausible, Newcomb's explanation has little experimental support, but there is a more intriguing hypothesis for the relationship between proximity and interpersonal attraction which is suggested by the work we will examine next. Briefly, it suggests that exposure to *any* stimulus is going to lead to increased attraction.

Mere Exposure: Familiarity Leads to Liking

When students in Rick Crandell's psychology courses came to class each day they found a few strange, non-English words written in the corner of the blackboard. Although they were clearly not part of the lesson being discussed, the words became an accepted part of the class environment. What varied was the frequency with which the words were seen. Some words only appeared once over the course of the semester, while others appeared as many as twenty-five times.

At the end of the semester, students in the class were surprised to be given a questionnaire that assessed their rating of favorability of a list of words. Embedded among the list were all the words that had appeared at one time or another on the blackboard during the semester. When the ratings were tabulated, the results were clear: the more frequently a word had been placed on the blackboard, the higher its favorability rating was. Increasing mere exposure to the words seemed to lead to increased positivity toward them; subjects "liked" more frequently seen words more than less frequently seen words (Crandall, 1972).

This class study demonstrated what has become a well-established finding known as the **mere exposure phenomenon.** Basically, the phenomenon shows that repeated exposure to any stimulus is sufficient to increase the positivity of the evaluation of the stimulus (Zajonc, 1968; A. A. Harrison, 1977). This phenomenon has occurred in a number of different areas, including evaluation of words, ratings of musical and other artistic stimuli, and even liking of other people. For example, there is correlational evidence that the more frequently a word appears in a given language, the more positively the word is rated.

In one study, Zajonc (1968) asked subjects to rate fruits, flowers, vegetables, and trees and found that, within a category, the more frequently a word appeared the more it tended to be liked. Thus, pine, apple, corn, and rose were liked most; acacia, mango, parsnip, and cornslip were liked least. Of course, such evidence is only correlational in nature. It is possible that increased ratings of liking are not due to the frequency with which the words appear in the language, but that the words appear more frequently because initially they are liked more.

More compelling evidence that mere frequency of exposure leads to liking comes from studies in which the frequency is experimentally manipulated. This can be done through the use of nonsense words with which an individual has no prior experience. Using a wide variety of exposures—ranging from seeing a word once for a fraction of a second to seeing the same word more than 240 times—has shown that repeated exposure increases attraction to stimuli. Similar results have been demonstrated for exposure to musical and other artistic stimuli: we tend to enjoy musical passages and pieces of art as they become more familiar.

Even rats exposed to particular pieces of music appear to enjoy them more if they have had prior experience with them. For instance, one experiment (Cross, Halcomb, & Matter, 1967) exposed groups of rats to selections from Mozart or Schoenberg for twelve hours a day over a fifty-two day period. After a fifteen-day rest period, the rats' musical preferences were tested by allowing them to shift their position in the cage in a way that would activate a switch to play music of either of the two composers. As would be expected from the mere exposure phenomenon, rats chose the music with which they were most familiar. And we should note that the specific musical selections played during the testing period were not the same as the ones played earlier. Thus, the animals' preferences involved a style of music, as opposed to specific pieces—pretty impressive, considering that we are talking about rats.

Given that repeated exposure to words and aesthetic stimuli results in increased attraction, we should not be too surprised that the same principle works with interpersonal attraction; it is clear that the more one person is exposed to another, the greater his or her attraction to that individual is—all other factors being equal. The phenomenon occurs when seeing photographs of someone, when meeting the person, and even when simply exposed to someone's name (A. A. Harrison, 1977).

We should note, however, that (as with many other things) one can get too much of a good thing. The effects of increased exposure are not consistently more and more positive. In fact, after some optimal level of exposure is reached, liking can actually decline with repeated exposure. Consider, for example, having to listen to your favorite record twice a day for a period of six months. The first few weeks would probably not be so bad, but after a while you might get sick of hearing the same music over and over again, and your liking for the record could taper off or cease entirely.

An explanation for both the increase and eventual decrease in attraction can be derived from learning theories. Both Berlyne (1970) and Stang (1973) suggest that two factors are at work in explaining the results of repeated exposure. According to them, the first factor consists of learning that occurs during repeated exposure to the stimulus. Because learning is a favorable experience, there is an increase in attraction for the object being learned about. But if too much exposure occurs, the second factor, satiation, occurs. In this stage, the stimulus no longer has any novel characteristics, and as the repeated exposure leads to boredom, the stimulus eventually becomes less favorable in its meaning.

Other researchers have put forward other models. For example, Birnbaum and Mellers (1979) suggest that increased frequency of stimulus exposure results in positive feelings of recognizability when frequently seen stimuli are encountered. These feelings of recognition in turn produce enhanced liking for the stimulus. At this point, although we cannot be sure of the precise explanation for the phenomenon of mere exposure, one thing remains clear: repeated exposure in and of itself generally results in enhanced attraction.

WHAT MAKES A PERSON ATTRACTIVE: FACTORS UNDERLYING INTERPERSONAL ATTRACTION

Why is it that some people seem thoroughly magnetic while others are disliked from the first moment we meet them? We turn now to approaches to interpersonal attraction that have sought to determine what specific characteristics and behaviors lead particular people to be liked—or disliked—by others. It is important to note before proceeding, however, that no single factor is likely to be of overriding importance in determining liking; instead, people are affected by a number of sources of information about others (Berg, 1984; Altman & Taylor, 1973).

Similarity: Do Birds of a Feather Flock Together?

As Michael ran through the almost obligatory list of questions that he always seemed to go through when meeting someone at a party— What dorm do you live in? What's your year in school? What's your major?—he was struck by the triteness of his queries. But he was also happy to find that he and his new acquaintance, Jessica, had a lot in common. They had the same major, were both juniors, and even lived in nearby dorms. What was more, they both had a passion for Italian food, liked foreign movies, and enjoyed piano and guitar music. In fact, the number of similar interests and opinions that they shared was remarkable. Michael was delighted that he finally had met someone with whom he shared so much, and he felt quite attracted to Jessica.

Although not necessarily representing "love at first sight," Michael's attraction to Jessica illustrates a clear principle derived from work on interpersonal attraction: oftentimes we like people who are similar to ourselves. We will discuss similarity across a number of dimensions— attitudinal, personality, and value similarity.

Attitude Similarity   Probably the clearest example of the relationship between similarity and interpersonal attraction resides in the area of attitude similarity. Since the early 1900s, researchers have known that people who like one another tend to share similar attitudes (Schuster & Elderton, 1906). The more challenging question became one of determining the direction of causality: does interpersonal attraction lead to the development of attitude similarity, or does attitude similarity lead to attraction? (We should also acknowledge a third possibility: that some other factor led to the mutual attraction and the attitude similarity.)

By experimentally manipulating the perceived degree of agreement between two individuals, researchers have found that similarity of attitudes can, in fact, cause interpersonal attraction. In the typical experiment (e.g., Byrne & Nelson, 1965), subjects are asked to respond to a series of questions regarding their attitudes toward topics, such as school and politics. The experimenter then collects the results, and under the guise of ascertaining subjects' impressions of a stranger on the basis of responses to a similar questionnaire, informs the subjects of the "stranger's" responses, which vary in their degree of agreement with the subject's own attitudes. The subject's attraction to the confederate is then

BOX 6-3   SPOTLIGHT ON METHODOLOGY

HOW DO I LOVE THEE? LET ME MEASURE THE WAYS

Most experimental research on interpersonal attraction employs traditional paper-and-pencil measures routinely used to measure attitudes in general. However, a number of clever, unobtrusive techniques for measuring interpersonal attraction have also been devised. Among the subtler (and better validated) are the following:

Eye Contact
The popular wisdom that lovers tend to gaze into each others' eyes is supported by research findings. The greater the length of time people spend looking at each other eye-to-eye, the greater the mutual attraction (Z. Rubin, 1970). There is an exception, however: unacquainted people who use too much eye contact may have their behavior interpreted as a hostile stare, something that results in dislike.

Body Orientation
The directness with which people orient their bodies toward one another and the degree to which they lean forward or back when interacting with each other are correlated with the degree of attraction between the pair. Facing someone directly and leaning toward that person are both signals of liking (Mehrabian, 1968).

Distance
The distance between two people who are interacting with each other is an indicant of attraction. There is a direct—and not surprising—relationship: the more they like each other, the closer they stand (Hall, 1966).

Pupil Dilation
In the same way that children's eyes widen when they see a big bar of candy, the pupils of adults become larger when they are in the presence of a liked person (and become smaller when viewing a disliked person). Interestingly, we tend to rate others more favorably when *they* have relatively larger pupils—everything else being equal (Hess, 1975).

In sum, if a person gazes at you, leans forward, sits close, and has dilated pupils when looking at you, you would be safe to assume that he or she is attracted to you.

---

assessed, using a paper-and-pencil measure (see Box 6-3 for subtler techniques that might be employed). Although quite simple and straightforward—albeit somewhat artificial—this experimental paradigm allows for some elegant hypothesis testing. For instance, the absolute number of perceived agreements and disagreements can be varied, as can the *proportion* of perceived agreements and disagreements. Moreover, the specific nature of attitudes can be varied (Byrne, 1971).

Results of a long line of studies indicate that a critical factor underlying the attitude similarity–attraction relationship is the proportion of agreements, and not the absolute number. For instance, you will like a person who is perceived to be similar to you on five out of ten attitudes (50 percent) less than the person who is perceived to agree with you on three out of four attitudes (75 percent), even though in the first case the absolute number of agreements (five) is greater than in the second case (three). This relationship is a mathematically linear one: the relationship between attraction and proportion of perceived attitude similarity forms a straight line when graphed (see Figure 6-4).

The effect of similar attitudes on liking has also been demonstrated

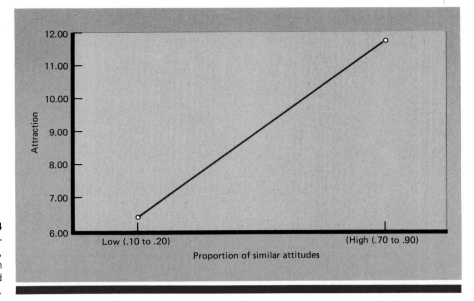

FIGURE 6-4
As the proportion of similar attitudes increased,
interpersonal attraction
rose. Source: Byrne and
Clore (1966).

in real-life settings. For instance, social psychologist Donn Byrne and his colleagues arranged for a computer date to be set up between males and females who differed either minimally or maximally on responses to a fifty-item attitude questionnaire (Byrne, Ervin, & Lamberth, 1970). After each couple was introduced, the partners were asked to spend thirty minutes together on a date. After the date, they independently completed a scale that assessed their attraction to each other. The results showed quite clearly that attraction was significantly related to similarity (as well as to physical attractiveness, which we will discuss later). In addition, measures taken at the end of the semester showed that attitude similarity was associated with a remembrance of the date's name, whether a pair had talked to one another since their first meeting, and the desire to go out with the other person in the future.

Value Similarity   Because similarity of attitudes leads so clearly to interpersonal attraction, it would not be surprising if similarity of values was also associated with liking—and this seems to be the case. For example, Hill and Stull (1981) studied same-sex college roommate pairs and found clear evidence that women who chose to be roommates had significantly greater similarity in terms of fundamental values pertaining to such subjects as religion and politics than those who had been assigned to be roommates. The greater the degree of value similarity measured at the start of the fall, the greater the likelihood that the pair would stay roommates in the spring, suggesting that value similarity enhanced liking. Although results for the male subjects were less clear (the only significant relationship for male pairs was in value similarity that was perceived to have existed, as opposed to actual value similarity and attraction), the results suggest that roommates who share basic values about the world are going to have more positive relationships than those who do not.

Personality Trait Similarity and the Need-complementarity Hypothesis

Another sphere in which similarity might be expected to relate to attraction is that of personality. Research dating back some time suggests that we are attracted to those who have personalities which are relatively similar to our own. For instance, in an early demonstration of the phenomenon Reader and English (1947) gave personality tests to pairs of friends and found higher correlations between their traits than in a control group consisting of nonfriend pairs.

Although the relationship between attraction and personality similarity is generally positive, it is considerably less strong than the attitude similarity–attraction relationship. It is reasonable to assume that almost everyone finds some personality traits—such as warmth and intelligence—attractive, whether or not they have those traits themselves. Moreover, it is plausible to assume that sometimes *dissimilarity* of personality will lead to increased interpersonal attraction—if those differences allow one partner to better fulfill the needs of the other.

The hypothesis that people are attracted to others who have significantly different personalities, but whose needs complement theirs, is known as the **need-complementarity hypothesis,** and it has been applied

We tend to be attracted to those who hold attitudes similar to our own—and assume that people we like have interests similar to ours. (Hugh Rogers/ Monkmeyer Press)

primarily to married couples. The hypothesis argues that husbands and wives are most compatible when the needs of one spouse are fulfilled through the needs of the other spouse (Winch, 1958). For example, a dominant wife may get along best with a submissive husband; or a husband and wife may differ in the degree to which they hold the same personality traits (the high-dominant husband with a low-dominant wife). In either instance, the needs of each fit together in the total context of the relationship.

The need-complementarity hypothesis is illustrated nicely by the comment made by someone discussing married life in a book on marriage: "Well, I've known a lot of couples where the rocks in *her* head seemed to fit the holes in *his*" (Howard, 1978). However, despite the fact that it sounds so reasonable, the need-complementarity hypothesis has not been notably successful when it comes to garnering experimental support. Despite initial support from Kerckhoff and Davis (1962)—who found that while value similarity was evident early in the history of a relationship, it was replaced later by need complementarity—subsequent research has been unsuccessful in supporting the notion of need complementarity (Levinger, Senn, & Jorgensen, 1970). For instance, Meyer and Pepper (1977) found that married couples who appeared to be best adjusted were the ones who were the most similar in their needs—not the most complementary. Although the need-complementarity hypothesis remains intriguing, it has not as yet produced experimental evidence in its favor.

Why Does Similarity Lead to Attraction?   We have seen that similarity, whether it be of attitudes, values, or personality, is consistently related to interpersonal attraction. But why should this be the case? Four explanations have been proposed (Huston & Levinger, 1978).

First, similarity may be directly reinforcing. For instance, we may have learned through prior experience that people with attitudes similar to our own are associated with rewarding circumstances or situations. Second, the fact that someone else has attitudes or qualities similar to our own may lead to a sense of confirmation of our views of the world. For example, if I feel that the arms race would be controlled best by a total nuclear arms freeze, I may be particularly attracted to someone else who shares my views because, in a sense, it validates my opinion by providing social support. Moreover, as we discussed in terms of social comparison theory, similar others allow us to evaluate our abilities and opinions more readily than dissimilar others.

A third explanation for the effects of similarity on liking is that learning the attitudes and values another person holds permits us to form an impression of what traits the other person has. If we perceive the traits to be positive—as would generally be the case for traits associated with oneself—the other will be perceived positively (Ajzen, 1974). Thus, according to this view, the inferred value of another's personality characteristics, and not the similarity per se, is rewarding.

One final possibility is that we like similar others because we infer that they are going to like us. As we shall see, knowing that someone else likes us generally leads to attraction toward the other person, a phenomenon known as reciprocity of liking. Thus, similarity may lead to inferences that the other likes us, and we in turn are attracted to them because they do.

It is likely that none of these explanations by itself is sufficient to explain the similarity–attraction relationship (Berscheid, 1984). Despite our inability to pinpoint the precise explanation, however, the notion that perceived similarity leads to attraction is well founded.

Reciprocity of Liking: I Like You Because You Like Me

As we mentioned earlier, there is a robust general finding regarding **reciprocity of liking**: we tend to like those who like us. Given information that another individual likes us, we tend to be attracted to that person. The converse process seems to hold true as well: when we like someone, we tend to assume that they like us in return (Mettee & Aronson, 1974; Burleson, 1984).

Although the reciprocity-of-liking rule has much support, there are exceptions, one of which relates to self-esteem. Recall from our discussion of attitudes in Chapter 4 that cognitive consistency theories in general, and balance theory in particular, predict that cognitions about ourselves and others generally fit together in consistent patterns. These theories can be applied to the area of interpersonal attraction.

Suppose, for instance, that Charlie has high self-esteem, which means, in a fundamental sense, that Charlie likes himself. Further assume that Charlie finds out that someone else (Rachel) likes him. In order to be consistent, it follows that Charlie will hold positive feelings toward Rachel, as in the balanced situation shown in the first half of Figure 6-5. This state of affairs produces the reciprocity-of-liking rule.

But suppose Charlie has low self-esteem, which can be conceptualized as a state of affairs in which Charlie dislikes himself. If Charlie learns that Rachel likes him, the situation can be in a state of balance only if Charlie decides he *dislikes* Rachel—the situation shown in the second half of Figure 6-5. Hence, according to balance theory, people with low self-esteem will not be susceptible to the reciprocity-of-liking rule: they are apt to *dislike* people they find liking them, since they don't like themselves—a prediction supported by a fair amount of research (Shrauger, 1975).

Another exception to the reciprocity-of-liking rule occurs when we suspect people are saying positive things about us to ingratiate themselves. **Ingratiation** is a deliberate effort to gain favor, often through flattery (E. E. Jones, 1964). If an employee tells the boss how much he likes her, the boss might feel that she is being flattered for an ulterior motive. Rather than forming a positive opinion of the employee, the boss may resist and begin to dislike the employee.

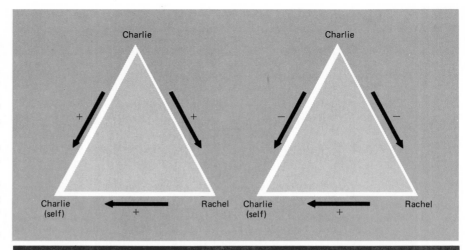

FIGURE 6-5
The way in which Charlie reacts to the knowledge that Rachel likes him depends on whether Charlie has a positive opinion of himself. In the first situation, Charlie has high self-esteem; balance occurs when Charlie likes Rachel. But in the second situation, Charlie's low self-esteem means that balance occurs when he dislikes Rachel. Source: Berscheid & Walster (1978).

However, aside from a few exceptions (such as people with low self-esteem and ingratiation attempts), expressing positive sentiments about someone is apt to produce reciprocated liking. As Berscheid and Walster (1978) note, Dale Carnegie once suggested that people should be "hearty in their approbation and lavish in their praise" in his classic self-help book, *How to Win Friends and Influence People*. He seems to have been right.

Positive Qualities: Liking the Good and Disliking the Bad

It is hardly surprising that people with meritorious qualities should be liked more than those with disagreeable qualities. For example, we like intelligent, warm, sincere, and competent people more than people who do not have those attributes (Kaplan & Anderson, 1973).

But sheer positivity is not the whole story. Sometimes we prefer people who display positive qualities that are a bit tarnished by negative ones over people who seem to be without flaw. An example of this was provided in a study by Aronson, Willerman, & Floyd (1966), who had either a very competent or an average individual commit or not commit a pratfall, which consisted of clumsily spilling a cup of coffee. The results showed that liking for the competent person increased after a pratfall, while liking tended to decrease for the average person. The explanation is straightforward. Very competent people who commit a blunder become more human and approachable and, thus, more attractive. On the other hand, the average person gains little from a blunder, since he or she is already seen as human enough.

Although later research has shown that the relationship between competence and attraction is also related to the self-esteem of the person doing the rating (Helmreich, Aronson, & LeFan, 1970), the basic fact remains: we tend to prefer competent people to incompetent ones.

212

Physical Attractiveness and Liking: It Doesn't Hurt to Be Beautiful

In an egalitarian and democratic society, most people would agree that people ought to be judged for what they are and what they do, rather than what they look like. Yet, despite general agreement with the old saying, "Beauty is only skin deep," it turns out that most people act as if physical attractiveness were a good indicant of how likable a person is. As Kathie Berlin indicated in her comments at the beginning of the chapter, the physical appearance of an individual can be an important aspect of how that person is viewed by others—however unwarranted such a bias may be.

People who are physically attractive are regarded more highly than unattractive ones with startling consistency, starting with nursery-school-age children and continuing into old age (Adams & Huston, 1975; Berscheid & Walster, 1974; Dion & Berscheid, 1974). Indeed, not only are they liked more, but people make more positive interpretations of the behavior of the physically attractive.

For example, Dion (1972) presented subjects with a description of a mild or severe instance of misbehavior by a 7-year-old and asked them to judge the typicality of the child's behavior. Included with the descriptions were a photograph of a child who had previously been judged to be either attractive or unattractive. When the misbehavior was of a mild nature, no effects due to the appearance of the child were detected. But when the misbehavior was severe, the physical attractiveness of the child affected how the behavior was interpreted. Subjects viewed attractive children's misbehavior as temporary, atypical incidents, unlikely to be repeated. Thus, an attractive girl who threw a rock at a sleeping dog was seen in this way by one subject:

> She appears to be a perfectly charming little girl, well-mannered, basically unselfish. It seems that she can adapt well among children her age and make a good impression. . . . She plays well with everyone, but like anyone else, a bad day can occur. Her cruelty need not be taken seriously.
>
> (Dion, 1972)

In contrast, similar incidents committed by unattractive children were judged much more harshly, being seen as examples of chronic misbehavior, symptomatic of an underlying behavior problem. For example, one subject wrote about an unattractive girl who threw the rock at the sleeping dog in this way:

> I think the child would be quite bratty and would be a problem to teachers. . . . She would probably try to pick a fight with other children her own age. . . . She would be a brat at home—all in all, she would be a problem.
>
> (Dion, 1972)

Clearly, the actions of the physically attractive child were viewed much more positively than those of the unattractive child. Judgments based on physical attractiveness extend to other areas as well; we expect physically attractive people to be more interesting, poised, sociable, kind, strong, outgoing, and sexually warm and responsive than less physically attractive people (Dion, Berscheid, & Walster, 1972). On the other hand, stereotypes regarding physical attractiveness are not uniformly positive, at least in terms of females. Dermer and Thiel (1975) found that people were more likely to view physically attractive females as vain and adulterous than unattractive ones.

Physical Appearance and Social Behavior

While the data regarding the relationship between attraction and physical appearance are clearly positive, the question of how appearance is related to subsequent behavior is more ambiguous. We might expect that since people tend to form more favorable impressions about the physically attractive, they will act more positively toward them. In turn, the physically attractive may develop more positive self-images and interpersonal styles, which lead them to become more effective during social interactions than less attractive people (Adams, 1977). Following this reasoning, we could expect physically attractive people to have a greater number of and more rewarding social encounters.

Most of the evidence that has been collected regarding the social encounters of the physically attractive has been in the context of dating behavior, and the results have been fairly consistent, showing that attractive people are chosen as dating partners more frequently than less attractive people. Moreover, self-reports of popularity are correlated with attractiveness (Walster, Aronson, Abrahams, & Rottman, 1966; Berscheid, Dion, Walster, & Walster, 1971).

There are some exceptions to these findings, however. Although the physically attractive may be preferred in the abstract, there is evidence that people tend to choose others during courtship and marriage who are similar to their own level of attractiveness. Known as the **matching hypothesis,** the idea is that an individual's own level of physical attractiveness affects the choices made in dating situations (Berscheid & Walster, 1974). The matching hypothesis has received a good deal of support (e.g., Price & Vandenberg, 1979), and it explains why most people eventually find partners they feel are satisfactory.

A second qualification to the physical attractiveness and social interaction relationship regards differences between males and females. There is some compelling evidence that despite a cultural belief that the appearances of females are more important than those of males, the opposite is true: physical attractiveness in males is more closely related to the amount and nature of social encounters than that in females.

This point was clearly illustrated in studies by Reis, Nezlek, and Wheeler (1980) and in a later follow-up (Reis, Wheeler, Spiegel, Kernis, Nezlek, & Perri, 1982). They had a group of college undergraduates keep a careful record of every social interaction of ten or more minutes'

The matching hypothesis suggests that people tend to choose as marriage partners those individuals who are similar to themselves in level of physical attractiveness. (Hazel Hankin)

duration that occurred during four 10-day periods over the course of a college year. Although this technique lacks some objectivity since it is based on subjects' recollections and perceptions of each social encounter, this deficit is offset by the wide range of situations covered—far more than could ever be obtained in a laboratory setting.

The results of the Reis et al. (1980) study showed a strong relationship between physical attractiveness and the quantity of social interaction, but only for males. As can be seen in Table 6-1, physical attractiveness in males correlated positively with quantity of opposite-sex interaction (the greater the man's attractiveness, the more opposite-sex interaction he had).

In contrast, the quantity of female interaction was not significantly associated with physical attractiveness. The explanation? It may be that attractive males are more assertive, having had a history of successful

TABLE 6-1 Correlations of Interaction Quantity with the Opposite Sex and Physical Attractiveness
Throughout the four measurement periods, the amount of interaction with the opposite sex was associated with physical attractiveness for males—but not for females.

	September	December	January	April
Males	.57*	.40*	.63*	.65*
Females	− .15	− .03	− .02	.10

*Statistically significant correlation.
Source: Adapted from Reis, Nezlek, & Wheeler, 1980.

encounters with females, and thus are more apt to approach women than unattractive males. This would result in the positive correlations shown in Table 6-1 for the males. But women may be culturally conditioned to avoid initiating opposite-sex interactions and thus "wait" for men to come to them. Furthermore, it is possible that men fear rejection from approaching highly attractive women, and thus tend to choose women across a relatively broad range of attractiveness as partners. This would mean attractive women would not have more opportunity for social interaction than unattractive women—thereby explaining the lack of correlation between female interaction quantity and physical attractiveness.

Results from the Reis et al. studies are complicated, and they show that the relationship between physical attractiveness and social behavior is a complex one. Attractiveness does not guarantee that one's social life will be an active one or that one will fare better in life generally than a person who is less attractive. Indeed, there is evidence that the social rewards that beauty is expected to bring can be illusory.

For instance, research examining the relationship between women's physical attractiveness in college and their adjustment and happiness twenty years later found a relationship—but in the opposite direction from what one might expect, given the other evidence regarding physical attractiveness. Women who had been attractive in college tended to be *less* happy and *less* well-adjusted in their later lives than those who had been relatively unattractive in college (Berscheid, Walster, & Campbell, 1974). It may be that aging is more devastating to someone who was initially very attractive than to someone who was less attractive early in life.

These findings reinforce an important point: although the effect of physical attractiveness is undeniable, many other factors help determine interpersonal attraction. Indeed, what people consider attractive is fleeting: even a pleasant facial expression brings about ratings of greater physical attractiveness than an unpleasant expression (Mueser, Grau, Sussman, & Rosen, 1984).

Moreover, physical attactiveness may be of greatest importance in the early stages of a relationship, when information about another is apt to be scanty. Standards of beauty also change drastically over time and across societies, so what is attractive in one time and place may evolve into something quite different. In sum, physical attractiveness does not ensure a lifetime of high-quality social relationships.

LOVE

I believe that 200 million other Americans want to leave some things in life a mystery, and right at the top of the things we don't want to know is why a man falls in love with a woman and vice versa. (Proxmire, 1975)

Love differs qualitatively
from "mere" attraction.
(Mary Ellen Mark/Archive
Pictures)

When Senator William Proxmire made the above statement in regard to the study funded by the National Science Foundation to examine the topic of romantic love, he was merely echoing many earlier sentiments, such as those of the social philosopher H. T. Finck (1902): "Love is such a tissue of paradoxes, and exists in such an endless variety of forms and shades, that you may say almost anything about it that you please, and it is likely to be correct" (p. 224).

Until not too long ago, many social psychologists would have agreed with at least the underlying message of such statements, for the study of romantic love was considered unscientific, primarily because the phenomenon was so difficult to observe in a systematic way. More recently, however, social psychologists have modified this view, and have offered a number of substantial theories to explain love. Given the importance love plays in people's most intimate relationships, as well as its influence on marriage and divorce, understanding love may prove to be of crucial importance to society.

Romantic Love

Most researchers involved in the study of romantic love argue that **romantic love** (or, as it is sometimes termed, **passionate love**) is not just a matter of liking that is of greater intensity than, say, typical friendship (Berscheid, 1984). Rather, it differs qualitatively from mere attraction in a number of respects. Romantic love includes relatively intense physiological arousal, as well as a strong psychological absorption and interest

BOX 6-4 SPOTLIGHT ON RESEARCH

LEVELS OF LIKING: UNDERSTANDING RELATIONSHIPS

In an important contribution to our understanding of the nature of relationships between people, George Levinger (1974) has suggested that there are three basic levels of relatedness: unilateral awareness, bilateral surface contact, and mutuality. This conception, which is illustrated graphically in Figure 6-6, serves to organize our understanding of how human beings relate to one another.

Awareness is the level at which most relatedness occurs. At this level we view others in terms of their outward characteristics, and those being perceived are not aware of the fact that they are being observed or judged.

With **surface contact**, the second level of pair relatedness, both people are aware of each other, and each forms attitudes and impressions of the other, as well as attitudes and impressions regarding the relationship itself. Most of our daily inter-

There are many different levels of relatedness between two people. (Michael Kagan/Monkmeyer Press)

FIGURE 6-6
Levels of relatedness. Source: G. A. Levinger (1974).

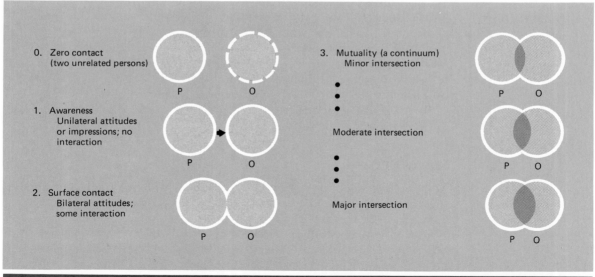

actions with others fall into this category. We see the same bus driver, building custodian, librarian, and bank teller very frequently, yet the depth and closeness of the relationship is minimal.

It is not until the relationship reaches the third stage, that of **mutuality**, that it becomes truly personal. No longer are interactions merely transitory or fixed within a restricted role relationship (such as bus driver–passenger). In mutual relationships, the individuals share knowledge about each other, feel a degree of responsibility for the other, and develop a set of personal norms informally regulating their relationship.

During the early stages of mutuality, referred to as **minor intersection** in Figure 6-6, individuals are hesitant and worry about disclosing information about themselves. But as the relationship progresses to the level of **moderate intersection** and **major intersection**, self-disclosure increases, and the partners will reveal intimate and important attitudes and feelings. Moreover, they learn the sources of the other person's happiness and satisfaction, and they begin to behave in a way that makes the relationship rewarding to the other person.

Levinger's three-level conception of relatedness provides a useful guide to the levels of interaction and attraction that can exist between two people. Moreover, it allows us to understand the nature of our own relationships and the categories into which they fall more fully.

in another individual. Romantic love also has been hypothesized to include a number of other characteristics which distinguish it from simple attraction, including the presence of romantic fantasies, ambivalent emotional states, and rapid swings of emotion.

Although there is general agreement on the nature of the characteristics that distinguish more superficial attraction from deeper romantic love, they remain somewhat difficult to quantify and make operational in scientific terms. One effort to provide an empirical differentiation between the two states has been carried out by Zick Rubin, who developed two paper-and-pencil scales to measure liking and loving. Each scale consists of a series of items (samples of which are shown in Figure 6-7) in which the respondent fills in the name of someone to whom he or she is attracted and then indicates agreement with each statement on a nine-point scale (Rubin, 1973).

As would be expected, couples who score high on the love scale behave differently from those who score lower. They tend to gaze into each other's eyes more, and their scores tend to predict whether the relationship will be maintained six months in the future (Rubin, 1973). It appears, then, that the loving and liking scales have some degree of

FIGURE 6-7
Samples of love-scale and liking-scale items. The greater the agreement with the statements within each of the scales, the greater the love or liking, respectively. Source: Rubin (1973).

Love Scale
I feel that I can confide in _____ about virtually everything.
I find it easy to ignore _____'s faults.
I would do almost anything for _____.

Liking Scale
I think that _____ is unusually well-adjusted.
I would highly recommend _____ for a responsible job.
I have great confidence in _____'s good judgment.

validity, and that they can differentiate reliably between feelings of liking and loving.

Why Do I Love Thee? Let Me Count the Reasons

Although it is possible to distinguish love from liking, this does not answer the question of *why* people fall in love. Although the answer is complicated, at least one social psychological theory has been put forward, based on Schachter's theory of emotion labeling (which we first encountered in our discussion of attribution theory in Chapter 2).

Building on Schachter's theory, Berscheid and Walster (1974) suggest that people experience romantic love when two things occur together: intense physiological arousal and situational cues that indicate that "love" is the appropriate label for the feelings they are experiencing. Thus, when physiological arousal (which might come from sexual arousal, excitement, or even negative emotions such as fear or anger) is labeled as being due to "falling in love" or "she's so wonderful" or "he's just right for me," the experience can be labeled "romantic love." What is particularly useful about this theory is that it explains why a person who keeps being hurt or rejected by someone else can still feel love for that person. The feelings of hurt or rejection can produce physiological arousal; if the arousal is labeled as being love-related, the attraction to the person will be maintained.

Although direct evidence for the theory has not been found, there is some intriguing indirect support, particularly for the notion that arousal of any sort can lead to the intensification of attraction. In one set of experiments (Dutton & Aron, 1974), researchers placed an attractive college-age woman at the end of a dangerous, swaying, 450-foot suspension bridge that spanned a canyon. The woman was ostensibly conducting a survey, and she asked men who had just managed to make it across the bridge a series of questions. She then offered to give the subjects more information about her survey if they desired, and wrote her telephone number on a small piece of paper so they could get in touch later. There were also a number of control conditions: in some instances the same female was at the end of a safe and sturdy bridge only 10 feet off the ground, and sometimes a male played the confederate role.

The experimenters predicted that the danger of the suspension bridge would lead to physiological arousal, and that this arousal would be labeled as attraction in the presence of the attractive woman. Just as predicted, men contacted the woman significantly more when the men had been in the dangerous situation; only a few made the call after crossing the nondangerous stable bridge. In addition, almost none of the male confederates was called, regardless of whether the bridge was safe or dangerous. These results suggest that the increased physiological arousal that may have occurred following the crossing of the dangerous bridge was related to the presence of the attractive woman.

The two-factor arousal-labeling theory also suggests a rationale for what has been called the "Romeo and Juliet effect" (Driscoll, Davis, & Lipitz, 1972). Couples who experience strong parental interference in their relationships tend to report greater love for one another than those with little interference. Consistent with the theory, parental interference may raise the general level of arousal among the two lovers, which then may be labeled as being due to enhanced passion for each other.

The arousal that precedes labeling need not be negative in nature, of course. A study by White, Fishbein, and Rutstein (1981) shows that when arousal was due to a positive stimulus (a tape of a Steve Martin comedy album) or even a neutral one (running in place), subjects subsequently liked an attractive confederate more than unaroused subjects did. Independent of the initial source of arousal, then, attraction can occur.

While the two-factor theory of love is itself an attractive (if not exactly lovable) theory, there has yet to be conclusive evidence for its support (e.g., Kenrick & Cialdini, 1977). Still, it is able to show quite clearly that romantic love is a fit topic for the science of social psychology and should not be restricted to poets and philosophers.

Sex and Love in Dating Relationships

Given the importance of physiological arousal in theories seeking to explain love, research on the role of sex in ongoing relationships holds particular significance. Although there is relatively little research in this area, one pioneering study has found three patterns that link sex and love in dating relationships among a sample of college-age students in the Boston area (Peplau, Rubin, & Hill, 1977). The three groups have been labeled sexually traditional, sexually moderate, and sexually liberal couples.

Sexually Traditional Couples   These couples, a minority of couples sampled, fit the traditional pattern of sexual behavior: sexual intercourse is reserved for marriage. The basic notion is that abstaining from intercourse prior to marriage indicates love and respect, although sexual practices short of actual intercourse are considered permissible. Couples in this category follow either a single standard (both men and women abstain) or a double standard (it would be permissible for the male to have sex if the woman consented).

Sexually Moderate Couples   Couples in this category feel that love is a prerequisite for sex, but a lifetime commitment is not required prior to having sexual intercourse. They typically begin sexual relations about six months after they start dating. Their lack of intercourse early in the relationship is due to their view that sex represents an expression of love that only comes with time and not because of moral principles against premarital sex.

Sexually Liberal Couples   The final grouping consists of couples whose sexual relationship began relatively early after they had met. They tend to adhere to a standard which is permissive, in which sexual intercourse can occur fairly casually without concern about whether they "love" their partner in the traditional sense. They view intercourse, in part, as a way of getting to know one another, or as an activity that is enjoyable in and of itself.

To study the role of sexual intimacy in dating relationships, Peplau, Rubin, and Hill (1977) surveyed individuals in a sample of 231 couples who had been dating steadily for about eight months. Using the typology described above, a number of differences emerged. For example, when the sample was divided by timing of first intercourse (which translates primarily into the sexually liberal versus sexually moderate groupings) it was clear that there were greater expressions of emotional closeness in the later intercourse group than in the early one, as shown in Table 6-2. Later sex couples more often report being in love, feeling more intimate ties, and being more likely to marry their partner. As would be expected, their sexual attitudes are less liberal than those of the early intercourse sample. They feel negatively about casual sex and they tend

TABLE 6-2   Couples Reporting Early and Later Sexual Intercourse
Differences in responses between people having sexual intercourse early and late in their dating relationship.

	MEN'S REPORTS		WOMEN'S REPORTS	
	Early Intercourse	Later Intercourse	Early Intercourse	Later Intercourse
Emotional Intimacy				
Love scale	6.7	7.3*	6.9	7.4*
Self-report of closeness	7.5	8.1*	7.6	8.1*
"How well do you know your partner?"	7.2	7.7*	7.4	7.8†
Couple is "in love" (% yes)	65%	84%*	65%	80%*
Probability of marrying partner (9 = 90–100% probability)	3.7	6.1*	4.5	6.1*
Sexual Attitudes				
Acceptability of intercourse for a woman with a casual acquaintance (9 = completely accept)	6.2	4.5*	5.4	3.4*
Importance of sex as a dating goal	6.4	5.2*	1.0	2.7*
How satisfying is intercourse with partner?	7.7	7.7	7.8	7.2*
Feel guilty about having intercourse with partner (1 = never, 9 = always)	1.5	2.2	1.9	2.8*

Note: All items are nine-point scales unless otherwise indicated: *N* = 90 early-sex couples and 92 later-sex couples. (Early = within one month of first date.)
* Significant difference between early and later figures.
Source: From Peplau, Rubin, & Hill (1977).

to feel greater guilt over their own sexual activities than the early intercourse group. This may account for the fact that they have sexual relations fewer times per week (two to three) than the early sex couples (four to five).

People in the sexually traditional group, in which the partners had abstained from sexual intercourse, tended to report considerably less serious relationships than couples in which intercourse had occurred. Only about half the respondents reported being in love, compared to about three-fourths of those who had had sexual intercourse. Of course, we cannot be sure whether the lower involvement of the relationships was the cause behind the lack of sexual intimacy or the result of lack of intercourse.

What Works Best?   Despite the major differences between many of the ratings of the sexually traditional, moderate, and liberal couples, there were *no* significant differences found in either general overall satisfaction with the relationship or its permanence over a two-year period. Despite discrepancies in reports of how much they loved each other, in the goals desired from the relationship, in the lifestyles of the respondents, and in their general attitudes toward sex, satisfaction with the relationship was quite high for members of all three groups. Moreover, the pattern of sexual behavior was not associated with the ultimate outcome of the relationship. A follow-up study conducted two years after the original survey showed that members of each group did not differ in the status of their relationships: they were equally likely to be still dating (34 percent), married to each other (20 percent), or no longer involved in the relationship (46 percent).

In sum, it appears from the results of this survey that no single pattern of sexual behavior results in more successful relationships than another. In the words of the survey authors, "We found no evidence that early sex necessarily short-circuits the development of lasting commitments, nor that sexual abstinence or moderation consistently increases or decreases the development of a lasting relationship" (Peplau, Rubin, & Hill, 1977, p. 103).

Deterioration of Interpersonal Attraction

The vast majority of work done by social psychologists on interpersonal attraction has concentrated on the issues involved in attraction toward others. Most social psychologists have examined only the initial encounter phase of relationships (Berscheid, 1984; Rusbult, 1983). However, anyone who is familiar with this country's divorce rate (approaching 50 percent) or who has suffered through a broken love affair is apt to be concerned with the processes involved in the opposite side of the coin: the deterioration of interpersonal attraction.

Unfortunately, there is relatively little research that directly examines the reasons behind the end of relationships (Gottman & Levenson,

1984). One exception is an examination of close heterosexual relationships in adults carried out by George Levinger (1983). He has speculated that a number of different processes contribute to the deterioration of a relationship. One involves changes in each partner's private judgments of the other person. Behavior that was once considered charming forgetfulness becomes labeled indifference, leading to a devaluing of the partner. There may also be difficulties in communication. For instance, each partner may become bent on justifying his or her point of view, as opposed to listening to the other person. Finally, people outside a relationship may provide social support for negative attitudes about the partner, as well as potentially fulfill needs that the partner cannot fulfill.

Clearly, many factors are involved in the deterioration and ending of relationships. One challenge for social psychologists is to identify these critical components in a manner that will allow couples to raise once-central relationships to their previous level of importance.

SUMMARY

Research on interpersonal attraction begins with the central fact that the presence of others is rewarding in and of itself. Two specific motivational needs are fulfilled through others: the need for affiliation and the need for social comparison. The need for affiliation is pronounced in fearful persons: people who are afraid desire the presence of others—particularly if the others are also in a fearful state. In addition, firstborns tend to have greater affiliative tendencies that later-borns.

People have a need for social comparison because they depend upon others for information about the social and physical world, and they use the views and opinions of others to evaluate their own behavior, abilities, expertise, and opinions. Generally, individuals are most apt to choose people who are fairly similar to themselves as comparison persons because they provide the most relevant information.

Certain factors of a situational nature also lead to interpersonal attraction. Proximity has an important effect upon whom people choose as friends. Moreover, the mere exposure phenomenon shows that repeated exposure to any stimulus is sufficient to increase the positivity of the evaluation of the stimulus. Hence, the more an individual is exposed to another person, the greater the attraction—although there are limits beyond which repeated exposure produces a reduction is liking.

One important approach to interpersonal attraction has been to determine what particular characteristics lead an individual to be liked or disliked by others. Similarity between people is one critical element. People who like one another tend to share similar attitudes, and learning that someone holds attitudes similar to one's own produces interpersonal attraction.

The important factor underlying the attitude similarity–attraction relationship concerns the proportion of shared attitudes, not the absolute number. Value and personality similarity also lead to attraction, although there has been some suggestion—not well-supported—that people choose partners in close relationships whose needs complement their own and who are, therefore, dissimilar. This latter hypothesis is known as the need-complementary hypothesis.

There are a number of explanations for why similarity leads to attraction. Similarity may be directly reinforcing; it may lead to a sense of confirmation of one's view of the world. People may view their own traits positively, and when they see the same traits in others, they react favorably. Or people may assume that similar others are going to like them, which makes the feeling mutual. This last explanation builds upon a well-established finding known as the reciprocity-of-liking phenomenon: people like others who they know like them.

Additional factors related to interpersonal attraction are the competence and physical attractiveness of an individual. Physical attractiveness is particularly important; its effects begin in nursery school and continue into adulthood.

Romantic or passionate love is qualitatively different from other forms of interpersonal attraction. People develop fantasies based on love objects; they have ambivalent emotional states, and attraction can vary drastically over relatively short periods of time. One theory of romantic love suggests that the experience of love is due to a combination of intense physiological arousal and situational cues that indicate that "love" is the appropriate label for the arousal.

The role of sex in ongoing dating relationships has also been examined. Three major patterns of sexual behavior in dating couples emerge: sexually traditional, wherein intercourse is reserved for marriage; sexually moderate, wherein sex is engaged in only after a relatively lengthy period of dating; and sexually liberal, wherein sex is engaged in soon after the first date. However, no one particular pattern is related to the success or lastingness of a relationship. Indeed, it is clear from work on deterioration of close relationships that the causes of the end of relationships are as complex as those of their development.

KEY TERMS

affiliation
anxiety
attitude similarity
comparison level
equity
ingratiation
interpersonal attraction
liking
loving
matching hypothesis
mere exposure phenomenon
mutuality

need-complementary hypothesis
need for social comparison
passionate love
proximity
reciprocity of liking
relatedness
sexually liberal couples
sexually moderate couples
sexually traditional couples
surface contact
value similarity

FOR FURTHER STUDY AND APPLICATION

Berscheid, E., & Walster, E. (1978). *Interpersonal attraction* (2nd ed.). Reading, MA: Addison-Wesley.
An excellent readable guide to the area of interpersonal attraction, from the least to the most meaningful kinds of relationships. Written by leading experts in the field.

Hatfield, E., & Walster, G. W. (1981). *A new look at love*. Reading, MA: Addison-Wesley.
For the reader interested in love (and who isn't?), this book offers everything one needs to know.

Huston, T. L. (Ed.). (1974). *Foundations of interpersonal attraction*. New York: Academic Press.
A series of technical chapters, written by eminent researchers, on the theoretical factors that underlie interpersonal attraction. Tough going, but worth the effort.

Hendrick, C., & Hendrick, S. (1983). *Liking, loving, and relating*. Monterey, CA: Brooks/Cole.
A current and clearly written guide to interpersonal attraction with particular attention paid to the rise and fall of relationships.

Rubin, Z. (1980). *Children's friendships*. Cambridge, MA: Harvard University Press.
A beautifully written examination of the development and maintenance of children's relationships. Very informative, with much of the material having clear implications for adult relationships.

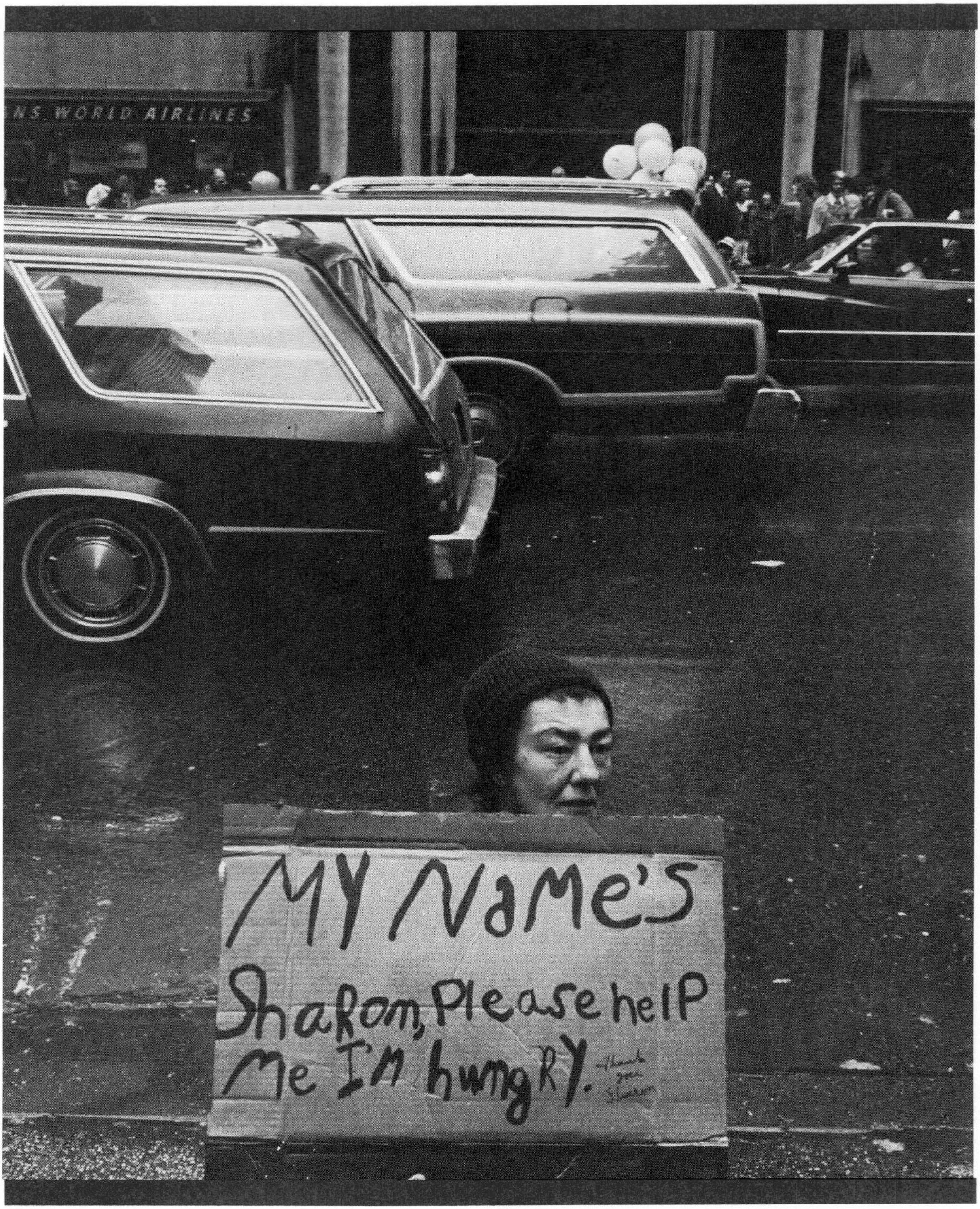
NS WORLD AIRLINES
MY Name's
Sharon, Please help
me I'm hungRY.

CHAPTER 7

PROSOCIAL BEHAVIOR: HELPING OTHERS

A CONVERSATION WITH . . .

Irving Reimer
Vice President, American Cancer Society

Of all the diseases that can strike an individual, probably none is feared more than cancer. It is not surprising, then, that efforts to prevent the disease should enlist the support of many people. The American Cancer Society, the chief organization designed to raise funds to support the eradication of the disease, is one of the most successful fund-raising organizations in the world, raising more than $150 million in a typical year and involving more than 1 million people as volunteers.

We discussed fund raising and volunteerism—critical examples of helping behavior, the topic of this chapter—with Irving Reimer, who is vice president for public information of the American Cancer Society. We began with a discussion of how the American Cancer Society differentiates itself from other equally worthy causes.

Q. There are numerous worthy charities that people can choose to support. How do you get people to be generous, both in terms of time and money, to your particular cause?

A. First of all, you have to establish a reputation so people know that you are an organization that can be counted upon to achieve some results. In the case of cancer, you also have to take the disease out of the closet and eliminate the terrible atmosphere of fear and the belief that only tragic consequences result from having cancer. You have got to have people believe that they can do something about it—because people want to associate their time and energies with some feeling that they are going to be successful. For example, some people don't want to link themselves with mental illness because they don't believe it is a curable problem. They don't like the victims, and they are more likely to see it as

partially the victim's fault. For these reasons, they are less willing to become involved with the problem.

Q. So you are saying that it is crucial that people have a relatively positive attitude toward the disease itself before they are willing to help out?

A. Right. In terms of cancer, our surveys show that the public believes that you can have realistic expectations of success with cancer—that is, if you find it early, you have a pretty good chance of being treated successfully—and this is a change that has taken place since the middle 1950s. So people are now willing to associate their time and energies as volunteer fund raisers with this organization.

Q. Is there anything else you can point to that makes people want to help out in the fight against cancer?

A. Another factor that has played to our advantage is that a lot of people are affected by cancer. They get angry at it. If they know a victim—a loved one, relative, friend, business associate—they want to fight back. They can do this by giving money, and they can do this by volunteering their time.

Q. Are there also personal benefits that an individual gets from volunteering his or her time? For example, I would guess that a volunteer gets involved in a social network with other volunteers and forms social relationships with others, which I'm sure is a big benefit.

A. Yes, we do encourage socialization. We have a lot of good meetings. The national volunteer gets to go to meetings in nice settings, because we think that the time the volunteer gives us is worth, in return, a good time and investment from our organization. People who put themselves out completely for you ought to receive some personal gain. People do a 100 percent job for us, but they gain recognition; they gain visibility; they learn some networking in the community.

Q. I can see that making volunteers and donors feel that the rewards are relatively high for participating in the activities of the American Cancer Society would increase help given to the organization. But there's another strategy that you might use, and that is to attempt to build empathy for the victim by making people feel that they themselves are potential victims. Do you use such a strategy?

A. What we do is build a communications program based on the fact that we are making progress, that there are close to 3 million people walking the streets of America cured of the disease, and that there are things you can do to protect yourself against the disease. We focus on lifestyles—the factors such as smoking, exposure to sun, having checkups, diet—that are related to increased risk. The tragic side of cancer does not have to be communicated by us; people see that. It's reported on in the press. John Wayne died of cancer; Steve McQueen died of cancer; that's there all the time. We've done enough surveys to learn that if you reinforce the negative, people walk away from it. What you have to do is present a positive framework of doing something about it.

Q. Do you perceive any general strategy for increasing helping behavior— not just for cancer, but increasing volunteerism in general?

A. First of all, I think we have to accept the fact that a large percentage of the American people are currently helping in all kinds of organizations. I understand that the number may be as high as 60 million people. That's a tremendous, unduplicated figure. I think what we can do to increase it even further is to bring the various helping organizations to the attention of people so they can make a selection of what they really want to do. I also think we've overlooked the potential of volunteerism from young people. The young people of the country are the most idealistic segment of the population, but they lose it when they go out into the real world. While they have such idealism, in high school and college, we ought to get them involved in helping.

OVERVIEW

Helping represents one of the noblest behaviors in the repertoire of human activities, and it is not surprising that it has attracted a good deal of attention from social psychologists. One of the most important reasons for this interest is that, in contrast to so many of the other topics we have discussed, people sometimes behave in a fashion that apparently goes against their own best interests. Moreover, the phenomenon of helping behavior raises a number of fundamental issues regarding social behavior, including how people develop a sense of responsibility for others and society, the relative contributions of situational and personality factors in causing behavior, and how members of society can promote positive social behavior.

In this chapter, we focus on the specific factors that underlie helping behavior. We begin by discussing the factors that enter into a person's decision that help is required in a given situation, and whether and how responsibility for helping is assumed and carried out. Next, we examine some of the specific variables which influence helping behavior, including the norms that guide an individual's behavior, feelings for the needy person, the mood of the potential helper, and the personality characteristics of the helper. Finally, the ways in which people learn and can be taught to engage in helping behavior are discussed.

Throughout the chapter, we will be using the terms **helping** and the more formal **prosocial behavior** interchangeably. Both refer to behavior that benefits other people. The help may be minor, such as picking up a hitchhiker, or it may be major, as in the case of the person who risks his life by repeatedly returning to icy waters to save shipwrecked passengers. It may be a deliberate, thoughtful series of actions, as when someone collects funds for a charity, or it may be impulsive, as when a person rushes into a burning building to help a screaming child. The common thread in these situations is the benefit that accrues to other people and to society in general from the helping behavior.

HELPING OTHERS IN TIMES OF NEED

Suppose you are talking with a small group of students, discussing personal problems associated with college life. Suddenly, you hear one of the discussants say the following, as he seems to lapse into an epileptic seizure:

> I-er-um-I think I-I need-er-if-if could-er-er-somebody er-er-er-er-er-er give me a little-er-give me a little help here because-er-I-er-I'm-er-er-er-h-h-having a-a-a real problem-er-right now and i-er-if somebody could help me out it would-it would-er-er s-s-sure be-sure be good . . . because-er-er-there-er-er-a cause I-er-I-uh-I've got a-a one of the-er seizure-er things coming on and-and-and I could really-er-use some help so if somebody would-er-give me a little h-help-uh-er-er-er-er c-could somebody-er-er-help-er-uh-uh-uh (choking sounds) . . . I'm gonna die-er-er-I'm . . . gonna die-er-help-er-er-seizure-er (chokes, then quiet).
>
> (Darley and Latané, 1968, p. 379)

Would you rush to the aid of the victim, or would you remain seated and assume that someone else would provide aid? The answer to that question is not simple, but one prediction can be made with confidence: the *greater* the number of other people present with you, the *less* likely you would be to help the victim.

The reason for such a prediction—which has been called the **bystander effect**—comes from the results of a series of experiments conducted by John Darley and Bibb Latané in the late 1960s (Darley & Latané, 1968; Latané & Darley, 1970). In their work, Darley and Latané found clear evidence for a phenomenon they termed **diffusion of responsibility**, which suggests that in cases in which there is more than

Helping behavior takes many forms ranging from that pictured here to less obvious types, such as donating blood or participating in community fund-raising activities. (Jack Prelutsky/Stock, Boston)

one witness to a situation requiring helping, responsibility for acting is felt to be diffused or shared among the bystanders. Thus, it could be predicted that the greater the number of bystanders present in such a situation, the less personally responsible each would feel, and the less likely that any one person would help—and this is just what they found.

For instance, in the case of the apparent seizure described above (which occurred as a manipulation in an experiment in which subjects were holding a discussion over an intercom with unseen confederates), 85 percent of the subjects sought help when they thought there were only two people present. But this figure dropped to 31 percent when they thought there were six persons present (see Figure 7-1). And not only did more subjects respond with fewer people present, but they responded more quickly than in the conditions with greater numbers of people.

The discovery of the diffusion of responsibility phenomenon, which has been replicated consistently (Latané & Nida, 1981), led Latané and Darley to develop a model to explain how situational factors—quite independent of the personality traits and characteristics of the people present—lead to helping in emergencies (Latané & Darley, 1970). Although the model, outlined in Figure 7-2, was proposed initially to account for helping in emergency situations only, it provides a useful guide for organizing much of the work on helping in nonemergency situations as well, and so we will discuss it in general terms. According to the model, the process of helping involves five basic steps: (1) notic-

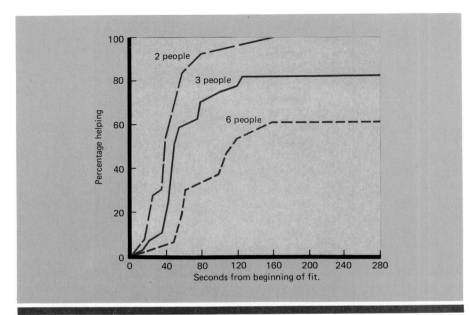

FIGURE 7-1
As the number of persons
present in an emergency
situation increased, it
took longer for the people
present to respond—and
fewer ultimately re-
sponded. Source: Latané
and Darley (1968).

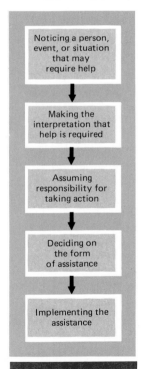

FIGURE 7-2
A model of helping be-
havior. Source: Based on
a model proposed by La-
tané and Darley (1970).

ing a person, event, or situation that may require help; (2) interpreting
the event as requiring help; (3) assuming responsibility for taking action;
(4) deciding on the form of assistance; and (5) implementing the assistance.

Noticing and Interpreting the Need for Help

The obvious first requisite in helping is for someone to notice the
potential need for assistance. But once an individual or situation has
come to the attention of a person, the interpretation placed on that
individual or situation is crucial. For example, one explanation for the
finding that the presence of greater numbers of people leads to less
helping is that the presence of passive others actually modifies a bystander's definition of the situation; what would have been interpreted
as an emergency had the person been alone is considered to be a
nonemergency because of the presence of inactive others.

The interpretation stage seems to reflect social comparison processes
in which the behavior of others is used as a guide for evaluating the
situation (Staub, 1980). Moreover, the greater the perception that the
situation represents a true emergency and requires immediate action,
the greater the likelihood that help will be offered. For instance, Shotland and Huston (1979) found that emergency situations are distinguished from other problems by the possibility that harm can worsen
with time, the lack of an easy solution to the problem, and the requirement that outside help be obtained. A child swallowing a razor blade,
a rape in progress, and a heart attack can all be considered emergencies,

while a cat stuck in a tree, a scraped knee, and a dropped tray of food at a party are not considered emergencies requiring immediate help. In situations *perceived* as emergencies, bystanders are considerably more likely to help than in nonemergency situations.

Assuming Responsibility for Taking Action

After a situation requiring help has been identified as such, the next step in the decision-making process regarding whether or not to intervene involves the assumption of responsibility. In essence, people try to determine whether they have any personal responsibility for taking action. It is at this point that diffusion of responsibility may occur and inhibit helping behavior.

In some cases, even when many others are present, responsibility is clear because of special expertise or roles that an individual holds. For instance, a doctor would be presumed to have greater expertise in dealing with an apparent epileptic seizure than a person without medical training and, therefore, would be expected to provide help regardless of the total number of bystanders present (Schwartz & Clausen, 1970). A field experiment supports this reasoning: Piliavin and Piliavin (1972) found that when an individual appeared to collapse on a subway car with blood trickling out of the corner of his mouth, bystanders were less apt to help when a person appearing to be an intern was close to the victim than when the "intern" was not present. It is likely that subjects thought they had less to offer—and hence less responsibility—than the highly trained intern.

It is also possible to increase people's feelings of responsibility through verbal requests. For instance, in one experiment, people sitting on the shore at Jones Beach, New York, were asked (by a confederate) to watch the confederate's possessions for a short time, while in a control condition no such request was made. After the confederate left, an apparent thief came by and started to pick up a radio that the confederate had left behind. Of the subjects who saw the theft, almost all (95 percent) of the experimental condition subjects tried to stop the theft, while only 20 percent in the control condition intervened (Moriarty, 1979). Simply making an individual's sense of responsibility salient may be sufficient, then, to increase helping behavior.

Deciding on and Implementing the Form of Assistance

Tallying Costs and Rewards   After a person determines that a situation requires helping and assumes responsibility for helping, he or she must decide on the form of assistance to offer. It is one thing to leave the scene of an accident to telephone the police and suggest that an ambulance be sent immediately, and quite another to pull a person out of a burning car and administer first aid to the victim immediately after a crash. In essence, then, helping may range from indirect forms—such as getting *others* to help—to more direct forms, in which aid is provided immediately. What determines which form of assistance is given relates to the rewards and costs surmised by the potential helper.

The general notion behind a rewards–costs approach to helping is that the rewards involved in helping generally must outweigh the costs if helping is to occur. In fact, as Irving Reimer of the American Cancer Society pointed out at the start of this chapter, often charities do attempt to increase the rewards of helping to ensure that the benefits outweigh the costs by, for instance, holding meetings in exotic and desirable locations.

Many experimental studies confirm that as the costs of helping increase, people are less likely to provide aid (e.g., Ungar, 1979; Midlarsky & Midlarsky, 1973). One of the clearest examples of the importance of how the costs of helping are reflected in offers of aid was provided in a study by Darley and Batson (1973). In the field experiment, the subject was a theology student who was about to give a talk either on the Good Samaritan parable—which relates how people should help one another—or on a nonhelping topic. The cost of helping was manipulated by controlling how late the subject was to give the talk.

On the way to the talk, the subject passed a confederate slumped in an alley who coughed and groaned as the subject walked by, and the measure of helping was the degree of aid given the apparent victim. The results of the study showed that whether the topic of the talk was relevant or irrelevant to helping had no effect on the degree of help provided by the subjects. What did matter was how late the subjects were: the greater the degree of tardiness, the less help they were apt to offer.

While it at first appears ironic that theology students on their way to recite the story of the Good Samaritan (who, according to the biblical tale, stops to help a fallen victim who has been robbed and beaten) were no more apt to help than those who were going to talk about something irrelevant to helping, later research suggests that the subjects may have perceived that the "greater good" lay in arriving at the talk in time—and thus helping a larger number of people—than in stopping to aid a single individual. In a follow-up study, Batson, Cochran, Biederman, Bloser, Ryan, and Vogt (1978) told half the subjects that their talk was very important, while the other half thought it was less important. Only those subjects who were in a hurry *and* who thought their mission was urgent showed a lower level of helping. In sum, it is clear that people weigh the potential costs of helping in making their decision to help or not.

The Benefits of Helping and the Concept of Altruism Although the costs of helping have received a good deal of attention and can be used to make reasonably accurate predictions of when helping will occur (e.g., Lynch & Cohen, 1978), the literature on the benefits of helping is considerably less complete. Part of this problem has to do with difficulties involved in conceptualizing and measuring the occurrence of helping behavior known as **altruism.**

Altruism refers to helping behavior that is beneficial to others but requires clear self-sacrifice on the part of the helper. Many forms of helping might be considered altruistic: running into a burning house to rescue a stranger's child, sheltering Jews in Nazi-occupied countries during World War II, saving a drowning person at great risk to life and limb. The costs are clearly high, and the outcomes of such altruistic acts appear to benefit only the recipient—not the helping individual.

Yet a closer examination reveals that it is ultimately possible to find a number of potential rewards even in what first seems to be the most altruistic act: enhancement of the altruistic individual's self-esteem and feelings of self-worth, accrual of praise and rewards from others, and gratitude from the victim. However, if this is the case, a definition of altruism that uses "self-sacrifice" as the major identifying characteristic is unwarranted since it can be argued that there are clear, if not immediate, rewards involved in altruistic behavior.

Further complicating the difficulties involved in defining altruistic behavior is the requirement that we be able to recognize altruism objectively. In many cases, simply observing behavior is not enough to infer an individual's intent. Suppose, for instance, that a rich person gives $500,000 to her alma mater. Although such a donation may appear at first to be an altruistic act, it is possible that the person's major motivation for giving is a wish to immortalize herself with a building named after her and to acquire a hefty tax deduction. Compare this with a poor person who gives just one dollar to a charity. The objective consequences of the two behaviors may be far lower for the poor person than for the rich one, but the self-sacrifice involved is much greater for the poor person.

We can see, then, that there are a number of difficulties involved in conceptualizing altruism—and even more when examining nonhumans, as we discuss in Box 7-1. Most researchers in the area have avoided the conceptual morass by concentrating on observable criteria and tending to ignore the underlying intentions of the altruistic individual. If there appear to be no external rewards and the act is not coerced by others, acts of helping can be considered altruistic.

NORMATIVE APPROACHES TO HELPING: DO UNTO OTHERS . . .

"Do unto others as you would have them do unto you." "Kindness is its own reward." "He who helps others helps himself." Platitudes such as these reflect society's general view that helping behavior is important, desirable, and virtuous. The vehicle by which this view is transmitted is known as a **norm,** which is a generalized expectation that is held

BOX 7-1   SPOTLIGHT ON THEORY

ALTRUISM AMONG THE ANIMALS

Although we have concentrated our discussion of altruism on human beings, it is fascinating to consider instances of true helping behavior among members of other species. Consider, for instance, the following examples reported by Rushton (1980):

- An injured adult dolphin is held to the surface of the water by a helping pair of dolphins, allowing its blowhole to be exposed to the air, and thereby avoiding suffocation.
- A fallen elephant, who otherwise would be unable to breathe because of its own weight, is helped to its feet by another elephant.
- A group of chimpanzees who have cooperatively hunted and killed a baby baboon divide and share the meat—even with other chimps who had taken no part in the kill.

Does such behavior represent true altruism? Sociobiologists, a group of biologists and social scientists who view social behavior as being largely genetically determined, would answer this question affirmatively (Wilson, 1975). They suggest that in many species behavior occurs that is beneficial to the species as a whole, and not merely to particular members of the species. Such behaviors include defense of other animals, rescue of others, cooperative hunting and food gathering, and sharing of food.

What is puzzling is how such altruistic behavior might be transmitted genetically according to the laws of natural selection proposed by Darwin (1871). Darwin suggested that behaviors which were most beneficial to a species would be the ones that would be most likely to be passed down to future generations, thus strengthening the species as a whole. Yet if one considers altruistic behaviors, it would seem that altruistic individuals might be the first to sacrifice themselves (as in defense of territoriality). If this were the case, they would tend to have fewer offspring, and therefore would be less likely to pass on the altruistic trait.

A solution to this problem has been suggested by Hamilton (1972). He noted that it is not just the production of direct offspring of an altruistic animal that helps transmit a trait, but the production of the offspring of relatives of the individual—who, to a certain extent, will share the genes of their altruistic ancestor. If an animal sacrifices itself to protect a relative, it will be protecting the transmission of the common genes that are shared. According to Hamilton, altruistic animal behavior is a way of ensuring the survival of at least part of that animal's genes and, ultimately, the survival of the species.

Altruistic behavior, then, can occur in species other than man. And when viewed in an evolutionary framework, altruistic behavior in human beings just may be in the best interests of *our* species.

---

regarding appropriate behavior in a given social situation. The extent to which a norm has been internalized is reflected in an individual's **personal normative structure,** a construct that has been studied extensively by social psychologists.

Although methodologically difficult to define precisely, the general structure of people's personal norms regarding helping can be determined. For instance, Schwartz (1977) constructed a series of questions that was designed to measure people's feeling of obligation in a variety of situations (summarized in Table 7-1). He found that certain norms were widely held, with relatively little variability among people. For instance, most people felt a fairly strong obligation to donate a heart (after their death) to a close relative who needed a heart transplant. On the other hand, there was much greater variability in response to a question asking about willingness to donate bone marrow to a stranger.

One implication of a normative view of helping is that there ought to be a clear relationship between norms espoused regarding helping behavior and subsequent helping. Also, the stronger and stabler the norms, the stronger the relationship should be. This hypothesis was confirmed in a study by Schwartz (1977), in which undergraduates completed a questionnaire containing items regarding personal norms about helping behavior at the start and end of a semester. Two months later, after they completed the questionnaire a second time, the students received a request asking that they volunteer a few hours a week to read to blind children. The results of the study showed that the more consistent an individual's normative structure was between the two time periods, the greater the relationship was between personal norms for helping and agreement to help. These results suggest that stable, consistent norms are predictive of the actual occurrence of helping behavior.

Although we have been discussing general helping norms, it is possible to conceptualize more specifically the norms that underlie helping behavior. These include norms of social responsibility, norms of equity, and norms of reciprocity. While all provide a reasonable explanation of helping behavior, each offers a different perspective on the phenomenon.

Norms of Social Responsibility: The Good Citizen Model

The most frequently invoked model of helping behavior based on normative considerations involves the **norm of social responsibility.** Basically, this norm suggests that there is an expectation that people will respond to the legitimate needs of others who are dependent upon them. Red Cross posters that say "be a good neighbor" to attract blood donors are using the norm of social responsibility to enhance the probability of helping behavior (Berkowitz, 1972).

One of the major factors that influences whether the norm of social responsibility will lead to helping behavior regards the potential helper's perception about the degree of dependency of the needy individual. In an experiment confirming this relationship (Berkowitz & Daniels, 1963), a subject was told that he would be acting as a "supervisor" to another student, who was called a "worker," in the construction of paper boxes. The two were separated and communicated with each other by notes, which were actually controlled by the experimenter. In these conditions, the dependency of the supervisor and the performance of the worker were stressed.

For instance, in the condition of highest dependency, the worker was told that the supervisor could win a prize if enough boxes were put together. Even though there was no social relationship between supervisor and worker—not only did they not know each other, but the worker was told that the supervisor would not find out how productive he or

TABLE 7-1 Examples of the Measurement of Personal Norms

Norms can be measured by finding the degree of agreement with a particular statement. Some statements (such as statement 2) elicit wide agreement; these would be considered widely held norms.

RESPONSE CATEGORIES AND DISTRIBUTIONS

Question	Obligation Not to Donate -1	No Obligation Either Way 0	1	2	3	4	Strong Obligation to Donate 5
1. If a stranger to you needed a bone marrow transplant and you were a suitable donor, would you feel a moral obligation to donate bone marrow?	12%	36%	12%	13%	8%	9%	10%
2. If a close relative of yours needed a heart transplant and you were a suitable donor, would you feel a moral obligation to arrange to donate your heart to him or her upon your death?	5%	11%	3%	7%	10%	16%	49%

Question	Strong Obligation to Refuse -3	-2	-1	No Obligation Either Way 0	1	2	Strong Obligation to Agree 3
3. How much of a moral obligation would you feel if the State Employment Service requested you to employ a delinquent youth with a police record?	11%	5%	5%	9%	13%	38%	19%

Question	Some Obligation Not to −1	No Obligation Either Way 0	Slight Obligation 1	Somewhat More Obligation 2	Strong Obligation 3
4. How much personal obligation do you feel to talk to a stranger in a movie theater?	39%	52%	7%	2%	7%
5. How much personal obligation do you feel to help other people in trouble?	.7%	4%	18%	45%	33%

Question	Obligation to Refuse −1	No Obligation Either Way 0	Weak Obligation to Agree 1	Obligation to Agree 2	Strong Obligation to Agree 3
6. If the School for the Blind asked you to read school books to blind children a few times a week in the afternoon or evening, would you feel a moral obligation?	.4%	12%	28%	41%	19%
7. If the President's Office for Voluntary Services asked you to work a few hours per week as an aide in a neighborhood day care center, would you feel a moral obligation?	6%	36%	24%	25%	9%
8. If a solicitor for the School for the Blind came to your door and requested a 1 lira contribution, would you feel a moral obligation?	.6%	2%	5%	29%	64%

Source: Schwartz (1977).

she was—it seemed the more the supervisor was dependent upon the outcomes, the more the worker produced. It seems clear from these studies that the greater dependency of one person on another's help, the more likely it is that help will be forthcoming.

On the other hand, the reason behind a person's dependence is also taken into consideration when someone is considering helping. For instance, in a field study by Piliavin, Rodin, and Piliavin (1969), a person on a subway train suddenly collapsed just after the subway car left the station for a seven and a half minute nonstop trip. Unless someone intervened, the man (a confederate, of course) would lay on the floor until the train reached the next station. There were two experimental conditions: In one, the man seemed to be drunk; he smelled of alcohol and carried a bottle of liquor. In the other, the man carried a black cane and appeared to be sober. Results of the study showed that helping was a function of the apparent cause of the collapse: subway riders spontaneously came to the aid of the confederate with the cane in 95 percent of the cases, while only 50 percent helped the "drunk." It seems, then, that people who are needy due to events beyond their own control are more apt to be the recipients of aid than those whose situations are seen as being voluntary and under their control (Berkowitz, 1969).

Another example of this phenomenon was found in an investigation of the pattern of contributions to the *New York Times' 100 Neediest Cases*. The greatest proportion of contributions went to victims who had little or no control over their problems, such as victims of child abuse or those needing medical aid. On the other hand, cases in which the victim had presumably relatively greater control—for example, instances of psychological illness and moral transgressions—received proportionally lower contributions (Bryan & Davenport, 1968).

Hence, as Irving Reimer of the American Cancer Society suggests, potential helpers are apt to consider the degree to which the victim is at fault, and the norm of social responsibility may be less salient when others' neediness is viewed as being due at least in part to their own actions. This implies that if, for example, the poor are seen as being poor because of their own laziness, they will be given less help than if they are seen as being poor by circumstances for which they are not responsible (Hatfield & Sprecher, 1983).

Norms of Equity and Reciprocity: I'll Help You so You'll Help Me

While the social responsibility norm suggests that helping behaviors ought to be motivated by feelings about the general good of others, without thought as to how or whether benefits to the helper will accrue, equity and reciprocity norms take a somewhat different view. As we shall see in greater detail in Chapter 13 on justice and the law, equity and reciprocity norms suggest that helping behavior might best be looked at in terms of justice and fairness to the needy—rather than taking a generalized view that helping the needy is an important social value (Hatfield & Sprecher, 1983; Gouldner, 1960; Greenberg & Cohen, 1982).

Basically, these norms postulate that people should be rewarded in proportion to their costs and should suffer in proportion to their transgressions. If a person is seen to be suffering disproportionately to what he or she deserves, then equity norms require that that person be helped in order to restore justice. Moreover, the norm of reciprocity suggests that prosocial behavior ought eventually to be reciprocated to the helper—and that in the future the helper ought to be able to derive some personal benefit for his or her prior helping. (The equity and reciprocity norms also suggest a related proposition, in which people tend to feel justified in hurting those who have harmed them. The ancient biblical dictum "an eye for an eye and a tooth for a tooth" exemplifies this notion.)

Instances of the operation of equity and reciprocity norms relating to helping behavior have been documented in both laboratory and field studies. The most direct evidence for the operation of reciprocity and equity comes from studies that show that helping behavior is directly related to the amount of prior helping that individuals have received (Wilke and Lanzetta, 1970). Moreover, the more help they previously received, the more help they later return to the people who had helped them. Interestingly, it also turns out that reciprocity is a general phenomenon. Not only do people reciprocate help to a specific individual who has helped them in the past, but they are more likely to give help to others in general if they have received help, although not necessarily as extensively as they tend to give to the specific person who has helped them (Staub, 1978).

It is also clear that reciprocity and equity norms affect how recipients of aid evaluate their helpers. For example, Gergen, Ellsworth, Maslach, and Seipel (1975) studied reciprocal and nonreciprocal exchanges of help in three different countries (the United States, Sweden, and Japan). In every country, subjects who were the recipients of a loan during a gambling game rated the donor more highly when the donor asked for the loan to be returned than when it was presented as a gift! Clearly, the aid recipient preferred to view the situation in terms of reciprocity and did not want to be in debt to the donor. (See Box 7-2 for further elaboration of this point.) Taking turns picking up the check when you go out to dinner frequently with friends provides another example of reciprocity norms in action.

Equity and reciprocity norms also come into play when a person inadvertently harms another person. When such harm occurs, there can be a tendency to attempt to restore equity by compensating the victim to make up, in a sense, for the earlier damage. But there are other ways in which equity can be restored in the eyes of the harm doer, many of which do not make up for the previous damage. For example, if someone trips over a rake that I left outside, I might try to blame the accident on the victim's clumsiness, thereby turning the accident into the fault of

BOX 7-2 SPOTLIGHT ON APPLICATIONS

REACTIONS OF RECIPIENTS TO RECEIVING HELP

As Sally Dogoode has her chauffeur maneuver her limousine onto the wrong side of the tracks to deliver her annual donation to the poorhouse, she finds that the recipients of her largess act downright ungrateful. "Why," she thinks to herself, "I've been giving to these poor folk for years. Why can't they just show a little gratitude?"

An answer to her question comes from an interesting line of work that indicates that although the social value of helping others typically goes unquestioned, in some cases recipients of aid may be psychologically worse off than before they received any help. For in many cases recipient self-esteem *drops* as a function of being an object of helping behavior (Fisher, Nadler, & Whitcher-Alagna, 1982; Fisher, Nadler, & DePaulo, 1983).

In one experiment, for example, subjects who had seen a companion succeed in a game but who had themselves failed to be successful experienced lower self-esteem and negative feelings when helped by the companion (Fisher & Nadler, 1976). Other work shows that when status or ability differences between donor and recipient are emphasized (with the recipient in a subordinate position), self-esteem tends to be reduced. Other factors that threaten a recipient's self-esteem include the inability of the recipient to reciprocate aid, threats to the recipient's feelings of autonomy and control over the environment, and helper motivation that is seen

as negative, such as aid that is given out of guilt.

On the other hand, a number of factors associated with the receipt of aid produce positive and nondefensive responses on the part of recipients. Among them are the following (Fisher, Nadler, & Whitcher-Alagna, 1982):

- Aid from donors with positive characteristics and motivation.
- Aid from donors who came from different social groups from that of the recipient.
- Aid that can be reciprocated by the recipient.
- Aid that does not threaten the recipient's autonomy and sense of control.
- Aid that is offered, rather than asked for.
- Aid that comes from donors with relatively low resources or expertise.

The factors cited above suggest that the most effective aid occurs when recipients feel that the donor likes and is interested in them and views them as autonomous. Moreover, it is critical for the help to be seen as eventually increasing the recipient's likelihood of future success.

These findings also suggest that the way in which help is given will have a crucial effect upon the recipient's self-esteem. In fact, it is likely that the ultimate success of the aid rests largely on the way the aid is offered and from whom it comes.

---

the victim. In this way, equity will be maintained, and no helping behavior or restitution is necessary. Also, I might fail to aid a victim by minimizing the victim's suffering and, after doing the harm, convincing myself that the victim really was not hurt very much.

Similar processes may occur when people do not cause the victim's suffering and merely act as observers. A number of studies have shown that people who fall victim to some harm—even through no fault of their own—can, in certain cases, be devalued and disliked by observers uninvolved in the situation (Lerner, 1970, 1974). For example, people who have lost a limb, been raped, or are the victims of some other sort of crime may receive hostile responses from others.

Is there life after cancer?

Some people think that even when a cancer is cured,
the patient will never live a normal life again.
The American Cancer Society knows better.
The Society offers cancer patients and their families extensive
service and rehabilitation programs with practical help and emotional
support. It helps people return to their homes and their jobs.
There *is* life after cancer. Two million people are living proof.
If you or anyone close to you needs help, call us.

American Cancer Society

This space contributed as a public service.

FIGURE 7-3
An example of an upbeat message from the American Cancer Society.

The reason? Lerner (1970) has argued that people like to feel the world is a fair and just place, but misfortunes which befall innocent victims contradict onlookers' intuitive notions that the world is just. In order to avoid feeling threatened and being forced to reject this notion, they derogate the victim instead, thereby serving their own view of the world as an equitable place. In accordance with this notion, the American Cancer Society tends to avoid emphasizing the suffering of the victims of cancer and instead stresses the fact that cancer is a curable disease, as Irving Reimer points out at the beginning of the chapter. An example of this approach is shown in the advertisement in Figure 7-3.

Normative Approaches in Perspective

Although the norms of social responsibility, equity, and reciprocity represent reasonable explanations for helping behavior, social psychologists have identified some difficulties with this type of reasoning. One problem is that norms tend to be relatively general, which limits their usefulness for predicting behavior in specific situations. Hence, while most people agree with the normative value of helping the needy, whether or not they contribute to the specific charity of, say, the Salvation Army, is not easily predicted. Second, some norms seem to be so universally ascribed to that their utility in describing particular instances of helping behavior, as well as individual differences in helping, may be limited.

Finally, one troubling finding relating to normative approaches to helping is the relatively low correlation that is typically found between helping norms and subsequent behavior.

For instance, in most studies the correlations between general helping norms and helping behavior rarely exceed .35, which is fairly modest. Although higher correlations can be found when more specific personal norms are used, the generally low correlations suggest that helping is quite sensitive to situational factors, such as those described earlier in the chapter, that enhance or inhibit the likelihood of helping. Still, norms provide at least part of the explanation of why people, even at great cost to themselves, behave in a helpful way.

EMOTIONAL RESPONSES TO HELPING: THE EFFECTS OF EMPATHY AND MOOD

One advertising technique sometimes used to increase gift giving to a charity is to employ a sad-looking, pathetic victim whose plight is described in such heart-wrenching detail that readers begin to feel the anguish and heartache of the victim themselves. The reasoning behind such advertising is that an emotional response is evoked, thereby increasing the reader's generosity.

Do such tactics work? The answer appears to be affirmative, for social psychologists have found that the keener a person's experience of another's neediness, the greater the likelihood of that person's providing aid. In addition, research shows that emotional states affect helping behavior in another way: the better the mood a person is in prior to being exposed to the victim, the more likely helping will occur. We examine findings relating to both kinds of situational factors below.

Empathy Approaches to Helping: Feelings for the Victim

An important determinant of helping behavior is the degree of empathy between a helper and a recipient of aid. **Empathy** occurs when someone experiences the emotions of another person. The basic notion is that helping behavior can be motivated by people's observation of the distress of a victim, because observers begin to put themselves in the place of the victim, feeling as if it were they who were suffering (Toi & Batson, 1982). In addition, some theories of empathy suggest that helping behavior may be caused by the anticipation of the victim's well-being and happiness following the termination of distress.

A fair amount of evidence indicates that increased empathy between a person and a victim is related to increased helping behavior. For example, Krebs (1975) had subjects observe a person similar or dissimilar to themselves receiving rewards or punishment while playing a roulette game. When the person was described as being similar—which should have led to greater empathy—subjects reacted to the observed experiences of the person more strongly on a number of physiological measures, including respiration and heart rate. Subjects also said they identified more with the similar model and felt worse about the model's punishment. Most importantly, when the subjects had to choose between helping themselves at a cost to the performer or helping the performer at a cost to themselves, subjects who had showed the greatest empathy earlier showed the most helping behavior toward the performer.

It seems, then, that feeling empathy for a victim will enhance probabilities of helping. But the exact mechanism by which empathy causes helping is not entirely understood (Rushton, 1980). When faced with a situation requiring help, an individual may not only experience the victim's emotions (empathy), but may also feel sorry for the victim, leading to a sympathetic reaction. It may be that the sympathetic reaction activates personal norms regarding appropriate helping behavior—as opposed to the empathy alone causing the helping. Still another explanation is viable: both empathy and personal norms may jointly explain instances of helping behavior.

Moods and Helping Behavior

A Good Mood Facilitates Helping

A Good Mood Facilitates Helping   Suppose your English professor has just returned a composition of yours which he had given a grade of A. As you walk out of the classroom building after class, feeling elated with your success, you notice that someone has dropped an expensively wrapped package on the ground. Would your glow of success lead you to rush past the package as you look for some friends with whom to celebrate, or would your happiness make you more likely to stop and try to find the owner of the package?

The results of a good number of studies suggest that you would be more likely to stop and help if you were in a good mood. Quite consistently, research indicates that people who are in a good mood are more likely to help than those who are in a neutral or negative mood (Rosenhan, Moore, & Underwood, 1976). And the magnitude of the experience which puts an individual in a good mood need not be great. For example, in one study subjects who found a dime in a phone booth coin return slot were more helpful than subjects who found no money (Isen & Levin, 1972). In the experiment, a confederate came up beside subjects after they had left the telephone booth and dropped a pile of papers on the ground. Subjects who had found a dime were more apt to stop and help the confederate pick up the papers than those who had not found any money. Other research finds that even pleasant weather—such as a bright and sunny day—puts people in a good mood that ultimately promotes helping behavior (Cunningham, 1979).

Of course, the effects of good moods on helping do not last forever, and—because the moods themselves may be transitory—the effects may be fairly fleeting. To investigate the temporal aspects of mood on helping behavior, Isen, Clark, and Schwartz (1976) conducted a study in which a sample package of stationery was dropped off at each of the subject's homes. Subjects later received a telephone call from a confederate who pretended to have misdialed. The request for aid was direct. The caller said she had used her last change, and she asked if the subject would call the number she had intended to reach initially and deliver a message.

In comparison with subjects who had not received the sample stationery, gift recipients were considerably more likely to help. But the effect of the gift varied according to the timing of the call. Helping behavior peaked when the call came four minutes after the gift had been delivered, but after twenty minutes had elapsed, there was no difference in the helping behavior between recipients and nonrecipients. The results, then, of this and other studies suggest that the effects of mood are transitory.

Why should being in a good mood evoke greater helping behavior? One explanation is that positive experiences influence the way in which people interpret the situation to determine whether assistance may be required (the second step in the model of helping behavior presented at the start of the chapter). Positive experiences may inspire pleasant moods, which in turn affect what people are thinking about and the nature of memories evoked by the situation. In turn, their decision to help is going to be affected by these positive recollections, and so helping is more likely to occur (Isen, Shalker, Clark, and Karp, 1978).

Negative Moods and Helping   Given the consistency and clarity with which positive moods are associated with greater helping, it is reasonable to suggest that negative or unpleasant moods might be associated with *decreases* in helping. However, the evidence for this proposition is considerably less consistent than for the relationship between good moods and increased helping. Some research supports the notion that bad moods promote reductions in helping behavior. For example, in one experiment a group of subjects watched movies that were judged to be sad (*Lady Sings the Blues* and *The Sterile Cuckoo*). After the movies, subjects were asked to contribute to a charity, and the results showed that they were less apt to donate than subjects in a control group who had seen a double feature judged to be neutral in character (Underwood, Berenson, Berenson, Cheng, Wilson, Kulik, Moore, & Wenzel, 1977).

On the other hand, other research contradicts the notion that helping is decreased when an individual is in a bad mood (e.g., Cialdini, Darby, & Vincent, 1973). One reconciliation of these conflicting findings has been suggested by Thompson, Cowan, and Rosenhan (1980). They propose that the nature of the relationship between helping and negative moods depends on whether people's attention is focused on themselves or on other individuals. When attention is focused on themselves (through failure due to their own lack of ability, or reflection on some past misfortune that befell them), negative moods are likely to produce less helping. On the other hand, when their attention is focused on the

TABLE 7-2   Measures of Helping Behavior
Subjects whose attention was focused on the victim helped to a greater extent than either control subjects or those whose attention was focused inward.

	Attention Focused on Other	Attention Focused on Self	Control
Percentage of subjects helping	83%	25%	25%
Mean time spent helping (in seconds)	657.3	254.3	244.6

Source: Adapted from Thompson, Cowan, & Rosenhan (1980).

problems of someone else (who may have failed or made a mistake, or who is experiencing some problem), the negative mood that is evoked may bring about increased helping behavior.

To test this formulation, subjects were asked to imagine that a close friend was terminally ill. In one condition, they were asked to pay attention to their own reactions; in the other, they were told to concentrate on the feelings of their dying friend. They then heard a graphic description of the course of the friend's disease, leading to an early and tragic death. Following these procedures subjects were given, as a measure of altruism, the opportunity to answer a set of 200 multiple-choice items anonymously, which they were told could help a graduate student in another department who was conducting a study.

The results were supportive of the hypothesis. As shown in Table 7-2, subjects whose attention had been focused on their sick friends were considerably more likely to help than either those whose attention had been focused on themselves or those in a control group who had heard a neutral scenario. The mean time spent answering the multiple-choice items was also significantly greater when attention was focused on the victim. It appears, then, in some instances that negative moods may actually increase altruism—at least in cases when the situation prompts an individual to focus attention on the plight of a needy person. Moreover, other research shows that those in a bad mood will be apt to help if the helping is easy to carry out and potentially of large benefit (Weyant, 1978), if they are responsible themselves for being in their bad mood (Rogers, Miller, Mayer, & Duvall, 1982), or if they think helping will relieve their bad mood (Manucia, Baumann, & Cialdini, 1984).

PERSONALITY CHARACTERISTICS AND HELPFUL BEHAVIOR: ARE THERE CONSISTENT GOOD SAMARITANS?

By definition, moods are fleeting and transitory, and as we have seen, the effects of mood fluctuations do not have a very lasting impact on people's helping behavior. We turn now to the opposite side of the coin by discussing whether there are long-term, enduring personality characteristics and individual differences that predict helping behavior. Basically, the question is whether or not certain traits or types of personalities are related to altruistic behavior consistently across different situations.

One approach used to answer this question is to study the lives of people who have displayed notable acts of altruism or helping behavior. One example is a study by London (1970), who interviewed people who had participated in an underground system for helping Jews escape from Nazi Germany. It turned out that there were a few consistencies in the backgrounds of these people (known as rescuers): they had a strong conscious identification with the moral values of their parents and a sense of adventurousness. But the specific situation in which they found themselves also influenced their altruism. They tended to be relatively marginal members of their community and not part of a cohesive, central social unit. Moreover, their initial decision to help was typically based on the desire to aid a specific individual with whom they were acquainted rather than an abstract group of potential victims, and it was only later that they became actively involved in helping increasing numbers. Thus, while certain traits did relate consistently to helping, these helpful tendencies were displayed only under specific sorts of situations.

Much of the work on helping behavior and personality traits has yielded a similar conclusion: personality factors and individual differences, without consideration of the situation, provide an insufficient explanation for helping behavior. In fact, most of the early research that sought to identify differences between helpers and nonhelpers was not successful. However, more recent work has shown that there are a few consistent individual differences. These include differences in empathy, and moral judgment sophistication.

Empathy as a Personality Characteristic

When we discussed empathy earlier, we viewed it as a situational factor which, relatively independent of the personality of the potential helper, affected whether that person ultimately helped someone else. But it also turns out that there are substantial individual differences between people's characteristic levels of empathy; some people are more empathetic than others, regardless of the situation.

It turns out that people who are characteristically high in empathy are more apt to provide help to someone experiencing distress than those low in empathy. The phenomenon goes even further: even when there is no real distress or strong emotion involved, highly empathetic people are more likely to offer help. For example, Eisenberg-Berg and Mussen (1978) found that male subjects who helped an experimenter by acting as subjects in a long, tedious experiment had significantly higher empathy scores, as measured by a written personality assessment, than nonvolunteers did.

Level 1: Preconventional morality At this level, concrete interests of the individuals are considered.
  Stage 1: Obedience and punishment orientation At this stage, people stick to rules in order to avoid punishment, and there is obedience for its own sake.
  Stage 2: Naive, hedonistic, and instrumental orientation At this stage, rules are followed only for one's own benefit. Obedience occurs because of rewards that are received.

Level 2: Conventional morality At this level, moral problems are approached as a member of society.
  Stage 3: "Good boy" morality Individuals at this stage show an interest in maintaining the respect of others and doing what is expected of them.
  Stage 4: Authority and social-order maintaining morality People at this stage conform to society's rules and consider that "right" is what society defines as right.

Level 3: Postconventional morality People at this level use moral principles which are seen as broader than any particular society.
  Stage 5: Morality of contract, individual rights, and democratically accepted law People at this stage do what is right because of a sense of obligation to laws which are agreed upon within society. They perceive that laws can be modified as a part of changes in an implicit social contract.
  Stage 6: Morality of individual principles and conscience At this final stage, a person follows laws because they are based on universal ethical principles. Laws that violate the principles are disobeyed.

FIGURE 7-4
Kohlberg's stages.

Of course, much of the evidence relating empathy and helping is correlational in nature—as is much of the work on individual differences and helping generally—and, therefore, we cannot be sure of the direction of causality. Thus, while it is tempting to assume that empathy *causes* more helping behavior, it is logically possible that engaging in a high level of helping behavior causes empathy—or that some third factor produces both empathy and helping. Therefore, correlations between individual differences and helping behavior must be interpreted with caution.

Moral Reasoning Level: Understanding Helping

The sophistication with which someone makes moral judgments is also related to that person's helping behavior. Lawrence Kohlberg has proposed a system consisting of six stages that distinguishes between different degrees of reasoning about what is and is not moral behavior. As shown in Figure 7-4, these six stages are divided into three levels. The system assumes that people proceed during development through the stages in a fixed order, but that many people never reach the highest levels of moral reasoning. To assess the level at which someone is operating, Kohlberg devised a series of moral dilemmas that person is asked to resolve. For example, consider the following scenario:

In Europe, a woman is near death from a special kind of cancer. There is one drug that the doctors think might save her. It is a form of radium that a druggist in the same town has recently discovered. The drug is expensive to make, but the druggist is charging ten times what the drug costs him to make. He paid $200 for the radium and he is charging $2000 for a small dose of the drug. The sick woman's husband, Heinz, goes to everyone he knows to borrow the money, but he can get together only about $1000. He tells the druggist that his wife is dying and asks him to sell the drug cheaper or let him pay later. The druggist says, "No, I discovered the drug and I'm going to make money from it." Heinz is desperate and considers breaking into the man's store to steal the drug for his wife.

(Kohlberg, 1969)

After reading about this situation, people are asked whether the husband should have broken into the store to steal the drug, and a carefully devised coding system assesses their level of moral reasoning based on their responses. For example, people at the lowest level of sophistication often argue that it is permissible to steal the drug since it is really only worth $200 and not $2000. In contrast, those at stage 6, the highest level, typically reason that the choice is one between the two evils of allowing someone to die and stealing, and that it is morally permissible to steal because saving a life is of greater importance to society (Kohlberg, 1969).

One assumption underlying Kohlberg's theory of moral reasoning is that moral judgments are reflective of general orientations to morality, and that such *judgments* ought to be related to actual, overt helping behavior in social situations. This assumption has received some—although by no means universal—support. In one experiment, Staub (1974) had subjects complete a series of questionnaires relating to moral values, among which was a measure based on Kohlberg's theory. Several weeks after filling out the questionnaires subjects returned, and while working on a task, heard a confederate in an adjoining room apparently moaning and complaining about stomach cramps. The confederate asked to lie down on a couch in the subject's room and eventually requested that the subject fill a prescription at a nearby drugstore that could relieve the pain, which was described as part of a chronic stomach ailment. The results of the study showed quite clearly that the subject's level of moral reasoning, as measured by Kohlberg's system, related to the degree to which he or she helped the confederate.

Although it appears from Staub's study that the level of moral reasoning behind an individual's judgments is indicative of the degree of helping behavior in which he or she engages, other evidence has been less supportive of Kohlberg's formulation. Indeed, the validity of the six-stage model of moral reasoning has not been established conclusively, with some critics questioning its universality (e.g., Gilligan, 1977). Still, there is a fair amount of evidence that people who are sophisticated in their moral judgments are apt to behave more helpfully than those with less sophistication when situations arise which require prosocial behavior.

Is There an Altruistic Personality?

We began this section by asking whether or not there were consistent Good Samaritans, people who tended to be helpful across situations.

While the evidence is not consistent and the question remains controversial, it does appear that there is some relationship between certain personality characteristics and the degree to which a person engages in prosocial behavior. Still, people who hold such personality characteristics are not universally helpful across all situations, and most social psychologists hold that situational factors are more predictive of helping behavior than personality variables. As was discussed earlier, the nature of a particular situation has an important effect on whether people in general choose to intervene, and it is unlikely that any one trait or set of traits will result in unvarying altruism.

LEARNING—AND TEACHING—HELPING BEHAVIORS

Throughout this chapter, we have been discussing the factors that lead people to behave in a prosocial manner. Although we described both situational variables and personality characteristics, one crucial area remains to be examined: how do people learn to be altruistic, and how can a society promote prosocial behavior? In this final section of the chapter, we will discuss some of the processes involved in learning prosocial behavior, and suggest some specific applications from the social psychological theory and research presented earlier that might be employed to increase the incidence of helping in our own society.

Reinforcement Approaches: Rewards, Punishments, and Helping

We mentioned earlier that part of the process that is related to the decision to help includes an assessment of the rewards and costs involved. This assessment process is based in part on the fact that people have learned, through various socialization experiences, that there are rewards inherent in helping. At the most basic level, parents reward their children for sharing behaviors and generosity, and they punish them for acting selfishly. But, as social learning theory suggests, children also learn to be helpful by observing others' behavior, vicariously experiencing the rewards and punishments that others receive, and ultimately modeling themselves after those behaviors that have been rewarded in others (Bandura, 1977).

Initially, children's moral behavior is guided through physical intervention. For example, a 2-year-old would not be allowed to explore his infant sister's face by touching her eyes and placing his fingers in her ears; instead, a parent would rapidly try to prevent such an incident by separating the children. At older ages, however, parents would begin to employ social rewards and sanctions and to use verbal commands to bring about moral behavior.

The importance of direct reinforcements of both a verbal and a tangible nature in increasing altruistic behavior has been shown in a number of studies. An early study demonstrated that candy provided when 4-year-old children shared a marble prompted an increase in sharing behavior (Fischer, 1963). Moreover, candy was more effective than verbal approval (in the form of "that's good" or "that's nice"). But verbal reinforcement is also effective, particularly with older children. In one experiment, for instance, there was an increase in 12-year-old children's donations to charity following verbal approval (Midlarsky, Bryan, & Brickman, 1973).

Just as positive reinforcement can promote increases in helping behavior, research indicates that punishment diminishes helping behavior in both adults and children. One example of this is provided by a field experiment in which a female confederate approached people on a street in Dayton, Ohio, and asked directions. In one condition, she provided punishment when the person responded by saying, "I can't understand what you're saying. Never mind, I'll ask someone else." Further down the street, a second confederate dropped a small bag, but continued walking, pretending not to notice that the bag had been dropped. Subjects who had been "punished" were significantly less apt to provide aid to the second confederate than those who were proferred gratitude from the first confederate (Moss & Page, 1972).

Modeling and Helping

While direct rewards and punishments play an important role in teaching prosocial behavior, probably an even greater source of information comes from the behavior of others. Children, as well as adults, observe the rewards and punishments that accrue to others for their behavior, and as a general rule will be apt to model behaviors on those for which others have been rewarded, and avoid those for which others have been punished.

One area in which the effects of modeling are particularly clear is contributions to charitable causes. In both children and adults, viewing another person behaving generously will lead to increased generosity on the part of the observer. On the other hand, if a model behaves selfishly, observers tend to become more selfish themselves (e.g., Rushton, 1975; Staub, 1971).

One now-classic example of the importance of modeling in helping behavior comes from a field study by Bryan and Test (1967). In one condition, subjects driving along a busy Los Angeles highway passed by a man who had apparently stopped to help a woman with a flat tire. About one-quarter mile down the road, subjects came across another woman who appeared to have a flat tire . . . actually, of course, a confederate. The dependent measure was how many people would stop, and this figure was compared with the figures in a control condition in which subjects were not exposed to a helpful model prior to coming across the woman in need. Bryan and Test reasoned that the observation of the helpful individual would provide a model and would increase helpfulness, which is just what happened. In the no-model condition just 35 of 4000 passersby stopped, while in the model condition more

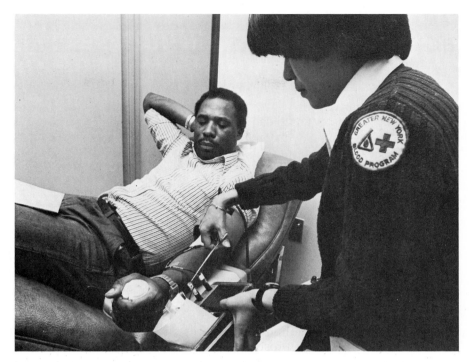

People who behave pro-
socially can act as mod-
els for others. How do you
feel when you find that
someone you know has
just given blood? (Irene
Bayer/Monkmeyer Press)

than twice as many (98) people stopped to offer aid. (We might note that under neither of the two conditions was much help offered.)

Other work tends to support these earlier findings. For instance, one experiment had female subjects who had just participated in and been paid for an experiment, ostensibly on social interaction, pass by a table surrounded by "Give Blood" posters (Rushton & Campbell, 1977). As a subject and a confederate went by, they were asked if they would be willing to give a pint of blood some time in the future. In one condition the confederate was asked first, in which case she agreed to donate. In the no-model condition, the subject was approached first. As would be expected from the Bryan and Test results, observing a model agree led to significantly greater agreement (67 percent) than not observing a model (25 percent). Of greater importance, however, were the long-term effects of viewing a model: a series of follow-up reminders were sent later to all those who had initially agreed to donate. In the no-model condition, none of the subjects actually donated, while in the model condition, one-third eventually gave blood.

The effects of modeling are so potent that the model's actions some-times do not even have to be seen for them to be effective in promoting helping behavior. This fact was shown graphically in a field experiment by Hornstein, Fisch, and Hommes (1968) in which the researchers dropped wallets in downtown New York City. Each wallet contained a letter which appeared to be from someone who had found the wallet a

BOX 7-3   SPOTLIGHT ON FIELD RESEARCH

ADDICTION TO ALTRUISM?

Could prosocial behavior be physically addictive, and thus lead to greater and greater amounts of altruism on future occasions? This surprising notion is suggested by results of a field study on habitual blood donors by Jane Piliavin and collaborators (Piliavin, Callero, & Evans, 1982; Piliavin, Evans, & Callero, 1984).

In the experiment, the researchers examined the subjective reactions of habitual blood donors at a Red Cross donation center, both before and after their donation. What they found was that the greater the number of times people had given blood before, the less negative the emotions they felt just prior to giving—and the stronger the postdonation positive emotions. Indeed, it seemed that after the third or fourth donation, the experience becomes so pleasurable that donors describe themselves as being "hooked."

Why should this be the case? An explanation comes from what has been called "opponent process theory" (Solomon, 1980). The theory suggests that when any strong emotional response occurs, an opponent process—an opposite emotional reaction—is activated which follows the initial reaction. If the initial response is negative (such as fear

and anxiety over donating), the opponent response will be positive (such as happiness and pleasure). Even more important, the theory suggests that repeated experiences tend to intensify the opponent process—even if the initial emotional reaction declines. The theory suggests, then, that the positive feelings that occur after giving blood become stronger and stronger with each consecutive donation—leading to the equivalent of an addiction to blood giving.

However, before we become concerned over finding people on neighborhood street corners staggering from one Red Cross blood donation center to another, we should note some of the limitations of these findings. For one thing, the results are essentially correlational in nature; we cannot know whether in fact it is the pleasurable affective experience that occurs subsequent to donation that actually brings about the return of the donors. Perhaps even more critical, the results shed little light on why people make the initial decision to donate—which is probably based on norms, empathy with the needy, and the other factors that we have discussed throughout the chapter. Still, the notion that helping can be addictive is intriguing.

---

first time, but had subsequently lost it before it could be returned to its owner. The nature of the letter varied according to experimental conditions. In the positive model condition, the letter said,

> I found your wallet, which I am returning. Everything is here just as I found it. I must say that it has been a great pleasure to be able to help somebody in the small things that make life nicer. It's really no problem at all and I'm glad to be able to help.

In the negative condition, the letter said:

> I found your wallet, which I am returning. Everything is here just as I found it. I must say that taking the responsibility for the wallet and having to return it has been a great inconvenience. I was quite annoyed at having to bother with the whole problem of returning it. I hope you appreciate the efforts that I have gone through.

Thus, in the positive model condition, the model viewed the experience favorably, while in the negative model condition, the model appeared to consider the experience of having to return the wallet as punishing. Social learning theory would suggest that people finding the wallet would experience the model's reinforcement or punishment vicariously, and that their subsequent helping behavior would be affected accordingly. The results convincingly confirmed this hypothesis. In the positive model condition, 51 percent of the wallets were returned, while in the negative model condition, only 25 percent were returned.

In sum, modeling is an important determinant of how people learn to behave in a prosocial manner. But modeling processes go beyond simply mimicking the behavior of others. For example, at higher levels of development, people learn to build abstract rules and principles through a process called **abstract modeling** (Bandura, 1977). Rather than always modeling other people's specific behaviors, people are capable of drawing generalized principles that underlie the behaviors they have observed. Hence, after observing a number of instances in which a model is rewarded for acting in a prosocial fashion, children can begin to learn or infer the meaning of such acts, and they are able to build and internalize their own model of behaving in an altruistic fashion.

The Reasons Modeling Works   There are a number of reasons models may affect helping behavior. As has been mentioned, one explanation is vicarious reinforcement. The rewards and punishments that we observe others receiving for particular behaviors can promote the acquisition of the same behaviors. Thus, if we view a model being rewarded for acting altruistically, we are more likely to be altruistic ourselves (Rushton & Sorrentino, 1981).

But modeling can be effective in promoting prosocial behavior for reasons other than vicarious reinforcement, because in many instances there is no apparent reward (or punishment) that accrues to the model following helping behavior. For instance, it is likely that models who engage in prosocial acts increase the range of alternate behaviors that appear to be applicable and relevant in a given situation as well as evoke norms relevant to prosocial behavior. In any particular situation, a number of possible behaviors are appropriate, but viewing a model behaving altruistically makes that particular mode of behavior more salient, and thus more likely to be imitated. Models also help to define the nature of a situation. Particularly when events are ambiguous, the emergency nature of a situation may not be apparent. By acting in a helpful manner, the model aids in clarifying that help is indeed necessary. Finally, models allow the observer to learn something about the probable consequences after help is provided (Krebs, 1970; Staub, 1978).

It should be noted that models are not always emulated. In fact, observing a model behaving in a socially inappropriate manner may lead to increases in prosocial behavior. This fact was illustrated in a study by Konečhni (1972), who had a confederate bump rudely into another confederate and knock some computer cards out of his hand. The confederate then walked away, without apologizing or attempting to pick the cards up. Subjects who viewed this incident showed a higher likelihood of helping when the confederate appeared to drop the computer cards again later. It seems as if feeling sympathy for someone who has recently been treated unjustly can lead to greater helping behavior— at least toward the ill-treated individual.

Teaching Moral Behavior: Do as I Say . . .

When parents admonish their children to do as they say (and not necessarily as they do), they are engaging in a fundamental form of moral education. People often use moral exhortations and preaching in an effort to promote altruistic and prosocial behavior in others. Indeed, this is one of the primary means by which charities operate.

Unfortunately, moral admonitions in and of themselves have not proven to be very effective in enhancing helping behavior. For example, one experiment found that compared with a model who *acted* generously, a model who *preached* generosity was significantly less effective in eliciting donations from an observer (Grusec & Skubiski, 1970). At the same time, preaching has, in some cases, been shown to be effective in producing increases in helping behavior. In one study using children (Grusec, Kuczynski, Rushton, & Simutis, 1978), two different types of moral exhortation were employed: preaching that was quite specific to the situation ("It's good to donate marbles to poor children.") or a more general admonition ("It's good to help children in any way one can."). Both the specific and the general exhortations produced greater charitable behavior, although the effects were not consistent across a number of measures that were taken.

Attribution theory may help to explain why such moral exhortations are not consistently effective. According to this explanation (Walters & Grusec, 1977), the effectiveness of preaching will depend upon the degree to which the preaching indicates that moral behavior is a sign of the target person's own moral character, instead of simply being a reaction to external pressure. To the extent that people are led to believe that moral behavior shows that they have high personal moral standards, they will be more likely to behave altruistically in the future. On the other hand, the extent to which they are led to attribute their altruistic actions to external situational pressures will make them less likely to behave helpfully in the future.

One test of this explanation was carried out by Grusec, Kuczynski, Rushton, and Simutis (1978). In the experiment, children were led to donate game winnings to a charity. They were then provided with one of two types of explanations for their behavior: they had donated for internal reasons (because they were the type of child who enjoyed helping others) or for external reasons (because they felt they were

Children who are led to believe that they are helpful because they are characteristically helpful people (an internal reason) are more likely to help in the future than those who are made to think that their past helping is due to factors external to themselves. (Suzanne Szasz/Photo Researchers)

expected to help others). Although not entirely consistent, the results showed that the children provided with the internal attribution and exposed to a generous model tended to donate more than those given an external attribution. As predicted, leading the subjects to believe that their behavior had been brought about through their own personal characteristics motivated them to be more helpful subsequently than those who felt that their earlier generous behavior could be attributed to situational factors independent of themselves.

Such research suggests that leading people to develop internal attributions for prosocial behavior may be an effective means of promoting more helping in the future. It is also consistent with techniques used by many charitable organizations, which sometimes attempt to obtain only a very small donation at first. For example, some charity campaigns have used slogans such as "even a dollar will help."

The notion behind such a strategy is twofold. First, once someone has given even a small amount, he or she is likely to experience the reinforcements that a charity dispenses to any giver: a thank-you note, a membership card, and an explanation of how useful a contribution will be to the needy. Second, the donation of even a small amount of money may be enough to shift a giver's attribution from an external one to an internal one. For both reasons, donors are more likely to increase the size of their donations later.

Formal Teaching of Morality: Values Clarification and Moral Reasoning Techniques

One of the primary reasons schools were first organized in the United States was to provide a vehicle by which moral values could be taught. Slowly, however, they have evolved to the point where formal schooling rarely contains any mechanism for the transmission of prosocial values. Two techniques have been developed, however, that have been used occasionally in school situations: values clarification and the promotion of moral reasoning. These techniques have been devised in an attempt to overcome the ineffectiveness of moral exhortations and preaching as means of promoting prosocial behavior.

The goal of values clarification is not so much to espouse a particular set of values or morality as it is to encourage an examination and understanding of the values that someone now holds. In fact, specific values are not taught; rather, it is hoped that clarifying a person's existing values will facilitate adoption of moral values (Simon, Howe, & Kirschenbaum, 1972).

The values clarification technique itself is straightforward. Individuals being trained in values clarification are given a series of exercises that are designed to make them aware of their own values and the relationship among them. For example, in one exercise, people are given an either-or forced choice question which is indicative of two opposing underlying values, such as, "Do you identify more with a Volkswagen or a Cadillac?" After a choice is made, people must explain their reasoning; through such a process, their understanding of the values behind their choice is enhanced. Presumably, values congruent with prosocial behavior will be reinforced through this process.

While values clarification promotes an awareness of one's values, it is not designed to espouse any particular point of view. An alternative technique, which is used in an attempt to motivate people to behave in a more moral fashion, is based upon Kohlberg's model of the development of moral reasoning. Using this method, moral reasoning is taught with the view that the level of moral development at which an individual is operating can be raised. The specific technique includes presenting moral dilemmas, creating cognitive conflict, and attempting to enhance people's perspective-taking abilities in order to teach them that moral issues involve many points of view that must be weighed simultaneously (Hersh, Paolitto, & Reimer, 1979).

Although both values clarification and enhancement of moral reasoning techniques have been successful in doing what they attempt to do, neither has demonstrated that they are useful in promoting more prosocial *behavior* (as opposed to prosocial values or reasoning). Indeed, there is evidence that although training may lead to a greater sense of morality, in some cases the sophistication of reasoning behind moral decisions is unaffected by such training (M. F. Kaplan, 1983). Still, given the links between attitude and behavior discussed in Chapter 4, it does seem reasonable that promoting values and reasoning regarding altruism would be at least a first step in leading people to behave in a more helpful and prosocial manner.

SUMMARY

Helping or prosocial behavior is behavior that benefits other people. For helping behavior to occur, people must first notice a person, event, or situation that may require help. Next, they must assume responsibility for taking action. Finally, they must decide on the form of assistance and implement the aid.

A number of situational factors affect whether the help will ultimately be implemented. For example, the phenomenon of diffusion of responsibility shows that, typically, the greater the number of bystanders viewing a situation in which help is required, the less personal responsibility each person will feel. Therefore, the more people present, the less likely that any one person will help. In addition, the assumption of responsibility for taking action is enhanced by the special expertise a person has or by verbal requests. The form the help will take involves an assessment of the rewards and costs, although as altruistic behavior shows, the costs of helping may sometimes far outweigh the apparent rewards.

Normative approaches to helping focus on the generalized expectations someone holds regarding appropriate behavior. Specific norms that relate to helping include norms of social responsibility, equity, and reciprocity. Although norms do appear to relate to helping behavior, the correlations are generally modest, indicating the importance of situational factors.

Feeling empathy (defined as one person's experience of the emotions of another) for a needy individual tends to result in greater helping to the needy person. Moreover, being in a good mood tends to facilitate prosocial behaviors, and—although the evidence is less consistent—being in a bad mood reduces helping behavior.

Research on personality and helping indicates that certain people are characteristically helpful and altruistic. Among the personality factors related to helping are general level of empathy and the sophistication of moral reasoning.

Reinforcement approaches to helping suggest that helping behavior is shaped through rewards and punishments—not only those an individual receives directly but also those experienced vicariously through the observation of the rewards and punishments that models receive. Social learning theory suggests that models are effective not only because of the vicarious reinforcement observers experience, but also because models can increase the range of alternate behaviors that are seen as relevant in the situation and because they can clarify the nature of the situation.

Helping behavior can also be taught through moral exhortation and preaching, although observation of actual helping behavior seems to be a more powerful technique for eliciting helping. Other techniques for promoting prosocial behavior include values clarification and enhancement of moral reasoning level. Although both techniques are effective in modifying values and moral reasoning, it has not been shown that they actually bring about increased prosocial behavior.

KEY TERMS

abstract modeling

altruism

bystander effect

diffusion of responsibility

empathy

norm

norm of equity

norm of reciprocity

norm of social responsibility

opponent process theory

personal normative structure

prosocial behavior

values clarification

vicarious

FOR FURTHER STUDY AND APPLICATION

Staub, E. (1978). *Positive social behavior and morality* (Vols. I–II). New York: Academic Press.
These two volumes represent a very comprehensive series of the work on helping behaviors. Written by an eminent researcher, the books are technical but readable. Highly recommended for anyone who holds a serious interest in the topic.

Musson, P., & Eisenberg-Berg, N. (1977). *Roots of caring, sharing, and helping: The development of prosocial behavior in children.* San Francisco: Freeman.
This book examines the development of helping behavior in children. It provides many suggestions for enhancing the development of greater prosocial behavior.

Latané, B., & Darley, J. M. (1970). *The unresponsive bystander: Why doesn't he help?* New York: Appleton Century-Crofts.
A report of the intriguing studies carried out in the late 1960s on helping and diffusion of responsibility that had a strong impact on the development of the study of helping behavior.

Fisher, J. D., Nadler, A., & DePaulo, B. M. (Eds.). (1983). *New directions in helping: Recipient reactions to aid.* New York: Academic Press.
Reviews the work on the reactions of aid recipients to being the targets of prosocial behavior. Contains chapters by some of the most experienced researchers in the field.

Nadler, A., Fisher, J. D., & DePaulo, B. M. (Eds.). (1983). *Applied research in help seeking and reactions to aid.* New York: Academic Press.
Describes current applied research relating to how people both seek out and react to aid in field settings.

Staub, E., Bar-Tal, D., Karylowski, J., & Reykowski, J. (Eds.). (1984). *Development and maintenance of prosocial behavior.* New York: Plenum.
This book provides a current overview of investigation and theory regarding a range of helping behavior, including kindness, generosity, cooperation, and other forms of prosocial behavior.

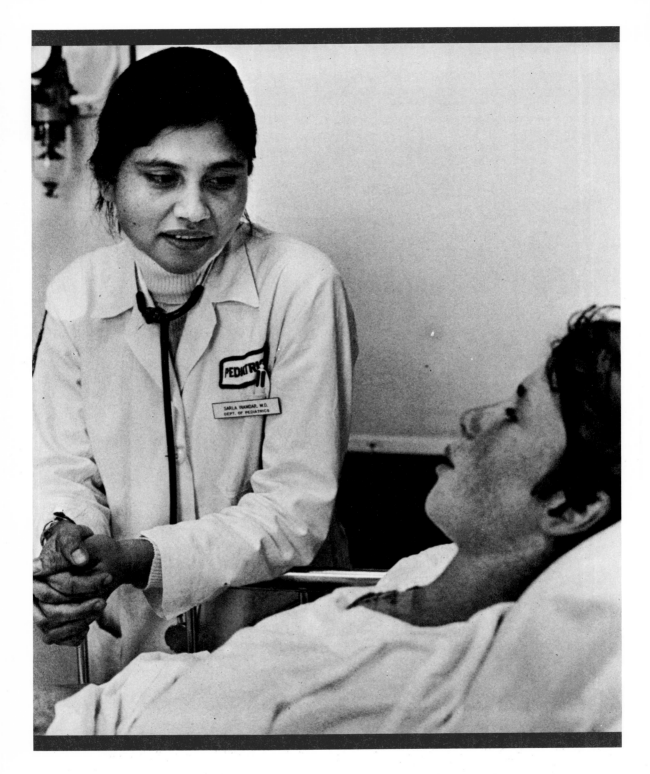

CHAPTER 8

SOCIAL PSYCHOLOGICAL INFLUENCES ON HEALTH: CARING FOR ONESELF AND OTHERS

A CONVERSATION WITH . . .

Tom Baranowski
Health Psychologist

One of the newest applications of social psychological principles and theory is within the health profession. Dr. Tom Baranowski, trained as a traditional social psychologist, now works at the University of Texas Medical School in Galveston, where he is involved in the training of physicians. We first discussed the kinds of activities he carries out on a day-to-day basis.

Q. Could you describe the kinds of things you do in your job?

A. I'm in the departments of pediatrics and preventative medicine and community health. As part of pediatrics, I teach first-year residents a course on patient education skills, focusing on something we call "regimen compliance." I also have two research projects that I direct. The major one is a heart disease prevention project, in which we are developing interventions that are useful for family groups. The second project is one on breast-feeding. We are looking at behavioral and nutritional factors in the mother's decision to breast-feed.

Q. In your class on regimen compliance, what are the kinds of things that you talk about? Are there specific things that you focus on?

A. First of all, it is not a class in the traditional sense. I work with first-year residents, and they are resistant to the kinds of educational experiences that you or I have had—they want to focus on clinical practice rather than sitting back and being lectured to.

I get all the first-year residents for one morning a week for eight weeks while they are doing their general pediatric clinic rotation. We discuss six issues that are related to patient compliance. These include identifying the patient's or the parents' agenda, determining what it is you want the patient to do, identifying how capable the patient is of carrying out the desired behavior, prioritizing what is most important for the patient to do, deciding how to educate the patient, and finally assessing whether the patients understand what has been communicated to them. As you can see, these are social psychological issues.

Q. How do the residents react to the program?

A. It varies a great deal. For many residents at this stage of their training, the major concern they have is harming a patient in some way. Given this fear, they focus on things that keep them from hurting patients. Getting patients to follow instructions is relatively low on the agenda of things the residents care about. At later stages of their residency, however, when they have greater confidence in their own abilities and have more experience in working directly with patients, they are more understanding of the importance of patient communication and find the information we provide to be valuable. After all, most physicians face life-and-death matters only infrequently; the majority of their practice revolves around colds, flu, and relatively minor aches and pains. Communicating effectively with patients can make a big difference in how successfully physicians can help their patients return to health.

Q. Do you do any direct care yourself of patients?

A. No, I've put my highest priority on research. But I have toyed with the idea of having an eating disorders clinic with a nutritionist, in which we could treat cases of obesity, bulimia, anorexia, and the like.

Q. What is it that social psychologists have to offer the field of medicine?

266

A. I think that their knowledge of communication skills, social influence processes, and a host of other basic social factors equips them to make a unique contribution to the health-care field—a contribution that is just beginning to be felt. And if social psychologists don't make that contribution, people from a variety of other behavioral service-based professions will.

OVERVIEW

As the discussion with Tom Baranowski suggests, it is only recently that social psychologists have begun to focus upon the social components of health care. In fact, a new area—known variously as the social psychology of health and illness, medical social psychology, and behavioral medicine—has developed which promises to help find solutions to one of the most critical problems facing society: the maintenance of good health. Work in this area has shown that social psychological factors such as interpersonal relationships, group membership, family and community social support, and social norms can be as important in determining a person's health as blood chemistry and metabolism. Most importantly, social psychological research has suggested new treatment approaches to ameliorate health problems and to prevent their occurrence in the first place.

In this chapter, we discuss social psychological influences on health and how people care for themselves and others. We begin by examining a specific health problem—heart disease—and discuss how it is associated with a fairly well-defined social behavior pattern. Next, we examine the social psychological nature of physician–patient relationships and how the interaction affects both the success of treatment and satisfaction with medical care. Finally, we discuss how social psychologists promote preventative health techniques, and focus on a model of health beliefs that has major implications for the way in which people care for themselves.

THE SOCIAL CAUSES OF ILLNESS: THE A'S AND B'S OF CORONARY HEART DISEASE

At the turn of the century, coronary heart disease was a relatively rare phenomenon. Now, however, coronary problems account for one-third of all deaths in Western society. How can we explain this phenomenal increase in the incidence of this health problem?

Many scientists suggest that the relatively recent high incidence of coronary heart disease can be attributed in part to changes in social factors (Chesney, Eagleston, & Rosenman, 1981; Ortega, 1983). As industrialization and the pace of life have quickened, so has the risk of

CARING AND UNCARING
BEHAVIOR: POSITIVE AND
NEGATIVE INTERACTION IN
A SOCIAL WORLD

People with so-called
Type A behaviors tend to
be tense, hard-driving,
and competitive and try to
do more than one thing at
a time—a behavior pat-
tern linked to coronary
heart disease. (Richard
Kalvar/Magnum)

succumbing to heart disease. In fact, a specific constellation of behaviors, referred to as the **Type A behavior pattern,** has been identified as
being associated with a higher risk of heart attack. Because there is no
better example of the way in which social psychological approaches to
health care have produced an impact on the understanding of medical
problems, we will consider this behavior pattern in detail.

According to the researchers who first identified the pattern, Type A
behavior is characterized primarily by "intense ambition, competitive
drive, constant preoccupation with occupational deadlines, and a sense
of time urgency" (M. Friedman & Rosenman, 1974, p. 1295). In a large,
eight-year study examining more than 3500 males, individuals who had
been identified at the start of the study as having a Type A behavior
pattern showed an incidence of heart disease twice as great as other
subjects, had twice as many fatal heart attacks, and had five times as
many recurring coronary events (Rosenman, Brand, Jenkins, Friedman,
Straus, & Wurm, 1975). Moreover, the risk due to the Type A behavior
was independent of any other factor that made people susceptible to
heart disease.

Although research has not found which of the *specific* behaviors associated with the Type A pattern is the critical link to coronary heart
disease (Matthews, 1982), the Type A behavior complex, as a whole,
has been well-defined and differentiated from traits associated with .
Type B behavior (a complex of behaviors nearly opposite those displayed by Type A personalities). As shown in Table 8-1, Type A individuals tend to speak rapidly and vigorously; they are tense; they inter-
rupt others, frequently hurrying questions along; and they are prone to
displays of hostility. Moreover, they tend to be dissatisfied with their

TABLE 8-1 Type A and Type B Behavior Patterns

Type A behaviors, taken together, have been found to be associated with higher rates of coronary heart disease than Type B behaviors.

Characteristics	Type A	Type B
Speech		
Rate	Rapid	Slow
Word production	Single-word answers: acceleration at the end of sentences	Measured: frequent pauses or breaks
Volume	Loud	Soft
Quality	Vigorous; terse; harsh	"Walter Mitty"
Intonation/inflection	Abrupt; explosive speech; key word emphasis	Monotone
Response latency	Immediate answers	Pauses before answering
Length of responses	Short and to the point	Long; rambling
Other	Word clipping; word omission; word repetition	
Behaviors		
Sighing	Frequent	Rare
Posture	Tense; on the edge of the chair	Relaxed; comfortable
General demeanor	Alert; intense	Calm; quiet attentiveness
Facial expression	Tense; hostile; grimace	Relaxed; friendly
Smile	Lateral	Broad
Laughter	Harsh	Gentle chuckle
Wrist clenching	Frequent	Rare
Responses to the interviewer		
Interrupts interviewer	Often	Rarely
Returns to previous subject when interrupted	Often	Rarely
Attempts to finish interviewer's questions	Often	Rarely
Uses humor	Rarely	Often
Hurries the interviewer ("yes, yes," "m-m," head nodding)	Often	Rarely
Competes for control of the interview	Wide variety of techniques—interruptions; verbal duets; extraneous comments; lengthy or evasive answers; questioning or correcting the interviewer	Rarely
Hostility	Often demonstrated during the interview through mechanisms such as boredom, condescension, authoritarianism, challenge	None
Typical content		
Satisfied with job	No, wants to move up	Yes
Hard-driving, ambitious	Yes, by own and others' judgments	Not particularly

(Continued)

TABLE 8-1 *(Continued)*

Characteristics	Type A	Type B
Feels a sense of time urgency	Yes	No
Impatience	Hates waiting in lines; will not wait at a restaurant; annoyed when caught behind a slow-moving vehicle	Takes delays of all kinds in stride and does not become frustrated or annoyed
Competition	Enjoys competition on the job; plays all games (even with children) to win	Does not thrive on competition and rarely engages in competitive activities
Admits to polyphasic thinking and activities	Often does or thinks two (or more) things at the same time	Rarely does or thinks two thinks at once
Hostility	In content and stylistics—argumentative responses; excessive qualifications; harsh generalizations; challenges; emotion-laden words; obscenity	Rarely present in any content

Source: Chesney, Eagleston, & Rosenman (1981).

jobs, hard-driving and ambitious, and intensely competitive, and they try to do more than one thing at a time. These behaviors stand in stark contrast to those associated with the easygoing Type B individuals who are relaxed, uncompetitive, patient, and rarely hostile.

Distinguishing A's from B's   A number of techniques have been devised to distinguish Type A and Type B individuals, including interviews and paper-and-pencil measures (e.g., Coleman, Klahr, Valentino, Ramsey, Caputo, & Winnick, 1984). Although the various measures are not always consistent among themselves (Matthews, 1982), one of the most frequently employed measures, the Jenkins Activity Survey (C. D. Jenkins, Zyzanski, & Rosenman, 1979), has good reliability and is a good predictor of coronary heart disease. The survey asks such questions as "Has your spouse or some friend ever told you that you eat too fast?" and "How would your wife (or closest friend) rate you?" to which "hard-driving and competitive" is a Type A response and "relaxed and easygoing" a Type B response. The survey enables researchers to identify self-reported behavioral differences between Type A and Type B individuals.

The differences between Type A and Type B individuals in their reactions to various situations are plentiful. For example, the sense of time urgency that Type A's experience result in their arriving early for appointments (Gastorf, 1980); they perform more poorly on tasks that require slow, methodical responses (the Type A's want to rush through the task; Glass, Snyder, & Hollis, 1974); they tend to estimate the lapse of one minute more quickly than Type B's (Burnam, Pennebaker, & Glass, 1975); and their systolic blood pressure rises more than Type B's when they are interrupted on a task (Napoli, Pardine, & Calicchia, 1984). Moreover, Type A's tend to persist at tasks even when they feel exhausted, and they work at top speed, even if there is no deadline involved (Carver, Coleman, & Glass, 1976; Yarnold & Grimm, 1982).

Research has even found that Type A individuals are more aggressive toward others than Type B individuals, at least when they are thwarted in their efforts to complete a task quickly and successfully. For instance, Carver and Glass (1978) asked subjects in a laboratory experiment to work on a puzzle. In one condition, a confederate made comments such as, "I don't know what's taking you so long; it's not that difficult" and "Hurry up or you'll never get finished," statements that clearly derogated and impeded their attempts to complete the puzzle. In the other condition, the confederate made no such comments. Subjects were then given the opportunity to administer (bogus) electric shocks to the confederate as part of a supposed teaching procedure (a frequently employed experimental technique that we will discuss in greater detail in Chapter 9).

The results of the experiment, which are displayed in Figure 8-1,

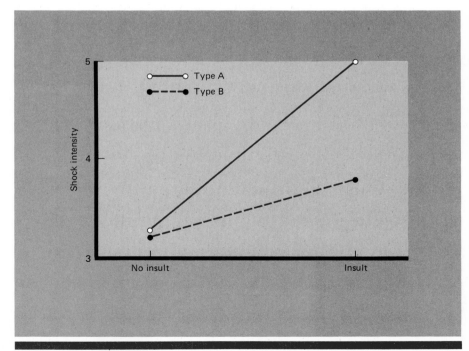

FIGURE 8-1
Aggression by Type A and Type B subjects. When not insulted, Type A's and Type B's gave the same low-level intensity shocks, but after being insulted, Type A's gave significantly higher shocks than Type B's. Source: Carver & Glass (1978).

reveal that neither Type A nor Type B individuals differed in the amount of aggression displayed toward the confederate when the confederate had made no insulting, deprecating comments. But when the confederate had challenged the subjects' sense of competence through his comments, there was a significant difference between Type A's and Type B's: Type A subjects gave significantly higher shocks than Type B subjects. Moreover, Type B subjects showed only a moderate—and, in fact, statistically nonsignificant—rise in the intensity of shocks they delivered over those given by noninstigated Type B's. Basically, then, the Type B subjects showed little overt reaction to the instigating confederate, while the Type A subjects reacted with increased aggressiveness.

We have been painting a fairly grim and unpleasant picture of Type A individuals: they are relatively hostile and aggressive, have a strong sense of time urgency, and exhibit high levels of competitiveness. Are there any redeeming qualities to such behavior? We can answer this question affirmatively, if we consider traditional success and achievement as a positive outcome, for it does appear that Type A's are more successful than Type B's (Carver & Humphries, 1982).

For example, one study that divided incoming college freshmen into Type A and B groups found that Type A's had higher grade-point averages than B's, and Type A characteristics were associated with the number of credits taken (Ovcharchyn, Johnson, & Petzel, 1980). Other research has shown that Type A college students earn more honors and plan to attend graduate school more frequently (Glass, 1977), and there is a significant relationship between Type A and occupational and socioeconomic status (Waldron, Zyzanski, Shekelle, Jenkens, & Tannenbaum, 1977).

But even in the area of success, being a Type A may have its drawbacks. Some researchers have argued that the driven characteristics of Type A individuals may result in output that, although quantitatively large, is of questionable quality (Friedman & Rosenman, 1974). Specifically, it is possible that the urgency that underlies their efforts may result in stereotyped, uncreative products. Moreover, it has also been found that Type A's prefer to work alone (Gastorf, Suls, & Sanders, 1980), and this voluntary isolation may reduce the positive influences and ideas that coworkers would bring. There are a number of reasons, then, why Type A's might want to behave more like Type B's (see Box 8-1).

THE TREATMENT AND MANAGEMENT OF ILLNESS: THE PHYSICIAN–PATIENT RELATIONSHIP

More than any other person, the physician has access to some of the most intimate aspects of our lives: our bodies (both inside and out) and details about our lifestyles. This unidirectional intimacy (how much do

BOX 8-1 SPOTLIGHT ON APPLICATION

CAN A'S BE B'S? CHANGING BEHAVIORAL PATTERNS

Although the relationship between Type A characteristics—taken as a whole—and heart problems is well established, a primary question remains to be resolved: whether or not changes in Type A behavior will result in a reduction of cardiac risk. There is some evidence—although by no means definitive—that the Type A behavioral pattern leads to an increase in cardiovascular responsiveness and sensitivity to stimulation and stress, and that it is this heightened responsiveness that leads to damage of the cardiovascular system—ultimately leading to heart disease (Carver & Humphries, 1982). If this sequence is correct, a reduction in the Type A individual's reactions to stress will ultimately reduce the possibility of heart damage. Such a reduction in stress reactions conceivably could occur either by changing people's perceptions of stressful stimuli or by attempting to decrease their physiological reaction to the stimuli.

The most extensive attempt to modify Type A behavioral patterns has been carried out in the San Francisco Bay area, where 600 men who have suffered heart attacks are participating in an ongoing study (Rosenman & Friedman, 1977; Friedman et al., 1984). The treatment consists of a variety of approaches which are intended to modify both the perception of stress and the reaction to stress.

Subjects have been taught to observe their own behavior, to change and manage their environment, and to attempt to cognitively restructure their thinking about once-stressful occurrences, making them neutral by interpreting them in ways that do not evoke stress. Thus, instead of fuming about the time they are wasting in a traffic jam, Type A's ought to think about the opportunity to contemplate their day's activities. They also have been told to adopt new, relaxing hobbies that are entirely separate from their careers, and they are learning procedures that will allow them to modify their physiological reactions through such techniques as deep muscle relaxation and learning to slow down physical activity.

A control group, consisting of 300 additional heart attack victims, is receiving standard medical treatment and information about heart attacks. Early results are encouraging, showing that techniques which specifically reduce Type A behaviors may be more effective than traditional medical practices. (Moreover, these techniques may be beneficial in reducing *all* medical problems—not just coronary heart disease.)

Still, there is no definitive evidence to date showing that reductions in Type A characteristics result invariably in a decrease in heart disease risk. Moreover, it is unclear just which aspect of Type A behavior is the crucial one, or whether it is a complex of several behaviors, all part of the Type A pattern, that is associated with the increased risk. In other words, we still do not know *specifically* what it is about Type A behaviors that leads to heart problems, and until we do, programs that attempt to decrease the risk must use relatively expensive and time-consuming procedures, modifying essentially *all* manifestations of the Type A pattern. Moreover, programs which emphasize the necessity of decreasing Type A behaviors run counter to the cultural norms of Western society, which emphasize the importance of work and achievement (Carver & Humphries, 1982). For these reasons, treatment programs that are designed to alter Type A behaviors may be facing an uphill battle.

Despite the difficulty in implementing treatment programs to reduce the Type A behavior pattern, such attempts illustrate quite clearly the role that social psychologists can play in the treatment of health problems.

most of us know about our physicians' day-to-day lives, let alone what they look like without their clothes?) may lead to a degree of emotional dependence upon the physician that is atypical of relationships with most other people with whom we interact. This dependency is compounded by the fact that illness serves to increase people's general feelings of neediness. Thus, perhaps more than in any other relationship, the physician–patient relationship can be laden with emotion.

Despite the clear importance of the social and emotional relationship between physician and patient, the physician and patient roles have typically been viewed in the context of the technical and physical aspects of their partnership. Although this is gradually changing—as our interview with Tom Baranowski points up—medical training today still emphasizes the physical and biological scientific and technological aspects of medicine and patient care, with relatively less concern for what a famous English physician, Sir William Osler, advised: "The practice of medicine is an art, not a trade; a calling, not a business; a calling in which your heart will be exercised equally with your head" (Osler, 1904, cited in H. S. Friedman & Di Matteo, 1979).

There is increasing evidence that the social and emotional aspects of physician–patient relationships not only affect the mutual interpersonal attraction felt between the two but also can result in more effective and satisfying medical care. Di Matteo and Friedman (1982) suggest that the nature of relationships has an effect on at least three critical areas: patient cooperation, treatment outcomes, and patient satisfaction.

Patient Cooperation

Often an individual will announce complete agreement with a physician's suggestion to stop smoking or to go on a strict diet and, soon after leaving the physician's office, light up a cigarette or stop for an ice cream cone. In fact, compliance with physicians' orders is a major problem in contemporary medical care, with estimates of noncompliance running from 4 to 92 percent of all patients. According to one expert (Stone, 1979), about one-third to one-half of all patients do not completely follow the medical regimens prescribed for them by their physicians. Although courses for physicians on increasing patient compliance (such as the one described by Tom Baranowski) are increasing in medical schools, the issue remains a serious one, since most physicians have had no formal training in how to deal with the problem.

Several studies have shown that the way in which the physician presents information to the patient has a clear impact on patient compliance (Ley, 1982). For example, written communications may be vague and lead to poor compliance. When a physician indicates that a tablet should be "taken with meals," the instructions may be translated in a variety of ways: before, during, or after meals.

Patient cooperation with instructions that are delivered verbally may be even lower, with some 60 percent of the patients in one study dis-

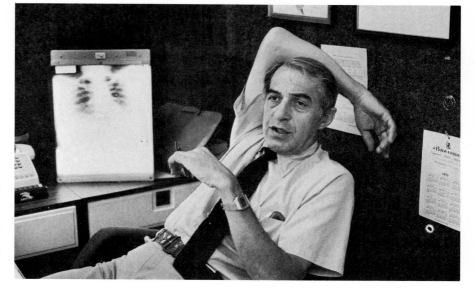

The manner in which physicians give information to their patients affects the way the patients comprehend and cooperate with treatment procedures. (John Mannaras/ Woodfin Camp)

playing errors in their understanding of how they should take medicine (Boyd, Covington, Stanaszek, & Coussons, 1974). Obviously, such misunderstanding will lead to lower compliance. And, as would be expected, greater clarity in instructions leads to higher compliance: Patients who can recall their physicians' instructions fully are more compliant than those who have errors in recall (Svarstad, 1976).

The *way* in which information is imparted may have an equally important effect upon patient cooperation. Physicians who are perceived as being aloof, antagonistic, or insensitive to a patient's needs are apt to produce lower rates of compliance than physicians who are viewed as being interested in the patient's psychological well-being as well as his or her medical health (M. S. Davis, 1968).

The reason that physicians are most successful in promoting compliance when they are interpersonally attractive, likable, and interested in the patient may be that such positive physician behavior tends to increase patients' feelings of choice and control over the situation. In turn, they come to feel that their behavior is being guided by their own self-motivated, internalized goals, as opposed to being guided by the controlling power of the physician. In fact, procedures to increase patient cooperation based upon this premise have been suggested by Rodin and Janis (1979). They include the following:

• Encouraging moderate patient self-disclosure
• Giving positive feedback, acceptance, understanding
• Making specific recommendations for the patient to carry out
• Eliciting patient commitment to the recommendations

- Communicating a sense that the patient has control over the situation and a sense of personal responsibility

Treatment Outcomes

Given that patient cooperation is influenced by the nature of the physician–patient relationship, it seems reasonable that the success of treatment will also be affected—and this does seem to be the case. A positive perception of physicians' affective behavior is related to confidence in the physicians' technical expertise, which leads to a reduction in patient fear and anxiety (Ben-Sira, 1976). For example, since patients' levels of fear and anxiety prior to surgery affect their recovery after the operation (Langer, Janis, & Wolfer, 1975), the amount of esteem in which a physician is held may have important postoperative consequences.

One study found that there was an increase in patients who died suddenly of heart attacks during or just after ward rounds in which a group of physicians hold a formal, impersonal discussion of a patient's condition within earshot (Jarvinen, 1955). The author suggests that the increase may be linked to the stress brought on by the rounds themselves, since it is possible that the anxiety and fear produced by the impersonal discussion led to the fatal heart attack.

Patient Satisfaction

When patients evaluate the quality of medical care they receive, the nature of the physician–patient relationship is crucial in determining the degree of satisfaction they express. This point was made clear in a large-scale study that examined the degree of satisfaction with medical care in a sample of 1000 families (Koos, 1955). A large majority of the families held that difficulty in the physician–patient relationship was their largest source of dissatisfaction with their medical care. More recent work confirms this finding; the way in which the physician and patient interact with one another has one of the largest effects on patient satisfaction (Doyle & Ware, 1977).

It is clear, then, that patient satisfaction with medical care depends largely on the kind of physician–patient relationship that exists. But up to now we have only considered the relationship from the point of view of the *patient*. Are the *physicians'* attitudes and behavior affected by the nature of the relationship? We turn to this question next.

PHYSICIANS AND PATIENTS: THE OTHER SIDE OF THE COIN

Consider the following:

Imagine that you are a young physician who has just completed a training program in primary care (general practice medicine). You

have taken a position in a city clinic, and this is your first week on
the job. Awaiting your next patient, you sit in a small examining room
that contains a chair, a stool, an examining table, and an instrument
table. Remember that there are 1304 formal disease entities noted in
a standard compilation (S. B. Berkowitz, 1967). Your challenge is to
decide whether the incoming patient has one or more of these diseases
or no medical problem whatsoever. You have twenty minutes (Mentzer
& Snyder, 1982, p. 161).

If we consider the problem facing the physician in purely medical
terms, we are oversimplifying the situation considerably, for the physician's quest for knowledge is also very much a social psychological one.
Just as patient cooperativeness and satisfaction are related to the way
in which the physician is perceived, the success of the physician depends at least partially on his or her social skills.

Self-disclosure: Getting Information from the Patient

In order to diagnose a patient's disease successfully, the physician must
first determine the symptoms the patient is experiencing and, perhaps
of equal importance, the symptoms the patient is *not* experiencing. To
do this, the physician must elicit full responses to a series of questions
that clarify what the complaint is and, ultimately, its source—not an easy
task, since the physician is faced with more than 1300 possible problems. And these are just the purely *physical* problems; problems of a
mental health nature are a further complicating factor (as we discuss in
Box 8-2).

Social psychological factors play an important part in determining the
success of this diagnostic quest. For example, the way in which patients
perceive and disclose their problems may be affected by their notion of
the role that the "good patient" ought to play (analogous to the role of
the "good subject" that we discussed in Chapter 1 relating to experimenter–subject interaction). For instance, S. E. Taylor (1979, 1982) has
suggested that patients are intimidated by the high social prestige and
power physicians have, may be reluctant to volunteer information
deemed trivial, or hesitate to admit to pain and discomfort that are
viewed as being unimportant.

Another deterrent to patient self-disclosure is the overly optimistic
view that many patients, particularly those of lower socioeconomic status, hold about their physicians' diagnostic prowess (Leigh & Reiser,
1980; Mentzer & Snyder, 1982). Some patients are so confident of their
physician's skill and power, they feel that their problems will be revealed through a physical examination analogous to the way a mechanic
can fix a motor simply by looking at it. If the patient holds such a view,
self-disclosure may seem irrelevant.

Laboratory research does suggest some ways in which self-disclosure
can be elicited. Jourard (1964) suggests that self-disclosure may, under

BOX 8-2   SPOTLIGHT ON RESEARCH

MENTAL HEALTH IS IN THE EYES OF THE BEHOLDER

When an individual is in poor health, there are usually clear physiological indicants of a problem: changes in the blood, muscles, blood vessels, cell structures—all things that are objectively discernible and upon which there is universal agreement that the person has a problem that requires a cure. But when we discuss mental health, it is far less obvious what should be considered healthy or unhealthy behavior. Indeed, what constitutes good mental health clearly requires reference to factors of a social psychological nature. Consider, for example, the following:

> When what hugs stopping earth than silent is
> more silent than more than much more is or
> total sun oceaning than any this
> tear jumping from each most least eye of a star
> and without was if minus and shall be
> immeasurable happenless unnow
> shuts more than open could that every tree
> or than all life more death begins to grow
> end's ending then these dolls of joy and grief
> these recent memories of future dream
> these perhaps who have lost their shadows if
> which did not do the losing spectres mime

Are these the ramblings of a madman? Or does the excerpt presented above simply indicate the depth of vision and clarity of thought of a highly sensitive, artistic individual?

In fact, the sample is taken from a poem ("#16") by the noted contemporary poet, E. E. Cummings (1981, p. 502). But the excerpt illustrates the difficulty that sometimes occurs in distinguishing normal from abnormal and how, in many respects, our view of the appropriateness of behavior is based on what is socially acceptable at a given point and in a given context.

The fragility of our definition of what constitutes abnormal behavior and its dependence on the situation in which behavior is viewed are shown by the results of a fascinating study by David Rosenhan (1973). Rosenhan and seven of his colleagues had themselves admitted to different mental hospitals across the United States. In every case, they voiced the same complaints: "I hear voices, unclear voices. I think they say 'empty,' 'hollow,' 'thud.' " Aside from this (and changing their real names and occupations), every other response to staff queries and psychological tests was truthful, and as soon as they entered the hospital, they said they no longer heard voices. Thus, each "patient" acted in a typically normal fashion.

Each patient was quickly diagnosed as suffering from a psychosis, with the majority being labeled schizophrenic. When released, most were still said to be schizophrenic, but in temporary remission—with the implication being that it could return at any time. The average time of commitment was nineteen days, and most releases occurred only after the intervention of someone outside the mental institution.

The fact that in *not one case* was the pseudopatient detected by hospital staff is disturbing, suggesting as it does the difficulties that even mental health professionals may have in distinguishing normal from abnormal behavior.

---

certain circumstances, be reciprocated, and physicians might try to present some degree of information about themselves to build rapport. Increasing the amount of time spent with the patient may also be enough to allow greater self-disclosure, as will nonverbal displays of warmth (Mentzer & Snyder, 1982). Even such mundane interventions as modifications in the environment may lead to changes in disclosure rate: A. L. Chaiken, Derlega, and Miller (1976) found that cozy surroundings are apt to elicit more self-disclosure than sterile and harshly lit environments (which are typical of medical examining rooms).

Patient Self-awareness

Another factor that enters into physician–patient relationships that may reduce the physician's ability to diagnose the true problem can be inferred from a theory of self-awareness proposed by Duval and Wicklund (1972; Wicklund, 1975). The theory suggests that certain situations bring about a state called **objective self-awareness,** in which an individual becomes more conscious of himself or herself and focuses on the discrepancies that may exist between the ideal self and the actual self. Typically, being in a state of objective self-awareness is a negative experience; people tend to feel uncomfortable when their self-consciousness is raised because it leads to heightened awareness of their shortcomings.

In the case of a physician–patient interchange, a state of objective self-awareness is a logical outcome of a process in which the physician is probing the patient for information of the most intimate sort. Indeed, the patient is likely to view himself or herself as an object that has some flaw (i.e., the illness or symptoms). This leads to an intensification of the discrepancy between the ideal and actual self which in turn can lead to an even greater decrease in perceived well-being (Mentzer & Snyder, 1982).

According to Wicklund (1975), there are two possible reactions to a state of objective awareness. First—and most likely—people will try to avoid the stimulus that brought about the self-consciousness. In the present case, this means that the patient may not respond effectively to the physician's questions because he or she is engaged in an active attempt to avoid the issue. However, a second strategy for dealing with a state of self-awareness is also possible: people may attempt to decrease the discrepancy between their actual and ideal selves. In the case of illness, this suggests that they will experience increased motivation to rid themselves of their diseased state, since this will bring them closer to their ideal selves. In turn, this motivation ought to make them particularly responsive to the information-gathering attempts of the physician if they believe that the result will be an increased likelihood of being cured.

The theory of objective self-awareness suggests that physicians ought to follow a two-pronged strategy in obtaining information from patients. First, the physician should stress facts that would reduce negative comparisons between ideal and actual self. For example, the fact that illness is part of most people's lives and is unrelated to issues of a person's worth may be helpful in avoiding ideal–real-self comparisons. Second, the physician should clarify for patients the importance of a precise and clear description of the symptoms for accurate diagnosis and try to make them feel that they are an intrinsic part of the diagnostic procedures (which, in fact, patients are). Such a strategy may capitalize upon patient attempts to decrease the discrepancy that may be perceived between their actual and ideal selves.

Keeping the Patient in the Dark: The MUM Effect

No one, including physicians, likes to deliver bad news—a phenomenon perhaps stemming from long ago when messengers who brought news of defeat in battle to Roman emperors were routinely killed by the unhappy recipients. Many surveys have shown that physicians generally do not want to tell dying patients that their illness is terminal and that the most anxiety-producing experience for first-year medical students is discussing fatal illness with patients who know that they are dying (Feifel, 1963; Saul & Kass, 1969).

The reluctance of people in general to transmit bad news has been labeled the **MUM effect** by Tesser and Rosen (1975), who have investigated the phenomenon extensively in laboratory experiments. They suggest that conveyers of information assume that recipients want to be told good news, not bad, and that the tendency to withhold information is rooted primarily in the desire to "protect" the recipient from unpleasant news. There may be other reasons for the MUM effect: people may feel guilty or anticipate feeling bad themselves when forced to deliver bad news, or they may fear that they themselves will be evaluated negatively by the recipient of bad news. Whatever the reason, there is strong experimental and laboratory support for the phenomenon.

If patients desired and benefited from being protected from bad news, the MUM effect would have a positive, or at worst a neutral, effect on physician–patient relationships. However, there is some evidence to the contrary: patients typically express a desire to hear the true state of their conditions, and some research even suggests that their health may benefit from information about the nature of their illness and its expected course.

Surveys of the general public show that some 80 percent of the public want to be informed of the nature of their illnesses, even if they are fatal (Blumenfield, Levy, & Kaufman, 1978, 1979). Moreover, reviews of procedures in which patients are given information about their upcoming surgery, the expected course of events, and the nature and degree of postsurgery pain and possible complications show that patients tend to recuperate more quickly and show less reliance on drugs for pain relief than when the patients have only limited knowledge.

An example of the importance of providing patients with information about anticipated painful stimuli comes from a study by Johnson and Leventhal (1974). In the field experiment, forty-eight hospitalized patients were given varying amounts and kinds of information about an upcoming endoscopic examination, an unpleasant and noxious procedure in which a tube is slowly snaked down a patient's throat to view the inside of the gastrointestinal system. Typically, physicians describe only the most salient parts of the process and tell patients basically that it will be tolerable but not particularly pleasant, omitting most of the details.

Johnson and Leventhal (1974) prepared two basic messages. One gave specific information about the sensory aspects of the procedure, such as gagging when the patient's throat was swabbed with anesthetic, the stick of a needle, and the feeling of fullness that would occur when air was pumped into the patient's stomach. Another message contained behavioral instructions which taught the subject to carry out various activities to reduce gagging and specific instructions on what to do to allow the tube to be inserted slowly and deliberately (such as rapid mouth breathing and panting). Using these two types of messages, they worked with four experimental groups: one group received both messages, one received just the sensory message, one just the behavioral message, and one received no message at all.

The results of the experiment showed many differences according to the nature of the information received, with the most effective information being a combination of the two types of messages. Among the most important reactions (shown in Table 8-2) was a reduction in gagging because of an increase in the deliberateness and control of the insertion of the tube (as measured by increased insertion time) in the combined message condition. Other data indicate that while the sensory information by itself tended to reduce signs of emotionality and the behavioral instruction alone reduced the intensity of the fear indicants, the most effective results came from a combination of the two types of messages.

The Johnson and Leventhal (1974) results suggest that physicians ought to provide their patients with precise information regarding what the treatment entails, what they should expect in terms of sensory experiences, and what they can do themselves to deal with their symptoms. This does not mean that patients should invariably be told every detail of their illnesses; in some cases, for instance, patients actively resist such information and forcing such knowledge on them may be detrimental (R. M. Kaplan, 1982; S. M. Miller & Mangan, 1983). More-

TABLE 8-2   Reactions of Patients to Different Types of Information
The combination of sensory description and behavioral instruction resulted in the most effective patient reactions. Note that lower amounts of gagging and longer insertion times (because of increased physician control over the procedure) are preferable.

	CONDITION			
	Control—No Information	Sensory Description Alone	Behavioral Instruction Alone	Combined Sensory Description and Behavioral Instruction
Occurrence of gagging	90%	46.2%	51.1%	36.4%
Time (in seconds) to pass tube into stomach	28.0	26.5	29.6	43.0

Source: Johnson & Leventhal (1974).

BOX 8-3   SPOTLIGHT ON THEORY

ON THE SELF-SERVING FUNCTION OF PATIENT COMPLAINTS

Most of us know at least one hypochondriac, someone who is preoccupied with health and bodily functions and who seems to fall prey to every illness that he or she has heard or read about. A study by Smith, Snyder, and Perkins (1983) suggests that the complaints and illnesses of hypochondriacs, while being an annoyance to those who must fend off their litany of complaints, may in fact serve an important self-protective function for such people.

Using theory based on Jones and Berglas's (1978) model of self-handicapping strategies, which we discussed in Chapter 2, the researchers reasoned that physical symptoms might be employed by hypochondriacs as a self-handicapping device by which the hypochondriac is provided with an excuse for potential failure. Because illness is generally thought of as being out of the control of the person suffering from it, the sick individual avoids being blamed for his or her poor performance. Moreover, if the sick person succeeds, the success is that much more impressive, since it occurred in spite of the handicap. Thus, no matter what happens, the self-esteem of the hypochondriac is preserved.

To test this reasoning, subjects who had previously been identified as hypochondriacs on a written personality measure were randomly assigned to one of three conditions in an experiment. In one condition, the subjects were told that they would take a test designed to measure their "social intelligence," which ostensibly was related to social attractiveness, interpersonal adjustment, job adjustment, and a host of other factors all related to general social desirability. It was assumed that self-handicapping strategies would be most likely to be employed in this condition. The second condition was identical, except that subjects were given the additional information that their performance on the test was *unlikely* to be affected by such "irrelevant" factors as physical health. This information was designed to discourage self-handicapping. Finally, in a third condition, subjects were given instructions that led them to believe that they would not be evaluated on the basis of their performance; this was the "no evaluation" condition. All subjects were subsequently given a battery of tests which included reports of current medical symptoms—the main dependent measure.

Results showed clear evidence of self-handicapping strategies being employed by the hypochondriacal subjects. The hypochondriacal subjects stated that they were currently suffering from more physical illness and symptoms when they thought they were going to be evaluated and when they thought that their poor health would provide an excuse than when they thought that poor health would not provide them with an acceptable excuse. In comparison, a control group of nonhypochondriacal subjects did not show this pattern; there was no attempt to use physical symptoms to excuse their performance.

The findings of the experiment suggest that hypochondriacs may employ their symptoms in a strategic fashion to protect both their self-image and the image they present to others. It suggests that physicians attempting to assess patient health problems should do so in as nonevaluative a manner as possible in order to discourage the employment of self-handicapping on the part of patients.

---

over, the specific way in which information is presented is an important factor (K. O. Anderson & Masur, 1983).

The MUM phenomenon, as well as the other work we have reviewed so far, provides suggestions based on social psychological research to health care workers on how to deal with patients who are already in ill health. (Also see Box 8-3.) We turn now to work focusing on how health problems can be prevented in the first place.

CARING FOR ONESELF: SOCIAL PSYCHOLOGICAL APPROACHES TO HEALTH MAINTENANCE

There is little disagreement on the importance of eating well, exercising regularly, maintaining an appropriate weight, getting enough sleep, brushing one's teeth, and so on . . . the list is seemingly endless. Yet many people do not adhere even to such straightforward rules, and avoidance of behaviors that will prevent many common health problems is frequent. The issue is not simply one of compliance to advice from a physician regarding specific medical problems, which we have already touched upon, but also compliance to health care regimens that, when followed, may result in the prevention of any number of illnesses (Masur, 1981). In the remainder of the chapter, we examine social psychological approaches to the prevention of disease and illness.

The Health Belief Model: Understanding Preventive Behavior

If a physician tells you to take a pill three times a day to remedy a specific medical complaint, you are considerably more likely to follow the suggestion than if he or she mentions that it would be reasonable to shed a few pounds. This conclusion is based on a good deal of survey research showing that medical suggestions that are viewed as being discretionary and not related to the specific amelioration of an illness are followed less rigorously than those that address a specific medical problem (S. E. Taylor, 1982; Croog & Levine, 1977).

One line of research that seeks to explain this phenomenon has been guided by the development of what is called the Health Belief Model or HBM (Rosenstock, 1966; Becker & Maiman, 1975). The HBM places heavy emphasis on factors of a cognitive nature, particularly those regarding perceptions of the severity of a disease and one's perceived susceptibility to it. As can be seen in Figure 8-2, the HBM has five major components that relate to the likelihood that an individual will follow a recommended action.

The first factor is the person's subjective state of readiness to take some action (component A), which is a function of the perceived susceptibility to and seriousness of the disease. The second factor refers to the individual's beliefs about the perceived benefits (component B). The perception of benefits is assumed to be based upon an individual's subjective appraisal of the degree of the preventive value (i.e., how likely is it that brushing my teeth will prevent tooth decay?), the availability of the procedure, and the feasibility of its implementation. The perceived barriers to preventive action are then theorized to be "deducted" from the benefits. Such barriers consist of the physical, psychological, and monetary costs of seeking treatment.

The Health Belief Model also incorporates two components that are labeled "modifying factors" (components C and D). One component (component C) is made up of demographic variables (such as age, sex,

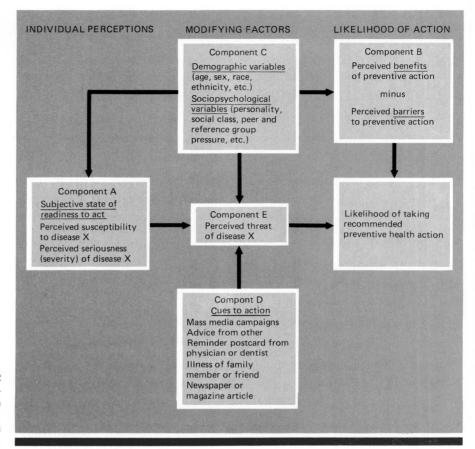

INDIVIDUAL PERCEPTIONS   MODIFYING FACTORS   LIKELIHOOD OF ACTION

Component C
Demographic variables
(age, sex, race,
ethnicity, etc.)
Sociopsychological
variables (personality,
social class, peer and
reference group
pressure, etc.)

Component B
Perceived benefits
of preventive action

minus

Perceived barriers
to preventive action

Component A
Subjective state of
readiness to act
Perceived susceptibility
to disease X
Perceived seriousness
(severity) of disease X

Component E
Perceived threat
of disease X

Likelihood of taking
recommended
preventive health action

Compont D
Cues to action
Mass media campaigns
Advice from other
Reminder postcard from
physician or dentist
Illness of family
member or friend
Newspaper or
magazine article

FIGURE 8-2
This figure shows the ma-
jor components of the
Health Belief Model.
Source: Becker & Maiman
(1975), copyright © 1975.

and race) and sociopsychological variables (such as personality and social class). Another component regarded as a modifying factor is labeled
"cues to action" (component D), and consists primarily of situational
influences that affect an individual's perception of the degree of threat
posed by the disease. These components are assumed to work indirectly
by modifying people's perceptions of their susceptibility to the disease
(component A), its perceived seriousness and threat (component E), and
the perceived benefits of action (component B).

Basically, the HBM suggests that the likelihood of taking preventive-
health measures is a direct function of two components: the perceived
threat of the disease and the perceived benefits (minus costs) of the
behavior. These two components can be affected by the other factors in
the model in the ways indicated in Figure 8-2. The theory does not
provide information on how to quantify the various components or
which (or whether) particular components should be weighted more
heavily than others. What it does suggest are predictions that are relative
to one another. For example, it suggests that people who perceive them-

selves as more susceptible to a disease are more likely to take preventive measures than those who perceive a lower susceptibility—theoretical suggestions fairly well supported by data (e.g., H. Leventhal, Hochbaum, & Rosenstock, 1960; M. H. Becker, Maiman, Kirscht, Haefner, Drachman, & Taylor, 1979).

A great deal of work in the health prevention field has been inspired by the HBM and, for the most part, its predictions have been upheld. To cite one example, the HBM was employed in a genetic screening program for Tay-Sachs disease, which is a rare but fatal disease affecting one in thirty children of a certain group of Jewish ancestry (M. H. Becker, Kaback, Rosenstock, & Ruth, 1975). Through a comprehensive educational approach (the "cues to action" component of the HBM), all members of the target population—couples in their child-bearing years—were reached. A group of 500 people who appeared for the genetic screening (the preventive health action in which blood samples were examined) and a sample of 500 who did not avail themselves of the screening were contacted and asked to complete a questionnaire. Results showed that, as one would predict from the model, participation in the screening was closely related to perceived susceptibility to the problem, and the model was supported in a number of other respects as well.

While most research shows the efficacy of the HBM, some results are not supportive (Sanders, 1982). For example, increasing the level of threat of a disease through the use of threatening communications does not always result in increased preventive actions (Stone, 1979). Moreover, the model does not stress the role of direct sensory experiences of symptoms and reactions to those symptoms (Safer, Tharps, Jackson, & Leventhal, 1984). Still, the Health Belief Model remains the major model of health-related preventive action, and its reliance on factors of a psychological nature illustrate the importance of social psychological theorizing to health care.

Promoting Good Health: A Social Learning Approach

While the Health Belief Model attempts to explain the factors underlying circumstances in which people will choose to take preventive steps to avoid illness and disease, some researchers have focused upon the nature of specific interventions that could be employed to increase compliance to behaviors that generally lead to better health. One of the best examples is the Stanford Heart Disease Prevention Program, carried out in three California communities over a three-year period. The program was designed to compare techniques of teaching people to modify their smoking, exercise, and dietary behavior to decrease their risks of heart disease (A. J. Meyer, Nash, McAlister, Maccoby, & Farquhar, 1980).

In the study, there were three conditions: media only, media plus face-to-face instruction, and no-treatment control condition. In the me-

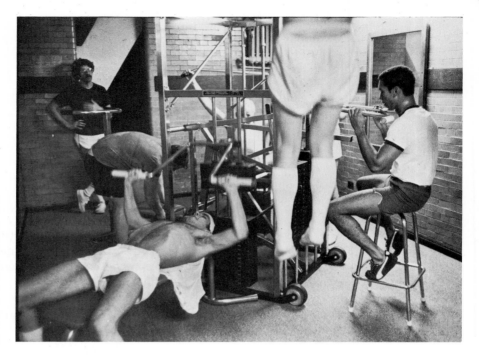

Demonstrations such as the Stanford Heart Disease Prevention Program have been successful in showing that educational techniques are able to bring about increases in behavior—such as exercise—that reduces the risk of future heart disease. (Gilles Peress/ Magnum)

dia-only condition, subjects were the recipients of an intensive media campaign that tried to bring about both awareness of the causes of heart disease and adoption of specific behaviors—such as weight reduction, cessation of smoking, and increase in exercise—that could reduce risk. Among the media materials employed were more than 150 radio and television spots, television and radio information shows, newspaper columns and ads, billboards, posters, and direct mailings.

In the media plus face-to-face instruction condition, not only were subjects exposed to the media campaign, but they also participated in a series of at least nine instructional sessions lasting for 1½ to 3½ hours each. During the instruction, which was usually held in group settings, techniques derived from social learning theory were employed. For example, instructors modeled appropriate behavior, and social reinforcement—both from the instructors and from other participants—was given for successful adherence to particular health-related practices during the previous week. The instruction was quite intensive, typically involving a group leader, an assistant, and a dietician at each session.

Finally, there was a no-treatment control condition, in which subjects merely completed a series of questionnaires and participated in interviews and medical examinations, as did the other subjects. It should be noted that because of the naturalistic, field nature of the study, there was the risk of subjects in the control condition being exposed to the media treatment. However, an attempt was made to control for this potential problem by assigning subjects in geographically separated communities to control and treatment conditions, respectively.

The results of this large, complex study were encouraging in showing reductions in behaviors associated with the risk of heart disease. Some significant decline in risk occurred over the three-year study for both treatment groups on a number of behavioral measures, and there was also an increase in knowledge of indicators of risk. Moreover, the media-plus-face-to-face instruction proved to be most effective on a number of other measures. For example, smoking cessation was significantly greater in the media-and-instruction condition than in the media-only condition.

While the results of the Stanford Heart Disease Prevention Program demonstrate that intensive educational techniques, based in part on social learning theory, can bring about significant changes in health-related behaviors, the study also illustrates the difficulty in designing effective, large-scale programs (Leventhal & Hirschman, 1982). The experimental treatments were essentially combined ''packages'' of disparate components, and we do not know which component was crucial in bringing about the decrease in risk-related behavior. Moreover, the study was enormously expensive and time-consuming to administer; it may be more difficult to bring about compliance to health-related behavior when less involved treatments are used. Finally, we do not yet have definitive data about whether there was an actual reduction in heart disease—only that the behavioral factors associated with it were modified.

Still, the study is clear in suggesting that social psychology has produced techniques that are applicable to the enhancement and maintenance of health. Moreover, current work is delineating more specifically conditions under which health problems can be ameliorated through attention to social psychological variables—a process which promises to enhance both our own and others' health and feelings of well-being.

SUMMARY

A new area of specialization has developed recently; it is known as the social psychology of health and illness, medical social psychology, or behavioral medicine. While a universal term has not emerged yet, topics such as the causes of disease, the development of prevention strategies, the treatment and management of illness, and the delivery of health care have been approached from a social psychological perspective.

One health problem that is clearly associated with a specific social behavioral pattern is heart disease. **Type A behavior** is characterized by strong ambition, competitiveness, and a sense of time urgency; persons with these traits tend to have a significantly higher rate of heart problems than **Type B** individuals, who do not have such traits. A recent study suggests that it is possible, however, to modify the Type A pattern and hence potentially reduce the incidence of heart disease.

Physician–patient interaction is another area that social psychologists have begun to investigate. When the physician and patient have a positive interpersonal relationship, patient cooperation is greater, treatment outcomes are more positive, and the degree of patient satisfaction with the medical treatment received tends to be higher. There are also several social psychological factors at work which affect a physician's ability to diagnose and treat illness successfully, including patient avoidance of self-disclosure, patient objective self-awareness, and the tendency to avoid telling patients unpleasant news about their conditions.

The Health Belief Model (HBM) has been developed to explain behavior related to prevention of potential disease. Among the most important factors are the way a person perceives his or her susceptibility to a disease, its seriousness, and the benefits and costs of preventive action. The model has been shown in field tests to predict preventive action reasonably well. Moreover, the Stanford Heart Disease Prevention Program has been useful in suggesting ways of modifying smoking, exercise, and dietary behavior that could lead to a decrease in the risk of heart disease.

KEY TERMS

cues to action
Health Belief Model (HBM)
hypochondriac
MUM effect
objective self-awareness

remission
self-disclosure
Type A behavior pattern
Type B behavior pattern

FOR FURTHER STUDY AND APPLICATION

Stone, G. C., Cohen, F., Adler, N. E. (1979). *Health psychology—A handbook.* San Francisco: Jossey-Bass.

Prokop, C. K., & Bradley, L. A. (Eds.). (1981). *Medical psychology: Contributions to behavioral medicine.* New York: Academic Press.

Both of these volumes provide a strong overview of the field of health psychology. They present a background of the area and discuss psychological aspects of illness and psychological approaches to improving health care. A good place to start.

DiMatteo, M. R., & Friedman, H. S. (1982). *Social psychology and medicine.* Cambridge, MA: Delgeschlager, Gunn, & Hain.

Sanders, G. S., & Suls, J. (Eds.). (1982). *Social psychology of health and illness.* Hillsdale, NJ: Lawrence Erlbaum Associates.

Eiser, J. R. (Ed.). (1982). *Social psychology and behavioral medicine.* New York: Wiley.

In contrast to the two books cited above, these volumes concentrate specifically on social psychological factors related to health. While the books are a bit technical, the informed nonexpert can find much of interest, particularly in terms of direct applications of social psychological theory to the practice of medicine and health care.

Pendleton, D., & Hasler, J. (1983). *Doctor–patient communication.* New York: Academic Press.

Provides a fine overview of how doctor–patient relationships affect the nature and quality of medical care. Discusses current trends in medical education for practitioners as well.

CHAPTER 9

AGGRESSION: HURTING OTHERS

A CONVERSATION WITH . . .

Patrick J. Murphy
*Chief, New York City
Police Department*

As the highest ranking uniformed police officer in New York City, Chief Patrick J. Murphy is in a unique position to comment on violence and other forms of aggression in today's society. Chief Murphy, a native New Yorker, began his career as a patrolman on the beat in 1955 and quickly rose through the ranks to a position in which he now commands a 25,000-person police force, the largest in the nation. We talked about his view of aggression and how it can be controlled and reduced.

Q. If you asked the average person in the street whether violence and aggression are problems, I think you would hear that, in fact, they are an important concern of most individuals. We are constantly reading about acts of violence, whether they are connected with crime or simply acts of wanton violence. Does the perception that violence is a problem match the reality?

A. Certainly this is true in a historical context. Back in the 1920s, we had about 300 homicides a year in New York. In recent years we have had in the neighborhood of 1800 homicides. Thus, there has been increased violence in terms of homicides, and in the case of violent robbery the numbers have also increased. Now, if you look at this on a year-to-year basis, the increase in violence doesn't seem so great. There's a conditioning effect, and I think people get used to it. But if they take a larger perspective, people would be surprised at the magnitude of the problem.

After President Kennedy or Martin Luther King was shot, someone made the comment that violence is as American as apple pie. I don't think that anyone would dispute that America is a violent country and that we have a violent society. And this is es-

pecially true when we look at violent crimes in other civilized countries throughout the world. In Japan, for instance, the rate of homicide is so small compared to ours that it is startling. Even in terms of Great Britain and other countries in Europe, our rate of violence is very high.

Q. This clearly argues against views suggesting that violence is instinctual in human beings, and suggests that something about the society or situation in the United States leads to violence. Do you agree?

A. Criminologists will tell you that when immigrants first came to this country, criminals among the first generation tended to commit crimes in the same way that they were committed in the old countries. But later generations started to commit the kinds of crimes that were committed by natives and people who had been here for a longer period of time. Succeeding generations were thus brought into the American crime culture.

Q. But why would the American crime culture be a more violent one than that found in other countries?

A. Some people will tell you it's the frontier heritage, in which the Caucasians came up against the Indians, violently subjugating and fighting for control of the land. We also have a history of subjugating black people to slavery, a condition that existed until 100 years ago. And, for the most part, it is always a violent subjugation of those people.

There is no doubt in my mind that the one thing which permits us to be a violent society is handgun proliferation. There is no other civilization in the world that has as much access to handguns as we do here in the United States.

Q. There is some evidence from social psychological research suggesting that the mere presence of guns can act to produce aggression. Do you think that handguns should be restricted in some way?

A. In my opinion, the first step to reduce violence would be, if not the outright banning of handguns, at least some kind of federal legislation on registration.

Q. But what about the argument that criminals would still be able to get hold of guns, even if they were banned?

A. Not if they are not manufactured or imported to the extent they are today. I think that the total number of people killed by handguns is probably 20,000 a year. That is a disgrace and a sad commentary on what is supposedly a civilized country.

Q. Of course, most people don't have or use handguns. What can the average law-abiding citizen do to combat violence?

A. People should pay attention to the small things of everyday life. People should pay their taxes. They should take responsibility for their own children. We find children out at ten, eleven, one o'clock at night. When you take them home their parents say, "See, I told you so. Okay, that's it; you're going to stay here because the police got you." Now, why do the parents wait for us? Common sense will tell you that it's not good for 10- and 11-year-olds to be out walking the streets late at night. We can't make the police the bad guys of society. People have to face up to their own responsibility. If children can't learn at home, then we're in trouble as a society.

OVERVIEW

Upon picking up almost any daily newspaper, even the most casual reader would be struck by the myriad instances of war, torture, assassination, invasion, and wanton destruction. And such acts of aggression do not occur only on a societal level; victimization by crime, rape, child abuse, and the fear of violence—the kinds of aggression faced daily by Chief Murphy—touch many people during at least some part of their lives. In fact, aggression (particularly in the form of warfare) can be considered *the* major social problem to afflict human society.

Is aggression innate, a "natural" part of the core of humankind? Or is aggression more reasonably viewed as a reaction to circumstances occasioned by the situations in which individuals find themselves? In this chapter we will attempt to answer these questions, drawing upon a large body of social psychological research and theory on aggression. We begin by attempting to provide a satisfactory definition of aggression by distinguishing it from situations in which people are unintentionally hurt or harmed. We also examine the three major theories of aggression: instinct theories, aggression as a reaction to frustration, and social learning theories. Then we discuss situational factors that affect aggression. Personality approaches, which view aggressive behavior as an enduring trait, will also be examined. Finally, we will discuss means of reducing and preventing aggression that are built upon social psychological theories and research.

UNDERSTANDING AGGRESSION: DEFINING THE TERM

Consider the following events:

- A soldier on the battlefront throws a hand grenade at an advancing squad of troops, killing five enemy soldiers.
- A physician carries out an emergency tracheotomy on a choking patient without anesthesia, causing excruciating pain, but even so is unable to save the patient's life.
- A member of the Gestapo tortures a prisoner to extract information.
- A child hits her classmate after not being able to play with the classmate's toy.
- A mother, in a fit of anger, tells her grown son that he has always been a disappointment to her and that she wishes that she had never had a child.

All of these situations involve some degree of injury or pain inflicted by one person on another, but whether we would consider them aggressive actions depends upon our definition of the term **aggression.** For instance, it is easy to conclude that the torturer is acting aggressively toward the prisoner. But what of the physician, who may cause just as much pain as the torturer? Clearly, one could argue that such behaviors are qualitatively distinct, although some theorists have contended that we should not distinguish between various forms of injury and pain. Arnold Buss (1961) suggests that aggression is any behavior that harms or hurts someone else. Using this definition, all five events would be considered aggressive.

In contrast, other researchers have suggested that such a conception is too simplistic, and that the *intent* of a person's actions must be taken into account before concluding that a particular behavior is or is not aggressive. The drawback with this sort of definition is that "intent" is difficult to establish; it is a hypothetical state that must be inferred indirectly. Moreover, if we want a broad definition of aggression—one that would be operative both with human beings *and* animals, for instance—intention is not a useful concept. How, for instance, does one establish intentionality with nonhumans?

Despite the conceptual difficulties that the use of "intention" entails, most social psychologists have felt it necessary to employ it when defining aggression in order to distinguish it from cases in which an individual hurts another person inadvertently. Hence, Leonard Berkowitz (1974) suggests that the term "aggression" should be used only for *intentional injury or harm to another person.* Given this definition—one which we will employ—we can see that it is possible to exclude the physician, since the pain caused by the tracheotomy clearly was not intentional. The other cases would, in contrast, be considered instances of aggression. (For ways in which aggression is *measured* by social psychologists, see Box 9-1.)

BOX 9-1   SPOTLIGHT ON METHODOLOGY

MEASURING AGGRESSION IN THE LABORATORY

The measurement of human aggression in laboratory experiments has represented a major challenge to social psychologists. Clearly, it would be neither desirable nor ethical to induce subjects to get into fistfights in the lab, no matter how compelling the data we could obtain from such activity would be. Instead, social psychologists have developed a number of alternate techniques.

By far, the most common technique employed today is one first devised by Arnold Buss (1961). In the procedure, two subjects arrive at an experiment and are told that one is to act as teacher and the other as learner. In order to teach the learner, the teacher is told he must administer nondangerous electric shocks to the learner whenever a mistake is made via an apparatus with buttons indicating ten levels of shock intensity.

In reality, the learner is a confederate who never receives any shocks—but the teacher, of course, doesn't know this. Prior to the administration of shocks, the experimental manipulation typically occurs. For example, the teacher may be angered or the stimuli in the environment modified in some way. Whatever the nature of the manipulation, the dependent measure is usually the intensity and duration of the shocks.

Although the Buss procedure or modifications of it are the primary means of measuring laboratory aggression, techniques as diverse as observing

horn-honking, cutting in line, and counting acts of violence have been employed. In addition, aggression toward inanimate objects has sometimes been measured. In some studies with children, subjects are given the opportunity to punch or kick an inflatable plastic Bobo doll (Bandura, Ross, & Ross, 1963). The drawback of such procedures is that, depending on one's definition, such behavior may not be considered aggression, since no human being is harmed.

Finally, verbal aggression has been used as a measure of aggressiveness. For example, some experiments require a subject to complete an evaluation of a target, and presume that negative evaluations will result in the target somehow being hurt (e.g., Ebbesen, Duncan, & Konečni, 1975). In other studies, conversation between subject and target is coded to determine the degree of verbal aggression presented toward the target.

None of the methods discussed above is foolproof, and none adequately takes into account the requirement that aggression reflect intentionality. Still, in hundreds of studies they have yielded useful data on human aggression. It should be noted, though, that each probably measures a slightly different form of aggression, and experiments that use multiple dependent measures are likely to yield the most valid findings when it comes to opportunities to generalize about human aggression.

THEORETICAL APPROACHES TO AGGRESSION

There are a number of broad models that have been put forward to explain the occurrence of aggression: instinct theories, frustration–aggression models, and social learning approaches. We will examine each in turn.

Instinct Theories of Aggression: It's All in the Genes

While sociobiological explanations of helping behavior have relatively few defenders, as we noted in Chapter 7, explanations of aggression that look to instinctual factors as the primary source of such behavior have no lack of proponents. The frequency and prevalence of aggression—in both human and animal behavior—have made explanations which posit that aggression represents an innate urge seem quite reasonable. However, instinct theories have also proven to be quite controversial.

There have been two major proponents of instinct theories: Sigmund Freud and Konrad Lorenz. Freud's view, which grew out of his work on psychoanalytic theory, was that human beings have an instinct known as **thanatos**—the death drive—which acts in opposition to **eros,** the life instinct (Freud, 1920). According to Freud, the energy of thanatos usually becomes directed toward others rather than toward the self, to avoid self-destruction. Basically, then, Freud sees aggression toward others as an inevitable and universal outcome of the rechanneling of the death instinct.

Freud's gloomy view of aggression is shared in many ways by the second major proponent of instinctual theories, Konrad Lorenz, although the underlying mechanisms differ in major respects since Lorenz sees aggression as adaptive rather than self-destructive. Lorenz's work is representative of the area of science known as **ethology,** which studies the behavior of animals. Lorenz (1966, 1974) argues that most animals share a fighting instinct, which serves a number of essential functions. For example, aggression allows animals to maintain their own particular territory, thus assuring a steady supply of food. It also serves to weed out weaker animals and allow only the strongest and most fit to reproduce, thus providing long-term evolutionary benefits to the species.

Although Lorenz's work concentrated on animals, it was his theorizing on human aggression that made him most controversial. Two extensions of his work are especially noteworthy: explanations of why human beings, unlike almost any other species, kill each other, and of how instinctual aggressive energy builds up and is periodically released.

Man as Killer   Lorenz's explanation for why human beings kill each other during aggressive encounters is based on his notion that there are basically two types of reactions to danger: fight or flight. Those animals that lack mechanisms to defend themselves effectively, such as birds and deer, tend to flee when encountering an enemy, while those with potent "weapons," such as long claws and sharp teeth, tend to fight. But Lorenz also suggests that the greater the fighting capabilities of an animal, the stronger are the innate inhibitions against aggressing against members of its own species. With relatively ineffective fighters, such inhibitions are particularly weak, since aggression against members of one's own species will not have much of an impact.

In the case of human beings, however, the pattern has broken down, according to Lorenz. Because human beings originally reacted to aggression with flight, as they lacked effective means to defend themselves, innate inhibitions against aggression toward other human beings are relatively weak. But the great technological advances in weaponry by human beings have allowed the development of great destructive power.

Are humans instinctually driven to be aggressive? Konrad Lorenz's theorizing suggests that aggressive behavior is innate. (Lookout Mountain Laboratory/Photo Researchers)

Because of the lack of inhibitory impulses, human beings, almost alone among all species, have become effective and relentless killers of each other.

Building up Aggression: An Energizing Model   A second major and controversial outcome of Lorenz's work with animals was his theorizing regarding the nature of instinctual aggressive energy. He, in a view congruent with that of Freud, suggested that aggressive energy is constantly being generated and slowly builds up within an individual over time. Such energy continues to build up until it is discharged in some way, usually because of the presence of some stimulus in the environment that elicits the aggression. The specific amount of aggression will be determined by the amount of energy that has been stored up. In fact, it is even possible for the energy to be released spontaneously if enough has been built up, even if no overt stimuli eliciting the aggression are present.

What is particularly noteworthy about this model is the implication that if aggressive energy can be discharged through some socially desirable means, there won't be sufficient energy left for it to be manifested in unacceptable ways. Thus, Lorenz suggested that society encourage "acceptable" fabricated forms of aggression—such as through sports and games.

Difficulties with Instinct Theories   Although the instinct theories of Freud and Lorenz seem sensible, most social psychologists have grave misgivings about their usefulness. For one thing, they provide little in the way of specific guidance about when and how people will aggress, other than contending that aggression inevitably will occur. More damning to instinct theories is the lack of experimental support. In some cases, such support is impossible to attain (how do we measure hypothetical energy such as thanatos?), while in other cases in which testable propositions can be put forward, the evidence generally is nonsupportive of instinctual theories.

Take, for example, Lorenz's notion that there is a reservoir of pent-up aggressive energy that, unless periodically drained, will manifest itself in aggressive behavior. The hypothesis that can be derived from this proposition is that participation in aggressive activities ought to reduce subsequent aggression. Unfortunately for instinct theories, there is evidence that directly contradicts the hypothesis.

Walters and Brown (1963) demonstrated that subjects who were rewarded for hitting an object were later no less aggressive—and sometimes *more* aggressive—than rewarded subjects who had not hit the object. Other research has *not* found evidence that those involved in sports, as participants or observers, are less likely to show subsequent aggression than those unexposed to such activities (L. Berkowitz, 1973; Goldstein & Arms, 1971). Thus, instinct theories have not fared well, and it is necessary to turn to other approaches to find more valid explanations of human aggression.

Aggression as a Reaction to Frustration: Frustration–Aggression Approaches

Consider the following situation:

> After being exposed to days of commercials extolling the virtues of a particular type of toy car, 6-year-old Jonathan convinces his mother to purchase one for him. Soon after he gets it home and after just a few minutes of play, Jonathan finds that his younger brother has broken the car. His mother tells him that it will have to be sent back to the manufacturer to be repaired and that he probably won't get it back for a few months. Jonathan reacts in a way that would surprise few of us: he goes over to his younger brother and hits him in the chest, knocking him over.

The scenario described above provides an example of one of the most durable hypotheses relating to human aggression: the frustration–aggression hypothesis. First put forward nearly fifty years ago (Dollard, Doob, Miller, Mowrer, & Sears, 1939), the hypothesis has entered our folklore as the cause that a layman would be most likely to choose to explain aggression. As stated initially, the hypothesis predicts two things: First, that frustration *always* leads to aggression of some sort; and second, that aggression is *always* the result of some frustration. By frustration, the hypothesis refers to the thwarting or blocking of some ongoing behavior directed toward a desired goal. Moreover, the hypothesis suggests that rather than frustration leading directly to aggression, the process is one in which frustration leads to a propensity to be aggressive and the arousal of an aggressive drive. This aggressive drive then leads to the actual aggression.

When such a direct hypothesis is put forward, one expects that it will be modified as the results of empirical research are accumulated, and the frustration–aggression hypothesis is no exception. Frustration often *does* lead to aggression, and in many instances some form of frustration precedes aggressive behavior. What has proven to be true, however, is that the links between frustration and aggression are much weaker than originally proposed: frustration does not inevitably lead to aggression, and aggression is not invariably preceded by frustration.

In the example cited at the beginning of this section, we might think of a number of alternate responses by Jonathan to the broken toy, such as begging his mother to go to the store to buy a replacement. Another alternative might be some form of cognitive dissonance reduction, in which Jonathan's attitude toward the toy is modified so that it becomes less positive ("I didn't really like it all that much"). Whatever the alternate response, it is clear that aggression is but one possible outcome of frustration.

Current Conceptions of the Frustration–Aggression Hypothesis   What, then, does influence the relationship between frustration and aggression? According to Leonard Berkowitz, one of the leading authorities on aggression today, the most reasonable way to view the frustration–aggression relationship is that frustration leads to a *readiness* to act aggressively due to the presence of anger caused by the frustration. Whether or not an individual responds aggressively depends on the presence of aggressive cues which trigger the actual occurrence of aggression. Such aggressive cues are learned stimuli that in the past have been associated with anger, aggression, or the instigators of aggression (Berkowitz, 1984).

A clear example of how even subtle aggressive cues can provoke aggression is illustrated in a study by Berkowitz and Geen (1966). In the experiment, subjects were introduced to a confederate who either angered them or acted neutrally. Following this, subjects were shown a violent scene from a movie—a boxing scene from *Champion*—and then, under an experimental ruse, were placed in a position where it was supposedly possible to administer electric shocks to the confederate.

To manipulate the presence of an aggressive cue, the name of the confederate was also varied: In one condition, he was named Kirk— which presumably evoked the fighter in the movie, played by Kirk Douglas. In the nonaggressive cue condition, the confederate was named Bob. The results displayed in Figure 9-1 show that aggression— as measured by the number of shocks given the confederate—was significantly higher when the subjects were angered than when they were

CARING AND UNCARING
BEHAVIOR: POSITIVE AND
NEGATIVE INTERACTION IN
A SOCIAL WORLD

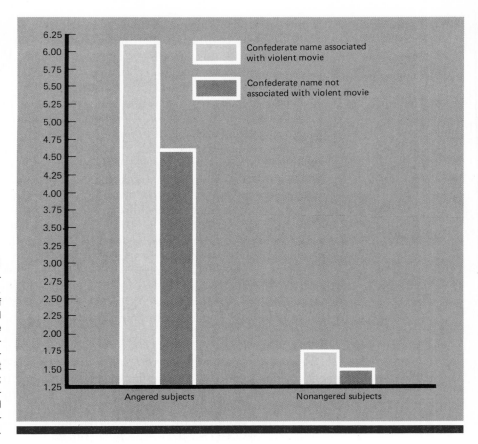

not. Even more significant was the fact that aggression toward the confederate was considerably higher when his name was associated with
the violent film than when it was not.

The Berkowitz and Geen study provides clear evidence for the importance of aggressive cues in eliciting aggressive behavior, and a great
deal of other research is supportive of this formulation. For example, in
one study a person introduced as a physical education major interested
in boxing evoked greater aggression than a speech major, and in another
the mere presence of a rifle and revolver sitting on a table was sufficient
to evoke greater aggression than when they were not present—a phenomenon that has been labeled the **weapons effect** (L. Berkowitz, 1965;
L. Berkowitz & LePage, 1967). On the other hand, the evidence that
aggressive cues are associated with increases in aggressive behavior is
not completely supportive—i.e., the weapons effect has proven difficult
to replicate—and the precise conditions under which aggressive cues
enhance aggression have yet to be specified (e.g., Buss, Booker, & Buss,
1972).

To sum up our discussion of the frustration–aggression hypothesis, it is clear that its original formulation contending that frustration always results in aggression and that instances of aggression are always preceded by frustration was too broad. It does appear that frustration and aggression are related and that the presence of aggressive behavior cues increases the probability and strength of overt aggression. But frustration does not always result in aggression, and aggression is not always preceded by frustration. Aggressive behavior has a variety of causes, of which frustration is only one.

Aggression as a Learned Behavior: Social Learning Approaches

Instinct theories view aggression as being guided primarily by internal, preprogrammed processes, while frustration–aggression theories suggest that there is an interplay between the internal motivation of aggressive drives and environmental cues that elicit aggression. In contrast, one approach that places relatively little emphasis on internal processes and concentrates instead on conditions within the external environment is that of the social learning theorists. They suggest that aggressive behaviors are basically *learned* behaviors, and that in order to understand these we should look at the rewards and punishments involved in the acquisition and maintenance of such behaviors (Bandura, 1973; Zillman, 1978).

If one were to take a social learning approach to the incident we discussed earlier in which Jonathan hit his brother when his new toy was broken, our analysis of the situation would be quite different from that taken by a frustration–aggression theorist. Rather than viewing frustration as the predisposing factor in causing the aggression, the social learning theorist would consider previous reinforcement that Jonathan had received for being aggressive. It is possible that he had learned that aggressive behavior would be an effective means of acquiring rewards, either by watching a model act aggressively or by being aggressive earlier and being rewarded for it.

According to social learning theory, the most basic mechanism for learning aggressive behaviors is through direct reinforcement and punishment. Children, for example, may learn that they can play with the best toys if they aggressively react to other children's requests for sharing, and hit men know that they will get paid only if they successfully murder their victims. The rewards and punishments need not be tangible; social approval and disapproval can also be effective as reinforcers. Chief Murphy's observation in the conversation at the start of the chapter that, ultimately, parents are responsible for controlling the aggressive behavior of their children is congruent with a social learning approach.

But even more important than direct reinforcement are the more indirect means. Albert Bandura, the main proponent of social learning approaches to aggression, suggests that a primary means of learning aggressive behaviors is through modeling processes—which we discussed in Chapter 7 with regard to helping behavior. A model is an individual whose behavior can be imitated by an observer. Social learning theory suggests that an individual who observes a model's actions and the subsequent consequences of those actions can learn the modeled behavior. If the consequences to the model are positive, the observer may (although not invariably will) imitate the behavior in a similar situation (Bandura, 1973).

A long list of research studies has shown that exposure to a live, aggressive model leads to enhanced aggression on the part of observers, but generally only if the observers have first been angered, insulted, or frustrated. For example, a classic study by Bandura, Ross, and Ross (1963) allowed nursery-school-age children to view an adult who played in a violent and aggressive manner with a Bobo doll—a large, inflatable plastic doll which always returns to an upright position after being pushed down—or, in another condition, played sedately with Tinker Toys.

Later, the children were given an opportunity to play with a number of toys, including a Bobo doll and Tinker Toys. The results were clear: when frustrated by the experimenter's refusal to allow them to play with a favorite toy, the children were considerably more aggressive after viewing the violent model than after viewing the nonviolent model. In fact, in many cases the children's aggressive behavior mimicked that of the adult model quite closely.

Modeling from Media Aggression   If observing a live model leads to increased aggression on the part of observers—a point that seems clear from a host of experiments—it is reasonable to ask whether viewing aggressive behavior in films and television will lead to increased aggression. The question is hardly a trivial one; as anyone who watches prime-time television or attends the movies knows, explicit aggression in large quantities is a staple element in many media productions.

Consider, for instance, the film *Indiana Jones and the Temple of Doom*, starring Harrison Ford, which includes such scenes as these:

- A priest pulls out the beating heart of a living man.
- A taskmaster is killed on a conveyor belt meant to crush rocks.
- One character burns another with a fiery torch.

But adult films and television are not the only source of media aggression. We need look no further than Saturday morning cartoon shows to find many instances of aggression, although most frequently in children's shows they are couched in the context of humor. In fact, one survey found that eight out of ten of all television programs contains physical violence and 60 percent of leading characters are involved in aggression. The average child views 13,000 violent deaths between the

Watching media aggression, even in cartoons, and participating in aggressive play with toy weapons have been associated with increases in actual aggression. (*Left,* Suzanne Szasz/Photo Researchers; *right,* John Garrett/Woodfin Camp)

ages of 5 and 15 (Gerbner, Gross, Jackson-Beeck, Jeffries-Fox, & Signoirelli, 1978).

Determining the effects of media violence on the aggression of viewers is no easy task, however. While it is relatively easy to demonstrate modeling in laboratory situations, media effects—particularly in naturalistic settings—are more difficult to uncover, and the methodological pitfalls are great (Ball, 1976; Kaplan & Singer, 1976). For example, in order to demonstrate that television aggression is linked to actual instances of aggression, the most obvious technique would be to observe naturalistically the type of television programming a given individual watched and then relate this to instances of aggressive behavior by that person.

Note that it is difficult to carry out a true experiment in which we assign subjects to watch particular aggressive or nonaggressive shows without being seriously intrusive in any naturalistic setting, although some attempts have been made (e.g., Parke, Berkowitz, Leyens, West, & Sebastian, 1977). We must turn instead to correlational studies, which can show if there is a relationship between viewing violent shows and subsequent aggression, but which are not able to show that televised violence *causes* aggression. Such correlational evidence cannot rule out alternative explanations—for instance, that both the viewing of aggressive television shows *and* subsequent aggression are caused by some third factor (perhaps, for instance, educational level—uneducated people may both be more violent and watch more aggressive shows). Moreover, as Eron (1982) suggests, the causal effects may be circular, with television violence affecting children's aggression, and aggressive children watching increasingly violent television. Hence, it is no simple task to demonstrate that viewing aggression is linked to later incidents of actual aggression.

A number of field studies have shown significant correlations between violent television programming and aggressive behavior (Eron, 1982).

For example, one such study found that subjects who watched more televised violence in the third grade tended to show more aggressive behavior when they were 19 years old than did those who had watched relatively little television in the third grade (Eron, Huesmann, Lefkowitz, and Walder, 1972). Coupled with the supportive results of true experiments carried out in both laboratory and field settings, studies such as this one (see, for instance, Box 9-2) suggest that viewing media violence can lead to increased aggression.

But it is also obvious that viewing aggression does not *always* lead to the acting out of violent behavior, and many recent investigations have focused on identifying the factors underlying the circumstances in which media violence is translated into actual aggression (Berkowitz, 1984). For example, aggression attributed to media violence may not be due just to simple modeling effects. Viewing televised aggression can lead an individual to think that aggression is a socially acceptable behavior and, in fact, people may learn *how* to aggress in a particular way from television programs and movies. One apparent example of such learning occurred in San Francisco, where a young girl was raped with a bottle, in apparent imitation of a similar scene in a television movie that had been aired just four days earlier. It is unlikely that this particular unusual and specific act would have occurred to the perpetrators without their having been given the idea from the movie.

The way in which an individual interprets the reasons behind observed aggression also has an important effect upon subsequent aggressive behavior on the part of the observer. When aggression is made to seem justified, it elicits more subsequent aggression than when it appears to be unjustified or random to the viewer. For example, T. P. Meyer (1972) showed subjects an actual news film in which a North Vietnamese soldier was stabbed to death by South Vietnamese soldiers. The context of the killing was manipulated: some subjects were told that it represented retaliation for atrocities by the victim against innocent civilians, while others were told that they had viewed a cold-blooded killing of a prisoner of war. Subjects later given the opportunity to aggress against a confederate were more aggressive when they had been told the killing they viewed was justifiable revenge than when offered the other description. Hence, observing aggression for which there appears to be some justification is more apt to facilitate later aggression than viewing acts of violence that lack a legitimate rationale.

Just as Chief Murphy suggested that people become conditioned to accept violence in society, there is evidence that a steady diet of media violence may lead viewers to become desensitized to the meaning of such aggression. One early experiment suggested that this could be the case: viewers of a series of graphic puberty rites carried out in a primitive culture showed a marked decrease in stress by the time they viewed the fourth cut in a young boy's genitals (Lazarus, Speisman, Mordkoff, & Davidson, 1962).

In a more direct test of the notion that viewing aggression leads to a

BOX 9-2　SPOTLIGHT ON APPLICATION

TELEVISION AND CRIME

Most of the research on the role of media violence and subsequent viewer aggression has been carried out on an individual level relating, for instance, how one person's television viewing is correlated with that individual's later aggressiveness. Recent approaches to the issue have examined the question from a societal level, and have found that the introduction of television seems to bear a relationship to aggression manifested through crime.

A pioneering study examined the impact of the introduction of television on FBI figures on violent crime, burglary (breaking and entering), auto theft, and larceny (Hennigan, DelRosario, Heath, Cook, Wharton, & Calder, 1982). Looking at changes in these figures over time, it was possible to estimate and plot the changes in criminal activity before, during, and after the introduction of television into an area. Moreover, because the Federal Communications Commission ordered a freeze on new television broadcasting licenses between late 1949 and

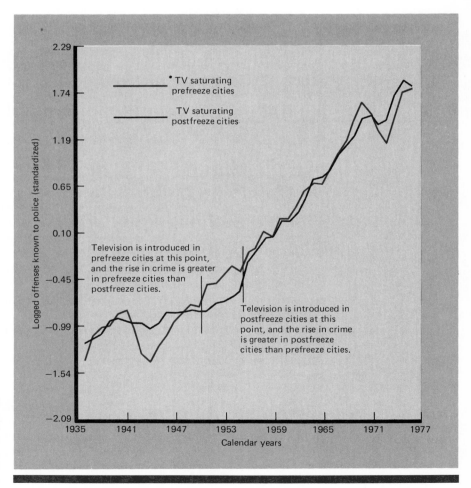

FIGURE 9-2
As television was introduced, larceny theft tended to rise. Source: Hennigan, DelRosario, Heath, Cook, Wharton, & Calder (1982).

305

mid-1952, only certain communities had access to television prior to the freeze (called prefreeze communities). This lag in introduction in some places meant that the level of crime in prefreeze communities should have risen faster than in comparable postfreeze communities just after the introduction of television in the prefreeze communities, if television was having such an effect. Likewise, the level of crime should have risen suddenly in the postfreeze communities shortly after *they* received television— and this rise should be significantly greater than in the prefreeze communities at that point in time.

Although results pertaining to violent crime, burglary, and auto theft did not show consistent effects related to the introduction of television, increases in larceny were consistently affected. As can be seen in Figure 9-2, in both sets of cities—prefreeze and postfreeze—the rate of larceny increased just after the introduction of television. Moreover, the rate of increase was much higher in the communities in which television was introduced recently than it was for the same period in the other set of communities.

While these findings are not definitive, they do suggest that the introduction of television was related to an increase in certain kinds of criminal activity. Why should this be so? Hennigan et al. (1982) suggest that it relates to the content of early television, which consisted primarily of middle- and upper-class, attractive, well-to-do characters, and which had many advertisements for consumer goods. Because the heaviest viewing of television occurs in poorer, less educated groups, it is possible that feelings of resentment and frustration developed over the viewers' inability to afford the lifestyles portrayed on television, ultimately leading to criminal activity on their part. Basically, then, this hypothesis suggests a variant of the frustration–aggression hypothesis—with frustration leading to aggression, which is manifested through criminal activity.

The lack of a relationship between the introduction of television and crimes other than larceny is puzzling, especially in view of the fact that there were relatively high amounts of violence in early television shows. One explanation is that the FBI criminal statistics are simply inadequate indicators of the aggression that follows from viewing media violence. It is clear that further research is required to answer definitively the question of how media violence is related to criminal aggression.

desensitization to its consequences, subjects in an experiment (Cline, 1973) were shown either an aggressive or an unaggressive movie (excerpts from a violent movie about a SWAT team or a scene from a volleyball game). Subsequently, subjects were led to believe that they were viewing an actual, live instance of aggression. Physiological measures of subjects' arousal (using galvanic skin responses) showed that individuals who had viewed the media aggression were *less* affected by the supposed actual example of aggression than those who had previously seen the movie showing a volleyball scene. It is possible, then, that frequent exposure to media violence can make people more insensitive to violence, unaware of its meaning and consequences. It is logical to assume that this insensitivity could ultimately lead to increased aggression on their part.

Social Learning Theories of Aggression: Some Final Comments   In examining the social learning view of aggression, we began by considering aggression that was observed in live models and proceeded to a consideration of aggression that is observed in media portrayals of aggressive behavior. Social learning theory is consistent, we have found, in suggesting that aggression is learned, instigated, and maintained through the observation of others' aggression and through the direct reinforcement of aggression.

What makes the social learning approach unique when compared with instinctual views of aggression and frustration–aggression approaches is the degree to which it views aggression as a modifiable or preventable phenomenon. Whereas instinctual views tend to look at aggression as an inevitable, genetically determined behavior, social learning approaches suggest that aggression can be unlearned in the same way that it is learned—or, under the appropriate circumstances, it may not be learned at all. And where the frustration–aggression hypothesis suggests that frustration is such a common occurrence for most people that its elimination (and thus the elimination of the aggression it causes) is unlikely, social learning theories are more optimistic. According to this approach, aggression can be reduced and potentially eliminated by controlling situational conditions. In the next section of the chapter, we discuss some of the major situational factors that have been related to aggression.

FACTORS AFFECTING AGGRESSION: THE SOCIAL AND PHYSICAL ENVIRONMENT

At one point or another, most of us have experienced frayed nerves and anger, and ultimately have acted aggressively during long, extremely hot periods of summer. In fact, it turns out that this is a fairly common occurrence; heat is but one factor of a situational nature that is related to increases in aggression.

In this part of the chapter, we will consider how situational factors affect aggression. First, the effect of physiological arousal caused by exercise, sex, alcohol, and drugs and the physical environment will be discussed. Then we will examine the role that anonymity and provocation from others plays in aggression.

Arousal as a Cause of Aggression

Just as Harry, hot and sweaty, finishes a long morning of strenuous work replanting his lawn, his son comes along and knocks over an expensive birdbath that Harry purchased recently and is planning to install. He reacts with verbal aggression, screaming at his son to stop being so clumsy.

Would his son have fared better if Harry had not been involved in physical exercise, but had spent the afternoon lolling about in the sun? The answer appears to be affirmative, because physical arousal has been linked to an increased propensity to behave aggressively in a number of studies (Rule & Nesdale, 1976). And physical activity is not the only source of arousal that may lead to increased aggression: arousal that is induced by sex, alcohol, and drugs may facilitate aggressive behavior.

Physical Arousal and Aggression: Does Sweat Lead to Swat?

Let us consider first physical exercise as a source of arousal. Clearly, when an individual exercises, a number of dramatic physiological changes occur: heart rate accelerates, there is an increase in galvanic skin response due to increased sweating, and various endocrinologic changes occur. Can these changes be linked to increased aggression? The answer is a modified "yes." Arousal due to exercise can facilitate aggression, but its effects are restricted primarily to persons who have been angered or frustrated and thus are predisposed to be aggressive. In cases in which the individual was not angered earlier, physical exercise by itself will not lead directly to increased aggression.

The prior conclusion was illustrated quite directly in a study by Zillmann, Katcher, and Milavsky (1972). In their experiment, subjects were either angered or not angered by a confederate. They then, according to condition, either participated in active physical exercise or carried out a more placid, nonarousing activity. When given the opportunity to act aggressively toward the confederate by ostensibly administering electric shocks, subjects gave significantly greater shocks when they had exercised only when they had been angered earlier by the confederate. Thus, physical exercise alone does not necessarily enhance aggressiveness.

Another restriction on the relationship between aggression and physical exercise relates to how an individual *attributes* his or her arousal. Generally, it appears that if the arousal can be attributed appropriately to physical exercise—or, for that matter, other sources of arousal—aggression will not be facilitated by the arousal. If, on the other hand, the source of the arousal cannot readily be identified, the arousal may be misinterpreted as due to anger, and the possibility of aggressive behavior may be increased.

In one experiment, angered subjects were given the opportunity to retaliate against a victim either immediately after strenuous exercise or a few minutes later (Zillman, Johnson, & Day, 1974). The experimenters reasoned that the arousal that angered subjects experienced immediately after exercise would be attributed directly to the exercise, compared to when a few minutes had passed—in which case the residual arousal would be less likely to be attributed to the exercise and more likely to be misattributed to the anger. Their results were consistent with this reasoning: angered subjects showed higher aggression a few minutes after exercising than immediately following exercise. As with the research on the labeling of emotions that we discussed in Chapter 2, then, how one identifies the source of arousal is critical in determining the nature of one's response. Depending on the circumstances, physical arousal may or may not result in heightened aggression.

Sexual Arousal and Aggression Forms of physical excitation other than exercise have also been linked to aggression. One dominant example is sexual arousal. Is there is a link between sexual arousal and aggression? The answer is apparently affirmative, although once again it must be qualified.

Early work on the issue of the link between sexual arousal and aggression seemed to show quite clearly that erotic stimuli (in the form of movies, pictures, or steamy passages describing sexual encounters) did enhance aggressive behavior. For example, Zillmann (1978) had subjects view a sexually explicit film (*The Couch*), or a nonarousing, although interesting, film about Marco Polo, and then led them either to be angered or not to be angered by a confederate. The results clearly showed that angered subjects gave the highest level of shocks to the confederate after viewing the sexually explicit film and lowest level after seeing the travel film. A prizefight film elicited an intermediate level of aggression. Seemingly, then, sexual arousal facilitated aggression—even more so than viewing an aggressive film.

However, later results examining the relationship between sexual arousal and aggression were not always consistent with these earlier findings. In fact, some research showed that exposure to mild forms of erotic stimuli actually produced *less* aggression than exposure to nonerotic stimuli (e.g., Baron & Bell, 1977). It now appears that the relationship between the strength of sexual arousal from erotic cues and subsequent aggressiveness is U-shaped when graphed, as shown in Figure 9-3.

Both nonerotic stimuli *and* highly erotic stimuli increase aggression,

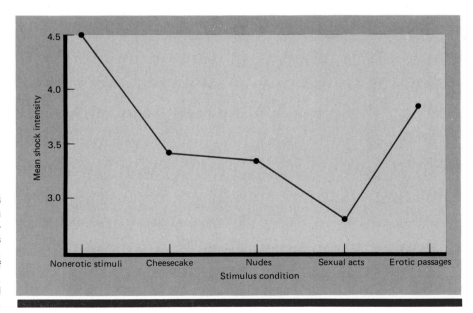

FIGURE 9-3
The relationship between sexual arousal and subsequent aggression forms a U-shape when graphed, according to the results of R. A. Baron and Bell. Source: Baron & Bell (1977).

then, while moderate levels of sexual arousal produce lower levels of aggression. The reason? Low levels of erotic stimuli, rather than producing arousal, seem to act primarily as a distraction from any angering or frustrating event that occurred earlier. In contrast, highly explicit erotic stimuli would be expected to produce high sexual arousal; the arousal then may produce higher levels of aggression analogous to the way in which arousal due to physical exercise can lead to increased aggression (Donnerstein, Donnerstein, & Evans, 1975).

Sexual Violence toward Women   Recent work on the relationship between sexual arousal and aggression has begun to examine the specific content of erotic stimuli, particularly as it pertains to the use of violence in pornographic material. Many individuals have argued that pornographic materials which incorporate acts of violence—usually against women—increase the likelihood of actual aggression, typically in the form of rape, toward women in real life. Indeed, if one examines the data, both violence against women *and* the incidence of aggressive pornography have increased in recent years (e.g., Malamuth & Spinner, 1980; Brownmiller, 1975). The question that arises from findings such as these is whether there is a causal link between the two.

Although the question cannot be answered on a societal level, experimental evidence clearly suggests that violence against women portrayed in pornography can lead to increased aggression. For example, in a study by Donnerstein and Berkowitz (1981), male subjects were angered by either a male or female confederate and then exposed to one of four different films: a neutral film of a talk-show interview; a purely erotic film that contained no aggressive sequence; a positive-outcome, aggressive, erotic movie (in which a female is slapped and sexually attacked by two men but ends up in the last thirty seconds smiling and apparently enjoying the sexual experience); and a negative-outcome, aggressive, erotic film (similar to the positive-outcome movie except for the final thirty seconds, at which point the woman appears to be suffering). Subjects were then given the opportunity to administer (bogus) shocks to the confederate, and results showed clear differences in level of aggression, depending upon the sex of the confederate and the movie to which they had been exposed.

As can be seen in Figure 9-4, aggression toward the male confederate differed little according to the film the subjects had seen. But for subjects who had a female target, the nature of the movie they had seen made a considerable difference. Although the purely erotic film did not produce greater aggression than viewing a neutral film, viewing either the positive- or negative-outcome film did produce a significant increase in aggression toward the female confederate. (There was no statistical difference between the positive- and negative-outcome films.) Basically, then, the aggressive erotic films produced a significant degree of aggression toward a female victim, although not toward a male victim.

There are a number of possible explanations for the findings, includ-

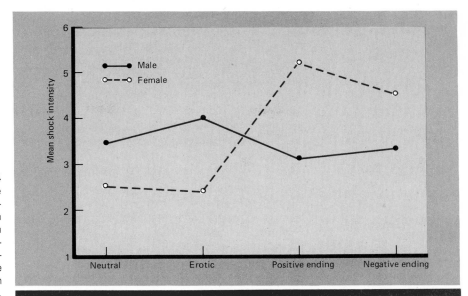

FIGURE 9-4
Aggression toward male targets differed little according to the film viewed; but aggression toward female targets varied significantly according to the nature of the film. Source: Donnerstein & Berkowitz (1981).

ing an increase in arousal level brought about by exposure to the aggressive and erotic movies, lowered inhibitions of observers to be aggressive because of exposure to the aggressive models, and the fact that when the victim was a female the film evoked learned stimulus-response

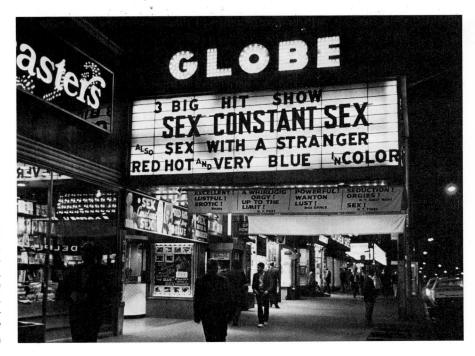

Pornography that contains aggressive content is associated with an increased readiness for men to act aggressively—including the act of rape—to women. (Jim Anderson/Woodfin Camp or Charles Gatewood/Magnum)

associations due to the similarity between the movie victim and the live victim. In fact, probably all of these factors played a role.

Regardless of the specific explanation, however, one fact emerged clearly: the inclusion of aggressive activities with sexual erotica can result in greater aggressive behavior by viewers than can erotic stimuli that do not include aggressive components. Moreover, other research (Malamuth & Check, 1982) has shown that individuals who are exposed to pornographic materials that include aggressive content are more apt to report willingness to commit rape than those who view nonaggressive pornographic materials. It is clear from findings such as these that evidence from laboratory studies supports the notion that the aggressive content of pornography may have particularly unfortunate effects. While it is too early to say conclusively that aggression against women results from exposure to aggressive pornography, the results of laboratory research are disturbing. (For a view of another part of the issue—on being a victim of sexual aggression—see Box 9-3.)

Arousal from Drugs and Alcohol: Getting High and Aggression   If you have ever had the unpleasant experience of being confronted at a party by a hostile drunk who earlier had been meek and mild-mannered in the best Clark Kent tradition, you may be convinced that alcohol can facilitate aggression. In contrast, a common stereotype holds that people become relaxed and mellow after smoking marijuana; such a view might lead you to infer that marijuana is an inhibitor or depressant of aggression.

In fact, both views are supported by experimental evidence. For example, in a series of experiments, Stuart Taylor and his colleagues (Taylor & Gammon, 1975; Taylor, Vardaris, Rawitch, Gammon, Cranston, & Lubetkin, 1976) gave subjects drinks that contained either a small or large dose of alcohol or THC (which is the active chemical in marijuana) or, in a control condition, drinks containing no alcohol or THC. Subjects were then given the opportunity to administer shocks to a competitor. As can be seen in Figure 9-5, subjects given large doses of alcohol showed increased aggression, while those given small amounts of alcohol actually showed levels of aggression that were below those of the no-alcohol control group. It seems as if the small amount of alcohol had a relaxing effect but did not produce so much relaxation that inhibitions against aggression were dropped—as seemed to occur with the large-dose-of-alcohol group. In terms of the THC, however, the pattern was very different. Small amounts of the THC had no appreciable effect upon aggression, while large doses led to a significant *decrease* in the amount of aggression displayed.

Results of the Taylor et al. research are at least suggestive that at high levels of ingestion alcohol facilitates aggression and marijuana inhibits aggression—conclusions supported by other research (e.g., Bailey, Leonard, Cranston, & Taylor, 1983). It seems, then, that the effects of alcohol

BOX 9-3   SPOTLIGHT ON FIELD RESEARCH

ON BEING A VICTIM: WHERE TO PLACE THE BLAME

The aftermath of a violent aggressive crime is often subtler than the objective property losses and bodily injury that are incurred. In fact, the psychological damage caused by such aggression is often far worse than any objective outcome, for almost all those involved in such crimes share to some degree a sense of **victimization**, the feeling that one has lost a measure of control over one's world. Because the sense of control over the occurrences in one's life is an important concomitant of a sense of well-being (Taylor, Lichtman, & Wood, 1984), loss of control can have important ramifications.

Among the crimes that bring about the greatest perception of loss of control is that of rape (Bard & Ellison, 1974). In fact, one of the most common reactions to rape is the development of self-blame in which the victim feels that she is somehow responsible for the event (Burgess & Holmstrom, 1974). Although in reality this is seldom true—the National Commission on the Causes and Prevention of Violence (1969) found that only 4.4 percent of rapes were brought about by the actions of the victim—the victim's perception that she is somehow at fault remains.

At first glance, the pervasive tendency for victims to blame themselves for their rapes is puzzling, given that it is simply not true in most cases. On reflection, however, the development of self-blame makes sense when viewed in light of the notion of perceived control. By blaming specific actions she has taken in a particular situation, a victim may increase her sense of control over the event and thus maintain a sense of mastery over the world in general. This type of self-blame, which has been termed **behavioral self-blame** (Janoff-Bulman, 1979), can thus be seen as a response which preserves victims' feelings that they are in control of their own lives.

Behavioral self-blame contrasts with **characterological self-blame**, in which the victims blame themselves because of internal personality failings—for being too trusting, gullible, or careless, for instance. Characterological self-blame is a less adaptive response to victimization, because it suggests that there is nothing the victim can do to alter the loss of control experienced from the rape.

In a survey of counselors at rape crisis centers, Janoff-Bulman (1979) found that the great majority (69 percent) of rape victims tended to adopt behavioral self-blame stategies. For instance, some frequent examples of reasoning were: "I shouldn't have let someone I didn't know into the house"; "I shouldn't have been out that late"; "I should not have walked alone in that neighborhood"; "I should not have hitchhiked"; "I should not have gone to his apartment"; "I shouldn't have left my window open" (Janoff-Bulman, 1979, p. 1806). On the other hand, a minority of victims—19 percent—displayed characterological self-blame, including: "I'm too trusting"; "I'm a weak person"; "I'm too naive and gullible"; "I'm the kind of person who attracts trouble"; "I'm immature and can't take care of myself" (p. 1806).

The finding that most rape victims seem to use behavioral self-blame strategies suggests that self-blame in many cases may actually be an adaptive response to victimization. It focuses the victim's attention on what she should do differently in the future to prevent a similar incident. On the other hand, forms of self-blame that focus on the unmodifiable basic character of the victim are less positive, because they suggest that the victim has little control over her environment and that she is, because of her personality, a likely victim again in the future.

In fact, counselors for victims of crime might make use of techniques that increase victims' sense of control as a therapeutic technique. By helping victims to see the way in which they can influence events in their lives, counselors may also be helping victims regain control of lives that have been severely disrupted.

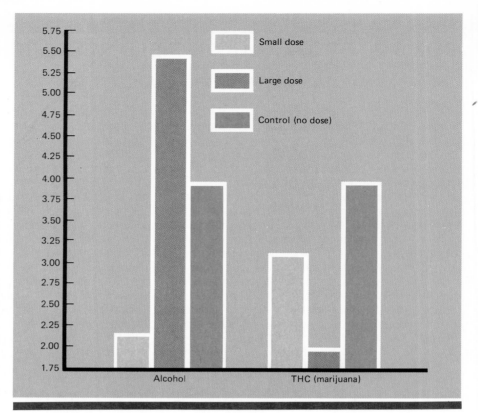

FIGURE 9-5
Effects of administration
of alcohol and THC on
length of shocks given
confederate. Although
large doses of alcohol increased aggression,
smaller amounts tended
to decrease it. Large
amounts of THC, in con-
trast, reduced aggression,
while a small dose had
only a minimal effect.
Source: S. P. Taylor, Vardaris, Rawitch, Gammon,
Cranston, & Lubetkin
(1976).

and drugs on aggression are quite specific to the particular type of
substance being ingested.

Heat and Noise: How the Physical Environment Affects Aggression

One of the most common explanations that could be found in the mass
media for the triggering of the massive urban riots that occurred in the
United States in the 1960s was the weather. According to the argument,
rioting tended to occur on days in which temperatures were unusually
hot, and in point of fact, it was obvious that in almost every case, riots
had tended to take place during the hottest summer months.

At first, social psychologists found such arguments reasonable, since
there was research suggesting that there ought to be a direct relationship
between aggression and temperature. For instance, some laboratory
studies found that as temperatures rose, animosity toward others tended
to increase (e.g., Griffitt & Veitch, 1971). But subsequent work showed
that the relationship was not always as clear-cut as first assumed. For
example, some studies showed just the opposite effect: Baron (1972)
found that subjects showed greater aggression against a confederate
when the temperature hovered around a comfortable 72° to 75°F than

when it was quite hot (91° to 95°F), and Baron and Ransberger (1978) found that rioting tended to escalate when the temperature was between 76° and 90°F—and then drop off at higher temperatures.

The most recent evidence regarding the relationships between aggression and temperature suggests that, as was first thought, aggression does tend to rise as a direct function of increasing heat. In a field study, Anderson and Anderson (1984) examined the incidence of the aggressive crimes of rape and murder that took place over a two-year period in the Houston, Texas, metropolitan area. As you can see in Figure 9-6, the incidence of aggressive crimes generally tended to rise as the temperatures rose—an increase that is statistically significant.

In sum, most evidence seems to suggest that heat is directly related to aggression: as the temperature rises, so does the likelihood of increased aggression. Moreover, it is not just obvious environmental factors such as the temperature of the air that lead to aggression; current work suggests that even such subtle influences as the presence of negative air ions can produce increased aggression (Baron, Russel, & Arms, 1984).

Noise as a source of aggression. We have discussed a number of instances in which increased physiological arousal leads to heightened aggression. When considering the factor of noise level, it seems reasonable that if excessive noise could be shown to lead to higher levels of arousal, it would also facilitate aggression. Indeed, most research seems to support such an interpretation, but with an important qualification: for noise to facilitate aggression, there must be some predisposing factor present, such as having viewed an aggressive film or having been angered by another individual (Konečni, 1975; Donnerstein & Wilson, 1976). On the other hand, if we consider the number of people who are

FIGURE 9-6
The relationship between temperature and aggressive crime. These data, based upon the results of a field study carried out in Houston, Texas, generally show that increasing levels of aggression are related to higher temperatures. Source: C. A. Anderson & Anderson (1984).

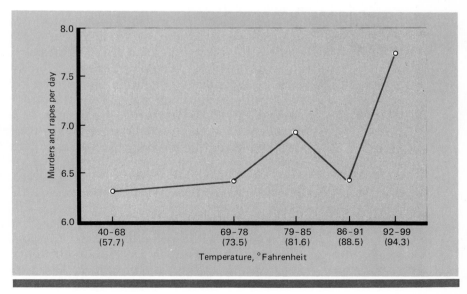

apt to have been angered for one reason or another prior to being exposed to high levels of noise—for example, in a noisy bus station filled with shoving commuters on their way home from work—instances of overt aggression due to the noise may not be infrequent.

Deindividuation: Anonymity Facilitates Aggression

If you have ever seen pictures of a Ku Klux Klan rally, you would probably agree that one of their striking characteristics is the white, hooded robes worn by the Klan members. No one's individual features can be discerned in such a costume; people blend into a mass of undifferentiated similarity.

While we would expect the Klan to explain its robes in terms of a uniform that sets members apart from nonmembers, social psychologists see another purpose such clothing serves: the anonymity of the custom produces a psychological state known as **deindividuation.** In deindividuation, self-awareness is reduced, fear of negative evaluation by others is diminished, and the individual is consequently more apt to engage in impulsive, antisocial, and nonnormatively sanctioned behaviors (Zimbardo, 1969; Diener, 1979). Deindividuation is also a potential cause of aggression, and this fact has been shown in a number of experiments.

One of the first demonstrations of deindividuation in the laboratory actually mimicked the example of the Ku Klux Klan. Philip Zimbardo devised a straightforward and simple manipulation: he had subjects wear a hood and a large laboratory coat so that they could not be identified (see Figure 9-7). He found that these deindividuated subjects were considerably more aggressive, as measured by bogus electric shocks delivered toward a disliked confederate, than subjects who were not anonymous (Zimbardo, 1969).

In a more recent study that examined not just the aggressive behavior but also the emotions experienced by deindividuated persons, Prentice-Dunn and Rogers (1980) manipulated whether subjects received individuated or deindividuated cues prior to administering shocks to another person in the guise of a behavior modification experiment. In the deindividuated condition, subjects were not addressed by name; they were told that the shock intensities they used would not be seen by the experimenter and that he would take full responsibility for their actions; they thought they would not meet the recipient of the shocks; and white noise was played loudly in the dimly lit room. In the individuated condition, the opposite was true: the subjects wore name tags and were addressed by name, the "unique reactions" of the subject were stressed, shock intensities were to be measured, the subject's responsibility for the well-being of the victim was emphasized, and the experiment was held in a brightly lit room, devoid of white noise.

The results showed that the deindividuation manipulation was effective in increasing aggression: subjects delivered shocks that on average were almost 50 percent greater in intensity in the deindividuation con-

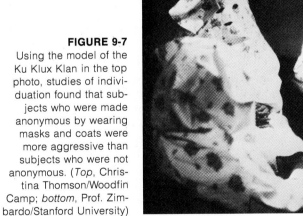

FIGURE 9-7
Using the model of the
Ku Klux Klan in the top
photo, studies of indivi-
duation found that sub-
jects who were made
anonymous by wearing
masks and coats were
more aggressive than
subjects who were not
anonymous. (*Top*, Chris-
tina Thomson/Woodfin
Camp; *bottom*, Prof. Zim-
bardo/Stanford University)

dition than in the individuation condition. Moreover, subjects in the
deindividuated condition reported experiencing a number of emotions
consistent with an internal state of deindividuation. They indicated that
their thinking and their emotions differed from normal in that they did
not feel responsible for causing harm, did not feel self-conscious, and
were less concerned with what both the experimenter and the victim
thought of them.

The results of this experiment and subsequent work on deindividuation (e.g., Prentice-Dunn & Rogers, 1983) suggest that increasing the individuation of members of groups such as the Ku Klux Klan and other uniformed organizations may act to decrease the incidence of aggression. Therefore, law enforcement agencies which may infiltrate the Ku Klux Klan, thereby becoming aware of the identities of the individual members, may be doing so in part with the intention of destroying the sense of deindividuation provided by the hoods and robes.

Direct Provocation as a Source of Aggression: If You Hurt Me, I'll Hurt You

One of the easiest ways to evoke aggression is to act aggressively toward another individual. What would a child's reaction be, for instance, to a classmate who made insulting remarks about his physical appearance and parental ancestry? Most likely his reaction would be one of anger. And if this bully continued to be abusive, a full-fledged fight might occur.

Such reactions to aggressive instigations are not limited to children. Adults, in fact, react in much the same way to insults and violence on the part of others. Let us consider verbal abuse and insults first. Many studies have shown that recipients of insulting and derogatory remarks show subsequent aggression toward the source of such abuse. And the retaliation is not necessarily in kind; verbal abuse is often followed by substantial physical aggression toward the instigator. In fact, there is some evidence that individuals exposed to verbal attack are more likely to display aggression to the insulting individual than when they are simply frustrated (Geen, 1968).

No less straightforward is the finding that physical aggression is a likely consequence of receiving a physical attack. When people are physically hurt, they tend to respond with aggression toward the source of pain. Moreover—as social learning theory would predict—they tend to match their level of retaliatory aggression to the level of pain they have received. For example, Taylor and Pisano (1971) placed subjects in a situation in which it appeared that a competitor kept increasing the level of shocks being given the subject. In return, most subjects tended to keep raising the level of their retaliatory shocks, thus matching their own general level of aggressiveness to that of their opponent.

Interestingly, simply being told that an opponent is *planning* in the future to be increasingly aggressive is sufficient to evoke retaliatory aggression at the higher level—even if the opponent does not act more aggressively (Greenwell & Dengerink, 1973). Apparently, it is not only the nature of physical discomfort that brings about a person's retaliatory aggression, but also the idea that the individual is planning an attack.

Basically, then, aggression is facilitated by exposure to the aggression of others. The aggressive party may serve as a model or may act directly to anger or frustrate the observer. In either case, if someone acts aggressively toward us, we are likely to retaliate. On the other hand, as

Berkowitz (1983) suggests, such retaliatory aggression is not inevitable; people can learn to overcome and restrain their aggressive tendencies.

AGGRESSION AS A WAY OF LIFE: IS THERE AN AGGRESSIVE PERSONALITY?

Throughout our discussion of aggression, we have been dealing with more-or-less "everyday" forms of aggression—the kind of aggression that occurs when psychopathology is not present and that follows some clearly defined, discriminable stimulus. We have also been assuming that the degree of aggression displayed by the aggressor is fairly proportionate to the degree of instigation experienced. Thus, in none of the experiments we have described has any subject gone beyond the constraints imposed by the experimenter and chased an obnoxious confederate with a hammer, rather than using the opportunity provided to administer electric shocks.

Outside the laboratory, however, aggression is not so tidily confined to discrete, relatively minor aggressive acts. In fact, there is a class of people known as **undercontrolled aggressors** who are responsible for a share of violent behavior far beyond their actual numbers (Megargee, 1966). These individuals employ aggression as a natural part of their lives; they react aggressively to stimuli which in others would provoke little, if any, reaction; and their lives may become centered around aggressive incidents.

Models of Violent People

The fullest description of such violent individuals comes from an extensive study carried out by Hans Toch (1969, 1975). He used a sample of seventy-seven people who had been imprisoned and had a history of unusually violent incidents. Through extensive interviews, Toch developed a set of ten categories into which each of the subjects fell (see Table 9-1) and these were validated through careful analysis by groups of judges. Among the major types were those termed "self-image promoters" (27.5 percent), "self-image defenders" (23 percent), and " 'rep' defenders" (14.5 percent).

A description of a few can provide the flavor of the category system. Self-image promoters are those with low self-esteem, and they seem to seek out violent situations to promote what they consider to be a more appropriate image. In contrast, self-image defenders, who also have low self-esteem, react violently to even the most benign situation or slightest affront in order to ensure that others will not come to a similar conclusion about their self-worth. "Rep" defenders are aggressive because of a social role that they feel has been assigned to them. Basically, they have a reputation to uphold because of their position within a social hierarchy, and their physical aggressiveness helps them to maintain their image as leaders.

TABLE 9-1   The Typology of "Violent Men" Proposed by Toch
These figures show the percentage of subjects who make up each of Toch's categories of violent people.

Type	Percentage
Self-image promoting	27.5
Self-image defending	13.0
"Rep" defending	14.5
Pressure removing	11.6
Exploiting	10.0
Bullying	5.8
Self-defending	5.8
Self-indulging	4.3
Norm enforcing	4.3
Catharsis producing	2.9

Source: Based on data from Toch (1969).

Each of the ten categories devised by Toch presents a quite disparate background and rationale for violence, and it is clear that no universal pattern can be used to explain all cases of violence. It also appears that, unlike "normal" aggressors, whose behavior is determined largely by situational factors, unusually violent people's aggression is more a function of their own personal characteristics and traits.

A Case of the Bad Seed?

An approach related to the study of aggressive individuals has been to examine the genetic makeup of people who are especially violent. In the early 1970s, evidence began to accumulate that certain male individuals who were born with an extra Y chromosome tended to display occasional episodes of violent behavior. Moreover, males with the extra Y chromosome, which is an extremely rare phenomenon occurring only once in more than 1000 births, were less intelligent than average and were unusually tall.

Most surprising was the finding that males with the extra Y chromosome were overrepresented in prison populations. In fact, one study found that prison inmates were fifteen times more likely to have the extra Y than the general population (Jarvik, Klodin, & Matsuyama, 1973). Such findings led some theorists to suggest that the presence of the additional Y chromosome could account for the violent and aggressive behavior of criminals. In fact, such a hypothesis has a strong intuitive appeal, and quite a few scientists, particularly those with a psychobiological orientation, and the mass media have popularized the notion.

It turned out, however, that there were a number of alternate explanations which began to cast doubt upon the efficacy of the extra-Y explanation. As Bandura (1973) pointed out, the greater incidence of extra-Y males in prison may be due directly to their tallness and lower intelligence—and these traits, in turn, may be why they are more likely to be criminals than individuals with a normal chromosome makeup. People with lower intelligence may be inept criminals, which may lead to their being caught more frequently. Lower intelligence may also preclude involvement in more intellectually challenging activities. Moreover, unusual height may allow them to be more aggressive toward others at an earlier age. Furthermore, if they are rewarded for such behavior, their general level of aggressiveness may be higher. Thus, rather than the extra Y chromosome being directly responsible for the aggression, the lower intelligence and unusual height may be the culprits.

Even more damning to the extra-Y explanation are demographic data that show that most people arrested and convicted of crimes do not have that chromosomal makeup, and that most people with the extra Y are never convicted of violent crimes (Witkin, Mednick, Schulsinger, Bakkestrom, Christiansen, Goodenough, Hirschorn, Lundsteen, Owen, Phillip, Ruben, & Stocking, 1976). It seems, then, as if the "bad seed" notion that aggressive behavior is predestined by an extra Y chromosome must be rejected.

On the other hand, there *is* evidence that abnormalities in the structure of the brain may be related to aggressive and violent tendencies. Work with animals has shown that aggression can be elicited by stimulation of particular areas of the brain (Delgado, 1969). Conversely, aggression in animals can be reduced by destroying certain portions of the brain. Moreover, occasional instances of extreme violence are found in individuals with brain abnormalities. For example, after Charles Whitman's 1966 shooting spree at the University of Texas, in which he killed fourteen people, shot at random on a clear, balmy afternoon, an autopsy revealed that he had a brain tumor in a part of the brain associated with aggression in animals. Still, in most instances of aggression there is no evidence of brain dysfunction, and brain dysfunction does not invariably lead to violent behavior. As with theories of chromosomal defects, then, explanations of aggressive behaviors that rely on brain abnormalities do not prove to be very useful.

PREVENTING AND REDUCING AGGRESSION

Given the magnitude of the problem of aggression in our society, enormous efforts have been put forth to attempt to prevent and reduce its occurrence. In the remainder of the chapter, we turn to some of the methods suggested by social psychological approaches to aggression that have been put forward to control aggression.

Cleansing the Body and Soul: The Catharsis Hypothesis

"Jack got into a fight again today on the playground," said the principal at a hurriedly called conference with Jack's parents. "We have got to do something about this pattern of aggressive behavior."

Jack's father replied, "I think I've got the answer. I've enrolled Jack in boxing lessons. I'm sure he'll be able to get his aggression out of his system in the ring."

The idea espoused above by Jack's father—that aggressive activities can release pent-up aggression—has been termed the **catharsis hypothesis.** This notion has been in vogue a very long time; one of the earliest proponents was Aristotle, who suggested that individuals who observed dramas could be purged of emotional feelings and impulses. Even today, many theorists using psychoanalytic and ethological theoretical approaches to aggression espouse some form of the hypothesis. For example, some writers taking a psychoanalytic approach suggest that hitting others with foam-covered bats (which actually produce no pain or injury to the victim) may have therapeutic qualities; it is assumed that subsequent aggression will be reduced (Bach & Wyden, 1968).

While the notion of catharsis is an appealing one, since it suggests a socially desirable vehicle for reducing aggressive impulses, the scientific evidence in its support is inconsistent. Indeed, there is a good deal of research suggesting that acts of aggression may actually *increase* subsequent behavioral and verbal aggressiveness (Geen, Stonner, & Shope, 1975; Ebbesen, Duncan, & Konečni, 1975).

There is, however, at least one clear set of circumstances under which later aggression *is* reduced through immediate aggression: when people who are angry are allowed to be physically aggressive against the individual who initially angered them, later aggression toward that person is reduced. For instance, in an experiment by Doob and Wood (1972), subjects were either angered or not angered by a confederate, according to condition. Next, half the subjects were given the opportunity to act aggressively by way of administering (bogus) electric shocks to the confederate, while the other half were required to wait by themselves in another room. Finally, all of the subjects participated in the final phase of the experiment, in which they were given the opportunity to administer (bogus) shocks against the confederate, this time in the context of reward and punishment for answers deemed to be noncreative.

The results of the Doob and Wood experiment were clear: for subjects who had been angered, the initial opportunity to act aggressively toward the source of the anger produced a significant reduction in later aggression, compared with those angered subjects who had not had the earlier opportunity to act aggressively. Unangered subjects showed no difference in later aggression according to whether or not they had had the opportunity to be aggressive earlier.

Subsequent research has confirmed that such catharsis effects are largely limited to cases in which a person's aggression is directed toward the individual who caused that person to be angry initially. Unfortunately, this hardly appears to be an effective means for curbing aggression, since catharsis in the form of reduced later aggression occurs only after the individual has had an initial opportunity to act aggressively. And more extreme forms of the catharsis hypothesis have not fared well at all. As we saw when we discussed the effects of media violence on aggression, viewing aggressive movies and television shows can actually increase aggressive behaviors. Thus, although catharsis may be effective in certain limited circumstances, participation in and exposure to aggression are not generally effective mechanisms for reducing later aggression.

Punishment as a Means of Controlling Aggression

It is conceivable that in our earlier example of the aggressive schoolboy, Jack, his father could have suggested to the principal that he be allowed to "beat the pants off him" as a way to control his aggression. Indeed, punishment of aggressive behavior is the means society most often chooses to control aggression: assaults, muggings, and rape lead to long prison terms, and murder is—in most parts of the world—punishable with death. On a lesser scale, it was not so long ago that corporal punishment—the use of physical pain—was legal in most of the schools in this country. And spankings remain an established socially acceptable child-raising practice.

Despite the prevalence of the use of punishment to deter aggression, there are a number of reasons its long-term efficacy is doubtful. First, physical punishments are likely to lead to anger and, as we saw earlier, ultimately to more aggression—if not necessarily to the person who produced the aggression, then to other, more vulnerable victims. Second, the individuals who mete out the punishment may act as aggressive models themselves and thus increase the likelihood of future aggression. Moreover, because administering punishment may be rewarding to the provider—since it usually leads to at least a temporary disruption of the aggression—the *provider* of punishment may be more likely to be aggressive in the future. Finally, the effects of punishment are often transitory; while they may temporarily prevent aggression, the reduction often does not last (Sulzer-Azaroff & Mayer, 1984).

The use of punishment, then, has not proven to be an effective, consistent means for reducing aggression. Although under certain conditions punishment can produce declines in aggression, the circumstances are fairly limited.

Social Learning Theory Approaches to Controlling Aggression

Social learning approaches to aggression suggest an alternative means of reducing aggression: the use of nonaggressive models. Data that show that aggressive models who are rewarded for their aggression elicit aggression from observers can also be used to infer that observation of nonaggressive models ought to reduce aggression. Moreover, the work on modeling effects on prosocial behavior (discussed in Chapter 7) also points to the conclusion that observation of nonaggressive models may be effective in controlling aggression.

In fact, there are laboratory data to support the notion that observation of nonaggressive models can lead to a reduction in aggression. For instance, in one study subjects who viewed a nonaggressive model were less aggressive to a peer than those who had viewed an aggressive one (Baron & Kepner, 1970). Unfortunately, given that most people are exposed to aggressive as well as nonaggressive models in their daily lives—even if only through media exposure—the observation of nonaggressive models may not be effective in a practical sense.

A more promising technique for reducing aggression has recently been developed by Huesmann, Eron, Klein, Brice, and Fischer (1983). Rather than being concerned with whether models act aggressively or nonaggressively, the emphasis is on the *interpretation* of the behaviors made by an observer. In the technique, which has been used in relation to exposure to media violence, an attempt is made to change people's attitudes toward the meaning of aggression that they view on television. They are taught that television violence is unrealistic, that aggressive behaviors do not have the same degree of acceptability in the real world that they do on television, and that aggressive behavior modeled by television characters is not appropriate. By changing attitudes about violence, it is assumed that the observation of aggression will have a smaller impact.

Do these notions hold up? A field study suggests that they do (Huesmann et al., 1983). A sample of first- and third-grade children who had a high incidence of exposure to television violence was exposed to two experimental treatments that were designed to reduce their imitation of violence viewed on television. The first treatment consisted of participation in three training sessions designed to teach that the behavior of the characters on violent shows does not represent the behavior of most people, that camera techniques and special effects provide only the illusion that aggression is occurring, and that most people use alternatives to aggression to solve their problems. A further treatment, administered nine months after the first, provided training that more explicitly taught the children that watching television violence was not desirable and that they should not imitate violent television programs.

The results were impressive. Compared with a control group who received training on issues unrelated to aggression, experimental group subjects were rated as significantly lower in aggression by their classmates. Moreover, subjects' attitudes toward watching television aggression became more negative.

It appears, then, that it is possible to decrease the effects of exposure to violence by altering people's perceptions and attitudes regarding the meaning of such aggression. Still, social learning theory suggests an even more direct way to reduce aggression: limiting exposure to aggressive models. If television and other media could reduce the violent content of programming, it seems reasonable that aggression could be reduced—especially when children spend more time watching television than they spend in school and probably in direct communication with their parents, as is the case in the United States (Singer, 1983).

In sum, social psychological approaches to aggression provide some direction toward preventing and reducing its occurrence. It remains for society to employ such techniques in a systematic manner in order to modify the perception—articulated by Chief Murphy at the start of this chapter—that violence is as American as apple pie.

SUMMARY

Although some theorists contend that aggression is any behavior that harms or hurts someone else, the predominant view is that aggression refers to the intentional injury or harm of another person. There are three broad models that seek to explain the occurrence of aggression: instinct theories, frustration–aggression approaches, and social learning theory.

Instinct theories argue that aggression represents an innate urge. Freud suggests that aggression is a manifestation of thanatos, the death instinct, that is directed toward others. Lorenz argues that human beings have a fighting instinct which causes their aggressive behavior, and that aggressive energy builds up over time until it is discharged in a socially desirable or undesirable way. Instinct theories in general lack experimental support.

The frustration–aggression hypothesis in its original form predicts that frustration always leads to aggression and that aggression is always the result of some frustration. Although too broadly stated, the basic notion has stood empirical testing. Refinements suggest, however, that frustration leads to a readiness to act aggressively, but whether the aggression actually occurs depends on the presence of aggressive cues in the environment.

Social learning theory suggests that aggressive behaviors are learned behaviors, shaped by rewards and punishments. A primary means of learning aggression is through the observation of models. Observing live models rewarded for acting aggressively clearly leads to increased aggression on the part of viewers, and this point suggests the hypothesis that observing television and movie media violence can result in heightened aggression. Although difficult to confirm experimentally, the hypothesis has received at least correlational support.

A number of situational factors in the social and physical environment are also related to aggression. Physiological arousal caused by exercise can facilitate aggression in angered individuals. Sexual arousal is linked to aggression, also, but in a more complicated fashion: both nonerotic and highly erotic stimuli increase aggression, while moderate levels of sexual arousal produce relatively lower levels of aggression. Moreover, violent pornography has been linked clearly to increased aggression toward women in laboratory experiments. Finally, arousal due to the ingestion of relatively large amounts of marijuana reduces aggression, while large amounts of alcohol produce greater aggression.

The physical environment is also related to aggression. Heat provokes greater aggression, according to the results of current research, as does noise level, at least when some predisposing factor relating to aggression has been present.

Deindividuation is a psychological state in which self-awareness is reduced, fear of negative evaluation by others is diminished, and, consequently, the individual is apt to engage in impulsive and antisocial activity—including increased aggression. Another cause of aggression relates to direct provocation. Either verbal or actual aggression directed toward a person is apt to provoke a physically aggressive response toward the instigator.

Some approaches to aggression have focused on individuals who are characteristically predisposed to violence. Categorizations of aggressive individuals show that there is no universal personality pattern or background that can be used to explain cases of violence. Likewise, results of studies of individuals with an extra Y chromosome, although showing a somewhat higher incidence of criminal activity than would be expected, do not definitively link increased aggression with genetic makeup.

Social psychological research has suggested a number of approaches to reducing aggression. The catharsis hypothesis suggests that aggressive activities can release pent-up aggression. However, the evidence in its support is very inconsistent. Punishment, although the means most frequently employed by society to control aggression, also has a number of drawbacks. The most promising approaches are based on social learning theories. The observation of nonaggressive models and modification of attitudes toward aggression both seem to be effective.

KEY TERMS

aggression
behavioral self-blame
catharsis hypothesis
characterological self-blame
deindividuation
desensitization
eros
ethology

fight-or-flight response
frustration–aggression theory
instinct theory of aggression
social learning theory of aggression
thanatos
victimization
weapons effect

FOR FURTHER STUDY AND APPLICATION

Bandura, A. (1973). *Aggression: A social learning analysis.* Englewood Cliffs, NJ: Prentice-Hall.

A readable guide and persuasive statement of social learning approaches to aggression. Provides a number of practical approaches to preventing and dealing with children's aggression.

Baron, R. A. (1977). *Human aggression.* New York: Plenum.

A well-written, comprehensive guide to research on aggression. Organized in a laudatory fashion and filled with insightful examples.

Hornstein, H. (1973). *Cruelty and kindness.* Englewood Cliffs, NJ: Prentice-Hall.

A fascinating integration of the topics of aggression and helping behavior. Readable and scholarly.

Geen, R. G., & Donnerstein, E. I. (1983). *Aggression: Theoretical and empirical reviews* (Vols. 1 and 2). New York: Academic Press.

Mummendy, A. (1984). *The social psychology of aggression.* New York: Springer-Verlag.

Zillman, D. (1978). *Hostility and aggression.* Hillsdale, NJ: Erlbaum.

Technical and comprehensive theoretical views of the work on aggression. Although written at a high level, they provide a good deal of detail useful to the person interested in aggression.

Malamuth, N. M., & Donnerstein, F. (Eds.). (1983). *Pornography and sexual aggression.* New York: Academic Press.

Written by the acknowledged experts in the field, this volume contains information on the relationship between rape and other types of sexual aggression and pornographic materials.

PART FOUR

SOCIAL INFLUENCE, GROUPS, AND ORGANIZATIONS

CHAPTER 10

SOCIAL INFLUENCE

A CONVERSATION WITH . . .

Shirley Chisholm
Politician

Shirley Chisholm, the first black woman elected to the U.S. House of Representatives, has had a long and distinguished career as a political leader. Serving for seven terms in the House—before choosing not to run for reelection—she has had national prominence as a political figure that has grown to large proportions. She was a member of the powerful Rules Committee and is a recognized expert in women's issues, labor, and education. Even now, although "officially" retired from politics and a professor of sociology at Mount Holyoke College, she commands large audiences during her frequent travels around the country, giving invited addresses. We began our conversation discussing her views of leadership:

Q. Social psychologists—along with philosophers, political scientists, and the like—have spent a good deal of time arguing about the nature of leadership. What, in your view as a politician, are the determinants of leadership?

A. To me, leadership implies the ability of a person to influence others on the basis of clear, precise, and concise enunciations of ideas, positions, and suggestions. That means that they must be able to articulate well and must be able to have their objectives and purposes clearly set in their own mind. In addition, not only is a leader attempting to impart a body of information to establish clear-cut positions to another, but the leader is also hoping to influence another's thinking. A leader also must, I think, have a sense of humor, a very important ingredient nowadays in attempting to influence others. People are so disturbed about so many things that unless you have certain factors that will help gain their atten-

tion or will help them to warm up to you, you could very well lose them along the way. And they also must not only be able to laugh, but they must be able to laugh at themselves.

Q. Many of those characteristics seem to fit President Ronald Reagan. He is certainly a good communicator of his policies, quite apart from any specific policies that one may or may not like. Do you consider him to be a good leader?

A. I think he fits many of those criteria. He is a very, very charming political personality. My ideology is almost the exact opposite of his, but you have to say he has strength. He enunciates clearly and precisely whatever it is he believes in. Nobody has to question where he's coming from and he's very clear-cut in terms of being able to talk about his objectives and purposes. He has his own kind of charisma. All of this, I think, has to be added up to a certain kind of leadership talent, whether or not you believe in what he's done.

Q. It seems as if you feel an individual can have leadership qualities quite apart from the specifics of a given situation. Does that mean you feel that leadership comes from a particular set of personality traits, independent of the situation?

A. I tend to feel that leadership capability is almost inborn. However, it is necessary for a person to be exposed to the appropriate stimuli and have the opportunity to develop that inborn, innate talent in order for him or her to actually become a leader. I don't think leadership is something that can really be learned or can be transferred from one person to another. I think a person has to have certain kinds of qualities or requisites within him, and, if given the proper milieu in which to develop, these talents will germinate and he or she will lead.

Q. To you, then—and this is something many social psychologists agree on—leadership is determined by both individual characteristics and situational factors.

A. Yes, I do have that feeling, based on my observations of effective leaders.

Q. You have mentioned quite a few characteristics that you feel are important in determining leadership. Are the leaders in the House of Representatives by and large individuals who fit your description of what makes a good leader?

A. Not at all. Built into the processes in the House are the requirements of longevity of service and tenure, who knows the right people, and who has the energy to get the votes behind

him or her. Excellence of leadership has little to do with it.

Q. You were one of the people with power in the House. Why did you retire from the political arena, and do you miss wielding the power that you had?

A. I said twenty-five years ago, when I entered the political arena, that I never intended to spend all of my creative and productive life in politics. It is a very, very rough life, particularly when one is as independent-minded as I am. I always knew I wanted to return to a more private existence and do some things for myself; and now I'm having a chance to do that. And, of course, I always considered that part of the power that I had was to educate others—and in my current role as professor and in my lectures around the country, I still am able to do that.

OVERVIEW

- At the urging of Reverend Jim Jones, more than 900 people stood patiently in line to take a deadly dose of cyanide, as those who preceded them lay on the ground moaning in agony as the poison did its work.

- Despite the fact that she really didn't think it a good idea, Sally nevertheless raised her hand to support twenty-four-hour male visitation rights in her dormitory. Because the voting was open, everyone would know how she voted—and what would her dorm mates think about someone who was so clearly on the "wrong" side of the issue?

Despite the obvious dissimilarities in the two prior incidents, a social psychological analysis would suggest some fundamental commonalities in the two situations—for both illustrate the power of **social influence** in people's lives. Social influence takes place when the actions of an individual or a group affect the behavior of others. The influence may be intentional—as in the case of Reverend Jim Jones, who actively urged a course of action on his followers—or it may be unintentional—as in the second scenario, in which Sally's mere anticipation of negative consequences for not conforming to the group is enough to affect her behavior. Either way, the outcome is a clear change in behavior due to other individuals.

In this chapter, we begin by examining social psychological approaches to conformity and compliance. **Conformity** refers to changes in behavior as a result of implicit group pressure, which may be real or imagined. It often involves private acceptance of the group's position, although this is not always the case. In contrast, **compliance** refers to behavioral changes due to explicit requests or demands from others. In the case of compliance, there is typically no underlying change in position; the person merely follows the group publicly but not privately.

Our examination of conformity and compliance will lead us to consider the processes that lead people to follow a majority point of view. But we will also discuss how individuals can be influenced by, and sometimes adopt, minority positions as well. We will then examine compliance to authority figures. This will lead us to the final part of the chapter, which concerns power and leadership. We will discuss the different kinds of power, and determine what it is that brings people—such as Shirley Chisholm—into leadership roles that allow them to exert influence over others.

CONFORMITY

To begin our discussion of social influence, put yourself in the following situation:

> You are among six new army recruits, listening to a lecture by a military officer. All of a sudden, you notice that your fellow recruits have stood up, removed their hats, and turned away from the lecturer, and they are starting to march out of the room—as the lecturer, seemingly unaware of what has happened, continues with his briefing. As the hapless sixth recruit, what are you likely to do under these conditions?

If you are like most people placed in this situation, your first reaction will be one of puzzlement and bafflement. But what is likely to happen soon is that you will follow the lead of the others, taking off your hat, standing up, and ultimately marching off to an unknown destination, just as they have done. The reason? You have been subject to strong and consistent pressures to conform, one of the phenomena of social life that plays a powerful role in determining our behavior.

The scenario described above is drawn from an episode of *Candid Camera*, the old television show in which people found themselves in ludicrous situations designed by the show's producers, only to be filmed by hidden cameras. In fact, the situation is quite similar to one devised by Solomon Asch in the 1950s to measure conformity to others in an experimental setting (Asch, 1951). In Asch's study, seven subjects were told that they were going to participate in a study of perception in which they would be asked to judge the length of lines. They were shown pairs of two cards, one of which contained a line called the standard, and one of which showed three additional lines. The subject's job was to identify which of three additional lines was identical in length to the standard.

For the first few sets of cards, all went well; one of the three lines was always the same length as the standard, and all the subjects were in agreement. But soon, something strange began to happen—at least from one subject's point of view. All of the other subjects, who each announced his or her choice aloud, in turn chose what appeared to be a clearly wrong alternative. In the same way that the lone recruit in the *Candid Camera* sequence was faced with either doing what he felt was reasonable or conforming to the group's behavior, the remaining subject was placed in the position of following his own sensory judgment or going along with the group. As you might have suspected, the group's puzzling behavior was actually controlled by the experimenter; there were five confederates, trained to give unanimously erroneous answers on certain trials, and just one actual subject.

In the same way that the army recruit joined with his fellow recruits in a series of bizarre behaviors, so did many of Asch's subjects. In fact, on about one-third of the trials subjects conformed to the unanimous but erroneous group decision, choosing an alternative that was clearly in error. However, Asch also found strong individual differences. Some of the subjects conformed to the group nearly all the time, while others remained totally independent of the pressure. But more than 75 percent of the subjects in the experiment conformed at least once to the others' judgments.

In both our examples, the individual's behavior yielded to the implicit influence of others. Indeed, this is the basic definition of conformity, which can be considered a change in public behavior or private belief as a result of real or imagined group pressure (Kiesler & Kiesler, 1969). Note that the changes in either public behavior or private belief are considered conformity; conforming behavior can occur even when people do not truly believe their public response. It was unlikely that most subjects in Asch's study felt that their perceptual experience was congruent with the group's erroneous responses; rather, subjects yielded to the group for more complicated reasons.

To understand why people conform to group pressure, we must examine a distinction between two types of social influence first cited by Deutsch and Gerard (1955)—normative and informational social pressure. **Normative social influence** is related to group norms, which are expectations held by those belonging to groups on how group members ought to behave (Rommetveit, 1955). Normative social pressure operates because of our attempts to meet the expectations of the group. One reason we conform, then, is because our experience has led us to believe that transgressors of group norms are punished by the other members of the group. Thus, someone may appear to agree with a majority decision about whether we should be allowed unlimited visitation in a dorm—as we mentioned in an earlier example—in order to avoid the anger that disagreement with such a position might bring about.

But there is another important reason groups can influence our behavior, related to **informational social influence.** Because we are unable to experience firsthand much of the world's phenomena, we rely on others' perceptions, experience, and knowledge. Other people, then, can provide information about the world to us. The use of others as resource persons provides an opportunity for groups to influence us through informational social influence. We may conform, therefore, because we think that the group members have information about the situation that we are lacking. Returning to our example, it is possible that someone might feel that other group members know more about the benefits of having unlimited visitation rights—perhaps it makes dorms safer by scaring off intruders—and conform because of this possibility.

In most situations in which people conform, it is likely that both normative and informational social influences are operating. For instance, in the Asch experiment, subjects who conformed to the group responses probably were doing so out of a desire to avoid contradicting group norms and potentially being laughed at, embarrassed, or punished in some other way by the group (normative social influence), as well as because they thought the other people might have had greater experience in the task or knew or saw something in the situation that they were missing (informational social influence).

The Autokinetic Phenomenon

A good deal of our knowledge of conformity has come from research that was inspired by an early series of studies done in the 1930s by Muzafir Sherif using a psychological phenomenon called the autokinetic effect. The **autokinetic effect,** which is the illusion that a small, stationary light in an otherwise darkened room appears to move, was used by Sherif to investigate the transmission of norms in groups.

The autokinetic effect is especially amenable to social influence because it is so ambiguous. Individuals making judgments by themselves vary widely in how much they perceive the pinpoint light (which is actually stationary) moving, with judgments ranging from less than an inch to more than a foot for some subjects. Interestingly, though, the judgments of subjects later brought together in groups and asked to announce their estimates aloud tend to converge, and subjects end up reporting that the light is moving the same amount (Sherif & Sherif, 1969). Even more important, when subjects are separated and again asked to make judgments by themselves, they tend to maintain the estimates that they made as a group.

The results of studies of the autokinetic effect and the way in which its perception is influenced by the presence of others has been used to trace the development of group norms. Prior to the group experience, individuals have no frame of reference in which to view the very ambiguous stimulus and thus make judgments that are relatively arbitrary in nature. However, the experience of making judgments with others allows the formation of an implicit group norm, which acts to define what is acceptable behavior. Hence, there is a convergence in the judgments of the group members.

Recent research has examined the persistence of the norms that develop in the group autokinetic situation. MacNeil and Sherif (1976) found that the greater the extremity of group norms from the original individual judgments of subjects, the less likely the norms would be accepted and transmitted by the group. To determine this, they planted confederates among naive subjects in groups making judgments about the degree of movement of the pinpoint light. The confederates manipulated the extremity of their judgments, thus causing variations in how extreme the initial group norms were. The subjects were asked to make judgments in successive groups, during which the confederates were gradually removed until only naive subjects were left. By the end of the series of judgments, groups in which the initial judgments of the confederates were extreme were far more likely to have moved away from the initial norms than groups in which the confederates caused the adoption of a more moderate norm initially.

MacNeil and Sherif interpret this finding as suggesting that the greater the extremity or arbitrariness of a norm, the greater the likelihood that the norm will be modified and eventually lost over the course of time. For example, it used to be customary in many colleges and universities for male students to wear jackets and ties to class. Given that there was no clear reason for this norm—there was certainly no evidence that people learned any better wearing a tie than a T-shirt—we might expect that it would be lost gradually and, of course, this is just what occurred. In sum, norms which have no clear rationale often tend to be transitory. This fact may help to explain why norms regarding fashions generally tend to show drastic shifts over the years.

Bringing About Conformity: How a Group Influences the Individual

Since the pioneering work of Sherif and Asch, literally hundreds of studies have investigated the phenomenon of conformity. We now know a great deal about the topic, and a few factors stand out that show how a group brings about conformity (Allen, 1965; Sanford & Penrod, 1984). We will discuss some of the major ones: the relationship between the individual and the group, how an individual is made to respond, the characteristics of the group's task, and the nature of the group.

Individual–Group Relationship   There are a number of ways in which individuals' relationship to the group will affect the degree to which the group can produce conformity. One of the major ones has to do with the principle that the more attractive the group and its members, the more people conform to the group. For instance, it is unlikely that we would ever see an advertisement for an automobile in which a group of sleazy, unshaven mobsters were shown extolling the virtues of the car. Rather—as we discussed in the chapter on attitudes—we are tempted by scenes of attractive celebrities who have chosen a particular make. The intent is to get us to conform to their view, and the advertisers are relying on the idea that we are more likely to conform to those we like. Although the basis for a person's attraction to the group may vary (it may be physical attractiveness, prestige, or competence), the result is basically the same: increased conformity.

Another factor relating to individuals' relationship to the group concerns the status of their position relative to the other members. **Status** refers to the social rank a person holds within a group. Generally speaking, lower-status individuals conform more to the group than higher-status individuals. On the other hand, certain theorists suggest that group leaders, who would generally be assumed to be high-status individuals, may conform more to group norms than others in order to maintain their position (Homans, 1950)—something we will discuss further when considering minority social influence later in this chapter.

Finally, conformity is greater in groups in which the members are similar to each other. The reason appears related to the notion that people seem to have a need to compare themselves to other, but relatively similar, people. According to this view, people who form the membership of a **reference group**—a group to which we belong or wish to belong and which provides standards and norms of appropriate behavior—can provide both explicit and implicit conformity pressure.

This phenomenon is illustrated by the changes that occur in the views of college students from the time they start their freshman year until they graduate. In a classic study, Newcomb (1961) showed that students who entered Bennington College, which could be characterized as quite politically, economically, and socially liberal, initially tended to be rather conservative, holding views similar to those of their parents. By the time they left Bennington, however, their views had become considerably more liberal. Newcomb attributed this change to a radical shift in reference groups. The freshmen initially tended to use their generally upper-class, conservative parents as reference group members but, as their time at Bennington increased, the reference group shifted to the more liberal juniors and seniors. Conformity therefore is related to the nature of an individual's reference group.

Response Conditions   Conformity is considerably higher when individuals must make public responses than when they can respond without the knowledge of the other group members. Similarly, a smaller degree of public commitment to a position is related to greater conformity; people who have previously made a strong public commitment to a position are less likely to be swayed by group pressure than those who have not committed themselves earlier on. Hence, a politician who early in her career took a strong stand in favor of military spending is unlikely to be easily convinced that military budgets should be cut, even when faced with strong pressures in that direction.

Task Characteristics   At least two factors relating to the characteristics of the group's task are related to conformity: the difficulty of the task and the individual's competence on it. The more difficult the activity in which the group is engaged and the less competent an individual is in performing the task, the greater his or her degree of conformity will be. The reason is probably related to the prevalence of informational social pressures to conform; we assume that a unanimous group is likely to have greater information and expertise (by virtue of their agreement) than we do.

Characteristics of the Group Members: Do Men or Women Conform More?   The characteristics of a group itself can have an important effect on the degree to which the group can influence its members. One factor that has attracted particular attention is the sex of the members of the group. Do men or women conform more?

Initial research seemed to suggest overwhelmingly that females conform at significantly higher levels than males. For instance, in a highly influential review of the literature, Allen (1965) concluded that "difference in amount of conformity for males and females has been repeatedly demonstrated, with females generally conforming more than males" (p. 159). However, more recent research has thrown that contention into doubt. A recent analysis by Alice Eagly and Linda Carli (Eagly, 1983; Eagly & Carli, 1981) employed a technique called meta-analysis, in which the results of numerous experiments are statistically combined to form an overall conclusion (see Box 10-1).

According to the results of the meta-analysis, Eagly and Carli also found support for the contention that women conform more in group pressure situations (and indeed were, in general, more persuadable than men). But they also found a potential biasing factor that could account for the difference: sex of the researcher. Almost 80 percent of the influenceability studies were carried out by males, and these male researchers tended to obtain larger sex differences (in the direction of greater female conformity) than female researchers did. In general, experiments authored by women showed no sex difference. It appears, then, that "sex differences" in conformity may be due not to actual differences between males and females, but rather to methodological difficulties.

Why should male researchers produce results that seem to favor men (if we consider a finding of less conformity and influenceability more favorable)? One reason may be that male and female experimenters differentially publish their findings in scholarly journals, with female experimenters choosing to report findings of no sex differences more

BOX 10-1   SPOTLIGHT ON METHODOLOGY

DOING SOCIAL PSYCHOLOGICAL RESEARCH:
COMBINING STUDIES THROUGH META-ANALYSIS

When trying to determine what prior work tells us regarding a research area, social psychologists traditionally have done what most people do when writing a term paper: they go to the library, examine a topic index such as *Psychological Abstracts,* read relevant previous research, and then synthesize the earlier research into some (hopefully) coherent summary.

This process clearly has some potential limitations, which are especially apparent to social psychologists. The most obvious difficulty relates to the point of view that a researcher brings to a problem area. Seldom do we have a completely unbiased view of an area that is of interest to us, and it is clear from much of the work that we have discussed earlier than people's attitudes are likely to color, if not totally distort, their interpretation of ambiguous information. Hence, it is difficult for even the most diligent researchers to avoid the possibility of responding to their own biases in interpreting research results.

The problem becomes even worse when we consider research areas that produce a set of contradictory findings. How is an observer supposed to reconcile literature that shows, for example, thirty-five studies that support one position and twenty-five studies that support another? Frequently, literature reviews attempt to invoke a voting procedure, in which results of studies are tallied, and the "winning" position is the one which has been demonstrated in the majority of studies. The problem here is that not all studies are comparable, and not all studies show results with some degree of strength and clarity. And this procedure becomes almost useless if the voting comes out close: what does one make of a situation in which twenty-five studies

support one position and twenty-five support another?

One answer to these problems of potential research bias in interpretation and difficulties in weighing research results has come in the form of a statistical technique labeled **meta-analysis** (G. V. Glass, 1976). Meta-analysis is a method for numerically combining the results of a set of studies to determine a statistical probability for a given conclusion. In addition, it provides a method for determining the combined statistical strength of effects of manipulations found in the studies of interest. Thus, rather than leaving the integration of findings to the subjective judgments of literature reviewers, meta-analysis provides an objective technique for ascertaining the joint outcomes of a set of studies. It is a powerful statistical tool, and it promises to upgrade the quality of our understanding of the large quantities of data that exist on just about any topic of interest to social psychologists.

Even with meta-analytic techniques, there are still problems in the interpretation of multiple studies. Foremost is what has been called the "file-drawer problem" (Rosenthal, 1979). Research that is carried out and does not produce statistically significant results tends not to be published. This means that for every study carried out which shows, for instance, a difference between male and female conformity levels, there may be many unpublished studies that show *no* difference—and because they were not published, researchers doing literature reviews will be unaware of the results and will not include them in the meta-analysis. Thus, even meta-analysis can have its problems, and results of meta-analyses must be evaluated critically.

than male experimenters. Another reason may be the choice of message topics used in the experiment. If researchers tend to use topics of a stereotypically "masculine" nature in their studies (for example, discussions of football), females may be prone to conform more because of their perceived lack of expertise in the subject matter. Indeed, a study by Sistrunk and McDavid (1971) found that varying the nature of the items used to elicit group pressure according to whether they were more familiar to men, women, or both resulted in differential sex findings. Males conformed most on the "feminine" items; females most on the "masculine" items; and there was no difference between males and females on the items that were equally familiar to both sexes. Although Eagly and Carli's (1981) meta-analysis did not find a statistically significant relationship between choice of materials and sex differences in conformity, it noted a trend in that direction, and the explanation remains a compelling one.

Size of Group You might expect that you would find yourself conforming more to a group of twenty individuals unanimously holding a position at variance with your own than a group of five opposing your point of view. In this case, however, most research suggests that once a unanimous majority increases in size much past three or four, conformity pressures reach their peak (Gerard, Wilhelmy, & Conolley, 1968; L. A. Rosenberg, 1961; Sanford & Penrod, 1984). Indeed, it appears that people's conformity may even decrease somewhat when more than three or four people oppose them.

The surprising finding that increased numbers of opponents does not necessarily lead to greater conformity is explained in part by an experiment by Wilder (1977). He suggested that one reason that group pressure does not become more influential as group size increases is that recipients of the pressure may begin to feel that they are in fact the target of a concerted effort to get them to change their minds and that the majority members do not necessarily all share the view they are expressing. To test this hypothesis, Wilder devised an experiment in which the influence of two groups of two people, both suggesting the same opinion, was compared with the influence of one group of four persons, who suggested identical opinions, over a target person's opinions. In line with this reasoning, the two groups of two people were more influential than the one group of four, presumably because the subject felt that members of two-person groups were expressing their own opinions and not being influenced by the other group members as much as when there were four members in the group. Thus, members of larger groups may be seen as less independent—and thus less influential—than members of smaller groups.

Group Unanimity: It Helps to Have a Social Supporter Up to this point we have been discussing social influence by groups in which the individual does not have a single ally. But what of the case in which targets of social influence do have someone, known as a **social supporter**, who shares their views? A large body of literature suggests that having even a single person who shares their views will allow most people to remain independent of the group (Allen, 1975). For instance, in Asch's classic studies, conformity in the presence of a social supporter was reduced to 15 percent of what it was when a partner was not present (Asch, 1952, 1955).

The importance of a social supporter in reducing conformity is illustrated by an experiment by Allen and Levin (1971). In the study, subjects were told they were to make visual judgments. The person who later became the subject's social supporter was presented as totally incompetent at the task. An individual wearing very thick glasses was given a vision test prior to the experiment in the presence of the subject, and it was clear that he had failed the test miserably. Subsequently, however, this same individual made visual judgments that were accurate and provided the subject with a potential social supporter against the rest of the group's supposed judgments, which, on most trials, were unanimously erroneous. Even though the social supporter's correct answers were seemingly due just to luck, because of his inability to see, subjects' conformity to the group dropped significantly compared with when no social supporter was present. However, conformity decreased even more in another experimental condition in which the social supporter had no apparent visual problems.

The results of this experiment suggest a number of explanations why having a social supporter can cause a significant drop in an individual's conformity. One reason is that the social supporter may provide an independent assessment of reality and can make the target of influence feel more confident in his or her own judgments. Another is that the social supporter's answers may simply break the apparent consensus of the group, which in turn may lead the subject to reject the majority as a valid reference group.

The presence of a social supporter may serve one other purpose as well. It is possible that the interpretation given to a stimulus presented to a subject may vary according to whether a unanimous—as compared with a nonunanimous majority—is present (Allen & Wilder, 1975a; Bohlander, Hartdagen, & Wychock, 1983). In other words, a person's perception and understanding of the meaning of a question or item may vary according to the responses of the various group members.

Take, for instance, the statement, "I am never hungry." Suppose you found that five members of a six-person group to which you belonged agreed unanimously with such a statement. One reaction you might have would be to say to yourself that the group must really be inferring something special about the word "hungry," and that the experimenter may mean "extremely hungry" when he presents such a statement.

On the other hand, the presence of a social supporter who disagreed with the statement might cause you to interpret the statement differently and allow you to maintain your independence from the group. In such a situation, the presence of a social supporter has caused you to restructure the meaning of the stimulus presented by the experimenter. According to this view, conformity can actually be seen as behavior that is congruent with one's "true" belief about a stimulus—true, at least, in terms of how one interprets the stimulus.

BOX 10-2 SPOTLIGHT ON APPLICATIONS

ASCH AND ABSCAM

While Solomon Asch carried out his classic studies on conformity long before the recent Abscam investigation, many of the elements of his research can be seen in the situation in which FBI men posed as Arab sheikhs in order to prove the corruptness of certain politicians. During the investigation, politicians were offered bribes by a supposed sheikh and his staff. The results were a number of indictments and convictions of some important political figures, and law enforcement officers have argued that the investigation revealed the underlying guilt of basically dishonest individuals.

The investigation has been controversial because those indicted have claimed that they were entrapped by the FBI, who lured them into criminal acts that they say they would not have committed had it not been for the presence of the supposed Arab sheikh. Indeed, psychologist Albert Levitt suggests that the FBI's tactics were no different from those used by Asch to evoke conformity in his subjects (McKean, 1982). Consider, for example, the following characteristics of the Abscam situation:

- Each politician was approached independently and brought into a room filled with a group of people (sometimes the sheikh, representatives of the sheikh, and a local lawyer), all of whom *unan-imously* urged him to take the bribe. The group norms were clearly in favor of taking the bribe, exerting normative social influence.
- The foreign, exotic background of the sheikh might also have provided informational social influence; the politician might have thought that in the sheikh's country the bribe was a standard way of doing business.
- Because no dissenters were present, no social supporter was able to provide an independent assessment of the situation.
- The FBI agents sometimes made legitimate business proposals, so that part of what they were saying was reasonable, although most was not. This is analogous to having the confederates in the Asch situation sometimes choose the correct response.

According to Levitt's view, we should expect that most people would conform to the demands of the situation, just as many of Asch's subjects did. In this way of looking at Abscam, then, the indicted politicians may be no more at fault than subjects who conform to the group in a conformity experiment—although such a defense is unlikely to stand up in a court of law.

Senator Harrison Williams was convicted for his participation in the Abscam bribery investigation, in which tactics were used that have been described as being similar to those in the classic Asch conformity situation. (AP/Wide World)

Clearly, then, the reasons social supporters reduce conformity are complex, and it appears that a number of possibilities underlie their effectiveness. The phenomenon is a clear one, however; unanimous groups are considerably more effective in producing conformity than nonunanimous ones.

Reducing Conformity: How a Minority Can Influence the Majority

We have, up to this point, been discussing how group majorities influence the dissenting group members. But group influence is not unidirectional, and there are many cases in which a minority in a group can influence and change the opinions held by the majority (Sanford & Penrod, 1984).

Consider, for instance, the case of Sigmund Freud and his theory of psychoanalysis. You probably know that Freud's theory, with its references to unconscious processes, infant sexuality, and libido, was initially greeted with skepticism and even derision by the scientific community. He had difficulty in getting his writings published and, in the words of one chronicler of those times, Freud and his disciples were thought of "not only as sexual perverts but also as either obsessional or paranoid psychopaths, and the combination was thought to be a real danger to the community" (E. Jones, 1961, p. 299). This was hardly an auspicious beginning for a theory that was to have one of the greatest influences of any set of ideas relating to human behavior.

However, Freud reacted to the hostile reaction from the majority of the scientific community simply by reiterating, refining, and expanding his theory. He never wavered in his convictions, and he presented a consistent (and persistent) view to the world. We all know the outcome: Freud's theory has far outlasted his initial critics, and in fact some of his harshest detractors eventually became supporters of his ideas.

While of course not the only reason for the rise in acceptance of the theory, Freud's technique of remaining consistent suggests a general procedure for persuading and influencing a disbelieving majority: engaging in a consistent demonstration of the minority's beliefs and behavior. Indeed, some social psychologists have suggested that unvarying consistency is the key to minority influence. Others, however, have felt that a more effective strategy for influencing a majority is for the minority to conform first and then to deviate from the group. We will examine the evidence for each of these strategies in turn.

Consistency: Never Waver A European social psychologist, Serge Moscovici, has presented compelling evidence for a theory that consistency on the part of a minority can lead to a change of opinion in the majority (Moscovici & Faucheaux, 1972; Moscovici & Mugny, 1983). He suggests that a minority's unyielding insistence on its own point of view creates a conflict which prevents the smooth functioning of a group. This, in turn, may cause the majority to rethink its position and eventually be swayed by the minority's position.

One experiment illustrates quite clearly the effect that a consistent minority can have on a majority (Moscovici, Lage, & Naffrechoux, 1969). In the study, groups of six female subjects were told that they would be making judgments about the color of a group of thirty-six slides. Unbeknownst to the subjects, all the slides were blue in color—although they did vary in intensity. In addition, the subjects did not know that two of the group members were confederates, who had been instructed to answer on every slide that the color was green (a clearly incorrect response). There was also a control condition, which consisted of groups of six naive subjects and no confederates.

After taking a public test for color blindness, the subjects were shown the series of thirty-six slides. For each slide, subjects answered sequentially and aloud. The results showed a clear influence of the (erroneous) minority upon the majority. In comparison to the control condition, in which just .25 percent of the responses were erroneous, more than 8 percent of the responses in the groups with confederates responded incorrectly by identifying the color they saw as green. In fact, about one-third of the experimental subjects answered incorrectly at least once.

Even more interesting is the subsequent finding that the consistent minority influenced the majority even after their part in the experiment had ended. After they had finished responding in their group of six, each subject was taken individually to another room and shown a series of sixteen disks, which this time did vary in color from very green, to blue-green, to very blue. Subjects were told to categorize each disk as blue or green but were not given the opportunity to make compromise judgments such as "blue-green." Most relevant are the colors chosen for the blue-green disks: subjects exposed to the consistent minority were more likely to say "green" than "blue" (as compared with subjects in the control condition), indicating that the effects of the minority persisted beyond their physical presence. And it turned out that those most likely to be affected by the group in the second procedure were those who had most ignored the minority during the first part of the experiment. Thus, even those subjects who appeared at first to remain independent of the minority were apparently influenced by their consistent responses.

Why should a consistent minority be able to influence a majority? We have already suggested that a consistent minority breaks the smooth functioning of a group and may lead the majority to rethink its position. But there is another factor beyond the mere disruption of the smooth functioning of the group (Moscovici & Nemeth, 1974): the minority, in its consistency, is perceived by the majority as having a strong position in which it believes and in which it is very confident. This certainty leads the majority to question its own point of view, and any lack of confidence on the part of the majority will be increased. In this way, the consistent minority can exert influence over and potentially change the majority position. Indeed, this is a tactic used by minority political parties—and religions—for generations.

An Alternate View: Conform, and Then Deviate As we have mentioned earlier, deviates in groups usually face a potential problem. They are often disliked, and frequently groups attempt to exclude them from future activities (e.g., Schachter, 1951). Given this possibility, the strategy of unyielding consistency for modifying the majority view suggested by the work of Moscovici and Faucheux presents a real danger. Rather than trying to understand the minority's position, the majority may simply reject it and ignore them. To deter such a possibility, Hollander (1980) suggests that a better strategy for the minority is initially to conform to the group and then, only after a period of conformity has established the "credentials" of the minority, to deviate from the group.

The mechanism underlying an individual's ability to espouse an unpopular view is something Hollander (1980) calls **idiosyncracy credit.** By showing a group that they are competent and can fulfill the expectations of the group regarding what is appropriate behavior, members of a minority accumulate idiosyncracy credit, similar to the accumulation of money in a savings account. Through the use of built-up credits, a minority is able to espouse deviant views without fear of sanction or rejection (analogous to the way in which a buildup of savings allows withdrawal of dollars from a savings account). Of course, at some point the idiosyncracy credit is going to be expended, and the minority must resume its adherence to the majority position if it is to maintain its position within the group.

The notion of idiosyncracy credits suggests a very different technique for influencing the group majority from that of the consistency theorists. If we follow the idiosyncracy view, it suggests that Freud should first have conformed to the predominant views of his era. Then, once he had established his credentials as a follower of the status quo, he would have been free—at least for a time—to present a deviant view. The difficulty with such a scenario is that it is hard to envisage how Freud would have been able to return adroitly to the majority view after his idiosyncratic credit was used up.

Still, there is experimental evidence in support of both the consistency and idiosyncratic credit theorists. Indeed, the most recent direct test of the two theories showed inconsistent findings for male and female subjects, with males supporting the idiosyncracy credit theory but females showing that both theories were equally effective (Bray, Johnson, & Chilstrom, 1982). Thus, while we cannot be sure which of the theories provides the best explanation, it is clear that minorities in groups can influence and sway the views of the majority. Moreover, recent work on social influence using computer simulations suggests that minority influence may follow principles similar to those of majority influence, although work along these lines is just beginning (Sanford & Penrod, 1984).

If this salesperson can get the potential purchaser to first agree to just a small favor, her chances of selling a vacuum cleaner are higher than if she asked for an order right off. (R. Solomon/Monkmeyer Press)

DIRECT COMPLIANCE: RESPONDING TO THE DIRECTIVES OF OTHERS

When we first discussed conformity, we mentioned that the pressures on the individuals to conform were generally implicit; there is no overt request or demand to yield to pressure. We turn now to situations in which there is direct, explicit pressure in the form of a request or demand to go along with a certain point of view or behavior which is meant to produce assent or agreement—behavior which is termed **compliance.** Although the distinctions between conformity and compliance are sometimes murky, we will examine two situations in which the resultant behavior can clearly be labeled compliance. First, we will discuss a method used by salespeople to increase customer compliance, termed the "foot-in-the-door" technique. Second, we will consider compliance as it relates to obedience to authority.

Putting Your Foot in the Door: Increasing Compliance

The foot-in-the-door strategy is a technique first developed by door-to-door salespeople and later studied by social psychologists as a more general procedure for producing compliance.

The technique works like this: rather than initially asking individuals to do what is really wanted of them, you first request that they agree to a smaller, but related, request. It turns out that compliance with the ultimate request increases significantly when the person first agrees to the smaller favor.

The foot-in-the-door phenomenon was first demonstrated in a study by Freedman and Fraser (1966). A number of experimenters went door-to-door, asking residents to sign a petition in favor of safe driving. Almost everyone complied with this small, benign request. However, a few weeks later, different experimenters recontacted the residents plus a control group who had not been asked to sign the petition previously and asked for a much larger request: that they erect a huge sign that said "Drive Carefully" on their front lawn. The results were clear: more than half (55 percent) of those who had signed the petition agreed to the request, while only 17 percent of those in the control group agreed.

More recent research has supported this early work (e.g., Snyder & Cunningham, 1975), and it shows that the larger the initial request, the more later compliance can be expected. Why does the foot-in-the-door phenomenon operate? We can suggest a number of reasons. One is that involvement with the small request leads to an explicit interest in an issue, and taking an action—any action—makes the individual more committed to the issue, thus increasing the likelihood of future compliance. Another explanation involves a possible change in people's self-image. After signing the petition initially, the residents may have begun to see themselves as social activists of a sort with a fairly strong interest in the topic of the petition. This change in perception could have increased their willingness to comply with the later, larger request.

While we cannot be certain of the reasons, placing a foot in the door generally seems to be effective, although a recent meta-analysis suggests that the phenomenon is relatively weak, and there are numerous exceptions (Beaman, Cole, Preston, Klentz, & Steblay, 1983). For instance, in cases in which the costs of the second request are very high, an earlier, smaller favor may be ineffective in producing higher subsequent compliance (Foss & Dempsey, 1979). The phenomenon, then, has its limits.

Obedience to Authority: Testing the Limits of Compliance

Place yourself in the following situation:

> A stranger comes to you, and asks you to help him out. He's interested in getting people to remember things better, and he has devised an interesting technique for improving memory. First he teaches people a list of words. Then he tells them to recall the words. Each time they make a mistake, they are to receive a painful electric shock. And the more mistakes they make, the more painful the shocks get, increasing up to 450 volts. The stranger shows you a sinister-looking shock generator for use in administering the shocks. The generator has a series of switches, starting at 30 volts and increasing to the maximum 450 volts. In addition, there are verbal designations under the switches, ranging from "slight shock," through "intense shock," through "danger: severe shock," all the way until there are three ominous red Xs at the top of the scale. Your role in all this? You are to administer the shocks, under the command of the stranger.

After such a presentation, you might feel that it is unlikely that the stranger would be apt to find any recruits willing to participate in his memory-enhancing scheme. But let's modify the situation a little. Suppose, now, that the stranger were a psychologist, and that you happened to be a participant in a psychological experiment. Furthermore, suppose that the experiment is described to you as one in which learning processes are being studied and you are told that your participation is crucial for the experiment to be successful. Under these modified circumstances, would you be more likely to participate? And if you agreed to participate, how severe a shock would you administer before you refused to continue?

Answers to these questions, which may appear to be entirely hypothetical to you, are suggested by the results of an actual experiment carried out by Stanley Milgram in the early 1960s (summarized in Milgram, 1974). Milgram devised an experiment similar to that described in the second scenario presented above. In actuality, however, the real topic of the experiment was obedience to authority, and the measure of interest—far from being recall of lists of words—was the degree to which individuals would follow the commands of the experimenter.

Most people feel that even when presented with the circumstances of the second situation, in which the rationale for the administration of electric shocks is apparently more legitimate, it would be the rare individual who would go very far up the scale in giving shocks. Indeed, Milgram asked a group of distinguished psychiatrists for their prediction, and they thought that only one in a thousand people would give the highest-level shock. The most prevalent opinion was that most people would not go beyond the 150-volt level. Other individuals, without any special training, were even more conservative, with many predicting that no shocks would be given by anyone.

In reality, neither distinguished psychiatrists nor untrained individuals were able to predict accurately how Milgram's subjects would perform. In fact, fully 65 percent of naive subjects placed in the experiment gave the highest-level shock of 450 volts. Although these startling results are tempered by the fact that in all cases the recipient was a confederate of the experimenter and did not receive *any* electric shocks, this is small solace, because the subjects did not know this. They thought that they were administering painful shocks at the behest of the experimenter.

Milgram tried a number of variants of his original study. For instance, in one experiment the physical proximity of the victim to the subject was varied. In one condition (remote), the victim could neither be seen nor heard; in another (voice feedback), he could not be seen, but his verbal protestations could be heard from the next room. In the two remaining conditions, the victim was in the same room as the subject. In the proximity condition, he was located a few feet away. In the final condition (touch proximity), the subject actually had to place the victim's hand on a shock plate in order for him to receive the shock. As you

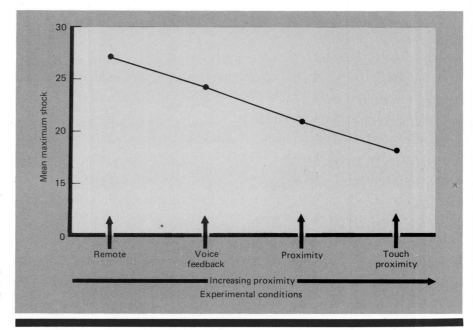

FIGURE 10-1
As the victim became
physically closer to the
subject, the mean level of
shock declined. Source:
Milgram (1974).

might guess, increasing proximity led to decreasing obedience (see
Figure 10-1). But what is most startling is that even when it was necessary physically to take the hand of the victim (who, at the 150-volt
level, demanded to be set free and would not voluntarily touch the
shock plate), a full 30 percent of the subjects were obedient to the
experimenter's wishes and gave the maximum shock level.

The results of Milgram's studies were startling, and they led to much
controversy. Some of the questions that were raised were methodological: did subjects really believe that they were giving shocks to the
confederate, and could the obedience observed be attributable to the
fact that subjects knew they were in the protected environment of a
psychological laboratory (Orne & Holland, 1968)? Moreover, some observers suggested that the obedience observed in the experiment did
not bear any resemblance to real-life instances of obedience.

While these criticisms cannot be answered with certainty, most evidence points to the fact that subjects were thoroughly drawn into the
experiment and were convinced that they actually were giving shocks
to the victim. Certainly, they displayed emotional reactions; many reported feeling anxious and upset. In addition, it is not hard to come up
with real-world analogies to the experiment: many of the defendants at
the Nuremberg trial after World War II used the excuse that they were
only following orders when they carried out various atrocities. More
recently, American soldiers in Vietnam complied in one instance with
orders from a superior officer to shoot all Vietnamese—men, women,

The My Lai massacre of civilians during the Vietnamese war provoked excuses from the soldiers involved in the killing that they were "only following orders" and therefore were not personally responsible. (AP/Wide World)

and children—on sight, an event that became known as the My Lai massacre. It seems, then, that the methodology of the Milgram experiments can be generalized beyond the experimental situation. (See also Box 10-3.)

More troubling is another sort of problem, which questions the ethicality of the experiments. Some observers suggested that it was unethical to place subjects in a situation in which they are pressed to carry out acts which normally would be unthinkable (Baumrind, 1964). Moreover, it is hardly reassuring to read descriptions of subjects' reactions while in the experiment itself; some subjects could be seen to "sweat, stutter, tremble, groan, bite their lips, and dig their fingernails into their flesh. Full-blown uncontrollable seizures were observed for three subjects" (Milgram, 1963, p. 375). It is not unreasonable to ask whether such extreme tension would have lasting consequences, despite Milgram's assurance that a full debriefing following the experiment eradicated any negative outcomes of participation. Long-term follow-ups also revealed no effects due to participation (Milgram, 1974). Nevertheless, the ethical issue remains an important, if unresolvable, one.

Independent of the ethicality issue, Milgram's studies revealed an important fact: authority figures can induce people to perform antisocial acts with relative ease. But what is the mechanism by which the authority is able to command such obedience? To answer this question, we need to consider the more general topic of social power.

BOX 10-3 SPOTLIGHT ON FIELD RESEARCH

THERE MAY BE A BURGLAR LURKING IN MANY OF US

Just as most of us feel that we'd never be like the subjects in Milgram's experiments, most of us probably think that we would never comply with a request to commit a burglary. Think again. A recent experiment suggests that, with the proper rationale and just a little prodding, we might in fact agree to participate in a full-scale burglary.

In an unusual field study designed to shed light on the motives of the participants in the notorious Watergate scandal, West, Gunn, and Chernicky (1975) asked college undergraduates—who had no idea that they were in an experiment—to participate in a burglary of a local advertising firm. The rationale for the crime varied according to experimental condition. In both of the first two conditions, subjects were told that the Internal Revenue Service wanted a microfilm of a set of records that the firm was keeping illegally and that had allowed the company to defraud the government of millions of dollars, but in one condition, subjects were led to believe they would receive immunity from prosecution if apprehended, while in the second condition, no immunity was offered.

In a third condition, subjects were told nothing of government involvement. Instead, the rationale for the burglary was business espionage: a competing advertising firm was offering $8000 for a copy of a set of designs, and the subject's share would be $2000 for participation. Finally, the fourth condition consisted of a control in which subjects were told simply that the purpose of the crime was to see if a set of burglary plans devised by the experimenter would succeed, and that nothing would be stolen (although the act of entering the advertising firm was already an illegal burglary).

All subjects were shown an elaborate set of plans which required three people to participate in the crime in addition to the subject. The plan was so comprehensive and detailed (including aerial photographs of the building and lists of local police cars) that subjects tended to be convinced that there was only a small chance of being apprehended.

The major dependent measure consisted of whether subjects agreed or refused to participate in the robbery. Overall, 20 percent of those approached agreed to join in the illegal burglary, but there were wide differences between conditions. Lowest compliance occurred in the fourth condition (10 percent), in which the only rationale was to help the experimenter, and in the non-immunity–IRS-sponsoring condition (5 percent). In the condition in which subjects could earn $2000 for participating, 20 percent agreed to participate. Highest participation occurred in the immunity–IRS-sponsored condition: 45 percent of the subjects approached agreed to participate.

Why would so many individuals agree to participate in a patently illegal venture? In a clear example of the fundamental attribution error we discussed in Chapter 2, a group of observers, questioned as to why they thought subjects agreed to participate, tended to attribute dispositional reasons for the subjects' acquiescence (i.e., that it had to do with the personality characteristics and traits of the subjects). However, compliant subjects themselves tended to explain their participation as due to the nature of the situation. In other words, they found the arguments and rationale for compliance compelling enough to go along with the recruiter.

As for our own participation in burglary: consider that, given the right cover story, 45 percent of the sample of undergraduates, probably not too different from the rest of us, agreed to do it.

SOCIAL POWER

The results of Milgram's studies on obedience to authority can be viewed as an example of the broader phenomenon of **social power,** which refers to a person's ability to control and shape another's behavior.

The bases of power that Adolph Hitler used include each of the six types of power identified by French and Raven. (The Bettmann Archive)

Social power represents the potential for social influence, in which individuals undergo an actual change in their behavior as a result of others. The Milgram obedience experiment represents a rather extreme and overt case of the wielding of power; in most cases power is used more subtly, and most often we are not even aware when our behavior has been influenced by the power of others. Yet, consider situations such as these:

- An employee of a corporation laughs enthusiastically at her boss's jokes, regardless of how funny they are.
- A child does not cross the street because he knows that his parents will spank him if he does.
- An individual joins the American Civil Liberties Union after learning that a much admired politician is a member of the organization.
- A Supreme Court justice resigns from the Court when the President tells him that he needs him to work in the United Nations.
- Despite her misgivings, your mother follows her physician's advice and receives a chest x-ray.
- The boss's secretary, who knows about an imminent shake-up in the company, is invited to lunch by a worried employee.

In each of the above cases, an individual's behavior has been influenced by the power of another person. However, each can be considered to be a somewhat different form of power, based on a different type of influence. French and Raven (1959), and later Raven (1974), identified six different bases of social power, which correspond to each of our examples. These bases have been labeled reward power, coercive power, referent power, legitimate power, expert power, and informational power.

Bases of Power

Reward Power   One way that individuals can influence others is through their ability to provide rewards when others comply with their wishes. Employees can be promoted, children can receive candy, and students can get good grades if their behavior conforms to the wishes of the powerful individual. It should be noted, though, that the contingencies that grant an individual reward power in one setting may not necessarily carry over into another setting. Thus, while employees may laugh uproariously at a boss's joke, in anticipation of being promoted, his next-door neighbor, who will not be concerned with his control over promotions, may not laugh so heartily at his jokes.

Coercive Power   The coercive base of power is the opposite side of the coin from reward power; it refers to the powerful person's ability to deliver punishments. While it can be an effective technique, it has some major drawbacks. For one, low-power individuals resent the use of coercive power and will tend to dislike the powerful person (J. Z. Rubin

353

& Lewicki, 1973). Moreover, use of coercive power leads individuals to try to end the relationship with the more powerful person. Finally, the use of coercion requires strict vigilance on the part of the powerful person in order to ensure that the influence wielded is effective. Generally speaking, then, the use of coercive power is a less preferable means of influencing others than alternate techniques. In particular, reward power is more effective than coercive power (Canavan-Gumpert, 1977; Sulzer-Azaroff & Mayer, 1984).

Referent Power When one person is very attractive to another, the admirer may attempt to behave like the attractive person. Indeed, if the attraction is strong enough, we can say that the individual identifies with the attractive other. **Identification** refers to cases in which an individual attempts to behave and even think in ways identical with another person. Referent power is the type of power that accrues to people with whom we identify. They have power over us because of our attempts to be like them. In our earlier example, then, the person who joins an organization because of an admired politician's membership is yielding to referent power.

A group can also be the source of referent power, if it is a group to which we are attracted and which provides standards and norms of appropriate behavior. Such groups are called reference groups, and as we mentioned earlier, they provide information—and social pressure—regarding what we should and should not do. A person who dyes his or her hair green in order to be accepted by other members of the punk rock movement (a social movement which enjoyed a degree of notoriety in some urban areas in the early 1980s) offers us an example of the referent power of the group to which he or she has aspirations for membership. It should be noted that *negative* reference groups can also wield referent power. Groups with which we want to avoid identification can lead us to modify our behavior in order to make us feel *less* similar to the group in question. Hence, a very conservative person might have had his hair cut in a crew cut in order to dissociate himself from the hippies in the late 1960s.

Legitimate Power Some kinds of power are wielded because of the formal position or role an individual occupies; this is known as legitimate power. Legitimate power is often couched in terms of "should" and "ought." For instance, children are sometimes told to listen to their parents not on the basis of reason but because "We're your parents, and you ought to listen to your parents."

One of the best examples of the use of legitimate power is presented by Milgram's studies of obedience. If you recall, we first described his experiment as being carried out by a "stranger" who had devised a technique to improve memory. The description was then modified to present the situation as it actually occurred, in the context of an experiment, and with the stranger as an experimenter. It is probable that the additional information changed your perspective on the legitimacy of

BOX 10-4 SPOTLIGHT ON APPLICATIONS

A DARK SIDE OF SOCIAL INFLUENCE PROCESSES: CHILD SEXUAL ABUSE

One of the country's most pressing social problems—yet one of its most secret—is child abuse. Recent estimates indicate that somewhere between 100,000 and 500,000 children are molested each year, and some studies indicate that 19 percent of all American women and 9 percent of all men were sexually molested at some time during their lives (*Newsweek,* 1984).

One of the most curious aspects of the problem relates to what are known as "sex rings"—groups of children who engage in sexual activities at the behest of an adult, who photographs them or exploits them sexually in some other way. In some cases, literally hundreds of children may be involved, yet few, if any, parents or other outsiders ever learn of the children's activities. In one recent case, for example, a group of teachers in a nursery school were accused of sexually molesting their students over a period of years. Although the sexual activities were apparently commonplace at the school, not one child spontaneously reported the abuse to his or her parents.

How can such activity take place for long periods without a child ever mentioning it to a parent or other responsible adult? One important reason, according to Ann Burgess, who studied children involved in group sex with adults, is the operation of social influence phenomena (Coleman, 1984). Among the examples she found were:

- An elaborate and explicit set or norms. The children were taught that the sexual activities in which they engaged were normal, and they learned that other members of the group would approve of their participation—as well as rewarding the fact that they keep their activities secret from others.
- Conformity to group activities. The children found it difficult to discontinue their participation because everyone else was going along with them.
- Power. The adult leaders used coercive power to maintain the participation of the children. They were threatened with physical, as well as psychological, punishment. For example, some children were told that pictures of them engaging in sexual activities would be shown to their parents if they did not go along with the group.
- The rewards of being part of a group. The children often had a sense of being special, of participating in a secret world of which their parents and other authority figures had no knowledge.
- Positive reinforcement. The adult ringleaders often provided powerful reinforcement, fulfilling children's needs for approval and attention as long as they participated in the group.

In sum, many of the processes of social influence found in group situations permitted children to remain secret participants in group sexual activities.

---

the request. In fact, we could continue modifying the description to make it sound even more compelling: suppose, for instance, that the situation were presented as a military one, in which the goal was to increase soldiers' ability to remember codes that could end a war earlier, and the stranger were the commander-in-chief of the armed forces instead of an experimenter. In this case, the legitimate power of the commander-in-chief would be likely to be much greater than that of a mere experimenter.

One of the unique characteristics of legitimate power is that its holder does not have to rely on rational arguments in order to convince others of his or her right to influence. Rather, the power flows inherently from the individual's position or role. It is also the case that the particular individual holding power is relatively less important than an individual with other bases of power. Presidents of the United States come and go, but the legitimate power of the presidency remains high, relatively independent of who is in office.

Expert Power   The dictum "knowledge is power" refers to the fact that we are influenced by those who are experts in an area relevant to our needs. For instance, we go to physicians when bothered by a health problem, and they are able to induce radical changes in our lifestyle through their suggestions. Even when physicians give advice that goes against our own opinions (as in the example cited earlier of the mother who gets an x-ray, despite her misgivings), we are apt to defer to the physician's greater knowledge. Indeed, physicians and other professionals are likely to use methods such as displaying their diplomas to increase their expert power.

Expert power is not held just by individuals with high prestige. A young child who is able to solve a Rubick's cube puzzle in thirty seconds holds a considerable amount of expert power when it comes to influencing adults who are attempting to solve the puzzle. But note that the expert power held by the child is highly situation-specific; we would not be influenced by the child's advice in other areas. Likewise, we generally would not accept our physician's advice on how to repair our automobile. Hence, expert power is limited to the area of expertise of its holder.

Informational Power   The most transitory type of power is informational power, which refers to power that is related to the specific content of an individual's information and which, once transmitted to another, causes the person to lose his or her power. For instance, when the boss's secretary in our earlier example discloses the nature of an upcoming company shake-up, she no longer holds any power, and it is unlikely that she will be invited to lunch with curious employees again. Thus, while the other bases of power that we described were more independent of the content of what an individual knows about a situation, informational power is grounded in the specific nature of some information. Once the information is revealed, future power is eliminated.

On the Virtues of Social Power

You may have received the impression from our discussion that there is something inherently "bad" about power. Indeed, in a society which venerates the concepts of equality and egalitarianism, the notion that some people have great power over others seems suspect. Yet it is also true that many of our societal institutions would operate badly or not at all if there were not at least some distribution of power. Large organizations are susceptible to breakdowns if clear lines of authority do not exist; teachers cannot teach without the power to discipline unruly children; politicians could not govern without the power given to them by the Constitution. Moreover, it is clear that the types of power described by French and Raven can facilitate ongoing social relationships (e.g., Raven & Haley, 1980).

However, although there is evidence showing that people with low power experience greater dissatisfaction than those with high power (Tannenbaum, 1974), recent work suggests that an individual's degree of power may have less impact in determining satisfaction in a social relationship than does the degree of competition between individuals. For example, Tjosvold (1981) created an experimental setting in which two people held unequal power, but operated in either a competitive or a cooperative setting. The degree of power held by a person proved relatively unimportant when the setting was cooperative. But when the context was made to appear competitive, both high- and low-power persons showed greater suspicion, more negative attitudes, and less ability to function effectively. Power disparities per se, then, are not necessarily detrimental to relationships and can act to promote effective social functioning—if the context calls for cooperation.

LEADERSHIP

One of the questions that has occupied political scientists, historians, and philosophers, no less than social psychologists, is what makes an individual a **leader.** Are some people "born leaders"? Is there something about an historical situation or set of circumstances that propels an individual toward leadership, relatively independent of the characteristics of that person? Or does the truth lie somewhere in-between—as suggested by Shirley Chisholm in our opening interview? These questions, have been the focus of a great deal of thought, not only by practicing politicians but by social psychologists as well.

Trait Approaches: The Great Person Theories

The well-known historian Thomas Carlyle put forth the premise that "the history of the world is the history of great men." Social psychologists followed this notion in their initial investigations of leadership by examining the personality traits of individuals identified as leaders in a variety of situations and attempting to develop a catalog of qualities that differentiate leaders from followers. This approach has come to be known as the **great person theory.**

While the theory is intuitively appealing, the results of literally hundreds of studies have yielded unimpressive findings. Although some traits do seem to correlate with leadership, the results are hardly astounding—and don't really provide us with much information. According to one influential review (Gibb, 1969), leaders tend to be taller and heavier; they are somewhat—but not too much—more intelligent; they are more extroverted and dominant; they show better adjustment; and they are more self-confident than nonleaders.

A more recent review expands upon this list in this way:

The leader is characterized by a strong drive for responsibility and task completion, vigor and persistence in the pursuit of goals, venturesomeness and originality in problem solving, drive to exercise initiative in social situations, self-confidence and sense of personal identity, willingness to accept consequences of decision and action, readiness to absorb interpersonal stress, willingness to tolerate frustration and delay, ability to influence other persons' behavior, and capacity to structure social interaction systems to the purpose at hand.

(Stogdill, 1974, p. 81)

There are certainly no surprises in such enumerations of the qualities of leaders, and when the magnitude of the correlations between a characteristic and leadership is considered, the relationship becomes even more tenuous. (The correlations generally range from about +.20 to +.30. While positive, these are relatively low.) Even more damning to the trait approach is the fact that there are many inconsistencies between studies. Even the findings that seem well-supported sometimes show a negative or no relationship with leadership in particular experiments. It also has been difficult to compare across studies, because many times researchers use different kinds of measures to tap what is supposed to be the same trait. Thus, differences in results across studies may be attributed to differences in measurement techniques.

Basically, then, the trait approach has not been effective in identifying universal characteristics of the "great person." The search for evidence supporting the notion that there exists one particular set of traits, common to all leaders, has not been successful—although it is still possible that traits play at least a partial role in determining leadership in particular situations and under specific conditions (Kenny & Zaccaro, 1983).

Situational Approaches: Are Individuals Thrust into Leadership Positions?

If trait and personality approaches to explaining leadership generally have not proved adequate, the next logical place to turn is to an examination of the situations in which a leader operates. In so doing we can ask if certain aspects of the environment lead an individual (independent of his or her personality or traits) to take on a leadership role. We all know of instances in which individuals with unsuspected leadership qualities get leadership thrust upon them, such as when Franklin Roosevelt died and Harry Truman became a decisive and, some say, great president.

The situational approach implies that a particular individual can be a leader in one setting and not another, because it is the characteristics of the situation and not the person that lead to leadership attainment. In a more extreme form, the situational hypothesis suggests that anyone can become the leader, since personality traits are unimportant. Although there is little evidence to support such an extreme hypothesis, there is a good deal of research that shows that, in terms of the specific task that must be done and the requirements of the group as a whole, the situation can have important consequences on who emerges as a leader (R. J. House & Baetz, 1979).

A number of studies have shown that group size has an important bearing on leadership emergence: the larger the group, the more likely it is that a leader will be required (Hemphill, 1950). Also related to leadership emergence is the nature of the group's membership. Groups that are homogeneous are more likely to produce a leader than groups that are relatively heterogeneous (Dyson, Godwin, & Hazelwood, 1976).

An individual's opportunities for communicating with others, as determined by the formal structure of the group, affect the probability that that person will become the leader. The greater the communicative opportunities, relative to other members, the higher the likelihood of the person becoming the group's leader (Guetzkow, 1968). One reason may be that people with greater communication opportunities feel that the other group members depend on them, prompting them to take more initiative in seeking leadership than the other members. Related to this notion is the finding that the greater the degree of importance in achieving a group goal, the more likely a leader will emerge (Crockett, 1955).

Another consideration that affects the choice of leader is the particular needs of a group's members and how well an individual can meet those needs. For example, in one elaborate experiment, subjects who owned local grocery stores were led to believe that a large chain of supermarkets was about to open a store in their town. The local grocers met in discussion groups in which they were told either that there was a good chance that a supermarket would open—the high-threat condition—or just a small chance—low-threat condition.

In the ensuing discussions among all groups, two confederates, each of whom supposedly owned a grocery store, played two different roles. One advocated a strong, aggressive response to the threat, while the other proposed a milder, more restrained course of action. The experimenters then arranged for an election to be held between the two confederates to determine the groups' leadership. It was clear that the degree of threat affected the grocer's choices. When the threat was high, they chose the aggressive individual; when the threat was low, they chose the milder member as leader (Mulder & Sterding, 1963). Hence, the needs of the members of the group lead them to choose as a leader an individual who is most apt to satisfy their needs.

Given that leaders are chosen on the basis of how well they satisfy a group's needs, it seems reasonable to assume that if a group's needs vary due to a change in circumstances, the person chosen as leader may well change. Support for this notion was found by Barnlund (1962), who showed that changes in the nature of a group's tasks, as well as shifts in the membership of a group, would lead to changes in leadership.

Indeed, individuals who desire to be leaders might be expected to manipulate a situation in order to create a need for their own skills and thus thrust themselves into leadership. And one study shows that persons in leadership roles sometimes place the group in a threatening or competitive situation in order to solidify their own leadership (Rabbie & Bekkers, 1976). As an example, many commentators have suggested that Argentina's invasion of the British Falkland Islands in 1982 was designed to promote support for the Argentinian ruling military junta, which was coming under increasing domestic criticism.

Situational Approaches to Leadership in Perspective We have seen a good deal of evidence that it is possible, to a degree, to predict under what conditions a leader will emerge. But it is also clear that there are drawbacks to purely situational descriptions of leadership. The greatest difficulty is that we are unable to specify which particular individual will be chosen as leader. While it is useful to know, for instance, that larger groups are more likely to develop leaders than smaller ones, our predictive power would be considerably greater if we could say which individual in the larger group is most apt to be chosen as leader. Moreover, when we are better able to predict who will become leader (as in the research showing that leaders tend to be those who fulfill the needs of the members), we must identify characteristics of the leader if we are to know if she or he can fulfill the members' needs. Indeed, it may be necessary to know something about the personal needs of the other group members, as well. In terms of predicting who is going to emerge as leader, then, a purely situational approach is inadequate.

Interactional Approaches to Leadership: It Depends on the Person and Situation

Although neither personality characteristics nor the situational factors alone fully explain leadership effectively, one view that has been shown to be useful is what has been termed the **interactional approach.** This view holds that under certain types of situations one kind of leader will be apt to emerge and be most effective, while under other circumstances an alternative leader might be more effective. Hence, there is an interaction between situational factors and the personality of the individual holding the leadership role (Beckhouse, Tanur, Weiler, & Weinstein, 1975; Hollander & Julian, 1969; Vroom, 1976).

Fiedler's Contingency Model The major theoretical model that has been built upon an interactional approach to leadership was developed by Fred Fiedler (Fiedler, 1978, 1981). The model, which has spawned more than 300 studies, is generally effective in identifying in what situations a particular type of leader would be appropriate.

Considering first the situational aspects of the theory, Fiedler suggests that there are three crucial characteristics of a situation that need to be examined. First the affective, emotional relationship between the leader and the followers must be assessed. In some situations, the group members are supportive, respectful, and loyal to the leader, while in others the opposite may be true. According to the model, the affective dimension is the most important. The second characteristic of the situation that must be considered is the degree of structure in the task with which the group is involved. The structure dimension is based upon the amount of clarity or ambiguity inherent in the task. Finally, the power

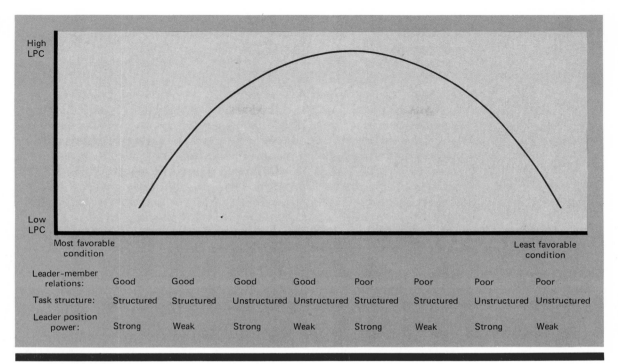

Leader-member relations:	Good	Good	Good	Good	Poor	Poor	Poor	Poor
Task structure:	Structured	Structured	Unstructured	Unstructured	Structured	Structured	Unstructured	Unstructured
Leader position power:	Strong	Weak	Strong	Weak	Strong	Weak	Strong	Weak

FIGURE 10-2

Optimal leadership style according to Fiedler's model. According to Fiedler's contingency model of leadership, the effectiveness of the leader varies according to the nature of leader–member relations, task structure, and the leader's position power. Source: Fiedler (1964).

position of the leader is the third aspect of the situation that affects leadership performance. The power position refers to the degree of power that the leader can assert over the other members of the group. Power, here, is defined as the degree of rewards and punishments that the leader is able to control.

The contingency model holds that the three factors relating to the situation determine the degree of favorability of the group to the leader. The most favorable situation is one in which the affective relations between the leader and the followers are positive, the task is highly structured, and the power position of the leader is strong, while the least favorable situation is one in which leader–member affective relations are poor, the task is unstructured, and the power position is weak. The model posits that other combinations of the three factors fall along a continuum of favorability as shown in Figure 10-2.

Recall, of course, that because the contingency model takes an interactional approach, it must also consider the personality of the leader. Fiedler has suggested that the most crucial variable to assess is the general motivational structure of the leader, which is usually either task-oriented (in which the completion of the task is of greatest importance) or relationship-oriented (in which the personal relations of the members is weighted more heavily).

According to the model, the most direct way of measuring this general orientation is to assess the leader's attitude toward the person referred to as the "least preferred coworker" or LPC. The LPC is the individual the leader identifies as the one person who was the most difficult to work with out of all the people he or she has ever known. The leader is then asked to rate that individual on a series of 18 eight-point scales that include such adjective pairs as pleasant–unpleasant, gloomy–cheerful, boring–interesting, and nasty–nice. It turns out that certain leaders rate even the LPC relatively generously, seeing strengths and positive qualities in the person they have liked working with least. In contrast, some leaders rate the LPC quite harshly, and so are considered low-LPC leaders.

By considering both the nature of the situation and the leader's attitude toward the LPC, the contingency model predicts the conditions for which a particular type of leader is best suited. As can be seen in Figure 10-2, situations that are either relatively favorable or unfavorable for the leader are best handled by a low-LPC leader, who is primarily task-oriented. On the other hand, situations of moderate leader favorability lead to optimum performance on the part of high-LPC leaders, who are more oriented toward maintaining positive relationships with the other members of the group.

The underlying logic of the model is apparent. Under conditions of low leader favorability, the leader–member relations tend to be poor, the task is unstructured, and the leader's power position is weak. In this case, an assertive, task-oriented leader who is very directive would clearly be of benefit to the group. On the other hand, in very favorable situations, in which the leader–member relations are positive, the task structure is clear, and the power position of the leader is strong, the group is already task-oriented and ready to be led. Thus, the group is receptive to the task-oriented low-LPC leader. It is under conditions of moderate leader favorability that a high-LPC leader excels. In this case, the relationship-oriented high-LPC leader, sensitive to the interpersonal needs of the group members, is most apt to be successful.

Does It Work? Happily, Fiedler and other researchers have amassed a good deal of supportive evidence for the contingency model. In settings as diverse as military academies, industry, and cross-cultural environments, the contingency model has proved a good predictor of leader effectiveness, and a recent meta-analysis of some 170 studies showed support for the theory in most cases (Strube & Garcia, 1981). On the other hand, support for the model is stronger in some respects than others. For instance, Fiedler relies heavily on examinations of the direction of correlations between LPC scores and group access *within* each of the eight situational favorability combinations, rather than the statistically significant differences *between* the correlations in each combination, which would be a stronger measure. Moreover, it is plausible that since LPC scores, leader–member relations, and group success are typically measured concurrently, the leader–member relations and LPC scores could be affected by the group's success—rather than vice versa, as the model suggests. Still, most evidence is highly supportive of the

Interactional approaches suggest that leadership is related to both situational and personality characteristics. (Mary Ellen Mark/Archive Pictures)

contingency model, and it remains our best model for determining leadership effectiveness (Rice & Kastenbaum, 1983).

Applying the Contingency Model   One intriguing outgrowth of the contingency model is its potential use as a means for training leaders to be more effective. Note that there are two possibilities for training inherent in the model: training leaders to modify their LPC level, or training leaders to change the degree of favorability of the situation. Traditionally, the first approach, in which leaders are taught to modify their behavioral styles, has been attempted, but the results have generally been disappointing except in laboratory experiments (Stogdill, 1974). In contrast, a more promising technique, based on the contingency model, has been to teach leaders to change the nature of the situation in which they are operating. In many ways, this approach may be more effective, because leaders may have greater control over the degree to which the situation can be structured than over their basic personalities and motivational structures.

Fiedler and colleagues have produced what is called the leader-match training program (Fiedler, Chemers, & Mahar, 1976), which includes a workbook that leaders can use to identify their own LPC level, and then to learn ways of measuring the degree of favorability of their present leadership position. Ultimately, leaders are taught techniques for modifying situations to optimize their success as leaders, given the nature of their LPC score and motivational structure. Results of such training do seem to be effective. For instance, Csoka and Bons (1978) found that West Point platoon leaders who had been trained using the leader-match program were more apt to be ranked first or second in their company than those who had not received training, and subsequent interviews revealed that the trained leaders tended to modify the situation according to tenets of the contingency model.

In sum, the contingency model has demonstrated its effectiveness in field settings as a means of improving leader effectiveness, although the evidence is not extensive. And we should note that the contingency model is not the only interactional theory of leadership (Forsyth, 1983). For instance, House and Baetz (1979) discuss the path–goal theory of leadership, which is concerned primarily with the way in which leaders can satisfy their subordinates' motivated goals. But the contingency model of leader effectiveness remains the best articulated, most comprehensive, and best supported of any of the models, and it clearly illustrates ways in which social psychological theories can be used to practical effect.

SUMMARY

Social influence, which refers to the ways in which the actions of an individual or group affects the behavior of others, results in conformity and compliance. Conformity consists of a change in public behavior or private belief that is the result of real or imagined group pressure. Both normative social influence (based upon one's expectations regarding appropriate group behavior) and informational social influence (based upon the premise that others may know more about the world than we do) lead to conformity.

The pioneering work of Asch, investigating conformity to groups, and that of Sherif, who examined the transmission of social norms, has led to a great deal of investigation of conformity. We now know that conformity is affected by the relationship between the individual and the group, the conditions under which responses are made, the characteristics of the task being carried out, the composition of the group, and the size of the group. Another critical factor is the degree of unanimity in the group. Specifically, the presence of just one social supporter brings about a significant reduction in conformity to the group.

Social influence is not unidirectional, for in some instances the minority can influence the majority. Two explanations have been suggested for minority influence: consistency, and initial conformity followed by deviance. Moscovici and Faucheux suggest that a minority can wield social influence by never wavering from its minority view. In contrast, Hollander posits that initial conformity to majority norms allows the buildup of idiosyncracy credits, through which an individual can deviate from the group with impunity.

Direct compliance to authority has been examined in a series of studies by Milgram, in which an experimenter led subjects to give electric shocks to another person. While most observers thought that almost no subjects would administer the maximum shock level (450 volts), about 65 percent of subjects did so. The experiments raised both ethical and methodological questions.

Obedience to authority rests upon an individual's social power, which refers to a person's ability to control and shape another's behavior. Six bases of power have been identified: reward power (based on reinforcement), coercive power (based on ability to punish), referent power (relating to identification with powerful others), legitimate power (based on role relationships), expert power (based on a person's superior knowledge), and informational power (based on specific information at a given time).

There are three main approaches to leadership: trait, situational, and interactional. Trait approaches, which attempt to identify particular personality characteristics and traits common to leaders, have generally been unsuccessful. Situational approaches have been fairly useful in determining how specific situation factors lead to leadership attainment, but they do not provide an adequate means of identifying exactly who will emerge as leader. The interactional approach looks at both the personality characteristics of an individual and the situation in which a group operates. The best example of the interactional approach is Fiedler's contingency model, which uses the degree of favorability of the group to the leader and the leader's personality (as measured by his or her rating of the least preferred coworker or LPC) to predict leader effectiveness. Interactional models provide the most reasonable approach to understanding leadership.

KEY TERMS

autokinetic effect
coercion
coercive power
compliance
conformity
contingency model of leadership
expert power
file-drawer problem
great person theory of leadership
idiosyncracy credit
informational power
informational social influence
interactional approach to leadership
leader

leader-match training program
least preferred coworker
legitimate power
meta-analysis
negative reference group
normative social pressure
reference group
referent power
reward power
situational approach to leadership
social influence
social power
social supporter
task characteristics

FOR FURTHER STUDY AND APPLICATION

Milgram, S. (1974). *Obedience to authority.* New York: Harper & Row.
A summary of Milgram's research on obedience, including some startling transcripts of actual experimental sessions.
Moscovici, S. (1976). *Social influence and social change.* London: Academic Press.
Presents a good overview of Moscovici's views on social influence, particularly regarding minority influence in groups.
Paulus, P. (1980). *Psychology of group influence.* Hillsdale, NJ: Erlbaum.
Paulus, P. (1983). *Basic group process.* Hillsdale, NJ: Erlbaum.
Each of these volumes contains a set of technical, but readable, chapters on the ways in which groups provide social influence.

Stogdill, R. M. (1974). *Handbook of leadership: A survey of theory and research.* New York: Free Press.
Fiedler, F. E., Chemers, M. M., & Mahar, L. (1976). *Improving leadership effectiveness: The leader match concept.* New York: Wiley.
The Stogdill volume provides all you ever wanted to know about leadership in a comprehensive review of decades of research. The Fiedler book is more applied, providing practical information on how to increase the effectiveness of leaders.
Cialdini, R. (1984). *Influence.* New York: Morrow.
In a well-written volume, Cialdini presents theory and applications relating to many social influence techniques.

CHAPTER 11

GROUP PROCESSES

A CONVERSATION WITH . . .

Joe Paterno
Coach

Joe Paterno, coach of the Pennsylvania State University football team, is one of America's best-known sports figures. Having one of the highest winning percentages of all coaches with more than ten years of service, he also holds an almost unique philosophy among college coaches: that academics should take precedence over football. How does he manage to field a consistently winning team? We began our talk with this question:

Q. Many coaches work with players as talented as yours, yet don't win nearly as many games. As a social psychologist, I'm particularly interested in how you take a group of individuals and mold them into a winning team. What's your secret of success?

A. That's not easily answered, but I'll do the best I can. I think it begins with the way you put your program together. You have to immediately build up some pride in being part of the organization. We do a lot of things here differently than other places. We talk all the time about not being afraid of being different, being unique. We demand more of people, from the time when we first begin recruiting. We tell recruits that they're not going to have a break from the classroom. We stress, all the time, the challenge of being a Penn State player. You may have noticed we don't have anything on our uniforms; they're very plain—no stripes, no names, nothing on the helmets. We wear black shoes; there are only about three or four major college teams that wear straight black shoes any more. There is a purpose for that. When our players put their uniforms on we want them to understand that they are part of a first-rate football team. Although they may not be better than other football players, they're

different, they're unique—not because of their individual strengths, but because they are part of a special Penn State team.

I build up a background in practice. We practice better than anybody; we practice harder than anybody; and we probably have higher pride than anybody. All this serves to create a kind of mystique about the situation which means that when they go out and play, there's more at stake than just fooball. It's the individual's pride and the commitment that he's made to the team.

Q. Then there are effects of being on the team that go beyond the football field?

A. Absolutely. In the dormitories, for instance, I want the dorm counselor to be able to count on the players because they're part of the team.

Q. I would guess that after being part of the team for a while, the football players would begin to internalize these standards themselves. It's not just a matter of doing what you say, is it?

A. Not at all. I try to develop leadership in the seniors and upperclassmen. They keep an eye on their teammates. I tell them they've got to be proud of the football team, and proud of their teammates.

Q. Is there a lot of competition within the team regarding, let's say, who's going to start?

A. A tremendous amount. I think it's one of the things that is most difficult in coaching. When it comes down to a youngster who really wants to play and feels that he's really good, then you have a problem. I don't know exactly how to solve it except to try to lean over backward to be fair to everybody. And I have a rule as a coach that it's not enough to *be* fair, you must *appear* to be fair. I think if you can get an individual to think that you really are concerned, you've got a chance to keep that youngster motivated. But it's a tough job.

Q. Do you ever have a problem getting especially talented players—the "stars"—to cooperate with the team?

A. Well, I have little sympathy for those people who don't. The best players have the most to gain by being cooperative. Football is so much a game of dependency. No matter how good you are, there are a lot of other people you're going to have to depend on.

Q. How do you maintain morale—group cohesiveness, a social psychologist would call it—consistently?

A. You can't create morale overnight, and once you have it's not easy to maintain but is something you've got to work at all the time. You've got a bunch of guys involved in a program who have got to feel responsible for each other. But we also try to understand each one of them as an individual, with individual problems, family problems, girlfriend problems, and all those kinds of things. Finally, we make a point of being concerned about the poorest football player on the squad. We're concerned about his morale and spend time to make sure he is treated fairly. I think it's important for every member of the team to feel that it's their team. It's not my team; it's their team.

OVERVIEW

- A "rap" session begins in your dormitory room, this time involving a heated discussion of the prevalence of cocaine use on campus.
- You help organize the college blood drive with a group of volunteers from the American Red Cross.
- Three couples go out to catch the latest Woody Allen movie, and then go for a pizza afterward.
- Your family gathers together to celebrate your grandfather's eighty-fifth birthday.

If you were to keep a diary of your daily activities for a few weeks, you would surely find that a large percentage of time is spent with others in the kinds of activities chronicled above. In fact, group participation represents an important aspect of most people's lives. Moreover, group membership has an important influence on everyday behavior, thinking, and emotional responses. Thus, as Coach Paterno suggested, groups have an influence that carries over into even nongroup activities.

In this chapter, we discuss groups, a topic that is at the heart of social psychology. We begin by formally defining a group. Next, we examine why people join groups. We then turn to the characteristics of groups themselves, including how they are structured and how they vary in attractiveness to their members. Finally, we discuss the consequences of belonging to a group for the group members. Whether the group is as intimate as a closely knit football team or as broad as membership in a throng of a half-million people demonstrating in front of the Washington Monument, groups have an important effect upon people's behavior.

WHAT IS A GROUP?

Although (or perhaps because) groups are so commonplace, there have been many approaches to defining what is meant by a group in formal, scientific terms. Various definitions have been put forward, most of which are related to a particular theoretical orientation. Rather than presenting one of these specific definitions, we will take a broader approach and suggest four criteria that seem to underlie most thinking about what makes a group.

1. *Interaction among group members.* At their most basic level, groups must permit some form of interaction among their members. It need not be physical, face-to-face interaction, however; verbal or written interaction may suffice.

2. *Perception of group membership.* Just as important as actual interaction among group members is the notion that individuals must view themselves as members of a group. For example, an aggregate or assemblage of people milling about at an airport gate waiting to board a plane would generally not be conceived of as a group because the individuals waiting would probably not perceive themselves as being associated with one another.

A corollary of the perception criterion is that persons in groups not only perceive themselves as group members, but usually are also perceived by others as being in a group. Thus, group membership can sometimes be thrust upon individuals who may not initially think of themselves as members of a group. Prime examples are ethnic, racial, and religious groups to which a person belongs. Although individuals may believe they are not affected by being members of a racial minority, for instance, other people may perceive them, and hence treat them, in a way that makes membership in the group a very real fact of life.

3. *Shared goals and norms.* One of the major reasons that people belong to groups is to achieve some goal whose attainment is facilitated by group membership. Thus, some of us might join the American Civil Liberties Union to promote freedom of speech, while others might join a chamber of commerce to promote the goals of free enterprise. Of course, some goals are less tangible and subtler. We might join a fraternity to meet other people, to avoid loneliness, or simply to be a part of some organization as a goal in and of itself. These affiliative goals can be sufficient to motivate our membership in a group and to act as shared goals by group members.

A related characteristic of formal groups is the existence of shared norms. Norms, as we have discussed before, refer to rules of behavior that are held by group members regarding what is—and is not—appropriate behavior. For instance, Joe Paterno remarked in our opening interview that the Penn State players learn to police themselves so that he does not have to enforce his rules and regulations about player conduct. What has happened, then, is that the players have adopted these norms and explicitly attempt to maintain them.

Norms have other effects as well. For example, Hargreaves (1963) showed that school achievement was actually determined, in part, by what students perceived as normatively appropriate. Thus, good students began to show decrements in performance when transferred to classes in which good scholastic behavior was not normatively sanctioned.

4. *Fate interdependence.* The final criterion regarding the characteristics of a group is the interdependence of fate of the group members. Events that affect one group member affect other members, and can affect the ability of the group to meet the goals for which it may have been formed. Clearly, for instance, if a football team is successful, all members share in the glory; when the team loses, it is a loss for the group as a whole. In a similar way, groups that are formed to meet the affiliation needs of members will be relatively successful if meetings are well-attended and there is a strong sense of enthusiasm about the group. In sum, the fate of each person in a group is affected by the group's outcomes as a whole, and the behavior of individuals within the group affects the success of the group itself.

WHY PEOPLE JOIN GROUPS

People do not have to form and participate in groups. Many activities that are typically carried out in groups could be done alone. Why, then, is group membership such a universal phenomenon? Group membership seems to provide a number of important features that lead it to be a part of most people's lives. Among them are attraction to the activities or goals of the group, liking for the members of the group, and needs for a group membership per se (Shaw, 1981). We will examine each in turn.

Attraction to Group Activities or Goals

A primary reason for group membership is to participate in the activities of the group or to attain some goal that is more apt to be achieved in a group than alone. Among the sorts of groups of this nature are work groups (formed to complete a task more efficiently and quickly through a pooling of resources and efforts), problem-solving groups (in which civic or other social problems are attacked), legislative groups (in which laws and regulations are formulated), and self-help groups (in which the group members attempt to improve themselves along some dimension; see Box 11-1).

One of the best examples of how group goals can influence group formation comes from a now-classic field study held in a boy's summer camp named Robber's Cave (Sherif, 1966). Two groups of middle-class 11- and 12-year-olds—none of whom knew that he was in an experiment—were settled in opposite sides of the camp. Each group was unaware of the other group's existence. To develop the two campsites

BOX 11-1   SPOTLIGHT ON APPLICATIONS

USING GROUPS TO PROMOTE PSYCHOLOGICAL CHANGE

To the mental health professional, groups represent an often-used therapeutic tool. Although groups are employed in many ways and by the therapists of diverse theoretical orientation, most reflect social psychologist Kurt Lewin's view that groups provide an effective means for learning new social skills (Lewin, 1951). The general goal behind the use of groups is to bring about positive changes in the individuals who choose to participate by harnessing the psychological processes that regularly occur in groups. These changes may be of a therapeutic nature (in which the goal is remediation of some personal problem), an increase in ability to experience and express emotions, or simply intellectual growth and understanding (Lomranz, Lakin, & Schiffman, 1972).

Among the most frequently used groups is the training group—or **T-group**. Although there is a diversity of goals underlying participation in T-groups, there are certain commonalities of method. Among the most important are the following (J. R. Gibb, 1975):

- The group typically has little structure, because there is no predetermined plan for group activities, which are determined solely by the group members.
- The group operates in relative isolation from outside environments such as family and work settings.
- Great emphasis is placed on the internal dynamics of the group and on the observation of the ongoing changes that occur as the group evolves.
- The focus in general is on the process of group interaction, rather than the specific content or nature of what is being discussed or decided. Hence, instead of being concerned with the specific nature of a group decision, the person holding the sessions would be interested in the processes underlying the way in which a group decision was arrived at.

In sum, then, T-groups attempt explicitly to harness group norms and processes in order to make individuals more aware of their own feelings, capabilities, and understanding of the world.

Do T-groups work? The question is difficult to answer. T-group programs are very heterogeneous and it is hard to do research using appropriate control groups. For instance, one cannot compare volunteers who participate in a T-group with nonvolunteers, who do not try to join one; the appropriate match is volunteers who participate with volunteers who do not participate. But in a review of 100 reasonably well-done studies, P. B. Smith (1975) reports positive changes in seventy-eight of them immediately after training. In the thirty-one studies that looked at changes one or more months after training, twenty-one found continued positive changes—as determined through self-reports (which of course hardly represent objective measures).

Still, it does seem that T-groups can have beneficial effects. However, these findings must be weighed against reports of "casualty" rates (referring to people who are clearly harmed by their participation) of anywhere from 1 to 7.5 percent (Lieberman, Yalom, & Miles, 1973). Participation in T-groups can represent a bit of a gamble, then, and potential participants should examine specific programs thoroughly before joining.

---

into groups, the experimenters arranged for the boys to engage in activities that could only be carried out by group efforts, such as carrying a heavy canoe into the water or cleaning a dirty beach so that it was suitable for use. Quite soon, each campsite evolved into what could clearly be called a group. They gave themselves names (the "Rattlers" and the "Eagles") and they developed particular patterns and standards of behavior unique to each group.

Once the two groups had been established, the experimenters tried to develop group competition. To do this, they devised a tournament of games in which the two groups competed for a series of prizes that only one group could win. The researchers got more than they bargained for: not only did the groups compete, but the competition soon went well beyond the tournament. The groups picked fights, raided each other's campsites, and generally behaved in a manner that led the researchers to feel that, to an outside observer, the children appeared as "wicked, disturbed, and vicious bunches of youngsters" (Sherif, 1966, p. 58).

In an attempt to reduce the intergroup conflict, the experimenters at first tried a number of strategies that proved ineffective. Arranging for pleasant experiences, such as watching a movie, only provoked more fighting as soon as the lights were dimmed. Moral exhortations proved useless. Even the introduction of a third group, which was supposed to act as a kind of common enemy, was ineffective. One thing did work, however: the introduction of a **superordinate goal**. Reasoning that it was common goals that led to the formation of the groups initially, the researchers thought that the introduction of goals that were common to both groups—superordinate goals—might be effective in uniting the two groups. This time, they were right.

The experimenters arranged for a series of apparent emergencies. For instance, the water supply broke down, and the boys had to work jointly if they wanted to have water to drink. After a number of such events, group hostility was eventually reduced, friendships developed across group lines, and the superordinate goals became effective in unifying the previously hostile groups.

The Robber's Cave study illustrates quite clearly the importance of the goals of a group in explaining group membership. Providing opportunities to attain goals and carry out activities of importance and interest to group members enhances the attractiveness of a group for its members.

Liking for Group Members

Another fundamental reason that people join groups is that they find the members themselves interpersonally attractive, independent of the goals and activities of the group. The variables that we identified in earlier chapters which promote attraction (such as similarity, physical attractiveness, and physical proximity) all can result not only in liking for individuals but in attraction to a group whose individual members are attractive.

Groups that form primarily on the basis of interpersonal attraction toward the group membership frequently form spontaneously (Cartwright & Zander, 1968). For instance, cliques of friends, street gangs, and social clubs usually develop as a result of inadvertent social interaction that in turn leads to more formal sorts of sustained activity on the part of the members.

The goals and nature of the activities of a group are important in determining the attractiveness of group membership. (Michael Philip Manheim/ Photo Researchers)

One of the clearest examples of how liking for individuals leads to the formation of groups comes from the field study carried out in a housing project that we discussed in our chapter on interpersonal attraction (Festinger, Schachter, & Back, 1950). In the study, as you may recall, the research found that architectural features of the project such as placement of sidewalks, stairways, halls, and mailboxes were an important determinant of who an individual's friends were. Once friendships had emerged, groups spontaneously arose, made up largely of persons attracted to one another.

Needs for Group Membership Per Se

One of the more intriguing hypotheses about why people join groups suggests that group membership can meet social and emotional needs of the members, quite independently of the nature of the group's activities or goals or the attractiveness of other members of the groups. As we mentioned in Chapter 2, Festinger (1954) suggested that people have a need for social comparison and will seek out others to compare their abilities, especially when clear-cut methods of assessing themselves are lacking. Moreover, he maintained that we will try to use people for comparison purposes who are relatively similar to ourselves in order to maximize the visibility of the evaluative information attained. Membership in groups, then, can provide the necessary pool of people against whom an individual could evaluate his or her abilities, according to Festinger's analysis.

Other researchers suggest that groups may directly satisfy needs for affiliation, as we discussed in Chapter 6 (Schachter, 1959). In sum, membership in groups can satisfy people's needs relating to group membership per se. In and of itself, group membership can be rewarding, relatively independent of the nature of the group, its activities, and its goals.

CHARACTERISTICS OF GROUP STRUCTURE

"Why is it," Peggy said to herself, "that I'm the one that's always asked to take the minutes at our meetings? Just for once I'd like to *run* things, the way Jessica always seems to do."

The complaint expressed by Peggy is a reflection of the fact that behavior in groups often evolves into regular, stable patterns, which are known as **group structure.** The structure of a group reflects the fact that not all group members do the same thing—there is differentiation in their activities and what members do to participate in the group. In the example cited above, for instance, Peggy's complaint suggests that she is usually called upon to take the minutes—a secretarial function—while Jessica usually takes charge of the group's activities—a leadership function. In an even more concrete example, work groups typically have executives, managers, and workers. Each of these positions has certain duties and responsibilities attached to it. The executives may make personnel decisions, the managers may keep the workers operating efficiently, and the workers may be the people who actually carry out the job at hand.

The behaviors that are associated with and expected of individuals in a given position are known as **roles.** In our initial example, Peggy would be expected to take clear, accurate notes, while Jessica would be expected to be decisive and assertive. The various roles played by group members are characterized by a status dimension, which indicates the evaluation of the role by the group. For instance, the leader role in our example is likely to be of higher status than the role of secretary.

Occupying a high-status role can make the individual in the role feel more attracted to the group and increase self-confidence and self-worth. For instance, children who are asked to play the role of teacher by tutoring a peer may feel more motivated, show more positive attitudes, and work harder as a consequence of occupying—even temporarily—a higher-status position than that of student (Gartner, Kohler, & Riessman, 1971; Allen, 1976). Clearly, then, role changes can have important consequences for people's behavior.

Origins of Group Structure

The type of structure that develops within a group is a consequence of three basic factors: the requirements for efficiency of performance, the abilities and motivations of the group members, and the environment within which the group is operating (Cartwright & Zander, 1968; Forsyth, 1983). The need for efficiency relates to the importance of completing the group's work within a specified period. Requirements for high efficiency often result in the specialization of tasks and the development of subgroups to perform various activities. The clearest example is the assembly line, where various subgroups of workers assemble parts which are later joined together to form a complete manufactured unit.

The types of abilities and motivations of the group members also have an impact upon the kind of structure that ultimately develops. For instance, one study has demonstrated that groups whose members were particularly concerned with their own personal sense of security and safety were most likely to develop a group structure in which there was greater role differentiation. In contrast, groups whose members were especially concerned with self-esteem tended to form groups in which there was more equality across roles (Aronoff & Messé, 1971). Similarly, groups in which certain members have significantly greater natural ability at a task than others are going to develop structures very different from those in which people have similar levels of ability. In both cases, the personality characteristics and expertise of the members lead to the development of group structure.

Both the physical and social environment in which the group operates can affect the structure that emerges. As we have mentioned before, for instance, Festinger, Schachter, and Back (1950) found that group structure was affected by architectural features such as the design of corridors and stairways in the physical environment within which a group is located. The social environment, as exemplified by an individual's socioeconomic status outside the group, also can have an effect upon an individual's status within a group situation. For example, juries tend to favor higher-status people—such as proprietors and skilled clerical workers—over lower-status unskilled workers when deciding who the jury foreman should be (Strodtbeck & Hook, 1961). In sum, the group structure that emerges often reflects the larger physical and social environment in which the group is located.

Group Cohesiveness

When a student leader says that a way must be found to increase school spirit, what he or she is really talking about is looking for a technique to change **group cohesiveness,** one of the fundamental dimensions on which group structure varies. Group cohesiveness refers to the extent to which members of a group want to continue as members of the group. Put another way, cohesiveness is a measure of how attractive a group is to its membership (see Box 11-2). Groups in which the members are committed to the group and are strongly attracted to the group are said to be high in cohesiveness; groups in which there is little attraction on the part of the members are said to be low in cohesiveness. In one sense, then, group cohesiveness is the social psychological equivalent of what Coach Joe Paterno meant when he discussed the kind of morale he tries to build with his football team: a feeling of commitment and liking for the group.

A number of factors affect cohesiveness. We will discuss the most important ones, including the ways in which the members' needs are met by membership in the group, the goals of the group, the attractiveness of the individuals making up the group, and the activities and leadership of the group.

Satisfaction of Needs

Underlying people's perceptions of how attractive a group is is the issue of how well the group can satisfy their needs. Because people have such diverse requirements regarding what is and is not important to them, all members of a group are not going to be equally attracted to it. Moreover, each individual in the group is not going to have his or her needs fulfilled equally well because of the necessity for role differentiation within the group. For instance, it is difficult to ensure that a third-string quarterback will be as attracted to a football team as the starting quarterback, simply because his needs for competition, activity, and recognition may not be well-satisfied. The greater the extent to which a group fulfills the needs of its members, the more cohesive the group will be.

Group Goals

Cohesiveness is clearly higher in groups in which the goals of the group are congruent with the goals of the members than in groups in which the members do not share the group's overall goals (Lott & Lott, 1965). For example, consider the plight of a pacifist who is drafted into a combat unit of the army. Undoubtedly, the pacifist is going to feel low attraction to the group. And, as more pacifists are drafted into the unit, cohesiveness is going to decrease.

We should note, however, that there are many goals around which a group may be organized. For instance, groups can fulfill task-oriented needs in which the major goal is to produce a product or bring about some event. An individual may believe the goal of membership in the local chamber of commerce is to promote the growth of business activity in a given town. But group members may also, and sometimes simultaneously, have social goals, such as the desire to meet and interact with others. Hence, some people may join the chamber of commerce just to be part of a social organization and may participate primarily to attain the goal of being with others.

Given that people in the same group may have joined it for many different reasons, even groups which are seemingly ineffective in meeting the goal for which they are organized can be high in cohesiveness. The reason? Other goals may become operative and displace the original goal as the underlying rationale for the group's existence. Thus, businessmen intent on promoting the business climate in a town may maintain their membership in an ineffective chamber of commerce because certain social goals are being met, thereby enhancing the cohesiveness of the group.

BOX 11-2   SPOTLIGHT ON METHODOLOGY

MEASURING COHESIVENESS

While social psychologists have developed a comprehensive understanding of both the causes and consequences of group cohesiveness, there is still no agreed-upon way of measuring cohesiveness. Some researchers simply ask group members to rate their attraction to the group as a whole, using, for instance, a 7-point scale, while others ask for ratings of each individual within the group and take the average rating as a general summary of the cohesiveness of the group. Although these two ways of measuring cohesiveness are usually correlated, sometimes they are not (Eisman, 1959). For instance, we could conceive of a situation in which a group's goals are very important to an individual (thus making the group, as a whole, attractive) but which has other members whom she dislikes.

Perhaps the most reasonable measurement of group cohesiveness comes through assessing sociometric choice (Moreno, 1953). In this technique, members of a group are asked to name the individual or individuals with whom they would most prefer to engage in an activity relevant to the group. The degree to which individuals choose other group members, as opposed to nongroup members, is taken as an indication of the degree of cohesiveness of the group. Groups in which the majority of choices are made outside the group would be rated

as lower in cohesiveness than groups in which most of the choices are other group members.

One of the most enlightening ways of dealing with sociometric choice data is to display them graphically in a sociogram. A sociogram—a sample of which is displayed in Figure 11-1—provides information on the nature of choice patterns within a group, which members make mutual choices, and whether any members are particularly popular or isolated. Moreover, the sociogram indicates the degree to which choices are made inside, as opposed to outside, the group, thus giving an overall indication of the cohesiveness of the group.

Although sociograms are quite effective in revealing patterns of attraction within a group, they do have their limitations. For one thing, the nature of the activity that is used to measure choices is critical: people might make very different sorts of decisions if the activity were repairing an automobile versus playing chess. In addition, sociograms work most effectively for small groups. When groups are much larger than five or six members, the maze of lines produced can become impossible to comprehend. Despite these limitations, however, sociograms can provide a clear and useful understanding of the degree of cohesiveness of a group.

FIGURE 11-1

A sociogram of a five-person group. In this example of a sociogram, group members Adam (A), Betsy (B), Charlie (C), David (D), and Ethel (E) have each made two choices, which are indicated by the direction of the arrows. Two persons (Adam and David) have chosen people outside the group (Quincy (Q) and Regina (R), respectively.) Ethel is clearly the most popular, being chosen by four others.

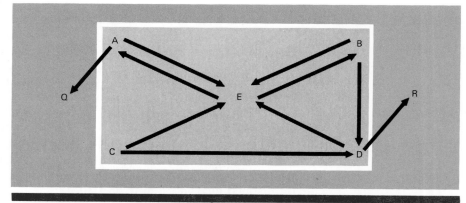

Member Attractiveness   At one time or another, most of us have belonged to a group that is not particularly successful. For instance, we
may have worked on a school newspaper that, because of limited resources, was generally unread and held in low esteem by the student
body. Or we might have been part of a team that had a consistently
losing season. Yet, despite the fact that the goals of such a group were
unmet, the group may have been highly attractive to its membership.
Why should this have been the case, given the importance of attainment
of goals in groups?

One answer may have resided in the other group members. If we find
them to be highly attractive, the fact that the group has not been able
to attain its goals becomes less important. The converse is also true,
however. In cases in which the other group members are disliked, group
cohesiveness is likely to suffer and group participation to dwindle—
even when attainment of the group's goals would be highly beneficial.
One early field study, for example, found that group cohesiveness was
low in a housing project in which the tenants were organizing a tenants'
organization which could have resulted in many improvements in the
project (Festinger & Kelley, 1951). The major reason for the lack of
cohesiveness—and for the subsequent difficulty in making the group
effective—was that the tenants thought of one another as "lower
class," and thus felt that interaction with each other was undesirable.
Therefore, the attractiveness of the group members (or lack of it) can
outweigh the importance of the group's goals in determining group
cohesiveness.

Group Activities and Leadership   Group cohesiveness is related closely
to the kinds of activities that one participates in as a group member. If
individuals are attracted to the group's activities, cohesiveness is likely
to be high. But it is not just a matter of liking what the group is engaged
in; it appears that group members must feel relatively successful at the
task in order for cohesiveness to be enhanced. One study of industrial
employees found that workers whose productivity was below the standards set by their work group tended to have a high rate of voluntary
terminations from the company, suggesting that cohesiveness was low
(Coch & French, 1948). Likewise, the introduction of "job enlargement,"
in which an employee's activities and responsibilities are expanded, has
as one rationale the notion that cohesiveness usually will increase in
work groups as the nature of an employee's activities becomes more
attractive (Hackman & Oldham, 1976).

The behavior of a group's leader is also related to cohesiveness:
generally, groups in which leadership is democratic and in which decision making involves participation of the group's members are more
cohesive than groups that have a strong, centralized, and authoritarian
leader (Cartwright, 1968). On the other hand, in some situations a very
directive leader can facilitate successful group performance and attainment of goals and hence indirectly increase group cohesiveness. Once

again, then, we see that situational factors—in this case, cohesiveness—relate to leader effectiveness.

Effects of Cohesiveness   We have seen what the major causes of group cohesiveness are. But what are the outcomes of cohesiveness? Let us consider a few of the consequences:

- *Maintenance of membership.* Members of groups in which there is high cohesiveness tend to maintain their membership longer than those in low-cohesive groups, almost by definition. If one is highly attracted to a group, maintenance of membership is the logical outcome. On the other hand, continuation of membership also depends upon the attractiveness of alternative groups that one might join. Thus, even a group high in cohesiveness could lose members if more attractive alternatives are at hand (Thibaut & Kelley, 1959).
- *Influence over members.* Groups that are higher in cohesiveness have greater influence and power over their members than groups in which cohesiveness is low. As we saw when we discussed conformity, high cohesiveness produces greater conformity to the group as a whole, as well as to the individual members of the group. For instance, members of religious cults and other highly cohesive groups often share decidedly uniform attitudes and behave in conformance with the standards of the group (Festinger, Schachter, & Back, 1950).
- *Self-esteem.* Members of groups that are high in cohesiveness tend to have higher self-esteem and display less anxiety than members of groups with less cohesiveness. It seems that high cohesiveness leads to greater acceptance and trust of the group's members, and this in turn allows each member to feel more secure and develop higher self-esteem (Julian, Bishop, & Fiedler, 1966). Because the group is attractive to the member, participation in group activities is rewarding, and we would therefore expect that there would be a consequent reduction in anxiety and increased sense of security while in the group. In fact, an experiment in which cohesiveness was experimentally manipulated illustrated this point. In the study, high- and low-cohesiveness groups were insulted by a nongroup member. There were marked differences in the group's responses. While the low-cohesive groups tended to ignore the hostile remarks, basically suffering in silence, the high-cohesive groups tended to react with verbal aggression against the insulting individual, supporting one another and dealing with the situation in a way that could reduce their own anxiety. Thus, membership in high-cohesive groups can have positive consequences in terms of anxiety reduction and enhanced self-esteem (Pepitone & Reichling, 1955).
- *Productivity and cohesiveness.* Should an employer interested in increasing his workers' productivity strive to keep them a cohesive group? The answer to this question is not entirely obvious. At first thought, we might expect that cohesive groups, given their propensity

to maintain membership and influence their workers, would be ideal to increase productivity. The difficulty with such an analysis, however, is that it overlooks the contribution of group norms in determining the effects of cohesiveness. Only if the group norm is such that high productivity is seen as desirable will there be a positive outcome due to cohesiveness. If group norms discourage production, productivity will actually decrease with higher cohesiveness (Zander, 1977).

Experimental evidence supports the prior reasoning. For example, in one study subjects were led to believe they were part of high- or low-cohesive groups before receiving (bogus) messages designed to establish performance norms. In one condition, the messages suggested that higher performance was desirable, while in another, the messages called for a slowdown. As predicted, the messages had a significantly greater effect in the high-cohesive groups than in those with low cohesiveness (Schachter, Ellertson, McBride, & Gregory, 1951).

GROUP BEHAVIOR: CONSEQUENCES OF GROUP MEMBERSHIP

Whenever Andrew found himself at one of his fraternity's parties, he wondered what came over himself. Not only did he begin to do stupid things—like trying out his imitation of Mick Jagger—but he became more aggressive and buffoonish. In retrospect, he felt like a first-class jerk. Since he didn't drink much, it wasn't the liquor. It was just that whenever he partied with friends, the same thing happened.

When people become members of a group, the group often has clear and immediate consequences on their behavior, as our illustration above exemplifies. In the remainder of the chapter, we discuss one of the major areas of the study of groups by social psychologists: the effects of group membership on an individual. We begin by examining a phenomenon known as social facilitation.

Social Facilitation

As any serious jogger could tell you, runners tend to make their best times when they are running with others, as compared with when they are running alone. An explanation for this can be traced back to one of the earliest findings from the discipline of social psychology: a study by Normal Triplett in the late 1800s (Triplett, 1897). Triplett was interested in the phenomenon which later became known as social facilitation, although he conceived of it as the study of competition. Triplett began his research by studying the results of bicycle races held under the auspices of the Racing Board of the League of American Wheelmen. He found that racing times were significantly faster for rides during com-

Social facilitation effects occur when the presence of others leads to improved performance. (Jim Anderson/Woodfin Camp)

petition with other riders than when a lone rider tried to beat the best time established for a particular track. Triplett thought that the presence of others might release riders' extra energy and thus cause them to pedal faster.

To test this hypothesis, Triplett carried out an experiment in which children were asked to turn reels that moved a marker around a 4-meter course. The reels were set up so that the children could either work alone or compete with another child. Triplett found that children moved the marker significantly faster when competing with a peer than when operating the reel by themselves, thereby confirming the results of the bicycle racers studies. Later research showed that the phenomenon was not restricted to competitive situations; even the presence of others as noncompeting spectators could lead to improved performance (Dashiell, 1930).

Although there were many demonstrations of the phenomenon, these really didn't explain the underlying reasons it should occur. Indeed, for many years the phenomenon that had become known as **social facilitation**—in which the presence of others improves performance—defied explanation. Even research findings pertaining to the effects of the presence of others proved to be inconsistent, because sometimes researchers found that the presence of others led to *decrements* in performance.

However, in the 1960s social psychologist Robert Zajonc devised an explanation that for the most part has proven surprisingly durable. Zajonc (1965) suggested that the presence of other individuals raises a person's level of emotional arousal, which, in turn, brings about changes in such physiological phenomena as heart rate, perspiration, and hormonal activity. Because work in learning psychology has shown that higher levels of arousal lead to better performance of well-learned responses and declines in performance of poorly learned responses, Zajonc reasoned that the performance of well-learned behaviors should be enhanced by the presence of others, while the performance of more poorly learned responses should become worse in the presence of others. Hence, the mere presence of others ought to be sufficient to bring about changes in performance, depending upon whether the response is well-learned or poorly learned.

While this explanation has, by and large, received subsequent support, we now know that the mere presence of others does not provide the whole explanation. For instance, some researchers have argued that it is not just the presence of others that affects performance, but the fact that others may be evaluating an individual's performance (Cottrell, 1972). This approach—known as an **evaluation apprehension** theory—suggests that when others are present but are not evaluating performance, social facilitation effects should be reduced.

Support for this latter position comes from a field study by Strube, Miles, and Finch (1981). They surreptitiously observed runners as they jogged around an indoor track. In one experimental condition, no spectators were present; in another, there was an inattentive spectator (a confederate), who appeared to gaze casually at the joggers and then turn away to do stretching exercises. In a third condition, however, an "attentive" spectator (confederate) maintained a constant gaze at the joggers and frequently established eye contact. Results, as measured by the speed at which the joggers ran the track, showed that mean speeds were significantly greater in the attentive spectator condition than in the no-spectator condition. However, the inattentive spectator condition produced no facilitation effects; there was no difference in running times between joggers who had no audience and those who had a nonattentive one. Thus, the presence of others is not sufficient for social facilitation effects to occur; the others must also be attentive to what the performer is doing.

One further explanation for social facilitation effects is known as **distraction/conflict theory** (Sanders, 1981). This theory basically suggests that the presence of others is distracting to the performer. While on simple tasks this distraction is inconsequential and simply raises drive levels—thus increasing performance—on more complex tasks the rise in drive is not sufficient to overcome the effects of distraction. In that case, performance declines.

Because—as it turns out—there is evidence to support each of the explanations put forward for the social facilitation effect (Bond & Titus, 1983), social psychologists have begun to reject the notion that one particular explanation is consistently viable. Instead, current research has been designed to test under what circumstances particular theories most effectively explain the data. Still, although there is disagreement over the explanation of the phenomenon, social facilitation effects themselves remain among the longest established findings in the field of social psychology, and have some tangible applications. Drawing on the findings, for instance, Robert Zajonc suggests—only half-facetiously—how the savvy student ought to prepare for a test: "Study all alone, preferably in an isolated cubicle, and arrange to take his examination in the company of many other students, on stage, and in the presence of a large audience. The results of his examination would be beyond his wildest expectations, provided, of course, he had learned the material quite thoroughly" (Zajonc, 1965, p. 274).

Social Loafing: Where More Is Less

More than fifty years ago, a German researcher named Ringelmann discovered a concrete example of the old maxim "many hands make light work." He asked his subjects to pull as hard as they could on a rope, and measured each subject's efforts while pulling alone and with one, two, or seven others. The results were unequivocal: the more people pulling, the less hard the average individual pulled. When alone, the subjects averaged a pulling strength of 63 kilograms, but this average fell to 53 kilograms with two co-pullers and only 31 kilograms per person with groups of eight.

Bibb Latané (1981) suggests that these results are indicative of a phenomenon known as **social loafing.** Social loafing occurs during a shared group activity when there is a decrease in individual effort due to the social presence of other persons. It happens because social pressure to perform is, in a sense, dissipated by the presence of others; an individual feels as if the pressure is shared by the other people (in a way analogous to the diffusion of responsibility concept we discussed in Chapter 7). Hence, people are apt to work less hard in groups due to the perception of reduced social pressure to produce.

In a series of experiments, Latané, Williams, and Harkins (1979) replicated the earlier findings pertaining to rope pulling. Subjects were asked to engage in the noncooperative task of shouting aloud and clapping, either alone or in groups of various sizes. The results were clear: the larger the group size, the lower the intensity of noise produced per person (see Figure 11-2). From this and other studies (e.g., Harkins & Petty, 1982), it is clear that social loafing is a well-established phenomenon.

Still, Latané's findings do not provide a clear explanation of *why* people should engage in social loafing, and there are several plausible alternative reasons. First, it is possible that people perceive that others in a group are less motivated or less skillful than themselves, and this leads them to reduce their own output. Second, social loafing may be caused by participants choosing goals that are less ambitious when others were present, working under the assumption that the task will be easier when others are involved. With lower goals, we would expect

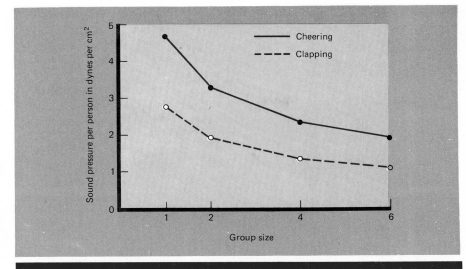

FIGURE 11-2
Intensity of noise pro-
duced according to group
size. As the group size
increased, the average
noise produced by a
group member declined.
Source: Latané, Williams,
& Harkins (1979).

less effort. Finally, a third explanation for social loafing rests on the assumption that individuals feel that their own efforts are less closely linked to any potential outcomes in a group setting than when they are alone. Hence, they would be less inclined to work at their maximum effort in a group situation than when working by themselves.

Given these possible explanations, how can we reduce the possibility of social loafing in collective situations? The most obvious solution is to structure group situations so that each group member feels personally responsible for the outcomes of the group as a whole. One specific technique would be to promote group norms that emphasize the individual's contribution to group performance, as Coach Paterno mentions in the discussion at the beginning of this chapter.

GROUP PROBLEM SOLVING: TWO (OR MORE) HEADS ARE USUALLY BETTER THAN ONE

If you had a thorny problem to solve, would you be better off working on the problem alone or working on it as part of a group? Years of research have yielded a consistent pattern of findings showing that groups typically produce more, and produce better, solutions to problems than the same number of individuals working alone (Steiner, 1972; G. Hill, 1982). For instance, a now-classic experiment by Shaw (1932) had groups or individual subjects attempting to solve problems involving conceptual and mathematical skills. In every case, the groups produced more correct solutions than the individuals. However, there was one important caveat to the finding of group superiority: the groups were considerably less efficient, when time was considered, than the

In most cases, group problem solving is both quantitatively and qualitatively superior to the performance of people working alone. (Bruce Davidson/Magnum)

individuals were. In other words, although groups produced more correct solutions, they did so at a cost of more time. In fact, much subsequent research has suggested that the advantage of groups in solving problems can be outweighed if efficiency in terms of time per person is a major criterion. Moreover, the performance of exceptionally talented individuals can be superior to that of a group.

As a general rule, though, group performance in problem-solving situations is qualitatively and quantitatively superior to the performance of the average individual working alone (Hill, 1982). There are a number of reasons groups are generally better at problem solving than individuals. One important explanation is that group members bring varied backgrounds and skills, which allows members with special abilities to compensate for other members' deficits. Groups present an opportunity, then, for the aggregation of individual expertise and contributions. Another reason is that the most able group member may influence the other members to come up with better solutions than they would have on their own. In addition, the group members can provide feedback regarding solutions that are incorrect. Finally, group membership may make the task more interesting and therefore spur greater effort and motivation to succeed (Forsyth, 1983).

Does participation in group problem-solving situations have lasting effects beyond the immediate group situation? At least one study suggests that this is not the case. Laughlin and Barth (1981) compared the performance of individuals who had first solved problems by themselves with their performance when they had first worked in groups and then tried to solve the problems alone. Results showed no transfer effects across situations: previous group experience did not improve subsequent individual performance, nor did previous individual experience

BOX 11-3 SPOTLIGHT ON RESEARCH

RECIPES FOR COLLECTIVE ACTION

In an imaginative exercise, Ivan Steiner, a noted expert on groups, has suggested that "recipes" for completing tasks in groups can be devised (Steiner, 1976). In much the same way that we follow a recipe to bake a cake—proceeding with a series of steps that lead to the final product—we can analyze group processes and determine how best to bring about the desired outcome. Here are some of Steiner's "recipes," based on specific kinds of group tasks.

Recipe 1: Additive tasks. An additive task is one in which each person's contribution is added to every other person's. For example, shoveling snow is additive: each person's accomplishments add to the total group's accomplishments. The recipe is straightforward: each member does as much as he or she can, while they all coordinate their activities with each other. The coordination is necessary to ensure that people don't impinge upon each other's activities and therefore reduce the total output.

Recipe 2: Disjunctive tasks. Disjunctive tasks are those which call for a single choice among several alternatives, one of which is right and the others wrong. The recipe: identify the most competent member of the group and present his or her solution to the group for approval. If the identity of the most competent member cannot be determined, all members should work simultaneously on the solution.

Each solution should then be presented to the group, and the best solution chosen.

Recipe 3: Compensatory tasks. Compensatory tasks are those in which the task cannot be divided into parts, the abilities of the individuals in the group cannot be determined, and the kinds of errors each individual has a tendency to make can be assumed to cancel each other out. The recipe in this case: Each individual should devise a solution of his own, and the statistical average of all solutions should be used as the group's final judgment.

Recipe 4: Conjunctive tasks. In a conjunctive task, the group can make a product that is no better than the one the least competent person in the group can make. The group must adjust its behavior to the least competent individual, as in the case of mountain climbers who can reach a summit only as fast as the slowest climber. The recipe: the least competent members should try their hardest, and all other group members should follow the lead of these persons.

The above four recipes are for the simplest group tasks; more complex tasks require more complex recipes. Still, Steiner's recipes provide an important way of looking at task-performing groups, in identifying both the nature of tasks and the approach that groups ought to take to carry them out.

---

affect later group performance. These findings suggest that although groups generally are better able to solve problems than individuals, participation in groups does not seem to have lasting effects beyond the immediate group situation. Rather than learn strategies that are useful in solving problems beyond the immediate group setting, participants in groups reach better solutions because of specific group conditions. (Also see Box 11-3.)

Making Decisions in Groups

While it is clear that groups are generally superior to individuals when considering problems that have a definite solution, many group tasks are more ambiguous and do not have a clear-cut solution. For instance, there is frequently no way of determining if a factory management group seeking to solve a problem, such as how to negotiate with an employee union, has reached the optimal solution; it is a matter of weighing options and determining what seems to be the best course of action. Although in such situations there is no single "right" answer, a number of important characteristics have been identified that distinguish group decisions from those decisions made by individuals acting alone. One of the most important characteristics concerning group decisions is the degree to which groups differ from individuals in the extremity of their decisions.

Choice Shifts   One management tool used in business is the use of groups to come to decisions. An often-stated rationale for group decision making is not just that groups may come to better solutions, but that they provide a conservative counterweight to more extreme solutions. In essence, this view suggests that less extreme (and, thus, presumably better) decisions would be more apt to be made if the decisions are made in group situations.

However, a large body of research produced by social psychologists in the late 1960s and early 1970s challenged this commonsense view by suggesting that in fact groups often tend to make riskier decisions than individuals solving the same problems on their own. This finding has been called the **risky shift,** which denotes the change that occurs in groups from more conservative decisions to more extreme ones. Although there were situations in which groups shifted toward more conservative decisions, most group situations were found to produce changes toward risk (Pruitt, 1971).

With literally dozens of experiments confirming the regularity of the risky shift, research soon shifted to trying to explain the reasons behind its occurrence, rather than demonstrate its existence. Three major explanations emerged:

1.   *Diffusion of responsibility.* The most direct explanation for the risky shift rests on the phenomenon of diffusion of responsibility, which we first considered in our discussion of helping behavior. The diffusion of responsibility theory suggests that people in groups become less conservative because any negative consequences for the decision are shared by the other group members. Each member has, in effect, less total responsibility for the negative consequences (Wallach, Kogan, & Bem, 1964).

Although it appears reasonable on the surface, there are several problems with this theory (Pruitt, 1971). For instance, it is difficult to understand why group members faced with hypothetical situations would feel responsible for equally hypothetical outcomes. Moreover, even subjects who simply watch others discussing the problem situations show a later shift to riskiness; it is unlikely that they could diffuse feelings of responsibility with others with whom they never even discuss the situation. There are, then, a number of arguments against the diffusion of responsibility explanation for the risky shift.

2. *Persuasion and leadership theory.* Another reasonable theory for the risky shift phenomenon rests on the assumption that individuals who make initially risky decisions tend to be more persuasive and influential in the group setting and may become de facto leaders of the group (Collins & Guetzkow, 1964; Vinokur & Burnstein, 1974). These people exert a disproportionate influence upon the group, and lead the others into making riskier decisions. A variant of this theory suggests that people who argue for riskier positions are more confident of their position and hence become more influential in the group setting.

Support for these explanations comes from work that shows that subsequent to group discussion, the more risk-taking group members and their riskier arguments are seen as most influential (Wallach, Kogan, & Burt, 1967). However, this is not very compelling support, because it may simply be a form of justification for a risk-taking shift that has already occurred, rather than a real reason.

3. *The cultural value of riskiness.* This explanation assumes that risk is something that is valued by members of our society. For instance, we tend to glorify people who have risked their fortunes on new ideas, procedures, or products. Hence, according to the first premise of the cultural value theory, there is a general tendency to admire people who take chances and to value risk-taking behavior.

The next part of the explanation assumes that most of us not only admire risk takers, but consider ourselves risk takers as well, or as least as daring as others in society. Therefore, when we make initial decisions about a choice, we tend to think of them as relatively nonconservative. However, when we get into a group situation and compare our responses with those of others, we may find that others are even riskier than we are. In order to maintain our view of ourselves as people inclined to take chances, then, we may wish to shift our answers in the direction of greater riskiness. In so doing, we end up as group members reaching a final decision that is riskier than our initial individual positions (R. Brown, 1965).

Choice Shifts in a Broader Context: Polarization   In all likelihood, the mechanisms underlying the three explanations for the risky shift that we have discussed—diffusion of responsibility, persuasion and leadership theory, and the cultural value of riskiness—all contribute to the phenomenon of group decisions generally being riskier than the decisions of their individual members. But recall that we mentioned that decisions occasionally became more *conservative* after group discussion. This finding suggested that it would be reasonable to view the risky shift as part of a broader context of choice shifts in which there is a movement not toward riskiness per se but toward extremity or polarization of group views—an approach that guides most current thinking on the topic.

The term **polarization** refers to the phenomenon in which group responses tend to be more extreme, although in the same direction, as the average of the individual responses made prior to group interaction (Myers & Lamm, 1976; Lamm & Myers, 1978). In other words, the concept of polarization encompasses shifts in the direction of both greater riskiness and greater conservativism.

There have been many demonstrations, apart from the work on the risky shift, that show group polarization at work. For example, instances both of prosocial and antisocial behavior tend to increase following group discussion. Results of specific experiments show that group discussion can increase the likelihood that individuals predisposed to suggest donations of time and money will do so (Schroeder, 1973), and individuals in groups may behave significantly more aggressively than individuals acting alone in situations in which aggressiveness is permissible (Wolosin, Sherman, & Mynatt, 1975).

Another example of group polarization comes from a study by Minix and Semmell (cited in Lamm & Myers, 1978) of groups of army officers, ROTC cadets, and non-military-affiliated university students. In discussion groups, each set of subjects came up with different solutions regarding action following a hypothetical international military crisis revolving around a threat to United States security. Both student groups were consistently more apt to suggest diplomatic alternatives than the army officers, who tended to recommend military action. More importantly, following discussion within their own groups, members of each group showed polarization by becoming more extreme in their attitudes than they were initially, and hence group differences were exaggerated.

Another relevant example of polarization processes can be seen in students as they progress through college. Attitudinal and behavioral differences that exist among students when they enter college and choose a specific major are amplified the longer they are in college. It seems as if students choose universities and majors which are populated by others who are similar to them, as well as participate in activities that are related to their initial interests. Their choices, in turn, reinforce and strengthen their early attitudinal and behavioral inclinations, resulting in polarization (Wilson, Gabb, Dienst, Wood, & Bavry, 1975). Hence, for example, students who choose English majors end up more like each other, while students majoring in military science behave more similarly to each other; at the same time, the differences between English and military science majors tend to increase.

Reasons for Group Polarization The explanations put forth initially for the risky shift have all been shown to be applicable to understanding the broader phenomenon of group polarization, and it is clear that the diffusion of responsibility, persuasion and leadership, and risk as a cultural valve theories provide partial explanations of group polarization. One other reason for the phenomenon that has received strong and consistent support involves the role of informational social influence, which, as we discussed in Chapter 10, refers to the fact that others may have more knowledge about an issue than a particular person has (Lamm & Myers, 1978). According to this view, the kinds of arguments that are made during a group discussion tend to support the position that is generally accepted. Because each individual within the group is not likely to have thought of all the previous arguments in support of his or her position, these new arguments—which are, in any case, supportive of most people's initial view—are likely to reinforce their initial position. Therefore, it is the new information that is presented that induces the group, as a whole, to take a more extreme position than the individuals making up the group took initially.

Although we cannot say for sure which of the explanations of the group polarization phenomenon is most appropriate—and, indeed, it is likely that all play a role in producing polarization to some degree—the phenomenon itself is clear: group discussion tends to produce changes in the attitudes of the group members toward a more extreme position than the initial, pregroup attitude expressed by the individual members.

We turn now to further examples of the powerful effect of groups in changing—and sometimes even distorting—the thinking of individuals as we consider a phenomenon called groupthink and, in Box 11-4, collective behavior.

Groupthink

The attempted Bay of Pigs invasion of Cuba has come to be recognized as one of the sorriest mistakes of recent American foreign policy. Planned and executed by President John F. Kennedy and his advisers in 1961, the abortive invasion was an immediate disaster and embarrassment to America. The plan called for a force of about 1400 Cuban exiles to land at the Bay of Pigs in Cuba and, with the help of the general Cuban populace (who were expected to revolt spontaneously against their president, Fidel Castro, at the start of the invasion), were to overthrow the Communist government. In actuality, things went wrong from the beginning. The exile force was poorly equipped, the Cuban air force, which was to have been destroyed in an attack, was able to mount a strong offensive, and within three days most of the invasion force had been captured by the vastly larger Cuban militia. Just about everything that could have gone wrong did go wrong. In President Kennedy's own words, the question was "How could we have been so stupid?"

An answer to this question was provided by social psychologist Irving Janis in the early 1970s. In an example of how social psychological principles can be adapted to explain political situations, Janis suggested that Kennedy and his advisers had been subject to a phenomenon that he termed groupthink. **Groupthink** refers to the "deterioration of mental efficiency, reality testing, and moral judgment that results from in-group pressures" (Janis, 1972, p. 9). Basically, groupthink is characterized by

BOX 11-4 SPOTLIGHT ON RESEARCH

GROUPS AS MOBS

[1789] Groups of French citizens, acting with strikingly single-minded determination, start through Paris killing government officials and destroying public property. The crowds that form seem to undertake wildly destructive actions, and eventually the government crumbles under the pressure of the rioting population.

[1979] A crowd in Cincinnati waiting for a concert to be given by the rock group The Who stampedes the entrance to the Coliseum. Eleven persons are literally trampled to death and many others are injured. An emergency-room supervisor comments: "The bodies were marked with multiple contusions and bruises and the victims had suffered hemorrhages."
(*Richmond News Leader,* December 5, 1979, p. 14, as cited in Forsyth, 1983, pp. 308–309).

The examples above illustrate the phenomenon of **collective behavior**—behavior that occurs in aggregates of people who are relatively unorganized yet who hold a sense of unity and may work toward similar goals. Although social psychologists interested in groups typically consider groups of ten or less, a sizable amount of research has concentrated on larger groups engaged in collective behavior.

The first work on collective behavior was done by the French sociologist Gustav LeBon (1895), who sought to explain why large groups seemingly took on a character that was quite different from the behavior of the individual members when they were not in the group situation. Citing instances in which mobs appeared to act in a uniformly violent fashion, LeBon suggested that participation in groups could cause a disappearance of one's overt, everyday personality and the formation of a **group mind** which led the participants to act in an intensely violent fashion. According to this view, which was adopted to a large extent by Freud (1922) in his later writings, there is a thin veneer of civilization that disappears when people find themselves in a large group. The crowd behavior becomes homogeneous, and normal social restraints are dropped as the group mind takes control. The mechanism by which this occurred was, according to LeBon, contagion; he felt that the behavioral characteristics of mobs spread through the crowd in the same way that diseases spread through a helpless populace.

A more recent formulation of contagion theory is known as **deindividuation theory,** which we discussed first in Chapter 9 (Diener, 1980; Zimbardo, 1969). According to this view, participation in large crowds reduces concerns about being evaluated by others and about maintaining a positive image. Crowd members feel anonymous and do not think of each other as individuals. Internalized norms regarding appropriate conduct do not come into play, and the individual feels free to engage in antisocial and violent behavior.

An alternative view, known as **emergent norm theory,** explains mob behavior in terms of the principles of small group behavior that we have been discussing in this chapter (Turner & Killian, 1972). Rather than the extreme behavior of crowds representing an atypical psychological state, emergent norm theory assumes that crowds begin with heterogeneous individuals who do not necessarily share similar motivation and behavior. However, once in the situation, norms regarding appropriate behavior develop and are communicated to the crowd members. Because of implicit pressures to conform to the norm, crowd members may behave in ways that are quite different from their typical conduct. The emergent norm theory also suggests that because social pressure is greatest in situations in which individuals are identifiable to one another, anonymity of crowd members ought to *reduce* antisocial behavior when norms favoring violent behavior have developed. Note how this prediction is just the opposite of what would be expected using contagion theory, which suggests that the anonymity *increases* antisocial behavior.

In an attempt to test the two theories, Mann, Newton, and Innes (1982) recently conducted a laboratory experiment in which they varied both the anonymity and nature of a norm regarding the administration of loud, crowdlike noise to a pair of discussants by groups of six to eight subjects. To manipulate anonymity, subjects either could see each other and know each other's names or could not be seen and were completely unknown to each other. To manipulate the norm, the group members were told that either an aggressive or a lenient norm (higher or lower noise levels) supposedly had been chosen by the group. In reality, the level bore no relation to what the group members actually chose; rather, it was manipulated by the experimenter.

The results of the study supported contagion theory and not emergent norm theory. Just as contagion theory suggests, subjects chose noise levels significantly higher when they were in the anonymous condition. Moreover, subjects within the anonymous condition chose levels of loudness irrespective of the nature of the group norm. Hence, the experiment suggests that contagion theory provides the most valid representation of crowd behavior. Of course, we cannot dismiss emergent norm theory on the basis of one study. The experiment provides a laboratory representation of an extreme real-world situation; thus, we must be cautious in our interpretations of the results. Until we have more research on the phenomenon of mob behavior, both contagion and emergent norm theory remain potentially viable explanations.

---

such strong pressures toward unanimity and endorsement of the leader's apparent position and by attraction to the group as a whole that critical analysis and evaluation of the situation become impossible.

According to this theory, groupthink has a number of important characteristics:

- The illusion develops that the group is invulnerable and cannot make important errors.
- There are efforts to rationalize and discount information that is contradictory to the predominant view of the group.
- Other groups are viewed stereotypically, resulting in the opinions of others being discounted.
- Pressures are placed on group members to adopt the majority view, thus helping to stifle minority opinions.
- Group members stifle their own misgivings, resulting in a kind of self-censorship.
- Because group members feel pressure to conform, there is an illusion of unanimity, thus reinforcing the dominant view.
- Individuals emerge, called **mindguards** by Janis, who act to protect the group from divergent or contradictory information.

In a thorough analysis of the Bay of Pigs incident, Janis (1972) demonstrates that these characteristics of groupthink were present. Indeed, a number of historical events bear all the hallmarks of groupthink, including such incidents as the attempt by the Nixon administration to cover up the Watergate break-in and the escalation of American involvement in Vietnam. In each of these cases, a small group of advisers who shared a strong attraction to the group was insulated from deviant opinions and did not have systematic procedures for considering views other than the ones apparently preferred by the group leader and majority.

The existence of groupthink has received support from a number of quarters. One approach has been to create laboratory simulations of situations producing conditions under which groupthink might be expected to occur. Thus, Flowers (1977) divided college students into high- and low-cohesiveness groups to solve a crisis problem. By varying whether the leader was nondirective or directive, Flowers was able to show that leaders who encouraged divergent opinions and emphasized the importance of reaching the optimal solution (the nondirective leaders) had groups that produced more solutions and used available information more effectively. (On the other hand, group cohesiveness had no significant effect upon the quality of decision making.) The results of the experiment at least partially support Janis's formulation.

A more direct test of the groupthink concept comes from a content analysis of public statements made by leaders involved in various crisis situations (Tetlock, 1979). Statements were thoroughly analyzed for their degree of complexity and the degree to which they reflected unequivocal positive references to the United States. Consistent with the groupthink formulation, situations in which groupthink was hypothesized to have occurred were associated with statements that were more simplistic and positive than situations without groupthink. Although there were not significantly more negative statements made about the enemies of the United States, as would have been expected under conditions of groupthink, the content analysis generally supported the groupthink hypothesis.

Given the existence of the groupthink phenomenon, how can it be avoided? Janis (1972) suggests several ways. One approach is to increase the quantity and quality of information available to the group. For instance, experts who represent a wide divergence of views could be brought into the deliberations of the group. Group members could be encouraged to play the role of devil's advocate.

Another approach to the prevention of groupthink revolves around how information available to the group is evaluated and synthesized. The group leader might encourage criticism and refrain from voicing his or her opinion early in the discussions. The group could also develop explicit procedures for dealing with and presenting divergent information. For instance, subgroups could be maintained to deal with and promote one particular position, and then be assigned the task of presenting that position to the group as a whole. Finally, after a tentative decision has been reached, a later meeting could be held to air any remaining doubts or to bring up any afterthoughts prior to making the decision final. Through techniques such as these, the potential development of groupthink can be prevented.

SUMMARY

The study of groups represents an integral part of the field of social psychology. Four criteria are necessary for an aggregate of people to be considered a group in a formal sense: (1) There must be interaction among group members. (2) The members of the group must perceive themselves as part of the group and generally be perceived by others as part of the group. (3) There must be shared goals and norms about appropriate behavior. (4) There must be interdependence of fates.

People join groups for a number of reasons, including attraction to the activities or goals of the group, liking for the specific members of the group, and needs for group membership per se. The importance of shared goals is suggested by the work of Sherif, in which superordinate goals led to a decrease in intergroup hostility. Needs for group membership have been demonstrated by work on need for social comparison and affiliation needs.

Group structure refers to the regular, stable patterns of activities and behavior in a group. One aspect of structure relates to the set of behaviors associated with a person in a given position, known as a role. Roles vary along a status dimension in a given group. The nature of the structure that emerges in a group is affected by the requirements for efficiency of performance, the abilities and motivations of the group members, and the environment within which the group operates.

Group cohesiveness—the degree to which members want to remain members of the group and are attracted to it—is a fundamental dimension of group structure. A number of factors affect group cohesiveness, including satisfaction of members' needs, the group's goals, member attractiveness, the nature of the group's activities, and the group's leadership. In turn, cohesiveness results in maintenance of membership, influence over the group's members, feelings of member self-esteem, and group productivity.

Once a group has been established, there are a number of consequences. Social facilitation, in which the presence of others improves performance, operates for well-learned activities because of increases in arousal due to the presence of attentive others. For poorly learned activities, arousal produces decrements in performance. Social loafing occurs when there is a decrease in individual effort due to the presence of other persons working jointly on a task. It occurs when the social pressure to perform is perceived as being shared by the coworkers.

Groups generally are more effective in solving problems than individuals working alone; groups tend to produce more and better quality solutions, although this is done at the expense of efficiency. Moreover, exceptionally talented individuals can outperform groups. Typically, though, groups are superior to the same number of individuals working alone.

Decision making in groups tends to show regular shifts to more extreme positions, a phenomenon known as polarization. Shifts toward greater riskiness (the risky shift) have been explained by the cultural value of riskiness, diffusion of responsibility, and persuasion or leadership theories. In addition, polarization can occur because group discussion airs arguments that are supportive of the generally accepted position, leading to reinforcement of the prevailing initial position and a less cautious approach that results in the ultimate acceptance of a more extreme group position.

A consequence of decision making in groups with strong pressures toward unanimity and endorsement of the leader's position and with strong attraction to the group is groupthink, which refers to a loss of rational decision making and critical abilities. Groupthink has occurred in a number of crisis situations. It can be avoided by increasing the quality and quantity of information available to the groups and by restructuring the ways in which information is evaluated and synthesized by the group members.

KEY TERMS

additive tasks
cohesiveness
collective behavior
compensatory tasks
conjunctive tasks
cultural value of riskiness
deindividuation
deviant
diffusion of responsibility
disjunctive tasks
distraction/conflict theory
emergent norm theory
evaluation apprehension
group
group cohesiveness
group mind

group structure
groupthink
job enlargement
legislative groups
persuasion and leadership theory
polarization
problem-solving groups
risky shift
self-help groups
social comparison
social facilitation
social loafing
status
superordinate goal
training groups (T-groups)

FOR FURTHER STUDY AND APPLICATION

Cartwright, D., & Zander, A. (Eds.). (1968). *Group dynamics: Research and theory* (3rd ed.). New York: Harper & Row.
This volume presents much of the seminal research and thinking in the area of group dynamics, with well-integrated chapter introductions.

Shaw, M. (1981). *Group dynamics: The psychology of small group behavior* (3rd ed.). New York: McGraw-Hill.
A thorough, comprehensive introduction to the field of group dynamics.

Steiner, I. (1972). *Group process and productivity.* New York: Academic Press.

Zander, A. (1977). *Groups at work.* San Francisco: Jossey-Bass.
Sophisticated, yet accessible, treatments of how groups operate and the factors affecting their productivity.

Janis, I. (1972). *Victims of groupthink.* Boston: Houghton Mifflin.
A fascinating analysis of the phenomenon of groupthink, with numerous historical examples.

Napier, R. W., & Gershenfeld, M. K. (1981). *Groups: Theory and experience* (2nd ed.). Boston: Houghton Mifflin.
Informative from both a theoretical and an applied point of view. As its title indicates, the book examines groups from a practical and scientific vantage.

Forsyth, D. (1983). *An introduction to group dynamics.* Monterey, CA: Brooks/Cole.
A readable, up-to-date introduction to current research, theory, and application regarding groups.

CHAPTER 12

SOCIAL PSYCHOLOGICAL APPROACHES TO ORGANIZATIONS AND THE WORKPLACE

A CONVERSATION WITH . . .

Joe Hankins (*top*)
and Chuck Clary
NASA Supervisors

The National Aeronautics and Space Administration—NASA—is an organization that is representative of the complexity of the United States government as a whole. In a conversation with Joe Hankins and Chuck Clary of NASA, whose jobs involve maintaining strict quality control in the production and launch preparation of space vehicles such as the space shuttle (which has been called the most complex piece of equipment ever made by man), we discussed some of the problems inherent in maintaining quality in an organization which involves thousands of individuals.

Q. From one perspective, what you do at NASA has such a clear and important goal, the successful operation of a space ship, that it must be easier to maintain motivation and morale than in an organization where people produce a less interesting product. Is that correct?

A. I do think that morale is very good and people are happy to be working at NASA. It can be irritating; at times we work seven days a week, ten hours a day. But basically it's easy to motivate people to work at a high level of competence.

Q. But I'd think that in an organization of this size there might be a problem with workers whose jobs are fairly low level and who can't see too clearly where the thing they are working on really fits into the overall project.

A. One thing that prevents that is the fact that everything anyone does is traceable to the person who actually performed that job. Every nut, every bolt can be traced to the individual who installed it. And in cases in which we've got, say, a panel with ten bolts in it, with two or three peo-

ple working together, one of the people will take charge and say that he or she attests to that particular panel or item being put together correctly. So ultimately one person has responsibility for every piece of equipment or procedure, and of course that motivates people to do the right kind of work.

Q. Then if something happens during a space flight, such as an equipment malfunction, you're able to go back to the people who made that particular piece of equipment and talk to them?

A. Right. As soon as there is a problem, we have people on the ground starting to look at what we had done which might help solve the problem. Our traceability goes back to when we first start putting an item together and to the source of the raw material. For instance, with aluminum we know where the original raw material was mined, where it was made into aluminum, and what kind of aluminum—all that is traceable.

Q. And everyone that works on space equipment is aware of this?

A. For everything we buy in the space shuttle program, we try to make the people aware that they're building space hardware—and we reward these people. For instance, we might have the astronauts go to a plant and give out special awards which only workers, not management, can get. Then we also have workers come here for launches as VIPs. There were about fifty here for the last shuttle flight, and we gave them a banquet where they could meet some astronauts. These types of awards dinners help performance.

Q. Is there anything else you do to try to keep people doing their best?

A. One other thing is that we have a policy that encourages people to admit if they've done something in error. We say that if you mess up and report it, not much is going to happen. If you've done something wrong, or broken something, you're not going to get criticized for it. Maybe we have to train you a little more, but we're not going to do anything to jeopardize your career; we're going to help you. But if you mess up and don't report it, a lot is going to happen if we find out.

Q. Basically, would you say you have less problems with quality than in other organizations?

A. I'm not really sure about other organizations, but I think we've got the best.

OVERVIEW

The task of coordinating the efforts of many individuals in an organization as large and complex as NASA is a challenging one. Social psychologists have begun to pay increasing attention to this challenge, for, as we will see in this chapter, many social psychological issues arise when we examine the operation of organizations and the workplace. For example, consider the following questions:

- What are methods for increasing motivation in organization members?
- Should workers participate in management decisions?
- How can organizational morale be raised?
- What is the most effective means to acclimate new members of an organization?
- How can organizational effectiveness and productivity be increased?

Each of these questions requires an answer that is, in large part, related to social psychological variables.

In contrast to work on group dynamics, which is concerned typically with small group behavior, work on organizations carried out by social psychologists has been directed toward understanding how large, complex systems of individuals, working toward a general common goal, operate. Most of this research has been carried out and applied to the workplace, particularly large-scale industrial and corporate organizations, since work in these kinds of settings provides employment for a large percentage of the populace.

In this chapter, we examine some of the social psychological factors that affect the behavior of individuals in organizations and the workplace. We first discuss the ways in which people's job performance is influenced by their peers and how social influence is communicated and enforced in organizations. Then we examine the decision-making processes and the communication structure of organizations. Finally, we consider techniques for making groups and organizations in the workplace more effective.

THE HAWTHORNE STUDIES

The Hawthorne plant of the Western Electric Company near Chicago was a major producer of telephone components in the early part of the twentieth century. It was also the site of one of the first research programs that identified the importance of social psychological factors in determining how productive workers could be, and, indeed, the work spawned a new approach to organizational study, known as the human relations model (Mayo, 1933; Whitehead, 1938; Roethlisberger & Dickson, 1939).

The initial studies conducted at the Hawthorne plant were designed simply to examine the effects of changes in illumination intensity on the productivity of workers assembling telephone components. Gradual increases in lighting were made, and each change brought increased productivity. Surprisingly, however, productivity increased even when the researchers went beyond a reasonable point and increased illumination to a level that was abnormally bright. Even more intriguing was the fact that when they began to decrease the lighting, productivity still rose slightly! It seemed clear that something other than illumination per se was playing a role in the workers' productivity.

A subsequent experiment at the Hawthorne plant shed some light on the reasons for the productivity increases. Using a small group of six women, the researchers made a number of changes in the working conditions, such as varying the rest pauses and rates of compensation. Once again, productivity increases occurred that were independent of the nature of the specific change. It almost seemed as if change itself could produce increases in productivity.

In fact, the explanation that the subjects themselves came up with was that the special attention they had received from the investigators, the fact that they were interested in the experimental results, and the uniqueness of their own situation as participants in the study all contributed to their increased productivity. The change and special attention, rather than the specific nature of the situational modifications, led to increases in productivity. This concept has become known as the **Hawthorne effect,** and it signifies that any time subjects know they are in an experiment their behavior may change simply as a function of the special attention they are receiving and not necessarily because of any of the experimental manipulations.

Although the Hawthorne studies have been criticized on methodological grounds (for instance, appropriate control groups were lacking; Parsons, 1974), the concept of the Hawthorne effect has proved durable and made an important contribution to the work on individuals in business settings. While it does not seem so revolutionary to us, the idea that social psychological factors must be taken into account in the workplace was a new one in the 1930s.

Michael Radler had a problem. As a supervisor at the Embryonic Production Corporation, he had difficulty in finding staff that would display the desired degree of initiative and innovation. It wasn't that his staff didn't have the right credentials; all of its members had received at least a master's degree in biology. And when they came for the job interview, they seemed bright, enthusiastic, and innovative. But after a month on the job, they fell into the same pattern as everyone else. They did things in the same way that employees had been doing them for years, and when he specifically asked them to come up with possible new procedures, they carefully told him that everything seemed to work fine the way it was being done, and that no major changes were likely to be as effective as the ones already in place.

What had happened to these new employees during their first month at work to make them act as if they had been entrenched members of the organization for years? One explanation is that strong social influence processes produced compliance to norms that contradicted what the employees' immediate supervisor was asking them to do. As we shall see, organizations influence their members through both formal and informal mechanisms, and the nature of this influence may be the greatest determinant of how productive and happy members are with their positions.

The process by which an individual comes to behave and hold attitudes similar to others in an organization is known as **organizational socialization.** First used to refer to how children learn customary and acceptable behaviors in a given culture, the concept of socialization has been adapted to the organizational context in the sense of "the process of learning the ropes, the process of being indoctrinated and trained, the process of being taught what is important in an organization or some subunit thereof" (Schein, 1968, p. 2). Organizational socialization, then, takes place on both formal and informal levels. Formal socialization occurs through the teaching and training of new members, while informal socialization occurs through interaction between older organizational members and newer ones, and results in an understanding of the norms of the organization. We will first discuss formal socialization practices: what the organization *wants* its members to know and do.

Formal Organizational Socialization

The process by which organizations carry out formal member socialization can be divided into three basic phases (Porter, Lawler, & Hackman, 1975; Van Maanen, 1978): prearrival, encounter, and change and acquisition.

Prearrival Phase   Even before an individual joins an organization, he or she is likely to have a set of attitudes and expectations regarding what the organization is like. These prior notions may be a result of previous experience with the organization (who, for instance, does not hold strong opinions about what the telephone company is like?), or they may be based upon rumors, guesses, or misinformation. Whatever the source of their expectations, individuals do not enter the organization as blank slates, but as people with ideas and notions about what is and is not appropriate behavior and what will be expected of them. From an organizational point of view, the goal of formal socialization is to modify or replace previous attitudes and behaviors that are inappropriate.

In our example of the Embryonic Production Corporation, it appears that the prearrival expectations and attitudes of employees matched those of the formal organization, at least as far as could be judged from the information available to supervisor Radler during the job interview with potential employees. Of course, one of the real difficulties in the interview process is that the underlying attitudes of the employees may not be expressed forthrightly. Employees may present themselves as favoring change and innovations, when in fact they do not. Thus, one of Radler's problems is to determine accurately prearrival attitudes of employees in order to optimize the likelihood of desired employee behavior.

Perhaps the easiest way to encourage socialization of new members of an organization is through the selection of members who already share the attitudes and behaviors desired by the organization. By choosing such people, the organization is assured that new members will fit in with minimal stress, both to themselves and to the organization. On the other hand, the organization may be losing opportunities for growth and change if it only chooses as members those individuals who are similar to its present membership (Schein, 1983).

Encounter   This phase of the socialization process refers to the actual interaction between the individual and the organization, and it occurs when the person joins the organization. The organization can employ three types of strategies to socialize its new members formally: reinforcement of preexisting attitudes and behaviors, direct teaching of new behaviors, and avoidance of reinforcement of nonvalued behavior or punishment of inappropriate behavior (Porter, Lawler, & Hackman, 1975). By reinforcing the attitudes and behavior that an individual has prior to entry into the organization, the organization builds upon what the person already knows and thinks. In a sense, it is a matter of bringing out the best, from the organization's point of view, of the person.

Direct teaching takes place through formal training programs, through the use of manuals about proper policies and procedures, and through supervisors and coworkers taking new employees under wing and showing them how to do the job. The most obvious source of an organization's ability to provide socialization experience resides in explicit training given to new members (Wanous, 1983). Some organizations use an alternative form of direct training; they appoint someone explicitly to socialize a newcomer. Arising out of the old tradition of apprenticeship, in which an individual learned a trade or skill from a master craftsman, this technique assumes that an individual will not only attempt to learn and evaluate the behavior of an established member of the organization, but will also eventually internalize the attitudes and values of that member. The person who provides this training is known as a **role model,** someone who provides an example of the behaviors associated with a particular position (Sarbin & Allen, 1968).

It should be noted that new organizational members may get mixed messages from an organization regarding what is appropriate behavior (see, for instance, Box 12-1). For instance, even if supervisors suggest the importance of innovative behavior and try explicitly to promote the behavior in their subordinates, other information that the new member receives can prove contradictory. Thus, a new organizational member might find that the employees who are most successful in the organization are those that follow the rules and don't rock the boat, avoiding innovation. These contradictory kinds of information, leading to different socialization outcomes, provide a possible explanation for the behavior of new employees in our example of the Embryonic Corporation (D. C. Feldman, 1983).

Change and Acquisition   After the encounter phase of socialization, new organizational members will generally modify their previous attitudes and behaviors and acquire new ones that are valued by the organization. The concept of socialization suggests that these changes may not be just a matter of behavioral compliance; rather, they may reflect underlying modifications in how an individual perceives that situation and what is understood to be appropriate behavior. Indeed, formal socialization processes may even produce a change in the self-image of a new member (Caplow, 1964). For example, staunch prounion workers who join a new firm in a management role may come to adopt antiunion sentiments held by other managers in the firm and view themselves—and what is considered appropriate behavior—quite differently from the way they did prior to joining the new organization. On the other hand, people who resist changes in attitudes may find themselves unhappy with their new situation and eventually terminate their involvement with the organization. (For the most contemporary kind of socialization problem, see Box 12-1.)

Socialization by Peers: How Organizational Members Influence One Another

We have been discussing the ways in which an organization, in a formal sense, can influence and bring about conforming behavior through its socialization practices. But in the same way that minorities in small

BOX 12-1 SPOTLIGHT ON APPLICATIONS

COMPUTERS IN ORGANIZATIONS: ENCOUNTERS WITH AN ALIEN CULTURE?

One of the most timely examples of informal socialization concerns what has been called the "computer culture" that exists in many organizations. Lee Sproull and Sara Kiesler (1983) have documented the computer culture in university settings, and their findings are relevant to the workplace and many other sorts of organizations as well.

According to Sproull and Kiesler, the culture of computers in college campuses has a number of characteristics:

- Tricks, pranks, and games are tolerated and, in some cases, encouraged.
- Individuals engage in mild forms of larceny, such as theft of computer time, copying software, and breaking into unauthorized systems.
- Social cooperation is deemphasized; individual performance is the norm. Moreover, status is confirmed through the "title" given to others: hackers, wizards, or losers.

Given these characteristics of the computer culture, how do newcomers react? In a survey of people's reactions as they first experienced the culture, Sproull and Keisler (1983) found that many experienced a degree of shock and disorientation. For instance, one person wrote:

I sat down at this computer and started hitting the buttons and it started making all this noise and people kept looking at me. I didn't know what I was doing. I didn't know it was on.

(Sproull & Kiesler, 1983, p. 6)

As people become more socialized into the culture, they tend to divide the world into two categories— we (those who don't know what they are doing) and they (those who do know). The negative perceptions of the "theys" outweigh their superior knowledge; they are seen as somewhat strange, as the following comment illustrates:

They can't relate to anything but the computer. They can't talk to a guy. Even when they talk, they talk computer language. It's like they've turned into a computer (p. 8).

Still, the evidence shows that newcomers can eventually be socialized into the computer culture in organizations. One thing that seems to make this transition possible is proper instruction on how to become acclimated to the computer. People who are formally socialized in this way tend to fare much better than those without comprehensive instruction, and their socialization can be relatively painless. Even so, the *social* aspects of computer use represents a relatively unresearched area and a future important area of investigation (e.g., Miura & Hess, 1983).

---

groups are sometimes able to influence the majority, important sources of socialization pressures are an individual's coworkers and organizational peer group. Pressures from these sources can be so powerful that they circumvent the formal socialization process that is relevant to the formal goals of the organization.

One of the best examples of how informal social influence can supplant formal socialization practices comes from one of the early Hawthorne studies. In one experiment, researchers became concerned with how a group's norms of what "appropriate" productivity means could affect the group's membership. Observing a group of workers in a switchboard wiring room, the researchers found that an informal norm of producing two switchboards a day existed (in contrast to manage-

Cohesiveness among workers can lead to increased productivity—if the workers' social norms value productivity. If not, high cohesiveness can sometimes lower productivity. (Abigail Heyman/ Archive Pictures)

ment's goal, based on time-and-motion studies, of two and a half switch-boards a day). Workers who either exceeded or did less than the informal goal of two per day received verbal abuse for their transgression. Underproducers were called "chiselers," and overproducers were called "speed kings" and "rate busters." The overproducers were even punished physically by being punched on the arm by their coworkers. In this way, the norm of productivity was maintained.

Why should workers adhere to norms about performance, even when their own rate of pay, dependent upon productivity, may suffer? One explanation is that the social relationships with their peers become of primary importance to the workers. As we mentioned in Chapter 11, this means that organizations with high cohesiveness among workers may actually have lower productivity than groups in which cohesiveness is lower if the norms of the group favor low productivity—because social pressure to conform to the norms will be stronger in the highly cohesive groups (Schachter, Ellertson, McBride, and Gregory, 1951; Berkowitz, 1954).

Given that the adherence to productivity norms is related to group cohesiveness, managers interested in increasing worker productivity seem to have a number of choices. One might attempt to decrease group cohesiveness, which could be expected to reduce the members' susceptibility to the group norms. The problem here would be that, as we discussed in the previous chapter, group cohesiveness is related to success in achieving goals (Shaw & Shaw, 1962). A more reasonable solution might be to change the norms regarding appropriate level of productivity. Although changing productivity norms is a difficult proposition, at least one technique seems useful: allowing workers to participate in the setting of formal production goals. This process can lead to greater worker acceptance of the goals, which should, in turn, lead to informal production norms that are congruent with the formal goals (Vroom & Yetton, 1973; Tuttle, 1983).

Returning one last time to the problem faced by our mythical supervisor at the Embryonic Production Corporation, we have at least one more explanation for the lack of innovativeness on the part of new workers after they have spent a month on the job. In all probability, the new employees adopted the norms and values of their coworkers rather than the official ones of the formal organization. It is possible that there was strong and consistent social pressure from other employees to avoid any radical changes in the nature of the job that might impact upon their positions, and new employees who wanted to have good relations with their fellow workers were apt to realize that espousing changes in established procedures might provoke the anger of their peers. Once again, the solution to this problem might be to try to foster acceptance of informal norms that are congruent with the formal goals of the organization. If this can be done, the organization will be considerably more effective in meeting its formal goals, and employee morale will be higher.

DECISION MAKING IN THE WORKPLACE: DEMOCRACY DOESN'T ALWAYS WORK

When we discussed decision making in small groups in our chapter on groups, we did it from the perspective of whether groups or individuals made the best decision, without regard to how (or even whether) the decision would be carried out. In the context of the workplace, however, the question is a bit more complicated, since decisions that are made ultimately do have to be put into effect. The question thus becomes one not only of whether group or individual decisions are better decisions, but also of whether the people that must implement the decision should participate in the decision-making process. While a democratic view of decision making would argue that everyone affected by the decision ought to be consulted before the decision is made, democratic processes may not always be appropriate (as our discussion of leadership effectiveness in Chapter 10 indicated).

Early work on the issue tried to answer the question of whether decisions should be made with group participation in an absolute manner; it was assumed that research could reveal whether participative decision making was or was not effective in all cases. It soon became clear, however, that such an approach was insufficient. For instance, Maier (1967) analyzed problem-solving capacities of groups, and found that they had both strengths and weaknesses. In terms of the assets of group problem-solving, Maier noted that groups could produce more knowledge and facts about the problem, have a broader perspective,

BOX 12-2   SPOTLIGHT ON THEORY

THE ORGANIZATION AS MACHINE

Nowhere is the need for a social psychological approach to organizations more apparent than when examining one of the classic models of workplace organizations, known as the bureaucratic model (Weber, 1952). According to this model, the ideal organization has a number of well-defined characteristics, including the following:

- Explicit rules, regulations, and procedures for every task.
- A rigid division of labor, in which individuals have well-specified and defined jobs that they can carry out with a high degree of competence and efficiency.
- Centralized decision making, in which decisions are passed down a chain of command.
- Strictly controlled lines of communication. Typically, messages should be communicated only to the position above and below one's own.

While in the abstract the characteristics of the bureaucratic model point to the smooth and efficient functioning of an organization, in practice it results in an authoritarian, repressive atmosphere for employees. Consider, for example, the following regulations for the employees of a Chicago department store in the early 1900s (reported in Mitchell, 1982):

1. Store must be open from 6 a.m. to 9 p.m.
2. Store must be swept; counters and base shelves dusted; lamps trimmed, filled, and chimneys cleaned; a pail of water, also a bucket of coal brought in before breakfast; and attend to customers who will call.
3. Store must not be open on the Sabbath day unless necessary and then only for a few minutes.
4. The employee who is in the habit of smoking Spanish cigars, being shaved at the barber shop, and going to dances and other places of amusement will surely give his employer reason to be suspicious of honesty and integrity.
5. Each employee must not pay less than $5 per year to the church and must attend Sunday school regularly.
6. Men employees are given one evening a week for courting and two if they go to prayer meeting.
7. After 14 hours of work in the store, the leisure time should be spent mostly in reading.

The difficulty with rules such as these, and the bureaucratic model on which they are based, is that there is an almost complete lack of attention to the social psychological aspects of a worker's environment (D. Katz & Kahn, 1978). As centralization and formalization increase, employees feel alienated from the organization. Worker norms contrary to formal management norms begin to take precedence, leading to inefficiency and organizational dysfunction. Because of the emphasis on rules, workers also become quite rigid, leading to difficulties in solving problems. In sum, by ignoring the social psychological aspects of work and the workplace, the bureaucratic model ultimately may create more problems than it solves.

---

consider more approaches, suggest more solutions, and provide greater member satisfaction support for the ultimate decision. On the other hand, group decision making was found to have a number of drawbacks, including a loss of efficiency, adoption of compromises that do not optimize effectiveness, potential domination of the group by a powerful individual or subgroup, and a loss of quick responsivity to urgent situations.

It became clear that group participation is not always an effective technique; the specifics of the situation must be taken into account. This

The specifics of a situation determine whether group participation in decision-making is better than decisions made by an organization and manager alone. (Sybil Shelton/Monkmeyer Press)

view is supported by an extensive review of the research literature that examined the bulk of the work done on the effects of participative decision making in workplace organizations (Locke & Schweiger, 1979). The researchers found that in terms of productivity, 22 percent of the studies showed a positive effect and 22 percent a negative effect; the remaining 56 percent showed no effect at all. Measures of member satisfaction came up with somewhat clearer results: 60 percent of the studies showed a positive effect, 9 percent a negative effect, and 30 percent no effect for participative decision making. Hence, while there is little support for the notion that productivity will increase through the use of participatory decision making, at least it seems that members of decision-making groups are more satisfied with the decisions that they ultimately come up with.

What seems clear from work on decision making in workplace organizations is that the question of whether participation is or is not better is inappropriate. Instead, we should be asking under what conditions participative decision making is effective. One well-articulated model that attempts to provide guidelines for determining when, and what kind of, participation is best is a contingency model developed by Vroom and Yetton (1973; Vroom, 1976). Analogous to the Fiedler leadership contingency model, the Vroom and Yetton contingency model takes into account a number of different factors that must be considered before the most effective decision-making strategy can be formulated.

The model begins by determining five major types of decision processes an organizational manager might employ:

● AI: The manager solves the problem alone.

- AII: Subordinates provide background information but not solutions, and the decision is made by the manager alone.
- CI: The manager asks for solutions from subordinates, although the subordinates do not meet as a group. Ultimately, the manager makes the decision.
- CII: The manager shares the problem with the group as a whole and gets the group's collective response. The manager ultimately makes the decision.
- GII: The group meets as a unit to generate and evaluate alternatives, and the decision is made by group consensus.

Given these possible outcomes, the Vroom and Yetton model goes on to specify seven properties of the problem that must be considered in a determination of which of the above techniques is most appropriate. The properties, shown in Figure 12-1, relate to questions which can be answered in the form of "yes" or "no," and are ones that managers seem to be able to use to diagnose a situation quickly and accurately.

The final step in the model is to relate the answers to the seven questions to a choice-of-decision process. Vroom and Yetton have devised a series of rules that are related to the quality of decision made and the acceptance of the decision by the group members. The use of these rules permits the development of the decision tree flowchart presented in Figure 12-2. By following a path along the flowchart and answering each of the questions sequentially, one can make a determination of the appropriate decision-making process.

Let's take a hypothetical example. Suppose manager Abercrombie is trying to decide whether or not her work crew should adopt a new widget manufacturing process. She sits down with the decision tree and answers each question in turn. First, is one solution going to be better than another? Answering "yes," she moves to question B: does she have sufficient information to make a good decision on her own? Answering "no," she goes to question C: is the problem structured? A "no" response brings her to question D, which asks if acceptance by subordinates is critical. Deciding the answer is no, she finds that the decision tree skips her past question E (not every question in the model needs to be answered), and on to question F (Do subordinates share the organiza-

FIGURE 12-1
Vroom and Yetton contingency model: questions to be answered by decision maker.

A. Is there a quality requirement such that one solution is likely to be more rational than another?
B. Do I have sufficient information to make a high-quality decision?
C. Is the problem structured?
D. Is acceptance of decision by subordinates critical to effective implementation?
E. If I were to make the decision by myself, is it reasonably certain that it would be accepted by my subordinates?
F. Do subordinates share the organizational goals to be attained in solving this problem?
G. Is conflict among subordinates likely in preferred solutions?

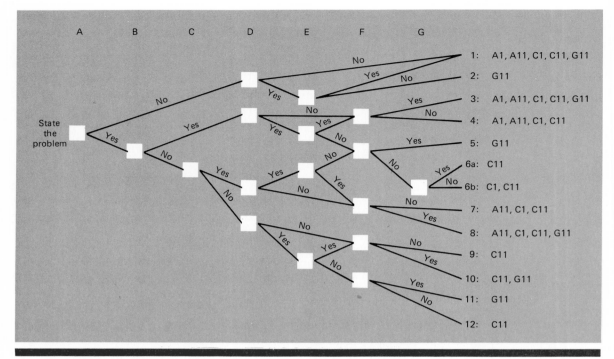

The decision tree diagram shows branches labeled A through G across the top, beginning from "State the problem" and branching through Yes/No decisions to the following outcomes:

1: A1, A11, C1, C11, G11
2: G11
3: A1, A11, C1, C11, G11
4: A1, A11, C1, C11
5: G11
6a: C11
6b: C1, C11
7: A11, C1, C11
8: A11, C1, C11, G11
9: C11
10: C11, G11
11: G11
12: C11

FIGURE 12-2

The Vroom and Yetton contingency model. The letters along the top of the page refer to the questions to be answered by the decision maker (listed in Figure 12-1). The outcomes refer to the five major types of decision processes as discussed in the list at the bottom of page 410 and the top of page 411. Source: Vroom & Yetton (1973).

tional goals?) Deciding that her subordinates do not necessarily share the goals of the organization—an increase in widget production, in this case—she finds that the model provides a solution. She should share the problem with her work crew and collectively obtain their input. Ultimately, however, manager Abercrombie should make the decision herself.

The Vroom and Yetton model of participation in decision making is complicated, and you could be forgiven for thinking that it is all so theoretical and complex that its relationship to the real world would be quite tenuous. However, there is a good deal of highly supportive evidence showing that the model predicts actual behavior of individuals in managerial roles. Using a series of model problems, the researchers asked several thousand managers to indicate the methods that they would use to make decisions regarding a problem that must be resolved (Vroom, 1976). Results clearly indicated the usefulness of the model in predicting the decision-making and problem-solving behavior of the managers. Moreover, managers trained in decision-making techniques were more effective in their positions.

It appears, then, that the Vroom and Yetton model provides an appropriate guide for when to employ groups in decision-making processes. Of course, it does not purport to provide the optimal solution in all situations, but it does indicate a preferred course of action in most cases.

412

The model is also important in that it illustrates the need to take multiple causative factors into account when examining decision-making and problem-solving groups. There does not appear to be a pat answer to the question of whether—and how—subordinates should be included in decisions (also see Box 12-3). Participation must depend on the nature of the specific situation and the needs for quality and acceptance of the solution.

COMMUNICATION STRUCTURE IN THE WORKPLACE

"Working through channels" is a phrase that is frequently heard in organizations. For instance, members of the secretarial pool with a grievance are not expected to communicate their problems directly to the president of a large company. They must transmit messages through their direct superior, who in turn may send them on to another person, until eventually—at least in theory—they may reach the company president. Similarly, in an organization such as NASA, difficulties are unlikely to reach a flight commander unless they have not been sucessfully resolved by lower-echelon staff.

Whether a complaint gets as far as the president or not, the movement of communicative messages through workplace organizations represents an important aspect of organizational structure. Generally, organizations are structured so that communications follow a particular pattern or arrangement. It turns out that the nature of such patterns can have a powerful effect upon the efficiency and satisfaction of the members of the organization.

Most work examining communication processes has been done in experimental settings in which a particular pattern, known as a communication network, is imposed on a group, and the effectiveness of that pattern is compared with that of others. What is generally manipulated in such experiments is the number of persons in the organization, the number of others each person can communicate with, and the number of persons who can communicate to each individual (Shaw, 1964, 1976; Bavelas, 1950). The possibilities inherent in even small groups are myriad; a few are presented in Figure 12-3. As we shall see, the position of individuals in a communication network has an important effect on who emerges as leader, the satisfaction of members of the organization, and the effectiveness and efficiency of the organization.

They Who Communicate, Lead

Examining the many possible patterns for communication channels, you will notice that they differ significantly in the degree to which one or more of the positions is central to the network. For instance, in the five-person circle, no single individual has the opportunity to communicate any more or less with the other members; the network is relatively

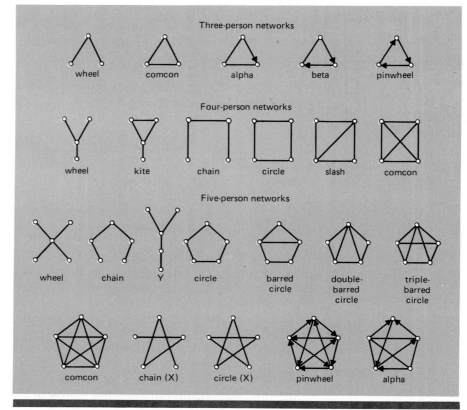

FIGURE 12-3
Communication networks.
These figures represent
communication networks
that might be found in organizations. The circles
stand for positions and
the lines for channels. Arrows indicate the direc-
tion through which com-
munications can flow.
Source: M. E. Shaw.
(1964).

decentralized. On the other hand, the five-person wheel is quite centralized, with the person in the center being able to communicate with
any of the other group members (while the others are able to send
messages only to the person in the center).

One of the major effects of such differences in the structure of the
networks is to influence who takes on a leadership role. Centralized
networks are considerably more apt to develop a leader, and the leader
is most likely to be the individual in the most central position (Shaw &
Rothschild, 1956; Shaw, 1964; Leavitt, 1951). On the other hand, decentralized networks are less apt to develop a particular leader, and if they
do, no single individual is more or less likely to become the leader.

The primary reasons that people with greater communication opportunities emerge as leaders are probably their greater knowledge of
events occurring within the group and their generally higher level of
information about the problem at hand. Indeed, if information is specifically provided to someone in a less central position and withheld
from those in more central positions, the leadership mantle is more
likely to fall upon the less central individual (Shaw, 1964). Hence,
leadership is affected by the nature of communications occurring within
a group structure.

Member Satisfaction

We might expect members of an organization who are relatively isolated from others in the organization insofar as their ability to transmit and receive communications goes to respond negatively to such a situation. Experimental results tend to support such a conclusion. The greater the opportunities to communicate with others, the higher the satisfaction of the individual members (Leavitt, 1951). In turn, this means that organizations that are decentralized are going to have higher general member satisfaction than those that are more centralized. It also suggests that there are going to be greater discrepancies between the degree of satisfaction of various group members in more centralized networks, where some members have high communicative opportunities and others relatively low opportunities, than in decentralized networks, in which all members have similar opportunities to communicate.

It should be noted that there are times when higher levels of communication lead to less member satisfaction; for example, when the nature of the communications is very negative in quality. Thus, if enhanced communication capabilities simply lead employees to hear more bad stories about the organization, working conditions, and mistakes of management, they may ultimately be less satisfied with the organization than if they had been less able to communicate.

Organizational Effectiveness and Communication Patterns

While the relationship between the nature of a communication network and the consequent effects on leadership emergence and member satisfaction is straightforward, the effects of an organization's communication network on productivity is more complex. In fact, it is necessary to consider the type of problem facing the group in order to make sense of the experimental literature.

Researchers have divided the types of tasks used to investigate group and organizational effectiveness into two broad categories: simple and complex. Simple problems are very basic and generally require nothing more than the assemblage of information; complex tasks require arithmetic operations, discussion, and construction of complicated solutions to problems. Quite consistently, it has been demonstrated that centralized networks are superior when considering simple problems. Simple problems are completed more quickly and with fewer errors in the centralized networks. On the other hand, decentralized networks are superior in solving more complex sorts of problems (Shaw, 1964; Porter & Roberts, 1976).

The reason for the discrepancy between simple and complex problems has to do with the phenomena of **independence** and **saturation.** Independence refers to the degree to which a group or organizational member can operate with freedom from the restrictions of others. In decentralized networks, there is greater independence of action and people can consult with one another more readily, leading to the superiority of decentralization in solving complex problems. In addition,

The nature of a job determines whether centralized or decentralized communication networks are most appropriate. (John Blaustein/Woodfin Camp)

their greater independence may account for the higher satisfaction of members of decentralized networks.

Saturation is the degree to which an individual or group is overloaded by the requirements of the group. An individual is said to be saturated when he or she is receiving or producing too many communications to perform effectively or the task being carried out is so complex that it places untenable demands upon that individual.

Saturation is useful in understanding the relative superiority of decentralized networks in completing complex tasks. When the task is simple, saturation is not likely, and a centralized pattern is effective in allowing the individual in the central position to handle and collect the relatively simple sorts of information involved in the task. In contrast, complex tasks can lead to the saturation of a person in a central position, thereby decreasing the efficiency and productivity of the group. In this case, then, a less centralized network will be most effective in dealing with the problem.

Implications for Organizational Design

It is clear from the work that we have described that no one communication network can be recommended for all organizations. Rather, the nature of the task must be considered. Routine and simple tasks seem to be done best in centralized networks, while complex and difficult tasks are done most successfully in decentralized structures. When satisfaction of group and organization members is considered, the findings become even more complex, and it is conceivable that what may be preferable from the point of view of productivity will be less desirable from a vantage point that considers group satisfaction.

We also need to consider that most of our knowledge regarding the effectiveness of one kind or another of communication network comes from work done in laboratory studies, which can be a far cry from the realities of large organizations. In actual organizations it is possible to circumvent formal communication patterns and communicate with people outside one's group. This point is illustrated by one study which found that members of centralized networks, who had the opportunity to communicate within their own group, tended to want to communicate more with people outside their group (Cohen, Robinson, & Edwards, 1969). In effect, this acted to weaken the effects of the structure of communications that had been formally set up.

In sum, it is necessary to view smaller groups and subunits within a larger organizational framework. Such groups do not exist in isolation; instead, they interact with others in a variety of settings and roles. Before we can design the "ideal" organizational structure, we must develop an understanding of how groups embedded in larger organizations are affected by their being part of a larger entity.

IMPROVING THE ORGANIZATION AND THE WORKPLACE

If one were to give advice to Joe Hankins and Chuck Clary, the NASA managers we talked to at the start of the chapter, regarding what social psychologists could offer to make NASA, and other organizations, more productive, efficient, and satisfying to employees, a number of specific techniques could be mentioned. In the remainder of the chapter, we discuss some of these suggestions.

Making Groups Work Better

Building on the literature and findings that were presented in the chapter on group processes, a number of techniques have been devised to enhance the quality and creativity of group decision, based on both laboratory and field study results.

Brainstorming **Brainstorming** works by harnessing the norms that typically restrain and inhibit new ideas and reversing them explicitly to encourage deviant thinking. In brainstorming, group participants are encouraged to express ideas without critically evaluating them and without considering their worth, and other group members are not permitted to make negative comments until all ideas have been presented. Participants are also encouraged to elaborate upon others' ideas and use them as a springboard for discussion and an impetus for new ideas. An atmosphere of freedom and openness is engendered, which can lead to the development of new and creative approaches to problems (Osborn, 1957).

Nominal Group Techniques   In contrast to brainstorming procedures, in which the conversation between group members is expected to elicit greater excitement and more ideas, the **nominal group technique** is more restrained and, in some senses, more controlled. In this method, the group members first privately produce a list of their ideas and write them down. Next, members methodically present one of their ideas to the group, acting as an advocate for the idea. After all ideas have been put forward, the group discusses and evaluates them as a group. Finally, there is a secret vote on each of the ideas. The voting is used to determine mathematically the "winner"—in this case what is presumably the best idea (Delberg, Van deVeu, & Gustafson, 1975).

There are a number of variants of the nominal group technique, including one known as the **Delphi method.** In the Delphi method, there is no actual physical group. Rather, a number of experts are contacted and requested to complete a detailed questionnaire on the topic of interest. Based on their written responses, a new questionnaire is developed to clarify any ambiguities or to get feedback on new issues that arose from the initial responses. Finally, the results are summarized and they are returned to the original respondents, who list the possible solutions in order of their worth. Ultimately, these results are combined mathematically to come up with the final solution that will be employed.

Brainstorming and the nominal group and Delphi techniques have a number of advantages over more traditional methods. In typical groups, the members may come to conclusions prematurely, and spend a good deal of time on issues that are unrelated to the task, such as maintenance of interpersonal relationships. In addition, persons in leadership positions can have an inordinate influence upon the group members, and subordinates can feel restrained in presenting their own views. The brainstorming, nominal group, and Delphi techniques, then, can all lead to decisions of higher quality by creating norms that enhance the likelihood of group members' participation and creativity.

Promoting Controversy   Although common sense might suggest that controversy in groups could lead to poor decisions and dissatisfaction among those in the group, some recent evidence suggests that controversy may actually enhance group decision-making capabilities—but only if the controversy is placed in the context of cooperation. Tjosvold (1982) placed experienced business managers in one of three conditions: an avoidance of controversy condition (in which opinion differences were to be smoothed over), a cooperative context controversy condition (in which the aim was a "frank discussion of differences"), and a competitive controversy condition (in which subjects were discussing their opinions openly, but also were to attempt to make their opinion prevail).

The results of the study showed quite clearly that the least effective approach was competitive controversy. Subjects had less awareness and understanding of the others' positions and tended to make decisions based only on their own point of view. In contrast, cooperative controversy resulted in increased understanding and acceptance of others' arguments, and the ultimate decisions were more complex and integrated. Results in the "no conflict" condition were not as favorable as in the cooperative controversy condition; while the managers did try to take the arguments of the others into account, the arguments were not understood very well.

Why, as the results of the Tjosvold (1982) study suggest, should the promotion of cooperative controversy be an effective technique for enhancing group effectiveness? One reason is that group members gain a better understanding of opposing views when cooperative controversy is encouraged, as we discussed in Chapter 11 with reference to the concept of groupthink (Maier, 1970; Tjosvold & Deewer, 1980). Moreover, uncertainty about the correct solution to a problem, which occurs when controversy about the problem is aroused, leads to an active search for more information, which can enhance the quality of the solution ultimately arrived at (D. W. Johnson & Johnson, 1979).

Structural Changes

One of the major ways in which people define themselves is in terms of the particular profession role they have and the way in which they are able to carry it out within the organization for which they work (Mares & Simmons, 1983). Social psychologists have attempted to capitalize on this fact by developing techniques that involve modifying the structure of the role and position that individuals within an organization hold. Two specific techniques include job or role changes and work unit changes.

Job or Role Changes   The most direct way to bring about organizational and workplace improvement is to start at the lowest level of analysis in the organization structure: the individual and the job or role that he or she performs. Some theorists have suggested that changing what an individual is required to do can bring about positive organizational results. Initially, this idea was broached solely to increase the efficiency of the individual doing a job. Thus, time-and-motion studies were done in which managers were asked to identify the physical components of an activity and determine the best (i.e., most efficient) method for physically carrying out the job, after which one, unique way for doing a job was defined (Mitchell, 1982). The difficulty with this approach was that it ignored the social psychological consequences of work. People per-

BOX 12-3   SPOTLIGHT ON APPLICATIONS

NOT ALL PARTICIPATION IS THE SAME: ASSESSING THE EFFECTS OF WORKER PARTICIPATION ON JOB SATISFACTION

Consider these two examples of worker participation:

> In David's auto plant, there is an auto-worker representative on the safety committee, grievance board, and board of directors. Although David himself isn't a member of any of these groups, the worker representative participates fully in each of these groups' deliberations, which have major authority over the operations of the entire plant.

> In the metal plant where she works, Marian is a member of a group of assembly-line workers who are involved in investigating and evaluating worker suggestions. Despite the fact that the group has a limited scope, considering only suggestions regarding sheet metal cutting procedures, the group's decisions are binding.

The two examples cited above illustrate some of the differences that can occur when we discuss the issue of worker participation in the making of decisions in the workplace. In the first illustration, the participation is relatively indirect; representatives of the employees, and not the employees themselves, have a role in the decision-making processes. In contrast, the second example shows a situation in which there is direct participation by the workers in decision making. Results of a recent field study conducted in Sweden, where worker participation is considerably more widespread than in this country, by Sigvard Rubenowitz, Flemming Norrgren, and Arnold Tannenbaum (1983) show that we might expect the results of the worker participation to be very different.

In their study, the researchers assessed the attitudes of workers in a group of manufacturing organizations, which varied in the degree to which they had indirect and direct worker participation in decision making. In *indirect* forms of participation, there were worker representatives on such bodies as the board of directors, union–management steering committee, safety committee, or grievance

TABLE 12-1   Reactions to Different Levels of Participation

The level of indirect participation makes little difference in employee attitudes, but the level of direct participation has significant effects.

	INDIRECT PARTICIPATION		DIRECT PARTICIPATION		
	Relatively High (N = 822)	Relatively Low (N = 827)	Relatively High (N = 360)		Relatively Low (N = 1289)
Perceived participation					
Individual level	2.12	2.15	2.33	*	2.08
Group level	2.02	2.03	2.29	*	1.95
Representative level	2.92	2.84	3.05	*	2.83
General commitment	3.32	3.36	3.51	*	3.30
Company spirit	3.75	* 3.66	3.85	*	3.65
Satisfaction with company policy	3.26	3.27	3.48	*	3.20
General job satisfaction	3.30	3.27	3.49	*	3.23

*Difference is significant.
Source: Rubenowitz, Norrgren, & Tannenbaum (1983).

boards. (In most cases, Swedish law mandates worker participation of this sort in plants over a certain size.)

In contrast, *direct* forms of participation included instances in which decision making occurred at the lowest possible level in the company in order to allow workers affected by the decision to participate. Although a group's supervisor generally retained the final authority, attempts were made to reach group consensus. Each group was also given a budget of its own in order to give it a sense of autonomy.

The results were clear. As shown in Table 12-1, whether or not the companies had high or low degrees of indirect participation made little difference in terms of a number of key attitudes, including perceived participation, commitment, satisfaction with company policy, and general job satisfaction— although there was a difference in terms of a measure of company spirit. In contrast, results were clear-cut in terms of distinctions between companies with high versus low levels of direct participation. On every measure, higher levels of direct participation resulted in more positive attitudes. Moreover, measures of absenteeism were related to employees' perceptions of participation; the greater the feelings of participation, the lower the rate of absenteeism.

In sum, these results show quite clearly that the nature of workers' participation in decision making is crucial in determining the effects on job satisfaction. Indirect participation—in which workers have representatives and various committees and boards, but do not themselves participate in decision making—is likely to be less important than direct participation by the workers in the decision-making process. It appears, then, that organizations that increase members' immediate participation in decisions are likely to get the most positive results (Lawler & Mohrman, 1984).

---

ceived themselves as an outgrowth of a machine, work was boring, and attrition was high.

Newer approaches to job and role modifications, known as job enrichment strategies, stress not just the physical and mental skills required to do a job properly, but the psychological requirements of the job (Katzell & Guzzo, 1983; also see Box 12-4). Recent work has suggested five dimensions to which job satisfaction is related (Hackman & Oldham, 1976):

1. *Skill variety:* the degree to which the job requires different skills underlying the activities that are part of the job.
2. *Task identity:* the degree to which an individual produces a whole, identifiable unit of work (versus completion of a small unit which is not an identifiable final product).
3. *Task significance:* the degree to which the job has an influence over others.
4. *Autonomy:* the degree to which an individual holding a job is able to schedule his or her activities and decide on the particular procedures to be employed.
5. *Feedback:* the extent to which clear, precise information about the effectiveness of performance is conveyed.

According to the model, each of the dimensions is associated with a particular psychological state, as shown in Table 12-2. In addition, enhancement of the job dimensions is associated with higher productivity, increased motivation and job satisfaction, high-quality performance, and

BOX 12-4 SPOTLIGHT ON RESEARCH

COMPENSATING WORKERS WITH TITLES INSTEAD OF MONEY

Instead of giving a raise when a worker's responsibilities increase, managers on tight budgets might consider awarding a new job title instead—for research based on equity theory suggests that the new title might work just as well as an increase in salary.

This conclusion comes from a study by Jerald Greenberg and Suzyn Ornstein (1983), who examined workers' reactions to the award of a new job title when their responsibilities increased. In the experiment, individuals acting as proofreaders were asked to take on additional responsibilities and work, but told that their pay would not be increased. However, in lieu of a raise, they were told that they would receive a change in job title to the more prestigious "senior proofreader."

The most crucial manipulation concerned whether subjects were told that the upgrading in job title was deserved or undeserved. In one condition, they were led to believe that the title was bestowed because of their superior performance and was therefore well deserved. But in a second condition, they were awarded the new title on a completely arbitrary basis, having nothing to do with their skills at proofreading. (In a control condition, some subjects were given more responsibilities—but no new title or money.)

Using equity theory, which we have discussed at a number of points throughout this book, the investigators reasoned that workers who experienced the outcome of a *deserved* job title would feel adequately compensated for the additional inputs required of them. They would feel equitably paid—and maintain their feelings of satisfaction and level of performance. In contrast, the investigators reasoned that a new job title that was seen as undeserved would not be perceived as a positive outcome and that therefore the workers would feel inequitably treated—leading to declines in satisfaction and performance. And workers who received not even a new title would probably respond most negatively.

The results of the study confirmed the equity theory predictions quite clearly. Individuals who received an earned new job title maintained their levels of job satisfaction and performance, while those with the undeserved title—although showing an initial improvement in performance due to feelings of overpayment—ultimately showed a sharp decline in performance and dissatisfaction with payment. Moreover, the bestowal of an earned job title produced significantly better effects than for the group of subjects who were given more responsibilities but not even a new title; the latter group's output declined significantly.

Generally, then, these results suggest that the bestowal of a new job title *is* an effective means for maintaining feelings of equitable compensation for greater work, even if more money is not forthcoming. But they also suggest that a new job title will be effective only if the recipient feels it is well deserved.

---

lower levels of absenteeism and turnover. For example, a division of Monsanto in Iowa found that productivity increased by 75 percent after the start of a job enrichment program (Mares & Simmons, 1983).

The Hackman and Oldham model has been shown to be useful in redesigning jobs to increase worker satisfaction (Umstot, Bell, & Mitchell, 1976). And, presumably, as positive changes occur in the nature of jobs, concomitant positive changes will occur in the organization as a whole.

Work Unit Changes The last technique that we will discuss regarding organizational effectiveness is related to the work unit in which an

TABLE 12-2 Job Characteristics and Resulting Psychological States and Job Outcomes (Hackman & Oldham's Model)

Job Dimensions	Psychological States	Outcomes
Skill variety Task identity Task significance	Meaningfulness of work	High motivation and satisfaction
Autonomy	Perceived responsibility	High-quality work
Feedback	Knowledge of results	Low absenteeism and turnover

Source: Based on Hackman & Oldham (1976).

individual carries out his job. Recall our discussion in Chapter 11 about the relationship between group cohesiveness and size of group; it was clear that the smaller the group, the greater the cohesiveness. Yet the average workers in a large industrial organization find themselves in a work group so large that they cannot possibly know all their fellow workers. Alternatively, their job may be on an assembly line consisting of one or two repetitious tasks, and they may feel estranged from any group membership at all. In either case, social psychologists have suggested that adjustments in the individual's perception of group membership can have positive benefits upon the worker's attitudes and performance.

In some automobile plants in Sweden, small groups of people in autonomous work groups assemble an entire unit, giving group members the opportunity to switch back and forth among different activities. (Lehtikova Oy/Woodfin Camp)

The most frequently used innovation along these lines is called the **autonomous work group.** Exemplified by its use in the production of Saab automobiles in Sweden, the autonomous work group replaces the assembly line with a system in which small groups of three or four people assemble an entire unit. Each person in the group is capable of carrying out the entire assembly alone, and the members of the team switch jobs. Thus, the nature of persons' jobs is constantly switching, and they have autonomy over scheduling and other decisions. The only constraint upon the work team's behavior is that it produce a certain minimum units in a given period of time. But once that quota is set, how the team reaches it is its own decision.

Evaluations of the effectiveness of autonomous work groups have been positive (Tichy, 1974; G. D. Jenkins & Gupta, 1983). There is greater job satisfaction, work quality is higher, and turnover and absenteeism are lower. Changes in the nature of work units, then, seem to be an effective technique for promoting organizational improvement.

Interpersonal Changes

The previous approach to organizational change stressed modifications in the way jobs and roles are structured. Another technique is to leave the job intact, but to effect changes in the individual's general psychological functioning. Some organizations have introduced sensitivity training, in which the goal is to increase individuals' awareness of themselves and others. Values are aired and discussed in order to increase tolerance toward others. Another approach is to develop communication skills in order to bring about more effective communication.

While theoretically appealing, techniques in which people's interpersonal skills are enhanced have not been demonstrated to be particularly effective in bringing about either individual or organizational change. Indeed, a cynic could argue that increased sensitivity on the part of supervisors might be associated with decreased organizational effectiveness—if supervisors become more sensitive to the feelings of others and less concerned with their productivity.

A FINAL NOTE

We have been discussing organizational effectiveness pretty much in terms of increased worker productivity and satisfaction on the job—as does much of the social psychological literature in the area (e.g., Perloff & Nelson, 1983). It should be clear, though, that what is meant by "effectiveness" is very much related to the goals of the organization. Because most of the literature and work on organizations have been on profit-making businesses, we have emphasized that particular type of organization. But, of course, other organizations, with very different sorts of goals (e.g., the Catholic church or the Democratic party), might not operate along the same lines, and their effectiveness might be measured by other criteria. Still, techniques for bringing about organizational change in nonbusiness settings would be similar.

Is It All Theoretical?

With much of the research on organizations based on laboratory experiments or simulations, the skeptical reader might reasonably ask whether social psychology has produced knowledge that is applicable to real-world organizational situations. One affirmative answer is provided in an interesting book by Marrow, Bowers, and Seashore (1967) which presents a comprehensive program of applications of social psychology theory to an intact, ongoing organization. The Harwood Manufacturing Company, with Marrow (who happened to have received training as a social psychologist) as chairman of the board, acquired a competing company of approximately equal size. Although the former competitor produced the same product, it was formally organized in radically different fashion from Harwood. Instead of a management system which encouraged participation in making decisions from a variety of levels of employees, the new company had a very traditional system in which a manager at a particular level independently made a decision; the manager's staff was expected to carry out the decision without having participated in the decision-making process.

Such differences in organizational style probably would not have mattered much to Marrow had not the new company been significantly inferior to Harwood on such measures as productivity, turnover, and waste. Therefore, Marrow instituted a series of measures designed to increase performance in the newly acquired company. Over a period of two years, a number of major organizational changes were made, including reorganization of the way in which work moved through the factory, new kinds of training programs, and sensitivity training for management and staff (Vroom, 1969).

Results of a comprehensive evaluation (carried out by a team of social psychologists consulting on the project) indicated that the changes were quite successful. Attitudes toward the company, fellow employees, and the salary scale became more favorable. Perhaps of greater interest (at least to Harwood's management) was the fact that production efficiency and return on invested capital rose markedly, while turnover and absenteeism decreased by 50 percent.

In sum, organizational changes based on social psychological principles were effective in producing concrete positive improvements in a real-world setting, and these principles are being employed ever more frequently in organizations today (e.g., Jenkins & Gupta, 1983). The work of social psychologists was not, then, just theoretical, but had very practical results. And as organizations become more sensitive to the social psychological implications of their practices and employ some of the techniques described in this chapter, we might expect that both productivity and worker satisfaction can be increased—with neither increase being at the expense of the other.

SUMMARY

Interest in social psychological factors related to organizations began with studies done in the Hawthorne assembly plant in the early 1920s. Among other things, these studies showed that anytime subjects know that they are in an experiment, their behavior may change just because of the special attention they are receiving, a phenomenon now known as the Hawthorne effect.

Organizational socialization refers to the process of learning the behaviors and norms characterized as appropriate by the organization. Socialization occurs formally through teaching and training, and informally through interaction with older organization members. There are three phases to formal socialization: prearrival, encounter, and change and acquisition. In the prearrival phase, individuals bring early ideas, attitudes, and behaviors relevant to the organization which may be modified or replaced through socialization. The encounter phase consists of interaction between the individual and the organization; socialization occurs through reinforcement of preexisting attitudes and behaviors, direct teaching of new behaviors, and avoidance of reinforcement or punishment of nonvalued behavior. Direct teaching of new behaviors is the most overt source of socialization, although training rarely includes explicit transmission of attitudes and values. The change and acquisition phase encompasses the modifications that occur in an individual's underlying attitudes and values.

Organizational socialization also occurs informally through an individual's peers. Production norms that deviate from formal quotas can influence the productivity of workers. Informal socialization can produce powerful conformity pressure, particularly when group cohesiveness is high.

The effectiveness of participative decision making and problem solving is contingent upon the nature of the situation. A comprehensive model has been developed by Vroom and Yetton, who have shown that the model accurately predicts individuals' decisions. The efficacy of participation depends on the specific situation and needs for quality and acceptance of the solution.

Organizations generally have specific communication networks, which are patterns imposed on a group restricting the flow of messages. Centralized networks are most likely to develop a leader, and the leader is apt to be the individual in the most central position. Decentralized networks, which present members with greater opportunities to communicate with others, lead to higher levels of member satisfaction than more centralized networks. Problem-solving success is also related to network configuration, with centralized networks working best for simple problems and decentralized best for complex problems.

There are a number of techniques used in organizations to increase the quality of group decisions. Brainstorming consists of encouraging members to express ideas without critically evaluating them in order to create an atmosphere of freedom and openness. In the nominal group technique, ideas are produced privately, presented to the group, and then voted on. In a variant of the nominal group technique, the Delphi method uses a series of questionnaires completed by experts. Finally, group decisions can be enhanced through the promotion of controversy, if it is done within a cooperative context.

Another approach to organizational improvement is through structural changes such as job or role changes. Modifications in such dimensions as skill variety, task identity, task significance, autonomy, and feedback have been shown to produce positive outcomes. Change in the operation of work units also is effective, including the institution of autonomous work groups, in which each person in a group can carry out a number of tasks interchangeably and the group determines who carries out what specific task as long as a certain minimum of production is maintained.

Finally, organizational improvement has been approached through attempts at increasing the level of a person's general psychological functioning, rather than through changes in the situation. Although not notably effective, sensitivity training and communication skill training have been used to enhance organizational members' interpersonal skills.

KEY TERMS

anticipatory socialization
autonomous work groups
brainstorming
communication networks
debasement
Delphi method
Hawthorne effect

nominal group technique
norms
organizational socialization
role model
socialization
Vroom and Yetton contingency model

FOR FURTHER STUDY AND APPLICATION

Katz, D., & Kahn, R. L. (1978). *The social psychology of organizations* (2nd ed.). New York: Wiley.
A broad, comprehensive overview of the ways in which social psychological theory impacts upon organizations.
Mitchell, T. R. (1982). *People in organizations: An introduction to organizational behavior.* New York: McGraw-Hill.

A readable, clear introduction to the general area of the psychology of organizations, with a particular emphasis on social psychological variables.
Marrow, A. J., Bowers, D. G., & Seashore, S. E. (1967). *Management by participation.* New York: Harper & Row.
An account of the use of social psychological principles in an actual organizational setting.

Mayo, E. (1933). *The human problems of an industrial civilization*. New York: Macmillan.

Parsons, H. M. (1974). What happened to Hawthorne? *Science, 183,* 922–932.

Two views of the results of the Hawthorne studies: the original, and a newer look at the data. Both sources highlight the potential impact of social psychological variables in industrial settings.

Baron, R. A. (1983). *Behavior in organizations.* Boston: Allyn & Bacon.

A comprehensive introduction to organizational behavior written by a social psychologist. Readable and interesting, and replete with many examples and applications.

PART FIVE

SOCIETY AND
THE SOCIAL AND
PHYSICAL WORLD

CHAPTER 13

THE SOCIAL PSYCHOLOGY OF THE LAW AND JUSTICE

A CONVERSATION WITH . . .

Archibald Cox
*Attorney and Former
Watergate Special
Prosecutor*

While the reputations of quite a few politicians were destroyed by the Watergate scandal and revelations, a few people emerged as genuine heroes. One such person was Archibald Cox, who served as special prosecutor until he was discharged by President Nixon in a move that marked the beginning of the end of Nixon's presidency.

A man of unimpeachable credentials and reputation, Cox has spent most of his career teaching at Harvard Law School. There have also been frequent stints in high-level government service. In addition to acting as Watergate special prosecutor, he was head of the Wage Stabilization Board during the Korean war, was an adviser to President John F. Kennedy, and served as solicitor general of the United States.

Our conversation centered around Cox's reflections on some of the legal and historical issues that are related to research done by social psychologists.

Q. I would like to ask you a few questions about the Watergate scandal that have special relevance to some of the work being done by social psychologists. One question pertains to the punishment that offenders receive for their offenses. Most research suggests that the average person feels that the greater the crime, the greater the punishment ought to be. Yet research also shows that many people believe a number of factors unrelated to the crime itself should be considered when determining the punishment of the offender, such as the degree of suffering the offender has already experienced.

To take a concrete example, one of the primary reasons that President Ford gave for pardoning President Nixon from Watergate-related crimes was that "President Nixon and his loved ones have suffered enough." In your view, was this fair and reasonable legal treatment?

A. I don't think it was appropriate when it came to pardoning President Nixon to take such things into account. I think equal justice requires that a President or former President answer and stand trial on charges of wrongdoing just like any ordinary person.

But when it comes to actual sentencing, there is an insoluble dilemma. On the one hand, there ought to be equality. If a white-collar, upper-class person is perceived as getting a light sentence, whereas a blue-collar, inner-city person is perceived as getting a heavier sentence, that seems like a departure from equal justice, which is certainly one ingredient of what is fair. On the other hand, I think it is probably true that the person who has grown up in a protected environment will find a short time in prison as punishing to him as a longer sentence would be to someone else, and to the extent that punishment is a deterrent against any future crime, the shorter sentence might suffice.

Q. Do you think that if President Nixon had gone to trial, he could have received a fair trial? Specifically, could a jury have been found that would have been capable of judging the evidence with no preconceptions?

A. Well, I take it from the experience in the cover-up cases of Haldemann, Erlichman, Mitchell, and the others that the prospective jurors chosen did give the answer, when questioned before the trial, that they had no preconceptions. I'm prepared to assume that this answer was honest in the sense of their conscious thoughts. But to some extent—ranging from possibly to probably—they may have been influenced by the atmosphere of the country at the time. Yet, if the prosecution didn't make a decent case, those preconceptions probably wouldn't have been enough to compel the results. On the other hand, they might have helped the prosecution just that necessary amount. It's hard to tell. I am convinced, however, that this risk is not reason enough either to bar such prosecutions of unfaithful public officials or to interfere with free reporting of developments prior to trial. Both the prosecutions and the discussion are necessary to honest, democratic government. Public officials who open themselves to such charges must take the risk of that much outside influence.

Q. Your answer relates to the issue of how juries are selected. Some researchers suggest that it is possible to determine from demographic or other characteristics whether a particular juror is going to be more sympathetic to the defense or prosecution. Using this knowledge, it would be possible to weed out jurors unsympathetic to a given side through the *voir dire** process. Is this a fair use of courtroom procedure?

A. I have misgivings about it. I suppose that if the jury is intended to be a cross section of the community, this approach rather tends to defeat the purpose. It troubles me. On the other hand, it is perfectly clear that in an intuitive sort of way lawyers have been doing it for years, so that this may be just a more sophisticated version of what has been done in the past.

* *Voir dire* refers to the questioning of potential jurors *before* they are actually assigned to the jury. Both prosecution and defense are allowed to exclude a certain number of potential jurors without having to state a reason.

Q. And, in fact, how often do you think juries actually are a cross section of the community?

A. In a way, it is hard to get twelve people who represent all the shades in a community, but I suppose the probabilities are that it's a little more representative if you leave it to the laws of chance than if you had certain types of people identified and excluded.

Q. Taking the Watergate experience as a whole, do you think that justice was served?

A. In considering it as a whole, the system seems to have worked. But one still doesn't know all the relevant facts. For one or two of the persons charged, I'm not sure I would have handled it the way it was handled. There was one case where I was startled by the leniency of the sentence. There were a couple of cases that weren't prosecuted where, on the basis of what I knew—which clearly wasn't everything—I wondered if *I* would have done that. But on the whole I would say that the system worked very well.

Q. Did you have difficulty with the concept of aggressively prosecuting a sitting President?

A. There were times when I was simply overwhelmed by the question, "Who am I to be challenging the President of the United States?" But my dominant concern was quite genuinely much more in terms of institutions and principles. I felt that in one sense our whole constitutionalism rested on whether the President would be forced to comply with Judge Siricca's orders to turn over the tapes. If any President could set himself above a court decree, this would negate in an important way any notions of constitutionalism, which in the end do rest on a combination of public support and voluntary compliance.

OVERVIEW

Archibald Cox has a unique perspective on the processes of the law in the United States, and his considered responses and observations illustrate the complexities of the issues raised in the interview about justice and the law. These issues—long of concern to the legal field—now represent a growing and important area for investigation by social psychologists, who bring to the field their unique perspective on the legal system as a social setting.

This chapter examines three of the major figures in courtroom trials—the defendant, judge, and juror—to learn how each is affected by social psychological variables. We will also consider three broad models of justice, discussing the factors underlying the perception of what is just and fair and how various legal situations call forth different conceptions of justice. As we shall see, social psychological approaches to justice and the law illustrate quite clearly how advances in theory, laboratory experimentation, and applied research are inextricably intertwined and can lead to a better understanding of society's most important institutions.

SOCIAL PSYCHOLOGICAL FACTORS IN THE COURTROOM

In the archetypal courtroom drama seen on film or television, the defendant is beautiful and demure, the prosecutor cold and callous, the defense attorney young and crusading, the judge distinguished and kind, and the jury attentive and interested. The case proceeds at a rapid pace, and in the end justice is served by the speedy acquittal of the defendant—who everyone knew was innocent from the start.

Actual courtroom trials bear little, if any, resemblance to this scenario. Like other institutions in our society the courts sometimes move ponderously, miscarriages of justice can occur, and mistakes are made. The precision with which the judicial system operates is limited by the fact that, despite carefully thought-out rules and procedures devised over centuries of practice, decisions made in courts are subject to distortions, biases, and errors of judgment. Above all, the decisions are *social* ones, made on the basis of numerous interacting factors of a social psychological nature. In this part of the chapter, three major players in courtroom settings—the defendant, judge, and juror—will be examined to illuminate how social psychological factors affect judicial decisions.

The Defendant

It Doesn't Hurt to Be Attractive—Most of the Time   In our description of the archetypal courtroom drama, the defendant was described as beautiful and demure. In the real world, or course, defendants vary a great deal in attractiveness, and research has shown that this fact may influence judicial decisions. Indeed, one of the major areas of research carried out by social psychologists on courtroom factors is how characteristics of the defendant relate to judicial outcomes.

One of the first experiments on defendant characteristics was carried out by Landy and Aronson (1969), who examined how a defendant's general social attractiveness related to the length of sentence awarded by mock jurors for the crime of vehicular homicide in which the defendant was negligent. In one condition, the defendant was described as a stable 64-year-old insurance adjuster who had been employed with the same firm for twenty-four years, whose wife had died of cancer, and who had been spending Christmas with his son and daughter-in-law. In the other condition, the defendant was described as an unstable 33-year-old janitor, twice divorced, who had been spending Christmas Eve with his girlfriend. The results were clear: the more attractive the general description of the defendant, the lighter the sentence. The insurance adjuster received a mean sentence of nine years, while the less socially attractive defendant received a mean sentence of twelve years.

Subsequent laboratory experiments have examined the components of social attractiveness more precisely and have found that such factors as attractiveness of personality and attire and even sheer physical attractiveness are related to sentence length, with greater attractiveness generally leading to more favorable treatment—all other factors being equal (Monahan & Loftus, 1982). In fact, trial lawyers often attempt to enhance the attractiveness of defendants in order to make a more positive impression (Saks & Hastie, 1978).

On the other hand, in certain situations attractiveness on the part of the defendant can actually have a detrimental effect. For instance, Sigall and Ostrove (1975) showed that if the defendant's physical attractiveness appears to have been used profitably during a criminal activity, jurors will give harsher sentences to more attractive defendants than to less attractive ones.

In the study, subjects were led to believe that an attractive or unattractive female defendant had been involved in one of two kinds of crimes: a burglary in which $2200 was stolen, or a swindle in which a bachelor was induced to invest $2200 in a nonexistent corporation. Acting as mock jurors, subjects gave the attractive burglar a more lenient sentence than the unattractive burglar (see Figure 13-1). But when the crime was a swindle, the attractive swindler held no advantage over the unattractive one and, in fact, received a somewhat harsher sentence than the unattractive swindler. It is plausible that the attractiveness of the swindler suggested to the jurors that she had used her beauty in the crime and that she would be more apt to transgress again in the future—therefore deserving a harsher punishment than the unattractive swindler.

It is important to note that although attractiveness of the defendant has been demonstrated over and over again to relate to sentencing, almost all of this evidence has come from laboratory experiments in

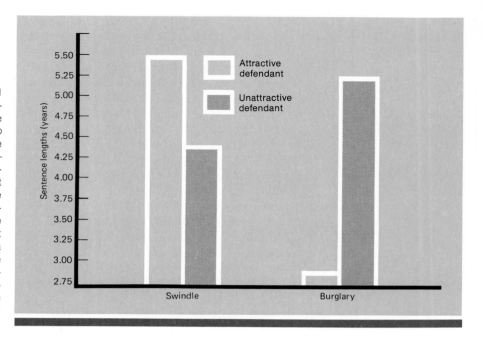

FIGURE 13-1
Sentences assigned to attractive and unattractive defendants according to type of crime. When the crime was a swindle—and the physical attractiveness of the defendant could have played a role in the crime—the sentence was higher for the attractive defendant. But when the crime was a burglary, unrelated to the defendant's attractiveness, the unattractive defendant received the higher sentence. Source: Sigall & Ostrove (1975).

which subjects act as mock jurors and make judgments in relatively artificial situations. The evidence is far less conclusive when examining results regarding defendant attractiveness in naturalistic settings. Some studies have found only a small effect (Kalven & Zeisel, 1966), while some naturalistic experiments have found none at all (Konečni & Ebbesen, 1982).

Indeed, the lack of nonlaboratory research supporting the experimental findings raises an important methodological issue: how well do laboratory analogues to courtroom settings represent actual judicial proceedings? Although laboratory procedures yield a high degree of control and precision, these virtues are often bought at the expense of generalizability to situations outside the laboratory. It is necessary, then, to keep in mind the limitations inherent in the type of methodology employed in a given study (Saks, 1983).

Other Defendant Characteristics   In most jurisdictions defendants' prior criminal records can be used as evidence only for determining their credibility, but not for determining their guilt or innocence. While theoretically such fine distinctions are possible, it seems unlikely that the average juror—or judge or attorney, for that matter—would be able to fine-tune his or her thinking in so precise a manner.

The reason hearkens back to our discussion of person perception in Chapter 2, in which we saw that people hold schemas and implicit personality theories that lead them to categorize people by putting them into a few discrete groupings. Such categorizations represent oversim-

Characteristics of the defendant unrelated to the crime—including physical appearance and socioeconomic status—enter into courtroom decisions. (Wayne Miller/Magnum)

plifications, and reveal a tendency to relate past and present behaviors in a target person more closely than is necessarily appropriate. Moreover, biases toward attributing the behavior of others to personality dispositions rather than to situational factors—the fundamental attribution error that we discussed in Chapter 2—also lead observers to perceive a closer link between past and present behaviors than may actually be the case. For these reasons, it would seem difficult for jurors to ignore someone's past criminal record when making decisions about that person's guilt or innocence with regard to a current accusation.

Although not extensive, research relating to a defendant's prior record and jurors' decisions tends to support such reasoning. For example, in one simulation study (Koza and Doob, 1975), a group of jurors were led to believe that a defendant was a habitual offender by learning that he was being held in custody, while another group was told that he was free on bail. Although legally such distinctions should not be taken into consideration, jurors rated the likelihood of a guilty verdict higher when they thought the defendant was in custody than when they thought him free on bail.

Even the way in which defendants argue for their own innocence can affect observers' judgments of guilt. An example illustrates this point: early in the Watergate investigation, the White House issued a denial of any involvement or wrongdoing. What was particularly surprising about the denial was the fact that up to that time, at least, no one had even suggested that the White House was involved. In fact, the denial itself helped provoke the very suspicions that the White House was trying to quash (Woodward & Bernstein, 1974). Former President Nixon's famous statement, "I am not a crook," had a similar effect.

Results of at least one study support the position that defendants who profess their innocence more strongly than an accusation warrants are likely to be viewed as guilty. Yandell (1979) had subjects listen to a target person who either had been accused or had not been accused of damaging a typewriter strongly deny that he had damaged it. Results showed that the target person was rated as considerably more guilty when his denial was spontaneous and did not follow an accusation than when it did follow an accusation. Subjects felt that the unaccused target appeared to be defensive and hence more likely to be guilty. It seems, then, that Shakespeare's observation in Hamlet that "the lady doth protest too much methinks" is taken by observers as an indication of guilt even today.

The Judge

While the stereotype of the courtroom judge is of an individual who is wise, understanding, and equitable and has keen insight into truth and justice, the reality frequently strays from this view. Although clearly the person in the courtroom with the most formal power, a judge—like other experts—is susceptible to biased judgments when making decisions (Slovic, Fischhoff, & Lichenstein, 1977).

One reason for this discrepancy between the stereotype and the reality is that the background of many judges is not particularly distinguished; some judges are elected and others appointed for purely political reasons. There is no guarantee that judges will possess special qualities that might set their behavior and decision-making abilities apart from those of laypersons. But even with appropriate training, research has found, most experts are apt to fall into the same attributional and judgmental traps as nonexperts; the decision-making processes of human beings are open to many sorts of errors, as we have seen throughout this book.

One example of judicial fallibility is provided by a study by Feldman and Rosen (1978), who examined the sentencing patterns of both judges and laypersons for criminals who acted alone or with others in carrying out a crime. According to legal tradition, individuals who commit a given act are generally presumed to be equally responsible for the outcome of the act, regardless of the number of others participating (Hart & Honore, 1959). But an equally compelling social psychological finding relating to the phenomenon of diffusion of responsibility suggests that this legal dictum might be difficult to carry out in practice. Work on diffusion of responsibility suggests that observers tend to perceive that individuals who carry out an activity alone are more responsible for subsequent outcomes than those who carry out the same activity with others (Mynatt & Sherman, 1975). This would suggest that the greater the number of participants in a criminal act, the less any individual

BOX 13-1 SPOTLIGHT ON RESEARCH

THE EYEWITNESS IN A SOCIAL PSYCHOLOGICAL CONTEXT

The lineup—the very term conjures up images of a frightened and angry victim, shrouded in darkness, who picks out her assailant from a group of seedy characters in a clear, confident voice, and then lapses into uncontrollable sobs at the memory of her attack.

While at least some aspects of such a scene may be accurate, the confidence of the victim may be misplaced, for work on eyewitness identification has shown that witnesses are notoriously prone to a considerable degree of error—a finding that should be of little surprise in light of the frequency of biases in person perception and attribution discussed in Chapter 2 (Levine & Tapp, 1982; Wells & Loftus, 1984).

Consider, for instance, an experiment that was conducted by Buckhout (1975) during a New York City television news program. Viewers were shown a twelve-second film of a mugging and then viewed a six-person lineup that included the actual assailant. Of the 2145 viewers that called the station after the program, only 15.3 percent were able to identify the assailant correctly, a figure which is just slightly higher than would be expected if the viewers had guessed randomly.

Early research on eyewitness perception showed similar results. In a review of findings, Gardner (1933) found that observers of criminal events staged by experimenters tended to show large variations in such details as height, age, and weight. For example, the estimations of height for the same person varied from 4 feet to 6.5 feet, with average estimation varying 8 inches from true height. The discrepancy from true age averaged eight years; hair color was missed 83 percent of the time; and 25 percent of the subjects left out more than half the details they had seen.

Why do eyewitnesses have such problems? Eyewitnesses are subject to the same sorts of perceptual biases to which any observer of others is susceptible. Consider, for example, these two major threats to accurate recall of criminal activity:

- *Social expectations and stereotypes.* The nature of the expectations about the way in which the world operates will affect how an individual perceives and remembers information. If people hold the stereotype that blacks are more prone to criminal activity than whites, they are going to perceive and remember events within this context. In a classic study, Allport and Postman (1945) showed a subject a drawing of a subway scene. Among the characters in the picture was an empty-handed black man who was shown conversing with a white man holding a razor. Subjects were asked to describe the picture to another person who had not seen the picture, who in turn recounted it to another person, and so forth. The typical story told by the last person in the chain had, as a major element, a black person holding a razor. Thus, events had been altered along the way to become congruent with the social expectations and stereotypes held by the observers.

- *Motivational and emotional states.* Eyewitnesses may be motivated to remember events in particular ways. Thus, the victim of a stabbing may not feel that he had provoked his assailant prior to being stabbed, and may well forget the angry words that were exchanged before the stabbing. Note that we are not talking about conscious deception here, but rather about instances in which individuals' motivational states lead them to perceive and remember events in a specific manner. Likewise, the emotional state of an eyewitness will affect accuracy. Highly aroused individuals are less likely to be accurate than individuals who are at low or moderate levels of arousal (Levine & Tapp, 1973). Since most criminal situations produce high levels of emotionality, eyewitness accuracy is likely to suffer.

There are other reasons that eyewitness reports suffer from inaccuracy, including the length of time between an event and its recall, the type of police questioning procedures that are employed, and even the number of times and way in which the material has been recounted prior to a final recall. On the other hand, not *all* eyewitness testimony is suspect—particularly when the victim knows the perpetrator or spends a relatively long time with the criminal (Wells & Loftus, 1984). Still, eyewitness accounts may easily be unreliable, and—given the strong influence of witnesses in judicial proceedings (e.g., Leippe, 1984; Whitley & Greenberg, 1984)—the courts would seem well advised to consider witness testimony carefully.

participant would be held personally responsible—and the lighter the sentence awarded.

Evidence in support of the prior reasoning was found in both a laboratory and a field experiment. In the laboratory study, college students acting as jurors rated a defendant who acted alone as significantly more responsible for the crime than a defendant who had acted with an accomplice. More interestingly, an examination of actual sentencing records for a two-year period showed an analogous finding. Jail sentences handed down by judges for a sample of 140 criminals who had committed a theft either alone or with other perpetrators showed evidence for diffusion of responsibility, despite the legal doctrine against such a phenomenon. Single perpetrators received a mean sentence of 9.06 years, while multiple perpetrators received a mean sentence of 7.67 years, a significant difference. Judges, like laypersons, appear to be susceptible to this bias in their decision-making processes.

Setting Bail   Another area in which judges' behaviors have been studied extensively involves the factors relating to the setting of bail for criminal defendants. One reason for this emphasis has been the amenability of bail setting to scientific study: in the typical case, judges make their decisions quickly on the basis of a short summary of the case, which includes such factors as the charges, the economic status of the defendant, and his or her ties to the local community and previous criminal record (M. S. Greenberg & Ruback, 1982). After hearing brief recommendations from prosecuting and defense attorneys, the judge makes a decision. Because the information is discrete and limited, it is relatively simple for social psychologists to simulate variations in the nature of information and ask subjects to make judgments of bail level. Moreover, it is also possible to be aware of, and thus control, all or most of the factors that enter into actual judges' decisions.

Perhaps the most far-reaching study of judges' bail decisions was done by Ebbesen and Konečni (1982). In the study, they asked actual judges to make decisions on a series of bogus cases about defendants who had been accused of stealing property with a value of about $900. Four factors were varied experimentally: the district attorney's bail recommendation, the defense attorney's recommendation, the extent of the defendant's community ties, and the nature of the defendant's prior criminal record. Analysis of the data showed that three of the four factors played a significant role in the judges' decisions; only the defense attorney's recommendations had no effect.

The experiments then examined judges' decisions in actual trial cases by analyzing the same four factors as in the simulation study plus the additional factor of severity of the crime. They were also able to obtain, of course, the bail figures that the judges ultimately recommended. After extensive analysis, they found that only two factors—the recommendations of the prosecuting and defense attorneys—had a direct effect on the judges' decisions. The other factors appeared to have had only an indirect effect or no effect on the decision-making process. The data suggest that the judges may have assumed that the severity of crime and the community ties of the defendant had already been taken into account by the defense and prosecuting attorneys when they made *their* recommendations, and that the judges allowed themselves to be influenced primarily by those recommendations.

The model of judicial decision making in bail cases has been termed a social-influence model by Ebbesen and Konečni (1982), since the judges appear to be conforming to the recommendations of others. But it should be noted that their findings cannot be considered definitive, since some factors that they did not measure—e.g., defendant socioeconomic status—might account for their results. Moreover, the discrepancies that emerge between the results of their initial simulation study and the later field results illustrate a point that must be emphasized: the results of even well-controlled simulations must be viewed cautiously before they are extrapolated outside the laboratory.

Judges' Communication: Instructing the Jury   Another aspect of judicial behavior that demonstrates the influence of social psychological factors is the nature of instructions given to jurors. Just prior to a jury's deliberations, a judge typically interprets the law that is relevant to the case, and the way in which the judge defines the legal issues has a large impact on juror behavior (Nagao & McClain, 1983). A number of studies have shown that very often such instructions are simply incomprehensible to the jurors (Charrow & Charrow, 1979; Forston, 1970). Moreover, even when jurors think they understand the instructions, they may misinterpret rules of law. For instance, Strawn and Buchanan (1976) found that only about half the jurors in a criminal case grasped the fundamental fact that the burden of proof rests on the prosecution, not the defense—even after they had been explicitly so informed.

Even more problematic are judges' instructions to jurors that inform them that they should disregard some information to which they have been exposed. As Attorney Cox suggested at the start of this chapter, such admonitions do not erase the recollection that, for instance, a defendant was previously convicted of a similar crime (information that is typically inadmissible) or memories of what one has heard regarding a trial prior to entering the courtroom.

One simulation study illustrated this fact clearly (Sue, Smith, & Caldwell, 1973). In the experiment, college students acting as jurors heard evidence about the defendant but were informed later that some of it should not be considered in their deliberations. It turned out, however, that the inadmissible evidence did have a significant effect upon the verdicts and sentence lengths arrived at, and this was particularly true when the evidence that was admissible was weak.

Perhaps the most surprising finding regarding judges' instructions pertains to an occasional "boomerang" effect in which not only are instructions not followed, but they result in decisions that are directly contrary to them. In a series of experiments, Borgida (1982) presented jurors with a description of a rape case in which some jurors were instructed explicitly that admissions made by the rape victim regarding her prior sexual experiences had no bearing on whether she had, in fact, consented to sexual intercourse with the defendant, as he claimed.

Instead of heeding these directions, jurors were more likely to find the accused rapist innocent (thus apparently using the victim's sexual history in coming to a verdict) when they received these instructions than when they had not been so instructed. It seems that the jurors interpreted the explicit instruction as a threat to their own decision-making freedom and reacted in a way that directly contradicted the judge's admonitions. (Alternatively, the explicit instructions may have drawn the juror's attention to the victim's sexual background.) For either reason, very explicit and precise instructions to a jury may sometimes backfire.

It should be noted that the law itself can be partially to blame for juror's disregard of judges' instructions; depending on the jurisdiction, the importance of the instructions varies dramatically. For example, in California the jury is told:

> It becomes my duty as judge to instruct you concerning the law applicable to this case, and it is your duty to follow the law as I shall state it to you.
>
> (Van Dyke, 1970, p. 17)

A far different charge is given by judges in Maryland:

> . . . In a criminal case, the jury are the judges of the law as well as the facts in the case. So whether I tell you about the law, while it is intended to be helpful to you in reaching a just and proper verdict in the case, it is not binding upon you as members of the jury and you may accept the law as you comprehend it to be the case.
>
> (Van Dyke, 1970, p. 20)

It is little wonder that judges' instructions present problems for juries when the legal establishment has not been able to develop uniform instructions.

The Juror

Making the Ultimate Decision

In the United States District Court in Chicago . . ., a 12-member jury listened for 15 weeks to dozens of witnesses and mountains of evidence in an antitrust suit brought by M.C.I. Communications Corporation against the American Telephone and Telegraph Company. The jurors then retired, deliberated for three days, and emerged to announce that they believed M.C.I. had been damaged; that they found A.T.&T.'s monopolistic practices to blame, and that they were awarding M.C.I $600 million. Since antitrust awards are automatically tripled for punitive purposes, the net due was $1.8 billion—the largest antitrust judgment in history. The attorneys at Jenner & Block, M.C.I.'s Chicago law firm, were delighted—but perhaps not entirely surprised. With the help of a new breed of specialists known as "jury researchers," they had already tried the case three times in varied forms before carefully constructed mock juries and had gleaned experimental evidence as to how things would go in court.

(Hunt, 1982, p. 70)

Is it, in fact, possible to predict with some degree of precision the nature of decisions that a jury will make? Increasing evidence from a variety of sources suggests a qualified "yes" to that question, for social psychologists have developed increasingly sophisticated and accurate models of jury decision-making processes.

Demographics and the Jury One of the primary theoretical tenets of the law is that accused parties are entitled to a jury composed of peers, representative of the community. In practice, this ideal has been difficult to reach because a jury of twelve or fewer individuals is hard put to match the range of social strata, ethnic origins, educational backgrounds, races, and ages typically found in any location, as we discussed with Archibald Cox at the beginning of the chapter. What this means in practice is that certain demograhic categories will be overrepresented in juries and, to the extent that defense and prosecuting attorneys have control over the composition of the jury, it may be possible to "stack" the jury either for or against the defendant. Because there is considerable leeway on the part of attorneys in excluding individuals who appear to be biased through the process known as *voir dire,* in which prospective jurors are questioned as to their impartiality and background, such an eventuality is at least theoretically possible.

In fact, some consistencies between particular demographic characteristics of jurors and their decision making have been found. For example, younger jurors are more apt to vote for acquittal than older jurors, while jurors with less education and those from lower socioeconomic

The racial and ethnic composition of a jury may bias the kinds of decisions that are made. (AP/ Wide World)

strata are more apt to vote for conviction (Nemeth, 1981). The political leanings of a juror also are correlated with judicial decisions. Political conservatives are more apt to convict defendants than liberals, and Democrats are more likely to favor the plaintiff than Republicans (Nemeth & Sosis, 1973; Hermann, 1970).

The results of research on sex and race of juror are somewhat less revealing of general consistencies. Depending on the study one examines, females have been found to be sometimes more and sometimes less conviction-prone than males. The only area in which a consistent sex difference has emerged involves rape trials, where females are more apt to favor conviction—and mete out harsher sentences—than males (Nemeth, 1981).

The results of research on race of juror are not definitive either. Most laboratory research has examined white jurors' differential conviction rates of white versus black defendants and found just a slight bias against black defendants (e.g., McGlynn, Megas, & Benson, 1976). On the other hand, survey research shows quite clearly that black defendants receive harsher treatment than white defendants in actual trial situations (Thornberry, 1973).

In general, demographic characteristics of jurors do not provide a terribly effective means of predicting jurors' decisions. What has proved to be a more accurate predictor, however, is the nature of the relationship between a juror's and a defendant's characteristics. Quite clearly, the greater the similarity between a juror and the defendant, the greater the leniency toward the defendant (Monahan & Loftus, 1982). This tendency may be caused by increased empathy between juror and defendant, or by heightened perceptions of attractiveness and likability for similar defendants (a phenomenon that we discussed in Chapter 6 in terms of interpersonal attraction). It is possible that such increased empathy or likability ultimately leads to greater juror leniency.

Juror Personality: Authoritarians Tend to Convict   Although juror demographic characteristics do not provide strong predictors of juror behavior, at least one personality factor—that of authoritarianism—has been shown to be strongly and consistently related to jury behavior. **Authoritarianism,** as noted in our discussion of prejudice (Chapter 5), refers to a complex of behaviors in which an individual displays rigidity, social and political conservatism, submissiveness to authority, conformity to conventional norms, and punitiveness and hostility toward those who deviate from such norms (Adorno, Frenkel-Brunswik, Levinson, & Sanford, 1950).

Research has shown repeatedly that persons high in authoritarianism, as measured through written personality scales, not only are more apt to convict defendants, but also tend to recommend longer sentences for those they consider guilty (Bray & Noble, 1978; V. L. Hamilton, 1976). Moreover, this tendency is even stronger when the authoritarian perceives that the defendant holds dissimilar attitudes to his or her own

(Mitchell & Byrne, 1973). There is one exception to these findings: as might be expected, authoritarians are *less* apt to vote in favor of conviction when the defendant is depicted as an authority figure or someone who was simply following the orders of an authority figure (V. L. Hamilton, 1976). This is, of course, consistent with the basic beliefs of the authoritarian.

Jury Structure and Procedure: Arriving at Group Consensus As we have discussed a number of times before, the particular group structure and procedure used by any group can have profound consequences for the nature of decisions reached by the group members, and jury groups are no different. Take, for instance, the size of the jury. Research on group dynamics has shown that groups tend to produce more and better solutions, although at the expense of time, than individuals produce (see Chapter 11). With more group members, groups theoretically contain greater resources—and, therefore, a larger group's solutions ought to be of higher quality. A conclusion from this line of reasoning is that larger juries will render more informed decisions than smaller ones.

Because in most cases the decisions that juries reach cannot be verified as either correct or incorrect, social psychologists have tended to use laboratory experiments and statistical simulations to determine the equivalence of various sized juries. The results are clear: quite consistently, twelve-person juries are superior to smaller juries. They are more likely to be more representative and accurate, less likely to convict an innocent person, and more apt to be unable to reach a unanimous decision than six-person juries (Nemeth, 1981; J. H. Davis, Bray, & Holt, 1977).

The positive nature of the latter point—that larger juries are more likely than smaller juries to be unable to make a unanimous decision, resulting in a "hung" jury—may at first seem obscure. But the reason that hung juries may not be undesirable is that unanimity, when it occurs, frequently indicates that a minority has abandoned its position in light of majority pressure. If the majority pressure is in favor of conviction, the acquiescence of a minority may result in the conviction of an innocent person. Larger juries, while increasing the potential size of both majority and minority, are more apt to provide dissenting jurors with at least one social supporter. And, as you may recall from our discussion of social influence processes in Chapter 10, conformity pressures are reduced dramatically by the presence of just one social supporter. Therefore, larger juries allow those holding dissenting opinions more opportunity to maintain their independence in the face of social pressure from others. Although this ultimately results in more hung juries, it presumably also results in fairer decisions.

The scientific findings have not been lost on the legal world. While legal decisions typically rely on legal precedents and not on social science evidence, a number of cases concerning the equitability of the use of smaller juries have made reference to research findings. In a 1978

BOX 13-2 SPOTLIGHT ON APPLICATIONS

APPLYING FORENSIC PSYCHOLOGY TO THE COURTROOM:
CAN THE JURY BE STACKED?

Much of this chapter has been devoted to a discussion of the ways in which social psychologists have identified factors that bias decision-making processes. We have seen that awareness of certain characteristics of defendants or jurors allows the prediction, with varying degrees of accuracy, of trial participants' behavior.

In fact, techniques and prescriptions have been devised to help attorneys systematically choose sympathetic jurors during *voir dire* proceedings (the purpose of which, theoretically, is to weed out jurors biased against the defense or prosecution). Typically, the procedure that has been followed involves administering a series of questionnaires to a sample of registered voters in the area in which a trial is being held. By asking pertinent questions about the trial, defendants, and prosecution, it is possible to relate general attitudinal patterns and demographic factors to a propensity to vote for acquittal or conviction. Then, when a jury is being chosen for the actual trial, potential jurors who hold similar attitudes and demographic characteristics to those who seem, from the survey results, most prone to acquit or convict the defendant can be identified. If this procedure is employed by attorneys for the defense, conviction-prone jurors can be preemptorily challenged and removed before they take their places on the jury—leading to a jury that is presumably inclined to vote acquittal (Bonora & Krauss, 1979).

Does it work? In a recent study, Moran and Comfort (1982) analyzed a large sample of jurors extensively, examining twenty-three demographic and personality variables and pre- and postdeliberation verdicts. Based on their data, they suggest that verdicts could be predicted with 87 percent accuracy just by knowing certain juror characteristics. But before one can say that scientific jury selection can be successful, it should be noted that their proce-

dure is much more direct than the typical process used by most jury researchers, who typically must rely on assessments of people who are *similar* to the jurors, and not the jurors themselves. Clearly, few lawyers are allowed the luxury of submitting personality questionnaires directly to potential jurors. The process of discerning demographic and personality characteristics, as well as attitudinal data, from the limited information available during juror selection is not simple (Patterson, 1984). Thus, social scientists are far from the stage at which they are able to stack the jury, either for or against a defendant.

However, an ethical issue still remains. Suppose, as one hopes will be the case, that social psychological predictions get more and more precise until we reach the day when juror behavior can be predicted with a great deal of accuracy. It has been argued that the result will be a *decrease* in justice as lawyers, along with their social scientist consultants, strive to create the "perfect" jury. In response to such criticism, Charlan Nemeth, an expert in applications of social psychology to the law, notes the following:

> . . . it is important to remember that the use of [preemptory challenges] does not allow the selection of favorable jurors. It provides for the excusing of unfavorable jurors. . . . Given that the law provides the defendant (and the prosecution) with the right to strike unfavorable jurors, it makes sense that the effective use of this right requires information and judgment. To the extent that social scientists offer this information and judgment, they help the system to operate more effectively.
>
> (Nemeth, 1981, p. 341)

As long as both sides in a jury trial have access to information obtained by social scientists, then, the judicial system is likely to benefit from increases in knowledge.

case regarding the distribution of obscene materials, the Supreme Court ruled that six-person juries are constitutional, but that five-person juries are not because "the purposes and functioning of the jury in a criminal trial are seriously impaired, and to a constitutional degree, by a reduction in size to below six members" (Ballew v. Georgia, 1978, p. 1030).

The Supreme Court used social science research showing that twelve-person juries are more appropriate than six-person juries to argue that six-person juries are constitutional and five-person juries are not. Although this extrapolation from the research findings may have been too extreme, it still represented a clear—and relatively rare—use of research findings to support a legal position. In a summary of the Court's opinion, Nemeth (1981) notes the arguments against reduced jury size made by Justice Blackman, who wrote the majority opinion. Blackman suggested that a reduction in size has some of the following effects:

> It lessens the likelihood of remembering each of the important pieces of evidence; it is less likely to overcome the biases of its members; the likelihood of convicting an innocent person increases . . . the variability of decisions is greater; the minority is less likely to be represented and, if represented, less likely to adhere to its position; fewer hung juries will occur; and the opportunity for meaningful and adequate representation of the community decreases.
>
> (Nemeth, 1981, p. 354)

In sum, the Supreme Court took into account a large body of data to support a point of law.

Jury Processes: Weighing the Evidence   In an ideal world, jurors would enter the courtroom untouched by prior opinions and biases, would weigh the evidence rationally, and would come up with a decision that strictly reflected the merits of the case. However, as you are probably well aware by now, the real world is not an ideal one. Still, there is some evidence that at the beginning of a trial jurors hold judgments of defendant guilt or innocence in abeyance and, in fact, may follow the dictum that defendants are presumed innocent until proven guilty.

In one interesting study, Saks, Werner, and Ostrom (1975) attempted to infer subjects' initial pretrial biases based upon the amount of information they received regarding a crime. They began by using a direct route. A group of subjects were asked what they thought their ultimate verdict would be in a situation in which they were jurors, the trial was about to begin, they had not heard any evidence, had not seen the defendant, and did not even know what the charges were. Given such a situation, the majority of subjects guessed that the probability of their judging the defendant guilty was exactly 50 percent. If these subjects held presumptions of innocence, it is certainly not apparent from that figure.

Pretrial publicity may affect the predispositions and expectations of jurors regarding the guilt or innocence of a juror. (Henri-Cartier Bresson/Magnum)

Had the study stopped at this point, it would have provided clear evidence that subjects do not enter trials with presumptions of innocence. But the researchers went further by using a statistical inferential technique in which subjects' assessments of guilt (measured by their ratings of probabilities of guilt) were determined by examining what their final judgments were when they had been presented differing levels of evidence. By plotting the data and forming algebraic equations, they could infer back to what subjects' initial probabilities of guilt were. As can be seen in Figure 13-2, the initial presumption of guilt can be inferred as being close to zero—in contrast to the guess of subjects that it is 50 percent. These results suggest that jurors may, in fact, adopt the notion that defendants are innocent until proven guilty—and once again that people are not always very accurate in the prediction or assessment of their own behavior.

Another factor that enters into juror decision making is the nature of the group discussion. As discussed in Chapter 11, group decisions tend to become polarized, with the initial tendencies of the individual group members becoming more pronounced (Myers & Lamm, 1976). As can be seen in the results of a study by Myers and Kaplan (1976) displayed in Figure 13-3, judicial decisions are no different from other sorts of decisions. In the experiment, simulated jurors were presented evidence that made the defendant look either highly guilty or relatively innocent. Ratings of defendant guilt taken before and after group discussion were more extreme after the discussion: initial ratings of guilt became even stronger and initial ratings of innocence moved toward the more inno-

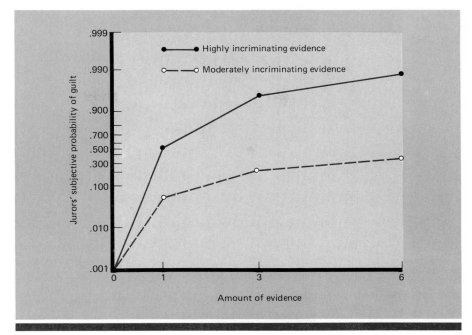

FIGURE 13-2
Jurors' ratings of defendant guilt. By determining
what jurors' final judg-
ments were when pre-
sented with differing levels of evidence, it is
possible to infer that the
subject's initial probabilities of guilt were close to
zero. Source: Saks, Wer-
ner, & Ostrom (1975).

cent end of the scale. In contrast, information that was not discussed
showed no change from before to after discussion. What these findings
and others suggest is that jury decisions tend to be determined largely
by the initial decisions of the individual group members made prior to
discussion—and not primarily by the cogency of arguments brought up
during the course of deliberations.

The Courtroom Revisited

We have examined three of the main characters in the courtroom: the
defendant, judge, and juror. As any crime buff would note, a number of
other players in legal proceedings have been left out, including the
police, defense lawyers, and prosecutor. Social psychologists are working to amass a body of knowledge about each of these participants as
well, in order to provide a full description of how social factors impact
upon the legal system. The ultimate goal of such work is not just to
develop an understanding of the legal system, but to provide methods
for making the system work more efficiently, effectively, and ultimately,
more just and fairer.

But what do we mean by "just" and "fair," concepts which, as we
discussed with Archibald Cox, are highly complex? In the remainder of
the chapter, we step out of the courtroom and examine approaches to
the broader question of what constitutes justice and fairness. We will
see that the answer cannot be determined without consideration of
social psychological concepts and principles.

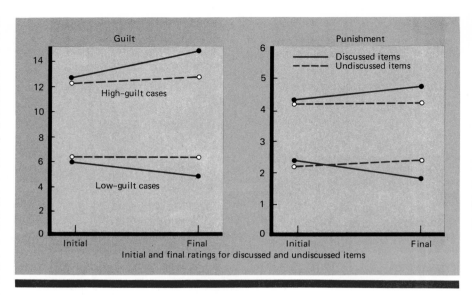

FIGURE 13-3
Ratings of defendant guilt and punishment. Both ratings of guilt and punishment length suggest that initially high judgments became even higher and initially low judgments became even lower after a group discussion—while judgments of undiscussed items remained basically unchanged. Source: D. G. Myers & E. F. Kaplan, Group induced polarization in simulated juries. *Personality and Social Psychology Bulletin,* Vol. 2, 1976, p. 65. Copyright © 1976 by the Society for Personality and Social Psychology, Inc. Reprinted by permission of Sage Publications, Inc.

MODELS OF JUSTICE

To the writers of the Declaration of Independence, the question of how to conceive of justice was encompassed by the phrase that all people "are created equal." Yet such a view of justice is one of many that might have been adopted by the founders of the United States. Consider, for instance, values such as these that might have been identified as requisites for just treatment (Deutsch, 1975).

- People should receive outcomes proportionate to their inputs.
- People should be rewarded according to their needs.
- People should receive outcomes according to their efforts.
- People should have equal opportunity to compete without favoritism or discrimination.
- People should receive outcomes according to supply and demand in the marketplace.

Many of these values clearly conflict with one another and, in fact, vary in their applicability, depending on the nature of a particular situation. But social psychologists have identified three basic models of justice underlying these seemingly disparate values: equality, equity, and relative needs. We will discuss each in turn.

Equality Models of Justice: Equalizing Outcomes

We would probably find few individuals who would argue against the abstract notion of equality. On closer examination, however, many as-

450

BOX 13-3   SPOTLIGHT ON FIELD RESEARCH

A CRIME REDUCTION EXPERIMENT

Throughout this chapter, the discussion of the legal system has centered around events that occur *after* a crime has been committed. However, some social psychologists have concentrated on the prevention of crime, working with the police to reduce the occurrence of criminal activities.

One of the best examples of the joint efforts of social scientists and the criminal justice system took place in the Asylum Hill section of Hartford, Connecticut. A poor area with a high crime rate, Asylum Hill provided an excellent field site to study the effects of various innovations on crime rates. Three key changes were made by those who implemented the program (Fowler, 1981). First, a police team was assigned on a permanent basis to the area. There were two reasons for this: it allowed the police to become familiar with the crime problem in the area and it strengthened the relationships between police and neighborhood residents.

A second major change that occurred as part of the implementation of the project related to traffic patterns. Some streets were closed to traffic altogether, while others were changed to one-way streets. This was done in order to emphasize the residential nature of the area and to give the residents a greater sense of control over their own environment. Finally, the third change was the formation of neighborhood organizations to participate in the crime reduction plans and in the physical changes that were being made as part of the program.

Although it took more than two years to implement the program, ultimately the changes appeared to be successful. Based on loose comparison group data—data that were collected from all other parts of the city except the area in question—the changes had a real and beneficial impact upon the Asylum Hill area. Burglary rates fell significantly. Perhaps of even greater importance, residents' perceptions of the likelihood that they would be a victim of burglary and of burglary as a neighborhood problem also decreased. Other street crimes appeared to drop somewhat, although to a lesser degree.

Thus, the program was a success—at least in the eyes of the people who put the program together and who evaluated its effects. On the other hand, residents of Hartford seemed to take a less favorable view. Among their concerns were the facts that "everyone knew that burglaries were still occurring in Asylum Hill" and that "everyone knew people who were afraid" (Fowler, 1981, p. 184). Indeed, the fact that there was an integrated, three-part program in place was not apparent to many critics. Thus, even though the program was a clear success on paper, many residents of the area viewed it as a failure. This fact demonstrates that what is convincing to a social scientist may not be to a resident of the nonscientific community. As Fowler (1981) notes, "as social scientists, we always need to be aware that the products of our imaginations and our abstract realities may not correspond at all with the way the world is experienced by those who are living with our abstractions" (p. 185).

---

pects of equality may not be looked upon with favor. For example, while most of us would agree that the citizenry should be fed, clothed, and sheltered according to some minimal standards, many would argue that above a certain minimal level variations in standard of living are not only tolerable but fair—if they are based on some reasonable criterion such as how hard the individual works or the amount of specialized training the individual has had. Yet the notion of equality makes no distinction in terms of the contribution of the individual; all that is considered is an equalization of the consequences to a person.

There is, in fact, some evidence from laboratory studies that the use of **equality models of justice** can be quite satisfying to participants. For example, leaders that apply the principle of equality to determine distributions of rewards to group members in laboratory settings tend to produce harmony and solidarity among group members, as well as higher levels of satisfaction (Bales, 1950). Moreover, research shows that people tend to believe that conflict among members of groups is least likely when equality in the distribution of rewards prevails (Leventhal, 1976).

On the other hand, applying equality in actual situations sometimes promotes dissatisfaction, particularly on the part of those whose contributions to the situation are considerably greater than those of others. Consider, for example, the factory worker who outproduces his peers by a ratio of two to one. An equality model might suggest that he receive the same amount of pay as his coworkers.

Other disconcerting applications of equality have been discussed by Sampson (1971). He mentions how, at the height of the hippie movement in the Haight-Ashbury district of San Francisco, a free bus service was set up between the district and Berkeley. As the bus would wend its way across San Francisco Bay, it would occasionally stop at "real" bus stops, where paying customers were waiting for the regular bus. The reaction of those waiting was typically one of astonishment and concern, and many refused a free ride, thinking that there must be *some* catch to a service that did not cost them anything.

Equity Models of Justice: Are the Outcomes Proportional to the Inputs?

Because of the limitations inherent in a strict interpretation of equality models, particularly the notion that rewards ought to be distributed equally to individuals regardless of their inputs, most Western governments—as well as most people—have adopted **equity models of justice.** As we first discussed in Chapter 6 in relation to interpersonal attraction, equity models suggest that the rewards that people receive should be proportional to the magnitude of their inputs. Individuals who contribute most to a given situation ought to receive the greatest benefits; those who contribute least ought to receive the least.

In typical equity models, inputs are defined as the contributions individuals make to a social situation that can be viewed as "entitling" them to an outcome consisting of rewards or costs. The inputs may consist of physical resources, such as money or effort expended, or of personal qualities such as physical attractiveness, intelligence, or cruelty. Outcomes are typically viewed as positive or negative consequences that individuals perceive they have incurred by their participation in the interaction (Walster, Walster, & Berscheid, 1978).

According to the major equity model proposed by Walster, Berscheid, & Walster (1976), four primary propositions can be made. First, people generally try to maximize their outcomes. Second, groups and societies tend to evolve systems based on equity models in allocating resources to their members, and they tend to reward members who treat others equitably and punish those who treat others inequitably. Third, when people find themselves in inequitable relationships, they feel distress proportionate to the inequity involved. Finally, people in inequitable relationships tend to attempt to restore equity, and the greater the inequity, the harder they will strive to restore it.

How can equity be restored? There are two major methods: direct tactics and defensive tactics. **Direct tactics** are those in which people directly alter either their own inputs and/or outcomes or the inputs and outcomes of others. To use an earlier example, a worker who is producing twice as much as his counterparts but is paid no differently could alter his inputs by reducing his production, thereby restoring equity. Conversely, he could ask for a raise to compensate for his higher productivity, thus altering his outcomes.

Defensive tactics for restoring equity involve psychological distortion of the way in which input–outcome ratios are perceived. Hence, our high producer could deny that a situation is inequitable by convincing himself that his productivity is really not all that great, or he could decide that his outcome—money, in this case—is really not that important to him and that other outcomes, such as his sense of accomplishment or competitiveness, are more germane.

Equity and the Law   Much of our legal system is based upon equity considerations. Consider, as one example, our system of matching severity of punishment with severity of crime. As was discussed with attorney Archibald Cox at the start of the chapter, in most cases part of the rationale behind length of sentencing rests on the idea of **retribution;** society attempts to make criminals suffer in a way that "pays back" some of the suffering they have caused. This being the case, it is possible that proof of a criminal's having suffered prior to being sentenced would tend to reduce the length of the sentence given. The reason? The inputs of such criminals will be viewed less negatively because of their prior suffering. In turn, their outcomes in the form of sentence length ought to be less negative.

It turns out that in both laboratory-simulated and actual cases, people acting as jurors do take into account the degree of suffering of the defendant (Austin, Walster, & Utne, 1976). In a comprehensive survey of jury trials, Kalven and Zeisel (1966) found that the perception of trial judges is that defendants who report deep remorse, who suffer during the commission of the crime, who have been in jail for a long time prior to the trial, or even who have had some tragedy unrelated to the crime befall them are apt to receive relatively lenient sentences. In fact, the invocation of a string of misfortunes is an accepted legal tactic. Consider, for example, the plea for leniency made before Congress of E. Howard Hunt, convicted of conspiracy for his involvement in the Watergate scandal:

FIGURE 13-4
This cartoon—drawn during the heat of the Watergate scandal—illustrates the notion that prior suffering should be considered in sentencing.

'YOUR HONOR, CAN WE JUST TAKE THE PARDON AND GO? . . . WE'VE SUFFERED ENOUGH ALREADY!'

Now I find myself confined under a sentence which may keep me in prison for the rest of my life. I have been incarcerated for six months. For a time, I was in solitary confinement. I have been physically attacked and robbed in jail. I have suffered a stroke. I have been transferred from place to place, manacled and chained, hand and foot. I am isolated from my motherless children. The funds provided me and others who participated in the break-in have long since been exhausted. I am faced with an enormous financial burden in defending myself against criminal charges and numerous civil suits.

Thus, evidence from nonlaboratory settings suggests a correlation between defendant suffering and actual or requested leniency.

Evidence from experimental studies carried out in laboratory settings shows a cause-and-effect relationship between defendant suffering and sentence length. Austin, Walster (Hatfield, and Utne (1976) report two studies in which subjects were given a description of either a minor crime (a purse snatching) or a major one (a purse snatching which included a severe beating of the victim). The descriptions also varied in degree of misfortune that had befallen the criminal attempting to leave the scene of the crime. In one condition, nothing happened; in the moderate suffering condition, the criminal broke some bones; while in the major suffering condition, the criminal became paralyzed from the neck down. For both the major and minor crime, the degree of suffering of the criminal had a significant effect on the length of sentences given by the subjects who were playing the role of presiding judge.

As can be seen in Figure 13-5, sentences became considerably shorter as the suffering of the criminal increased. The more the criminal had appeared to suffer, the less severe the punishment assigned by the subjects.

In sum, equity theory suggests that individuals implicitly weigh and balance the inputs and outcomes derived from a criminal's activity and use these factors in determining what is just punishment. Such a view entails a fairly thoughtful, logical view of the processes involved in decision making. However, there is at least one related approach to justice that illustrates that sometimes people engage in biased decision-making activities; this approach is based upon what has been called the **just-world hypothesis.**

The Just-World Hypothesis: People Get What They Deserve and Deserve What They Get   According to Melvin Lerner, an important factor in how most people view the justice of a given situation is their underlying belief in a just world (Lerner, Miller, & Holmes, 1976). At the heart of this model is the notion that people get out of life pretty much what they deserve and, conversely, people tend to deserve what happens to them.

This belief presumably begins to develop in early childhood, when we are taught that the rules provided by our parents are *the* correct ones, and that rewards and punishments automatically follow, respectively, from good and bad behavior. Many adults continue to hold this notion to a degree, feeling that their own and others' behavior results in the rewards and punishments they incur. Moreover, the concept is embellished to the degree that people tend also to feel that, almost by definition, people who receive rewards are good and people who are punished are bad.

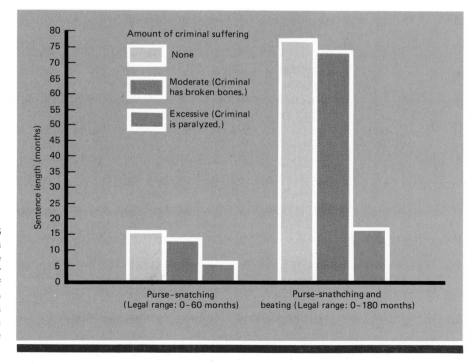

FIGURE 13-5
Mean number of months sentence in prison. The greater degree of prior suffering on the part of the criminal, the lower the sentence he or she was given. Source: Austin Walster (Hatfield), & Utne (1976).

While a formal logician would cringe at such reasoning, there is a good deal of supportive evidence showing that just-world notions do color people's explanations for why certain events happen to particular individuals. This tendency presents little difficulty when good things happen to people, since the judgment is generally that they deserved them. But when the event is undesirable, such as an assault or an accident, observers' judgments that the person must have deserved to be punished can have very unfortunate implications.

For instance, one survey has shown that victims of crimes such as kidnapping, rape, and assault typically are queried by acquaintances about what it was that *they* did to bring on the misfortune (Symonds, 1975). They were asked why they were in a bad area of town, or what they did to entice the rapist, or if they flaunted the watch they had been wearing before a robbery. The reason behind such queries appears to be questioners' desire to receive assurance that the victim's misfortune was caused by the victim's behavior—thereby maintaining a sense that the world is good.

A few studies have attempted to show how just-world considerations affect judicial judgments. In one laboratory experiment with subjects acting as jurors, Jones and Aronson (1973) tested the hypothesis that when disaster strikes a respectable person, he or she will be judged *more* at fault than when a less respectable individual is involved in a disaster. This counterintuitive prediction is derived directly from just-world considerations, as we can see from an example.

Suppose that a narcotics pusher who deals in child pornography is hit by a car while crossing the street. Most observers viewing the situation would say that the pusher got what was coming to him, thus confirming just-world notions. But if the victim were a saintly man crossing the street to bring food to a poor family, observers' just-world notions would be threatened, and they would need to do something to restore their beliefs. According to Jones and Aronson, their most likely response would be to blame the victim, saying that perhaps he had not been paying attention or had been distracted in some way. By making such a response, the observers are able to view the accident as the victim's fault.

To test these notions, subjects in the Jones and Aronson study were asked to judge the degree of fault of a rape victim. They were presented with one of three descriptions of the rape, in which an attempt was made to vary the victim's respectability. She was presented as either married or a virgin (both judged by subjects to be relatively high in respectability) or as divorced (judged by subjects to be relatively lower in respectability). After reading the case they were asked to judge the degree of fault of the victim. As shown in Table 13-1 the judgments followed the predictions. When the victim was said to be married or an unmarried virgin, the fault of the victim was considered significantly greater than when the victim was divorced. On the other hand, when subjects were asked to recommend the number of years the defendant

TABLE 13-1   Ratings of Victim and Defendant

Measure	VICTIM CHARACTERISTICS		
	Married	Virgin	Divorced
Fault of victim (the more negative the score, the less fault attributed to the victim)	−2.44	−3.60	−5.46
Number of years of imprisonment recommended for defendant	15.03	13.70	11.13

Source: Based on Jones & Aronson (1973).

should be jailed, defendants received higher sentences when the victim was married or a virgin than when the victim was divorced. Even though the divorced victim was judged less at fault, then, the perpetrator of a crime was given a lighter sentence than when the victim was supposedly "more respectable."

Although there is some evidence to the contrary (e.g., Aderman, Brehm, & Katz, 1974), most research seems to support the notion that people act in accordance with the just-world hypothesis. Why is it so pervasive? One reason seems to be that it acts as a self-protective mechanism (Lerner, 1966). It is highly threatening to admit that negative events might happen just on the basis of chance. In order to protect

Do people get what they deserve and deserve what they get? "Just-world" notions hold that this is the case. (Bruce Davidson/Magnum)

themselves against this idea, people tend to view negative outcomes as being deserved.

Because of just-world notions, in many cases innocent victims are devalued and blamed for their unfortunate circumstances. Thus, presuming that the world is just may also lead to insensitivity about suffering in general. Lerner (1977) suggests that people's major concern is with maintaining their view that they themselves will not be treated unjustly, and believing this leads them to be relatively insensitive to the injustice that others face. In a concrete sense, they may actively avoid learning facts that clarify the injustices that do abound through a process of selective inattention. Hence, people may avoid viewing television shows discussing social problems or noticing that others are displaying signs of poverty such as shabby clothing or malnutrition.

Relative Needs Models of Justice: Outcomes According to Needs

The final model of justice that social psychologists have studied is that of **relative need.** The relative need principle suggests that resources should be allocated to those with the greatest need, regardless of the amount of contribution that they make to a social situation or society. The corollary of the rule also holds: those who transgress the most should receive the greatest punishment, without regard to extenuating circumstances.

Although justice based on relative needs is probably the least frequently followed model—particularly in capitalistic societies—there are a number of instances in which it can be found. Notions prevalent in most countries that no one should go hungry and that all should receive some minimal level of assistance are based on relative needs models which suggest that, up to a certain level, those in greatest need should receive the greatest amount of assistance. Moreover, as Rawls (1971) points out, providing the needy with help permits the development of trust among members of groups, institutions, and society as a whole.

Comparing Models of Justice

Having discussed the three major models of justice (equality, equity, and relative needs), we turn now to the conditions under which each works most effectively. Morton Deutsch (1975) has suggested general principles to explain when each model is most likely to be used, at least in settings in which people try to cooperate with one another in the distribution of resources. The determining factor in each case is the goal regarding the primary outcome of the interaction:

• If the primary goal is economic productivity, *equity* (as opposed to equality or need) is likely to be the primary principle of justice employed. Equity models tend to produce the highest outcomes from a given input, which is particularly important when the inputs that are available are limited.

- If the primary goal is the fostering or maintenance of positive social relationships, *equality* will tend to be the primary determinant of justice. Equality models of justice tend to foster the belief that all participants in a social system have equal worth and merit and that they warrant mutual respect and esteem. In contrast, equity models suggest that individuals should be evaluated on the strength of their inputs, leading to the likelihood of relatively large disparities between the outcomes of individuals.
- If the major goal in cooperative situations is to promote the personal development and personal welfare of the participants, *relative need* is apt to be the primary model of justice. The reason has been well stated by Deutsch:

> It is apparent that individuals' needs fluctuate and it is unlikely that the needs of members [of a group or society] will always be equal to one another or proportionate to their relative contributions. Thus, if at a particular time an individual has a need that is important to his survival, development, or well-being, he must have access to the resources for satisfying his need independently of whether doing so is socially equitable or equal in the short run.
> (Deutsch, 1975, p. 147)

A Final Perspective on Justice

It is clear that questions regarding the appropriateness of a particular model of justice cannot be answered without making reference to the values and goals that a society holds (Knight & Dubro, 1984). Although Western society has a decidedly economic orientation in many respects, thereby leading to a predominance of equity models of justice, in some instances other models of justice hold. Moreover, in societies in which cooperation is valued most highly, one could expect equity models to predominate. Hence, no model of justice is "better" than any other; different models simply reflect the differing, and sometimes contradictory, goals of society.

SUMMARY

Social psychologists have examined a number of factors relating to the courtroom, including the roles of defendant, judge, and juror. Research on defendants shows that their general social attractiveness is related to sentence length, at least in laboratory studies. Specifically, it appears that attractiveness of personality and attire, and even physical attractiveness, produces more jury and judge leniency. On the other hand, if the physical attractiveness of a suspect is used profitably during criminal activity, jurors are apt to give harsher sentences to more attractive defendants than to less attractive ones. Another defendant characteristic regards defendants' prior records and the degree to which defendants argue for their own innocence. Defendants with prior records tend to be judged guilty more readily, and those who argue their innocence without being accused tend to be viewed as guilty.

Judges also are susceptible to biases due to social psychological factors. For example, they sentence multiple offenders more lightly than sole perpetrators, despite legal dictums against such behavior, and bail setting is, in part, a function of social influence coming from defense and prosecuting attorneys. In addition, their legal instructions to jurors may be incomprehensible or may sometimes result in decisions that are directly contrary to the instructions.

There are a number of consistencies between juror demographic characteristics and their decision making. Younger jurors are more apt to vote for acquittal than older jurors, while jurors with less education, jurors from lower socioeconomic strata, political conservatives, and authoritarians are more apt to vote for conviction. Of greatest importance is the degree of similarity between juror and defendant; preceived similarity leads to greater lenience.

An area in which social psychological research on legal factors has had an important impact relates to jury size. Research has consistently shown that twelve-person juries tend to be more representative and accurate, are less likely to convict an innocent person, and are less apt to reach a decision than six-person juries. Using these findings, the Supreme Court extrapolated the point that six-person juries are constitutional while five-person juries are not.

Research suggests that jurors are able to follow the legal dictum that defendants are presumed innocent until proven guilty. On the other hand, group decisions tend to be determined largely by the initial decisions of the individual group members made prior to discussion, and less to the nature of the arguments brought up during the course of deliberations.

Three major approaches to justice are based on equality, equity, and relative needs models. Equality models ignore the contributions made by people and instead consider just the equalization of outcomes. In contrast, equity models suggest that the rewards or outcomes that people receive should be proportional to the magnitude of their inputs or contributions. Equity theory suggests that people try to maximize their outcomes, that groups and societies tend to evolve systems based on equity models, that people in inequitable relationships feel distress which is proportionate to the degree of inequity experienced, and that people in inequitable relationships attempt to restore equity. Equity can be restored either through direct tactics—in which inputs and/or outcomes are overtly modified—or through defensive tactics—psychological distortions of inputs and/or outcomes. Many legal doctrines are based on equity considerations. For example, sentence length is based in part on the notion of retribution, by which society attempts to make criminals suffer in an amount congruent with the degree of suffering that they have caused.

An approach to justice that is related to equity theory is based on the just-world hypothesis. This hypothesis suggests that people tend to feel that others (and they themselves) receive rewards and punishments that they deserve, and that they deserve what they receive. This suggests that people who suffer misfortunes are apt to be thought of as deserving such outcomes.

The third major model of justice is based on relative needs. The relative needs model suggests that resources should be allocated to those with the greatest need, regardless of the degree of contribution that they have made to a group or to society.

Depending on the goal of cooperative situations, particular models of justice are apt to be used. If the primary goal is economic activity, equity is likely to be the primary principle of justice employed. If the major goal is the fostering or maintenance of positive social relationships, equality will tend to predominate. Finally, if the major goal is to promote personal development and the welfare of individuals, relative need is apt to be the primary model of justice.

KEY TERMS

authoritarianism
bail
defendant
equality model of justice
equity model of justice
eyewitness
judge
juror

jury
jury size
jury structure
justice
just-world hypothesis
relative needs model of justice
retribution
voir dire

FOR FURTHER STUDY AND APPLICATION

Saks, M. J., & Hastie, R. (1978). *Social psychology in court.* New York: Van Nostrand.
A fine, interesting introduction to the realm of social psychology and the law. Provides useful and practical guidelines for applying social science to the courtroom, and synthesizes the research in meaningful ways.

Greenberg, M. S., & Ruback, R. B. (1982). *Social psychology of the criminal justice system.* Monterey, CA: Brooks/Cole.
Reviews the criminal justice system, starting from the reporting of crimes and ending with prison and parole for convicted offenders. A bit technical, and theoretically sophisticated: the authors apply a cohesive framework to the entire justice system.

Lipsitt, P., & Sales, B. (Eds.). (1979). *New directions in psycholegal research.* New York: Van Nostrand Reinhold.
A series of technical chapter written by experts in the field. Provides a good overview of different research programs relating to psychology and the law.

Konečni, V. J., & Ebbesen, E. B. (Eds.). (1982). *The criminal justice system: A social psychological analysis.* San Francisco: Freeman.
A series of chapters, written at a relatively high level, that provide a current sampling of topics. Includes a particularly interesting chapter on bail-setting processes and a comparison between laboratory and field study results.

Wells, G. L., & Loftus, E. A. (1984). *Eyewitness testimony: Psychological perspectives.* New York: Cambridge University Press.
A well-written overview of what is known regarding eyewitness testimony. Includes chapters on lie detection, hypnosis, and legal reforms relating to the use of eyewitnesses in trials.

CHAPTER 14

SOCIAL EXCHANGE AND BARGAINING

A CONVERSATION WITH . . .

Paul Warnke
U.S. Arms Negotiator

Paul Warnke, a Washington, D.C., attorney, was the chief negotiator at the Strategic Arms Limitation Treaty (SALT) talks with the Soviet Union during the 1970s. The main purpose of the negotiations was to produce an agreement to limit the development of nuclear weapons in both the United States and the Soviet Union. An agreement was reached, and it proved to be the capstone of a long career in negotiations for Mr. Warnke. His experience includes labor negotiations, arbitrations, contract negotiations, settlement negotiations, and legal proceedings as well as international negotiations. Clearly, he is an expert on the topic of bargaining.

We began our discussion by asking about the SALT negotiations.

Q. How did the SALT negotiations differ from other sorts of negotiations in which you have been involved?

A. The difference in the SALT negotiations is that there is no way of enforcing the result. And, therefore, you have got to be sure the result is one with which both sides can live. In an arms control agreement, for example, there is always an escape clause which provides that either side can renounce the treaty if it finds that its supreme interest is jeopardized by its continuation.

Q. One could ask what the point of the exercise is if that is the case.

A. Well, there *is* no point to it unless you feel that there is some result which is going to be desirable for both sides. Then both sides will feel that they are better off sticking with the bargain. The most dramatic illustration of this point is the SALT II treaty, which was never ratified by Congress. But even though it may not be legally binding, both sides have found it in their own interests to abide by its provisions.

Q. Can you describe in general terms what it is like to be negotiating with the Russians—to sit down and negotiate this very weighty subject?

A. It is, of course, tremendously interesting because the issue is so important. You have the tremendous advantage of being able to devote full time to that one question. It is also part of a continuing process, so you do have the advantage—or disadvantage—of years and years of prior negotiations on earlier treaties. There is an awful lot of "institutional memory" on both sides. You must try to fit arms control into an overall security policy, so you have to be conscious of what it is you need in the way of military forces, how nuclear forces interact with conventional forces, and so on. You have a whole variety of constituencies—not only the various groups in the U.S. government, but also your allies. Thus, you have to be concerned not only with how an arms control proposal fits into your own picture of what your defense force structure should look like, but also how it's going to work with your allies.

Basically, then, you not only have to negotiate with the Russians, but you have to negotiate with the executive branch, the Congress, and our western European allies as well. So you are running a whole set of negotiations simultaneously.

Q. During the SALT talks, were there many times when you were surprised with the course of the negotiations?

A. I was unusually surprised by the fact that having debated an issue over a long, long period of time, sometimes the Soviets just totally collapsed. Rather than coming up with an intermediate position, sometimes we'd have a total clash and eventually they would just accept our position. I tried to figure out why this was true. I think it was because their decision-making process is more difficult than ours. We had interagency working groups that could work out most things. But I don't think that concept exists within the Soviet bureaucracy. So a position is formulated by each of the separate branches in the ministry of defense, ministry of foreign affairs, KGB, or whatever. And then all this goes up to the top, where all the differences must be reconciled. What this means is that sometimes it is very difficult for them to come up with a compromise, and rather than try they sometimes just give up.

Q. What do you think about the idea of a nuclear freeze as a negotiating strategy?

A. As an objective, it is fine. But if the idea is an immediate total nuclear freeze, it is not negotiable. It is an instance of the best being the enemy of the good. If you try to get too much done with one bite, you're not going to get anything done. There are just too many things that have to be taken into account. So you have to take it apart and take it on a step-by-step basis. If you do it that way, you have manageable issues.

Q. What about an arms buildup as a negotiating strategy? There is a good deal of talk in this country about the strategy of negotiating from a position of strength.

A. Obviously you have to have a position of strength. Otherwise, no one is going to take you seriously. But the argument being made now is that you have to have a position of superiority, and that won't work. The other side is then not going to bargain. If we say we want to have a superior bargaining position so we can force them to submit to our will, they will say that they will wait until they are back on an equal footing. If we say that we want to have a bargaining advantage, the other party will say we can't have a bargaining advantage. Why should they go into negotiations at a disadvantage? The records show that the Soviets were not willing to bargain until they thought they had reached a position of rough parity. And that is always going to be the case. So efforts to gain a superior bargaining position will result in no bargain.

OVERVIEW

Although few of us will ever get the opportunity to bargain face-to-face with Soviet negotiators over arms control, bargaining is a frequent occurrence in everyone's life. Consider, for instance, the following situations:

- At the end of each month, three roommates sit down to figure out how much money they spent on food, the number of meals that each of them ate at the apartment, and whether anyone owes or is owed additional money.
- You and two neighbors decide to maintain a joint vegetable garden; you will each help to plant and will share equally in the crop.
- A woman places a bid on an antique headboard at a country auction, but is outbid by the person standing next to her.
- Two divorcing parents agree to joint custody of their three children.

What these situations have in common is that they all involve what has been called **social exchange.** Social exchange refers to interactions in which individuals exchange something, trade items, or divide a set of rewards. The exchange may involve something as concrete as dollars and cents, or it may be as intangible—in the case of the divorcing parents—as love and affection for one's children. The important point is that each party can potentially contribute something to the exchange and at the same time hopes to get something from it.

In this chapter, we first discuss the general topic of social exchange. We next turn to work on bargaining, a form of social exchange in which individuals try to settle an issue through negotiation. We will discuss practical strategies for shaping and coming to agreements between two or more people. Finally, we discuss bargaining in the context of arms negotiating, one of the major social issues confronting the world today. Social psychologists have found that many of the same threads run through different kinds of bargaining situations, whether they are between two people deciding what movie to see or between heads of state negotiating issues of war and peace.

SOCIAL EXCHANGE: SOCIAL INTERACTION AS AN ECONOMIC ACTIVITY

As developed by John Thibaut and Harold Kelley (1959; Kelley and Thibaut, 1978), social exchange theory suggests that human interaction can be viewed as a kind of joint economic activity. Each participant in a social interaction obtains certain rewards from the interaction, but also accrues certain costs. According to the theory, in order to understand how lasting and satisfying the relationship is, it is necessary to identify and place values upon its rewards and costs, which may be in the form of status, money, love, services, goods, or information (Foa & Foa, 1976). After the rewards and costs are assessed, the theory predicts that an individual will figure what he or she nets from the situation—the outcome—by simply subtracting the costs from the rewards; hence, the formula, Rewards − Costs = Outcome. In a general sense, if the resulting outcome figure is positive, the participant will want to continue the interaction, but if it is negative, the individual will try to end the relationship.

But there are some complicating factors. Consider, for example, two individuals, each of whom agrees to purchase similar vacant lots from a real estate salesman for $20,000. If we consider just the objective costs, each will pay the same amount and receive the same reward (the lot). Therefore, if we simply subtract costs from rewards, we might assume that the two would share identical outcomes and hence would be equally satisfied. But this may not be true if we consider the separate prior histories of the two people. Suppose one of the people has an annual income that averages $15,000, while the other is a millionaire.

The value placed on the lot is likely to be significantly higher for the less affluent individual than for the millionaire.

The same reasoning explains why two individuals who experience identical rewards and costs from a social interaction may view the interactions with differing levels of satisfaction. To account for this, Thibaut and Kelley (1959) introduced the concept of **comparison level** (CL), the level to which the outcome of a particular relationship is compared. The CL is the outcome that individuals feel is appropriate, reasonable, and deserved from a relationship, based upon their prior experience in other relationships as well as their perception of how satisfied others are with their similar relationships.

Thus, if most of my friends have bad marriages, with frequent major confrontations and infidelities, the comparison level with which I compare the degree of satisfaction I am getting from my own marriage will be relatively low—and I may be relatively satisfied with my marriage even if my wife and I fight a lot. On the other hand, if I perceive that my friends have flawless marriages and never fight, I may believe that my own occasional quarrels are indicative of a very weak marriage. Hence, the satisfaction I experience in my marriage is relative to my comparison level, and the theory suggests that if I view my relationship as below my CL, I am likely to terminate it.

However, we all know of relationships in which the participants are very dissatisfied, and yet the relationships linger on. To account for this phenomenon, Thibaut and Kelley (1959) suggest that one must also consider the **comparison level for alternatives** (CL_{Alt}). The CL_{Alt} refers to the outcomes that an individual feels could be obtained from the best alternative interaction available. If the outcome of a given relationship is lower than the CL_{Alt}, the individual will leave the relationship; but if the outcome is higher than the CL_{Alt}, the individual will remain in the relationship—even if in absolute terms the person is dissatisfied. Thus, many unhappy marriages stay afloat simply because the alternatives seem even worse.

Depicting Outcomes: The Payoff Matrix

One of the innovations developed by social exchange theorists concerns the use of the **payoff matrix** to represent social relationships. The matrix provides a means for representing the various alternative responses that an individual can make in a given situation, as well as those of the person with whom they are interacting. Most important, it shows the outcomes that each participant would receive should a given combination of choices be made by the participants.

Consider, for instance, the hypothetical payoff matrix depicted in Figure 14-1. Wendy and Karl are trying to decide what to do on their first date, which Karl has promised to pay for. For the sake of argument, let's say their choices are limited to two: either seeing the old Humphrey Bogart movie *The Maltese Falcon* or going to a fancy restaurant for

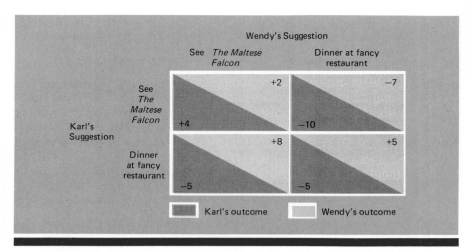

FIGURE 14-1
A sample payoff Matrix. The numbers in this payoff matrix are hypothetical, varying along a "satisfaction" scale ranging from −10 (least positive) to +10 (most positive).

dinner. Further assume that Karl prefers to go to the movies (to save money), while Wendy prefers dinner out, although she'd settle for the movie. The situation is complicated by the fact that Karl does not want to seem stingy, while Wendy does not want to appear extravagant.

Each specific *combination* of choices brings a specific outcome. If, for example, they *both* suggest going to *The Maltese Falcon*, the outcome is positive for each, although more positive for Karl. If Wendy suggests going to see *The Maltese Falcon*, while Karl suggests going to dinner (something he doesn't really want to pay for), his outcome is moderately negative—at least he seems generous even if he really doesn't want to spring for dinner—while Wendy's outcome is quite positive. On the other hand, if *she* suggests going to dinner while Karl suggests the movies, he is seen as stingy while she seems extravagant. In other words, they both lose. Finally, if they both suggest dinner, Karl's outcome is moderately negative (he still has to pay for the cost of dinner) while Wendy's outcome is relatively positive.

Given the various outcome combinations, which is most likely? Because both benefit moderately when they suggest going to see the movie, this is the option most likely to be chosen—assuming that each wants the relationship to continue. If Wendy really doesn't like Karl, the figures representing her outcomes would change radically. Moreover, it should be noted that the figures are totally hypothetical; they merely illustrate that each combination of choices in an exchange situation brings its own particular outcomes.

The Prisoner's Dilemma The most extensive use, by far, of payoff matrices to investigate social exchange is a situation known as the "Prisoner's Dilemma." It can best be understood by placing yourself in the following situation:

You have chosen a life of crime. Unfortunately, however, you are not very successful at it. Indeed, at this very moment you are sitting in the county jail, a suspect in a robbery. In the next cell is your partner in crime. The district attorney is sure that you are both guilty, but he doesn't have enough evidence to convict you at a trial. He takes you aside, and tells you that you have two alternatives: either you confess or you don't confess. And you know that your partner has the same alternatives.

The district attorney then goes on to tell you that if neither of you confesses, he is going to prosecute you on trumped-up charges which he knows will stick, and you'll both end up in jail with a small but significant sentence of one year in prison. If you *both* confess, you will both go to jail, but for somewhat less than the maximum permitted by law—eight years each. But if just one of you confesses and the other does not, the confessor will have a very short term for turning states' evidence (three months), while the nonconfessor will receive the maximum sentence allowed by law—ten years.

What are you going to do?

The problem posed by this situation, known as the "Prisoner's Dilemma," has formed the basis for one of the most fertile areas of research on social exchange (Luce & Raiffa, 1957). Consider your options, which are schematized in Figure 14-2. From a joint cooperative point of view, the best option clearly is for neither of you to confess; in that case, each ends up with just one year in jail. On the other hand, it is probably very tempting to confess and hope that your partner does not. In this case, you get off easy, with just three months in jail, while your partner ends up with ten years. (You're likely to need a new partner as well.) But— and here is the catch—if your partner also decides to confess, you'll both go to jail for a very long time. Of course, there's still one worse situation, from your point of view: if you don't confess and he does, he'll get just three months—and you'll get ten years.

Because of the ease with which variables associated with cooperation

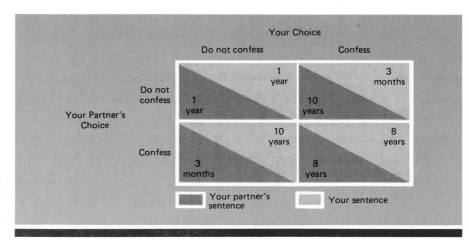

FIGURE 14-2
An example of the payoff matrix used in the typical Prisoner's Dilemma situation.

and competition—such as sentence length, degree of feedback, and availability of communication—can be manipulated, the Prisoner's Dilemma situation has formed the basis for hundreds of studies on social exchange and bargaining. Indeed, many of the generalizations that we make in this chapter are based upon Prisoner's Dilemma-type experiments, and the technique has been useful in providing a good deal of information on specific factors associated with bargaining behavior.

The Prisoner's Dilemma situation tends to evoke a fairly regular pattern of behavior (Rubin & Brown, 1975). When people first play the game, their response is likely to be unconcerned with possible future retaliatory behavior on the part of their partner, and they tend to act exploitatively. But if they see that their exploitative behavior is going to bring about retaliation—which ultimately means that *both* parties lose—the most rational choice becomes the cooperative one. Neither party will win much, but losses will be kept to a minimum.

Of course rationality is not always a strong point of human nature, and typically what happens is that after a long string of cooperative choices, one or the other partner will decide to make a noncooperative choice, and that partner will win big—but at the expense of the other. As soon as this occurs, the most likely consequence is that on the following turn, both players will make noncooperative choices, ensuring that both lose. And the pattern of noncooperative choices is likely to continue into consecutive trials. However, this noncooperative pattern may be broken on occasion—if one partner unilaterally begins to make a cooperative choice and keeps on making it, even if he or she has continued losses in the face of the partner's gains. The typical outcome of such a strategy is to bring the noncooperative partner around into a more cooperative framework; cooperation will tend to persist after it has been restored.

Methodological Drawbacks   Although much has been learned by researchers employing the Prisoner's Dilemma game, the experimental procedure has been criticized severely (Nemeth, 1972; Sommer, 1982). Because of methodological constraints, it may not be a terribly close approximation to real-life bargaining behavior such as that encountered by arms negotiator Paul Warnke. For example, subjects generally have no way of communicating their goals or motivations to their partner, and interaction between parties is kept to a minimum. Inevitably, subjects may come to feel that they are interacting not with another person but with an abstract payoff matrix.

Indeed, the use of payoff matrices raises a broader criticism of research on social exchange. While it is relatively easy to represent rewards, costs, and outcomes when they are couched in terms of years or dollars and cents, when we talk about "love" or "status" or "information"—all possible units of exchange—things become murky. Even worse is the necessity for assigning equivalent units to costs (for instance, time or money) and rewards (for instance, "affection") in order to derive an individual's outcomes mathematically. What this has meant is that most research has been conducted in situations in which the payoffs can be quantified unequivocally in terms of either money or points in games. (Also see Box 14-1.)

Another drawback to the use of payoff matrices is that they provide a fairly rational, economic analysis of exchange, putting relatively little emphasis on the specifically social aspects of the situation. For example, partners in an exchange may, over time, begin to operate under any of the norms of justice that we discussed in detail in Chapter 13: equality, equity, or relative needs. The equality norm implies that there ought to be equal outcomes for all participants in an exchange situation—regardless of the resources that an individual contributes. Equity norms suggest that a fair exchange has occurred when one party perceives that the rewards he or she receives are proportional to the magnitude of the costs incurred, and that the reward–cost ratio is similar for the other party. Finally, the relative needs norm says that resources should be distributed according to which party has the greatest need, without regard to the resources he or she initially brings to the situation. Regardless of whether equality, equity, or relative needs norms evolve in an exchange situation, each increases the complexity of the exchange in a way that one-dimensional payoff matrices are hard put to capture.

Other Approaches to Social Exchange and Bargaining: Acme, Bolt, and the Road to and from Cooperation

Although approaches that use the Prisoner's Dilemma and payoff matrices have predominated research on social exchange and bargaining, other techniques have been devised. One classic method is the Acme–Bolt trucking game, first used by Morton Deutsch and Robert Krauss (1960). In this game, each participant is assigned the role of manager of a trucking company—either Acme or Bolt—that is trying to deliver some goods in opposite directions along the set of highways shown in Figure 14-3. While most of the roadways have two lanes, the most direct route includes a stretch of one-lane highway that can only be used by one truck at a time. Subjects are told that when the merchandise is delivered, each company will receive payment of $.60; but they are also required to deduct operating expenses at the rate of $.01 per second. Hence, the shorter the trip, the greater the profit—and if the trip takes *too* long, they can actually end up losing money.

The shortest, and only profitable, route is the one-lane road shared by the two companies, and therefore it is the natural choice to take initially. However, since it is a one-lane road, only one company can use it at a time. If the two trucks meet head-on, it is necessary for one to back up and allow the other to pass first. If this is done, both companies can make money, although one would do better than the other.

BOX 14-1 SPOTLIGHT ON METHODOLOGY

THE DILEMMA OF THE COMMONS

What do the following situations have in common?

- Overuse of energy resources
- Near extinction of the whale
- World overpopulation
- Air pollution
- Depletion of fresh drinking water

While each of these situations represents a very real social problem, they are also indicative of a phenomenon known as the "Dilemma of the Commons." The **Commons Dilemma** is a situation in which each person, using a finite resource, can choose to cooperate and have less personal use of the resource or choose not to cooperate and have greater personal use of the resource. The catch is that if enough people choose not to cooperate, the resource will eventually be depleted—and everyone will suffer.

The Commons Dilemma was first used in reference to the commons found in New England villages in the eighteenth century. The general practice was to put aside a certain area that was commonly owned for residents to graze their cattle. The system worked fine if individuals limited the number of cattle they grazed. And even if one or two people grazed a few more than usual, the commons could

generally continue to serve the needs of the town. Problems arose, however, when more than a few people decided to augment their personal gain by increasing the number of cattle grazing. At that point, the system came crashing down; the vegetation died out from overuse, and eventually all the cattle starved to death.

In essence, the Commons Dilemma is that short-term personal gains result in long-term disaster. In fact, this dilemma is similar to that facing a person playing a Prisoner's Dilemma game, and over the last few years the use of scenarios involving the Commons Dilemma has come to be the paradigm that is employed most frequently to study the issues that were formerly investigated with Prisoner's Dilemma games. The Commons Dilemma has several advantages over other types of games. It seems to be somewhat more realistic, since it can involve more than two participants. There are also more strategies, more possibilities for communication during the game, and more possible outcomes. Finally, given the nature of important social problems that can be investigated with the Commons Dilemma—such as energy resources, overpopulation, and pollution—the games result in more involvement on the part of players (Edney & Harper, 1978).

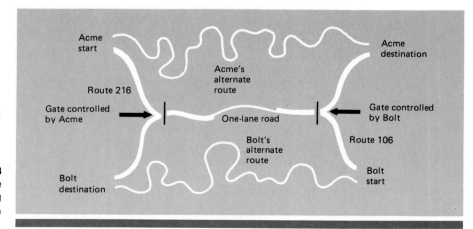

FIGURE 14-3
Road map used in the Acme–Bolt trucking game. Source: Deutsch & Krauss (1960).

472

But if they cooperate and take turns using the road, in the end each side will end up making similar profits.

To study the effects of having weapons and threats on cooperation, a variant of the game was devised. Acme was given a gate that it could use on the one-lane road which could block Bolt's passage. In this unilateral threat condition, Acme could stop Bolt from ever using the one-lane road. In still another variant, there was an opportunity for bilateral threat; *both* companies were allowed to use a gate blocking the one-lane road.

To Deutsch and Krauss, the question of greatest interest was the degree to which allowing the use of threat would affect the winnings of each player. The results were clear. In the no-threat condition, both companies ended up earning about $1 over the course of twenty trials. But in both the unilateral and bilateral threat conditions, *both* companies lost money. When Acme had the opportunity to block Bolt, its losses were a little over $1, while Bolt lost close to $3. And when they both had gates, they each lost relatively large amounts, well over $4 each. In sum, the results were clear in indicating that threat worked to neither party's advantage; whether just one or both companies had the capability of employing a "weapon," both were less successful than they would have been without the opportunity to use that weapon. These results are congruent with work using Prisoner's Dilemma situations.

Other research looking into cooperation and competition has built upon this early work of Deutsch and Krauss (1960). For instance, in one variation, the degree of conflict between Acme and Bolt was manipulated by varying the percentage of the most direct route that the one-lane road covered, making it 20 percent, 50 percent, or 90 percent (Deutsch, Canavan, & Rubin, 1971). It was hypothesized that the greater the proportion of one-lane highway, the greater the conflict between the two participants would be, and the experimental results bore out this reasoning. More threats were made and the gates were used more frequently when the one-lane road was proportionately larger than when it was relatively shorter.

It is tempting to generalize beyond the experimental work of Deutsch and his colleagues to real-world conflict, in which the availability of threats and weapons is high and the potential degree of conflict seems almost limitless. Still, such generalizations must be made cautiously, given that the experimental results were obtained under conditions in which the stakes for the players themselves were relatively small (Gallo, 1966). It is one thing to lose a few imaginary dollars in a trucking game experiment and quite another to suffer the consequences of full-scale war due to one's failure to cooperate with an opponent.

But there is a consistency in the results of experiments investigating threat: the greater the opportunity to threaten using weapons, the more likely it is that the degree of cooperation between two parties will decline (Deutsch, 1973). Moreover, even when cooperation is clearly the most rational choice, people will frequently choose to compete with

U.S. President Jimmy Carter and Soviet leader Leonid Brezhnev square off at the start of the negotiations of the SALT II talks. (UPI/Bettmann)

one another. One explanation for displays of competitiveness comes from a recent study by Riskind and Wilson (1982), who hypothesize that competitiveness may have interpersonal advantages. In their research, a group of subjects were given information leading them to believe that a person was either high or low in competitiveness. In subsequent ratings of that person, competitive individuals were liked more and seen as generally more attractive than those who were presented as uncompetitive. It seems that, at least in Western society, cultural norms favor competitive behavior.

THE BARGAINING PROCESS

Most of us can probably envision the following conversation:

Used-car dealer: Now here's a real beauty. Only 92,000 miles, in great condition, and a steal at $1150.

Potential purchaser: But look at the blue smoke that comes out of the exhaust when you turn it on. And all those dents in the fender make it look awful. I'll give you $500.

Used-car dealer: I'd be killing myself to take that. But look, I want to move this off my lot because I'm getting in some new ones tomorrow. Write me a check for $950 right now, and you can drive home.

Potential purchaser: Make it $900 and it's a deal.

Used-car dealer: OK—it's a deal.

Similar types of situations occur constantly in everyday life, on the level of both whether the United States and the Soviet Union can agree to arms limitations talks and whether a husband or wife should take out the garbage. Despite the differences in the level of importance of such interchanges, they share a number of common elements found in all bargaining situations. Bargaining typically involves two major parties; it is possible that the parties will reach an agreement in which each party will be better off—or at least no worse off—than if no agreement had been reached; there is more than one agreement that can be reached; and each party has conflicting preferences regarding the agreement (Deutsch, 1960; C. E. Miller & Crandall, 1980).

Social psychologists have approached the topic of bargaining by breaking it down to its bare essentials in the laboratory. In the typical experiment in bargaining, two people are presented with a scenario, such as the one we presented earlier, in which one will act as the seller and the other the buyer of a used car. Next, they are given a set of possible outcomes for themselves and their partner, depending on the nature of the agreement they reach. In some cases, they may actually be given money based on their agreement. The experiment involves exchanging offers back and forth until an agreement is reached.

As you can see, there are many possible variables that can be manipulated within this situation: the kinds of bargains that are allowed, the nature of the outcomes, the kinds of communication possible, and so forth. Indeed, the ease with which these factors can be varied has made bargaining a very popular area within social psychology, with literally thousands of studies being conducted that employ bargaining paradigms. Much of this research has been directed toward identifying the factors that underlie successful negotiations, in which both parties end bargaining feeling that they concluded the best deal possible. Other work has taken a different tack, examining the strategies that one party can use to make the optimum deal for his or her own benefit (e.g., Greenhalgh, Gilkey, & Scott, 1983). We will discuss some of the major factors relating to bargaining success by considering work that has been directed toward determining how various types of outcome or payoff combinations affect bargaining.

The Payoff: Maximizing Profits and Minimizing Losses

Because each person in a bargaining situation will be motivated to maximize his or her profits—a basic assumption underlying bargaining research—the range of the profits permitted typically has an important effect on how the bargainers interact with one another. There are basically two kinds of situations with respect to payoffs: **zero-sum,** in which a gain to one person is a loss to the other, and **variable-sum,** in which both parties may benefit (or lose) from a bargain that is struck. In an example of a zero-sum situation, when the car seller raises his price by $100, he gains that money ($+100$), while the buyer loses it (-100). The

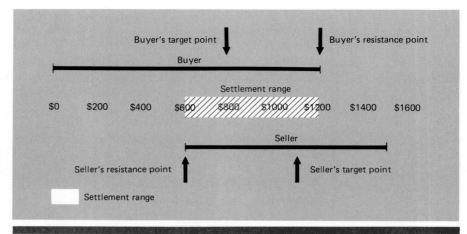

FIGURE 14-4
Settlement range of buyer
and seller of used car.
Note that the range of a
possible agreement (the
settlement range) is ac-
tually fairly large.

term "zero-sum" comes from the fact that the two figures, when added
together, always equal zero (in our example, $+\$100 + (-\$100) = 0$). In
an example of a variable-sum situation, two people might agree to buy
and share textbooks jointly for a semester; in this bargain, each person
gains. Similarly, arms negotiation pacts that are effective tend to operate
as variable-sum situations; as Paul Warnke pointed out, successful arms
reduction agreements are made when both sides feel they have gained
something by coming to an agreement.

It is assumed that typical bargaining situations have a range of possible agreement values which are preferable to no settlement. Thus, in
the example of a car buyer and seller, there is a range, known as the
settlement range, along which buyer and seller potentially can agree
(see Figure 14-4). At some point in the range, the buyer will be more
pleased than the seller with the outcome; at other points, the opposite
will hold. The point beyond which a party is not prepared to move is
known as the **resistance point,** which is the worst deal to which the
bargainer is willing to agree. People involved in negotiations also have
a sense of what they expect to end up with; this point is known as the
target point.

Learning what an opponent's resistance and target points are can have
a crucial effect upon the success of a negotiation from the point of view
of the individual possessing the information. For example, if the car
dealer knows that the potential buyer is willing to spend as much as
$1200, he is unlikely to be very forthcoming in terms of reducing the
price beyond his initial price of $1500. On the other hand, if the poten-
tial buyer knows that the salesperson is willing to go as low as $600
(the seller's resistance point), he is unlikely to accept a price much
higher than that.

Because information regarding an opponent's resistance point is so
crucial, both parties in a negotiation are apt to try to infer them from

the opponent, using the opponent's initial offer and later concessions to determine the true resistance point. At the same time, the opponent is attempting both to hide his or her own resistance point and to try to infer the partner's point. And bargaining situations hold even more complications than these; monetary outcome is just one dimension upon which negotiation rests. Bargainers may also be concerned with presenting themselves well, with concluding a negotiation within a given time period (e.g., the buyer needs a car to get to work the next day), and with a host of other factors. Nonetheless, focusing upon the numeric payoffs of the two parties has led to a well-substantiated, fairly consistent set of findings regarding bargaining, and a number of generalizations about effective bargaining strategies can be made.

The Initial Offer: Make It Extreme

In most cases, the strategy of making an extreme initial offer appears to pay off well in the end, compared with situations in which more moderate offers are made initially (Hamner & Yukl, 1977; Yukl, 1974). The reason for this seems to be that the initial offer is used by the opponent as an indication of the offerer's resistance and target points which, due to the extremity of the offer, may be perceived as being more extreme than is actually the case. In turn, this may modify the opponent's target point in a direction more favorable to the person who made the initial offer.

Another reason high initial demands are apt to lead to better final settlements is that the later demands made by an individual are apt to be perceived as being relatively generous—at least in terms of the extremity of the initial offer. Moreover, an extreme initial offer allows an individual to make more concessions during later negotiations. Because the norm of reciprocity (which we discussed in Chapter 7 in terms of helping behavior) suggests that opponents may try to reciprocate concessions, it is possible that the opponent will be more forthcoming during later bargaining (Cialdini, Vincent, Lewis, Catalan, Wheeler, & Darby, 1975).

In a field demonstration of the importance of initial extremity in bargaining, Cialdini, Bickman, and Cacioppo (1979) visited a Chevrolet dealer to ask the price of a Monte Carlo. In one condition, they first asked the price of *another* car and then rejected it, saying the price was too high. But in another condition, they did not first strike a tougher stance; instead, they simply asked the price of the Monte Carlo initially. In this weaker condition, the prices they were quoted were some $200 higher on an average than the prices quoted when they had appeared more aggressive initially.

On the other hand, an extreme initial offer does not always affect the eventual outcome of the bargaining (Benton, Kelley, & Liebling, 1972). When bargainers are aware through direct knowledge of, or are highly confident of their influence on the resistance and target points of their opponent, an opponent's extreme initial offer will have little or no effect on the eventual outcome of the negotiations. Indeed, there might well be a boomerang effect, in which the opponent responds with a very extreme bargaining line, leading ultimately to a lack of settlement or a breakdown in negotiations. Moreover, extreme offers, if they are too extreme, may be taken as a sign that the bargainer is not negotiating seriously, again preventing any sort of settlement from being negotiated.

Producing Concessions

Just as research has suggested ways of making concessions that are most apt to produce a favorable settlement, there is also work on ways of producing concessions from one's opponent. Pruitt (1981) has outlined a number of techniques, including the imposition of time pressures on one's opponent, increasing the opponent's perception of one's firmness, producing a reduction in the opponent's resistance to making concessions, and improving the opponent's mood or strengthening the social relationship with the other. We will discuss each in turn.

Imposing Time Pressures   When the Soviet Union and the United States confronted each other during one of the periodic crises over Berlin, one of the threats that the Soviet premier, Nikita Khruschev, made was that the Soviet Union would sign a separate peace treaty with East Germany after six months unless the United States capitulated on a number of key demands. Although the deadline was removed by the Soviet Union relatively soon after it was made, it had the desired effect of demonstrating the seriousness of the situation to the United States.

As this example illustrates, one technique for producing concessions is to impose a deadline beyond which one will either refuse to negotiate or will carry out some undesirable action, such as—with an economic transaction—turning to an alternate supplier or, in the field of labor relations, calling a strike. In a higher stakes situation, opponents might threaten to attack the adversary if agreement is not reached within a certain time frame (G. H. Snyder & Diesing, 1977).

The difficulty with using threats of time deadlines is that in order to be credible they must be carried out. This means that if a deadline is imposed upon an opponent, it is possible that negotiations will have to be broken off when the deadline comes up even if continuation is desired by the party making the threat.

Looking Tough: Increasing the Perception of Firmness   Another tactic that is apt to produce favorable settlements is increasing one's appearance of firmness. As we have already mentioned, one technique that is generally successful is to begin with relatively extreme demands. But whether an initial offer is extreme or moderate, it is unlikely to be acceptable to one's opponent. The next question that arises, then, is

Purchasing a used car
can involve a compli-
cated round of negotia-
tions. (Sam Pierson Jr./
Photo Researchers)

how to move from the initial offer into the settlement zone in which an acceptable compromise can be reached. In order to do this, it is necessary for each partner to make concessions from their initial position.

The strategy that seems to be most effective in producing favorable final offers for a bargain is one in which the concessions made are relatively small in size and few in number (Komorita & Brenner, 1968; Yukl, 1973). It is also helpful to make concessions on the basis of reciprocal concessions made by one's opponent, rather than conceding unilaterally. Finally, it is useful to explain and justify the reasons behind each concession to an opponent. For example, the car salesman in our earlier example justified his lowering the price because he was getting some new cars in the next day and needed more space on his lot.

Jervis (1970) suggests that concessions made by a bargainer should be *decoupled* from the notion that they are a sign of weakness and that future concessions are apt to be made. He suggests three specific strategies for decoupling. First, bargainers can explicitly deny that a concession will be repeated (I'll do it this once, but I can't go down in price another penny"). Second, they can try to show that a concession is a result of some unique circumstance (I'll lower my price since I have so many new cars coming onto the lot tomorrow that I need the space"). Finally, a concession can be coupled with a move that contradicts the perception of weakening in a bargaining position. (For instance, "I'll lower my price, but I won't be able to give you a warranty.") In each of these cases, concessions are paired with other actions that suggest that they should not be taken as a sign of weakening in the bargainer's position.

While the strategies of making just small concessions, or concessions that are coupled with actions that strengthen one's position, suggest a rather tough bargaining stance, once again we find that negotiating behavior that is *too* extreme (i.e., granting very small concessions) will not be effective in producing reciprocal concessions from opponents (G. Yukl, 1974). Moreover, if bargainers are aware of their opponents' resistance and target points, the favorability of the final settlement is unaffected by the size of the concessions made.

Reducing the Opponent's Resistance to Making Concessions   Another approach to producing favorable settlements involves modification of an opponent's resistance and target points. When using such an approach, the basic aim is to reduce the opponent's resistance to making concessions.

Perhaps the most successful form of producing concessions is to provide persuasive arguments for why a concession should, on logical grounds, be made. Thus, a buyer of a used car who says that the price should be lowered because of the money he will have to spend on repairs might convince the salesman enough to lower the price. Likewise, many countries have argued that increases in U.S. military aid are necessary to avoid a Communist takeover. The factors that we discussed in relation to attitude change in Chapter 4—such as the use of one-sided rather than two-sided arguments and appeals to fear—are applicable here.

Explicit threats are another means by which bargainers can reduce the resistance of their opponents (Pruitt, 1981). Threats inform opponents that there will be retaliation or punishment if they do not concede—and implicitly suggest that punishment will *not* occur if the concession is made. One of the best examples of the use of high-stakes threats was President John Kennedy's threat to prevent any Soviet ship from reaching Cuba during the Cuban missile crisis.

As with many of the other tactics we have discussed, too strong a threat may produce resistance rather than compliance. There are, however, ways in which resistance to threats can be reduced. It might be possible to suggest that the source of the threat is not under the control of the bargainer. For example, a union negotiator might suggest that a strike threat must be made in order to placate the union members he represents, and that he personally would rather not make the threat. Likewise, threats may be couched as warnings; rather than *committing* oneself to an action if a concession is made, one could *predict* that the action would have to be carried out if certain concessions were not made (G. H. Snyder & Diesing, 1977). In one example of this, Robert Kennedy labeled the demand that Cuba renounce Russian missiles during the Cuban missile crisis as a "statement of fact" rather than an "ultimatum." Rather than coming across as a direct threat, it was communicated indirectly.

The opposite side of the coin from using threats is promising some reward for conceding. Thus, the car salesman who promises to throw in a new seat cover if his price is accepted is using reward as a tactic. Likewise, legislators often promise to support colleagues' bills in order to get votes for their own projects. Of course, implicit in many promises is the hint of threat; if a legislator fails to support a bill, instead of voting for that legislator's measure later (the promised reward), a colleague may vote against it (a punishment). Whether an anticipated action is perceived as a reward or a punishment depends primarily on how the recipient perceives the statement (Pruitt, 1981). If recipients see compliance as resulting in a loss to themselves, it is viewed as a threat; if compliance is viewed as bringing about a gain, it will be perceived as a promise.

Compliance to a request may vary significantly according to whether it is perceived as a threat or a promise. In an interesting laboratory experiment, J. Z. Rubin and Lewicki (1973) presented subjects with a request that was worded one of eight different ways, and asked them to presume the degree of compliance that would be elicited by each request. Different types of threats produced significant variations in level of compliance. For example, threats that compelled the opponent to do something ("If you do not agree to work on my topic, I will not write up the report") were viewed as less persuasive than threats in which the partner was asked not to do something ("If you insist on working on your topic, I will not write up the report"). Considerably greater compliance was predicted when the statement was worded as a promise ("If you do not insist on working on your topic, I will write up the final report").

The finding that promises were seen as more effective in eliciting compliance than threats is congruent with the work on power that we discussed in Chapter 10. There, you will recall, it was clear that power tactics based on reward typically resulted in higher compliance than power tactics based on coercion.

Modifying the Social Relationship between Bargainers   A final set of tactics suggested by Pruitt (1981) for bargaining successfully concerns changing the nature of the social relationship that exists between the bargainers. Rather than dealing with the specific issues, such tactics suggest that a bargainer should try to promote a friendly atmosphere and a good mood during bargaining. Just as the research on the effects of moods on helping behavior indicates (see Chapter 7), placing an opponent in a more positive mood during negotiations ought to produce higher levels of helpfulness—presumably indicated by a greater willingness to make concessions.

Of course, if the bargainer appears to be *too* friendly and the opponent perceives it as an attempt at ingratiation or some devious impression management technique, the tactic may backfire. Thus, as with the other tactics for successful bargaining that we have been discussing, their employment must not be too heavy-handed.

Coalition Formation and Bargaining

Up to now, we have been viewing bargaining as a one-to-one enterprise in which two people get together to work out their differences. In the real world, situations are frequently not quite as simple, since issues are often decided by many interested parties (see Box 14-2). Indeed, this is one of the difficulties that has kept the Middle East in turmoil for the last fifty years. Rather than an Israeli–Arab conflict, as the situation is commonly referred to, it consists of the problems of Israel, Egypt, Lebanon, Syria, Jordan, Saudi Arabia, and at least ten other separate countries—plus the Palestine Liberation Organization. Each of these parties has its own interests and motives, and a peaceful solution to Middle East problems requires that each be satisfied to some degree.

To study multiparty bargaining, investigators have turned to experimental game situations, in which a group of individuals is given a goal and each person is given a limited set of resources through which the goal can potentially be obtained. The question that has been researched most often is how **coalitions** are formed among the members. Coalitions consist of people who join together to achieve common objectives against competing parties. Such coalitions increase the probability that its members will achieve the goal and decrease the likelihood that the remaining parties will be successful.

Coalitions may be formed in a variety of situations. For example, in the mideast, a number of countries could form an alliance that would provide them with an advantage over the remaining, unorganized countries. Or a number of small businesses could band together in order to win a major contract from another firm—something they could not have done if they had acted independently. In each of these situations, the critical defining characteristic is that they involve three or more parties, two or more of whom agree to use their resources jointly in an attempt to influence the outcome (Gamson, 1964). At least four major theories have been used to account for coalition formation: minimum resource theory, minimum power theory, weighted probability theory, and bargaining theory.

Minimum Resource Theory: Strength through Weakness Consider the simplest conditions under which a coalition might form: three people with different resources and rules for winning such that no person can win alone. Given this situation, the questions are how two of the people will join together to form a winning coalition and how the winnings will be distributed between the two winning coalition members.

According to *minimum resource theory,* a coalition will form in which the total resources brought to the coalition are as small as possible—but are sufficient to allow the two members joining the coalition to win (Gamson, 1964). A concrete example illustrates this. Suppose the resources in a game are distributed so that Al has two chips, Bill has three chips, and Cassandra has four chips. A total of at least five chips is

BOX 14-2 SPOTLIGHT ON RESEARCH

USING THIRD-PARTY INTERVENTION TO REDUCE CONFLICT

When Henry Kissinger employed his famous "shuttle diplomacy" during the Israeli–Arab conflict, flying back and forth between the various capitals of the involved countries, he was engaging in a form of conflict resolution known as third-party intervention. Third-party intervention differs from the phenomenon of bargaining and negotiating that we have been discussing up to now in that it involves not just the interested parties directly associated with a dispute, but a third party who intervenes to help identify the important issues or to attempt to resolve the conflict (McGillicuddy, Van Slyck, & Pruitt, 1984).

Jeffrey Rubin (1980), who has investigated the use of third-party intervention in both laboratory studies and historical analyses, has put forward three major propositions to explain the circumstances under which third parties can effect conflict resolution.

First, third parties allow the involved parties to make concessions without losing face. Concessions that one would be reluctant to make directly to an adversary, because they could be construed as a sign of weakness, may be made at the request of the third party. Because a fundamental quality of bargaining is that it involves compromise, third parties who facilitate concession making can thereby aid the cause of the negotiations.

A second generalization that can be made about third-party intervention is that techniques that are effective when conflicts are relatively mild may not only be ineffective at higher intensities of conflict, but may actually make things worse. For example, some of the approaches that typically make third parties effective in mild conflicts—such as introducing communication between the parties and identifying, defining, and sharpening issues on which the parties agree and disagree—may lead the participants to feel that they are further apart than before the intervention of the third party if the disagreements between them are particularly strong. It is as if the third party makes the disagreements that do exist more salient under conditions of strong conflict.

A final generalization that Rubin draws is that the parties directly involved in a conflict often see third-party intervention in a negative light; frequently, they would prefer to resolve their differences themselves than have a third party injected into the dispute. Interestingly, though, resistance of disputants to third-party intervention may actually have a desirable consequence; the two sides may try more diligently to resolve their differences on their own, thereby making at least the *threat* of third-party intervention ultimately effective. Third parties, then, are often effective in increasing disputants' motivation to reach an equitable agreement and for this reason alone may be helpful in conflict resolution.

---

needed to win. Hence, no one can win alone. Potentially, any combination of two would work: Al and Bill, Bill and Cassandra, or Al and Cassandra. But what happens is that Al and Bill (the two weaker parties) are most apt to form a coalition.

The reason, according to minimum resource theory, is that the participants implicitly follow a norm of equity which assumes that outcomes should be proportional to inputs. By joining up with a weaker partner, participants assume that their outcome will be larger than if they had joined with a more powerful ally. Hence, if I am Bill, with three chips, I have my choice of forming a coalition with Al (two chips) or Cassandra (four chips). If I join with Cassandra, who has greater resources or inputs than I do, I am likely to assume that her share of the joint outcomes we win will be greater than my share—since she has brought more re-sources. On the other hand, if I join with the weaker Al, I can expect to end up with a proportionally larger share of the winnings.

Following this reasoning, the coalitions that are most apt to form are among the bargainers who have the weakest resources—but who, when joining together, can profit most from their coalition formation. In some cases, then, it seems that there is strength through weakness, at least in terms of coalition formation.

Minimum Power Theory Rather than focusing on the *amount* of each bargainer's resources, as does minimum resource theory, minimum power theory concentrates on the *number* of coalitions an individual's resources can change from a losing one to a winning one (Gamson, 1964). The greater the number of winning coalitions that can be formed with a player's resources, the greater the power of that person. This power is not based on the amount of a player's resources, but on the number of times that the use of the resources produces a winning combination.

According to **minimum power theory,** participants in a bargaining situation will tend to divide rewards on the basis of power, on the assumption that more powerful players deserve a greater proportion of the rewards. This outlook implies that one would seek out coalition partners with minimal power in order to maximize one's own rewards. As with minimum resource theory, this theory suggests that weakness will result in strength. But there is a crucial difference. If we look at our earlier example of Al (with two chips), Bill (with three), and Cassandra (with four), all three have the same amount of power because each person is equally able to bring about a victory by joining with any other person. Hence, this theory predicts that all three combinations of two are equally likely to occur and—since all three have the same amount of power—in any coalition that forms, the resources are likely to be divided equally.

Weighted Probability Theory The third theory of coalition formation that we shall mention is known as **weighted probability theory** (Komorita, 1974). Not only does this theory attempt to predict which coalition is most likely to emerge—as do minimum resource and minimum power theories—but it also tries to provide the exact probabilities of occurrence for every coalition that could possibly be formed (C. E. Miller & Crandall, 1980). The details of the theory are mathematically sophisticated. In general, the theory determines the number of possible winning minimal coalitions that can be formed and the number of members of each winning coalition. Each of these winning coalitions is then assigned a probability of occurrence, and the likelihood of a given coalition being formed is determined.

Bargaining Theory The final and most complicated of the four proposed theories explaining coalition formation is bargaining theory (Komorita & Chertkoff, 1973). Once again, the details are complex, but the basic principles can be explained fairly simply. **Bargaining theory** suggests that individuals in bargaining situations initially estimate the payoff they would receive in a given coalition if the payoff were to be divided according to an equity norm (the resources they bring to the coalition) as well as to an equality norm (divided equally, regardless of an individual's initial resources). The theory then suggests that the estimated payoff for a given coalition is halfway between these two initial estimates, and the person will prefer to join the coalition that promises the highest expected payoff.

Since all members are going through the same process, this theory predicts that the coalition which eventually forms will be the one that allows each member to obtain his or her respective maximum expected payoff. The theory also predicts that during extended gaming situations, the nature of the coalitions will vary as the individuals have an opportunity to offer concessions and are more willing to be part of coalitions that they might not otherwise have found acceptable.

Evaluating the Theories: Choosing the Situation with Care When we evaluate the theories, no one theory stands out; some theories provide precise predictions in certain settings and experimental tests, and some are superior in others. Generalizations can be made, however, which point to the conditions under which the processes underlying each theory would be demonstrated (C. E. Miller & Crandall, 1980):

- When there is a great deal of conflict over something of great value, communication possibilities are low, and the norm of equity is particularly salient, minimum resource theory would provide a particularly accurate assessment.
- When it is so important to win something that the exact amount of the winnings is unimportant, equity norms are likely to fall by the wayside. Under these conditions, minimum power theory is apt to allow particularly effective prediction.
- If the overall size of a group is relatively large, weighted probability theory provides better predictions than either the minimum resource or the minimum power theory.
- When norms of equity *and* equality are particularly salient and bargaining continues over many trials, bargaining theory provides a fairly accurate assessment.

Can a general statement about which theory is most accurate by made? Miller and Crandall (1980) suggest that, all other things being equal, bargaining theory "does a better job than any of the other three theories in predicting both how the payoff will be divided and which coalition will form" (p. 361). Still, even though this assessment appears unequivocal, we should remember that it is based upon the results of laboratory game situations, many employing such tasks as playing a board game like Parcheesi or Risk. As always, we must consider the nature and limitations of the evidence before applying the findings in everyday contexts—although analyses of actual instances of coalition formation (such as coalitions that arise after elections in European parliaments) show fairly good convergence with laboratory findings (Jackson, 1984).

Bargaining in Perspective

The view of bargaining that has been presented here has emphasized the competitive nature of the activity. This has been done in recognition of the fact that the most crucial sorts of bargaining being done today—such as those carried out by Paul Warnke involving arms negotiations—have typically been performed with little spirit of cooperation, but instead with a deep sense of mutual distrust. It should be noted, however, that bargaining need not be an unrelenting competitive struggle. Negotiations in which each party acts cooperatively, in a spirit of mutual gain, may bring about the most effective and ultimately most satisfying negotiations. Social psychologists need to address ways in which such norms of cooperation can be encouraged.

APPLICATIONS OF BARGAINING IN THE WORLD ARENA

While the results of laboratory studies are able to provide us with clear generalizations—as well as myriad examples of the difficulties in negotiating rational, equitable settlements—the limitations of such research are particularly important to note. In most laboratory studies, the individuals represent only themselves and not a larger group, as they would in union–management negotiations or in international bargaining. Thus, there is no constituency to answer to in individual negotiation studies, and bargainers are free to make deals on the basis of what they perceive as their own personal interests.

When bargainers are acting as representatives of an organization or country, there is often tangible pressure to produce a favorable settlement—or run the risk of losing one's job (Blake & Mouton, 1961, 1979). For example, a union leader who is seen as being too "soft" toward management is likely to be replaced with someone who appears to be tougher. A similar instance was President Reagan's 1983 firing of a member of the U.S. Nuclear Disarmament Commission for reportedly being too yielding to the Soviet Union during arms negotiations.

The fact that international negotiations take place under public scrutiny can also bring pressures on bargainers that are absent from more private negotiations. Research has shown that negotiators want to pre-

Union negotiators must be responsive to the desires and demands of their fellow union members and must bargain with these views in mind. (Hazel Hankin)

sent themselves publicly as strong and competent, and that they feel the way to do this is to take a firm and relatively unyielding position— at least in public (B. R. Brown, 1968; Breaugh & Klimoski, 1981). Because of these social pressures, negotiators may be less efficient in producing a bargain than they would be if they were free of public scrutiny. Moreover, the one-sided perceptions about the opposing side that negotiators (as well as the general public) may have are going to influence the course of negotiations (see Box 14-3).

Another difficulty inherent in real-world negotiation that is typically absent from laboratory analogues is the need for a considerable degree of communication between negotiators and the parties they represent. For example, as Paul Warnke mentioned in his interview, one frustration in the SALT treaty negotiations was the Soviet negotiators' need to check out points with their government at home frequently which kept the negotiations moving at a snail's pace. Thus, if negotiators are not empowered to make decisions of their own, the ultimate shape of an agreement may not be the same and the negotiations will certainly require more time.

Social Psychological Approaches to Arms Reduction

Probably no social issue was of greater prominence in the United States in the early 1980s than that of nuclear arms control. Most proponents suggested the implementation of a nuclear freeze, in which the world's political superpowers would pledge to build no new nuclear weapons— which already existed in sufficient quantities to destroy the world many times over. After the freeze took hold, advocates reasoned, the superpowers would be able to hold arms reduction talks to decrease the size of their nuclear arsenals.

BOX 14-3 SPOTLIGHT ON APPLICATIONS

MISPERCEPTIONS IN INTERNATIONAL RELATIONS

Russians want war and Americans want peace. The Arabs want war and the Israelis want peace. The North Vietnamese wanted war and the South Vietnamese wanted peace. Right?

You are probably thinking that such broad generalizations are at best inaccurate and more likely meaningless and deceptive—and of course you are correct. But views such as these continue to dominate the thinking of many people as they look at the world situation. In a trenchant analysis of a number of international crises that eventually led to war, Ralph White (1966, 1970, 1977) has shown that several common elements of a social psychological nature are related to misperceptions and misattributions of the enemy and its behavior. For example, he cites the following distortions experienced by many Americans that may have affected decisions regarding American entry into the war in Vietnam:

- *An image of the enemy as diabolical.* Americans viewed the Vietcong as an inscrutable, deceptive people who were capable of horrible atrocities and fiendish aggression.
- *A virile self-image.* Americans saw themselves and their military policy as determined, correct, and strong.
- *Military overconfidence.* Having never "lost" a war, Americans believed they could win any confrontation in which they participated. It always seemed that just one more battle would be the one to bring a final victory.

- *Lack of empathy.* There was no clear understanding of what the enemy felt, how it perceived the situation, or even why it was fighting.
- *Selective inattention.* The United States consistently ignored facts and events that might have changed its position or understanding of the war. For instance, the widespread corruption of the South Vietnamese government and its undemocratic policies were ignored because it was on "our" side.
- *A moral self-image.* The United States viewed itself not only as militarily superior but morally superior as well.

Such misperceptions are characteristic of a number of wars that White has analyzed. And such misperceptions of enemies are not limited to the United States; it is likely a similar analysis could be carried out from the perspective of the Vietcong.

While misperceptions do not necessarily *cause* war, they may lead to an escalation of aggression and fighting far beyond what an objective view of a situation would bring about. And since it would not be unreasonable to expect that negotiators—charged with reaching settlements with an enemy—might share the same sort of misperceptions of the enemy, such stereotypic thinking would be bound to complicate, and perhaps even derail, negotiations that might otherwise prevent or end hostilities.

The notion of a weapons "freeze" runs counter to the strategy of **deterrence** that the superpowers traditionally have employed, as alluded to by Paul Warnke. Deterrence is the notion that threats of large-scale retaliation against an enemy attacker are the most effective means of preventing the attack in the first place. According to this view, the most suitable means of defense is through arms *increases* in order to ensure that retaliation against an attack would be so great that the attacking country would not survive (Morgan, 1977).

Does deterrence work? The question is difficult to answer, given the impossibility of doing controlled, experimental research in a highly complex field situation. Moreover, what is being examined in such research is the behavior of abstract entities—countries—which are, in reality, made up of the behaviors of many individuals. Finally, it is difficult to re-create retrospectively the base of knowledge from which the decision makers were working.

Despite these difficulties, careful analyses of historical instances of deterrence suggest that it has not been terribly effective in preventing military conflict. For example, an analysis that considered 2000 years of history found that countries that used a military buildup as a means of preventing war were more likely to become involved in wars than countries that were not so prepared (Naroll, Bullough, & Naroll, 1974). Moreover, it seems that the ready availability of weapons brought about by an arms race can lead policy makers to incorporate military action into their options when confronted with crises considerably more readily than if so many arms were not available.

In sum, the presence of an arms buildup can act as a self-fulfilling prophecy: a country may expect to need arms to resolve international crises and, to meet this expected need, produce and stockpile huge quantities of arms. Later, the presence of the arms results in the perception that arms are a viable option for resolving foreign policy disputes. Ultimately, this perception increases the probability that the arms will be used, until at some point the arms are actually employed. Hence, the initial expectation that arms may be necessary results in their being used.

Raising the Stakes: The Arms Race   Another aspect of the use of deterrence and threat is the need for each side in a conflict to increase the size of its threat continually in response to the arms buildup of the other side. In order to pose a credible threat, a country's arsenal must be at least as effective as—and, in fact, somewhat *more* effective than—that of its enemy. Each time a new weapon is developed, the opponent must produce an even more powerful one in order to deter the use of the first. In sum, the stakes keep being raised.

Both politicians—of varying political beliefs—and social scientists have suggested a number of strategies for reducing arms buildups. One technique that theoretically might be employed is **unilateral disarmament,** in which one country determines that it simply will no longer participate in the arms buildup and will reduce the size of its existing arsenal. For example, the United States might announce that, given its present capability to destroy the Soviet Union many times over, it would destroy a certain number of weapons and no longer produce new ones. It would be hoped that the Soviet Union would follow suit, but the disarmament would not be contingent upon expected responses.

For practical reasons, the strategy of unilateral disarmament is unlikely. Most political leaders would find it impossible to put their country in a position in which it appeared to be weakening its strength relative to another power. Moreover, there is a risk inherent in unilateral

Social psychological re-
search has suggested a
number of strategies for
limiting the arms race.
(David Burnett/Contact)

disarmament in that an enemy would perceive the country that is dis-
arming as being particularly vulnerable to attack and the very act of
unilateral disarmament might make an enemy feel less inhibited to act
aggressively. Finally, laboratory research suggests that strength in bargaining position is a factor in producing favorable settlements—which,
in this case, may be conceptualized as a containment of warfare.

Limiting the Arms Buildup with SALT   Another approach to limiting the
arms race is exemplified by the extensive negotiations held between
the United States and the Soviet Union in the late 1970s. Paul Warnke,
chief negotiator of the SALT talks, indicated in his comments that the
major goal of the SALT talks was to put a ceiling on the number of
certain classes of nuclear weapons. This is a much more modest goal, it
should be noted, than disarmament, in which there is an actual reduction
in arms. Despite the fact that the treaty was never ratified by the U.S.
Senate, both parties appear to be adhering to the basic tenets of the
agreement. The difficulty with SALT, however, is that it allows the
development of even more sophisticated weapons that do not fall under
the very specific and limited constraints of the treaty. Moreover, the
weapons themselves are highly complex, and it is almost impossible to
compare different weapons systems to determine whether reduction in
one system is equivalent to reduction in another (Granberg, 1978).

Limiting the Arms Buildup with GRIT   While SALT has proven to be an
initial step in the direction of arms control, it is a fairly limited approach.
An alternative and specific strategy for reducing the arms buildup has
been proposed by social psychologist Charles Osgood (1962, 1979). It

is called the **graduated and reciprocated initiative in tension reduction strategy,** or GRIT. Despite its formidable nomenclature, the idea behind it is really quite simple. According to the plan, one side in an international conflict announces—and then carries out—a unilateral but relatively minor reduction in armament, or makes some other small concession. The concession should be small enough not to leave the party vulnerable to attack, but it should be large enough to put pressure on the other side to make a concession of its own.

GRIT begins to take hold if the sequence is repeated, with each side making reciprocal concessions of its own in response to the other side's concessions. According to the procedure, each response is carefully thought out and should take place over a relatively lengthy period of time in order to avoid the appearance of pushing the other side too strongly. Giving the other side ample time also increases the likelihood of some sort of favorable response.

How effective is GRIT as a procedure for provoking concessions? The most unequivocal data come from research done in the laboratory. For example, in some studies subjects in Prisoner's Dilemma-type situations are told to use specific aspects of GRIT, such as announcing that they intend to act cooperatively or to make concessions (Lindskold, 1979). Most results confirm the efficacy of GRIT in producing more cooperation on the part of adversaries.

The more important question is whether or not GRIT can work outside the laboratory. Although the results cannot be as firm as those derived from more controlled situations, there is at least anecdotal support from a number of converging sources of evidence. First, simulations in which participants act out the role of negotiators of particular countries with certain levels of armament tend to reinforce the finding that GRIT is an effective strategy (Lindskold, 1979). Second, and more convincing, content analyses of actual historical confrontations show that strategies in which the countries involved reciprocate concessions—a crucial part of the GRIT procedure—were effective in preventing war (Leng & Wheeler, 1979).

Probably the best real-world example of the employment of GRIT is what has been called the "Kennedy experiment" (Etzioni, 1969). In a major speech on June 10, 1963, President John Kennedy announced that the United States was unilaterally going to stop testing nuclear weapons in the atmosphere. He said the tests would not be started again *unless* any other country began them first. He also suggested that American attitudes toward the Soviet Union should be reexamined and that Americans should do all that they could to try to get the Soviet Union to coexist in peace with the United States.

This speech marked the start of a series of reciprocal moves on the parts of the Soviet Union and the United States. The Soviet Union responded rapidly—and positively—to Kennedy's overture by praising his speech and by agreeing to an American request to allow observers from the United States to intercede in a war that was occurring in Yemen.

The United States responded to this move with a reciprocal easing of its foreign policy by giving full recognition to the Soviet-backed United Nations delegation from Hungary. Ultimately, reciprocation through a number of steps resulted in the Soviet Union's decision to end production of strategic bombers and in the signing of a limited nuclear test ban treaty.

The "experiment" ended prematurely with the assassination of President Kennedy, and the war in Vietnam clouded and ultimately prevented further reciprocal concessions on the part of both the United States and the Soviet Union. Still, it appears that the basic strategies of GRIT had brought about a successful reduction in tension and armament, at least for a limited period of time.

Could the United States implement a similar strategy based on GRIT today? Donald Granberg (1978) has outlined a hypothetical series of prescriptive steps that the United States could take to bring about a reduction in tensions. He suggests that the first step would be for the President to make a conciliatory speech—similar to the one Kennedy made in 1963—in which GRIT is explicitly described and a series of concrete unilateral measures are announced, such as a reduction in a certain type of missile or the decision to cancel production of a new weapon system. The President would then call for some specific measures to be taken by the Soviet Union. Another tactic might be to announce a phased withdrawal of troops from a sensitive area, such as Korea, in which each withdrawal is linked to a corresponding withdrawal by the other side. Whether or not systematic application of GRIT can lead to a long-term reduction in hostilities between the superpowers is an open question, but it is clearly worth speculating on, and potentially implementing, the process.

SUMMARY

Social exchange theory concerns interactions in which individuals exchange something, trade items, or divide a set of rewards. The theory views human interaction as a kind of joint economic activity in which each participant obtains certain rewards, but also accrues costs. Outcomes are calculated by subtracting costs from rewards and are measured against two comparison levels—one comparing components of other relationships and one comparing the best possible alternative available. If an outcome of a given relationship is lower than the comparison level for alternatives, a relationship will be terminated; but if the outcome is higher, the individual will remain in the relationship—even if, in absolute terms, the person is dissatisfied.

A payoff matrix represents the various alternative responses that an individual can make in a given situation, as well as those of the person with whom that individual is interacting. It shows the outcomes that each participant would receive if a given combination of choices was made by the participants. While payoff matrices suggest a simple method for representing social exchange, it is difficult to assign numerical values to costs and rewards that are social in nature—such as love, status, or information.

The Prisoner's Dilemma game has been used frequently to study bargaining behavior. There are three general types of motivational orientations that a player typically brings to the game: cooperative, competitive, and individualistic. Other approaches to bargaining have employed the Acme–Bolt trucking game, a classic situation devised by Deutsch and Krauss.

Bargaining typically involves two major parties; it is possible that the parties will reach an agreement in which neither will be better off—or at least not worse off—than if no agreement had been reached; there is more than one agreement that can be reached; and each party has conflicting preferences regarding the agreement. Basically, two kinds of situations exist in terms of payoffs: zero-sum, in which a gain to one person is a loss to the other, and variable-sum, in which both parties may benefit (or lose) from a bargain. In most situations there is also a settlement range—a range of possible agreement values which are preferable to no settlement. The point beyond which a party is not prepared to move is known as the resistance point, while the expectation of where the negotiations will be consummated is the target point.

Social psychological research has revealed a number of generalizations regarding effective bargaining strategies. Usually, for instance, it is best to make extreme initial offers. There are also a number of techniques that tend to produce concessions, including imposing time pressures, increasing the perception of firmness, making small and few concessions that are decoupled from the appearance that future concessions will be made, reducing the opponent's resistance to making concessions, and modifying the social relationship between bargainers.

Some research has examined how coalitions, or alliances between members of multiparty bargaining situations, are formed. Four theories have been used to account for coalition formation: minimum resource theory, minimum power theory, weighted probability theory, and bargaining theory. In general, bargaining theory provides the most accurate predictions, although there are many exceptions to this generalization.

Bargainers in international negotiations have many pressures on them that cannot be re-created in the laboratory; thus, applications from laboratory research must be made cautiously. However, a number of approaches to arms reduction have come out of work by social psychologists, although none has been satisfactorily tested. One suggestion for arms reduction has been the employment of GRIT, a graduated and reciprocated initiative in tension reduction strategy. The plan suggests that each side in a conflict make a minor unilateral concession, but publicly link the move with a concession from the opposing side. A series of small linked moves might result in major progress.

KEY TERMS

bargaining theory
bilateral
coalition
coercion
Commons Dilemma
comparison level
comparison level for alternatives
competitive motivational orientation
compliance
concession
cooperative motivational orientation
decoupling
deterrence
equality norms
equity norms
individualistic motivational orientation

minimum power theory
minimum resource theory
negotiation
payoff matrix
reciprocity
relative needs norm
resistance point
settlement range
social exchange
target point
third-party intervention
unilateral
variable-sum
weighted probability theory
zero-sum

FOR FURTHER STUDY AND APPLICATION

Kelley, H. H., & Thibaut, J. W. (1978). *Interpersonal relations: A theory of interdependence.* New York: Wiley.

An update of the authors' views on social exchange. Far from easy reading, but worth the effort.

Maynard, D. W. (1984). *Inside plea bargaining.* New York: Plenum.

In this book, patterns of bargaining in actual judicial settings are explored. Over fifty cases are described from the perspective of prosecutor, defense attorney, and judge.

Rubin, J. Z., and Brown, B. R. (1975). *The social psychology of bargaining and negotiation.* New York: Academic Press.

A well-written, interesting overview of the literature on bargaining. Provides a fine practical guide to bargaining, as well as covering the literature well.

Rubin, J. Z. (Ed.). (1981). *Dynamics of third party intervention: Kissinger in the Middle East.* New York: Praeger.

A series of chapters on third-party intervention, written by experts, using Henry Kissinger's shuttle diplomacy as a case study.

Pruitt, D. G. (1981). *Negotiation behavior.* New York: Academic Press.

Provides a comprehensive overview and critique of the work on bargaining, with particular emphasis on the experimental literature.

CHAPTER 15

THE PHYSICAL WORLD: THE ENVIRONMENT AND SOCIAL BEHAVIOR

A CONVERSATION WITH . . .

Joan Goody
Architect

Joan Goody is a principal partner in the firm of Goody, Clancy & Associates, Inc., a nationally known architectural firm based in Boston. Goody has received national recognition for a wide range of projects, ranging from the planning and development of residential communities to the restoration and reuse of historic buildings. She has also played a major role in the design of college dormitories at such places as MIT and Tufts University.

We spoke initially about the way in which architects take social psychological factors into account in the design of new buildings:

Q. How do you consider the social needs of the individuals who will be using a building when you sit down to design a new building?

A. I think there are three general influences on a design, only one of which is overtly social. First, there is the physical context—the nature of the physical surroundings, whether it is an open field or a dense city block—and the way you relate to the landscape or the neighboring structures. In some ways this involves how the building appears to the passerby, as opposed to the user, though it also expresses the relationship of the buildings' users to their surroundings.

The second influence is the social context of the building—or what architects refer to as the "program" of the building. A program tells you exactly what the building is supposed to do: for instance, a building which will house 500 students, single and double bedrooms with shared baths and common living rooms to be used in the months of September through June, and so forth. Using a program, one tries to understand what is going to take place in a building. The kind of design one ultimately arrives at is

a function of what is going to take place inside a building. Something that is right for, say, housing the elderly, in terms of scale, color, texture, and lighting, would be totally inappropriate for gatherings of large crowds of teenagers.

The third influence on design is the kind of materials that are available. Availability of materials and economics dictate that buildings will incorporate particular design features.

Q. Is it possible for you to simply look at a building and determine whether it works or doesn't work?

A. After a building is occupied, there are telltale sorts of things. For instance, if we included meeting places in the corridors of student housing and they are stripped of all furniture shortly after the building opens, it probably means that people aren't using them and that they prefer to have furniture in their rooms—and that the architect did something wrong. If a place is deserted or abused, chances are high that you misjudged what the appropriate space or its location was. I always admonish architects in my office that it is not the occupants' fault if they do not use the building the way we want them to; it's *our* fault. If the occupants are sticking notices on the door, it means we forgot to put bulletin boards in the right place. Of course, because building is such a long procedure, no matter how carefully you plan, the use of the building may change from the time it is designed to the time it is occupied.

Q. I know that you have had a good deal of experience in designing dormitories. How do you reconcile the competing demands of students to have their own private spaces, on one hand, and their desires to socialize with each other on a frequent basis?

498

A. That is an interesting question because it opens another issue. One of the ways we like to develop the program for a building is to work with a representative group of users; in the case of a dorm, these would be students, administrators, and faculty. I have had a lot of experience working with groups of students, and they will invariably express the desire for privacy very clearly: almost all students want private rooms, whether they are off the corridor or part of a suite. They are less articulate about expressing the desire for sociability, which turns out to represent very important needs. The lesson from that is that you cannot find out everything by simply interviewing—you also have to observe the behavior of people who are actually using a building with a similar program, a building that works the way in which it was intended.

Q. One of the topics of concern to social psychologists is territoriality, the notion that people develop feelings of ownership over particular areas. Is territoriality something that architects generally take into account?

A. My understanding of territoriality in the context of our discussion is that if you can do something to make a temporary resident, such as a student living in a dorm for a school year, feel as if the place is his or her own, it has a better chance of being well-liked and well-maintained. So we go to some lengths to try to create situations where there is room for user participation in terms of shaping the environment. Take, for instance, window coverings: we tried very hard to come up with a kind of curtain rod on which you can put any number of different kinds of curtains so that the students could put up something of their own. Similarly, we have devised a custom design system so that the students can rearrange bookshelves on the wall. And we try to allocate a specific piece of wall where they can glue, or tape, or do anything they want.

Q. Are there rules of thumb you follow in terms of how much space is necessary to prevent a person from feeling crowded in a dormitory room?

A. Not in terms of square footage. We consider the furniture that we're going to use, rather than the total square footage. The other factor to consider is that students love odd shapes. When I was renovating older dorms, rooms that I considered a problem because of their shapes turned out to be the most popular. People liked them because they were special. So even if a room is tiny, people will accept it—if it possesses some unique attribute which compensates for its size.

OVERVIEW

Where are you at this moment? You may be in the library, in your dormitory room, sitting on a grassy knoll, or riding a bus to school. Wherever it is, it is surely the case that you are being influenced by the physical environment around you.

As our interview with Joan Goody suggests, the nature of an individual's environment provides an important influence on behavior in a particular setting. A relatively new branch of psychology, known as **environmental psychology,** is directed at understanding the relationship between the environment and behavior. This chapter examines a number of key issues from environmental psychology which are of particular interest to social psychologists, who have found that the physical world has a large impact on social behavior.

We first discuss the notion of territoriality in human beings, a phenomenon in which feelings of ownership develop over a particular geographic area. Next, personal space—the area around a person's body into which other people may not enter—is examined. We also consider the notion of crowding, noting both the reasons for and consequences of what is generally an aversive psychological state. Finally, the chapter examines the way in which people come to perceive and understand their environment. As you will see, the physical environment plays an important role in our everyday social interactions, as well as influencing our behavior even when we are alone.

TERRITORIALITY

Imagine that, as a university undergraduate, you tend to do most of your studying in the library. In fact, you have found a quiet corner of the reserve reading room which you like to use. Since the room is generally uncrowded, you are able to sit at the same table each time. In fact, over the course of the semester, you come to think of the table and chair as yours, even though you know it's a public place. However, one day just before final exams, when the whole library is much more crowded, you find someone sitting not just at "your" table but in "your" chair. Feeling angered, you go over to the intruder. You are about to tell her that she ought to move—but you stop, feeling that you really have no right to complain; after all, you don't own that space, do you?

This scenario is played out in one form or another many times in many places. People feel protective of an area that they use habitually, be it a library table, a park bench, an office, a parking spot, a home. The concept of **territoriality,** borrowed from research on animal behavior, has been used to label the feelings of ownership that develop over a particular geographic area. Although many definitions have been proposed, one of the most complete is suggested by Holahan (1982). According to him, territoriality is behavior associated with the ownership or occupation of a place or area which frequently involves personalizing the place and defending it against intrusions.

Three general types of territories have been identified (I. Altman, 1975; R. B. Taylor & Stough, 1978):

1. **Primary territories** are under the complete, long-term control of their users, and are perceived as such both by their owners and by others. Intrusions by others are regarded as serious normative errors and may

even present a threat to a person's identity. The best examples of a primary territory are a person's home and, to a lesser degree, his or her office.

2. **Secondary territories** are under less personal control. The use of secondary territories is not permanent, and any one individual is not the only user over the course of a day. The territories may be personalized while being occupied, but the personalization ends when the owner leaves the area. Our earlier description of a particular seat in a library is a good example of a secondary territory. Observers will perceive that a user has temporary ownership, but that the area can legitimately be used by others at other times.

3. **Public territories** are areas which any member of the public has the right to use. Areas such as beaches, parks, telephone booths, and buses all represent public territories. They are not owned in either a formal or an informal sense, but rather are open to anyone who wants to use them. However, while an individual is using them, they do take on aspects of ownership by the occupant—although on a temporary basis. Thus, a person sitting on a park bench will not be asked to leave by another person; the bench occupant, by his or her mere presence, takes temporary control of the territory. But as soon as the first person leaves, the second is legitimately entitled to claim the space.

It is important to distinguish between these three types of territoriality because the reactions of individuals to violations of territory differ markedly according to the type of territory in question. For example, violations of primary territories may readily produce aggression—sometimes at extreme levels. Indeed, local laws frequently sanction the killing of an intruder in someone's home; people who commit that act are rarely prosecuted. On the other hand, violations of secondary and public territories are relatively unlikely to evoke overt aggression.

A field study by Stephen Worchel and Margaret Lollis (1982) shows that there are also cultural differences in how various types of territories are defended. The study examined the responses of home dwellers in the United States and Greece to contamination by bags of litter of primary, secondary, and public territories. The investigators hypothesized that litter would be disposed of more rapidly when it was found on primary and secondary territories—areas which the residents controlled most directly—than on public territories—which were not under their personal control.

In the study, an experimenter placed litter on the front yard, on the sidewalk in front of the residence, or on the street curb in front of a home, and the speed with which the litter was removed was measured. (If the litter had not been removed within twenty-four hours, the experimenter picked it up.) As can be seen in Figure 15-1, there was little difference in speed of removal according to culture when the litter was put in the residents' yards. In contrast, the litter was removed faster from the sidewalk and curb areas in the United States than in Greece.

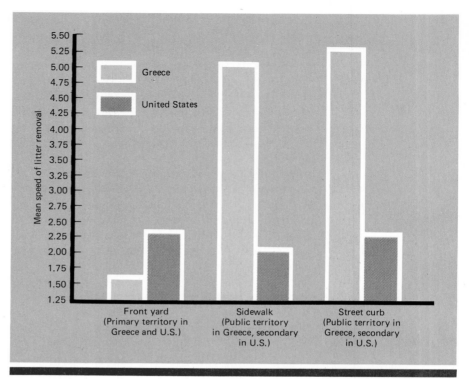

FIGURE 15-1
When litter was placed in front yards, there was little difference in the speed of litter removal. But cultural differences emerged with the litter on sidewalks and street curbs, which are public territories in Greece and secondary territories in the United States. Source: S. Worchel and M. Lollis, Reactions to territorial contamination as a function of culture. *Personality and Social Psychology Bulletin*, Vol. 8, No. 2, June, 1982, p. 373. Copyright © 1982 by the Society for Personality and Social Psychology, Inc. Reprinted by permission by Sage Publications, Inc.

These results suggest that the two areas are differentially perceived by the members of the two cultures. In Greece, both the sidewalk and the curb are thought of as public territories, while in the United States they are more likely to be considered secondary territories. These results also suggest an interesting strategy for increasing public responsibility for litter removal: a change in the perception of territorial control may make individuals come to feel more responsible for caring for particular areas.

Besides evoking attempts at defense, territories also produce positive responses. In a demonstration of what might be called the "home, sweet home" effect (Bell, Fisher, & Loomis, 1978), Edney (1975) asked pairs of subjects to interact in one member of the pair's dormitory room. Thus, one person was a visitor, while the other was operating in his home territory. Subjects who were visitors rated their resident partners as being more relaxed than the resident subjects rated their visitor partners. In addition, residents viewed their rooms as pleasanter and more private places than the visitors did. Similarly, R. B. Taylor and Lanni (1981) held three-person discussion groups in one of the group members' rooms. Regardless of the personality of the group members, the dominant member of the group turned out to be the person to whom the room belonged.

In an analogous demonstration of the importance of being in one's own territory, sports teams frequently perform better during their home games than when they are on the road (Altman, 1975). The reason? It is likely that the home team's knowledge of the idiosyncrasies of their own field, wind patterns, fans, and the like proves advantageous. This knowledge may help members to feel more relaxed or generally positive about playing at home—ultimately leading to better performance.

Marking a Territory: Staking Out Your Turf

One of the ways in which people maintain territoriality is through the use of markers which delineate the boundaries of the territory. Although animal territories are often marked by physiological means, as those of us with male dogs know, human beings employ physical markers such as fences, walls, and hedges, or "no trespassing" signs.

In general, primary territories are apt to be the most overtly demarcated, while markers in secondary and public territories tend to be far subtler. Suppose, for instance, you wanted to maintain your favorite spot at the library and keep others from sitting at "your" table. One way might be to choose a position that was most likely to transmit your feelings of territoriality. Which position at the table would be most effective? Sommer and Becker (1969) asked a group of subjects to indicate where they would sit if they actively wanted to defend their position. As shown in Figure 15-2, they tended to select the middle chair. In contrast, a decision to retreat was indicated by choice of a corner position.

In a subsequent field experiment, Sommer and Becker then left various personal possessions, such as books or clothing, in front of a vacant

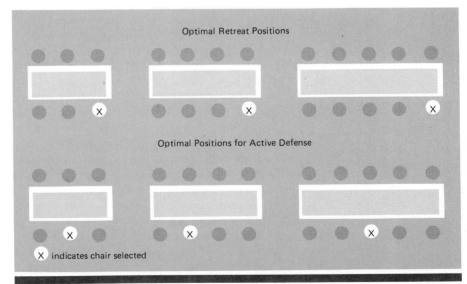

FIGURE 15-2
Choice of seating position for retreat or defense. Seating position varies according to desire to maintain or retreat from territorial possession at a table. Source Sommer & Becker (1969).

Territorial markers act to reserve and defend particular areas. (Randy Matusow)

chair in a crowded or uncrowded public area. Results showed that the type of item left had no effect on whether the seat was taken by someone under uncrowded conditions; just about any sort of item was effective in preventing someone from taking the seat. But when the area was crowded, only very personal items—such as jackets and sweaters—were effective in preventing territorial violation.

In some cases, territorial markers used in public places may be of such great subtlety that a casual observer might miss them. For example, Brown and Altman (1981) suggest that when people are unable to use physical markers, they may use bodily markers such as touch to establish a territory and subsequently maintain control over it. A contemporary example of this phenomenon can be seen in game arcades. In a study of territorial control of particular electronic games at a public arcade, Werner, Brown, and Damron (1981) observed that players who had just approached a machine spent significantly more time touching the machine when a stranger appeared to be watching them start to play than when a friend was watching. It seems as if the stranger's observation led to feelings of territorial threat and thus to the need to provide the marker of touching, while the presence of the observing friend did not necessitate marking.

Is touch an effective marker? In a follow-up study, Werner, Brown, and Damron (1981) found that, in fact, it was. A confederate who touched a machine was approached considerably less by strangers than one who did not touch the machine but simply stood in front of it.

The Functions of Territoriality

Why should territoriality be so pervasive a phenomenon? A number of functions served by territoriality have been suggested by social psychologists.

Territoriality as a Support for Social Interaction   The major reason for the pervasiveness of territoriality seems to be that it serves a number of psychological functions that support social interaction. First, and most basic, maintaining territories allows us to organize our daily lives. To take the extreme case, if we had no territory in which we could restrict the presence of others, people could be wandering through our homes at any time of the day or night.

Territoriality also provides us with a convenient way of organizing and understanding the world. We are able to predict, with a good deal of confidence, what activities will be going on in a given area because certain territorial areas are designed for specific activities. Thus, we know that cooking is going on in the kitchen or that the shower is being used to wash up. On a more specific level, each family member often has a particular chair and place at the table that he or she generally uses, rather than having to decide at every meal who is going to sit where (Edney, 1975).

Territoriality and Social Organization   A second major function of territoriality is to develop, clarify, and maintain social organization (Edney, 1975). Groups in which social status, dominance, and roles are highly differentiated use territoriality to indicate the position an individual

People usually have specific places where they sit during mealtime; this serves to add to the predictability of the social world. (Thomas Hopker/ Woodfin Camp)

holds within the group. For example, individuals with high personal needs for dominance tend to make higher territoriality demands than those with lower needs for dominance. Similarly, high-status individuals often choose to sit at the head of the table during meetings (DeLong, 1970, 1973).

Territoriality as a Source of Group and Personal Identity The first questions you are apt to ask someone at an initial encounter are the old standards, "Where do you live?" and "Where were you raised?" The frequency with which these questions are asked points out a third major function of territoriality: it allows the development of a sense of group and personal identity (Edney, 1975). Individuals who share a territory often share similar experiences and develop a common base of knowledge; they use the same stores, their children attend the same schools, they may share the same frustrations with their local government's inability to keep the streets clean and the snow plowed (also see Box 15-1). These sorts of common experiences lead individuals to develop a common group identity. This identity can be manifested in many ways, including similar ways of dressing, the use of language, and celebration of particular holidays.

In the most extreme cases of territoriality, even what would normally be public territory space is usurped by residents of an area, with outsiders being discouraged and even harassed for entering an area that is claimed by another group. For example, when street gangs have well-defined areas that belong to them, intruders from other gangs understand that violence is likely to ensue if they cross a territorial boundary. In fact, in many cases the territories are marked by graffiti on walls and buildings that indicate where one gang's territory begins and another's stops (Ley & Cybriwsky, 1974).

While it may seem, on the face of it, that the extreme territoriality of groups leads to intergroup hostility, in fact it may do just the opposite. Ley and Cybriwsky (1974) found that street gangs were caught up in more violence when the boundaries of territories were not well-defined than when they were unambiguous. By clearly demarcating which area belongs to which group, territorial markers seem to prevent intergang violence. Interestingly, the same phenomenon holds true when we look at animals; there is more fighting prior to establishment of firm territories than when the boundaries have been well-defined (Lorenz, 1966).

In addition to promoting a sense of group identity, territories also lead to a sense of personal identity. As we noted earlier, people tend to identify themselves on the basis of where they live ("I'm a New Yorker") or where they grew up ("I was raised in Texas"). Knowing where a person comes from often leads to a stereotypic labeling process; for instance, someone might assume that people who choose to live in Greenwich Village in New York are going to be more avant-garde and sophisticated than people living on farms in Kansas.

As Joan Goody discussed in the interview at the beginning of the chapter, people generally appreciate uniqueness in their territories, and they may try to personalize them to distinguish them from others. Think of a dormitory, which is typically a series of identical cubicles with the same furniture and function at the start of a school year. What is the first thing students do when moving in in the fall? Typically, they put up pictures and posters, rearrange the furniture, and otherwise act to make the space more personalized to reflect their own interests, attitudes, and values. And as the school year goes on, the amount of personalization in dormitory rooms increases (Hensen & Altman, 1976).

Territoriality may also allow people to maintain a feeling of personal protection that is absent when they do not have a sense of territoriality. In an interesting demonstration of this phenomenon, A. H. Patterson (1978) interviewed elderly home owners who had territorial markers in front of their homes such as "no trespassing" signs or fences. While one might think at first that such markers would be a sign of exceptional defensiveness and inordinate fear of crime, the truth was just the opposite. Compared with a group of home owners who had no such territorial markers in front of their homes, those who had markers tended to have less fear of personal injury and property loss.

Because the study is correlational in nature, it is impossible to conclude that displaying territorial markers leads to a greater sense of security—though that may be the case. There is another equally plausible explanation: perhaps those who already feel secure and in control of their environment are the people who end up erecting territorial markers. Although either explanation might be correct, these results at least suggest that territoriality is linked to a sense of personal safety.

Making Territories Work: Applications and Design Implications of Territoriality

Can architects and environmental planners make use of the work that has been done on territoriality? Although in actual practice knowledge of territoriality obtained from social psychological research has not been applied systematically to design issues, a number of general principles can be derived (Holahan, 1982; Altman, 1975).

Rather than designing particular areas and letting usage patterns determine the kind of territory, it would seem important to design areas that are specifically meant to be primary, secondary, and public territories. For instance, one of the major failings of residential housing projects is that secondary territories—such as halls and play areas—function instead as public territories. In such instances, crime tends to be unusually high (Newman, 1972). This suggests that design features which keep secondary territories from becoming more public—such as the use of territorial markers, the restriction of nonresident visitors, and the creation of private entrances—can all add to residents' positive feelings about their environment.

The best design strategy might be one which takes into account peo-

BOX 15-1   SPOTLIGHT ON RESEARCH

PERCEIVING ONE'S TERRITORY: COGNITIVE MAPS

If you were asked to sketch a map of your hometown, chances are you would be able to do so readily. But it is also true that your map would hardly be like the one that Rand-McNally would produce; the shape, scale, landmarks, and streets that you included would probably be more representative of your own experience and view of the town than that which an objective cartographer would produce.

It turns out that the maps people draw of the territories that they inhabit represent an important clue to the way in which they interact with and use their environment. In fact, a good deal of research has been carried out on what is termed **cognitive mapping,** which is the way that spatial information is acquired, perceived, stored, and used in the understanding of one's physical environment (Stea, 1974).

Cognitive maps are a person's organized representation of the geographic environment, which is typically stored in terms of visual images. Such cognitive maps serve a number of important functions. For one thing, they provide individuals with a way of organizing what might otherwise be a confusing and overstimulating environment. By producing their own representations of an environment, people are able to feel more secure and to be less confused in their perception of the environment.

Cognitive maps serve an additional, more utilitarian function: they allow individuals to adapt to their environment by identifying where certain important features are and how to get from one place to another (Downs & Stea, 1977). Thus, some of the important features that are apt to be part of a person's cognitive map are road maps and other paths (such as subway lines) that allow an individual to travel from place to place.

One important determinant of the accuracy of people's cognitive maps is their familiarity with an area (G. W. Evans, 1980). For instance, Holahan & Dobrowolny (1978) asked University of Texas students to produce maps of the campus. An analysis of the maps showed that the more frequently the students passed through a given area during their school day, the greater the detail of the map. In general, it appears that the precision with which an area is mapped is a function of how familiar a person is with the area (Holahan, 1982).

Another important factor that relates to cognitive mapping is socioeconomic status (SES). One clear effect of SES is the size of the area included in people's cognitive maps: quite consistently, people at higher socioeconomic levels tend to include more differentiated maps than people at lower levels. In one dramatic example, wealthy residents of Los Angeles were found to show greater familiarity with up to 1000 times as much of the city as poorer residents. As would be expected, this knowledge was reflected in more accurate and objective cognitive maps being produced by the higher SES residents (Gould & White, 1974; see Figure 15-3).

Why should this be the case? One reason appears to be the greater mobility available to the higher SES people. Rather than being limited to public transportation, wealthier people are able to travel via private automobile, which gives them greater access to large parts of the city. Indeed, it has been found that when lower SES people are given more opportunities for transportation around a city, their cognitive maps begin to resemble those of higher SES individuals more closely (Appleyard, 1976; Michelson, 1976).

---

ple's needs for control over their environment in terms of social interaction and stimulation (Altman, 1975). Hence, territories in which people control their environment, allowing them to feel that *they* determine the use of space, public or private, and its performance of ownership, are apt to be the most effective in providing a sense of environmental quality.

508

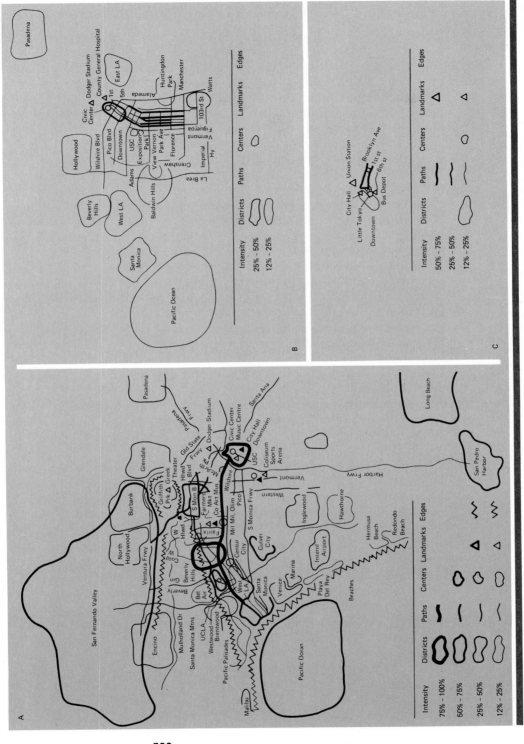

FIGURE 15-3

Three cognitive maps. In the cognitive maps depicted here, Los Angeles is represented
through the eyes of (a) an upper-middle-class white living in the Westwood area of the
city, (b) a lower SES black from Avalon, and (c) a lower SES Spanish-speaking resident of
Boyle Heights. Source: Orleans (1967).

PERSONAL SPACE: OUR BUBBLE OF TERRITORY

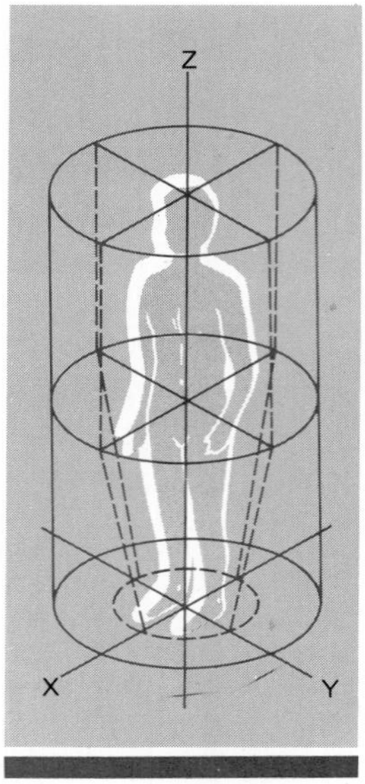

When we discussed territoriality, we were primarily interested in the feelings of ownership that extend to particular geographic areas. The concept of personal space extends notions of territoriality to a person's own body. Specifically, **personal space** refers to the area around a person's body into which others may not enter. This space is like a bubble which surrounds individuals, "protecting" them from intrusions by others in the same way that territoriality protects them.

The bubble analogy is a bit too simple, however. Hayduk (1978) has suggested a three-dimensional model of personal space—displayed in Figure 15-4—which takes into account the fact that different areas of the body may have different spatial requirements. According to this view, personal space is greatest for the top half of the body, but tapers below the waist toward the floor. Moreover, personal space is not rigid; it grows and shrinks, according to the situation, the individuals with whom one is interacting, and one's personality characteristics.

We already mentioned one of the most important effects of personal space zones in Chapter 3 in discussing nonverbal communication processes: the maintenance of normatively appropriate distances between individuals. But personal space zones vary for a number of other reasons. For instance, zone size may reflect feelings of anxiety. People who are feeling anxious tend to maintain more personal space between themselves and others than when they are not as anxious (Hayduk, 1978). There are also a number of sex differences that have emerged, although the data are not entirely consistent (Hayduk, 1983). Men tend to have larger personal space zones than women (Wittig & Skolnick, 1978). When two men interact with each other, they keep a significantly larger distance from one another than two women interacting with each other do. Interestingly, a man and woman who are well acquainted tend to maintain even less personal space than do same-sex pairs of either sex. The reason seems to be that the female of the pair reduces her personal space zone and simply moves closer to the male—who responds by maintaining the closer distance (Edwards, 1972).

One of the most interesting lines of research examining personal space zones has been done with chronic schizophrenics. Arrowitz (1965, 1968) found that when both schizophrenics and normal persons were asked to approach another person until they reached a point at which they no longer felt comfortable, the schizophrenics stayed farther away than the normals, indicating that they had a larger personal space zone. But there was large variability, with some of the schizophrenics standing much closer than the normals. In addition, other research has confirmed that schizophrenics tend to show greater variability in their personal space, and can be insensitive to the personal space zones of others by invading them. One reason for this nonnormative use of personal space may rest on the fact that some schizophrenics have an ill-defined sense of where their own bodies end and where the rest of the world begins.

FIGURE 15-4
A three-dimensional model of a typical person's personal space zones. Source: Hayduk (1978).

510

Use of personal space also develops systematically as children grow older; typically, interaction distances increase as children age (Aiello & Aiello, 1974; Hayduk, 1983). In fact, this finding holds across different cultural groups. For example, Pagan and Aiello (1982) observed Puerto Rican children at the first-, sixth-, and eleventh-grade levels who were interacting in same-sex pairs. Children in both New York and Puerto Rico were observed. The results, displayed in Figure 15-5, show clear developmental differences that are similar regardless of the subjects' geographic location, with older children using larger interaction distances than younger ones.

Understanding the Use of Personal Space

We have seen a number of ways in which personal space functions. But why do people maintain a "bubble" of protection around themselves? A number of reasons have been suggested, based on different theoretical orientations.

Personal Space and Information Overload   When others stand very close to us, their voices seem louder, we may feel (and smell) their hot breath, we may notice wrinkles in their skin. In other words, we are bombarded with sensory stimulation, all of which must be processed cognitively. The **overload** model of personal space builds upon this possibility by suggesting that we maintain personal space in order to reduce the potential "overload" on our information processing systems (G. W. Evans, 1974). By keeping others at a distance, we are able to maintain control over the stimulation that we would otherwise be forced to process.

Some evidence exists to support this model, but it is largely indirect.

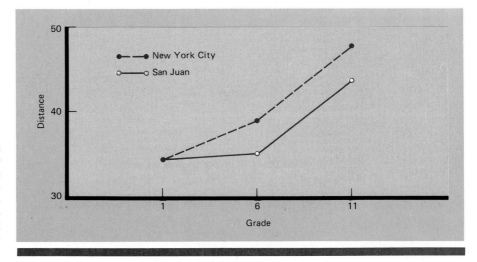

FIGURE 15-5
Interaction distance of Puerto Rican children at three grade levels. Children at older ages tend to interact at greater distances both in New York and Puerto Rico. Source: Pagan & Aiello (1982).

For example, Nesbit and Steven (1974) suggested that if the overload model were viable, people who were experiencing high levels of sensory stimulation would be likely to stand farther apart than those experiencing lower levels of stimulation. In support of this reasoning, they found that individuals in an overstimulating amusement park spaced themselves farther away from each other than people in a less stimulating environment. Still, this is correlational data and as such does not provide definitive support.

Personal Space as Protection   An alternative—although not mutually exclusive—approach to explaining the functions of personal space suggests that personal space zones serve to protect us from stress. This model, known as **stress theory,** says that personal space can shield us from stressful stimuli that may be present when others come too close to us. What are these potential stressors? G. W. Evans (1979) suggests an important one is potential aggression that may come from others. If we allow other people to get too close to us, an act of aggression can have serious consequences. On the other hand, if we maintain our distance, an aggressive act will have less significance. Similarly, maintenance of personal space zones allows us to fend off high levels of noise that may emanate from other people. In sum, personal space may afford us protection from unwanted stressful stimuli.

Once again, there is evidence, albeit indirect, which supports the stress model of personal space. This research shows that invasions of personal space result in a rise in physiological arousal. For example, invasions of personal space result in higher levels of galvanic skin response (GSR), a measure of anxiety that reflects changes in the electrical conductance of the skin (G. W. Evans & Howard, 1972). Other research supporting the stress model is described in Box 15-2.

Personal Space as a Communication Channel: Getting the Message Across   One final explanation for the use of personal space is as a channel of communication. As we discussed in detail in Chapter 3, interpersonal spacing can reflect the nature of the relationship between two individuals, and is also related to other nonverbal behaviors such as eye contact and body orientation. Thus, maintenance of personal space zones can be conceptualized as largely a matter of controlling the type of message individuals want to communicate to others with whom they are interacting.

Personal Space in Perspective: Applications and Design Implications

As with many other topics we have discussed, research has so far not revealed which of the major approaches—information overload, stress reduction, or the communication model—is most successful in explaining the functioning of personal space zones. In fact, given that none of

BOX 15-2 SPOTLIGHT ON METHODOLOGY

INVASIONS OF PERSONAL SPACE—OR WAS IT INVASIONS OF SUBJECT PRIVACY?

A naturalistic field study which has been quite controversial—for ethical reasons—illustrates the stressful nature of invasions of personal space. Middlemist, Knowles, and Matter (1976) studied both the amount of time it took unsuspecting subjects to begin urinating in a men's room and the length of their urination under differing degrees of invasion of personal space. Why, you may ask, would investigators interested in personal space zones spend their time in a men's room? It turns out that both the rapidity with which urination begins and the length of urination in males are sensitive measures of stress; higher degrees of stress tend to increase the delay of onset of urination and decrease the amount of time it takes to empty the bladder. Hence, the use of these measures makes sense if you want an unobtrusive measure of stress reactions to invasions of personal space zones.

In the experiment, subjects were forced to use the leftmost of three urinals. In the close invasion condition, a confederate would enter and stand in front of the urinal directly next to the subject. In the moderate invasion condition, the confederate would stand at the rightmost urinal; the two people were thus separated from one another by a urinal. Finally, in the third, no-invasion control condition, subjects were allowed to urinate in solitude. But in every condition, subjects' behavior was monitored by a confederate hidden in a toilet stall and equipped with a periscope.

The results of the Middlemist et al. study were as one would expect from the stress model of personal space. The greater the degree of invasion of personal space, the slower the onset of urination and the quicker urination was completed.

While the results of the study are clear in supporting the notion that invasion of personal space is stressful, the experimental procedure brought a good deal of criticism from psychologists concerned with the ethics of the situation. For example, Koocher (1977) argued that the methodology violated the human dignity of subjects and presented the potential of extreme psychological discomfort to subjects if they had stumbled upon the fact that their bathroom behavior was being observed. The original investigators countered that the question being asked by the research was worthy and that the procedure was an acceptable one, given that available alternatives offered no better means of investigating the issue (Middlemist, Knowles, & Matter, 1977). Like most matters of an ethical nature, the issue remains controversial. What is clear is that the study confirms that personal space invasion is related to increases in physiological stress; thus, an important function of maintenance of personal space zones may be to protect people from excessive stress.

---

the models is mutually exclusive, it is probable that each operates to a greater or lesser degree, depending on the parameters of the situation.

The research on personal space can be used to make some concrete suggestions regarding the design of architectural features of buildings. For example, some studies have shown that the more enclosed an area is, the more personal space is wanted by those using it. Thus, as room size or ceiling height is decreased, people want to maintain a greater amount of personal space (Savinar, 1975; M. White, 1975). Moreover, people try to maintain greater personal distance when they are located in corners of rooms than when they are at its center (Tennis & Dabbs, 1975). The implications of these results are clear: architects wanting to

Architectural arrange-
ments, like the seats
shown here, are some-
times designed without
regard to the require-
ments of social interac-
tion. (Raymond Depardon/
Magnum)

decrease interaction distance among residents of a particular building should design larger, more open spaces.

Moreover, architectural features that force people to interact with others at an inappropriate distance are likely to be found aversive. Thus, fixed seating arrangements, such as those often found at airports and other waiting rooms, are apt to discourage social interaction if they do not take into account people's personal space zones. The importance of this point has been shown in a series of studies of airport waiting rooms carried out by Robert Sommer (1974). In his research, he found that seats were usually bolted to the floor, facing the ticket counters, or arranged back-to-back. It was almost impossible to hold a conversation except with persons immediately to an individual's left or right. Moreover, even when talking to their adjacent neighbor, people tended to contort their bodies in order to get into a more comfortable position. Interestingly, airport designers are often aware of the negative effects of such architectural features (Sommer, 1974). They employ them in order to *prevent* socialization; they prefer that people spend as little time as possible in their seats and instead spend money at the airport concessions!

Direct manipulation of personal space can also be used to influence the nature of social relationships between two people. Thus, research on patient behavior in therapeutic settings has shown that patients become more open and comfortable when clinicians seat themselves close to the patient than when they are farther away (Jourard, 1970). Moreover, counselors who seat themselves across a table from their clients are apt to be viewed less positively than counselors who are seated corner-to-corner at a table (Widgery & Stackpole, 1972). Environments, then, can be managed to bring about more effective use of personal space.

THE EXPERIENCE OF CROWDING

With 50 percent of the United States population living on just 1 percent of the land, the phenomenon of crowding represents an important fact of many people's daily lives. Images conjured up by the term "crowding" come to mind readily: people riding a subway car during rush hour, a small ghetto apartment in which a large family is living, a standing-room-only performance at a theater.

But while such images are easily conjured up, a precise scientific definition of crowding is considerably more difficult to produce. Amount of space by itself is clearly insufficient; people may feel crowded in a bus but not at a party in someone's living room, even if the square footage is identical. Likewise, the number of people per se is not a sufficient criterion to define crowding. Fifty thousand people at a football game may not experience crowding at all—if the stadium is built to a capacity of 100,000.

Clearly, then, definitions of crowding that rely on space and numbers of people alone are insufficient. Most researchers now feel that a crucial aspect in understanding crowding is a person's psychological experience related to both number of people and available space (e.g., Stokols, 1978). It is necessary, then, to distinguish between density and crowding. **Density** refers to the purely physical and spatial aspects of a situation—the number of people per spatial unit. **Crowding,** in contrast, refers to the psychological or subjective factors in a situation—how an individual perceives a given number of people in a particular space.

According to this conceptualization, high density per se does not inevitably lead to the experience of crowding. Rather, additional factors of a social psychological nature must be present before high density is experienced as crowding. It should be noted, though, that this view— though it is the most popular—has been a point of contention among researchers in the area. For example, Jonathan Freedman (1975) has argued that the distinction between crowding and density is unnecessary and that the use of the separate terms has led to an overemphasis on studying something hypothetical—crowding—and a consequent underemphasis on the physical aspects of environments and behavioral responses to those aspects.

One resolution to the controversy surrounding the conceptualization of density and crowding has been offered by Bell, Fisher, and Loomis (1978). They suggest that high density should be seen as a physical state that produces the potential of physical and/or psychological inconvenience. Whether the inconvenience is salient to an individual in a high-density physical situation depends on individual differences, situational conditions such as time in the setting and presence of other stressors, and social conditions such as the nature of the person's relationship with others. According to this conceptualization, if the inconvenience caused by the high density is not made salient to the individual, negative effects are not likely to occur; but if the high density is made salient to the person, crowding will be experienced. Crowding, then, is viewed as a psychological state that is stressful and that motivates attempts to bring about its cessation or reduction.

Why High Density Leads to Aversive Consequences

What are the potential problems of high density that can lead to the experience of crowding? At least four models have been suggested by researchers to try to answer this question: stimulus overload, loss of control, ecological models, and focus of attention approaches (Stokols, 1976). There are insufficient data at this point to say which model provides the best explanation for when high density leads to crowding; in fact, each may contribute to the experience of crowding.

High Density as Excessive Stimulation   The stimulus overload approach suggests that, just as any physical stimulus in excess is aversive, high density results in a negative psychological state because it overwhelms and, ultimately, overloads people. The presence of others is viewed by this model as not particularly different from any sort of excessive stimulation, be it noise, heat, or light. In order to reduce this excessive stimulation, people seem to try to escape from it, either by actually leaving the area or by psychologically "tuning out" the presence of others.

Loss of Control Models of Crowding   A second model that attempts to explain why high density can lead to the experience of crowding is the issue of control that we first discussed in Chapter 8. Excessive numbers of people in a relatively small area can lead a person to feel that his or her behavioral control and freedom have been reduced. While at first individuals will try to gain control of a situation in which they experience loss of control, ultimately they may experience a sense of learned helplessness, feeling that no matter what actions they take they will be unable to change the situation (Burger, Oakman, & Bullard, 1983; Rodin & Baum, 1978; Seligman, 1975; Epstein, 1981).

The efficacy of the loss of control model is suggested by the results of a study by Rodin (1976). In one experiment, Rodin found that children who lived in chronically high-density environments were less apt to attempt to assert control over reinforcement than children who lived in lower-density households. What this suggests is that the children from high-density homes had learned to accept their environment passively—in other words, had learned to be helpless—and that this passive acceptance had generalized beyond their home environment. Moreover,

We are apt to experience crowding in high-density situations if our attention is focused on others—such as would be the case in a filled subway car where there is little else to do but watch other people. (David M. Grossman/Photo Reseachers)

subjects from the high-density homes did significantly worse on an experimental task in which there was a contingency between performance and outcome. Such results suggest that high density can lead to a generalized sense of lack of control over one's environment and a passive acceptance of one's world.

Ecological Models Another approach to explaining why high density can lead to the experience of crowding is the ecological model. This approach suggests that high density is aversive because of the scarcity of resources to carry out what one is trying to do. Resources might be anything from actual materials that are being used to construct something to roles that people play in a given situation. Thus, if there are too many people in a group that is constructing a float for a parade, certain people may be left out or have nothing to do. These people may experience a sense of crowding—whereas others, who are able to be more involved in the task, will not perceive the situation in an aversive light. According to the ecological model, then, the way a person defines the situation determines whether or not he or she will feel crowded.

Focus of Attention as a Determinant of Crowding The final approach to crowding that we will discuss considers the stimuli to which people attend. Worchel and Brown (1984; Worchel and Yohai, 1979) suggest that the focus of people's attention may shift when they are in high-density situations, and the nature of this shift determines whether a sense of crowding will be experienced. If attention is focused on other people, we are likely to experience crowding. On the other hand, if attention is focused on some other aspect of a situation, crowding will not be felt. As mentioned earlier, we may feel quite crowded in a noisy subway; since there is so little else to attend to, our attention is likely to be focused primarily on the multitude of other people. On the other hand, we may feel relatively uncrowded in a situation of equal density, such as a party in which our attention is focused on a specific conversation with one other person.

Responses to Crowding

While it is still too early in the history of environmental psychology to pinpoint the exact causes of the perception of crowding, a good deal is known about people's responses to the state. Probably the most common initial reaction to crowding is a change in affective state: people report feeling unhappy, anxious, fearful, or angry in crowded environments (G. W. Evans, 1980). There are many examples of this finding, which appears consistently in both laboratory and field studies. For example, Saegert, MacIntosh, and West (1975) asked subjects to carry out a series of tasks in a setting such as a railway station that was either crowded or uncrowded at the time. Subjects reported feeling considerably more anxious under crowded conditions. Even anticipating that an environment will be crowded is sufficient to produce negative emotional states (Baum & Greenberg, 1975).

Interestingly, there seems to be a consistent sex difference in reactions to crowding, with females reacting relatively less negatively to crowding than males (Aiello, Nicosia, & Thompson, 1979). Why should this be the case? One explanation rests on differential socialization processes in our culture; females may be taught to be more affiliative than males, and thus may find crowding less aversive, while males are socialized to show greater competitiveness and crowding may arouse these competitive tendencies. It is also possible that since men tend to have larger personal space distances than women, only the males truly experience crowding. Although the specific explanation is not yet clear, the finding is consistent.

Psychological Reaction to Crowding   Given the link between emotional experience and physiological arousal, it would not be surprising to find that crowding can result in physiological arousal, and numerous studies bear this out (e.g., Evans, 1974, 1979). For instance, crowding causes increases in heart rate and blood pressure (Evans, 1979), and one study even found that the level of adrenaline in the circulatory system was correlated with the level of density on rush-hour trains (Lundberg, 1976). Automobile commuters also seem to have physiological reactions to traffic density; one series of field studies found that traffic tie-ups were related to changes in the blood pressure of drivers (Novaco, Stokols, Campbell, & Stokols, 1979).

Given the physiological reactions that occur due to the presence of

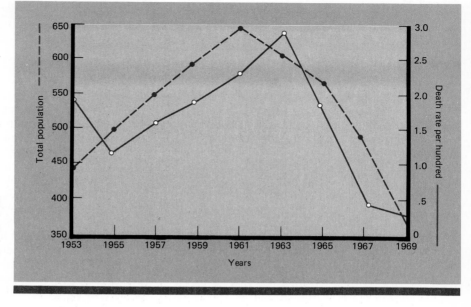

FIGURE 15-6
Number of deaths com-
pared with population
size. As population den-
sity increased, the num-
ber of deaths rose.
Source: Paulus, McCain,
& Cox (1978).

crowding, it would not be surprising to find that higher rates of illness
are also associated with crowding, and this, too, has proven to be true.
For example, a comprehensive study of crowding in prisons revealed
that those prisoners living in crowded housing units had a higher number of complaints of illness (Cox, Paulus, McCain, & Schkade, 1979). In
a revealing field study, Baron, Mandel, Adams, and Griffen (1976) examined records of students who visited the student health center on a
college campus. The records showed that students living in dormitories
of high social density made more visits than those from low-density
dormitories.

Perhaps the most striking research examining the relationship between crowding and health was carried out by Paulus, McCain, and Cox
(1978). In the study, they examined death rates for inmates in a state
psychiatric prison over a sixteen-year period. In that time the population
ranged from a low of about 375 to a high of about 650. At the same time,
the death rate ranged from .7 to about 3.0 per hundred prisoners. What
is most interesting about these figures is the close correspondence at
any given time between population and death rate. As shown in Figure
15-6, as the population rose and fell, so did the death rate.

Results such as these have been supported in a number of studies
(e.g., Schaeffer, Baum, & Paulus, 1984; Paulus & McCain, 1983). Of
course, the studies we have mentioned—and most others investigating
the relationship between crowding and physical illness—are correlational in nature, and all that has been demonstrated is an association
between crowding and illness or death. We still are not able to infer
that crowding itself *causes* illness, only that there is a relationship; it is

BOX 15-3 SPOTLIGHT ON APPLICATIONS

NOISE AND SOCIAL BEHAVIOR

Consider the plight of the students in a public school in New York City some years ago. The school was located directly adjacent to an elevated railroad track on which trains screeched by every 4.5 minutes. When a train was passing by, teachers could not be heard without screaming—for a thirty-second period.

What were the effects of such periodic high levels of noise? As you might guess, there were clear impacts on student performance. An examination of reading achievement showed that students in the classrooms closest to the railroad had significantly lower reading scores than students who were in classes in the opposite side of the building, where the noise levels were somewhat lower (Bronzaft & McCarthy, 1975).

These results illustrate quite dramatically the aversive effects of high levels of noise. Indeed, although the negative qualities of crowding have been studied most extensively, other environmental stimuli can have equally unpleasant effects on social behavior. Noise, in particular, has been shown to have undesirable effects. For example, high noise levels lead to less helping behavior and more aggression toward others (Siegel & Steele, 1979; Konečni, 1975). Moreover, there is clear evidence from laboratory research that task performance declines at high levels of noise (Gulian, 1974; Loeb, Holding, & Baker, 1982). Noise can have particularly detrimental effects if it cannot be controlled by the individual experiencing it or if it is completely unpredictable (D. C. Glass, Singer, & Friedman, 1969).

The negative effects of high levels of noise suggest that its reduction could bring about positive results—and this point was well illustrated by the findings of a follow-up study carried out at the school next to the elevated railroad tracks. After years of complaints by teachers and students, the classrooms closest to the tracks were outfitted with sound-reducing material and rubber cushioning was added to the tracks themselves. The result? The following year, achievement levels rose to match those of pupils on the other, previously quieter side of the building (Goldman, 1982).

---

entirely possible—and perhaps even probable—that some other factor associated with crowding is the underlying cause of poor health. For example, it is plausible that high social density leads to poor sanitation, and it is the poor sanitation that ultimately leads to the higher incidence of illness. Thus, correlational studies of crowding must be interpreted with caution.

Liking for Others: Finding that Stranger Across a Crowded Room An old Rodgers and Hammerstein lyric from *South Pacific* speaks of glimpsing a stranger across a crowded room, who turns out to be a once-in-a-lifetime love. What the lyricists may not have known is that if the room were *too* crowded, it would have been unlikely that such positive attraction would even have developed. Research findings are clear in suggesting that interpersonal attraction is negatively related to social density.

Some of the most compelling evidence along these lines comes from a study of attraction to roommates under crowded and uncrowded conditions. Baron et al. (1976) asked students who were housed three to a room in dormitories built to house two in each room how much they liked their roommates, and compared their responses with those of students who were housed two to a room in rooms meant for two. Not only were roommates liked less under the crowded conditions, but they were viewed as being less cooperative.

Recent research suggests that even rooms designed for three people seem to produce negative interpersonal feelings. Aiello, Baum, and Gormley (1980) found that, on the average, residents of triple rooms felt more crowded, were less attracted to their roommates, and experienced greater social tension and more negative emotions than residents of double rooms. The reason? It appears that in triple rooms there was a tendency for two of the three roommates to form a relatively close relationship, which left the third roommate isolated—and unhappy with the situation. Moreover, follow-up research showed that third roommates often experienced a direct sense of loss of control over their environment (Aiello, Vautier, & Bernstein, 1983). These research findings are consistent with the comments of architect Joan Goody, who mentioned students' strong preference for single rooms. (Refer to Box 15-4 for a further look at research on dormitory preferences in college students.)

Helping and Hurting Others: Prosocial Behavior, Aggression, and Crowding   Up to now, the effects of crowding that we have discussed have been uniformly negative. It should come as no surprise, then, that prosocial behavior diminishes and aggression increases under crowded conditions.

The evidence regarding helping behavior and density, while not completely consistent, generally shows that helping is lower in areas of high density. For example, residents of high-, medium-, and low-density university dormitories differed in the frequency with which they mailed stamped, addressed envelopes that had apparently been dropped; residents in lower-density dormitories were much more likely to return the letters than those living in higher-density dorms (Bickman, Teger, Gabriele, McLaughlin, Berger, & Sunaday, 1973). Similarly, people were less likely to help a confederate find a lost contact lens when a shopping mall was crowded than when it was relatively uncrowded (Cohen & Spacapan, 1978). One probable explanation for this finding is that there is greater diffusion of responsibility under conditions of greater crowding.

While most research is clear in suggesting that high-density environments lead to reductions in prosocial behavior, the evidence is not entirely consistent. The exception comes from research that has examined urban/rural differences. Although the first studies done indicated that urbanites, living under higher-density conditions, were less helpful than rural dwellers (e.g., Korte & Kerr, 1975), more recent research suggests that this may not be accurate (e.g., Holahan, 1977; House & Wolf, 1978). Indeed, it appears that lower levels of helping sometimes found in urban areas are due to fears for personal safety rather than a generalized unhelpfulness on the part of city dwellers.

BOX 15-4 SPOTLIGHT ON APPLICATIONS

IN SEARCH OF THE PERFECT DORMITORY

Although it is frequently contended that "people are social animals," this does not mean that being with others is something we want to do twenty-four hours a day. Indeed, as architect Joan Goody asserted at the beginning of the chapter, college students almost invariably state that they would prefer a single room over any other type.

Unfortunately, it is considerably more costly for schools to provide all or even mostly singles, so in most cases dormitories consist predominantly of double, and sometimes even triple and quadruple, rooms. But even though students tend to be less than pleased about the necessity of sharing a room with others, there are things that can be done to make the situation pleasanter—for it turns out that the configuration of a dormitory has an important bearing on student satisfaction.

In an ongoing series of field experiments, Andrew

FIGURE 15-7

Floor plans of traditional corridor-style and suite-style dormitories. Although similar in square footage, the configurations of the two floor plans had dramatic effects upon the occupants. Source: Baum & Valins (1977).

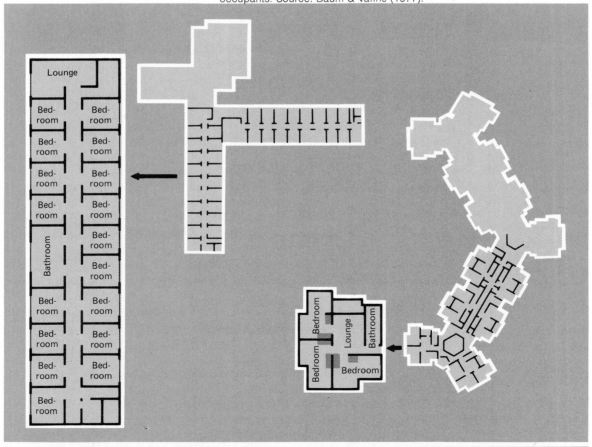

Baum and Stuart Valins (1977, 1979) investigated various dormitory floor plans at the State University of New York at Stony Brook. The major comparison was between residents assigned to dormitories arranged in a typical pattern—a series of bedrooms located along a long corridor, with a central bathroom and shared lounge—versus residents assigned to dormitories in which three to four bedrooms were arranged in a suite, with a bath and living room shared only by the occupants of the few bedrooms (see Figure 15-7).

Although the floor plans varied greatly, each resident had virtually identical square footage. But, as you might suspect, the effects on the occupants were dramatic. Residents of the corridor-style dormitory reported feeling significantly greater crowding, felt they had less privacy, and reported the desire to avoid others considerably more frequently than residents of the suite-style dormitories. In addition, while suite dwellers reported no differences in perceptions of crowding according to which room they had in the suite, there were strong differences in reported crowding according to the location of corridor style dorm dwellers. Students who lived near the bathroom or the lounge reported feeling considerably more crowded than those further away

from those two areas. Finally, corridor residents felt that they were forced into interactions with others much more frequently, they were less sure of what their neighbors thought about them, and they were less apt to perceive similarity in attitudes between themselves and their neighbors.

Perhaps the most intriguing finding to emerge from this series of studies is the fact that the effects of residence lingered even after the students left the dormitory. When residents participated in a laboratory study outside of the dorm, residents of the corridor-style dormitory tended to sit further away from a confederate and looked at him or her less often. They also performed worse than suite residents on a task that required cooperation—and better when the task called for an inhibition of personal involvment.

Why should suite residents come out so far ahead of corridor residents? The major reason seems to be that corridor residents have far less control over their social interactions with others. Thus, in order to cope with the situation, corridor residents tend to withdraw from social interaction with their peers.

For those of you living on campus, you might consider these data as you contemplate your choice of living quarters next semester.

When we look at aggression, the findings are also somewhat equivocal, although the general pattern of results suggests that there is a positive relationship between density and overt aggression, at least at moderate levels of crowding, and especially for males (Paulus, 1980). For example, Stokols, Rall, Pinner, & Schopler (1973) found that groups of males felt more aggressive—and thought others were more aggressive—in small rooms. Interestingly, though, the opposite was true for females in the same situation. It is possible that females may interpret the lowered intimacy of uncrowded conditions as somewhat aversive and thus be more inclined to act aggressively.

While it appears that aggression increases as crowding increases, there are limits to this pattern—and at very high levels of crowding, aggression actually drops (Loo, 1978). It appears that at high levels of crowding, aggression may make people feel *more* involved with others—when what they really want is to develop some sense of control or territoriality. In order to develop this sense of control, they may try to reduce their social interaction (Paulus, 1980). If this is the case, people would be most likely to withdraw from the scene, rather than act aggressively.

Task Performance and Crowding: Can You Do Your Best in a Crowd?
If you had your choice of taking a test in an isolated, uncrowded room

or in a room that was crowded with others, which would you choose? Based on our previous discussion of the many negative factors associated with crowding, it seems that the obvious choice would be to take the test under uncrowded conditions.

However, based on theoretical work on task performance, you might be making a mistake—depending on the nature of the test. If the test were relatively simple, you might actually perform better in a more crowded situation. On the other hand, if the test were complicated, you would be likely to perform best when taking the test alone. The reason for this differential prediction is the old Yerkes–Dodson law, a model that relates arousal to task performance. According to the law, arousal facilitates performance on simple tasks, but decreases performance on complex tasks. What this means is that when arousal is high and crowding does appear to increase arousal, complex task performance will suffer. But when the task is simple, crowding not only should not hurt performance, but may even act to improve it.

Congruent with this formulation, many studies show no effects of crowding on task performance—but in general such studies have used very simple tasks (e.g., Freedman, Levy, Buchanan, & Price, 1972; Stokols, Rall, Pinner, & Schopler, 1973). But in experiments in which the tasks are complex, crowding has a definite negative effect upon performance (e.g., Paulus & Matthews, 1980). Moreover, crowding can have lingering effects upon task performance. For example, Sherrod (1974) asked groups of students to sit together under either very crowded or uncrowded conditions and work on a variety of simple tasks for two hours. Later, they were all taken to a large uncrowded room and given a test designed to measure tolerance for frustration. Interestingly, the students who had initially been in the crowded room became frustrated much more quickly than those who had worked under uncrowded conditions.

In sum, the effects of crowding on performance are complicated, but a few generalities have emerged. Performance on simple tasks seems largely unaffected by crowding. However, complex task performance clearly suffers in a crowded situation, and there may be detrimental aftereffects as well.

Controlling the Consequences of Crowding: Applications and Design Suggestions

We have seen a number of different effects of crowded conditions, including physiological arousal, decreased interpersonal attraction, decreased helping, increased aggression, and frequent decrements in task performance—all in all, a fairly sorry lot. Can these aversive reactions to crowding be alleviated or in any way controlled?

If we return to the four models of crowding that we discussed initially in this section—stimulus overload, loss of control, ecological models, and focus of attention approaches—some suggestions for design and

Design features should take into account the kinds of activities that occur in a given area. (Hugh Rogers/Monkmeyer Press)

situational improvements may be made. For example, to reduce stimulus overload, the initial designs of buildings should allow ample space for the users. Control approaches (in agreement with architect Joan Goody's comments) would suggest that areas be designed to give residents a choice in how they use the space and the activities in which they engage. In concrete terms, this suggests that walls and partitions might be movable and furniture should be easy to rearrange.

The ecological approach suggests that designers should construct spaces in which the perception of involvement in the ongoing activities for which the space was designed is enhanced. In contrast, the focus of attention approach implies that the use of bright colors, pictures and posters on walls, and other visual distractions would lead to less attention being paid to other people and more to the environment, something that ought to lower perceptions of crowding.

While none of these suggestions is a cure-all for the negative consequences of crowding, they do provide some concrete steps that may be taken to alleviate what can be a very debilitating phenomenon. They also illustrate some of the ways in which theory and research carried out by social psychologists can have a beneficial effect on everyday life—a theme that we have been sounding throughout this book.

SUMMARY

Environmental psychology studies the relationship between the physical environment and social behavior. The term "territoriality" has been used to label the feelings of ownership that develop over a particular geographic area. There are three general types of territories: primary territories, which are under the complete, long-term control of their users; secondary territories, which are under temporary control; and public territories, areas which any member of the public has the right to use. People use markers, such as fences, walls, hedges, and signs, to maintain territories. Territories serve a number of functions. They allow us to organize our daily lives; they develop, clarify, and maintain social organization; and they act as a source of group and personal identity.

Personal space is the area around a person's body into which others may not enter. Maintenance of personal space may prevent information overload, may serve as protection from stressful stimuli, and may act as a communication channel.

Crowding is a psychological state that is stressful and motivates attempts to bring about its reduction or cessation. In contrast, high density is a state that is related to the physical and spatial aspects of a situation. At least four explanations have been suggested for why high density can lead to the experience of crowding. These include stimulus overload, loss of control, ecological models, and focus of attention approaches. Among the responses to crowding are negative affective states, physiological arousal, decreases in interpersonal attraction, decreases in helping behavior, increases in aggression, and general decrements in performance.

KEY TERMS

cognitive maps
crowding
density
ecological model of crowding
environmental psychology
focus of attention
information overload
loss-of-control model of crowding

marker
personal space
primary territory
public territory
secondary territory
stimulus overload
stress theory
territory

FOR FURTHER STUDY AND APPLICATION

Altman, I. (1975). *The environment and social behavior.* Monterey, CA: Brooks/Cole.

Holahan, C. J. (1982). *Environmental psychology.* New York: Random House.

Two good introductions to the field of environmental psychology. Altman's book, in particular, has an excellent section on territoriality.

Proshansky, H. M., Ittelson, W. H., & Rivlin, L. G.

(Eds.). (1976). *Environmental psychology: People and their physical settings.* New York: Holt, Rinehart & Winston.

A fine set of chapters by distinguished authors. Fairly technical, but accessible.

Sommer, R. (1969). *Personal space.* Englewood Cliffs, NJ: Prentice-Hall.

Although some of the work reported here has been

superseded by more current research, the book remains a classic in the field. Chock full of ingenious experiments.

Evans, G. W. (Ed.). (1983). *Environmental stress.* New York: Cambridge University Press.

In this book, work on five kinds of environmental stress is examined: stress caused by noise, heat, air pollution, crowding, and poor architectural design.

Baum, A., & Valins, S. (1977). *Architecture and social behavior: Psychological studies of social density.* Hillsdale, NJ: Erlbaum.

Describes the extensive work done on crowding in dormitories at the State University of New York at Stony Brook. Makes for interesting reading.

GLOSSARY

abstract modeling As contrasted with direct modeling, occurs when individuals draw general principles underlying behavior observed (7).*

adaptors In kinesics, specific behaviors which served a particular function at some point in a person's development, but are no longer part of that person's behavioral repertoire (3).

additive model of impression formation Suggests that bits of information are added together to form a judgment about another person (2).

additive tasks Tasks on which each member's contribution is added to every other member's. Coordination is necessary to ensure against impinging on another to impede total output (11).

adjacency pair In verbal communication, two partners taking sequential turns where the second is in response to the first (3).

affective relationships In balance theory, relationships related to the nature of liking between the elements. With an unstable cognitive state, the perceiver seeks balance by making a change in the nature of the relationship (4).

* Indicates chapter in which term is introduced.

affiliation A tendency to desire others' company in order to obtain comfort, consolation, and reassurance (6).

ageism Negative attitudes toward older people and the aging process; discrimination against the aged and institutional policies that maintain stereotypes of aging (5).

aggression Intentional injury or harm to another (9).

altruism Helping behavior that is beneficial to others but requires clear self-sacrifice on the part of the helper (7).

anticipatory socialization Occurs when an individual adopts the attitudes and behaviors of a group to which he or she does not yet belong (12).

archival research Analysis of existing records or documents in an attempt to confirm a hypothesis (1).

attribution Understanding of and judgments about the causes underlying people's behavior (2).

attribution theory The systematic study of how observers determine the causes of behavior (1).

authoritarian personality A personality syndrome

in which individuals who developed hostility against authority figures displace their hostility toward groups perceived as weak or unconventional and therefore display prejudice and discrimination (5).

autokinetic effect An illusion in which a stationary light appears to move. Provides a method of investigating the transmission of norms in groups (10).

autonomous work groups A system whereby a small work group assembles an entire unit while filling a quota (allows for interchanging jobs) (12).

averaging model of impression formation Suggests that separate bits of information are mathematically averaged to derive a general impression of a person (2).

balance theory Proposed by Heider; concerned with how people make consistent their attitudes toward people and an attitudinal object (4).

behavioral self-blame Victim's assumption of responsibility for specific actions which helps preserve their sense of control (9).

brainstorming Technique for explicitly reversing norms that typically restrain and inhibit novelty to encourage deviant thinking and creativity. Participants present ideas spontaneously, with no critique until after the session (12).

brainwashing The use of coercion to bring about attitude change (4).

catharsis hypothesis Asserts that participation in such activities as sports or drama can be a means of reducing aggression (9).

central route of persuasion Persuasion which occurs due to an individual's thoughtful consideration of issues related to persuasive attempt (4).

central traits Those particular traits which are used to organize an impression of and provide a framework for the interpretation of subsequent information in determining an impression of another (2).

classical conditioning Learning through the pairing of a previously neutral stimulus and an unconditioned stimulus to evoke a response (1).

coercive power Power based on the ability to deliver punishment as a consequence of noncompliance (10).

cognitive dissonance A state of psychological tension, aroused when an individual holds two cognitions that contradict one another (4).

cognitive mapping The way that spatial information is acquired, perceived, stored, and used in the understanding of one's physical environment (15).

cognitive theories Theories that emphasize how people subjectively understand, interpret, and experience the world (1).

collective behavior Behavior occurring in relatively unorganized aggregates of people who nevertheless have a sense of unity and perhaps work toward a common goal (11).

Commons Dilemma A situation where each person, using a set of finite resources, can choose to cooperate and personally use less of the resource or not cooperate and use more. The dilemma emerges from the fact that if too many do not cooperate, the resource will be depleted (14).

communication channel Path along which messages flow (e.g., eye gaze, posture, and verbal channel, or tone of voice) (3).

communication networks (in organizations) Patterns imposed on a group restricting the flow of messages (12).

comparison level The outcome that individuals feel is appropriate and deserved from a relationship, derived from prior experience as well as the perception of others' satisfaction in similar relationships (14).

comparison level for alternatives The outcomes that an individual feels could be obtained from the best alternative interaction available (14).

competitive motivational orientation In a bargaining situation, where a bargainer is motivated to attempt to do better than his partner (14).

consensus In Kelley's attribution theory, the degree to which others react similarly in a given situation (2).

contingency model Model of leadership based on match between leader and task characteristics; devised by Fiedler (10).

control group That group used in scientific experiments in which researcher does not manipulate the variable being studied to contrast effects of a manipulation in another group (1).

cooperative motivational orientation In a bargaining situation, where bargainers have a positive interest in their partners' outcome as well as their own (14).

correlational research Tests whether changes in one factor are associated with changes in another factor (1).

correspondent inferences The process by which people attempt to attribute a behavior or action to a specific underlying intention, trait, or disposition consistent with the behavior (2).

covariation principle Suggests that we try to analyze the relationships among a multitude of possible cause-and-effect variables inherent in a situation to pinpoint a cause of behavior (2).

crowding In contrast to density, refers to psychological or subjective factors; how an individual is affected by the perception of a given number of people in a particular space (15).

cues to action Component of Health Belief Model, consisting mainly of situational influences that affect perception of degree of threat posed by the disease (7).

debasement A concept suggesting that individuals who experience an enlightening event that portrays some inadequacy within themselves become unusually susceptible to social influence (12).

defensive tactics of restoring equity A method of restoring equity involving psychological distortion of the way in which input–outcome ratios are perceived (13).

deindividuation A psychological state where self-awareness is reduced and fear of negative evaluation by others is diminished, resulting in an increased tendency to engage in impulsive, antisocial, inappropriate behavior (9).

Delphi method Variant of the nominal group technique, using questionnaires to elicit experts' responses to a topic, ultimately to obtain their assessment of the optimal solution (12).

demand characteristics The cues that subjects obtain in an experiment that provide information regarding what is expected or appropriate behavior (1).

density In contrast to crowding, refers to the objective state and number of people per spatial unit (15).

dependent variable That factor in an experiment expected to change as a result of changes in the independent variable (1).

diffusion of responsibility Suggests that when there is more than one witness to a situation requiring helping, responsibility for acting is felt to be diffused or shared among the bystanders, thereby reducing the likelihood of an individual's tendency to help (7).

direct tactics of restoring equity Those tactics in which people directly alter their own, or others', inputs and/or outputs (13).

discrimination Behavioral manifestation of prejudice (5).

display rules Implicit rules that govern a situation or interpersonal relationship on the appropriateness of showing a particular emotion via facial expressions (3).

distinctiveness In Kelley's attribution theory, the extent to which the same behavior occurs in relation to other people or stimuli (2).

ecological model of crowding Suggests that high density is aversive because of the scarcity of resources to carry out what one is attempting (15).

emblem In kinesics, a behavior which serves to replace verbal communication, with a shared common meaning within a culture (3).

emergent norm theory Assumes that heterogeneous individuals, once in a crowd, develop common motives and norms relevant to the immediate situation (11).

empirical research The systemic collection of data and observation to test ideas (1).

environmental psychology The area of social psychology directed at understanding the relationship between the environment and social behavior (15).

equality models of justice Suggest that contributions made by people should be ignored; instead, contend that there should be equalization of outcomes (13).

equilibrium theory of nonverbal behavioral channels Suggests that increases in intimacy in one nonverbal channel are accompanied by a compensatory decrease in another nonverbal channel (3).

equity models of justice Suggest that the rewards people receive should be proportional to the magnitude of their contributions (13).

equity theory Considers social exchange to be fair when an individual's own outcomes and those perceived for a partner are balanced, along with costs of each partner (6).

Eros Freud's term for the life instinct (9).

evaluation apprehension Subject's concern that another person will evaluate him or her (4).

experimental research Aimed at discovering causal relationships between various factors, where a change in one factor causes a change in the other (1).

experimenter expectancy effect Occurs when an experimenter emits unintentional cues to subjects regarding the way in which they are to behave in a given condition (1).

expert power Power wielded by one who exceeds others in a particular area of knowledge; the power is limited to its particular area of expertise (10).

facial affect program View which asserts that each primary emotion has a characteristic muscular activation which results in a particular facial expression (3).

facial feedback hypothesis Asserts that facial expressions not only reflect emotion but are also important in determining how people actually experience and label emotion (3).

field experiment Research done in "natural" settings but including appropriate controls and manipulations, allowing cause-and-effect relationships to be determined (1).

field study A research study done in a naturally occurring environment (1).

fight-or-flight response Mechanism by which an organism prepares to defend itself from danger either by fighting or by fleeing (9).

file-drawer problem Cases in which research not proven statistically significant is not published, thereby possibly introducing bias by not being considered in meta-analysis and literature reviews (10).

focus of attention approach to crowding Suggests that a person's focus may shift in high-density situations; the nature of this shift determines whether crowding is experienced (13).

forewarning A technique for increasing resistance to persuasion in which people are given information that they will be receiving; a message discrepant from their current attitude, giving them the opportunity to develop counterarguments (4).

frustration–aggression theory Suggests that frustration, resulting from blocked goal attainment, leads to a readiness to be aggressive (9).

frustration theory of prejudice From psychodynamic view, suggests that prejudice is a manifestation of displaced hostility due to frustration (5).

fundamental attribution error Observers' tendency to overestimate the degree to which actors' personal dispositions cause behavior and underestimate the effect of situational factors (2).

generalization The ability to apply the results of a study to settings and subject populations beyond those immediately employed in the experiment (1).

genetic theories Suggest that social behavior has its roots in biologically determined causes (1).

great person theory An approach to leadership which examines personality traits of "leaders" in an attempt to develop a set of qualities to differentiate leaders from followers (10).

group An aggregate of individuals in which there is (1) interaction among members, (2) perception of membership, (3) shared goals and norms, and (4) fate interdependence (11).

group cohesiveness The extent to which members want to continue as a group; provides measure of how attractive the group is to its membership (11).

group dynamics An area of social psychology concerned with small-group behavior (11).

group mind Notion suggesting that participation in groups can cause the disappearance of one's overt, everyday personality and the incorporation of a uniform way of thinking and set of ideas (11).

group structure The regular, stable patterns of behavior which evolve in groups (11).

groupthink Deterioration of mental efficiency, reality testing, and moral judgment resulting from in-group pressure (11).

halo effect The inference of uniformly negative or positive traits based on an initial judgment regarding the presence of negative or positive traits (2).

Hawthorne effect A subject's change in behavior simply as a function of the attention received rather than of the experimental manipulations themselves (2).

Health Belief Model (HBM) Developed to explain behavior related to prevention of potential disease (7).

hypothetical constructs Abstract concepts not existing in a directly observable way (4).

idiosyncracy credit In Hollander's theory, the mechanism underlying an individual's ability to espouse an unpopular view accomplished by accruing credit or group approval through an initial display of competence and fulfillment of group expectations (10).

illustrator In kinesics, a well-defined type of body behavior which acts to modify and augment spoken messages (3).

implicit deception Occurs when the experimental situation is so different from what subjects expect that they behave under incorrect assumptions (1).

impression management Methods by which people try to create specific impressions about themselves (1).

independent variable In an experiment, that factor being manipulated by researcher to learn the effects of the manipulation (1).

individualistic motivational orientation When bargainers are concerned only with maximizing their own outcomes (14).

informational power Power based on the specific content of an individual's information (10).

informational social influence Brings about conformity due to the fact that others sometimes have more knowledge and information about the world (10).

inoculation theory Suggests that people's attitudes are made more resistant to persuasion by earlier exposure to samples of opposing arguments and refutational strategies (4).

instinct theories of aggression View aggression as determined by innate, biological, preprogrammed processes (9).

interactional approach to leadership Asserts that neither personality nor situational characteristics alone can explain leadership emergence sufficiently; their interaction must be considered (10).

interpersonal attraction The area of social psychology that deals with the way in which people form and maintain social relationships and develop liking for one another (6).

job enlargement A technique by which an employee's activities and responsibilities are expanded; meant to increase job interest and cohesiveness (11).

just-world hypothesis A model of justice based on the notion that one's behavior produces the rewards and punishments one incurs. Consequently, those rewarded are thought to be good; those punished are thought to be bad (13).

kinesics Study of how movements of body parts are related to communication (3).

least-preferred coworker (LPC) In Fiedler's theory of leadership, individual identified by leader as "most difficult to work with." Used in attempts to predict most appropriate type of leader for a given situation (10).

legitimate power Power wielded due to formal position or role which an individual occupies (10).

Likert scale Direct method of measuring an individual's evaluation of an attitudinal object, typically using a 7-point scale on which degree of agreement is indicated (4).

linguistic competence An individual's highest level of linguistic ability (reflected in the initial formulation of a message) (3).

loss of control models of crowding Suggest that excess numbers of people in relatively small areas lead a person to feel a reduction in his or her behavioral control and freedom (15).

matching hypothesis Suggests that an individual's choices of potential partners are influenced by his or her own level of physical attractiveness (6).

mere exposure phenomenon Phenomenon in which repeated exposure to any stimulus tends to increase the positivity of evaluation of the stimulus (6).

message formulation Process by which a message is encoded to match specific characteristics of the recipient (3).

meta-communicative content The underlying meaning that is an unspoken part of a message (3).

minimum power theory Asserts that participants in a bargaining situation will tend to divide rewards on the basis of power wielded (14).

minimum resource theory Asserts that a coalition

will form in a bargaining situation whereby the total resources brought to the coalition are as small as possible but large enough to allow the members to win (14).

minority group From a social psychological standpoint, a minority is determined by psychological factors as opposed to strictly numerical characteristics, with the salient defining characteristic being the amount of power wielded by each group (5).

MUM effect The reluctance of individuals to transmit bad news in a desire to protect the recipient (17).

need-complementary hypothesis Asserts that people are attracted to others with significantly different personalities but complementary needs (6).

negative reference groups Those groups which affect one's behavior due to motivation to avoid similarity or identification with members of the group (10).

nominal group technique A method designed to produce innovation and participation in organization. After participants advocate ideas, they are discussed and evaluated; then a final majority vote is taken (12).

nonparticipant observation Done by recording people's behavior without intervening in the situation (1).

norm A generalized expectation regarding appropriate behavior in a given situation (4).

normative social influence Conformity based on an attempt to meet the expectation of others and group norms (10).

operant conditioning A kind of learning in which reinforcement which follows a response leads to changes in the likelihood of the response occurring again (1).

operationalization The way in which abstract concepts of the hypothesis are translated into actual procedures used in a research study (1).

opponent process theory A phenomenon in which the presence of a strong emotional response triggers an opposite emotional process after the initial reaction (8).

organizational socialization Process of being indoctrinated and trained regarding what is important in an organization (12).

overjustification effect Phenomenon in which there is a loss of intrinsic value in performing a task when external reinforcements are offered (4).

overload model of personal space Suggests that people maintain personal space in order to reduce potential overload of their information-processing systems (15).

participant observation Where researcher participates in ongoing activities of the people being observed (1).

path-goal theory of leadership Interactional theory concerned primarily with the way in which leaders satisfy subordinates' motivated goals (10).

payoff matrix A means of representing various alternative responses that one can make in a given situation, as well as those of the person with whom one is interacting, and the potential outcomes (14).

peripheral route (of persuasion) Use of noncontent information in acceptance of the message of persuasion (4).

person perception The way in which particular traits are used in forming an overall impression of others (2).

person positivity bias Refers to the tendency to rate others in a predominantly positive way (2).

personal normative structure A reflection of the extent to which norms have been internalized in an individual (8).

personal space Refers to the area around a person's body into which others may not enter (15).

power semantic The power or status level that a conversant holds, suggesting that higher authority be addressed with greater formality (3).

prejudice Positive or negative evaluations of members of a particular group based primarily on membership in the group rather than characteristics of the individual (5).

primary territories Geographic areas under the complete, long-term control of their users; they are perceived as such by both the owners and others (15).

prosocial behavior Behavior which benefits other people (8).

proxemics Refers to the regularities that occur in interpersonal spacing (3).

psychodynamic approach to prejudice Contends

that deficits in an individual's level of psychological functioning lead to prejudice (5).

public territories Geographic areas any member of the public has a right to use (15).

random assignment Use of the laws of probability in assigning subjects in an experiment to a given condition, so that each subject has an equal probability by being assigned to a condition (1).

recency effect When later information received is given more credence than earlier information in person perception (2).

reciprocity norm Suggests that prosocial behavior ought eventually to be reciprocated to the helpers (8).

reciprocity of liking Phenomenon in which knowledge of someone's admiration for us tends to result in the other being held in positive regard in return (6).

reference group A group to which one belongs, or wishes to belong, and which provides standards and norms of appropriate behavior. Reference groups can provide both explicit and implicit conformity pressure (10).

referent power Power attributed to individuals or groups (reference groups) with whom identification occurs. These individuals or groups provide standards of appropriate behavior (10).

reinforcement theory of attitude formation Suggests that attitudes are learned through reward and punishment (4).

relative needs model of justice Suggests that resources be allocated according to greatest need without regard to the degree of contribution (13).

relative needs norm Suggests that resources should be distributed according to need without regard to initial amounts of resource contributions from each party (14).

resistance point The worst deal to which the bargainer is willing to agree (14).

reward power Power based on the ability to provide rewards, increasing influence in a specific setting (10).

risky shift Phenomenon by which group decisions are riskier and less conservative than individuals' decisions (11).

role A set of behaviors associated with a position (1).

role deception Occurs when other participants in a study are misrepresented (1).

role model An individual who provides an example of behaviors associated with a particular position or status (12).

role taking The understanding that others have different points of view and perceptions and that messages need to take account of this (3).

role theory Asserts that behavior is shaped by the roles that society provides for individuals to play. (1).

Sapir–Whorf hypothesis Proposes that language tends to influence and perhaps determine how people view and understand the world (3).

secondary territories Geographic areas under less personal control than primary territories. Usage is not permanent and any one individual is not the sole user over the course of a day; only temporary ownership is perceived (15).

self-fulfilling prophecy Phenomenon whereby the expectation about the possibility of future events or behaviors acts to increase the likelihood that those events or behaviors will occur (5).

self-handicapping strategy Where a person sets up circumstances to accommodate future failures and to cast blame on external rather than internal causes (2).

self-perception theory Builds on attribution theory; suggests that people can form attitudes by observing their own behavior and inferring attitudes from the behavior (4).

semantic differential scaling Method which uses bipolar adjectives to obtain a direct measure of evaluation of an attitudinal object (4).

settlement range The scale along which a buyer and seller can potentially agree (14).

situational approach to leadership Implies that the characteristics of a situation, not the individuals involved, determine leadership emergence (10).

situational approach to prejudice Emphasizes ways in which the immediate environment is related to prejudicial attitudes (5).

sleeper effect An increase in the persuasive impact of a message occurring after time has elapsed from the initial exposure to the persuasive message (4).

social cognition The way in which people think about and understand their social world (2).

social communicative competence The degree to which individuals take into account the characteristics of their audience and produce a message formulated for the audience understanding (3).

social comparison theory Asserts that people are dependent on others for information about the social and physical world around them and to evaluate their own behavior, abilities, expertise, and opinions (2).

social exchange theory Views human interaction as a kind of joint economic activity where rewards and costs involved are assessed to determine the value of continuing the relationship (14).

social facilitation Phenomenon in which the presence of others may lead to increased productivity or performance (11).

social influence Where actions of an individual or group affect the behavior of others, intentionally or unintentionally (10).

social learning theory Focuses on social behavior from learning theory perceptions; the emphasis is on how rewards and punishments affect the acquisition and maintenance of behavior (1).

social loafing Phenomenon occurring when the presence of others results in a decrease of individual effort (11).

social power Power based on the ability to shape and control another's behavior; representative of potential for social influence (10).

social psychology The discipline that examines how a person's thoughts, feelings, and actions are affected by others. A science which seeks to predict and understand social behavior (1).

social reality Refers to people's judgments of how others generally think, feel, and view the world (2).

social responsibility norm Suggests that there is an expectation that people will respond to the legitimate needs of those dependent on them (8).

social supporter In a social influence situation, an individual who agrees with the target of conformity pressure, and who allows the target to remain independent (10).

sociobiology Area of study which suggests that, through a process of natural selection, certain social behaviors have evolved to provide the human species with survival advantages (1).

sociocultural approach to prejudice Suggests that the impact of society operates in various ways to influence individuals' prejudice (5).

solidarity semantic The degree of shared social experience between two individuals relating to verbal communication processes (3).

status Evaluation of a role by the group in which the role is contained or defined (11).

stereotype Cognitions and expectations assigned to members of groups simply on the basis of their membership in the group (5).

stimulus overload approach to crowding Suggests that high density results in negative psychological states because too many stimuli overwhelm people and cannot be processed (13).

stress theory Says that personal space can shield us from stressful stimuli (such as aggression or noise) that may be presented when others come too close (15).

survey research Research in which a representative group of people (respondents) are asked a series of questions regarding their behavior, attitudes, or beliefs (1).

target point The notion (in negotiating) that people have of what they expect to end up with (14).

technical deception Occurs when equipment and procedures of an experiment are misrepresented (1).

territoriality Behavior associated with the ownership or occupation of a place; frequently involves personalizing the area and defending it against intrusion (15).

Thanatos Freud's term for the death drive (working in opposition to Eros) (9).

Thurstone scale An equal-appearing interval scale which validates the assumption of mathematically equal intervals between points on the scale (4).

tokenism Behavior in which an individual's relatively unimportant acts toward a minority allow avoidance of tasks of greater value (5).

training group (T-group) Group in which the objectives are to attempt to harness explicitly group norms and processes in order to make individuals more aware of their feelings, capabilities, and understanding of the world (11).

treatment group In an experiment, that group

which receives some kind of procedure provided by an investigator (1).

Type A behavior pattern Behavior syndrome associated with a higher risk of coronary heart disease; characterized primarily by intense ambition, competitive drive, preoccupation with occupational deadlines, and time urgency (7).

Type B behavior pattern Behavior syndrome associated with a lower risk of coronary heart disease; characterized by easygoing attitudes and relaxed, uncompetitive, patient, and rarely hostile behaviors, in contrast to Type A behaviors (7).

ultimate attributional error Prejudiced person's tendency to attribute negative actions of minority to dispositional characteristics of the target of prejudice (5).

unit relationships In balance theory, the degree to which elements are perceived as belonging together due to similarity, ownership, or similar membership in a class (4).

values clarification technique A method for examining and understanding the values currently held by an individual (8).

variable-sum situation A bargaining situation in which both parties simultaneously may benefit or lose from a bargain struck (14).

vicarious learning Learning due to the observation of others receiving rewards and punishments (4).

Vroom & Yetton contingency model Attempts to provide guidelines for determining when and what kind of participative decision making is most effective (12).

weapons effect A phenomenon in which the mere presence of weaponry is believed sufficient to evoke a readiness to act aggressively (9).

weighted probability theory Assigns a probability of occurrence and determines the number of possible winning minimal coalitions and numbers of members of each (14).

zero-sum bargaining situation Where a gain to one person in a bargaining situation is a loss to another (14).

BIBLIOGRAPHY

Adams, G. R. (1977). Physical attractiveness research: Toward a developmental social psychology of beauty. *Human Development, 20,* 217–239.

Adams, G. R., & Huston T. L. (1975). Social perception of middle-aged persons varying in physical attractiveness. *Developmental Psychology, 11,* 657–658.

Aderman, D., Brehm, S. S., & Katz, L. B. (1974). Empathic observation of an innocent victim: The just world revisited. *Journal of Personality and Social Psychology, 29,* 342–347.

Adorno, T. W., Frenkel-Brunswik, E., Levinson, R. N., & Sanford, R. N. (1950). *The authoritarian personality.* New York: Harper & Row.

Aiello, J. R., & Aiello, T. D. (1974). The development of personal space: Proxemic behavior of children six through sixteen. *Human Ecology, 2,* 177–189.

Aiello, J. R., Baum, A., & Gormley, F. P. (1980). *Social determinants of residential crowding stress.* Unpublished manuscript, Rutgers University, New Brunswick, NJ.

Aiello, J. R., Nicosia, G., & Thompson, D. E. (1979). Physiological, social, and behavioral consequences of crowding on children and adolescents. *Child Development, 50,* 195–202.

Aiello, J. R., & Thompson, D. E. (1980). Personal space, crowding, and spatial behavior in a cultural context. In I. Altman, J. F. Wohlwill, & A. Rapoport (Eds.), *Human behavior and environment: Vol. 4. Environment and culture.* New York: Plenum Press.

Aiello, J. R., Vautier, J. S., & Bernstein, M. D. (1983, August). *Crowding stress: Impact of social support, group formation, and control.* Paper presented at the meeting of the American Psychological Association, Anaheim, CA.

Ajzen, I. (1974). Effects of information on interpersonal attraction: Similarity versus affective value. *Journal of Personality and Social Psychology, 29,* 374–380.

Ajzen, I., & Fishbein, M. (1980). *Understanding attitudes and predicting social behavior.* Englewood Cliffs, NJ: Prentice-Hall.

Ajzen, I., Timko, C., & White, J. (1982). Self-monitoring and the attitude-behavior relation. *Journal of Personality and Social Psychology, 42,* 426–435.

Allen, V. L. (1965). Situational factors in conformity. In L. Berkowitz (Ed.), *Advances in Experimental Social Psychology* (Vol. 2). New York: Academic Press.

Allen, V. L. (1975). Social support for nonconformity. In L. Berkowitz (Ed.), *Advances in experimental social psychology* (Vol. 8). New York: Academic Press.

Allen, V. L. (Ed.). (1976). *Children as teachers: Theory and research on tutoring.* New York: Academic Press.

Allen, V. L., & Atkinson, M. L. (1981). Identification of spontaneous and deliberate behavior. *Journal of Nonverbal Behavior, 5,* 224–237.

Allen, V. L., & Feldman, R. S. (1973). Learning through tutoring: Low achieving children as tutors. *Journal of Experimental Education, 42,* 1–5.

Allen, V. L., & Levine, J. M. (1971). Social support and conformity: The role of independent assessment of reality. *Journal of Experimental Social Psychology, 7,* 48–58.

Allen, V. L., & Wilder, D. A. (1975a). Categorization, belief similarity, and intergroup discrimination. *Journal of Personality and Social Psychology, 32,* 971–977.

Allen, V. L., & Wilder, D. A. (1975b). Cognitive restructuring induced by social support. Unpublished manuscript. Cited in V. L. Allen, Social support for nonconformity. In L. Berkowitz (Ed.), *Advances in experimental social psychology* (Vol. 8). New York: Academic Press.

Allport, F. H. (1924). *Social psychology.* Boston: Houghton Mifflin.

Allport, G. (1968). The historical background of modern social psychology. In G. Lindzey & E. Aronson (Eds.), *The handbook of social psychology* (2nd ed.). Reading, MA: Addison-Wesley.

Allport, G. W. (1935). Attitudes. In C. Murchison (Ed.), *Handbook of social psychology* (pp. 798–884). Worcester, MA: Clark University Press.

Allport G. W. (1954). *The nature of prejudice.* Cambridge, MA: Addison-Wesley.

Allport, G. W., & Postman, L. J. (1945). The basic psychology of rumor. *Transactions of the New York Academy of Sciences, 8* (Series II), 61–81.

Altman, I. (1975). *The environment and social behavior.* Monetery, CA: Brooks/Cole.

Altman, J. S., & Taylor, D. A. (1973). *Social penetration: The development of interpersonal relationships.* New York: Holt, Rinehart and Winston.

Amir, Y. (1976). The role of intergroup contact in change of prejudice and ethnic relations. In P. Katz (Ed.), *Towards the elimination of racism.* New York: Pergamon.

Amir, Y., & Sharan, S. (1984). *School desegregation.* Hillsdale, NJ: Erlbaum.

Anderson, C. A., & Anderson, D. C. (1984). Ambient temperature and violent crime: Tests of the linear and curvilinear hypotheses. *Journal of Personality and Social Psychology, 46,* 91–97.

Anderson, K. O., & Masur, F. T. III. (1983, August). *Psychological preparation for cardiac catheterization.* Paper presented at the 91st annual convention of the American Psychological Association, Anaheim, CA.

Anderson, N. H. (1965). Averaging versus adding as a stimulus-combination rule in impression formation. *Journal of Experimental Psychology, 70,* 394–400.

Anderson, N. H. (1974). Cognitive algebra integration theory applied to social attribution. In L. Berkowitz (Ed.), *Advances in experimental social psychology* (Vol. 7, pp. 1–101). New York: Academic Press.

Andrews, C. R., & Debus, R. L. (1978). Persistence and causal perception of failure: Modifying cognitive attributions. *Journal of Educational Psychology, 70,* 154–166.

Andrews, K. H., & Kandel, D. B. (1979). Attitude and behavior: A specification of the contingent consistency hypothesis. *American Sociological Review, 44,* 298–310.

Appleyard, D. (1976). *Planning a pluralistic city.* Cambridge, MA: M.I.T. Press.

Archibald, W. P. (1974). Alternative explanations for the self-fulfilling prophecy. *Psychological Bulletin, 81,* 74–84.

Argyle, M., & Cook, M. (1976). *Gaze and mutual gaze.* Cambridge, England: Cambridge University Press.

Argyle, M., & Dear, J. (1965). Eye-contact, distance and affiliation. *Sociometry, 28,* 289–304.

Argyle, M., Ingham, R., Alkema, F., & McCallin, M. (1974). Social skills training and psychotherapy: A comparative study. *Psychological Medicine, 4,* 435–443.

Argyle, M., Trower, P., & Bryant, B. (1974). Explorations in the treatment of personality disorders and neuroses by social skills training. *British Journal of Medical Psychology.* 47, 63–72.

Aronoff, J., & Messé, L. A. (1971). Motivational determinants of small-group structure. *Journal of Personality and Social Psychology, 17,* 319–324.

Aronson, E., & Bridgeman, D. (1979). Jigsaw groups and the desegregated classroom: In pursuit of common goals. *Journal of Personality and Social Psychology, 5,* 438–446.

Aronson, E., & Golden, B. W. (1962). The effect of relevant and irrelevant aspects of communicator credibility on attitude change. *Journal of Personality, 30,* 135–146.

Aronson, E., Stephan, W., Sikes, J., Blaney, N., & Snapp, M. (1978). *Cooperation in the classroom.* Beverly Hills, CA: Sage.

Aronson, E., Willerman, B., & Floyd, J. (1966). The effect of a pratfall on increasing interpersonal attractiveness. *Psychonomic Science, 4,* 227–228.

Asch, S. E. (1946). Forming impressions of personality. *Journal of Abnormal and Social Psychology, 41,* 258–290.

Asch, S. E. (1951). Effects of group pressure upon the modification and distortion of judgments. In H. Guetzkow (Ed.), *Groups, leadership, and men.* Pittsburgh, PA: Carnegie Press.

Asch, S. E. (1952). *Social psychology.* Englewood Cliffs, NJ: Prentice-Hall.

Asch, S. E. (1955). Opinions and social pressure. *Scientific American, 193,* 31–55.

Asch, S. E., & Zukier, H. (1984). Thinking about persons. *Journal of Personality and Social Psychology, 46,* 1230–1240.

Ashmore, R. D. (1970). Prejudice: Causes and cures. In B. E. Collins (Ed.), *Social psychology.* Reading, MA: Addison-Wesley.

Austin, W., Walster (Hatfield), E., & Utne, M. K. (1976). Equity and the law: The effect of harmdoer's "suffering in the act" on liking and assigned punishment. In L. Berkowitz & E. Walster (Eds.), *Advances in experimental social psychology* (Vol. 9, pp. 163–190). New York: Academic Press.

Bach, G., & Wyden, P. (1968). *The intimate enemy: How to fight fair in love and marriage.* New York: Avon.

Bagozzi, R. P., & Burnkrant, R. E. (1979). Attitude organization and the attitude–behavior rela-

tionship. *Journal of Personality and Social Psychology, 37,* 913–929.

Bailey, D. S., Leonard, K. E., Cranston, J. W., & Taylor, S. P. (1983). Effects of alcohol and self-awareness on human physical aggression. *Personality and Social Psychology Bulletin, 9,* 289–295.

Bales, R. F. (1950). *Interaction process analysis.* Reading, MA: Addison-Wesley.

Ball, S. (1976). Methodological problems in assessing the impact of television programs. *Journal of Social Issues, 32,* 8–17.

Ballew v. Georgia, 46 LW4217 (1978).

Bandura, A. (1965). Vicarious processes: A case of no-trial learning. In L. Berkowitz (Ed.), *Advances in experimental social psychology* (Vol. 2, pp. 1–55). New York: Academic Press.

Bandura, A. (1973). *Aggression: A social learning analysis.* Englewood Cliffs, NJ: Prentice-Hall.

Bandura, A. (1977). *Social-learning theory.* Englewood Cliffs, NJ: Prentice-Hall.

Bandura, A., Ross, D., & Ross, S. (1963). Vicarious reinforcement and imitative learning. *Journal of Abnormal and Social Psychology, 67,* 601–607.

Baratz, J. C. (1969). Teaching reading in an urban Negro school. In J. C. Baratz and R. W. Shay (Eds.), *Teaching black children to read.* Washington, DC: Center for Applied Linguistics.

Bard, N., & Ellison, K. (1974). Crisis intervention and investigation of forcible rape. *The Police Chief, 41,* 68–73.

Barnlund, D. C. (1962). Consistency of emergent leadership in groups with changing tasks and numbers. *Speech Monographs, 29,* 45–52.

Baron, R. A. (1972). Aggression as a function of ambient temperature and prior anger arousal. *Journal of Personality and Social Psychology, 21,* 183–189.

Baron, R. A., & Bell, P. A. (1977). Sexual aggression and aggression by males: Effects of type of erotic stimuli and prior provocation. *Journal of Personality and Social Psychology, 35,* 79–87.

Baron, R. A., & Kepner, C. R. (1970). Model's behavior and attraction toward the model as determinants of adult aggressive behavior. *Journal of Personality and Social Psychology, 14,* 335–344.

Baron, R. A., & Ransberger, V. M. (1978). Ambient

temperature and the occurrence of collective violence: The "long, hot summer" revisited. *Journal of Personality and Social Psychology, 36,* 351–360.

Baron, R. A., Russell, G. W., & Arms, R. L. (1984). Negative ions and behavior. *Journal of Personality and Social Psychology.* In press.

Baron, R. M., Mandel, D. R., Adams, C. A., & Griffen, L. M. (1976). Effects of social density in university residential environments. *Journal of Personality and Social Psychology 34,* 434–446.

Baron, R. M., & Rodin, J. (1978). Perceived control and crowding stress. In A. Baum, J. E. Singer, & S. Valins (Eds.), *Advances in environmental psychology.* Hillsdale, NJ: Erlbaum.

Barret, F. M. (1980). Sexual experience, birth control usage, and sex education of unmarried Canadian university students: Changes between 1968 and 1978. *Archives of Sexual Behavior, 9,* 367–390.

Bar-Tal, D. (1978). Attributional analysis of achievement-related behavior. *Review of Educational Research, 48,* 259–271.

Bateson, G., Jackson, D. D., Haley, J., & Weakland, J. (1956). Toward a theory of schizophrenia. *Behavioral Science, 1,* 251–264.

Batson, C. D., Cochran, P. J., Biederman, M. F., Blosser, J. L., Ryan, M. J., & Vogt, B. (1978). Failure to help when in a hurry: Callousness or conflict? *Personality and Social Psychology Bulletin 4*(1), 97–101.

Baum, A., & Greenberg, C. I. (1975). Waiting for a crowd: The behavioral and perceptual effects of anticipated crowding. *Journal of Personality and Social Psychology, 32,* 667–671.

Baum, A., & Valins, S. (1977). *Architecture and social behavior: Psychological studies of social density.* Hillsdale, NJ: Erlbaum.

Baum, A., & Valins, S. (1979). Architectural mediation of residential density and control: Crowding and the regulation of social contact. In L. Berkowitz (Ed.), *Advances in experimental social psychology* (Vol. 12). New York: Academic Press.

Baumeister, R. F., & Darley, J. M. (1982). Reducing the biasing effect of perpetrator attractiveness in jury simulation. *Personality and Social Psychology Bulletin, 8,* 286–292.

Baumrind, D. (1964). Some thoughts on the ethics of reading Milgram's "Behavioral study of obedience." *American Psychologist, 19,* 421–423.

Bavelas, A. (1950). Communication patterns in task-oriented groups. *Journal of the Acoustical Society of America, 22,* 725–730.

Beaman, A. L., Cole, C. M., Preston, M., Klentz, B., & Steblay, N. M. (1983). Fifteen years of foot-in-the-door research: A meta-analysis. *Personality and Social Psychology Bulletin, 9,* 181–196.

Becker, H. S. (1973). *Outsiders: Studies in the sociology of deviance* (rev. ed.). New York: Free Press.

Becker, M. H., Kaback, M., Rosenstock, I. M., & Ruth, M. (1975). Some influences of public participation in a genetic screening program. *Journal of Community Health, 1,* 3–14.

Becker, M. H., & Maiman, L. A. (1975). Sociobehavioral determinants of compliance with health and medical care recommendations. *Medical Care, 13,* 10–24.

Becker, M. H., Maiman, L. A., Kirscht, J. P., Haefner, D. P., Drachman, R. H., & Taylor, D. W. (1979). Patient perceptions and compliance: Recent studies of the health belief model. In R. Haynes, D. Taylor, & D. Sackett (Eds.), *Compliance in health care.* Baltimore, MD.: Johns Hopkins University Press.

Beckhouse, L., Tanur, J., Weiler, J., & Weinstein, E. (1975). . . . And some men have leadership thrust upon them. *Journal of Personality and Social Psychology, 31,* 557–566.

Beckman, L. (1970). Effects of students' performance on teachers' and observers' attributions of causality. *Journal of Educational Psychology, 61,* 76–82.

Bell, P. A., Fisher, J. D., & Loomis, R. J. (1978). *Environmental psychology.* Philadelphia, PA: W. B. Saunders.

Bem, D. (1972). Self-perception theory. In L. Berkowitz (Ed.), *Advances in experimental social psychology* (Vol. 6, pp. 1–62). New York: Academic Press.

Bem, D. J. (1967). Self-perception: An alternative interpretation of cognitive dissonance phenomena. *Psychological Review, 74,* 183–200.

Ben-Sira, Z. (1976). The function of the professional's affective behavior in client satisfaction: A revised approach to social interaction theory. *Journal of Health and Social Behavior, 17,* 3–11.

Benton, A., Kelley, H. H., & Liebling, B. (1972). Effects of extremity of offers and concession rate on the outcomes of bargaining. *Journal of Personality and Social Psychology, 24,* 78–83.

Berg, J. H. (1984). Development of friendship between roommates. *Journal of Personality and Social Psychology, 46,* 346–356.

Berger, J., Cohen, B. P., & Zelditch, M., Jr. (1973). Status characteristics and social interaction. In R. J. Ofshe (Ed.), *Interpersonal behavior in small groups* (pp. 194–216). Englewood Cliffs, NJ: Prentice-Hall.

Berger, M. M. (1970). *Videotape techniques in psychiatric training and treatment.* New York: Brunner, Mazel.

Berger, S. M. (1962). Conditioning through vicarious instigation. *Psychological Review, 69,* 450–466.

Berkowitz, L. (1954). Group standards, cohesiveness, and productivity. *Human Relations, 7,* 509–519.

Berkowitz, L. (1965). Some aspects of observed aggression. *Journal of Personality and Social Psychology, 2,* 359–369.

Berkowitz, L. (1969). Resistance to improper dependency relationships. *Journal of Experimental Social Psychology, 5,* 282–294.

Berkowitz, L. (1972). Social norms, feelings, and other factors affecting helping and altruism. In L. Berkowitz (Ed.), *Advances in experimental social psychology* (Vol. 6). New York: Academic Press.

Berkowitz, L. (1973). Control of aggression. In B. M. Caldwell & H. Riccinti (Eds.), *Review of child development research* (Vol. 3, pp. 95–140). Chicago, IL: University of Chicago Press.

Berkowitz, L. (1974). Some determinants of impulsive aggression: The role of mediated associations with reinforcements for aggression. *Psychological Review, 81,* 165–176.

Berkowitz, L. (1983). Aversively stimulated aggression: Some parallels and differences in research with animals and humans. *American Psychologist, 38,* 1135–1144.

Berkowitz, L. (1984). Some effects of thoughts on anti- and prosocial influences of media events: A cognitive-neoassociation analysis. *Psychological Bulletin, 95,* (3) 410–427.

Berkowitz, L., & Daniels, L. R. (1963). Responsibility and dependency. *Journal of Abnormal and Social Psychology, 66,* 429–436.

Berkowitz, L., & Geen, R. G. (1966). Film violence and the cue properties of available targets. *Journal of Personality and Social Psychology, 3,* 525–530.

Berkowitz, L., & LePage, A. (1967). Weapons as aggression-eliciting stimuli. *Journal of Personality and Social Psychology, 7,* 202–207.

Berkowitz, S. B. (1967). *Differential diagnosis.* Springfield, IL: Thomas.

Berlyn, D. E. (1970). Novelty, complexity, and hedonic value. *Perception and Psychophysics, 8,* 279–286.

Berlyn, D. E. (Ed). (1974). *Studies in new experimental aesthetics: Steps toward an objective psychology of aesthetic appreciation.* New York: Halsted Press.

Bernstein, B. (1972). A socio-linguistic approach to socialization with some references to educability. In J. J. Guwperz and D. Hymes (Eds.), *Directions in sociolinguistics.* New York: Holt, Rinehart and Winston.

Berscheid, E. (in press). Interpersonal attraction. In G. Lindzey (Ed.), *Handbook of social psychology* (3rd ed.). Reading, MA: Addison-Wesley.

Berscheid, E., Dion, K. K., Walster, E., & Walster, G. W. (1971). Physical attractiveness and dating choice: A test of the matching hypothesis. *Journal of Experimental Social Psychology, 7,* 173–189.

Berscheid, E., & Walster, E. (1974). Physical attractiveness. In L. Berkowitz (Ed.), *Advances in experimental social psychology* (Vol. 7, pp 157–215). New York: Academic Press.

Berscheid, E., & Walster, E. (1978). *Interpersonal attraction* (2nd ed.). Reading, MA: Addison-Wesley.

Berscheid, E., Walster, E., & Campbell, R. (1974). Grow old with me. Cited in E. Berscheid & E. Walster, Physical attractiveness. In L. Berkowitz (Ed.), *Advances in experimental social psychology* (Vol. 7). New York: Academic Press.

Bettelheim, B., & Janowitz, M. (1950). *The dynamics of prejudice: A psychological and sociological study of veterans.* New York: Harper.

Bickman, L. (1980). Introduction. *Applied Social Psychology Annual, 1,* 7–18.

Bickman, L., Teger, A., Gabriele, T., McLaughlin, C., Berger, M., & Sunaday, E. (1973). Dormitory density and helping behavior. *Environment and Behavior, 5,* 465–490.

Biddle, B. J., & Thomas, E. J. (Eds.). (1966). *Role theory: Concepts and research.* New York: Wiley.

Billig, M., & Tajfel, H. (1973). Social categorization and similarity in intergroup behavior. *European Journal of Social Psychology, 3,* 27–52.

Birnbaum, M. H., & Mellers, B. A. (1979). Stimulus recognition may mediate exposure effects. *Journal of Personality and Social Psychology, 37,* 391–394.

Blake, R. R., & Mouton, J. S. (1961). Loyalty of representatives to ingroup positions during intergroup competition. *Sociometry, 24,* 177–183.

Blake, R. R., & Mouton, J. S. (1979). Intergroup problem solving in organizations: From theory to practice. In W. G. Austin & S. Worchel (Eds.), *The social psychology of intergroup relations* (pp. 20–32). Monterey, CA: Brooks/Cole.

Blanchard, F., Adelman, L., & Cook, S. (1975). The effect of group success and failure upon interpersonal attraction in cooperating interracial groups. *Journal of Personality and Social Psychology, 31,* 1020–1030.

Block, J., & Lanning, K. (1984). Attribution therapy requestioned: A secondary analysis of the Wilson–Linville study. *Journal of Personality and Social Psychology, 46,* 705–708.

Blumenfield, M., Levy, N. B., & Kaufman, D. (1978). Do patients want to be told? *New England Journal of Medicine, 299,* 1138.

Blumenfield, M., Levy, N. B., & Kaufman, D. (1979). The wish to be informed of a fatal illness. *Omega, 9,* 323–326.

Blumstein, P. W., & Schwartz, P. (1977). Bisexuality: Some social psychological issues. *Journal of Social Issues, 33,* 30–45.

Bogart, L. (1967). *Strategy in advertising.* New York: Harcourt.

Bohlander, R. W., Hartdagen, S. E., & Wychock, S. G. (1983, April). The role of the cognitive set in the social support situation. Paper presented at the meeting of the Eastern Psychological Association.

Bond, C. F., Jr., & Titus, L. J. (1983). Social facil-itation: A meta-analysis of 241 studies. *Psychological Bulletin, 94,* 265–292.

Bonora, B., & Krauss, E. (Eds.). (1979). *Jurywork: Systematic techniques.* Berkeley, CA: National Jury Project.

Borgida, E. (1982). Legal reform of rape laws: Social psychological and constitutional considerations. In L. Bickman (Ed.), *Applied Social Psychology Annual, 2.*

Bossard, J. H. S. (1932). Residential propinquity as a factor in mate selection. *American Journal of Sociology, 38,* 219–224.

Bowman, C. H., & Fishbein, M. (1978). Understanding public reaction to energy proposals: An application of the Fishbein Model. *Journal of Personality and Social Psychology, 3,* 319–340.

Boyd, J. R., Covington, T. R., Stanaszek, W. F., & Coussons, R. T. (1974). Drug defaulting, II. Analysis of noncompliance patterns. *American Journal of Hospital Pharmacy, 31,* 485–491.

Bray, R. M., Johnson, D., & Chilstrom, J. T., Jr. (1982). Social influence by group members with minority opinions: A comparison of Hollander and Moscovici. *Journal of Personality and Social Psychology, 43,* 78–88.

Bray, R. M., & Noble, A. M. (1978). Authoritarianism and decisions of mock juries: Evidence of jury bias and group polarization. *Journal of Personality and Social Psychology, 36,* 1424–1430.

Breaugh, J. A., & Klimoski, R. J. (1980). Social forces in negotiation simulation. *Personality and Social Psychology Bulletin, 7,* 290–295.

Breed, G. (1972). The effect of intimacy: Reciprocity or retreat? *British Journal of Clinical and Social Psychology, 11,* 135–142.

Brehm, J. W. (1956). Post-decision changes in desirability of alternatives. *Journal of Abnormal and Social Psychology, 52,* 384–389.

Brehm, J. W., & Cohen, A. R. (1959). Re-evaluation of choice alternatives as a function of their number and qualitative similarity. *Journal of Abnormal and Social Psychology, 58,* 373–378.

Brennan, T. (1982) Loneliness at adolescence. In L. A. Peplav & D. Perlman (Eds.), *Loneliness: A sourcebook of current theory, research, and practice,* New York: Wiley. (pp. 269–290).

Brewer, M. (1979). The role of ethnocentrism in

intergroup conflict. *The social psychology of intergroup relations*. Monterey, CA: Brooks/Cole.

Bronzaft, A. L., & McCarthy, D. P. (1975). The effect of elevated train noise on reading ability. *Environment and Behavior, 7*, 517–527.

Broverman, I. K., Vogel, S. R., Broverman, D. M., Clarkson, F. E., & Rosenkrantz, P. S. (1972). Sex-role stereotypes: A current appraisal. *Journal of Social Issues, 28*, 59–78.

Brown, B. B., & Altman, I. (1981). Territoriality and residential crime. A conceptual framework. In P. J. Brantingham & P. L. Brantingham (Eds.), *Urban crime and environmental criminology*. Beverly Hills, CA: Sage.

Brown, B. R. (1968). The need to maintain face in interpersonal bargaining. *Journal of Experimental Social Psychology, 4*, 107–122.

Brown, R. (1965). *Social Psychology*. Glencoe, IL: Free Press.

Brown, R. (1976). Reference: In memorial tribute to Eric Lennenberg. *Cognition, 4*, 125–153.

Brown, R., & Gilman, A. (1960). The pronouns of power and solidarity. In T. A. Sebeok (Ed.), *Style in language* (pp. 253–276). Cambridge, MA: M.I.T. Press.

Brown, R., & Lennenberg, E. H. (1954). A study of language and cognition. *Journal of Abnormal and Social Psychology, 454–462.*

Brownmiller, S. (1975). *Against our will: Men, women, and rape*. New York: Simon & Schuster.

Bryan, J. H., & Test, M. A. (1967). Models and helping: Naturalistic studies in aiding behavior. *Journal of Personality and Social Psychology, 6*, 400–407.

Buck, R. (1976). A test of nonverbal receiving ability: Preliminary studies. *Human Communications Research, 2*(2), 162–171.

Buckhout, R. (1975). Eyewitness testimony. *Scientific American, 231*, 23–31.

Buckhout, R. (1980). Nearly 2000 witnesses can be wrong. *Bulletin of the Psychonomic Society, 16*(4) 307–310.

Bugental, D. E., Love, L. R., Kaswan, J. W., & April, C. (1971). Verbal–nonverbal conflict in parental messages to normal and disturbed children. *Journal of Abnormal Psychology, 77*, 6–10.

Bullough, V., & Bullough, B. (1977). *Sin, sickness, and sanity*. New York: New American Library.

Bureau of Labor Statistics. (1981). *Employment and earnings. Washington, DC: U.S. Government Printing Office.*

Burger, J. M., Oakman, J. A., & Bullard, N. G. (1983). Desire for control and the perception of crowding. *Personality and Social Psychology Bulletin, 9*, 475–479.

Burgess, A. W., & Holmstrom, L. L. (1974). *Rape: Victims of crisis*. Bowie, MD: Robert J. Brady.

Burleson, J. A. (1984, April). *Reciprocity of interpersonal attraction within acquainted versus unacquainted small groups*. Paper presented at the annual meeting of the Eastern Psychological Association, Baltimore, MD.

Burnam, M. A., Pennebaker, J. W., & Glass, D. C. (1975). Time consciousness, achievement striving, and the Type A coronary-prone behavior pattern. *Journal of Abnormal Psychology, 84*, 76–79.

Burnstein, E., & Schul, Y. (1982). The informational basis of social judgements: Operations in forming an impression of another person. *Journal of Experimental Social Psychology, 18*, 217–234.

Buss, A. H. (1961). *The psychology of aggression*. New York: Wiley.

Buss, A. H., Booker, A., & Buss, E. (1972). Firing a weapon and aggression. *Journal of Personality and Social Psychology, 22*, 296–302.

Butler, R. N. (1980). Ageism: A foreword. *Journal of Social Issues, 36*, 8–29.

Byrne, D. (1969). Attitudes and attraction. *Advances in experimental social psychology* (Vol. 4, pp. 35–89). New York: Academic Press.

Byrne, D. (1971). *The attraction paradigm*. New York: Academic Press.

Bryne, D., & Clore, G. L. (1970). A reinforcement model of evaluative responses. *Personality: An International Journal, 1*, 103–128.

Byrne, D., Ervin, C. R., & Lamberth, J. (1970). Continuity between the experimental study of attraction and "real life" computer dating. *Journal of Personality and Social Psychology, 16*, 157–165.

Byrne, D., & Nelson, D. (1965). Attraction as a linear function of proportion of positive reinforcement. *Journal of Personality and Social Psychology, 1*, 659–663.

Cacioppo, J. T., & Petty, R. E. (1979). Attitudes and cognitive response: An electrophysiological approach. *Journal of Personality and Social Psychology, 37,* 2181–2199.

Cairns, H. S., & Cairns, C. E. (1976). *Psycholinguistics: A cognitive view of language.* New York: Holt, Rinehart and Winston.

Calder, B. J., Insko, C. A., & Yandell, B. (1974). The relation of cognitive and memorial processes to persuasion on a simulated jury trial. *Journal of Applied Social Psychology, 4,* 62–93.

Caldwell, D. F., O'Reilly, C. A., & Morris, J. H. (1983). Responses to an organizational reward: A field test of the sufficiency of justification hypothesis. *Journal of Personality and Social Psychology, 44,* 506–514.

Campbell, A. (1981). *The sense of well-being in America: Recent patterns and trends.* New York: McGraw-Hill.

Campbell, A., Converse, P. E., & Rodgers, W. L. (1976). *The quality of American life: Perceptions, evaluations and satisfactions.* New York: Russel Sage Foundation.

Campbell, D. T. (1967). Stereotypes and the perception of group difference. *American Psychologist, 22,* 817–829.

Cantor, N., & Mischel, W. (1977). Traits as prototypes: Effects on recognition memory. *Journal of Personality and Social Psychology, 35,* 38–48.

Cantor, N., & Mischel, W. (1979). Prototypes in person perception. In L. Berkowitz (Ed.), *Advances in experimental social psychology* (Vol. 12). New York: Academic Press.

Caplow, T. (1964). *Principles of organization.* New York: Harcourt, Brace & World.

Carlsmith, J. M., & Anderson, C. A. (1979). Ambient temperature and the occurrence of collective violence: A new analysis. *Journal of Personality and Social Psychology, 37,* 337–344.

Carlsmith, J. M., Ellsworth, P. C. & Aronson, E. (1976). *Methods of research in social psychology.* Reading, MA: Addison-Wesley.

Cartwright, D. (1968). The nature of group cohesiveness. In D. Cartwright & A. Zander (Eds.), *Group dynamics: Theory and research* (3rd ed.). New York: Harper & Row.

Cartwright, D., & Zander, A. (1968). *Group dynamics: Research and theory.* New York: Harper & Row.

Carver, C. S., Coleman, A. E., & Glass, D. C. (1976). The coronary-prone behavior pattern and the suppression of fatigue on a treadmill test. *Journal of Personality and Social Psychology, 33,* 460–466.

Carver, C. S., DeGregorio, E., & Gillis, R. (1980). Field-study of an ego-defensive bias in attribution among two categories of observers. *Personality and Social Psychology Bulletin, 6,* 44–50.

Carver, C. S., & Glass, D. C. (1978). Coronary-prone behavior pattern and interpersonal aggression. *Journal of Personality and Social Psychology, 36,* 361–366.

Chaiken, A. L., & Derlega, V. J. (1979). Nonverbal mediators of expectancy effects in black and white children. *Journal of Personality and Social Psychology, 37,* 897–912.

Chaiken, A. L., Derlega, V. J., & Miller, S. J. (1976). Effects of room environment on self-disclosure in a counseling analogue. *Journal of Counseling Psychology, 23*(5), 479–481.

Chaiken, S. (1980). Heuristic versus systematic information processing and the use of source versus message cues in persuasion. *Journal of Personality and Social Psychology, 39,* 752–766.

Chapanis, N. P., & Chapanis, A. C. (1964). Cognitive dissonance: Five years later. *Psychological Bulletin, 61,* 1–22.

Charrow, R. P., & Charrow, V. R. (1979). Making legal language understandable: A psycholinguistic study of jury instructions. *Columbia Law Review, 79,* 1306–1374.

Check, J. V. P., & Malamuth, N. M. (1983). Sex role stereotyping and reactions to depictions of stranger versus acquaintance rape. *Journal of Personality and Social Psychology, 45,* 344–356.

Cherry, F., & Byrne, D. (1977). Authoritarianism. In T. Blass (Ed.), *Personality variables in social behavior* (pp. 109–133). Hillsdale, NJ: Erlbaum.

Chesney, M. A., Fagleston, J. R., & Rosenman, R. H. (1981). Type A behavior: Assessment and intervention. In C. K. Prokop & L. A. Bradley (Eds.), *Medical psychology: Contributions to behavioral medicine* (pp. 20–37). New York: Academic Press.

Cialdini, R. (1984). *Influence.* New York: Morrow.

Cialdini, R., Darby, B., & Vincent, J. (1973). Transgression and altruism: A case for hedonism. *Journal of Experimental Social Psychology, 9,* 502–516.

Cialdini, R. B., Bickman, L., & Cacioppo, J. T. (1979). An example of consumeristic social psychology: Bargaining tough in the new car showroom. *Journal of Applied Social Psychology, 9,* 115–126.

Cialdini, R. B., Vincent, J. E., Lewis, S. K., Catalan, J., Wheeler, D., & Darby, B. L. (1975). Reciprocal concessions procedure for inducing compliance: The door-in-the-face technique. *Journal of Personality and Social Psychology, 31,* 206–215.

Clark, H. H., & Clark, E. V. (1977). *Psychology and language.* New York: Harcourt, Brace, Jovanovich.

Clark, K. B., & Clark, M. P. (1947). Racial identification and preference in negro children. In T. M. Newcomb & E. L. Hartley (Eds.), *Readings in Social Psychology.* New York: Holt.

Clore, G. L., Bray, R. M., Itkin, S. M., & Murphy, P. (1978). Interracial attitudes and behavior at summer camp. *Journal of Personality and Social Psychology, 36,* 107–116.

Coch, L., & French, J. R. P., Jr. (1948). Overcoming resistance to change. *Human Relations, 11,* 512–532.

Cohen, A. M., Robinson, E. H., & Edwards, J. L. (1969). Experiments in organizational embeddedness. *Administrative Science Quarterly, 14,* 208–221.

Cohen, S., & Spacapan, S. (1978). The aftereffects of stress: An additional interpretation. *Environmental Psychology and Nonverbal Behavior, 3,* 43–57.

Coleman, D. A., Jr., Klahr, S., Valentino, C., Ramsey, P. R., Caputo, D. V., & Winnick, W. A. (1984, April). *A multidimensional analysis of Type-A personality.* Paper presented at the annual meeting of the Eastern Psychological Association, Baltimore, MD.

Collett, P. On training Englishmen in the nonverbal behavior of Arabs: An experiment on intercultural communication. *International Journal of Psychology, 6,* 209–215.

Collins, B. E., & Guetzkow, H. (1964). *A social psychology of group processes for decision-making.* New York: Wiley.

Collins, G. (1982, June 30). Is the violence in "Blade Runner" a socially destructive element? *New York Times.*

Conner, R. (1982). Random assignment of clients in social experimentation. In J. Siebert (Ed.), *Ethics of social research surveys and experiments* (pp. 57–78). New York: Springer-Verlag.

Conolley, E. S., Gerard, H. B., & Kline, T. (1978). Competitive behavior: A manifestation of motivation for ability comparison. *Journal of Experimental Social Psychology, 14,* 123–131.

Converse, J., Jr., & Cooper, J. (1979). The importance of decisions and free-choice attitude change: A curvilinear finding. *Journal of Experimental Social Psychology, 15,* 48–61.

Cook, S. W. (1969). Motives in a conceptual analysis of attitude-related behavior. In W. J. Arnold & D. Levine (Eds.), *Nebraska symposium on motivation* (Vol. 17). Lincoln: University of Nebraska Press.

Cook, S. W. (1976). Ethical issues in the conduct of research in social relations. In C. Sellitz, L. C. Wrightson, & S. W. Cook (Eds.), *Research methods in social relations* (3rd ed.). New York: Holt, Rinehart and Winston.

Cook, T. D., Gruder, C. L., Hennigan, K. M., & Flay, B. R. (1979). History of the sleeper effect: Some logical pitfalls in accepting the null hypothesis. *Psychological Bulletin, 86,* 662–679.

Cooper, H. M. (1979). Pygmalion grows up: A model for teacher expectation communication and performance influence. *Review of Educational Research, 49,* 389–410.

Cornbleth, C., Davis, O. L., & Button, C. (1974). Expectations for pupil achievement and teacher–pupil interaction. *Social Education, 38,* 54–58.

Cotton, J. L. (1981). A review of research on Schachter's theory of emotion and the misattribution of arousal. *European Journal of Social Psychology, 11,* 365–397.

Cottrell, N. B. (1972). Social facilitation. In C. G. McClintock (Ed.), *Experimental social psychology* (pp. 185–236). New York: Holt.

Cottrell, N. B., & Epley, S. W. (1977). Affiliation, social comparison, and socially mediated stress reduction. In J. M. Suls & R. L. Miller (Eds.), *Social comparison processes.* New York: Wiley.

Cox, V. C., Paulus, P. B., McCain, G., & Schkade, J. K. (1979). Field research on the effects of crowding in prisons and on offshore drilling platforms. In J. R. Aiello & A. Baum (Eds.), *Residential crowding and design.* New York: Plenum.

Crandall, R. (1972). Field extension of the frequency-affect findings. *Psychological Reports, 31,* 371–374.

Crane, D. A. (1961). Lynch: The image of the city—review. *Journal of the American Institute of Planners, 27,* 152–155.

Crockett, W. (1955). Emergent leaders in small decision-making groups. *Journal of Abnormal and Social Psychology, 51,* 378–383.

Croog, S. H., & Levine, S. (1977). *The heart patient recovers.* New York: Human Sciences.

Crosby, F., Bromley, S., & Saxe, L. (1980). Recent unobtrusive studies of black and white discrimination and prejudice: A literature review. *Psychological Bulletin, 87,* 546–563.

Cross, H. A., Halcomb, C. G., & Matter, W. W. (1967). Imprinting and exposure learning in rats given early auditory stimulation. *Psychonomic Science, 10,* 223–234.

Croyle, R. T., & Cooper, J. (1983). Dissonance arousal: Physiological evidence. *Journal of Personality and Social Psychology, 45,* 782–791.

Csoka, L. S., & Bons, P. M. (1978). Manipulating the situation to fix the leader's style—two validation studies of Leader Match. *Journal of Applied Psychology, 63,* 295–300.

Cummings, E. E. (1981). *Complete poems.* 1910–1962 (Vol. 2). London: Grenada Publishing.

Cunningham, M. R. (1981). Weather, mood and helping behavior: Quasi-experiments with the Sunshine Samaritan. *Journal of Personality and Social Psychology, 37,* 1947–1956.

Cutrona, C. E. (1982). Transition to college: Loneliness and the process of social adjustment. In L. A. Peplau & D. Perlman (Eds.), *Loneliness: A sourcebook of current theory, research, and therapy.* New York: Wiley.

Darley, J. M., & Aronson, E. (1966). Self-evaluation use. Direct anxiety reduction as determinants of the fear-affiliation relationship. *Journal of Experimental Social Psychology* (Suppl. 1), 66–79.

Darley, J. M., & Batson, C. D. (1973). "From Jeruselem to Jericho": A study of situational and dispositional variables in helping behavior. *Journal of Personality and Social Psychology, 27,* 100–108.

Darwin, C. (1871). *The descent of man.* London: Murray.

Dashiell, J. F. (1930). An experimental analysis of some group effects. *Journal of Abnormal and Social Psychology, 25,* 190–199.

Davidson, A. R., & Jaccard, J. J. (1979). Variables that moderate the attitude–behavior relation: Results of a longitudinal survey. *Journal of Personality and Social Psychology, 37,* 1364–1376.

Davis, J. H., Bray, R. M., & Holt, R. W. (1977). The empirical study of decision processes in juries: A critical review. In J. L. Tapp & F. J. Levine (Eds.), *Justice and the individual in society: Psychological and legal issues.* New York: Holt, Rinehart and Winston.

Davis, M. S. (1968a). Physiologic, psychological, and demographic factors in patient compliance with doctors' orders. *Medical Care, 6,* 115–122.

Davis, M. S. (1968b). Variations in patients' compliance with doctors' advice: An empirical analysis of patterns of communication. *American Journal of Public Health, 58,* 274–288.

Dean, L. M., Willis, F. N., & Hewitt, J. (1975). Initial interaction distance among individuals equal and unequal in military rank. *Journal of Personality and Social Psychology, 32,* 294–299.

Delberg, A. L., Van de Veu, A. H., & Gustafson, D. H. (1975). *Group techniques for program planning.* Glenview, IL: Scott, Foresman.

Delgado, J. M. R. (1969). Offensive–defensive behavior in free monkeys and chimpanzees induced by radio stimulation of the brain. In S. Garattini & E. G. Sigg (Eds.), *Aggressive behavior.* New York: Wiley.

Dembroski, T. M., MacDougall, J. M., Herd, J. A., & Shields, J. L. (1983). Perspectives on coronary-prone behavior. In D. S. Krantz, A. Baum & J. E. Singer (Eds.), *Handbook of Psychology and Health, 3,* Hillsdale, NJ: Erlbaum.

DePaulo, B. M., & Fisher, J. D. (1980). The costs of asking for help. *Basic and Applied Social Psychology, 1,* 23–35.

DerKarabetran, A., & Smith, A. (1977). Sex-role stereotyping in the United States: Is it changing? *Sex Roles, 3,* 193–198.

Dermer, M., & Thiel, D. L. (1975). When beauty may fail. *Journal of Personality and Social Psychology, 31,* 1168–1176.

Deutsch, M. (1958). Trust and suspicion. *Journal of Conflict Resolution, 2,* 265–279.

Deutsch, M. (1960). The effect of motivational orientation upon trust and suspicion. *Human Relations, 13,* 123–139.

Deutsch, M. (1973). *The resolution of conflict: Constructive and destructive processes.* New Haven, CT: Yale University Press.

Deutsch, M. (1975). Equity, equality, and need: What determines which value will be used as the basis of distributive justice? *Journal of Social Issues, 31,* 137–149.

Deutsch, M., Canavan, D., & Rubin, J. (1971). The effects of size of conflict and sex of experimenter upon interpersonal bargaining. *Journal of Experimental Social Psychology, 7,* 258–267.

Deutsch, M., & Gerard, H. B. (1955). A study of normative and informational social influence upon individual judgment. *Journal of Abnormal and Social Psychology, 51,* 629–636.

Deutsch, M., & Krauss, R. M. (1960). The effect of threat upon interpersonal bargaining. *Journal of Abnormal and Social Psychology, 61,* 181–189.

Diener, E. (1979). Deindividuation: The absence of self-awareness and self-regulation on group numbers. In P. Paulus (Ed.), *The psychology of group influence.* Hillsdale, NJ: Erlbaum.

Dillehay, R. C. (1973). On the irrelevance of the classical negative evidence concerning the effect of attitudes on behavior. *American Psychologist, 28,* 887–891.

DiMatteo, M. R. (1979). A social-psychological analysis of physician–patient rapport: Toward a science of the art of medicine. *Journal of Social Issues, 35*(1), 12–33.

DiMatteo, M. R., & Friedman, H. S. (1982). *Social psychology and medicine.* Cambridge, MA: Oelgeschlager, Gunn and Haig.

Dion, K. K. (1972). Physical attractiveness and evaluations of children's transgressions. *Journal of Personality and Social Psychology, 24,* 207–213.

Dion, K. K., & Berscheid, E. (1974). Physical attractiveness and peer perception among children. *Sociometry, 37,* 1–12.

Dion, K. K., Berscheid, E., & Walster, E. (1972). What is beautiful is good. *Journal of Personality and Social Psychology, 24,* 285–290.

Dittes, J. (1959). Attractiveness of groups as a function of self-esteem and acceptance by group. *Journal of Abnormal and Social Psychology, 59,* 77–82.

Dittmann, A. T. (1972). *Interpersonal messages of emotion.* New York: Springer.

Dollard, J., Doob, L., Miller, N., Mowrer, O. H., & Sears, R. R. (1939). *Frustration and aggression.* New Haven, CT: Yale University Press.

Dong, T. L., Zingle, H. W., Patterson, J. G., Ivey, A. E., & Haase, R. T. (1976). Development and validation of a microcounseling skill discrimination scale. *Journal of Counseling Psychology, 23,* 468–472.

Donnerstein, E., & Berkowitz, L. (1981). Victim reactions in aggressive erotic films as a factor in violence against women. *Journal of Personality and Social Psychology, 41,* 710–724.

Donnerstein, E., Donnerstein, M., & Evans, R. (1975). Erotic stimuli and aggression: Facilitation or inhibitions. *Journal of Personality and Social Psychology, 32,* 237–244.

Donnerstein, E., & Wilson, D. W. (1976). The effects of noise and perceived control upon ongoing and subsequent aggressive behavior. *Journal of Personality and Social Psychology, 34,* 774–781.

Donnerstein, M., & Donnerstein, E. (1977). Modeling in the control of interracial aggression: The problem of generality. *Journal of Personality, 45,* 100–116.

Doob, A. N., & Wood, L. (1972). Catharsis and aggression: The effects of annoyance and retaliation on aggressive behavior. *Journal of Personality and Social Psychology, 22,* 156–172.

Downing, L. L., & Monaco, N. R. (1982, April). *Ingroup–outgroup bias as a function of differential contact with ingroups and outgroups and authoritarian personality.* Paper presented at the meeting of the Eastern Psychological Association, Baltimore, MD.

Downs, R. M., & Stea, D. (1977). *Maps in minds: Reflections on cognitive mapping.* New York: Harper & Row.

Doyle, B. J., & Ware, J. E. (1977). Physician conduct and other factors that affect consumer satisfaction with medical care. *Journal of Medical Education, 52,* 793, 801.

Driscoll, R., Davis, K. E., & Lipitz, M. E. (1972). Parental interference and romantic love: The Romeo and Juliet effect. *Journal of Personality and Social Psychology, 24,* 1010.

Dusek, J. B., Hall, V. C., & Neger, W. J. (1984). *Teacher expectancies.* Hillsdale, NJ: Erlbaum.

Dutton, D., & Aron, A. (1974). Some evidence for heightened sexual attraction under conditions of high anxiety. *Journal of Personality and Social Psychology, 30,* 510–517.

Dutton, D. G., & Lennox, V. L. (1974). Effect of prior "token" compliance on subsequent interracial behavior. *Journal of Personality and Social Psychology, 29,* 65–71.

Duval, S., & Wicklund, R. A. (1972). *A theory of objective self-awareness.* New York: Academic Press.

Dweck, C. S. (1975). The role of expectations and attributions in the alleviation of learned helplessness. *Journal of Personality and Social Psychology, 31,* 647–685.

Dweck, C. S., Bush, E. S. (1976). Sex differences in learned helplessness: I. Differential debilitation with peers and adult evaluators. *Developmental Psychology, 12,* 147–156.

Dyson, J. N., Godwin, P. H., & Hazlewood, L. A. (1976). Group composition, leadership orientation and decision outcomes. *Small Group Behavior, 7,* 114–128.

Eagly, A. H. (1978). Sex differences in influenceability. *Psychological Bulletin, 85,* 86–116.

Eagly, A. H. (1983a). Gender and social influence: A social psychological analysis. *American Psychologist, 38,* 971–981.

Eagly, A. H. (1983b, April). *Who says so? The processing of communicator cues in persuasion.* Paper presented at the meeting of the Eastern Psychological Association, Philadelphia, PA.

Eagly, A. H., & Carli, L. L. (1981). Sex of researchers and sex-typed communications as determinants of sex differences in influenceability: A meta-analysis of social influence studies. *Psychological Bulletin, 90,* 1–20.

Eagly, A. H., & Himmelfarb, S. (1978). Attitudes and opinions. In M. R. Rosenzweig & L. W. Porter (Eds.), *Annual Review of Psychology, 29.*

Eagly, A. H., & Steffen, V. (1984). Gender stereotypes stem from the distribution of women and men into social roles. *Journal of Personality and Social Psychology, 46,* 735–754.

Eagly, A. H., & Warren, R. (1976). Intelligence, comprehension, and opinion change. *Journal of Personality, 44,* 226–242.

Eagly, A. H., Wood, W., & Chaiken, S. (1978). Causal inferences about communicators and their effect on opinion change. *Journal of Personality and Social Psychology, 36,* 424–435.

Ebbesen, E. B., Duncan, B., & Konečni, V. J. (1975). Effects of content of verbal aggression on future verbal aggression: A field experiment. *Journal of Experimental Social Psychology, 11,* 192–204.

Ebbesen, E. B., & Konečni, V. J. (1982). An analysis of the bail system. In V. J. Konečni & E. B. Ebbesen (Eds.), *The criminal justice system: A social-psychological analysis* (pp. 191–229). San Francisco: Freeman.

Edney, J. J. (1975). Territoriality and control: A field experiment. *Journal of Personality and Social Psychology, 31,* 1108–1115.

Edney, J. J., & Harper, C. S. (1978). Heroism in a resource crisis: A simulation study. *Environmental Management, 2,* 523–527.

Edwards, D. J. A. (1972). Approaching the unfamiliar: A study of human interaction distances. *Journal of Behavioral Sciences, 1,* 249–250.

Ehrlich, D., Guttman, I., Schonbach, P., & Mills, J. (1957). Post-decision exposure to relevant information. *Journal of Abnormal and Social Psychology, 54,* 98–102.

Eisenberg-Berg, N., & Mussen, P. (1978). Empathy and moral development in adolescence. *Developmental Psychology, 14,* 185–186.

Eisman, B. (1959). Some operational measures of cohesiveness and their correlations. *Human Relations, 12,* 183–189.

Ekman, P. (1972). Universals and cultural differences in facial expressions of emotion. In J. Cole (Ed.), *Nebraska symposium on motivation* (Vol. 19). Lincoln: University of Nebraska Press.

Ekman, P. (1973). Cross-cultural studies of facial expression. In P. Ekman (Ed.), *Darwin and facial expression: A century of research in review* (pp. 169–222). New York: Academic Press.

Ekman, P., & Friesen, W. V. (1968). Nonverbal behavior in psychotherapy research. In J. Schlien (Ed.), *Research in psychotherapy* (Vol. 3, pp. 468–472). Washington, DC: American Psychological Association.

Ekman, P., & Friesen, W. V. (1971). Constants across cultures in the face and emotion. *Journal of Personality and Social Psychology, 17*(2), 124–129.

Ekman, P., & Friesen, W. V. (1974). Detecting deception from the body or face. *Journal of Personality and Social Psychology, 29*(3), 288–298.

Ekman, P., & Friesen, W. V. (1975). *Unmasking the face: A guide to recognizing emotions from facial clues.* Englewood Cliffs, NJ: Prentice-Hall.

Ekman, P., Friesen, W. V., & Ellsworth, P. (1972). *Emotion in the human face.* Elmsford, NY: Pergamon Press.

Ekman, P., Levenson, R. W., & Friesen, W. V. (1983). Autonomic nervous system distinguishes among emotions. *Science, 221,* 1208–1210.

Elashoff, J. R., & Snow, R. E. (1971) *Pygmalion reconsidered.* Worthington, OH: Charles A. Jones.

Ellsworth, P. C., & Carlsmith, J. M. (1968). Effect of eye contact and verbal content on affective response to a dyadic interaction. *Journal of Personality and Social Psychology, 10,* 15–20.

Ellsworth, P. C., Carlsmith, J. M., & Henson, A. (1972). The stare as a stimulus to flight in human subjects: A series of field experiments. *Journal of Personality and Social Psychology, 21,* 302–311.

Englis, B. G., & Lanzetta, J. T. (1984, April). *The effects of group categorization of observers' vicarious emotional responses.* Paper presented at the annual meeting of the Eastern Psychological Association, Baltimore, MD.

Epstein, Y. M. (1981). Crowding, stress and human behavior. *Journal of Social Issues, 37,* 126–144.

Erdmann, G., & Janke, H. (1978). Interaction between physiological and cognitive determinants of emotions: Experimental studies on Schacter's theory of emotions. *Biological Psychology, 6,* 61–74.

Eron, L. D. (1982). Parent–child interaction, television violence, and aggression of children. *American Psychologist, 37,* 197–211.

Eron, L. D., Huesmann, L. R., Lefkowitz, M. M., & Walder, L. O. (1972). Does television violence cause aggression? *American Psychologist, 27,* 253–263.

Etzioni, A. (1969). Social psychological aspects of international relations. In G. Lindzey & E. Aronson (Eds.), *Handbook of social psychology* (2nd ed., Vol. 5). Reading, MA: Addison-Wesley.

Evans, G. W. (1974). An examination of the information overload mechanism of personal space. *Man–Environment Systems, 4,* 61.

Evans, G. W. (1979). Crowding and human performance. *Journal of Applied Social Psychology, 9,* 27–46.

Evans, G. W. (1980). Environmental cognition. *Psychological Bulletin, 88,* 259–287.

Evans, G. W., & Howard, R. B. (1972). A methodological investigation of personal space. In W. J. Mitchell (Ed.), *Environmental design: Research and practice* (EDRA 3). Los Angeles: University of California.

Evans, N. J., & Dovido, J. F. (1983, April). *Evaluative processing of racial stereotypes.* Paper presented at the 54th annual meeting of the Eastern Psychological Association, Philadelphia, PA.

Exline, R. V., & Winters, L. C. (1965). Affective relations and mutual glances in dyads. In S. S. Tomkins & C. W. Izard (Eds.), *Affect, cognition and personality.* New York: Springer.

Farber, M. A. (1982, October 18). Crime victims tell of fear, despair, and emotional scars. *New York Times,* p. B1.

Fazio, R. H. (1979). Motives for social comparison: The construction–validation distinction. *Journal of Personality and Social Psychology, 37,* 1683–1698.

Fazio, R. H., Cooper, J., Danson, K., & Johnson, M. (1981). *Personality and Social Psychology Bulletin, 7,* 97–102.

Fazio, R., & Zanna, M. (1978). Attitudinal qualities relating to the strength of the attitude–behavior relationship. *Journal of Personality and Social Psychology, 14,* 398–408.

Fazio, R. H., Zanna, M. P., & Cooper, J. (1977). Dissonance and self-perception: An integrative view of each theory's proper domain of application. *Journal of Experimental Social Psychology, 13,* 464–479.

Feifel, H. (1963). In N. L. Farberow (Ed.), *Taboo topics* (pp. 8–21). New York: Atherton.

Feldman, D. C. (1983). A socialization process that helps new recruits succeed. In J. R. Hackman, E. E. Lawler, III, & L. W. Porter (Eds.), *Perspectives on behavior in organizations* (pp. 170–190). New York: McGraw-Hill.

Feldman, R. S. (Ed.). (1982). *Development of nonverbal behavior in children.* New York: Springer-Verlag.

Feldman, R. S., & Donohoe, L. F. (1978). Nonverbal communication of affect in interracial dyads. *Journal of Educational Psychology, 70,* 979–987.

Feldman, R. S., & Prohaska, T. (1979). The student

as Pygmalion: Effect of students' expectancy on the teacher. *Journal of Educational Psychology, 71*, 485–493.

Feldman, R. S., & Rosen, F. P. (1978). Diffusion of responsibility in crime, punishment and other adversity. *Law and Human Behavior, 4*, 313–322.

Feldman, R. S., & Theiss, A. J. (1982). The teacher and student as Pygmalions: The joint effects of teacher and student expectation. *Journal of Educational Psychology, 74*, 217–223.

Festinger, L. (1954). A theory of social comparison processes. *Human Relations, 7*, 117–140.

Festinger, L. (1957). *A theory of cognitive dissonance.* Stanford, CA: Stanford University Press.

Festinger, L., & Carlsmith, J. M. (1959). Cognitive consequences of forced compliance. *Journal of Abnormal and Social Psychology, 58*, 203–210.

Festinger, L., & Kelley, H. (1951). *Changing attitudes through social contact.* Ann Arbor, MI: Research Center for Group Dynamics.

Festinger, L., Schachter, S., & Back, K. W. (1950). *Social pressure in informal groups.* New York: Harper.

Fiedler, F. E. (1976). Validation and extension of the contingency model of leadership effectiveness: A review of empirical findings. *Psychological Bulletin, 76*, 128–148.

Fiedler, F. E. (1978). The contingency model and the dynamics of the leadership process. In L. Berkowitz (Ed.), *Advances in experimental social psychology* (Vol. II). New York: Academic Press.

Fiedler, F. E. (1981). Leadership effectiveness. *American Behavioral Scientist, 24*, 619–632.

Fiedler, F. E., Chemers, M. M., & Mahar, L. (1976). *Improving leadership effectiveness: The leader match concept.* New York: Wiley.

Fiedler, F. E., Mitchell, R., & Triandis, H. C. (1971). The culture assimilator: An approach to cross-cultural training. *Journal of Applied Psychology, 55*, 95–102.

Finck, H. T. (1902). *Romantic love and personal beauty: Their development, causal relations, historic and national peculiarities.* London: Macmillan.

Fischer, W. F. (1963). Sharing in pre-school children as a function of amount and type of reinforcement. *Genetic Psychology Monographs, 68*, 215–245.

Fishbein, M., & Ajzen, I. (1975). *Belief, attitude, intention and behavior: An introduction to theory and research.* Reading, MA: Addison-Wesley.

Fisher, J. D., & Nadler, A. (1976). Effect of donor resources on recipient self-esteem and self-help. *Journal of Experimental Social Psychology, 12*, 139–150.

Fisher, J. D., Nadler, A., & DePaulo, B. M. (Eds.). (1983). *New directions in helping: Recipient reactions to aid.* New York: Academic Press.

Fisher, J. D., Nadler, A., & Whitcher-Alagna, S. (1982). Recipient reactions to aid. *Psychological Bulletin, 91*, 27–54.

Fiske, S. T. (1980). Attention and weight in person perception: The impact of negative and extreme behavior. *Journal of Personality and Social Psychology, 38*, 889–906.

Fiske, S. T., & Taylor, S. E. (1983). *Social cognition.* Reading, MA: Addison-Wesley.

Flavell, J. H., Botkin, P. T., Fry, C. K., Wright, J. C., & Jarvis, P. E. (1968). *The development of role-taking and communication skills in children.* Huntington, NY: Frieger.

Flowers, M. (1977). A laboratory test of some implications of Janis's groupthink hypothesis. *Journal of Personality and Social Psychology, 35*, 888–896.

Foa, E., & Foa, V. (1976). Resource theory of social exchange. In J. Thibaut, J. Spence, & R. Carson (Eds.), *Contemporary trends in social psychology.* Morristown, NJ: General Learning Press.

Foot, H. C., Chapman, A. J., & Smith, J. R. (1977). Friendship and social responsiveness in boys and girls. *Journal of Personality and Social Psychology, 35*, 401–411.

Forston, R. F. (1970). Judge's instructions: A quantitative analysis of jurors' listening comprehension. *Today's Speech, 18*, 34–38.

Forsyth, D. R. (1983). *An introduction to group dynamics.* Monterey, CA: Brooks/Cole.

Foss, D. J., & Hakes, D. T. (1978). *Psycholinguistics.* Englewood Cliffs, NJ: Prentice-Hall.

Foss, R. D., & Dempsey, C. B. (1979). Blood donation and the foot-in-the-door technique: A limiting case. *Journal of Personality and Social Psychology, 37*, 580–590.

Freed, B. (1980). Foreign talk, baby talk, native talk. *International Journal of the Sociology of Language, 28*, 2.

Freedman, J. L. (1969). Preference for dissonance

information. *Journal of Personality and Social Psychology, 2,* 287–289.

Freedman, J. L. (1975). *Crowding and behavior.* San Francisco: W. H. Freeman.

Freedman, J. L., & Fraser, S. C. (1966). Compliance without pressure: The foot-in-the-door technique. *Journal of Personality and Social Psychology, 4,* 195–202.

Freedman, J. L., Levy, A. Buchanan, R. W., & Price, J. (1972). Crowding and human aggressiveness. *Journal of Experimental Social Psychology, 8,* 528–548.

French, J. R. P., Jr., & Raven, B. H. (1959). The bases of social power. In D. Cartwright (Ed.), *Studies in social power.* Ann Arbor: University of Michigan Press.

Freud, S. (1920). *A general introduction to psychoanalysis.* New York: Boni & Liveright.

Freud, S. (1922). *Group psychology and the analysis of the ego.* London: Hogarth Press.

Freud, S. (1930). *Civilization and its discontents.* London: Hogarth Press.

Frey, D., & Wicklund, R. A. (1978). A clarification of selective exposure: The impact of choice. *Journal of Experimental Social Psychology, 14,* 132–139.

Friedman, H. S., & DiMatteo, M. R. (1979). Health care as an interpersonal process. *Journal of Social Issues, 35,* 1–11.

Friedman, L. (1981). How affiliation affects stress in fear and anxiety situations. *Journal of Personality and Social Psychology, 40,* 1102–1117.

Friedman, M., & Rosenman, R. H. (1974). *Type A behavior and your heart.* Greenwich, CT: Fawcett.

Friedman, M., Thoresen, C. E., Gill, J. J., Ulmer, D., Leonti, T., Powell, L., Price, V., Elek, S. R., Robin, D. D., Breall, W. S., Piaget, G., Dixon, T., Bourg, E., Levy, R. A., & Tasto, D. L. (1984). Feasibility of altering Type A behavior pattern after myocardial infarction. *Circulation, 66,* 83–92.

Frieze, I., Whiteley, B., Hanusa, B., & McHugh, M. (1982). Assessing the theoretical models for sex differences in causal attributions for success and failure. *Sex roles: A journal of research, 8,* 333–344.

Fyans, L. J., & Maehr, M. L. (1979). Attributional style, task selection and achievement. *Journal of Educational Psychology, 71,* 499–507.

Gallo, P. S. (1966). Effects of increased incentives upon the use of threat in bargaining. *Journal of Personality and Social Psychology, 4,* 14–20.

Gallup, G. (1972). *The sophisticated poll watcher's guide.* Princeton, NJ: Princeton Opinion Press.

Gamson, W. A. (1964). Experimental studies of coalition formation. In L. Berkowitz (Ed.), *Advances in experimental social psychology* (Vol. 1). New York: Academic Press.

Gartner, A., Kohler, M. C., & Riessman, F. (1971). *Children teach children: Learning by teaching.* New York: Harper.

Gastorf, J. W. (1980). Time urgency of the Type A behavior pattern. *Journal of Consulting and Clinical Psychology, 48,* 299.

Gastorf, J. W., Suls, J., & Sanders, G. S. (1980). The Type A coronary-prone behavior pattern and social facilitation. *Journal of Personality and Social Psychology, 38,* 773–780.

Gatchel, R. J., & Baum, A. (1983). *An introduction to health psychology.* Reading, MA: Addison-Wesley.

Gay, G. (1975). Teachers' achievement expectations of and classroom interactions with ethnically different students. *Contemporary Education, 46,* 166–172.

Geen, R. G. (1968). Effects of frustration, attack, and prior training in aggressiveness upon aggressive behavior. *Journal of Personality and Social Psychology, 9,* 316–332.

Geen, R. G., Stonner, D., & Shope, G. L. (1975). The facilitation of aggression by aggression: Evidence against the catharsis hypothesis. *Journal of Personality and Social Psychology, 31,* 721–726.

Geller, D. Deception. In J. Siebert (Ed.), *Ethics of social research surveys and experiments.* New York: Springer-Verlag.

Gerard, H. B. (1983). School desegregation: The social science role. *American Psychologist, 38,* 869–877.

Gerard, H. B., Wilhelmy, R. A., & Conolley, E. S. (1968). Conformity and group size. *Journal of Personality and Social Psychology, 8,* 79–82.

Gerber, G., Gross, L., Jackson-Beeck, M., Jeffries-Fox, S., & Signorielli, N. (1978). Cultural indicators; Violence profile No. 9. *Journal of Communication, 28,* 176–207.

Gergen, K. J., Ellsworth, P., Maslach, C., & Seipel, M. (1975). Obligation, donor resources, and reactions to aid in three cultures. *Journal of*

Personality and Social Psychology, 31, 390–400.

Gibb, C. A. (1969). Leadership. In G. Lindzey & E. Aronson (Eds.), *Handbook of social psychology*. Reading, MA: Addison-Wesley.

Gibb, J. R. (1975). The training group. In K. D. Benne, L. P. Bradford, J. R. Gibb, & R. O. Lippitt (Eds.), *The laboratory method of changing and learning: Theory and application*. Palo Alto, CA: Science and Behavior Books.

Gilbert, G. M. (1951). Stereotype persistence and change among college students. *Journal of Abnormal and Social Psychology*, 245–254.

Gilligan, C. (1977). In a different voice: Women's conceptions of self and morality. *Harvard Educational Review, 47*, 481–517.

Gladstein, G. A. (1974). Nonverbal communication and counseling/psychotherapy: A review. *Counseling Psychologist, 4*, 34–52.

Glass, D. C. (1977). *Behavior patterns, stress, and coronary disease*. Hillsdale, NJ: Erlbaum.

Glass, D. C., Singer, J. E., & Friedman, L. N. (1969). Psychic cost of adaptation to an environmental stressor. *Journal of Personality and Social Psychology, 12*, 200–210.

Glass, D. C., Snyder, M. L., & Hollis, J. F. (1974). Time urgency and the Type A coronary-prone behavior pattern. *Journal of Applied Social Psychology, 4*, 125–140.

Glass, G. V. (1976). Privacy, secondary and meta-analysis of research. *Educational Researcher, 5*(10), 3–8.

Glenn, N. D., & Weaver, C. N. (1979). Attitudes toward premarital, extramarital, and homosexual relations in the U.S. in the 1970s. *The Journal of Sex Research, 15*, 108–118.

Goethals, G. R., & Darley, J. M. (1977). Social comparison theory: An attributional approach. In J. M. Suls & R. L. Miller (Eds.), *Social comparison processes: Theoretical and empirical perspectives*. Washington, DC: Hemisphere/Halsted.

Goldman, A. L. (1982, April 26). Scores rise at school after nearby subway is quieted. *New York Times*.

Goldstein, J. H., & Arms, R. L. (1977). Effects of observing athletic contests on hostility. *Sociometry, 34*, 83–90.

Goleman, D. (1984, April). Complex coercion binds sex rings using children. *New York Times, 133*, C1–C5.

Gottman, J. M., & Levenson, R. W. (1984). Why marriages fail: Affective and physiological patterns in marital interaction. In. J. C. Masters & K. Yorkin-Levin (Eds.). *Boundary areas in social and developmental psychology* (pp. 67–106). New York: Academic Press.

Gould, P., & White, R. (1974). *Mental Maps*. New York: Penguin.

Gouldner, A. W. (1960). The norm of reciprocity: A preliminary statement. *American Sociological Review, 25*, 161–178.

Granberg, D. (1978). GRIT in the quarter: Reversing the arms race through unilateral initiatives. *Bulletin of Peace Proposals, 9*, 210–221.

Greenberg, J., & Cohen, R. L. (1982). *Equity and justice in social behavior*. New York: Academic Press.

Greenberg, J., & Ornstein, S. (1983). High status job title as compensation for underpayment: A test of equity theory. *Journal of Applied Psychology, 68*, 285–297.

Greenberg, M. (1974). A concept of community. *Social Work, 19*, 64–72.

Greenberg, M. S., & Ruback, R. B. (1982). *Social psychology of the criminal justice system*. Monterey, CA: Brooks/Cole.

Greene, L., & Riess, M. (1984, April). *The role of gaze in managing impressions of dominance and submission*. Paper presented at the annual meeting of the Eastern Psychological Association, Baltimore, MD.

Greenhalgh, L., Gilkey, R. W., & Scott, A. (1983, August). *Effects of personality, skill and tactics on outcomes of negotiations*. Paper presented at the meeting of the American Psychological Association, Anaheim, CA.

Greenwald, A. G. (1975). On the inconclusiveness of "crucial" cognitive tests of dissonance vs. self-perception theories. *Journal of Experimental Social Psychology, 11*, 490–499.

Greenwald, A. G., & Ronis, D. L. (1978). Twenty years of cognitive dissonance: Case study of the evolution of a theory. *Psychological Review, 85*, 53–57.

Greenwell, J., & Dengerink, H. A. (1973). The role of perceived versus actual attack in human physical aggression. *Journal of Personality and Social Psychology, 26*, 66–71.

Griffitt, W., & Veitch, R. (1971). Hot and crowded: Influences of population density on interpersonal affective behavior. *Journal of Personality and Social Psychology, 17,* 92–98.

Gruder, C. L., Cook T. D., Hennigan, K. M., Flay, B. R., Alessis, C., & Halamaj, J. (1978). Empirical tests of the absolute sleeper effect predicted from the discounting cue hypothesis. *Journal of Personality and Social Psychology, 36,* 1061–1074.

Grusec, J. E., Kuczynski, L., Rushton, J. P., & Simutis, Z. M. (1978) Modeling, direct instruction, and attributions: Effects on altruism. *Developmental Psychology, 14,* 51–57.

Grusec, J. E., & Skubiski, S. L. (1970). Model nurturance, demand characteristics of the modeling experiment, and altruism. *Journal of Personality and Social Psychology, 14,* 352–359.

Guetzkow, H. (1968). Differentiation of roles in task-oriented groups. In D. Cartwright & A. Zander (Eds.), *Group dynamics: Research and theory* (3rd ed.). New York: Harper & Row.

Gulian, E. (1974). Psychological consequences of exposure to noise: Facts and explanations. In U.S. Environmental Protection Agency, *Proceedings of the International Congress on Noise as a Public Health Problem.* Washington, DC: U.S. Government Printing Office.

Hackman, J. R., & Oldham, G. R. (1976). Motivation through the design of work: Test of a theory. *Organizational Behavior and Human Performance, 16,* 250–279.

Hager, J. C., & Ekman, P. (1981). Methodological problems of Tourangeau and Ellsworth's study of facial expression and experience and emotion. *Journal of Personality and Social Psychology, 40*(2), 385–392.

Hall, E. T. (1966). *The hidden dimension.* Garden City, NY: Doubleday.

Hamilton, D. L. (1979). A cognitive-attributional analysis of stereotyping. In L. Berkowitz (Ed.), *Advances in experimental social psychology* (Vol. 12). New York: Academic Press.

Hamilton, J. C., & Ekman, P. (1981). Methodological problems in Tourangeau and Ellsworth's study of facial expression and experience of emotion. *Journal of Personality and Social Psychology, 40,* 358–362.

Hamilton, V. L. (1976). Individual differences in ascriptions of responsibility, guilt, and appropriate judgment. In G. Berman, C. Nemeth, & N. Vidmar (Eds.), *Psychology and the Law.* Lexington, MA: Heath.

Hamilton, W. D. (1972). Altruism and related phenomena, mainly in social insects. *Annual Review of Ecology and Systematics, 3,* 193–232.

Hamner, W. C., & Yukl, G. A. (1977). The effectiveness of different offer strategies in bargaining. In D. Druckman (Ed.), *Negotiations: Social psychological perspectives.* London: Sage.

Harary, F. (1983). Consistency theory is alive and well. *Personality and Social Psychology Bulletin, 9,* 60–64.

Hargreaves, D. H. (1967). *Social relations in a secondary school.* New York: Humanities Press.

Harkins, S. G., & Petty, R. D. (1982). Effects of task difficulty and task uniqueness on social loafing. *Journal of Personality and Social Psychology, 43,* 1214–1229.

Harrison A. A. (1977). Mere exposure. In L. Berkowitz (Ed.), *Advances in experimental social psychology* (Vol. 10). New York: Academic Press.

Harrison, R. P. (1974). *Beyond words: An introduction to nonverbal communication.* Englewood Cliffs, NJ: Prentice-Hall.

Hart, H. L. A., & Hornore, A. M. (1959). *Causation in the law.* Oxford: Clarendon Press.

Harvey, J. H., Town, J. P., & Yarkin, K. C. (1981). How fundamental is "the fundamental attribution error"? *Journal of Personality and Social Psychology, 40,* 346–349.

Hastie, R. (1984). Causes and effects of causal attribution. *Journal of Personality and Social Psychology, 46,* 456.

Hatfield, E., & Sprecher, S. (1983). Equity theory and recipient reactions to aid. In J. D. Fisher, A. Nadler, & B. M. DePaulo (Eds.), *New directions in helping: Vol. 1. Recipient reactions to aid.* New York: Academic Press.

Hayduk, L. A. (1978). Personal space: An evaluative and orienting overview. *Psychological Bulletin, 85,* 117–134.

Hayduk, L. A. (1983). Personal space: Where we now stand. *Psychological Bulletin, 94,* 293–335.

Heider, F. (1946). Attitudes and cognitive organization. *Journal of Psychology, 21,* 107–112.

Heider, F. (1958). *The psychology of interpersonal relations.* New York: Wiley.

Heimann, R. A., & Heimann, H. M. (1972). Nonverbal communication and counselor education. *Comparative Group Studies, 3*, 443–460.

Helmreich, R., Aronson, E., & LeFan, J. (1970). To err is humanizing—sometimes: Effects of self esteem, competence, and a pratfall on interpersonal attraction. *Journal of Personality and Social Psychology, 16*, 259–264.

Hemphill, J. (1950). Relations between the size of the group and the behavior of "superior" leaders. *Journal of Social Psychology, 32*, 11–22.

Hendrick, C., Bixenstine, V., & Hawkins, G. (1971). Race versus belief similarity as determinants of attraction. *Journal of Personality and Social Psychology, 17*, 250–258.

Hennessy B. (1981). *Public opinion* (4th ed.). Monterey, CA: Brooks/Cole.

Hennigan, K. M., DelRosario, M L., Heath, L., Cook, T. D., Wharton, J. D., & Calder, B. J. (1982). Impact of the introduction of television on crime in the United States: Empirical findings and theoretical implications. *Journal of Personality and Social Psychology, 42*, 461–477.

Hensen, W. B., & Altman, I. (1976). Decorating personal places: a descriptive analysis. *Environment and Behavior, 8*, 491–504.

Hermann, P. J. (1970). Occupations of jurors as an influence on their verdict. *The Forum, 5*, 150–155.

Hersh, R. H., Paolitto, D. P., & Reimer, J. (1979). *Promoting moral growth.* New York: Longmans.

Heslin, R., and Patterson, M. L. (1982). *Nonverbal behavior and social psychology.* New York: Plenum.

Hess, E. H. (1975). *The tell-tale eye.* New York: Van Nostrand-Reinhold.

A hidden epidemic. (1984, May 14). *Newsweek, 53*, 30–36.

Hill, C. T., & Stull, D. E. (1981). Sex differences in effects of social and value similarity in same-sex friendship. *Journal of Personality and Social Psychology, 41*, 488–502.

Hill, G. (1982). Group versus individual performance: Are N + 1 heads better than one? *Psychological Bulletin, 91*, 517–539.

Himmelfarb, S., & Eagly, A. H. (1974). Orientations to the study of attitudes and their change. In S. Himmelfarb & A. H. Eagly (Eds.), *Readings in attitude change.* New York: Wiley.

Hoffman, M. L. (1977). Sex differences in empathy and related behaviors. *Psychological Bulletin, 84*, 712–722.

Holahan, C. J. (1977). Urban-rural differences in judged appropriateness of altruistic responses: Personal vs. situational effects. *Sociometry, 40*, 378–382.

Holahan, C. J. (1982). *Environmental psychology.* New York: Random House.

Holahan, C. J., & Dobrowolny, M. B. (1978). Cognitive and behavioral correlates of the spatial environment: An interactional analysis. *Environment and Behavior, 10*, 317–334.

Hollander, E. P. (1980). Leadership and social exchange processes. In K. J. Gergen, M. Greenberg, & R. Willis (Eds.), *Social exchange: Advances in theory and research.* New York: Plenum.

Hollander, E. P., & Julian, J. W. (1969). Contemporary trends in the analysis of leadership process. *Psychological Bulletin, 71*, 387–397.

Homans, G. C. (1950). *The human group.* New York: Harcourt, Brace.

Homans, G. C. (1958). Social behavior and exchange. *American Journal of Sociology, 63*, 597–606.

Hornstein, H. A., Fisch, E., & Holmes, M. (1968). Influence of a model's feelings about his behavior and his relevance as a comparison on other observers' helping behavior. *Journal of Personality and Social Psychology, 10*, 222–226.

Hort, H. L. A., & Honore, A. M. (1959). *Causation in the law.* Oxford: Clarendon Press.

House, J. S., & Wolf, S. (1978). Effects of urban residence on interpersonal trust and helping behavior. *Journal of Personality and Social Psychology, 36*, 1029–1043.

House, R. J., & Baetz, M. L. (1979). Leadership: Some empirical generalizations and new research directions. *Research in Organizational Behavior, 1*, 341–423.

Hovland, C., Janis, I., & Kelley, H. H. (1953). *Communication and persuasion.* New Haven, CT: Yale University Press.

Hovland, C. I., & Weiss, W. (1951). The influence of source credibility on communication effectiveness. *Public Opinion Quarterly, 15*, 635–650.

Howard, J. (1978). *Families*. New York: Simon & Schuster.

Hoyt, M. F., & Raven, B. H. (1973). Birth order and the 1971 Los Angeles earthquake. *Journal of Personality and Social Psychology, 28,* 123–128.

Huesmann, L. R., Eron, L. D., Klein, R., Brice, P., & Fischer, P. (1983). Mitigating the imitation of aggressive behaviors by changing children's attitudes about media violence. *Journal of Personality and Social Psychology, 5,* 899–910.

Hunt, M. (1974). *Sexual behavior in the 1970s.* Chicago: Dell.

Hunt, M. (1982, November 28). Putting juries on the couch. *New York Times Magazine.*

Hurt, H. T., Scott, M. D., & McCroskey, J. G. (1978). *Communication in the classroom.* Reading, MA: Addison-Wesley.

Huston, T. L., & Levinger, G. (1978). Interpersonal attraction and relationships. In M. R. Rosenzweig & L. W. Porter (Eds.), *Annual Review of Psychology, 29.*

Hutchinson, J. B. (Ed.). (1978). *Biological determinants of sexual behavior.* New York: Wiley.

Insko, C. A., & Adewole, A. (1979). The role of assumed reciprocation of sentiment and assumed similarity in the production of attraction and agreement effects of p-o-x triads. *Journal of Personality and Social Psychology, 37,* 790–808.

Insko, C. A., & Cialdini, R. B. (1969). A test of three interpretations of attitudinal verbal reinforcement. *Journal of Personality and Social Psychology, 12,* 333–341.

Insko, C. A., & Melson, W. H. (1969). Verbal reinforcement of attitude in laboratory and nonlaboratory contexts. *Journal of Personality, 37,* 25–40.

Isen, A. M., Clark, M., & Schwartz, M. F. (1976). Duration of the effect of good mood on helping: "Footprints on the sands of time." *Journal of Personality and Social Psychology, 21,* 384–388.

Isen, A. M., & Levin, P. F. (1972). Effect of feeling good on helping: Cookies and kindness. *Journal of Personality and Social Psychology, 21,* 384–388.

Isen, A. M., Shalker, T. E., Clark, M., & Karp, L. (1978). Affect, accessibility of material in memory and behavior: A cognitive loop? *Journal of Personality and Social Psychology, 36,* 1–13.

Ivey, A. E. (1971). *Microcounseling: Innovations in interview training.* Springfield, IL: Charles C. Thomas.

Izard, C. E. (1977). *Human emotions.* New York: Plenum.

Jaccard, J., Knox, R., & Brinberg, D. (1979). Prediction of behavior from beliefs: An extension and test of a subjective probability model. *Journal of Personality and Social Psychology, 37,* 1239–1248.

Jackson, J. M. (1984, April). *European cabinet creation and coalition formation theories.* Paper presented at the annual meeting of the Eastern Psychological Association, Baltimore, MD.

Jaffe, D. T., & Kanter, R. M. (1976). Couple strains in communal households: A four-factor model of the separation process. *Journal of Social Issues, 32,* 169–191.

Janis, I. (1971). Groupthink. *Psychology Today, 5,* 43–46, 74–76.

Janis, I. (1972). *Victims of groupthink: A psychological study of foreign-policy decisions and fiascoes.* Boston: Houghton-Mifflin.

Janis, I. L., & Feshbach, S. (1953). Effects of fear-arousing communications. *Journal of Abnormal and Social Psychology, 48,* 78–92.

Janis, I. L., & Rodin, J. (1979). Attribution, control, and decision making: Social psychology and health care. In G. C. Stone (Ed.), *Health psychology—A handbook.* San Francisco: Jossey-Bass.

Janoff-Bulman, R. (1979). Characterological versus behavioral self blame: Inquiries into depression and rape. *Journal of Personality and Social Psychology, 37,* 1798–1809.

Janoff-Bulman, R., & Marshall, G. (1982). Mortality, well being, and control: A study of a population of institutionalized aged. *Personality and Social Psychology Bulletin, 8,* 691–698.

Jarvik, L. F., Klodin, V., & Matsuyama, S. S. (1973). Human aggression and the extra Y chromosome: Fact or fantasy. *American Psychologist, 28,* 674–682.

Jarvinen, K. A. J. (1955). Can ward rounds be a danger to patients with myocardial infarction? *British Medical Journal, 1,* 318–320.

Jemmott, J. B., III, Pettigrew, T. F., & Johnson, J. T. (1983, August). *The effects of in-group ver-*

557

sus out-group membership in social perception. Paper presented at the 91st Annual Convention of the American Psychological Association, Anaheim, CA.

Jenkins, C. D., Zyzanski, S. J., & Rosenman, R. H. (1979). *Jenkins' activity survey.* New York: Psychological Corporation.

Jenkins, G. D., Jr., & Gupta, N. (1983, August). *Successes and tensions in a "new design" organization.* Paper presented at the meeting of the American Psychological Association, Anaheim, CA.

Johnson, D. W., & Johnson, R. T. (1979). Conflict in the classroom: Controversy and learning. *Review of Educational Research, 49,* 51–70.

Johnson, J. E., & Leventhal, H. (1974). Effects of accurate expectations and behavioral instructions on reactions during a noxious medical examination. *Journal of Personality and Social Psychology, 29,* 710–718.

Jones, C., & Aronson, E. (1973). Attribution of fault to a rape victim as a function of respectability of the victim. *Journal of Personality and Social Psychology, 26,* 415–419.

Jones, E. (1961). *The life and work of Sigmund Freud.* New York: Basic Books.

Jones, E. E. (1964). *Ingratiation: A social psychological analysis.* New York: Appleton-Century-Crofts.

Jones, E. E., & Berglas, S. (1978). Control of attributions about the self through self-handicapping strategies: The appeal of alcohol and the role of under-achievement. *Personality and Social Psychology Bulletin, 4,* 200–206.

Jones, E. E., & Davis, K. E. (1965). A theory of correspondent inferences: From acts to dispositions. In L. Berkowitz (Ed.), *Advances in experimental and social psychology* (Vol. 2). New York: Academic Press.

Jones, E. E., Gergen, K. J., & Davis, K. E. (1961). Role playing variations and their informational value on person perception. *Journal of Abnormal and Social Psychology, 63,* 302–310.

Jones, E. E., & Goethals, G. R. (1972). *Order effects in impression formation: Attribution context and the nature of the entity.* Morristown, NJ: General Learning Press.

Jones, E. E., Wood, G. C., & Quattrone, G. A. (1981). Perceived variability of personal characteristics in in-groups and out-groups: The role of knowledge and evaluation. *Personality and Social Psychology Bulletin, 7,* 523–528.

Jordan, N. (1953). Behavioral forces that are a function of attitudes and of cognitive organization. *Human Relations, 6,* 273–287.

Jourard, S. M. (1964). *The transparent self.* Princeton, NJ: Van Nostrand.

Jourard, S. M. (1970). Experimenter–subject distance and self disclosure. *Journal of Personality and Social Psychology, 15,* 278–282.

Jourard, S. M. (1971). *Self-disclosure.* New York: Wiley.

Judd, C. M., & Krosnick, J. A. (1982). Attitude centrality, organization, and measurement. *Journal of Personality and Social Psychology, 42,* 436-447.

Julian, J. W., Bishop, D. W., & Fiedler, F. E. (1966). Quasitherapeutic effects of intergroup competition. *Journal of Personality and Social Psychology, 5,* 321–327.

Kahle, L. R., & Berman, J. J. (1979). Attitude causes behaviors: A cross-lagged panel analysis. *Journal of Personality and Social Psychology, 37,* 315–321.

Kalven, H., & Zeisel, H. (1966). *The American jury.* Boston: Little Brown.

Kanouse, D. E., & Hanson, L. R., Jr. (1972). Negativity in evaluations. In E. E. Jones, D. E. Kanouse, H. H. Kelley, R. E. Nisbett, S. Valins, & B. Weiner (Eds.), *Attribution: Perceiving causes of behavior.* Morristown, NJ: General Learning Press.

Kaplan, M. F. (1975). Information integration in social judgement: Interaction of judge and informational components. *Human judgement and decision processes.* New York: Academic Press.

Kaplan, M. F. (1983, May). *Effect of training on reasoning in moral choice.* Paper presented at the meeting of the Midwestern Psychological Association, Chicago.

Kaplan, M. F., & Anderson, N. H. (1973). Information integration theory and reinforcement theory as approaches to interpersonal attraction. *Journal of Personality and Social Psychology, 28,* 301–312.

Kaplan, R. M. (1982). Coping with stressful medical exams. In H. S. Friedman and M. R. DiMatteo (Eds.), *Interpersonal issues in health care.* New York: Academic Press.

Kaplan, R. M., & Singer, R. D. (1976). Television

violence and viewer aggression: A re-examination of the evidence. *Journal of Social Issues, 32,* 35–70.

Karlins, M., & Abelson, H. I. (1979). *How opinions and attitudes are changed.* New York: Springer.

Karlins, M., Coffman, T. L., & Walters, G. (1969). On the fading of social stereotypes: Studies in three generations of college students. *Journal of Personality and Social Psychology, 13,* 1–16.

Katz, D., & Braly, K. (1933). Racial stereotypes of one hundred college students. *Journal of Abnormal and Social Psychology, 28,* 280–290.

Katz, D., & Kahn, R. L. (1978). *The social psychology of organizations* (2nd ed.). New York: Wiley.

Katz, D., & Stotland, E. (1959). A preliminary statement of a theory of attitude structure and change. In S. Koch (Ed.), *Psychology: A study of a science* (Vol. 3). New York: McGraw-Hill.

Katz, P. A. (Ed.). (1976). *Towards the elimination of racism.* Elmsford, NY: Pergamon Press.

Katzell, R. A., & Guzzo, R. A. (1983). Psychological approaches to productivity improvement. *American Psychologist, 38,* 468–472.

Kelley, H. H. (1950). The warm–cold variable in first impressions of persons. *Journal of Personality, 18,* 431–439.

Kelley, H. H. (1967). Attribution theory in social psychology. *Nebraska Symposium on Motivation, 15,* 192–238.

Kelley, H. H. (1978). *Interpersonal relations: A theory of interdependence.* New York: Wiley-Interscience.

Kelley, H. H. (1979). *Close relationships: Their structures and processes.* Hillsdale, NJ: Erlbaum.

Kendall, P., & Wolf, K. (1949). In P. Lazarsfeld & F. Stanton (Eds.), *Communications research, 1948–1949.* New York: Harper & Row.

Kenny, D. A., & Zaccaro, S. J. (1983). An estimate of variance due to traits in leadership. *Journal of Applied Psychology, 68*(4), 678–685.

Kenrick, D. T., & Cialdini, R. B. (1977). Romantic attraction: Misattribution versus reinforcement explanations. *Journal of Personality and Social Psychology, 35,* 381–391.

Kerckhoff, A. C., & Davis, K. E. (1962). Value consensus and need complementarity in mate selection. *American Sociological Review, 27,* 295–303.

Kerlinger, F. N. (1973). *Foundations of behavioral research* (2nd ed.). New York: Holt, Rinehart and Winston.

Kiesler, C. A., Collins, P. E., & Miller, N. (1969). *Attitude change: A critical analysis of theoretical approaches.* New York: Wiley.

Kiesler, C. A., & Kiesler, S. B. (1969). *Conformity.* Reading, MA: Addison-Wesley.

Kinsey, A. C., Pomeroy, W. B., & Martin, C. E. (1948). *Sexual behavior in the human male.* Philadelphia, PA: Saunders.

Klan gains momentum as the economy soars. (1982, June 18). *Daily Hampshire Gazette,* Northampton, MA.

Kleinke, C. L., Meeker, F. B., & LaFong, C. (1974). Effects of gaze, touch, and use of name on evaluation of "engaged" couples. *Journal of Research in Personality, 7,* 368–373.

Kluger, R. (1976). *Simple justice.* New York: Knopf.

Knight, G. P., & Dubro, A. F. (1984). Cooperative, competitive, and individualistic social values: An individual regression and clustering approach. *Journal of Personality and Social Psychology, 46,* 98–105.

Koffka, K. (1935). *Principles of gestalt psychology.* New York: Harcourt Brace.

Kogan, N., & Wallach, M. A. (1967). Risk taking as a function of the situation, the person, and the group. In G. Mandler, P. Mussen, N. Kogan, & M. A. Wallach (Eds.), *New directions in psychology III.* New York: Holt, Rinehart and Winston.

Kohlberg, L. (1969). Stage and sequence: The cognitive-developmental approach to socialization. In D. Goslin (Ed.), *Handbook of socialization theory and research.* Chicago: Rand McNally.

Komorita, S. S. (1974). A weighted probability model of coalition formation. *Psychological Review, 81,* 242–256.

Komorita, S. S., & Brenner, A. R. (1968). Bargaining and concession making under bilateral monopoly. *Journal of Personality and Social Psychology, 9,* 15–20.

Komorita, S. S., & Chertkoff, J. M., (1973). A bargaining theory of coalition formation. *Psychological Review, 80,* 149–162.

Konečni, V. J. (1972). Some effects of guilt on

compliance: A field replication. *Journal of Personality and Social Psychology, 23,* 30–32.

Konečni, V. J. (1975). Annoyance, type and duration of post-annoyance activity, and aggression: The "cathartic" effect. *Journal of Experimental Psychology, 104,* 76–102.

Konečni, V. J. (1982). An analysis of the sentencing system. In V. J. Konečni & E. B. Ebbesen (Eds.), *The criminal justice system: A social-psychological analysis.* San Francisco: Freeman.

Konečni, V. J., & Ebbesen, E. B. (Eds.). (1982). *The criminal justice system: A social-psychological analysis.* San Francisco: Freeman.

Koocher, G. P. (1977). Bathroom behavior and human dignity. *Journal of Personality and Social Psychology, 35,* 120–121.

Koos, E. (1955). Metropolis—what city people think of their medical services. *American Journal of Public Health, 45,* 1551–1557.

Korte, C., & Kerr, N. (1975). Responses to altruistic opportunities under urban and rural conditions. *Journal of Social Psychology, 95,* 183–184.

Koza, P., & Doob, A. N. (1975). Some empirical evidence of judicial interim release proceedings. *Criminal Law Quarterly, 17,* 258–272.

Krasner, L., Knowles, J. B., Ullman, L. P. (1965). Effect of verbal conditioning of attitudes on subsequent motor performance. *Journal of Personality and Social Psychology, 1,* 407–412.

Krebs, D. L. (1970). Altruism—an examination of the concept and a review of the literature. *Psychological Bulletin, 73,* 258–302.

Krebs, D. L. (1975). Empathy and altruism. *Journal of Personality and Social Psychology, 32,* 1134–1146.

Krumboltz, J., Varenhorst, B., & Thoresen, C. (1967). Nonverbal factors in the effectiveness of models in counseling. *Journal of Counseling Psychology, 14,* 412–418.

Labov, W. (1973). The logic of nonstandard English. In N. Keddie (Ed.), *Tinker, tailor. . . . The myth of cultural deprivation* (pp. 21–66). Harmondsworth, England: Penguin Education.

Lamm, H., & Myers, D. G. (1978). Group-induced polarization of attitudes and behavior. In L. Berkowitz (Ed.), *Advances in experimental social psychology* (Vol. II, pp. 145–195). New York: Academic Press.

Landis, D., Day, H. R., McGrew, P. L., Thomas, J. A., & Miller, A. B. (1976). Can a black "culture assimilator" increase racial understanding? *Journal of Social Issues, 32,* 169–184.

Landy, D., & Aronson, E. (1969). The influence of the character of the criminal and his victim on the decisions of simulated jurors. *Journal of Experimental Social Psychology, 5,* 141–152.

Langer, E., Blank, A., & Chanowitz, B. (1978). The mindlessness of ostensibly thoughtful action: The role of "placebo" information in interpersonal interaction. *Journal of Personality and Social Psychology, 36,* 335–342.

Langer, E. J., Janis, I. L., and Wolfer, J. A. (1975). Reduction of psychological stress in surgical patients. *Journal of Experimental Social Psychology, 11,* 155–165.

LaPiere, R. T. (1934). Attitudes and actions. *Social Forces, 13,* 230–237.

Larkin, J., D'Eredita, T., Dempsey, S., McClure, J., & Pepe, M. (1983, April). *Hope for late bloomers: Another look at the primacy effect in ability attribution.* Paper presented at the annual meeting of the Eastern Psychological Association, Baltimore, MD.

Larson, R., Csikszentmihalyi, N., & Graef, R. (1982). Time alone in daily experience: Loneliness or renewal? In L. A. Peplau & D. Perlman (Eds.), *Loneliness: A sourcebook of current theory, research and therapy.* New York: Wiley.

Latané, B. (1981). The psychology of social impact. *American Psychologist, 36,* 343–356.

Latané, B., & Darley, J. M. (1968). Group inhibition of bystander intervention. *Journal of Personality and Social Psychology, 10,* 215–221.

Latané, B., & Darley, J. M. (1970).*The unresponsive bystander: Why doesn't he help?* New York: Appleton-Crofts.

Latané, B., & Nida, S. (1981). Ten years of research on group size and helping. *Psychological Bulletin, 89,* 308–324.

Latané, B., Williams, K., & Harkins, S. (1979). Many hands make light the work: The causes and consequences of social loafing. *Journal of Personality and Social Psychology, 37,* 822–832.

Latané, B., & Wolf, S. (1981). The social impact of majorities and minorities. *Psychological Review, 88,* 438–453.

Laughlin, P. R., & Barth, J. M. (1981). Group-to-individual and individual-to-group problem-solving transfer. *Journal of Personality and Social Psychology, 41,* 1087–1093.

Lawler, E. E., III, & Mohrman, S. A. (1984). *Quality circles: A self-destruct approach?* Center for Effective Organizations Publication G84-1. Los Angeles: University of Southern California School of Business Administration.

Lazarus, R. S., Opton, E. M., Jr., Nomikos, M. S. & Rankin, N. O. (1965). The principle of short-circuiting of threat: Further evidence. *Journal of Personality, 33,* 622–635.

Leavitt, H. J. (1951). Some effects of certain communication patterns on group performance. *Journal of Abnormal and Social Psychology, 46,* 38–50.

LeBon, G. (1896). *The crowd: A study of the popular mind.* London: Ernest Benn.

Leigh, H., & Reiser, M. F. (1980). *The patient.* New York: Plenum.

Leng, R. J., & Wheeler, H. G. (1979). Influence strategies, success, and war. *Journal of Conflict Resolution, 23,* 655–684.

Lepper, M. R., Greene, D., & Nisbett, R. E. (1973). Undermining children's intrinsic interest with extrinsic rewards: A test of the overjustification hypothesis. *Journal of Personality and Social Psychology, 28,* 129–137.

Lerner, M. J. (1966, September). *The unjust consequences of the need to believe in a just world.* Paper presented at the meeting of the American Psychological Association, New York.

Lerner, M. J. (1977). The justice motive: Some hypotheses as to its origins and forms. *Journal of Personality, 45,* 1–52.

Lerner, M. J., Miller, D. T., & Holmes, J. G. (1976). Deserving versus justice: A contemporary dilemma. In L. Berkowitz & E. Walster (Eds.), *Advances in experimental social psychology* (Vol. 12). New York: Academic Press.

Leventhal, G. S. (1976). Fairness in social relationships. In J. W. Thibaut, J. T. Spence, & R. C. Carson (Eds.), *Contemporary topics in social psychology.* Morristown, NJ: General Learning Press.

Leventhal, H. (1970). Findings and theory in the study of fear communications. In L. Berkowitz (Ed.), *Advances in experimental social psychology* (Vol. 5, pp. 119–186). New York: Academic Press.

Leventhal, H. (1974). Attitudes. In C. Nemeth (Ed.), *Social psychology: Classic and contemporary integration.* Chicago: Rand-McNally.

Leventhal, H., Hochbaum, G., & Rosenstock, I. (1960). Epidemic impact on the general population in two cities. In U.S. Department of Health, Education and Welfare, *The impact of Asian influenza on community life: A study in five cities* (Public Health Service Publication No. 766). Washington, DC: U.S. Government Printing Office.

Levin, R. J. (1975, October). The Redbook Report on Premarital and Extramarital Sex: The end of the double standard? *Redbook,* pp. 38–44, 190–192.

Levine, F. J., & Tapp, J. (1973). The psychology of criminal identification: The gap from Wade to Kirby. *University of Pennsylvania Law Review, 121,* 1079–1131.

Levine, F. J., & Tapp, J. L. (1982). Eyewitness identification: Problems and pitfalls. In V. J. Konečni & E. B. Ebbesen (Eds.), *The criminal justice system: A social-psychological analysis* (pp. 99–127). San Francisco: W. H. Freeman.

Levine, R. A., & Campbell, D. T. (1972). *Ethnocentrism: Theories of conflict, ethnic attitudes and group behavior.* New York: Wiley.

Levinger, G. (1983). Development and change. In H. H. Kelley, E. Berscheid, A. Christensen, J. Harvey, T. Huston, G. Levinger, E. McCintock, L. A. Peplau, & D. R. Peterson (Eds.), *Close relationships.* San Francisco: W. H. Freeman.

Levinger, G., Senn, D. J., & Jorgensen, B. W. (1970). Progress toward permanence in courtship: A test of the Kerckhoff–David hypothesis. *Sociometry, 33,* 427–443.

Levinger, G. A. (1974). A three-level approach to attraction: Toward an understanding of pair relatedness. In T. L. Huston (Ed.), *Foundations of interpersonal attraction.* New York: Academic Press.

Lewin, K. (1951). *Field theory in social science.* New York: Harper.

Lewin, K., Lippitt, R., & White, R. K. (1939). Patterns of aggressive behavior in experimentally created "social climates." *Journal of Social Psychology, 10,* 271–299.

Ley, D., & Cybriwsky, R. (1974). Urban graffiti as territorial markers. *Annals of the Association of American Geographers, 64,* 491–505.

Ley, P. (1982). Giving information to patients. In J. R. Eiser (Ed.), *Social psychology and behavioral medicine.* New York: Wiley.

Lieberman, M. A., Yalom, I. D., & Miles, M. (1973). *Encounter groups: First facts.* New York: Basic Books.

Likert, R. (1932). A technique for the measurement of attitudes [Special issue]. *Archives of Psychology.* (140).

Lindskold, S. (1979). Managing conflict through announced conciliatory initiatives backed with retaliatory capacity. In W. G. Austin & S. Worchel (Eds.), *The social psychology of intergroup relations.* Monterey, CA: Brooks/Cole.

Linville, P. W. (1982). The complexity-extremity effect and age-based stereotyping. *Journal of Personality and Social Psychology, 42,* 183–211.

Locke, E. A., & Schweiger, D. M. (1979). Participation in decision-making: One more look. In B. Staw (Ed.), *Research in organizational behavior* (Vol. 1). Greenwich, CT: JAI Press.

Loeb, M., Holding, D. H., & Baker, M. A. (1982). Noise, stress and circadian arousal in self-paced computation. *Motivation and Emotion, 6,* 43–48.

Lomranz, J., Lakin, M., & Schiffman, H. (1972). Variants of sensitivity training and encounter: Diversity and fragmentation? *Journal of Applied Behavioral Science, 8,* 399–420.

London, P. (1970). The rescuers: Motivational hypotheses about Christians who saved Jews from the Nazis. In J. Macaulay & L. Berkowitz (Eds.), *Altruism and helping behavior.* New York: Academic Press.

Loo, C. M. (1978). Density, crowding, and preschool children. In A. Baum & Y. Epstein (Eds.), *Human response to crowding.* Hillsdale, NJ: Erlbaum.

Lorenz, K. (1966). *On aggression.* New York: Harcourt, Brace.

Lott, A. J., & Lott, B. E. (1965). Group cohesiveness as interpersonal attraction: A review of relationships with antecedent and consequent variables. *Psychological Bulletin, 64,* 259–309.

Lott, A. J., & Lott, B. E. (1974). The role of reward in the formation of positive interpersonal attitudes. In T. L. Huston (Ed.), *Foundations of interpersonal attraction* (pp. 171–189). New York: Academic Press.

Lott, D. F., & Sommer, R. (1967). Seating arrangements and status. *Journal of Personality and Social Psychology, 7,* 90–94.

Love, K. D., & Aiello, J. R. (1980). Using projective techniques to measure interaction distance: A methodological note. *Personality and Social Psychology Bulletin, 6,* 102–104.

Luce, R. D., & Raiffa, H. (1957). *Games and decisions.* New York: Wiley.

Luchins, A. S. (1957). Experimental attempts to minimize the impact of first impressions. In C. I. Hovland (Ed.), *The order of presentation in persuasion* (pp. 62–75). New Haven, CT: Yale University Press.

Lucker, G. W., Rosenfield, D., Sikes, J., & Aronson, E. (1977). Performance in the interdependent classroom: A field study. *American Research Journal, 13,* 115–123.

Lundberg, U. (1976). Urban commuting: Crowdedness and catecholamine excretion. *Journal of Human Stress, 2,* 26–32.

Luthans, F. (1981). *Organizational behavior* (3rd ed.). New York: McGraw-Hill.

Lynch, J. G., Jr., & Cohen, J. L. (1978). The use of subjective expected utility theory as an aid to understanding variables that influence helping behavior. *Journal of Personality and Social Psychology, 36,* 1138–1151.

Maass, A., & Clark, R. D., III (1984). Hidden impact of minorities: Fifteen years of minority influence research. *Psychological Bulletin, 95*(3), 428–450.

MacNeil, M. K., & Sherif, M. (1976). Norm change over subject generations as a function of arbitrariness of prescribed norms. *Journal of Personality and Social Psychology, 34,* 762–773.

Maier, N. R. F. (1967). Assets and liabilities in group problem solving: The need for an integrative function. *Psychological Review, 47,* 239–249.

Maier, N. R. F. (1970). *Problem solving and crea-*

tivity in individuals and groups. Monterey, CA: Brooks/Cole.

Malamuth, N., & Check, J. (1982). Penile tumescence and perceptual responses to rape as a function of victim's perceived reactions. *Journal of Applied Social Psychology.*

Malamuth, N., & Spinner, B. (1980). A longitudinal content analysis of sexual violence in the best-selling erotica magazines. *Journal of Sex Research, 16,* 226–237.

Mann, L., Newton, J. W., & Innes, J. M. (1982). A test between deindividuation and emergent norm theories of crowd aggression. *Journal of Personality and Social Psychology, 42,* 260–272.

Manucia, G. K., Baumann, D. J., & Cialdini, R. B. (1984). Mood influences on helping: Direct effects or side effects? *Journal of Personality and Social Psychology, 46,* 357–364.

Marrow, A. J., Bowers, D. G., & Seashore, S. E. (1967). *Management by participation.* New York: Harper & Row.

Marshall, G. D., & Zimbardo, P. G. (1979). Affective consequences of inadequately explained physiological arousal. *Journal of Personality and Social Psychology, 37,* 970–988.

Maslach, C. (1979). Negative emotional biasing of unexplained arousal. *Journal of Personality and Social Psychology, 37,* 953–969.

Masters, W. H., & Johnson, V. E. (1979). *Homosexuality in perspective.* Boston: Little, Brown.

Masur, Frank T., III (1981). Adherence to health care regimens. *Medical Psychology—Contributions to Behavioral Medicine,* 441–470.

Matlin, M., & Stang, D. (1978). *The Pollyanna principle: Selectivity in language, memory, and thought.* Cambridge, MA: Schenkman.

Matthews, K. A. (1982). Psychological perspectives on the Type A behavior pattern. *Psychological Bulletin, 91,* 293–323.

Maykovich, M. K. (1975). Correlates of racial prejudice. *Journal of Personality and Social Psychology, 32,* 1014–1020.

Mayo, E. (1933). *The human problems of an industrial civilization.* New York: Macmillan.

Mazzula, J. M., Lasagna, L., & Griner, P. F. (1974). Variation in interpretation of prescription instructions. *Journal of the American Medical Association, 227,* 929–931.

McArthur, L. A. (1972). The how and what of why: Some determinants and consequences of causal attribution. *Journal of Personality and Social Psychology, 22,* 171–193.

McArthur, L. Z. (1981). What grabs you? The role of attention in impression formation and causal attribution. In E. T. Higgins, C. P. Herman, & M. P. Zanna (Eds.), *Social cognition: The Ontario Symposium.* Hillsdale, NJ: Erlbaum.

McCauley, C., & Stitt, C. L. (1978). An individual and quantitative measure of stereotypes. *Journal of Personality and Social Psychology, 36,* 929–940.

McDougall, W. (1908). *Introduction to social psychology.* London: Methuen.

McGillicuddy, N. B., Van Slyck, M. R., & Pruitt, D. G. (1984, April). *Effects of third party intervention on negotiation outcome.* Paper presented at the annual meeting of the Eastern Psychological Association, Baltimore, MD.

McGlynn, R. P., Megas, J. G., & Benson, D. H. (1976). Sex and race as factors affecting attribution of insanity in a murder trial. *Journal of Psychology, 93,* 93–99.

McGuire, W. J. (1964). Inducing resistance to persuasion. In L. Berkowitz (Ed.), *Advances in experimental social psychology* (Vol. 1). New York: Academic Press.

McGuire, W. J. (1969). The nature of attitudes and attitude change. In G. Lindzey & E. Aronson, *Handbook of social psychology* (2nd ed., Vol. III). Reading, MA: Addison-Wesley.

McKean, K. (1982). Did Abscam manipulate its targets? *Discover, 3,* 80–83.

Mead, M. (1928). *Coming of age in Samoa.* New York: Morrow.

Megargee, E. I. (1966). Undercontrolled and overcontrolled personality types in extreme antisocial aggression [Special issue]. *Psychological Monographs, 80*(611).

Mehrabian, A. (1968a) Inference of attitude from the posture orientation and distance of a communicator. *Journal of Consulting and Clinical Psychology, 32,* 296–308.

Mehrabian, A. (1968b). Relationship of attitude to seated posture, orientation, and distance. *Journal of Personality and Social Psychology, 10,* 26–30.

Mentzer, S. J., & Snyder, M. L. (1982). The doctor and the patient: A psychological perspective.

In G. S. Sanders & J. Suls (Eds.), *Social psychology of health and illness* (pp. 161–181). Hillsdale, NJ: Erlbaum.

Mettee, D. R., & Aronson, E. (1974). Affective reactions to appraisal from others. In T. L. Huston (Ed.), *Foundations of interpersonal attraction* (pp. 235–283). New York: Academic Press.

Mewborn, C. R., & Rogers, R. W. (1979). Effects of threatening and reassuring components of fear appeals on psychological and verbal measures of emotion and attitudes. *Journal of Experimental Psychology, 15,* 242–253.

Meyer, A. J., Nash, J. D., McAlister, A. L., Maccoby, N., & Farquhar, J. W. (1980). Skills training in a cardiovascular education campaign. *Journal of Consulting and Clinical Psychology, 48,* 129–142.

Meyer, J. P., & Pepper, S. (1977). Need compatibility and marital adjustment in young married couples. *Journal of Personality and Social Psychology, 35,* 331–342.

Meyer, T. P. (1972). The effects of sexually arousing and violent films on aggressive behavior. *Journal of Sex Research, 8,* 324–331.

Michelson, W. (1976). *Man and his urban environment: A sociological approach.* Reading, MA: Addison-Wesley.

Middlemist, R. D., Knowles, E. S., & Matter, C. F. (1976). Personal space invasion in the lavatory: Suggestive evidence for arousal. *Journal of Personality and Social Psychology, 33,* 541–546.

Middlemist, R. D., Knowles, E. S., & Matter, C. F. (1977). What to do and what to report: A reply to Koocher. *Journal of Personality and Social Psychology, 35,* 122–124.

Midlarsky, E., Bryan, J. H., & Brickman, P. (1973). Aversive approval: Interactive effects of modeling and reinforcement on altruistic behavior. *Child Development, 44,* 321–328.

Midlarsky, E., & Midlarsky, M. (1973). Some determinants of aiding under experimentally induced stress. *Journal of Personality, 41,* 305–327.

Milgram, S. (1963). Behavioral study of obedience. *Journal of Abnormal and Social Psychology, 67,* 371–378.

Milgram, S. (1974). *Obedience to authority.* New York: Harper & Row.

Milgram, S. (1977). *The individual in a social world: Essays and experiments.* Reading, MA: Addison-Wesley.

Milgram, S., Greenwald, J., Kessler, S., McKenna, W., & Waters, J. (1972). A psychological map of New York City. *American Scientist, 60,* 194–200.

Miller, C. E., & Crandall, R. (1980). Experimental research on the social psychology of bargaining and coalition formation. In P. B. Paulus (Ed.), *Psychology of group influence* (pp. 333–374). Hillsdale, NJ: Erlbaum.

Miller, D. T., & Ross, M. (1975). Self-serving biases in the attribution of causality: Fact or fiction? *Psychology Bulletin, 82,* 213–225.

Miller, G. R., Bauchner, J. E., Hocking, J. E., Fontes, N. E., Kaminski, E. P., & Brandt, D. R. (1981). "... and nothing but the truth": How well can observers detect deceptive testimony? *Perspectives in law and psychology: Vol. II. The trial process.* New York: Plenum.

Miller, G. R., & Burgoon, J. K. (1982). Factors affecting assessment of witness credibility. In N. N. Kerr & R. Bray (Eds.), *The psychology of the courtroom* (pp. 176–177). New York: Academic Press.

Miller, S. M., & Managan, C. E. (1983). Interacting effects of information and coping style in adapting to gynecologic stress: Should the doctor tell all? *Journal of Personality and Social Psychology, 45,* 223–236.

Mitchell, H. E., & Byrne, D. (1973). The defendant's dilemma: Effects of jurors' attitudes and authoritarianism on judicial decisions. *Journal of Personality and Social Psychology, 25,* 123–129.

Mitchell, T. R. (1982). *People in organizations: An introduction to organizational behavior* (2nd ed.). New York: McGraw-Hill.

Miura, I., & Hess, R. D. (1983, August). *Sex differences in computer access, interest and usage.* Paper presented at the 91st annual convention of the American Psychological Association, Anaheim, CA.

Moe, J. L., Nacoste, R. W., & Insko, C. A. (1981). Belief versus race as determinants of discrimination: A study of southern adolescents in 1966 and 1979. *Journal of Personality and Social Psychology, 41,* 1031–1050.

Monahan, J., & Loftus, E. F. (1982). The psychology of law. *Annual Reviews, 33,* 441–475.

Montague, A. (1971). *Touching*. New York: Harper & Row.

Moore, G. T. (1974). Developmental variations between and within individuals in the cognitive representation of large-scale spatial environments. *Man–Environment Systems, 4,* 55–57.

Moran, G., & Comfort, J. C. (1982). Scientific juror selection: Sex as a moderator of demographic and personality predictors of impaneled felony juror behavior. *Journal of Personality and Social Psychology, 43,* 1052–1063.

Moreno, J. (1953). *Who shall survive?* (2nd ed.). Beacon, NY: Beacon House.

Morgan, M. (1981). The overjustification effect: A developmental test of self-perception interpretation. *Journal of Personality and Social Psychology, 40,* 809–821.

Morgan, P. M., (1977). *Deterrence: A conceptual analysis*. Beverly Hills, CA: Sage.

Moriarty, T. (1975). Crime, commitment, and the responsive bystander: Two field experiments. *Journal of Personality and Social Psychology, 31,* 370–376.

Moscovici, S., & Faucheaux, C. (1972). Social influence, conformity bias, and the study of active minorities. In L. Berkowitz (Ed.), *Advances in experimental social psychology* (Vol. 6). New York: Academic Press.

Moscovici, S., Lage, E., & Naffrechoux, M. (1969). Influence of a consistent minority on the responses of a majority in a color perception task. *Sociometry, 32,* 365–380.

Moscovici, S., & Mugny, G. (1983). Minority influence. In P. B. Paulus (Ed.), *Basic group processes*. New York: Springer-Verlag.

Moscovici, S., & Nemeth, C. (1974). Social influence II: Minority influence. In C. Nemeth (Ed.), *Social psychology: Classic and contemporary integrations*. Chicago: Rand McNally.

Moss, M. K., & Page, R. A. (1972). Reinforcement and helping behavior. *Journal of Applied Social Psychology, 2,* 360–371.

Mueser, K. T., Grau, B. W., Sussman, S., & Rosen, A. J. (1984). You're only as pretty as you feel: Facial expression as a determinant of physical attractiveness. *Journal of Personality and Social Psychology, 46,* 469–478.

Mulder, M., & Sterding, A. (1963). Threat, attraction to group, and need for strong leadership. *Human Relations, 16,* 317–334.

Myers, D. G., & Kaplan, M. F. (1976). Group-induced polarization in simulated juries. *Personality and Social Psychology Bulletin, 2,* 63–66.

Myers, D. G., & Lamm, H. (1976). The group polarization phenomenon. *Psychological Bulletin, 83,* 602–627.

Mynatt, C., & Sherman, S. J. (1975). Responsibility attribution in groups and individuals: A direct test of the diffusion of responsibility hypothesis. *Journal of Personality and Social Psychology, 4,* 197–216.

Nadler, A., Shapira, R., & Ben-Itzhak, S. (1982). Good looks may help: Effects of helper's physical attractiveness and sex of helper on males' and females' help-seeking behavior. *Journal of Personality and Social Psychology, 42*(1), 90–99.

Nagao, D. H., & McClain, L. (1983, May). *The effects of judge's instructions concerning reasonable doubt on mock juror's verdicts*. Paper presented at the annual meeting of the Midwestern Psychological Association, Chicago, IL.

Nahemon, L., & Lawton, M. P. (1975). Similarity and propinquity in friendship formation. *Journal of Personality and Social Psychology, 32,* 204–213.

Napoli, A., Pardine, P., & Calicchia, J. (1984, April). *Task interruption and the coronary-prone behavior pattern*. Paper presented at the annual meeting of the Eastern Psychological Association, Baltimore, MD.

Naroll, R., Bullough, V. L., & Naroll, F. (1974). *Military deterrence in history: A pilot cross-historical survey*. Albany: State University of New York Press.

National Commission on the Causes and Prevention of Violence (1969). *Crimes of violence* (Vol. 2). Washington, DC: U.S. Government Printing Office.

Nemeth, C. (1972). A critical analysis of research utilizing the prisoner's dilemma paradigm for the study of bargaining. In L. Berkowitz (Ed.), *Advances in experimental social psychology* (Vol. 6). New York: Academic Press.

Nemeth, C. (1981). Jury trials: Psychology and law. *Advances in Experimental Social Psychology, 14,* 309–367.

Nemeth, C., & Sosis, R. (1973). Simulated jury study: Characteristics of the defendant and the jurors. *Journal of Social Psychology, 90,* 221–229.

Nesbit, P., & Steven, G. (1974). Personal space and stimulus intensity at a southern California amusement park. *Sociometry, 37,* 105–115.

Newcomb, T. M. (1956). The prediction of interpersonal attraction. *American Psychologist, 11,* 575–586.

Newcomb, T. M. (1961). *The acquaintance process.* New York: Holt, Rinehart and Winston.

Newman, O. (1972). *Defensible space: Crime prevention through urban design.* New York: Macmillan.

Newtson, D. (1974). Dispositional inference from effects of actions: Effects chosen and effects forgone. *Journal of Experimental Social Psychology, 10,* 489–496.

Ng, C. A. (1975). The educational background of the adult Chinese student. *TESL Talk, 6,* 36–40.

Nisbett, R. E., Caputo, C., Legant, P., & Maracek, J. (1973). Behavior as seen by the actor and as seen by the observer. *Journal of Personality and Social Psychology, 27,* 154–165.

Nisbett, R. E., & Ross, L. (1980). *Human inference: Strategies and shortcomings of social judgment.* Englewood Cliffs, NJ: Prentice-Hall.

Noller, P. (1982). Channel consistency and inconsistency in the communications of married couples. *Journal of Personality and Social Psychology, 43,* 732–741.

Norman, W. T. (1963). Toward an adequate taxonomy of personality attributes: Replicated factor structure in peer nomination personality ratings. *Journal of Abnormal and Social Psychology, 66,* 574–583.

Norvell, N., & Worchel, S. (1981). A re-examination of the relation between equal status contact and intergroup attraction. *Journal of Personality and Social Psychology, 41,* 902–908.

Novaco, R. W., Stokols, D., Campbell, J., & Stokols, J. (1979). Transportation, stress, and community psychology. *American Journal of Community Psychology, 7,* 361–380.

Oddou, G., & Clavijo, F. (1983, August). *Teaching culture: The effects on attitude change and perceived similarity.* Paper presented at the meeting of the American Psychological Association, Anaheim, CA.

Olsen, M. E. (1981). Consumers' attitudes toward energy conservation. *Journal of Social Issues, 37,* 108–131.

Olson, J. M., Ellis, R. J., & Zanna, M. P. (1983). Validating objective versus subjective judgments: Interest in social comparison and consistency information. *Personality and Social Psychology Bulletin, 9,* 427–436.

Orleans, P. (1967). Differential cognition of urban residents: Effects of social scale on mapping. *Science, engineering and the city* (Publication 1498). Washington, DC: National Academy of Engineering.

Orne, M. T., & Holland, C. C. (1968). On the ecological validity of laboratory deceptions. *International Journal of Psychiatry, 6,* 282–293.

Ortega, D. F. (1983, August). *The Type A coronary-prone behavior pattern: Some recent research on behavioral characteristics.* Paper presented at the 91st annual convention of the American Psychological Association, Anaheim, CA.

Orvis, B. R., Cunningham, J. D., & Kelley, H. H. (1975). A closer examination of causal inference: The role of consensus, distinctiveness and consistency information. *Journal of Personality and Social Psychology, 32,* 605–616.

Osborn, A. F. (1957). *Applied imagination.* New York: Scribner.

Osgood, C. E. (1962). *An alternative to war or surrender.* Urbana: University of Illinois Press.

Osgood, C. E. (1979). GRIT for MBFR: A proposal for unfreezing force-level postures in Europe. *Peace Research Reviews, 8,* 77–92.

Osgood, C. E., Suci, G. J., & Tannenbaum, P. (1957). *The measurement of meaning.* Urbana: University of Illinois Press.

Osgood, C. E., & Tannenbaum, P. H. (1955). The principle of congruity in the prediction of attitude change. *Psychological Review, 62,* 42–55.

Oskamp, S. (1984). *Applied social psychology.* Englewood Cliffs, NJ: Prentice-Hall.

Pagan, G., & Aiello, J. R. (1982). Development of personal space among Puerto Ricans. *Journal of Nonverbal Behavior, 7,* 59–68.

Page, M. M. (1969). Social psychology of a classical conditioning of attitudes experiment. *Journal of Personality and Social Psychology, 11,* 177–186.

Palamarek, D. L., & Rule, B. G. (1979). The effects of ambient temperature and insult on the motivation to retaliate or escape. *Motivation and Emotion, 3,* 83–92.

Park, B., & Rothbart, M. (1982). Perception of out-group homogeneity and levels of social categorization: Memory for the subordinate attributes of in-group and out-group members. *Journal of Personality and Social Psychology, 42,* 1051–1068.

Parke, R. D., Berkowitz, L., Leyens, J. P., West, S. G., & Sebastian, R. J. (1977). Some effects of violent and nonviolent movies on the behavior of juvenile delinquents. In L. Berkowitz (Ed.), *Advances in experimental social psychology* (Vol. 10). New York: Academic Press.

Parsons, H. M. (1974). What happened at Hawthorne? *Science, 183,* 922–932.

Patterson, A. H. (1978). Territorial behavior and fear of crime in the elderly. *Environmental Psychology and Nonverbal Behavior, 2,* 131–144.

Patterson, A. H. (1984, April). *Scientific jury selection: An empirical evaluation.* Paper presented at the annual meeting of the Eastern Psychological Association, Baltimore, MD.

Patterson, M. L. (1973). Compensation in nonverbal immediacy behaviors: A review. *Sociometry, 36,* 237–252.

Patterson, M. L. (1976). An arousal model of interpersonal intimacy. *Psychology Review, 83,* 235–245.

Patterson, M. L. (1983). *Nonverbal behavior: A functional perspective.* New York: Springer-Verlag.

Patterson, M. L., Jordan, A., Hogan, M. B., & Frerker, D. (1981). Effects of nonverbal intimacy on arousal and behavioral adjustment. *Journal of Nonverbal Behavior, 5,* 184–198.

Paulus, P. B. (1980). *Psychology of group influence.* Hillsdale, NJ: Erlbaum.

Paulus, P. B. (1983). *Basic group processes.* New York: Springer-Verlag.

Paulus, P. B., & Matthews, R. W. (1980). When density affects task performance. *Personality and Social Psychology Bulletin, 6,* 119–124.

Paulus, P. B., & McCain, G. (1983). Crowding in jails. *Basic and Applied Social Psychology, 4,* 89–107.

Paulus, P. B., McCain, G., & Cox, V. C. (1978). Death rates, psychiatric commitments, blood pressure, and perceived crowding as a function of institutional crowding. *Environmental Psychology and Nonverbal Behavior, 3,* 107–116.

Pepitone, A., & Reichling, G. (1955). Group cohesiveness and the expression of hostility. *Human Relations, 8,* 327–337.

Peplau, L. A., & Perlman, D. (Eds.). (1982). *Loneliness: A sourcebook of current theory, research and therapy.* New York: Wiley.

Peplau, L. A., Rubin, Z., & Hill, C. T. (1977). Sexual intimacy in dating relationships. *Journal of Social Issues, 33*(2), 76–109.

Perloff, R., & Nelson, S. D. (1983). Economic productivity and the behavioral sciences. *American Psychologist,* 451–453.

Pettigrew, T. F. (1979). The ultimate attribution error: Extending Allport's cognitive analysis of prejudice. *Personality and Social Psychology Bulletin, 5,* 461–476.

Petty, R. E., & Cacioppo, J. T. (1977). Forewarning, cognitive responding, and resistance to persuasion. *Journal of Personality and Social Psychology, 35,* 645–655.

Petty, R. E., & Cacioppo, J. T. (1979). Effects of forewarning of persuasive intent and involvement on cognitive responses and persuasion. *Personality and Social Psychology Bulletin. 5,* 173–176.

Petty, R. E., & Cacioppo, J. T. (1981). *Attitudes and persuasion: Classic and contemporary approaches.* Dubuque, IA: Wm. C. Brown.

Petty, R. E., & Cacioppo, J. T. (1984). The effects of involvement in response to argument quantity and quality: Central and peripheral routes to persuasion. *Journal of Personality and Social Psychology, 46,* 69–81.

Piliavin, I., Rodin, J., & Piliavin, J. A. (1969). Good Samaritanism: An underground phenomenon? *Journal of Personality and Social Psychology, 13,* 289–299.

Piliavin, J. A., Callero, P. L., & Evans, D. E. (1982). Addiction to altruism? Opponent-process theory and habitual blood donation. *Journal of Personality and Social Psychology, 43,* 1200–1213.

Piliavin, J. A., Evans, D. E., & Callero, P. (1984). Learning to "give to unnamed strangers": The process of commitment to regular blood donation. In E. Staub, D. Bar-Tal, J. Karylowski, & J. Reykowski (Eds.), *The development and maintenance of prosocial behavior: International perspectives.* New York. Plenum.

Piliavin, J. A., & Piliavin, I. M. (1972). Effect of blood on reactions to a victim. *Journal of Personality and Social Psychology, 23,* 353–361.

Porter, L. W., Lawler, E. E., III, & Hackman, J. R. (1975). *Behavior in organizations.* New York: McGraw-Hill.

Porter, L. W., & Roberts, K. H. (1976). Communication in organizations. In M. D. Dunnette (Ed.), *Handbook of industrial and organizational psychology.* Chicago: Rand McNally.

Pratkanis, A. R., & Greenwald, A. G. (1983, May). *Towards a reliable sleeper effect in persuasion.* Paper presented at the meeting of the Midwestern Psychological Association, Chicago, IL.

Prentice-Dunn, S., & Rogers, R. W. (1980). Effects of deindividuating situational cues and aggressive models on subjective deindividuation and aggression. *Journal of Personality and Social Psychology, 39,* 104–113.

Prentice-Dunn, S., & Rogers, R. W. (1983). Deindividuation in aggression. In R. Green & E. Donnerstein (Eds.), *Aggression: Theoretical and empirical reviews.* New York: Academic Press.

Price, R. A., & Vandenberg, S. G. (1979). Matching for physical attractiveness in married couples. *Personality and Social Psychology Bulletin, 5,* 398–400.

Proxmire, W. (1975). Press release, U.S. Senate Office.

Pruitt, D. G. (1971). Choice shifts in group discussion: An introductory review. *Journal of Personality and Social Psychology, 20,* 339–360.

Pruitt, D. G. (1981). *Negotiation behavior.* New York: Academic Press.

Rabbie, J. M., & Bekkers, F. (1976). Threatened leadership and intergroup competition. *Nederlands Tijdschrift de Psychologie en haar Grensgebieden, 31,* 269–283.

Rajecki, D. W. (1982). *Attitudes: Themes and advances.* Sunderland, MA: Sinauer.

Raven, B. H. (1974). The comparative analysis of power and power preference. In J. Tedeschi (Ed.), *Perspectives on social power.* Chicago: Aldine-Atherton.

Raven, B. H., & Haley, R. W. (1980). Social influence in a medical context. In L. Bickman (Ed.), *Applied Social Psychology Annual, 1,* 255–278.

Rawls, J. (1971). *A theory of justice.* Cambridge, MA: Harvard University Press.

Reader, N., & English, H. B. (1947). Personality factors in adolescent female friendships. *Journal of Consulting Psychology, 11,* 212–220.

Reis, H. T., Nezlek, J., & Wheeler, L. (1980). Physical attractiveness in social interaction. *Journal of Personality and Social Psychology, 38,* 604–617.

Reis, H. T., Wheeler, L., Spiegel, N., Kernis, M. H., Nezlek, J., & Perri, M. (1982). Physical attractiveness in social interaction: Why does appearance affect social experience? *Journal of Personality and Social Psychology, 43,* 979–996.

Reisenzein, R. (1983). The Schachter theory of emotion: Two decades later. *Psychological Bulletin, 94,* 239–264.

Reiss, I. L. (1980). *A guide for researching heterosexual relationships.* Minneapolis: University of Minnesota, Minnesota Family Study Center.

Rice, R. W., & Kastenbaum, D. R. (1983). The contingency model of leadership: Some current issues. *Basic and Applied Social Psychology, 4,* 373–392.

Riecken, H. (1952). Some problems of consensus development. *Rural Sociology, 17,* 245–252.

Rinn, W. E. (1984). The neuropsychology of facial expression: A review of the neurological and psychological mechanisms of producing facial expressions. *Psychological Bulletin, 95,* 52–77.

Riordan, C. A., & Tedeschi, J. T. (1983). Attraction in aversive environments: Some evidence for classical conditioning and negative reinforcement. *Journal of Personality and Social Psychology, 44,* 683–692.

Riskind, J. H., & Wilson, D. W. (1982). Interpersonal attraction for the competitive person: Unscrambling the competition paradox. *Journal of Applied Social Psychology, 12,* 444–452.

Rodin, J. (1976). Crowding, perceived choice and response to controllable and uncontrollable outcomes. *Journal of Experimental Social Psychology, 12,* 564–578.

568

Rodin, J., & Baum, A. (1978). Crowding and helplessness: Potential consequences of density and loss of control. In A. Baum and Y. Epstein (Eds.), *Human response to crowding*. New York: Halsted.

Rodin, J., & Janis, I. L. (1979). The social power of health care practitioners as agents of change. *The Journal of Social Issues, 35,* 60–81.

Rodin, J., & Langer, E. (1977). Long-term effects of a control-relevant intervention with the institutionalized aged. *Journal of Personality and Social Psychology, 35,* 897–902.

Rodin, J., & Langer, E. (1980). Aging labels: The decline of control and the fall of self-esteem. *Journal of Social Issues, 36,* 12–29.

Rodrigues, A. (1967). Effects of balance, positivity, and agreement in triadic social relations. *Journal of Personality and Social Psychology, 5,* 472–476.

Roethlisberger, F. J., & Dickson, W. V. (1939). *Management and the worker.* Cambridge, MA: Harvard University Press.

Rogers, M., Miller, N., Mayer, F. S., & Duvall, S. (1982). Personal responsibility and salience of the request for help: Determinants of the relation between negative affect and helping behavior. *Journal of Personality and Social Psychology, 43,* 956–970.

Rogers, R. W. (1975). A protection motivation theory of fear appeals and attitude change. *Journal of Psychology, 91,* 93–114.

Rokeach, M. (1960). *The open and closed mind: Investigations into the nature of belief systems and personality systems.* New York: Basic Books.

Rokeach, M. (1971). Long-range experimental modification of values, attitudes, and behavior. *American Psychologist, 26,* 453–459.

Rommetveit, R. (1955). *Social norms and roles.* Minneapolis: University of Minnesota Press.

Rose, A. (1948). Anti-semitism's root in city hatred. *Commentary, 6,* 374–378.

Rosenberg, L. A. (1961). Group size, prior experience, and conformity. *Journal of Abnormal and Social Psychology, 63,* 436–437.

Rosenberg, M. J. (1965). When dissonance fails: On eliminating evaluation apprehension from attitude measurement. *Journal of Personality and Social Psychology, 1,* 28–42.

Rosenberg, S., & Gara, M. A. (1983). Contemporary perspectives and future directions of personality and social psychology. *Journal of Personality and Social Psychology, 45,* 57–73.

Rosenhan, D. L. (1973). On being sane in insane places. *Science, 179,* 250–258.

Rosenhan, D. L., Moore, B. S., & Underwood, B. (1976). The social psychology of moral behavior. In T. Lickona (Ed.), *Moral development and behavior: Theory, research, and social issues.* New York: Holt, Rinehart and Winston.

Rosenkrantz, P. S., & Crockett, W. H. (1965). Some factors influencing the assimilation of disparate information in impression formation. *Journal of Personality and Social Psychology, 2,* 397–402.

Rosenman, R. H., Brand, R. J., Jenkins, C. D., Friedman, M., Straus, R., & Wurn, M. (1975). Coronary heart disease in the Western Collaborative Group Study: Final follow-up experience of 8 1/2 years. *Journal of the American Medical Association, 233,* 872–877.

Rosenman, R. H., & Friedman, M. (1977). Modifying Type A behavior pattern. *Journal of Psychosomatic Research, 21,* 323–331.

Rosenstock, I. M. (1966). Why people use health services. *Milbank Memorial Fund Quarterly, 44,* 94–127.

Rosenthal, R. (1979). The "file drawer problem" and tolerance for null results. *Psychological Bulletin, 86,* 638–641.

Rosenthal, R., & Jacobson, L. (1968). *Pygmalion in the classroom: Teacher expectation and pupils' intellectual development.* New York: Holt, Rinehart and Winston.

Rosenthal, R., & Rosnow, R. L. (1975). *The volunteer subject.* New York: Wiley.

Rosenthal, R., & Rosnow, R. L. (1984). Applying Hamlet's question to the ethical conduct of research: A conceptual addendum. *American Psychologist, 39,* 561–563.

Roskies, E. (1983). Modification of coronary-risk behavior. In D. S. Krantz, A. Baum, & J. E. Singer (Eds.), *Handbook of psychology and health, 3,* Hillsdale, NJ: Erlbaum.

Ross, E. A. (1908). *Social psychology.* New York: Macmillan.

Ross, L., Greene, D., & House, P. (1977). The "false consensus effect": An egocentric bias in social perception and attribution processes. *Journal of Experimental Social Psychology, 13,* 279–301.

Ross, L., Rodin, J., & Zimbardo, P. (1969). Toward an attribution therapy: The reduction of fear through induced cognitive-emotional misattribution. *Journal of Personality and Social Psychology, 12,* 279–288.

Ross, L. D. (1977). The intuitive psychologist and his shortcomings: Distortions in the attribution process. In L. Berkowitz (Ed.), *Advances in experimental social psychology* (Vol. 10). New York: Academic Press.

Rubenowitz, S., Norrgren, F., & Tannenbaum, A. S. (1983). Some social psychological effects of direct and indirect participation in ten Swedish companies. *Organization Studies, 4,* 243–259.

Rubin, J. Z. (1980). Experimental research on third-party intervention in conflict: Toward some generalizations. *Psychological Bulletin, 87,* 379–391.

Rubin, J. Z., & Brown, B. R. (1975). *The social psychology of bargaining and negotiation.* New York: Academic Press.

Rubin, J. Z., & Lewicki, R. J. (1973). A three-factor experimental analysis of promises and threats. *Journal of Applied Social Psychology, 3,* 240–257.

Rubin, Z. (1970). Measurement of romantic love. *Journal of Personality and Social Psychology, 16,* 265–273.

Rubin, Z. (1973). *Liking and loving: An invitation to social psychology.* New York: Holt, Rinehart and Winston.

Rule, B. G., & Nesdale, A. R. (1976). Emotional arousal and aggressive behavior. *Psychological Bulletin, 83,* 851–863.

Rumelhart, D. E. (1984). Schemata and the cognitive system. In R. S. Wyer, Jr., & T. K. Siull (Eds.), *Handbook of social cognition.* Hillsdale, NJ: Erlbaum.

Rusbult, C. E. (1983). A longitudinal test of the investment model: The development (and deterioration) of satisfaction and commitment in heterosexual involvements. *Journal of Personality and Social Psychology, 45,* 101–117.

Rushton, J. P. (1975). Generosity in children: Immediate and long-term effects of modeling, preaching, and moral judgment. *Journal of*

Personality and Social Psychology, 31, 459–466.

Rushton, J. P. (1980). *Altruism, socialization, and society.* Englewood Cliffs, NJ: Prentice-Hall.

Rushton, J. P., & Campbell, A. C. (1977). Modeling, vicarious reinforcement and extraversion on blood donating in adults. Immediate and long-term effects. *European Journal of Social Psychology, 7,* 297–306.

Rushton, J. P., & Sorrentino, R. M. (Eds.). (1981). *Altruism and helping behavior: Social, personality, and developmental perspectives.* Hillsdale, NJ: Erlbaum.

Sacks, H., Schegloff, E. A., & Jefferson, G. (1974). A simplest systematics for the organization of turn-taking for conversation. *Language, 50,* 696–735.

Saegert, S., Macintosh, E., & West, S. (1975). Two studies of crowding in urban public spaces. *Environment and Behavior, 1,* 159–184.

Safer, M. A., Tharps, Q. J., Jackson, T. C., & Leventhal, H. (in press). Determinants of three stages of delay in seeking care at a medical clinic. *Medical Care.*

Saks, M. J. (1983, August). *Social psychology and the law: The state of the art.* Paper presented at the meeting of the American Psychological Association, Anaheim, CA.

Saks, M. J., & Hastie, R. (1978). *Social psychology in court.* New York: Van Nostrand.

Saks, M. J., Werner, C. M., & Ostrom, T. M. (1975). Jury size and consensus requirements: The laws of probability vs. the laws of the land. *Journal of Contemporary Law, 1,* 163–173.

Sampson, E. E. (1971). *Social psychology and contemporary society.* New York: Wiley.

Sanders, G. S. (1981). Driven by distraction: An integrative review of social facilitation theory and research. *Journal of Experimental Social Psychology, 17,* 227–251.

Sanders, G. S. (1982). Social comparison and perceptions of health and illness. In G. S. Sanders & J. Suls (Eds.), *Social psychology of health and illness.* Hillsdale, NJ: Erlbaum.

Sarbin, T. R., & Allen, V. L. (1968). Role theory. In G. Lindzey & E. Aronson (Eds.), *Handbook of social psychology* (Vol. 1, pp. 223–258). Reading, MA: Addison-Wesley.

Sarnoff, I., & Zimbardo, P. G. (1961). Anxiety, fear, and social facilitation. *Journal of Abnormal and Social Psychology, 62,* 597–605.

Saul, E. V., & Kass, T. S. (1969). Study of anticipated anxiety in a medical school setting. *Journal of Medical Education, 44,* 526.

Savinar, J. (1975). The effect of ceiling height on personal space. *Man–Environment Systems, 5,* 321–324.

Schachter, S. (1951). Deviation, rejection, and communication. *Journal of Abnormal and Social Psychology, 46,* 190–207.

Schachter, S. (1959). *The psychology of affiliation.* Stanford, CA: Stanford University Press.

Schachter, S., Ellertson, N., McBride, D., & Gregory, D. (1951). An experimental study of cohesiveness and productivity. *Human Relations, 4,* 29–238.

Schaeffer, M. A., Baum, A., & Paulus, P. B. (1984, April). *Hormonal effects of crowding in prison.* Paper presented at the annual meeting of the Eastern Psychological Association, Baltimore, MD.

Schein, E. H. (1956). The Chinese indoctrination program for prisoners of war. *Psychiatry, 19,* 149–172.

Schein, E. H. (1957). Reaction patterns to severe chronic stress in American army prisoners of war of the Chinese. *Journal of Social Issues, 13*(3), 21–30.

Schein, E. H. (1968). Organizational socialization and the profession of management. *Industrial Management Review, 9,* 1–16.

Schein, E. H. (1983). Entry into the organizational career. In J. R. Hackman, E. E. Lawler, III, & L. W. Porter (Eds.), *Perspectives on behavior in organizations* (pp. 138–146). New York: McGraw-Hill.

Scherer, K. R., & Ekman, P. (1982). *Handbook of methods in nonverbal behavior research.* New York: Cambridge University Press.

Schiffenbauer, A., & Schiavo, R. S. (1976). Physical distance and attraction: An intensification effect. *Journal of Experimental Social Psychology, 12,* 274–282.

Schlenker, B. R. (1980). *Impression management: The self-concept, social identity, and interpersonal relations.* Monterey, CA: Brooks/Cole.

Schoeneman, T. J., & Rubanowitz, D. E. (1983, August). *Attributions in the advice columns: Actors and observers, causes and reasons.* Paper presented at the meeting of the American Psychological Association, Anaheim, CA.

Schofield, J. (1978). School desegregation and intergroup relations. In D. Bar-Tal & L. Saxe (Eds.), *Social psychology of education: Theory and research.* New York: Wiley.

Schofield, J. W. (1982). *Black and white in school: Trust, tension, or tolerance?* New York: Praeger.

Schroeder, H. E. (1973). The risky shift as a general choice shift. *Journal of Personality and Social Psychology, 27,* 297–300.

Schuman, H., & Johnson, M. P. (1976). Attitudes and behavior. *Annual Review of Sociology, 2,* 161–207.

Schuster, E., Eldeston, E. M. (1907). *The inheritance of ability.* London: Dulav & Co.

Schwartz, S. H. (1977). Normative influences on altruism. In L. Berkowitz (Ed.), *Advances in experimental social psychology* (Vol. 10). New York: Academic Press.

Schwartz, S. H., & Clausen, G. T. (1970). Responsibility, norms, and helping in an emergency. *Journal of Personality and Social Psychology, 16,* 299–310.

Scott, R. L. (1977). Communication as an international, social system. *Human Communication Research, 3,* 258–267.

Sears, D. O. (1968). The paradox of de facto selective exposure without preferences for supportive information. In R. P. Abelson (Ed.), *Theories of cognitive consistency.* Chicago, IL: Rand McNally.

Sears, D. O. (1982). The person-positivity bias. *Journal of Personality and Social Psychology, 44,* 233–250.

Segal, M. W. (1974). Alphabet and attraction: An unobtrusive measure of the effect of propinquity in a field setting. *Journal of Personality and Social Psychology, 30,* 654–657.

Seligman, M. E. P. (1975). *Helplessness.* San Francisco: W. H. Freedman.

Serber, M. (1972). Teaching the nonverbal components of assertive training. *Journal of Behavior Therapy and Experimental Psychiatry, 3,* 179–183.

Shannon, C., & Weaver, W. (1949). *The mathematical theory of communication.* Urbana: University of Illinois Press.

Sharan, S. (1984). *Cooperative learning in the classroom: Research in desegregated schools.* Hillsdale, NJ: Erlbaum.

Shatz, M., & Gelman, R. (1977). Beyond syntax:

The influence of conversational constraints on speech modifications. In C. E. Snow & C. A. Fergusun (Eds.), *Talking to children: Language input and acquisition.* Cambridge, England: Cambridge University Press.

Shaver, K. G. (1983). *An introduction to attribution processes.* Hillsdale, NJ: Erlbaum.

Shaver, P., & Klinnert, M. (1982). Schachter's theories of affiliation and emotion: Implications of developmental research. In L. Wheeler (Ed.), *Review of personality and social psychology* (Vol. 3). Beverly Hills, CA: Sage.

Shaw, M. E. (1932). A comparison of individuals and small groups in the rational solution of complex problems. *American Journal of Psychology, 44,* 491–504.

Shaw, M. E. (1964). Communication networks. In L. Berkowitz (Ed.), *Advances in experimental social psychology* (Vol. 1, pp. 111–147). New York: Academic Press.

Shaw, M. E. (1981). *Group dynamics: The psychology of small group behavior.* New York: McGraw-Hill.

Shaw, M. E., & Costanzo, P. R. (1982). *Theories of social psychology* (2nd ed.). New York: McGraw-Hill.

Shaw, M. E., & Rothschild, G. H. (1956). Some effects of prolonged experiences in communication networks. *Journal of Applied Psychology, 40,* 281–286.

Shaw, M. E., & Shaw, L. M. (1962). Some effects of sociometric grouping upon learning in a second grade classroom. *Journal of Social Psychology, 57,* 453–458.

Sheatsley, P. B., & Feldman, J. J. (1964). The assassination of President Kennedy: A preliminary report on public attitude and behavior. *Public Opinion Quarterly, 28,* 189–215.

Sherif, M. (1935). A study of some social factors in perception. *Archives of Psychology* (187).

Sherif, M. (1966). *In common predicament: Social psychology of intergroup conflict and cooperation.* Boston, MA: Houghton-Mifflin.

Sherif, M., Harvey, O. J., White, B. J., Hood, W. E., & Sherif, C. W. (1961). *Intergroup conflict and cooperation: The Robber's Cove experiment.* Norman: University of Oklahoma Book Exchange.

Sherif, M., & Sherif, C. W. (1969). *Social psychology* (rev. ed.). New York: Harper & Row.

Sherrod, D. R. (1974). Crowding, perceived control and behavioral aftereffects. *Journal of Applied Social Psychology, 4,* 171–186.

Shetty, Y. K. (1978). Managerial power and organizational effectiveness: A contingency analysis. *Journal of Management Studies, 15,* 178–181.

Shotland, R. L., & Huston, T. L. (1979). Emergencies: What are they and do they influence bystanders to intervene? *Journal of Personality and Social Psychology, 37,* 1822–1834.

Shrauger, J. S. (1975). Responses to evaluation as a function of initial self-perceptions. *Psychological Bulletin, 82,* 581–596.

Siegel, J. M., & Steele, C. M. (1979). Noise level and social discrimination. *Personality and Social Psychology Bulletin, 5,* 95–99.

Sigall, H., & Ostrove, N. (1975). Beautiful but dangerous: Effects of offender attractiveness and nature of the crime on juridic judgment. *Journal of Personality and Social Psychology, 31,* 410–444.

Sillars, A. L. (1982). Attribution and communication: Are people "naive scientists" or just naive? In M. E. Roloff & C. R. Berger (Eds.), *Social cognition and communication* (pp. 73–106). Beverly Hills, CA: Sage.

Silverman, B. I. (1974). Consequences, social discrimination, and the principle of belief congruence. *Journal of Personality and Social Psychology, 29,* 497–508.

Simmons, J., & Mares, W. (1983). *Working together.* New York: Knopf.

Simon, S. B., Howe, L. V., & Kirschenbaum, H. (1972). *Values clarification: A handbook of practical strategies for teachers and students.* New York: Hart.

Simpson, G. E., & Yinger, J. M. (1972). *Racial and cultural minorities: An analysis of prejudice and discrimination.* New York: Harper & Row.

Singer, D. G. (1983). A time to reexamine the role of television in our lives. *American Psychologist, 38,* 815–843.

Sistrunk, F., & McDavid, J. W. (1971). Sex variable in conformity behavior. *Journal of Personality and Social Psychology, 17,* 200–207.

Skrypnek, B. J., & Snyder, M. (1982). On the self-perpetuating nature of stereotypes about women and men. *Journal of Experimental Social Psychology, 18,* 277–291.

Slovic, P., Fischhoff, B., & Lichenstein, S. (1977).

Cognitive processes and societal risk taking. In J. S. Carroll & J. W. Payne (Eds.), *Cognition and social behavior*. Hillsdale, NJ: Erlbaum.

Smedley, J. W., & Bayton, J. A. (1978). Evaluative race–class stereotypes by race and perceived class of subjects. *Journal of Personality and Social Psychology, 36,* 530–535.

Smith, E. R. (1984). Attributions and other inferences: Processing information about the self versus others. *Journal of Experimental Social Psychology, 20,* 97–115.

Smith, P. B. (1975). Controlled studies of the outcome of sensitivity training. *Psychological Bulletin, 82,* 597–622.

Smith, T. W., Snyder, C. R., & Handelsman, M. M. (1982). On the self-serving function of an academic wooden leg: Test anxiety as a self-handicapping strategy. *Journal of Personality and Social Psychology, 42,* 314–321.

Smith, T. W., Snyder, C. R., & Perkins, S. C. (1983). The self-serving functions of hypochondriacal complaints: Physical symptoms as self-handicapping strategies. *Journal of Personality and Social Psychology, 44,* 787–797.

Snow, R. (1969). Unfinished Pygmalion. *Contemporary Psychology, 14,* 197–199.

Snyder, G. H., & Diesing, P. (1977). *Conflict among nations*. Princeton, NJ: Princeton University Press.

Snyder, M., & Cantor, N. (1979). Testing hypotheses about other people: The use of historical knowledge. *Journal of Experimental Social Psychology, 15,* 330–343.

Snyder, M., & Cunningham, M. R. (1975). To comply or not to comply: Testing the self-perception explanation of the "foot in the door" phenomenon. *Journal of Personality and Social Psychology, 31,* 64–67.

Snyder, M., & Swann, W. B., Jr. (1978). Behavioral confirmation in social interaction: From social perception to social reality. *Journal of Experimental Social Psychology, 14,* 148–162.

Snyder, M., & Tanke, E. (1976). Behavior and attitudes: Some people are more consistent than others. *Journal of Personality and Social Psychology, 44,* 501–517.

Solomon, R. (1980). The opponent-process theory of acquired motivation: The costs of pleasure and the benefits of pain. *American Psychologist 35,* 691–712.

Sommer, R. (1974). *Tight spaces: Hard architecture and how to humanize it*. Englewood Cliffs, NJ: Prentice-Hall.

Sommer, R. (1982). The district attorney's dilemma: Experimental games and the real world of plea bargaining. *American Psychologist, 37,* 526–532.

Sommer, R., & Becker, F. D. (1969). Territorial defense and the good neighbor. *Journal of Personality and Social Psychology, 11,* 85–92.

Sproull, L. S., & Kiesler, S. B. (1983, August). *Encounters with the alien culture*. Paper presented at the meeting of the American Psychological Association, Anaheim, CA.

Staats, A. W. (1975). *Social behaviorism*. Homewood, IL: Dorsey Press.

Staats, A. W., & Staats, C. K. (1958). Attitudes established by classical conditioning. *Journal of Abnormal and Social Psychology, 57,* 37–40.

Stang, D. J. (1973). Six theories of repeated exposure and affect. *Catalog of Selected Documents in Psychology, 126.*

Stang, D. J. (1974). *An analysis of the effects of political campaigning*. Paper presented at the 66th annual meeting of the Southern Society for Philosophy and Psychology, Tampa, FL.

Staub, E. (1971). A child in distress: The influence of nurturance and modeling on children's attempts to help. *Developmental Psychology, 5,* 124–133.

Staub, E. (1974). Helping a distressed person: Social, personality, and stimulus determinants. In L. Berkowitz (Ed.), *Advances in experimental social psychology* (Vol. 7). New York: Academic Press.

Staub, E. (Ed.). (1978). *Positive social behavior and morality: Vol. 1. Social and personal influences*. New York: Academic Press.

Stea, D. (1974). Architecture in the head: Cognitive mapping. In J. Lang, C. Burnette, W. Moleski, & D. Vachon (Eds.), *Designing for human behavior*. Stroudsberg, PA: Dowden, Hutchinson, & Ross.

Steele, C. M., Southwick, L. L., & Critchlow, B. (1981). Dissonance and alcohol: Drinking your troubles away. *Journal of Personality and Social Psychology, 41,* 831–846.

Steiner, I. (1972). *Group process and productivity*. New York: Academic Press.

Steiner, I. (1976). Task-performing groups. In J. W. Thibaut, J. T. Spence, & R. C. Carson

(Eds.), *Contemporary topics in social psychology.* Morristown, NJ: General Learning Press.

Steiner, I. D., & Spaulding, J. (1966). Perference for balanced situations. Unpublished manuscript, University of Illinois, Urbana.

Stephan, W., Berscheid, E., & Walster, E. (1971). Sexual arousal and heterosexual perception. *Journal of Personality and Social Psychology, 20,* 93–101.

Stephan, W. G. (1978). School desegregation: An evaluation of predictions made in *Brown v. Board of Education. Psychological Bulletin, 85,* 217–238.

Stewart, R. H. (1965). Effect of continuous responding on the order effect in personality impression formation. *Journal of Personality and Social Psychology, 1,* 161–165.

Stogdill, R. M. (1974). *Handbook of leadership: A survey of theory and research.* New York: The Free Press.

Stokols, D. (1976). The experience of crowding in primary and secondary environments. *Environment and Behavior, 8,* 49–86.

Stokols, D. (1978). A typology of crowding experiences. In A. Baum and Y. M. Epstein (Eds.), *Human response to crowding.* Hillsdale, NJ: Erlbaum.

Stokols, D., Rall, M., Pinner, B., & Schopler, J. (1973). Physical, social, and personal determinants of the perception of crowding. *Environment and Behavior, 5,* 87–117.

Stone, G. C. (1979). Patient compliance and the role of the expert. *Journal of Social Issues, 35*(1), 34–59.

Storms, M. D., & Nisbett, R. E. (1970). Insomnia and the attribution process. *Journal of Personality and Social Psychology, 16,* 219–328.

Strawn, D. V., & Buchanan, R. W. (1976). Jury confusion: A threat to justice. *Judicature, 59,* 478–483.

Strong, S. R., Taylor, R. G., Bratton, J. C., & Loper, R. A. (1971). Nonverbal behavior and perceived counselor characteristics. *Journal of Counseling Psychology, 18,* 554–561.

Strube, M. J., & Garcia, J. E. (1981). A meta-analytic investigation of Fiedler's contingency model of leadership effectiveness. *Psychological Bulletin, 90,* 307–321.

Strube, M. J., Miles, M. E., & Finch, W. H. (1981). The social facilitation of a simple task: Field

tests of alternative explanations. *Personality and Social Psychology Bulletin, 7,* 701–707.

Sue, S., Smith, R. E., & Caldwell, C. (1973). Effects of inadmissible evidence on the decisions of simulated jurors: A moral dilemma. *Journal of Applied Social Psychology, 3,* 345–353.

Suedfeld, P., & Borrie, R. A. (1978). Sensory deprivation, attitude change, and defense against persuasion. *Canadian Journal of Behavioral Science, 10,* 16–27.

Sulzer-Azaroff, B., & Mayer, G. R. (1984). *Achieving educational success: Effective behavioral strategies.* New York: Holt.

Sussman, N. (1976). Sex and sexuality in history. In B. J. Sadock, H. I. Kaplan, & A. M. Freedman (Eds.), *The sexual experience* (pp. 7–70). Baltimore, MD: Williams & Wilkins.

Svarstad, B. (1976). Physician–patient communication and patient conformity with medical advice. In D. Mechanic (Ed.), *The growth of bureaucratic medicine.* New York: Wiley.

Symonds, M. (1975). Victims of violence: Psychological effects and after effects. *The American Journal of Psychoanalysis, 35,* 19–26.

Taguiri, R. (1958). Social preference and its perception. In R. Taguiri & L. Petrullo (Eds.), *Person, perception, and interpersonal behavior* (pp. 316–336). Stanford, CA: Stanford University Press.

Tajfel, H., Billig, M. G., Bundy, R. P., & Flament, C. (1971). Social categorization and intergroup behavior. *European Journal of Social Psychology, 1,* 149–178.

Tanford, S., & Penrod, S. (1984). Social influence model: A formal integration of research on majority and minority influence processes. *Psychological Bulletin, 95,* 189–225.

Tannenbaum, A. (1974). *Hierarchy in organizations.* New York: Wiley.

Taylor, D. M., & Jaggi, V. (1974). Ethnocentrism and causal attribution in a south Indian context. *Journal of Cross-Cultural Psychology, 5,* 162–171.

Taylor, R. B., & Lanni, J. C. (1981). Territorial dominance: The influence of the resident advantage in triadic decision-making. *Journal of Personality and Social Psychology, 41,* 909–915.

Taylor, R. B., & Stough, R. R. (1978). Territorial cognition: Assessing Altman's typology. *Jour-*

nal of Personality and Social Psychology, 36, 418–423.

Taylor, S. E. (1979). Hospital patient behavior: Reactance, helplessness, or control? Journal of Social Issues, 35, 156–184.

Taylor, S. E. (1982). Social cognition and health. Personality and Social Psychology Bulletin, 8, 549–562.

Taylor, S. E., & Crocker, J. (1981). Schematic bases of social information processing. In E. T. Higgins, C. P. Herman, & M. P. Zanna (Eds.), Social cognition: The Ontario Symposium (Vol. 1). Hillsdale, NJ: Erlbaum.

Taylor, S. E., & Fiske, S. T. (1978). Salience, attention, and attribution: Top of the head phenomena. In L. Berkowitz (Ed.), Advances in experimental social psychology (Vol. 11). New York: Academic Press.

Taylor, S. E., Lichtman, R. R., & Wood, J. V. (1984). Attributions, beliefs about control, and adjustment to breast cancer. Journal of Personality and Social Psychology, 46, 489–502.

Taylor, S. P., & Gammon, C. B. (1975). Effects of type and dose of alcohol on human physical aggression. Journal of Personality and Social Psychology, 32, 169–175.

Taylor, S. P., & Pisano, R. (1971). Physical aggression as a function of frustration and physical attack. Journal of Social Psychology, 84, 261–267.

Taylor, S. P., Vardaris, R. M., Rawitch, A. B., Gammon, C. B., Cranston, J. W., & Lubetkin, A. I. (1976). The effects of alcohol and Delta-9-tetrahydrocannabinol on human physical aggression. Aggressive Behavior, 2, 153–161.

Taysor, G. R. (1954). Sex in history. New York: Vanguard.

Tennis, G. H., & Dabbs, J. M. (1975). Sex, setting, and personal space: First grade through college. Sociometry, 38, 385–394.

Tesser, A., & Rosen, S. (1975). Why subjects say they would or would not communicate affectively toned messages. Paper presented at the meeting of the Southeastern Psychological Association, Atlanta, GA.

Tetlock, P. E. (1979). Identifying victims of groupthink from public statements of decision makers. Journal of Personality and Social Psychology, 37, 1314–1324.

Thibaut, J. W., & Kelley, H. H. (1959). The social psychology of groups. New York: Wiley.

Thompson, W. C., Cowan, C. L., & Rosenhan, D. L. (1980). Focus of attention mediates the impact of negative affect on altruism. Journal of Personality and Social Psychology, 38(2), 291–300.

Thornberry, T. P. (1973). Criminology, race, socioeconomic status and sentencing in the juvenile justice system. Journal of Criminal Law and Criminology, 64, 90–98.

Thurstone, L. L. (1928). Attitudes can be measured. American Journal of Sociology, 33, 529–554.

Tichy, N. M. (1974). Organizational innovations in Sweden. Columbia Journal of World Business, 18–22.

Tjosvold, D. (1981). Unequal power relationships within a cooperative or competitive context. Journal of Applied Social Psychology, 11, 137–150.

Tjosvold, D. (1982). Effects of approach to controversy on superiors' incorporation of subordinates' information in decision making. Journal of Applied Psychology, 67, 189–193.

Tjosvold, D., & Deewer, D. K. (1980). Effects of controversy within a cooperative or competitive context on organizational decision-making. Journal of Applied Psychology, 65, 590–595.

Toch, H. (1969). Violent men. Chicago: Aldine.

Toch, H. (1975). Men in crisis: Human breakdowns in prison. Chicago: Aldine.

Toi, M., & Batson, C. D. (1982). More evidence that empathy is a source of altruistic motivation. Journal of Personality and Social Psychology, 43, 281–292.

Tomkins, S. S. (1962). Affect, imagery, consciousness: Vol. 1. The positive affects. New York: Springer.

Tourangeau, R., & Ellsworth, P. C. (1979). The role of facial response in the experience of emotion. Journal of Personality and Social Psychology, 37, 1519–1531.

Triandis, H. C. (1972). The analysis of subjective culture. New York: Wiley.

Triandis, H. C., & Davis, E. (1965). Race and belief as determinants of behavioral intentions. Journal of Personality and Social Psychology, 2, 715–725.

Triandis, H., Loh, W., & Levin, L. (1966). Race, status, quality of spoken English, and opinions about civil rights as determinants of interpersonal attitudes. *Journal of Personality and Social Psychology, 3,* 468–472.

Triandis, H. C., & Vassiliou, V. (1967). Frequency of contacts and stereotyping. *Journal of Personality and Social Psychology, 7,* 316–328.

Triplett, N. (1897). The dynamogenic factors in pacemaking and competition. *American Journal of Psychology, 9,* 507–533.

Trope, Y. (1980). Self assessment, self enhancement, and task performance. *Journal of Experimental Social Psychology, 16,* 116–129.

Turiel, E. (1983). *The development of social knowledge.* Cambridge, England: Cambridge University Press.

Turner, R. H., & Killian, L. M. (1972). *Collective behavior* (2nd ed.). Englewood Cliffs, NJ: Prentice-Hall.

Tuttle, T. C. (1983). Organizational productivity: A challenge for psychologists. *American Psychologist, 38,* 479–486.

Umiker-Sebeok, D. J. (1976). *The conversational skills of preschool children.* Unpublished doctoral dissertation, Indiana University.

Umstot, D. D., Bell, C. H., & Mitchell, T. R. (1976). Effects of job enrichment and task goals on satisfaction and productivity: Implications for job design. *Journal of Applied Psychology, 61,* 379–394.

Underwood, B., Berenson, J. F., Berenson, R. J., Cheng, K. K., Wilson, D., Kulik, J., Moore, B. S., & Wenzel, G. (1977). Attention, negative affect, and altruism: An ecological validation. *Personality and Social Psychology Bulletin, 3,* 54–58.

Ungar, S. (1979). The effects of effort and stigma on helping. *Journal of Social Psychology, 107,* 23–28.

U.S. Commission on Civil Rights. (1983, January). *Intimidation and violence: Racial and religious bigotry in America* (Clearinghouse Publication 77). Washington, D.C: U.S. Government Printing Office.

Valins, S. (1966). Cognitive effects of false heart-rate feedback. *Journal of Personality and Social Psychology, 4,* 400–408.

Van Der Pligt, J., & Eiser, J. R. (1983). Actors' and observers' attributions, self-serving bias, and positivity bias. *European Journal of Social Psychology, 13,* 95–104.

Van Dyke, J. M. (1970, March). The jury as a political institution. *Center Magazine,* pp. 17–26.

Van Maanen, J. (1978). People processing: Strategies of organizational socialization. *Organizational Dynamics,* (summer).

Verplanck, W. S. (1955). The control of the content of conversation: Reinforcement of statements of opinions. *Journal of Abnormal and Social Psychology, 51,* 668–676.

Vinokur, A., & Burnstein, E. (1974). Effects of partially shared persuasive arguments on group-induced shifts: A group problem solving approach. *Journal of Personality and Social Psychology, 29,* 305–315.

Vinokur-Kaplan, D. (1978). To have—or not to have—another child: Family planning attitudes, intentions, and behavior. *Journal of Applied Social Psychology, 8,* 29–46.

Vroom, V. H. (1969). Industrial social psychology. In G. Lindzey & E. Aronson (Eds.), *Handbook of social psychology* (Vol. 5). Reading, MA: Addison-Wesley.

Vroom, V. H. (1976). Leadership. In M. D. Dunnette, *Handbook of industrial and organizational psychology.* Chicago: Rand McNally College.

Vroom, V. H., and Yetton, P. W. (1973). *Leadership and decision making.* Pittsburgh, PA: University of Pittsburgh Press.

Wagley, C., & Harns, M. (1958). *Minorities in the new world.* New York: Columbia.

Waldron, I., Zyzanski, S. J., Shekelle, R. B., Jenkins, C. D., & Tannenbaum, S. (1977). The coronary-prone behavior pattern in employed men and women. *Journal of Human Stress, 3,* 2–19.

Wallace, M. D. (1979). Arms race and escalation: Some new evidence. *Journal of Conflict Resolution, 23,* 3–16.

Wallach, M. A., Kogan, N., & Bem, D. J. (1964). Diffusion of responsibility and level of risk taking in groups. *Journal of Abnormal and Social Psychology, 68,* 263–274.

Wallach, M. A., Kogan, N., & Burt, R. (1967). Group risk taking and field dependence–independence of group members. *Sociometry, 30,* 323–339.

Wallston, B. S., DeVellis, B. M., & Wallston, K. (1983). Licensed practical nurses' sex role stereotypes. *Psychology of Women Quarterly, 7,* 199–208.

Walster (Hatfield), E., Aronson, V., Abrahams, D., & Rottman, L. (1966). Importance of physical attractiveness in dating behavior. *Journal of*

Personality and Social Psychology, 4, 508–516.

Walster (Hatfield), E., Berscheid, E., & Walster, G. W. (1976). New directions in equity research. In L. Berkowitz & E. Walster (Hatfield) (Eds.), *Advances in Experimental Social Psychology, 9,* 1–42.

Walster (Hatfield), E., & Walster, G. W. (1978). *Love.* Reading, MA: Addison-Wesley.

Walster (Hatfield), E., Walster, G. W., & Berscheid, E. (1978). *Equity: Theory and research.* Boston: Allyn and Bacon.

Walters, G. C., & Grusec, J. E. (1977). *Punishment.* San Francisco: W. H. Freeman.

Walters, R. H., & Brown, M. (1963). Studies of reinforcement of aggression. III. Transfer of responses to an interpersonal situation. *Child Development, 34,* 536–571.

Wanous, J. P. (1983). The entry of newcomers into organizations. In J. R. Hackman, E. E. Lawler, III, & L. W. Porter (Eds.), *Perspectives on behavior in organizations* (pp. 159–167). New York: McGraw-Hill.

Warner, L., & DeFleur, M. (1969). Attitude as an interactional concept: Social constraint and social distance as intervening variables between attitudes and action. *American Sociological Review, 34,* 153–169.

Watkins, M. J., & Pegnircioğlu, Z. F. (1984). Determining perceived meaning during impression formation: Another look at the meaning change hypothesis. *Journal of Personality and Social Psychology, 46,* 1005–1016.

Watson, D. (1982). The actor and the observer: How are their perceptions of causality divergent? *Psychological Bulletin, 92,* 682–700.

Watson, O. M., & Graves, T. D. (1966). Quantitative research in proxemic behavior. *American Anthropologist, 68,* 971–985.

Waxer, P. H. (1977). Nonverbal cues for anxiety: An examination of emotional leakage. *Journal of Abnormal Psychology, 86,* 306–314.

Weber, M. (1952). The essentials of bureaucratic organization: An ideal-type construction. In R. K. Merton et al. (Eds.), *A reader in bureaucracy.* Glencoe, Ill: Free Press.

Weber, R., & Crocker, J. (1983). Cognitive processes in the revision of stereotypic beliefs. *Journal of Personality and Social Psychology, 45,* 961–977.

Weigel, R. H., & Newman, L. S. (1976). Increasing attitude–behavior correspondence by broadening the scope of the behavioral measure. *Journal of Personality and Social Psychology, 33,* 793–802.

Weiner, B. (Ed.). (1974). *Achievement motivation and attribution theory.* Morristown, NJ: General Learning Press.

Weiner, B. (1979). Theory of motivation for some classroom experiences. *Journal of Educational Psychology, 71,* 3–25.

Weiner, B. (1980, April) *The role of affect in rational (attributional) approaches to human motivation.* Paper presented at the annual meeting of the American Educational Research Association, Boston.

Weiner, B., Frieze, I., Kukla, A., Reed, L., Rest, S., & Rosenbaum, R. M. (1972). Perceiving the causes of success and failure. In E. E. Jones, D. E. Kanouse, H. H. Kelley, R. E. Nisbett, S. Valins, & B. Weiner (Eds.), *Attribution: Perceiving the causes of behavior* (pp. 95–120). Morristown, NJ: General Learning Press.

Wells, G. L., & Harvey, J. H. (1978). Naive attributors' attributions and predictions: What is informative and when is an effect an effect? *Journal of Personality and Social Psychology, 36,* 483–490.

Wells, G. L., & Loftus, E. A. (Eds.). (1984). *Eyewitness testimony: Psychological perspectives.* New York: Cambridge University Press.

Werner, C. M., Brown, B. B., & Damron, G. (1981). Territorial marking in a game arcade. *Journal of Personality and Social Psychology, 41,* 1094–1104.

West, S. G., Gunn, S. P., & Chernicky, P. (1975). Ubiquitous Watergate: An attributional analysis. *Journal of Personality and Social Psychology, 32,* 55–65.

Weyant, J. M. (1978). Effects of mood states, costs, and benefits on helping. *Journal of Personality and Social Psychology, 36,* 1169–1176.

Wheeler, L. (1974). Social comparison and selective affiliation. In T. L. Huston (Ed.), *Foundations of interpersonal attraction* (pp. 309–328). New York: Academic Press.

White, G. L., Fishbein, S., & Rutstein, J. (1981). Passionate love and the misattribution of arousal. *Journal of Personality and Social Psychology, 41,* 56–62.

White, M. (1975). Interpersonal distance as affected by room size, status, and sex. *Journal of Social Psychology, 95,* 241–249.

White, R. K. (1966). Misperception and the Vietnam war. *Journal of Social Issues, 22*(3), 1–164.

White, R. K. (1970). *Nobody wanted war: Misperception in Vietnam and other wars.* Garden City: Doubleday.

White, R. K. (1977). Misperception in the Arab-Israeli conflict. *Journal of Social Issues, 33*(1), 190–221.

Whitehead, T. N. (1938). *The industrial worker.* Cambridge, MA: Harvard University Press.

Whitley, B. E., Jr., & Greenberg, M. S. (1984, April). *The role of eyewitness confidence in juror perceptions of credibility.* Paper presented at the annual meeting of the Eastern Psychological Association, Baltimore, MD.

Whorf, B. L. (1956). *Language, thought, and reality.* New York: Wiley.

Wicker, A. W. (1969). Attitudes versus actions: The relationship of verbal and overt behavioral responses to attitude objects. *Journal of Social Issues, 25,* 41–78.

Wicklund, R. A. (1975). Objective self awareness. In L. Berkowitz (Ed.), *Advances in experimental social psychology* (Vol. 8). New York: Academic Press.

Wicklund, R. A., & Brehm, J. W. (1976). *Perspectives on cognitive dissonance.* Hillsdale, NJ: Erlbaum.

Widgery, R., & Stackpole, C. (1972). Desk position, interviewee anxiety, and interviewer credibility: An example of cognitive balance in a dyad. *Journal of Counseling Psychology, 19,* 173–177.

Wilder, D. A. (1977). Perception of groups, size of opposition, and social influence. *Journal of Experimental Social Psychology, 13,* 253–268.

Wilder, D. A. (1984). Intergroup contact: The typical member and the exception to the rule. *Journal of Experimental Social Psychology, 20,* 177–194.

Wilke, H., & Lanzetta, J. T. (1970). The obligation to help: The effects of amount of prior help on subsequent helping behavior. *Journal of Experimental Social Psychology, 6,* 483–493.

Wilson, E. (1975). *Sociobiology: The new synthesis.* Cambridge, MA: Harvard University Press.

Wilson, E. (1978). *On human nature.* Cambridge, MA: Harvard University Press.

Wilson, R. C., Gabb, J. G., Dienst, E. R., Wood, L., & Bavry, J. L. (1975). *College professors and their impact on students.* New York: Wiley.

Wilson, T., & Linville, P. (1982). Improving academic performance of college freshmen: Attribution therapy revisited. *Journal of Personality and Social Psychology, 42,* 367–376.

Wilson, T. D., & Linville, P. N. (in press). Improving the performance of college freshmen with attribution techniques. *Journal of Personality and Social Psychology.*

Winch, R. F. (1958). *Mate selection: A study of complementary needs.* New York: Harper & Row.

Witkin, H. A., Mednick, S. A., Schulsinger, F., Bakkestrom, E., Christiansen, K. O., Goodenough, D. R., Hirschhorn, K., Lundsteen, C., Owen, D. R., Phillip, J., Ruben, D. B., & Stocking, M. (1976). Criminality in XYY and XXY men. *Science, 193,* 547–555.

Wittig, M. A., & Skolnick, P. (1978). Status versus warmth as determinants of sex differences in personal space. *Sex Roles, 4,* 493–503.

Wolinsky, J. (1983). Research crumbles stereotypes of age. *APA Monitor, 14,* 26–28.

Wolosin, R. J., Sherman, S. J., & Mynatt, C. R. (1975). When self-interest and altruism conflict. *Journal of Personality and Social Psychology, 32,* 752–760.

Woodward, B., & Bernstein, L. (1974). *All the President's Men.* New York: Simon & Schuster.

Worchel, P. (1979). Trust and distrust. In W. Austin & S. Worchel (Eds.), *The social psychology of intergroup relations.* Monterey, CA: Brooks/Cole.

Worchel, S., Andreoli, V., & Folger, R. (1977). Intergroup cooperation and intergroup attraction: The effect of previous interaction and outcome of combined effects. *Journal of Experimental Social Psychology, 13,* 131–140.

Worchel, S., & Brown, E. H. (1984). The role of plausibility in influencing environmental attributions. *Journal of Experimental Social Psychology, 20,* 86–96.

Worchel, S., & Lollis, M. (1982). Reactions to territorial contamination as a function of culture. *Personality and Social Psychology Bulletin, 8,* 370–375.

Worchel, S., & Sigall, H. (1976). There is no place like home, unless. ... *The ACC basketball handbook.* Charlotte, NC: VMI Publications.

Worchel, S., & Yohai, S. M. L. (1979). The role of

attribution in the experience of crowding. *Journal of Experimental Social Psychology.*

Word, C. O., Zanna, M. P., & Cooper, J. (1974). The nonverbal mediation of self-fulfilling prophecies in interracial interaction. *Journal of Experimental Social Psychology, 10,* 109–120.

Yandell, B. (1979). Those who protest much are seen as guilty. *Personality and Social Psychology Bulletin, 5,* 44–47.

Yarnold, P. R., & Grimm, L. G. (1982). Time urgency among coronary-prone individuals. *Journal of Abnormal Psychology, 91,* 175–177.

Yogev, S. (1983). Judging the professional woman: Changing research, changing values. *Psychology of Women Quarterly, 7,* 219–234.

Yukl, G. (1974). Effects of the opponent's initial offer, concession magnitude, and concession frequency on bargaining behavior. *Journal of Personality and Social Psychology, 30,* 323–335.

Yukl, G. A. (1973). Effects of the opponent's initial offer and concession magnitude on bargaining outcomes. *Proceedings of the 81st Annual Convention of the American Psychological Association, 8,* 143–144.

Zajonc, R. B. (1965). Social facilitation. *Science, 149,* 269–274.

Zajonc, R. B. (1968). The attitudinal effects of mere exposure. *Journal of Personality and Social Psychology, 9,* Part 2, 1–27.

Zajonc, R. B (1970, February). Brainwash: Familiarity breeds comfort. *Psychology Today, 13,* 32–35, 60–62.

Zander, A. (1977). *Groups at work.* San Francisco, CA: Jossey-Bass.

Zanna, M., Goethals, G. R., & Hill, J. (1975). Evaluating a sex-related ability: Social comparison with similar others and standard setters. *Journal of Experimental Social Psychology, 11,* 86–93.

Zanna, M. P., Kiesler, C. A., & Pilkonis, P. A. (1970). Positive and negative attitudinal affect established by classical conditioning. *Journal of Personality and Social Psychology, 14,* 321–328.

Zanna, M. P., Olson, J. M., & Fazio, R. H. (1981). Self-perception and attitude–behavior consistency. *Personality and Social Psychology Bulletin, 7,* 252–256.

Zanna, M. P., & Pack, S. J. (1975). On the self-fulfilling nature of apparent sex differences in behavior. *Journal of Experimental Social Psychology, 11,* 583–591.

Zareh, F., & Mayer, S. (1983, August). *Cognitive complexity and liking for in-group and out-group members.* Paper presented at the 91st annual meeting of the American Psychological Association, Anaheim, CA.

Zillman, D. (1978). *Hostility and aggression.* Hillsdale, NJ: Erlbaum.

Zillman, D., Johnson, R. C., & Day, K. D. (1974). Attribution of apparent arousal and proficiency of recovery from sympathetic activation affecting activation transfer to aggressive behavior. *Journal of Experimental Social Psychology, 10,* 503–515.

Zillman, D., Katcher, A., & Milavsky, B. (1972). Excitation transfer from physical exercise to subsequent aggressive behavior. *Journal of Experimental Social Psychology, 8,* 247–259.

Zimbardo, P. G. (1969). The human choice: Individuation, reason, and order versus deindividuation, impulse, and chaos. In W. J. Arnold & D. Levine (Eds.), *Nebraska symposium of motivation* (Vol. 17). Lincoln: University of Nebraska Press.

Zimbardo, P. G., & Formica, R. (1963). Emotional comparison and self-esteem as determinants of affiliation. *Journal of Personality, 31,* 141–162.

Zuckerman, M. (1971). Physiological measures of sexual response in the human. *Psychological Bulletin, 75,* 297–329.

Zuckerman, M. (1976). Sexual attitudes and behavior in college students. In W. W. Oaks, G. A. Melchiode, & I. Ficher (Eds.), *Sex and the life cycle.* New York: Grune and Stratton.

Zuckerman, M. (1978). Use of consensus information in prediction of behavior. *Journal of Experimental Social Psychology, 14,* 163–171.

Zuckerman, M., DePaulo, B. M., & Rosenthal, R. (1981). Verbal and nonverbal communication of deception. *Advances in Experimental Social Psychology, 14,* 1–59.

Zuckerman, M., & Nass, R. A., Jr. (1982, April). *After the revolution: Comparisons of sexual attitudes and experiences among college students in the 1970's and 1980's.* Paper presented at the annual meeting of the Eastern Psychology Association, Baltimore, MD.

ACKNOWLEDGMENTS

Citation in Chapter 1. Racially motivated attack in Sheepshead Bay. Copyright © June 23, 1982, The New York Times Company. (Citation 1)

Citation in Chapter 1. Subway altruism. Copyright © December 21, 1982, The New York Times Company. (Citation 2)

Citation in Chapter 1. Attack of military headquarters in Beirut. Copyright © October 25, 1983, Los Angeles Times Company. (Citation 3).

Citation in Chapter 1. U.S. and Russian arms negotiations. Copyright © 1983, Chicago Sun Times. (Citation 4)

Citation in Chapter 1 from McFadden, "Passenger Saves Blind Man's Life on IND Tracks. Copyright © 1982 by The New York Times Company. Reprinted by permission.

Fig. 1-1 from Deutsch, M. and Krauss, R. M., *Theories in Social Psychology*. Copyright © 1965 by Basic Books, Inc., Publishers. Reprinted by permission of the publisher.

Citation in Chapter 1 from McFadden, "Passenger Saves Blind Man's Life on IND Tracks." Copyright © 1982 by The New York Times Company. Reprinted by permission.

Fig. 2-2 from Cantor, N., and Mischel, W., *Advances in experimental social psychology*, vol. 12, 1979. Copyright © by Academic Press. Adapted by permission.

Fig. 2-3 from Langer, E., Blank, A., and Chanowitz, B., *Journal of Personality and Social Psychology*, 1978. Copyright © by the American Psychological Association. Adapted by permission of the authors.

Fig. 2-4 from Weiner, B., Frieze, I., Kukla, A., Reed, L., Rest, S., & Rosenbaum, R. M. *Attribution: Perceiving the causes of success and failure.* Copyright © 1971, by Silver Burdett Company. Reproduced by permission.

Fig. 2-5 from Bar-Tal, D., Affective and cognitive reactions in situations of success and failure as a function of attributions. *Review of Educational Research*, vol. 48, 1978. American Educational Research Association. Reproduced by permission.

Fig. 2-6 from Smith, T. W., Snyder, C. R., & Handelsman, M. M., Means for self-reports of anxiety. *Journal of Personality and Social Psychology*, vol. 42. Copyright © 1982 by the American Psychological Association. Adapted by permission of the author.

Table 2-1 from Luchins, A. S., *The order of presentation in persuasion.* Copyright © 1957 by Yale University Press. Adapted by permission of the author.

Table 2-3 from Wilson, T., and Linville, P., Improving the academic performance of college freshmen: Attribution therapy revisited. *Journal of Personality and Social Psychology*, 42, no. 2. Copyright © 1982 by the American Psychological Association. Adapted by permission of the authors.

Citation in Chapter 3 from Labov, W., *Tinker, Tailor. . . The Myth of Cultural Deprivation.* Copyright © 1973 by Penguin Education Books, Ltd. Adapted by permission.

Photographs in Chapter 3 from Ekman, P., and Friesen, W. V., New Guinea data on facial expression of emotion, *Journal of Personality and Social Psychology*, vol. 17. Copyright © 1971 by the American Psychological Association. Adapted by permission of the authors.

Fig. 3-8 from Patterson, M. L., An arousal model of interpersonal intimacy. *Psychological Review*. Copyright © 1976 by the American Psychological Association. Adapted by permission of the author.

Fig. 3-9 from Noller, P., Channel consistency and inconsistency in the communications of married couples. *Journal of Personality and Social Psychology*, vol. 43. Copyright © 1982 by the American Psychological Association. Adapted by permission of the author.

Table 3-1 from Ekman, P., and Friesen, W. V., New Guinea data on facial expression of emotion. *Journal of Personality and Social Psychology*, 17. Copyright © 1971 by the American Psychological Association. Adapted by permission of the authors.

Fig. 4-4 from Chaiken, S., Heuristic vs. systematic information processing and the use of source vs. message cues in persuasion. *Journal of Personality and Social Psychology*. Copyright © 1980 by the American Psychological Association. Adapted by permission of the author.

Table 4-1 from Festinger, L., and Carlsmith, J. M., Cognitive consequences of forced compliance. *Journal of Abnormal and Social Psychology*. Copyright © 1959 by the American Psychological Association. Adapted by permission of the authors.

Table 4-2 from Hennessy, E., *Public Opinion*, 4th ed. Copyright © 1981 by Brooks/Cole Publishing Co. Adapted by permission.

Citation in Chapter 5 from Associated Press, "KKK Gains Momentum as the Economy Sours," June 18, 1982. Adapted by permission.

Dialogue in Chapter 5 from Allport, G. W., *The Nature of Prejudice*, 1954, Addison-Wesley Publishing Co. Adapted by permission.

Citation in Chapter 5. "Racial murderer (KKK)." Copyright © June 3, 1982 by the Washington Post. (Overview—citation 1)

NAME INDEX

Ostrove, N., 435–436
Owen, D. R., 321

Pack, S. J., 164–165
Pagan, G., 511
Page, M. M., 123
Page, R. A., 254
Paolitto, D. P., 260
Pardine, P., 271
Park, B., 173
Parke, R. D., 303
Parsons, H. M., 402
Patterson, A. H., 446, 507
Patterson, M. L., 99, 101, 102
Paulus, P. B., 519, 523, 524
Pennebaker, J. W., 271
Penrod, S., 337, 341, 344, 346
Pepe, M., 50
Pepitone, A., 380
Peplau, L. A., 196, 221–223
Pepper, S., 210
Perkins, S. C., 282
Perlman, D., 196
Perloff, R., 424
Perri, M., 214–216
Pettigrew, T. F., 168–170
Petty, R. D., 384
Petty, R. E., 142, 145, 147
Peynircioğlu, Z. F., 48
Phillip, J., 321
Piliavin, I. M., 235, 242
Piliavin, J. A., 235, 242, 256
Pilkonis, P. A., 123
Pinner, B., 523, 524
Pisano, R., 318
Porter, L. W., 403, 404, 415
Postman, L. J., 439
Powell, L., 273
Pratkanis, A. R., 140
Prentice-Dunn, S., 316–317
Preston, M., 348
Price, J., 524
Price, R. A., 214
Price, V., 273
Prohaska, T., 75
Proxmire, W., 216
Pruitt, D. G., 388, 478, 480, 481,
483

Quattrone, G. A., 173

Rabbie, J. M., 359
Raiffa, H., 469
Rajecki, D. W., 121
Rall, M., 523, 524
Ramsey, P. R., 270
Ransberger, V. M., 314–315
Raven, B. H., 199, 353, 356
Rawitch, A. B., 312, 314
Rawls, J., 458

Reader, N., 209
Reed, L., 67–68
Reichling, G., 380
Reimer, J., 260
Reis, H. T., 214–216
Reisenzein, R., 65
Reiser, M. F., 277
Reiss, M., 94
Rest, S., 67–68
Rice, R. W., 362–363
Riessman, F., 375
Rinn, W. E., 92
Riordan, C. A., 123
Riskind, J. H., 474
Roberts, K. H., 415
Robin, D. D., 273
Robinson, E. H., 417
Rodin, J., 67, 163, 242, 275–276,
516
Rodrigues, A., 130
Roethlisberger, F. J., 402
Rogers, M., 249
Rogers, R. W., 142, 316–317
Rokeach, M., 172, 184
Rommetveit, R., 335
Ronis, D. L., 137
Rosen, A. J., 216
Rosen, F. P., 438
Rosen, S., 280
Rosenbaum, R. M., 67–68
Rosenberg, L. A., 341
Rosenberg, M. J., 19, 133
Rosenhan, D. L., 247, 248, 278
Rosenkrantz, P. S., 50, 163
Rosenmann, R. H., 267–270, 272,
273
Rosenstock, I. M., 283, 285
Rosenthal, R., 33, 34, 71, 73, 74,
86, 91, 166, 340
Rosnow, R., 33, 34
Ross, D., 302
Ross, L., 19, 55, 62, 67
Ross, M., 63
Ross, S., 302
Rothbart, M., 173
Rothschild, G. H., 414
Rottman, L., 214
Ruback, R. B., 440
Rubanowitz, D. E., 59
Ruben, D. B., 321
Rubenowitz, S., 420–421
Rubin, J. Z., 353–354, 470, 473,
481, 483
Rubin, Z., 93, 207, 219–223
Rule, B. G., 307
Rumelhart, D. E., 51
Rusbult, C. E., 223
Rushton, J. P., 238, 247, 254, 255,
257–259
Russell, G. W., 315
Ruth, M., 285
Rutstein, J., 221
Ryan, M. J., 236

Sacks, H., 108
Safer, M. A., 285
Saks, M. J., 435, 447–449
Sampson, E. E., 452
Sanders, G. S., 285, 383
Sanford, R. N., 16, 174, 337, 341,
344, 346, 444
Sarbin, T., 17
Sarnoff, I., 198
Saul, E. V., 280
Savinar, J., 513
Saxe, L., 167
Schachter, S., 64–65, 194–198, 200,
202–203, 220, 346, 374, 376,
380, 381, 407
Schaeffer, M. A., 519
Schegloff, E. A., 108
Schein, E. H., 145, 403, 404
Schiavo, R. S., 97
Schiffenbauer, A., 97
Schiffman, H., 372
Schkade, J. K., 519
Schlenker, B., 17
Schoeneman, T. J., 59
Schofield, J., 180, 182
Schonbach, P., 137
Schopler, J., 523, 524
Schroeder, H. E., 390
Schulsinger, F., 321
Schuman, H., 148
Schwartz, M. F., 247–248
Schwartz, S. H., 235, 238–239, 241
Schweiger, D. M., 410
Scott, A., 475
Scott, M. D., 106
Scott, R. L., 105
Sears, D. O., 61, 137
Sears, R. R., 298, 299
Seashore, S. E., 425
Sebastian, R. J., 303
Segal, M. W., 203
Seipel, M., 243
Seligman, M. E. P., 516
Senn, D. J., 210
Shalker, T. E., 248
Shannon, C., 104
Sharan, S., 180, 182
Shatz, M., 105
Shaver, P., 197
Shaw, L. M., 9, 407
Shaw, M. E., 371, 385–386, 407,
413–415
Sheatsley, P. B., 198
Shekelle, R. B., 272
Sherif, C. W., 180, 336
Sherif, M., 19, 180, 336, 337, 371–
373
Sherman, S. J., 390, 438
Sherrod, D. R., 524
Shope, G. L., 322
Shotland, R. L., 234–235
Shrauger, J. S., 211
Siegel, J. M., 520

SUBJECT INDEX